THE WAR OF
THE AMERICAN REVOLUTION

WARS OF THE UNITED STATES
(Editor: Richard L. Blanco)
Vol. 1

GARLAND REFERENCE LIBRARY
OF SOCIAL SCIENCE
Vol. 154

THE WAR OF
THE AMERICAN REVOLUTION
A Selected Annotated Bibliography
of Published Sources

Richard L. Blanco

GARLAND PUBLISHING, INC. • NEW YORK & LONDON
1984

Library of Congress Cataloging in Publication Data

Blanco, Richard L.
  The War of the American Revolution.

  (Wars of the United States ; v. 1) (Garland refer-
ence library of social science ; v. 154)
  Bibliography: p.
  Includes indexes.
  1. United States—History—Revolution, 1775–1783—
Bibliography. I. Title. II. Series. III. Series:
Garland reference library of social science ; v. 154.
  Z1238.B55 1984 [E208] 016.9737   82-49168
  ISBN 0-8240-9171-X

Cover design by Laurence Walczak

Printed on acid-free, 250-year-life paper
Manufactured in the United States of America

I dedicate this book to Renée—my wonderful wife for twenty-two years—who has been my delightful companion at archives and libraries from Halifax, Nova Scotia, to Atlanta, Georgia.

CONTENTS

PREFACE

In this bicentennial year of the end of the American Revolution, it is timely and appropriate that this volume be available. Although much information exists about our struggle for independence from Great Britain two centuries ago, we have lacked a compact, readable, select, annotated bibliography about the 1775–1783 era that is suitable for a broad reading audience. This volume is a selection of the best printed literature in English concerning the War of American Independence. I have blended items about traditional military, naval, and diplomatic subjects with topics representative of the newer "social" history, such as crowd behavior, prisoners of war, and women in the Revolution.

With this volume, Garland Publishing, Inc., launches a new series of annotated bibliographies known as "The Wars of the United States." Between 1983 and 1987, specialists will publish works on the following aspects: the French and Indian War; the War of the American Revolution; the War of 1812; the Mexican War; the Civil War: the North; the Civil War: the South; the Indian Wars of the West; the Spanish-American War; World War I; World War II: Europe; the War against Japan; the Korean War; the War in Vietnam; and the Small Wars of the United States. These works will be unmatched by any other comparable collection of reference volumes in scope, depth, and, I hope, degree of usefulness for researchers.

For over three decades, historians have been increasingly aware that military history is not merely a compilation of battles and campaigns. Thus, though half of this study concentrates on relatively familiar themes about men in combat on land and sea, the remainder of the book contains a broad listing of fresher subjects (cartography, espionage, crowd behavior, class tensions, etc.) that have greatly enhanced our knowledge of the Revolution. Such themes demonstrate that armies and navies are obviously extensions of a society, that the eight-year war influenced virtually every national institution in the United States, and that an intrinsic relationship exists between the experiences of a country fighting for its national identity and the political-social-economic foundations that it creates for the future of mankind.

There is much "Americana" covered in this reference work. High-school students, college undergraduates, graduate students, military and naval "buffs," social scientists, those with a curiosity about their national heritage, and, especially, readers who want "a good book" or article about Bunker Hill, Valley Forge, John Paul Jones, George Washington, or life in the Continental army will find abundant citations about the birth of the United States in these pages.

INTRODUCTION

This work is a classified, selective, annotated bibliography of over 3,700 entries related to the American Revolutionary War. It includes citations and descriptions about books, journals, magazines, dissertations, and official documents.

Believing that the more entries one could list, the more useful the book would be, I compressed information about publications into terse sentences. In general, I summarized an article in one sentence and a standard book in a few sentences. For a key work, I wrote a longer paragraph. Whenever possible, I stressed that a particular volume or essay is either readable for adults, helpful for youngsters, suitable for college students, or written for specialists. With this book, undergraduates, in particular, should have little difficulty in compiling material for a "term paper" on the Revolution.

Inasmuch as no recent, satisfactory topical organization on the war existed, I devised my own outline. To aid the reader to locate references quickly, the entries are arranged in fourteen broad categories. Although some excellent studies on the Revolution have appeared in the past three years, my "cut-off" date is 1980. To my knowledge, no other volume in print contains a list of published material on the Revolution to so recent a date. Because this work was designed for a popular audience, it includes less primary source material (such as papers, memoirs, correspondence, and autobiographies).

I kept the amount of cross-references to a minimum. An excessive amount of the recent writing on the war (it appears to me) tends to be polemical about some historical "school" of interpreting the Revolution. On the assumption that the average reader would not be particularly fascinated, for example, by the critics or the defenders of Carl Becker's thesis (that a social upheaval transpired within a military-political revolution), I did not select many essays or books that are argumentative about another historian's work, rather than substantive or informative. Hence, comments that usually abound in some annotated bibliographies that read: "For a different viewpoint, see . . . ," are absent here. Virtually the only cross-referencing in this work occurs when I cite an essay from a book of articles, such as entry 855, with the full bibliographic data. Thereafter, when I list another essay from the same book, as in entry 884, I explain: "See 855, pp. 132-158."

I could not have completed this study without assistance. Mrs. Brenda Peake, Secretary of the History Department, State University College at Brockport, Brockport, New York, very cheerfully and efficiently typed the manuscript. I remain awed at how—in addition to her many office duties—she managed to copy from my drafts and to master the bibliographic techniques. Renée Blanco, my spouse, merits special praise. Not only has my wife been a steady source of encouragement, but she proofread the manuscript several times, wrote the periodical list, and compiled the author and subject indexes. To Brenda, and especially to Renée, I extend my deepest gratitude.

PERIODICALS CITED

AGRIC HIST	Agricultural History
AHR	American Historical Review
ALA HIST	Alabama History
ALA HIST Q	Alabama History Quarterly
ALA REV	Alabama Review
AMER ANTIQ SOC PROC	American Antiquarian Society Proceedings
AMER ARCH	American Archeologist
AMER BOOK COLL	American Book Collector
AMER COLL	American Collector
AMER ECON REV	American Economic Review
AMER HERITAGE	American Heritage
AMER HIST ASSOC ANN REP	American Historical Association Annual Report
AMER HIST ILLUS	American History Illustrated
AMER J ECON SOC	American Journal of Economics and Sociology
AMER J LEGAL HIST	American Journal of Legal History
AMER JEW HIST SOC PUB	American Jewish History Society Publications
AMER MERCURY	American Mercury
AMER MONTHLY	American Monthly
AMER NEP	American Neptune
AMER PHIL SOC PROC	American Philosophical Society Proceedings

AMER POL SCI REV	American Political Science Review
AMER Q	American Quarterly
AMER SCAN REV	American Scandinavian Review
AMER STUDIES	American Studies
AMERICAS	Americas
ANN AMER ACAD POLITICS SOC SCI	Annals American Academy of Politics and Social Science
ANN MED HIST	Annals of Medical History
ARMED FORCES SOC	Armed Forces and Society
ARMY Q DEF REV	Army Quarterly Defense Review
ATL MONTHLY	Atlantic Monthly
ATLANTA HIST J	Atlanta Historical Journal
BAPTIST HIST HERITAGE	Baptist History Heritage
BERKS CTY HIST REV	Berks County Historical Review
BOSTON PUB LIB Q	Boston Public Library Quarterly
BOSTONIAN SOC PROC	Bostonian Society Proceedings
BUFF HIST SOC PUB	Buffalo Historical Society Publications
BULL BIB	Bulletin of Bibliography
BULL HIST MED	Bulletin of the History of Medicine
BULL INST HIST RES	Bulletin of the Institute of Historical Research
BULL JOHNS HOPKINS HOSP	Bulletin of Johns Hopkins Hospital
BUS HIST REV	Business History Review
BY VALOUR AND ARMS	By Valour and Arms

CAN ETHNIC STUD	Canadian Ethnic Studies
CAN HIST REV	Canadian Historical Review
CAN J ECON POL SCI	Canadian Journal of Economics, Politics, and Science
CAN J HIST	Canadian Journal of History
CAN REV AMER STUD	Canadian Review of American Studies
CATH HIST REV	Catholic Historical Review
CENTENNIAL REV	Centennial Review
CHIC HIST	Chicago History
CHURCH HIST	Church History
CITHARA	Cithara
COL SOC MASS PUB	Colonial Society of Massachusetts Publications
COL U Q	Columbia University Quarterly
COLLECTOR	Collector
CONCORDIA HIST INSTIT Q	Concordia Historical Institute Quarterly
CONN HIST	Connecticut History
CONN HIST SOC BULL	Connecticut Historical Society Bulletin
CONN HIST SOC COLL	Connecticut Historical Society Collections
CONN REV	Connecticut Review
CONTEMP REV	Contemporary Review
DALHOUSIE REV	Dalhousie Review
DAR MAG	Daughters of the American Revolution Magazine
DEL HIST	Delaware History
DIP HIST	Diplomatic History
DOWN EAST	Down East
DUQUESNE REV	Duquesne Review
DURHAM U J	Durham University Journal
E TENN HIST	East Tennesse History

EARLY AMER
  LIT   Early American Literature
ECON HIST
  REV   Economic Historical Review
EIGHTEENTH
  CENTURY   Eighteenth Century
EIRE-IRELAND   Eire-Ireland: A Journal of Irish Studies
ENG HIST
  REV   English Historical Review
ESSEX INST
  HIST COL   Essex Institute Historical Collections
EXPLORATIONS
  IN ECONOMIC
  HISTORY   Explorations in Economic History
FIDES ET
  HISTORY   Fides et History
FIELD ART J   Field Artillery Journal
FILSON CLUB
  Q   Filson Club Quarterly
FLA HIST Q   Florida Historical Quarterly
FORT TIC
  MUS BULL   Fort Ticonderoga Museum Bulletin
FRANCO-
  AMER REV   Franco-American Review
FRIENDS HIST
  ASSOC BULL   Friends Historical Association Bulletin
FOUNDATIONS   Foundations
GA HIST Q   Georgia History Quarterly
GA MA   Georgia Magazine
GA REV   Georgia Review
GA SOC SCI J   Georgia Social Science Journal
GEN MAG
  HIST
  CHRON   Genealogical Magazine and History Chronicle
GRANITE
  MONTHLY   Granite Monthly
GRANITE
  STATE   Granite State
GRANITE
  STATE MAG   Granite State Magazine
GREATER
  PHIL   Greater Philadelphia
HALVE MAEN   Halve Maen

HISP AMER	
HIST REV	Hispanic American Historical Review
HIST J	Historical Journal
HIST J WEST	
MASS	Historical Journal of Western Massachusetts
HIST MAG	Historical Magazine
HIST MAG	
PROT EPIS	Historical Magazine of the Protestant Episcopal
CHURCH	Church
HIST NH	Historical New Hampshire
HIST PAP LAN	
CTY HIST	Historical Papers of the Lancaster County
SOC	Historical Society
HIST	
REFLECTIONS	Historical Reflections
HIST SOC DEL	
PAP	Historical Society of Delaware Papers
HIST	
TEACHER	History Teacher
HIST TODAY	History Today
HISTORIAN	Historian
HISTORY	History
HUNT LIB Q	Huntington Library Quarterly
IND MAG	
HIST	Indiana Magazine History
IND MILT	
HIST J	Indiana Military History Journal
IND SOC	
STUD Q	Indiana Social Studies Quarterly
INF J	Infantry Journal
INTER HIST	
REV	International Historical Review
INTER REC	
MED	International Record of Medicine
INTER-AMER	
REV BIB	Inter-American Review of Bibliography
IRISH SWORD	Irish Sword
J AMER	
FOLKLORE	Journal of American Folklore
J AMER	
PHARM	Journal of the American Pharmaceutical
ASSOC	Association
J AMER STUD	Journal of American Studies

J BRIT STUD	Journal of British Studies
J CHURCH STATE	Journal of Church and State
J ECON HIST	Journal of Economic History
J ECON BUS HIST	Journal of Economic and Business History
J GEN ED	Journal of General Education
J HIST IDEAS	Journal of the History of Ideas
J HIST MED ALLIED SCI	Journal of the History of Medicine and Allied Sciences
J HIST STUD	Journal of Historical Studies
J ILL STATE HIST SOC	Journal of the Illinois State Historical Society
J IMP COM HIST	Journal of Imperial and Commonwealth History
J INTERDISP HIST	Journal of Interdisciplinary History
J IRISH AMER SOC	Journal of the Irish American Society
J LONG ISLAND HIST	Journal of Long Island History
J MED SOC NY	Journal of the Medical Society of New York
J MICH STATE HIST SOC	Journal of the Michigan State Historical Society
J MILT INST	Journal of the Military Institute
J MISS HIST	Journal of Mississippi History
J NEGRO EDUC	Journal of Negro Education
J NEGRO HIST	Journal of Negro History
J PRESBY HIST	Journal of Presbyterian History
J SOC HIST	Journal of Social History
J SPORTS HIST	Journal of Sports History
J URBAN HIST	Journal of Urban History
J WEST	Journal of the West
JAH	Journal of American History (1907–35)
JAH	Journal of American History (1964–)
JAMA	Journal of the American Medical Association
JOURN HIST	Journalism History
JOURN Q	Journalism Quarterly

JSAHR	Journal of the Society for Army Historical Research
JSH	Journal of Southern History
KENT HIST SOC REG	Kentucky Historical Society Register
LA HIST	Louisiana History
LA HIST Q	Louisiana History Quarterly
LA STUD	Louisiana Studies
LABOR HIST	Labor History
LAT AMER RES REV	Latin American Research Review
LIB CONG INFO BULL	Library of Congress Information Bulletin
LONG ISLAND HIST FORUM	Long Island History Forum
MAG AMER HIST	Magazine American History
MAG HIST	Magazine of History
MAINE HIST SO Q	Maine Historical Society Quarterly
MAINE HIST SOC COLL	Maine Historical Society Collections
MAINE HIST SOC PROC	Maine Historical Society Proceedings
MANUSCRIPTS	Manuscripts
MARINE CORPS GAZ	Marine Corps Gazette
MASS HIST SOC PROC	Massachusetts Historical Society Proceedings
MASS HIST SOC PUB	Massachusetts Historical Society Publications
MASS REV	Massachusetts Review
MD HIST MAG	Maryland Historical Magazine
MD HISTORIAN	Maryland Historian
MENNON HIST BULL	Mennonite History Bulletin
MENNON Q REV	Mennonite Quarterly Review
METH HIST	Methodist History
MICH HIST	Michigan History

MICH HIST COLL	Michigan Historical Collections
MICH HIST MAG	Michigan History Magazine
MID-AMER	Mid-America
MIDWEST Q	Midwest Quarterly
MILT AFF	Military Affairs
MILT COLL HIST	Military Collector and Historian
MILT ENG	Military Engineer
MILT REV	Military Review
MILT SURG	Military Surgeon
MINN HIST	Minnesota History
MISS HIST SOC BULL	Mississippi Historical Society Bulletin
MISS HIST SOC PUB	Mississippi Historical Society Publications
MISSOURI HISTORY	Missouri History
MM	Mariner's Mirror
MONT CTY HIST SOC BULL	Montgomery County Historical Society Bulletin
MORE BOOKS	More Books
MVHR	Mississippi Valley Historical Review
NAT GEO MAG	National Geographic Magazine
NAT MUS BULL	National Museum Bulletin
NAUT RES J	Nautical Research Journal
NAVAL CHRONICLE	Naval Chronicle
NAVAL WAR COLL REV	Naval War College Review
NC HIST REV	North Carolina Historical Review
NE GALAXY	New England Galaxy
NE HIST GEN REG	New England Historical and Genealogical Register
NE SOC STUD BULL	New England Social Studies Bulletin
NE SOC STUD J	New England Social Studies Journal
NEGRO HIST BULL	Negro History Bulletin

NEQ	New England Quarterly
NEW BRUNS HIST SOC	New Brunswick Historical Society
NEW HAVEN HIST SOC COLL	New Haven Historical Society Collection
NEWPORT HIST	Newport History
NH HIST SOC COLL	New Hampshire Historical Society Collections
NH HIST SOC PAP	New Hampshire Historical Society Papers
NH HIST SOC PROC	New Hampshire Historical Society Proceedings
NH PROFILES	New Hampshire Profiles
NIAG FRONTIER	Niagara Frontier
NJ HIST	New Jersey History
NJ HIST SOC PROC	New Jersey Historical Society Proceedings
NORTH JERSEY HIGHLANDER	North Jersey Highlander
NOVA SCOTIA HIST	Nova Scotia History
NOW AND THEN	Now and Then
NW OHIO Q	Northwest Ohio Quarterly
NY FOLKORE Q	New York Folkore Quarterly
NY HIST	New York History
NY HIST SOC COLL	New York Historical Society Collections
NY HIST SOC PROC	New York Historical Society Proceedings
NY PUB LIB BULL	New York Public Library Bulletin
NY STATE HIST ASSOC PROC	New York State Historical Association Proceedings
NY STATE HIST ASSOC Q J	New York State Historical Association Quarterly Journal

NY STATE LIB BULL	New York State Library Bulletin
NY STATE MED J	New York State Medical Journal
OHIO ARCH HIST Q	Ohio Archeological Historical Quarterly
ONTARIO HIST SOC PAP	Ontario Historical Society Papers
ONTARIO HISTORY	Ontario History
PA HIST	Pennsylvania History
PA MENNONITE HERITAGE	Pennsylvania Mennonite Heritage
PA MHB	Pennsylvania Magazine of History and Biography
PAC HIST REV	Pacific Historical Review
PAP BIB SOC AMER	Papers of the Bibliographical Society of America
PAP GER SOC PROC	Papers of the German Society Proceedings
PAP MICH AC SC ART LET	Papers of the Michigan Academy of Science, Arts, and Letters
PARAMETERS	Parameters
PAST AND PRESENT	Past and Present
PERSP AMER HIST	Perspectives in American History
POL AMER STUD	Polish American Studies
POL SCI Q	Political Science Quarterly
POLISH REV	Polish Review
PRESBY HIST SOC J	Presbyterian Historical Society Journal
PRINCETON U LIB CHRON	Princeton University Library Chronicle
PROC WEST SOC FR HIST	Proceedings of the Western Society of French Historians
PROLOGUE	Prologue
Q J LIB CONG	Quarterly Journal of the Library of Congress
Q J SPEECH	Quarterly Journal of Speech
QUAKER HIST	Quaker History

REV AMER HIST	Reviews in American History
REV POL	Review of Politics
RI HIST	Rhode Island History
RI HIST MAG	Rhode Island Historical Magazine
RI HIST SOC COLL	Rhode Island Historical Society Collections
RI HIST SOC PUB	Rhode Island Historical Society Publications
RI HIST TRACTS	Rhode Island Historical Tracts
RI JEW HIST NOTES	Rhode Island Jewish History Notes
RI JEW HIST SOC	Rhode Island Jewish Historical Society
RICHMOND CTY HIST	Richmond County History
ROCH HIST SOC PUB	Rochester History Society Publications
ROYAL SOC CAN TRANS	Royal Society of Canada Transactions
RURAL SOC	Rural Sociology
RUSS REV	Russian Review
S ATL Q	South Atlantic Quarterly
S CAL Q	Southern California Quarterly
SAT EVE POST	Saturday Evening Post
SC HIST ASSOC PROC	South Carolina Historical Association Proceedings
SC HIST ILLUS	South Carolina History Illustrated
SC HIST MAG	South Carolina Historical and Genealogical Magazine
SCOTTISH HIST REV	Scottish Historical Review
SCRIBNER'S MAG	Scribner's Magazine
SLAVIC REV	Slavic Review
SMITHSONIAN	Smithsonian
SOC SCI Q	Social Science Quarterly
SOC STUD	Social Studies
SOCIETAS: A REVIEW OF SOCIAL HISTORY	Societas: A Review of Social History

SOUTHERN STUDIES	Southern Studies
SOUTHWEST HIST Q	Southwest Historical Quarterly
STUDIES IN EIGHTEENTH CENTURY CULTURE	Studies in Eighteenth Century Culture
TECH CULT	Technology and Culture
TENN HIST Q	Tennessee History Quarterly
TRANS MORAVIAN HIST SOC	Transactions of the Moravian Historical Society
TRANS MORAVIAN SOC	Transactions of the Moravian Society
TRANS STUD COLL PHYS PHIL	Transactions and the Studies of the College of Physicians of Philadelphia
TRINITY COLL HIST PAP	Trinity College Historical Papers
TYLER' S Q HIST GEN MAG	Tyler's Quarterly Historical and Genealogical Magazine
UNI BUFF STUD	University of Buffalo Studies
US CATH HIST SOC REV	United States Catholic Historical Society Review
USNIP	United States Naval Institute Proceedings
VA CAV	Virginia Cavalcade
VA HIST SOC COLL	Virginia Historical Society Collections
VA MHB	Virginia Magazine of History and Biography
VA Q R	Virginia Quarterly Review
VT HIST	Vermont History
VT HIST Q	Vermont Historical Quarterly
VT HIST SOC	Vermont Historical Society
VT HIST SOC PROC	Vermont Historical Society Proceedings
VT LIFE	Vermont Life

I

CAUSES OF THE WAR

A. GENERAL BACKGROUND

1. Adams, Randolph G. POLITICAL IDEAS OF THE AMERICAN REVOLUTION: BRITANNIC-AMERICAN CONTRIBUTIONS TO THE PROBLEMS OF IMPERIAL ORGANIZATION, 1765-1775. Durham: Trinity College Press, 1922.

   Examining Anglo-American relations in the pre-war decade, the author claims that if the British had not insisted on re-taining sovereignty and had not refused to delegate authority in the colonies, American independence would not have occurred. Coherent, gracefully written, and based on a wide range of material, this volume has some enlightening chapters.

2. Adams, Thomas R. AMERICAN INDEPENDENCE: THE GROWTH OF AN IDEA: A BIBLIOGRAPHICAL STUDY OF THE AMERICAN POLITICAL PAMPHLETS PRINTED BETWEEN 1764 AND 1776 DEALING WITH THE DISPUTE BE-TWEEN GREAT BRITAIN AND HER COLONIES. Providence: Brown University Press, 1965.

   This key work contains 231 entries about pamphlets that were influential in the revolutionary debate. The book is an es-sential tool in tracing the development of political concepts. A single printing of a pamphlet may have had greater influence than several editions of another. This invaluable book sug-gests where the items can be located.

3. Bailyn, Bernard. EDUCATION IN THE FORMING OF AMERICAN SOCIETY. NEEDS AND OPPORTUNITIES FOR STUDY. Chapel Hill: The Univer-sity of North Carolina Press, 1960.

   Here is a fine summary of developments in colonial education as a contributing factor in the formation of American character. The author traces the English background, dissenting academics, English missionaries, the quality and transplantation of culture, the financing of education, and the role of education in the Revolution.

4. Barrow, Thomas C. TRADE AND EMPIRE; THE BRITISH CUSTOMS SER-VICE IN COLONIAL AMERICA, 1660-1775. Cambridge: Harvard University Press, 1967.

   Barrow dramatically illustrates the conflict between central authority and local attitudes in the colonies as the constant

3

source of contention. This was the first definitive monograph
on the judicial handling of the Navigation Acts and their
enforcement. Nicely written, fully annotated, this study is
highly recommended.

5. Bell, Herbert C. "The West Indian Trade Before the American
    Revolution." AHR, 22 (1918), 272-287.

    Here is a good examination of the importance of flour and
    rum in the commerce of a great mercantile system.

6. Bridenbaugh, Carl. CITIES IN REVOLT: URBAN LIFE IN AMERICA,
    1743-1776. New York: Alfred A. Knopf, 1955.

    The author examines society in Boston, Newport, New York,
    Philadelphia, and Charleston to provide a thoughtful summary of
    social-cultural life on the eve of the revolution. The cities
    provided the political leadership for the turmoil in 1775.
    This is a lively, cogent, and nicely organized volume that
    explains much about Americans.

7. Broeze, Frank J.A., Peter D. McClelland, Gary M. Walton,
    and David J. Loschky. "The New Economic Theory, the Navi-
    gation Acts, and the Continental Tobacco Market, 1770-1790,"
    ECON HIST REV, 26 (1973), 668-678.

    Here are four thoughtful articles centered on the theme of
    the influence of a major commodity in imperial trade.

8. Carter, Clarence E. "The Significance of the Military Office
    In America, 1763-1775." AHR, 28 (1923), 457-488.

    By the eve of war, the Commander-In-Chief of British forces
    had acquired increasing judicial, administrative, and geo-
    graphic responsibilities.

9. Clark, Dora Mae. "The British Treasury and the Administration
    of Military Affairs in America, 1754-1774." PA HIST, 2
    (1935), 197-204.

    The Treasury was highly influential in controlling policies
    for British troops in North America.

10. ———. THE RISE OF THE BRITISH TREASURY: COLONIAL ADMINIS-
     TRATION IN THE EIGHTEENTH CENTURY. New Haven: Yale Uni-
     versity Press, 1960.

     This classic work demonstrates that financial affairs were
     dominant in the Colonial Office by placing the Grenville
     program into clearer perspective. The book shows the influ-
     ence of lesser officials like Charles Jenkinson and John
     Robinson in formulating policies for the government. Some-
     what ponderous and occasionally dull, nevertheless, this
     study sheds light on London officialdom.

11.   Cole, W.A. "Trends in Eighteenth Century Smuggling." ECON
      HIST REV, 10 (1957-58), 395-410.

      The stress here is on the lucrative contraband in tea.

12.   Dickerson, Oliver M. THE NAVIGATION ACT AND THE AMERICAN REV-
      OLUTION. Philadelphia: University of Pennsylvania Press,
      1951.

      Incorporating in this seminal work his wide-ranging inter-
      ests, Dickerson finds the Act imposed few hardships before
      1763, except on tea and molasses. The Customs was well en-
      forced, and few objections surfaced in the colonies; the Acts
      were "the cement of empire" binding the colonists to England.
      The changes came with the Sugar Act (1764), a separate Board
      of Customs at Boston (1767), and the Townshend Acts which
      caused wide-spread resentment. As the British strove to
      invigorate their trade controls and imposed stricter penalites
      for violations, the Act became a target of revolutionary
      ideology.

13.   ————. "Writs of Assistance as a Cause of the Revolution,"
      in Richard B. Morris, ed. THE ERA OF THE AMERICAN REVOLU-
      TION: STUDIES INSCRIBED TO EVARTS B. GREENE. New York:
      Columbia University Press, 1939, pp. 40-75.

      Dickerson traces the evolution of the judicial device in the
      colonies to enforce compliance to Customs regulations.

14.   Ernst, Joseph Albert. MONEY AND POLITICS IN AMERICA, 1755-
      1775: A STUDY IN THE CURRENCY ACT OF 1768 AND THE POLITICAL
      ECONOMY OF REVOLUTION. Chapel Hill: University of North
      Carolina Press, 1976.

      Claiming that a fundamental conflict of interests between
      British and American commercial classes existed, Ernst pro-
      vides a sound economic interpretation of the Revolution. The
      amount of research about the Board of Trade, paper currency
      issues, and exchange rates is awesome. Somewhat vague in
      key passages, this work is not for novices.

15.   Gipson, Lawrence H. THE BRITISH EMPIRE BEFORE THE AMERICAN
      REVOLUTION. 15 vols. Vols. 1-3. Caldwell, Idaho: The
      Caxton Printers, Ltd., 1935. Vols. 4-15. New York: Alfred
      A. Knopf, 1939-70.

      This magisterial work is the best study about the British
      Empire in the eighteenth-century. Volumes 1-3 survey the
      Empire prior to 1748; volumes 4-8 treat the Seven Years War;
      volumes 9-12 cover the coming of the Revolution; volume 13
      is a summary of the series; volume 14 is a bibliographic guide
      of published works; and volume 15 is a bibliographic guide of
      manuscripts. This work shows a superb sweep of history, an
      unsurpassed knowledge of source material, and a sparkling
      prose style. Gipson stressed the fact that the American

Revolution should be viewed from an "imperial" context. The
mercantile order seemed sturdy and reliable. Hence, Gipson
sought to discover why only the thirteen colonies seceded.
There are many answers provided here, but basic is that after
1763 the Americans were unable to convince the Crown that
British policy was inimical to colonial interests. Furthermore, Britain was unwilling to adjust to an empire of
autonomous units.

16.   ———. THE COMING OF THE REVOLUTION, 1763-1775. New York:
       Harper and Brothers, 1954.

Gipson demonstrates the results of a research career devoted to examining the intricate British-colonial relationships. This work is convincing, judicious and especially
valuable for graduate students and specialists. Gipson was
particularly astute in explaining the imperial viewpoint
while simultaneously clarifying the colonists' attitudes.
The book is formidable to read, but it is essential to comprehend the long-range causes of the war.

17.   Goebel, Dorothy Borne. "The 'New England Trade' and the
       French West Indies, 1763-1774. A Study in Trade Policies."
       WMQ, 20 (1963), 331-372.

French efforts to modify British regulations (at two
Caribbean ports) had significant implications for the American procurement of war material after 1775.

18.   Greene, Jack P. "'A Posture of Hostility': A Reconsidera-
       tion of Some Aspects of the Origins of the American Revo-
       lution." AMER ANTIQ SOC PROC, 87 (1977), 27-68.

The British imperial reforms in 1748-56 were central to the
causal pattern of growing American resistance as Crown officials tended to stifle opposition.

19.   ———. "An Uneasy Connection. An Analysis of the Pre-
       Conditions of the American Revolution." In Stephen G.
       Kurtz, and James H. Hutson, eds. ESSAYS ON THE AMERICAN
       REVOLUTION. Chapel Hill: The University of North Carolina
       Press, 1973, pp. 33-80.

Greene provides a superb synthesis of the many factors
(increase in wealth, the power of elites, development of
local governments) to explore the long-range causes of the
rebellion.

20.   ———. "Autonomy and Stability: New England and The
       British Colonial Experience in Early Modern America."
       J SOC HIST, 7 (1974), 171-194.

Greene reviews four recent works to examine the meaning of
New England sectionalism and uniqueness.

THE WAR OF
THE AMERICAN REVOLUTION

VT Q	Vermont Quarterly
VERMONTER	Vermonter
W TENN HIST SOC PAPER	West Tennessee Historical Society Papers
W VA HIST	West Virginia History
WASAGA THE IND HIST	Wasaga, the Indian Historian
WEATHERWISE	Weatherwise
WESLEYAN HIST SOC PROC	Wesleyan Historical Society Proceedings
WESLEYAN Q REV	Wesleyan Quarterly Review
WEST HIST	Western History
WEST HIST Q	Western Historical Quarterly
WEST PA HIST MAG	West Pennsylvania Historical Magazine
WIS MAG HIST	Wisconsin Magazine of History
WIS STATE HIST SOC PROC	Wisconsin State Historical Society Proceedings
WMQ	William and Mary Quarterly
WORLD POL	World Politics
YALE REV	Yale Review

21. ———. "Changing Interpretations of Early American
     Politics," in Ray A. Hungtington, ed. THE REINTERPRETATION
     OF EARLY AMERICAN HISTORY. San Marino, California: The
     Huntington Library, 1966, pp. 151-184.

     Here is a fascinating commentary about the formation of
     colonial political elites.

22. ———. "The Flight from Determinism: A Review of the Re-
     cent Literature on the Coming of the American Revolution."
     S ATL Q, 61 (1962), 235-257.

     Greene notes the influence of the "Namieristic" stress on
     the structure of British politics in contrast to several
     other historical viewpoints with more sophistication and
     less economic emphasis.

23. ———. "The Plunge of Lemmings: A Consideration of Recent
     Writings on British Politics and the American Revolution."
     S ATL Q, 67 (1968), 141-175.

     In an excellent survey of interpretations, Greene notes
     that the Revolution was "a conservative and defensive move-
     ment against recent provocations by the mother country."

24. ———. "The Seven Years' War and the American Revolution:
     The Casual Relationship Reconsidered." J IMP COM HIST,
     8 (1980), 85-105.

     The conflict caused an awareness of American interests and
     increased colonial post-war expectations.

25. ———. "The Social Origins of the American Revolution: An
     Evaluation and an Interpretation." POL SCI Q, 88 (1973),
     1-23.

     This is a key article which deftly summarizes the schools
     of historic thought about the Revolution's origins - the
     Progressives, Namierites, Imperialists, neo-Whigs, and
     several others interpretations; Greene opts for the current
     theory of "modernization."

26. ———· "Virginia Political Culture in the Era of the Ameri-
     can Revolution," VA Q R, 44 (1968), 302-310.

     Greene stresses the ideals of order, justice, and an open
     society of virtuous men as a major theme of Virginia's lead-
     ers.

27. Hacker, Louis M. "The First American Revolution." COL U Q,
     27 (1935), 259-283.

     Hacker concentrated on the viewpoints of the American mer-
     chant class and stressed economic issues.

28. Harper, Lawrence A. THE ENGLISH NAVIGATION LAWS, A SEVEN-
     TEENTH-CENTURY EXPERIMENT IN SOCIAL ENGINEERING. New York:
     Oxford University Press, 1940.

     This Herculean task of assessing the laws and amendments
     of complex legislation merits praise. Showing exceptions to
     the law, citing conflicting evidence about key decisions,
     Harper discourses about the regulations on trade and ship-
     ping, concluding that the exact effectiveness of the Acts
     remains in doubt. Thoroughly documented, highly readable,
     this essential work is a model of clarity.

29. Henretta, James A. "SALUTARY NEGLECT": COLONIAL ADMIN-
     ISTRATION UNDER THE DUKE OF NEWCASTLE. Princeton:
     Princeton University Press, 1972.

     Examining the Duke's role as chief architect of colonial
     policy and the neglect of enforcement by English official-
     dom, Henretta questions why more reforms failed to occur.
     There is much data here about domestic politics, Crown
     patronage, and imperial programs. The work has detailed
     footnotes, and an ample bibliography. It should be con-
     sulted by specialists.

30. Humphreys, R.A. "British Colonial Policy and the American
     Revolution, 1763-1776." HISTORY, 19 (1934-35), 42-48.

     Commenting on Namier's influence on history, Humphreys as-
     serts that more study of the 1770-1774 period is needed.

31. Jensen, Merrill. THE FOUNDING OF A NATION; A HISTORY OF
     THE AMERICAN REVOLUTION. New York: Oxford University
     Press, 1968.

     In a lengthy narrative of excellent political history,
     Jensen almost suggests that the war merely consolidated
     changes in society that were accomplished or were being com-
     pleted. Major events are covered briefly; here is an ex-
     cellent selection of contemporary literature; and there are
     ample details on some key events. But Jensen leaves the
     reader uncertain of his standards of judgment, and what
     audience he aims for is unclear. Yet this work shows a vast
     knowledge of the field, it provides penetrating insights
     into many realms of thought, and it demonstrates massive
     research. The opinions rendered in the important study are
     lucid, judicious, and demonstrate an impressive knowledge
     of the source materials.

32. Kammen, Michael G. A ROPE OF SAND; THE COLONIAL AGENTS,
     BRITISH POLITICS, AND THE AMERICAN REVOLUTION. Ithaca:
     Cornell University Press, 1968.

     Here is a scholarly study of agents who lobbied for their
     colonies in London. This is not easy reading, and the
     expositions are long and are sometimes rambling. The

author carefully probes the intricacies of British politics
and the decline of the influence of these agents by 1774.
The biographical data accumulated is impressive, and the
presentation of the agents as a coherent interest group
is well-handled.

33. Kellogg, Louise Phelps. "A Footnote to the Quebec Act,"
    CAN HIST REV, 13 (1932), 147-156.

    This is a good summary of the problems the British had
    with French Canadians in the Illinois Country.

34. King, Joseph E. "The Real Quebec Act." MID-AMERICA, 34
    (1952), 14-41.

    This is one of the best analysis of the controversial
    legislation that had ramifications in religion, Indian re-
    lationships, political jurisdictions, and as a cause of
    the Revolution.

35. Knollenberg, Bernhard. ORIGINS OF THE AMERICAN REVOLUTION,
    1759-1776. New York: Macmillan Publishing Co., 1960.

    The author uses original sources to demonstrate that
    little sentiment for independence existed to 1763. In 1759
    trouble began with British military triumphs, and Ministe-
    rial reluctance to placate the colonists. The author cites
    a number of famous incidents, their ramifications in com-
    merce, justice, church affairs, and land claims which all
    heightened the friction. The issue of taxation and relations
    with the army are carefully noted here. While much of
    this pre-Stamp Act tension is familiar, this is a cogent
    and analytical summary of developments written by a master
    historian.

36. Labaree, Leonard W. ROYAL INSTRUCTIONS TO BRITISH COLONIAL
    GOVERNORS, 1670-1776. New York: D. Appleton-Century Co.,
    1935.

    Here are the replicas of the commissions and instructions
    by the Crown to its American governors, providing them,
    thereby, with a constitutional guide. The author has col-
    lated some 1,100 items covering areas from Nova Scotia to
    the Barbados. Superbly indexed and cross-referenced, this
    work is a useful guide, and the result of prodigious re-
    search.

37. Lockridge, Kenneth A. "Social Change and the Meaning of
    the American Revolution," J SOC HIST, 6 (1973), 403-439.

    In a highly theoretical essay, the author examines
    aspects of colonial society undergoing changes that led to
    the Revolution.

38. Lokken, Roy N. "The Concept of Democracy in Colonial Poli-
     tical Thought." WMQ, (1959), 568-580.

     The colonial assemblies were the counterpart of the House
     of Commons, and "democracy" already existed before 1775.

39. Lucas, Paul. "A Note on the Comparative Study on the
     Structure of Politics in Mid-Eighteenth Century Britain
     and its American Colonies." WMQ, 28 (1971), 301-309.

     Comparing the approaches of Bernard Bailyn and Jack
     Greene, Lucas is convinced that Greene's stress on "new
     men" in colonial politics is the key.

40. McIlwain, Charles Howard. AMERICAN REVOLUTION; A CON-
     STITUTIONAL HISTORY. New York: Macmillan Publishing
     Co., 1923.

     After an involved and learned comparison of the conflict-
     ing constitutional claims of America and Britain, the
     author supports the colonial claim of freedom from Parlia-
     mentary control. Written mainly from the angle of con-
     stitutional law, McIlwain demonstrated an impressive flair
     for summarizing complex issues and in transmitting his
     enthusiasm. Here one finds a thesis clearly defined,
     arguments cogently explained, and a firm grasp of the
     documentation demonstrated.

41. Maier, Pauline. FROM RESISTANCE TO REVOLUTION; COLONIAL
     RADICALS AND THE DEVELOPMENT OF AMERICAN OPPOSITION TO
     BRITAIN, 1765-1776. New York: Alfred A. Knopf, 1972.

     In a seminal contribution to the literature, the author
     focuses on the radical Sons of Liberty to examine why and
     how they functioned. Usually obscure men, they informed
     the populace in a hundred places about British tyranny.
     Maier is especially clever, in this very readable work,
     in tracing the network of their membership, and how they
     presented their concepts of liberty. They believed in
     "ordered resistance" and their support came from the
     "crowd." The evidence is carefully mustered, the ap-
     pendices list memberships in the radical clubs, and the
     bibliography is extensive.

42. Martin, Alfred S. "The King's Customs: Philadelphia,
     1763-1774." WMQ, 5 (1948), 200-216.

     An account by John Swift, a revenue collector, demon-
     strates the erosion of the British Customs service by
     1774.

43. Metzger, Charles Henry. THE QUEBEC ACT, A PRIMARY CAUSE
     OF THE AMERICAN REVOLUTION. New York: E.P. Herbermann,
     1936.

The author has meticulously compiled an interesting summary from contemporary evidence (sermons, newspaper, town
meetings, colonial assemblies) to demonstrate the degree of
bigotry and religious intolerance that typified Protestant
colonials in response to the Act. Unfortunately, Metzger
overstated his thesis, tended to ignore other factors that
led to revolution, and, he did not demonstrate if the Act
was actually a primary influence. However, this is a well-
researched volume that should be perused.

44. Miller, John Chester. ORIGINS OF THE AMERICAN REVOLUTION.
     New York: Atlantic Monthly Press, 1943.

     This is one of the best works for beginners on the pre-
     1775 era. It is witty, lively, and replete with thoughtful
     passages. There are vivid portraits here of key British
     and American political figures that are blended in a con-
     cise and spirited narrative. The book provides many
     penetrating insights about the breakdown of imperial re-
     lationships with the colonies in well-organized chapters.

45. Morgan, Edmund S. "The American Revolution: Revisions in
     Need of Revision." WMQ, 14 (1973), 3-15.

     In a major article, Morgan summarizes various interpre-
     tations and calls for a closer study of local institutions
     in America for clues about the causes.

46. Nettels, Curtis P. "British Mercantilisms and the Economic
     Development of the Thirteen Colonies." J ECON HIST, 12
     (1952), 105-114.

     This is a good summary of the views of Lawrence A. Harper
     and Oliver M. Dickerson on the effects of the Navigation
     Acts upon the colonies.

47. Ritcheson, Charles R. BRITISH POLICIES AND THE AMERICAN
     REVOLUTION. Norman: University of Oklahoma Press, 1954.

     This is a fine account which breaks the stereotype views
     of Burke, North, and George III, and it illuminates the
     efforts of Grenville to reform the British colonial system.
     The material on peace proposals is lucid as is the material
     about how the Crown's Ministers attempted to cope with suc-
     cessive crises. Though the writer overlooked some per-
     tinent studies on this topic, nevertheless, he examined a
     mass of public and private papers to present a readable
     and intimate picture of British politics.

48. Rossiter, Clinton L. SEEDTIME OF THE REPUBLIC, THE ORIGINS
     OF THE AMERICAN TRADITION OF POLITICAL LIBERTY. New
     York: Harcourt, Brace and Co., 1953.

     Here is an excellent background study about the develop-
     ment of liberty in the colonies, the evolution of political

theories, and the influence of these themes in practice.
Rossiter has compiled a neat compendium of American liter-
ate opinion on politics which shows enormous research. This
work is for specialists who will appreciate that, even with
imprecisions here about the meaning of natural law and
natural rights, it is engrossing and thoughtful about the
political ideas of the era.

49. Savelle, Max. SEEDS OF LIBERTY, THE GENESIS OF THE AMERI-
     CAN MIND. Seattle: University of Washington Press, 1965.

     Savelle searched for colonial attitudes to demonstrate
     "the American way of life," and a pattern of American cul-
     ture. His summary of how common ideals and attitudes
     emerged by the 1760s is refreshing. This very cogent work
     is stimulating, nicely written, and it explains much about
     the formation of a distinct American character.

50. Shade, William G., ed. "Lawrence Henry Gipson: Four Dim-
     ensions." PA HIST, 36 (1969), 7-79.

     Here is a fine summary of Gipson's seminal volumes on the
     British empire.

51. Smelser, Marshall. "An Understanding of the American
     Revolution." REV POL, 38 (1976), 297-312.

     This article would be useful for high-schoolers.

52. Sosin, Jack M. AGENTS AND MERCHANTS, BRITISH COLONIAL
     POLICY AND THE ORIGINS OF THE AMERICAN REVOLUTION, 1763-
     1775. Lincoln: University of Nebraska Press, 1965.

     If one desires a book with information of how Whitehall
     viewed American problems, then this volume is recommended.
     Sosin provides an excellent summary of how Secretaries of
     State and other key figures formulated and implemented
     policies. The data on lobbies and colonial agents is
     especially useful. Very good on British sources and
     perspectives, the work is weak on American attitudes.

53. ------. "Imperial Regulation of Colonial Paper Money, 1764-
     1773." PA MHB,   88, (1964), 174-198.

     The British regulation of provincial currency exacerbated
     tension; the Currency Act of 1764 defined Parliamentary
     supremacy in such matters.

54. Warren, Winslow. "The Colonial Customs Service in Mass-
     achusetts in Its Relation to the American Revolution."
     MASS HIST SOC PROC, 46, (1912-13), 440-474.

     Arguments over revenue matters from 1650 to 1775 demon-
     strated a continuous debate between the colonies and London.

B. AMERICAN RESISTANCE BEFORE THE STAMP ACT

55. Andrews, Charles M. "The American Revolution: An Inter-
     pretation." AHR, 31 (1926), 219-232.

     The author faults Britain's ruling class and claims that
     the colonists were justified in revolting.

56. ———' THE COLONIAL BACKGROUND OF THE AMERICAN REVOLU-
     TION. New Haven: Yale University Press, 1924.

     Andrews viewed the Revolution as part of man's inevitable
     march toward progress. The author saw Americans as a chosen
     people whose desire to terminate the tyranny of George III
     was reinforced by environmental factors. Though this work
     may now seem outdated, it has an interesting perspective
     and was soundly written.

57. Appleby, Joyce. "The Social Origins of American Revolu-
     tionary Ideology." JAH, 64 (1978), 935-958.

     This is an excellent critique of the views of numerous
     historians who have commented on the colonial mercantilistic
     movement.

58. Bailyn, Bernard. "Political Experience and Enlighten-
     ment Ideas in Eighteenth Century America." AHR, 67
     (1962), 339-351.

     Because so many institutional reforms had occurred by
     1775, the Revolution was basically a matter of doctrine
     and ideas.

59. ———. THE IDEOLOGICAL ORIGINS OF THE AMERICAN REVOLU-
     TION. Cambridge, Harvard University Press, 1967.

     There are brilliant chapters here about colonial con-
     ceptions of power and liberty, the rationale for rebel-
     lion, and the vision of a self-governing republic. Bailyn
     shows the impact of ideology on slavery, religion, the
     rise of democracy, and the erosion of differential social
     practices. Avoiding cliches and stereotypes in this fine
     synthesis about the influence of ideas, Bailyn perceives
     the nature of the rebellion. The work is fully documented,
     well-conceived, and it demonstrates a commendable attempt
     to comprehend the political rhetoric of the eighteenth-
     century.

60. ———. "The Origins of American Politics." PERSP. AMER
     HIST, 1 (1967), 9-120.

     Here is a masterly summary of colonial political theory
     that is one of the best articles of its kind on "political
     theory".

61. Barrow, Thomas C. "A Project For Imperial Reform: Hints
    Respecting the Settlement for Our American Province,
    1763." WMQ, 24 (1967), 108-126.

    This proposal was written by William Knox, Under-Secre-
    tary of State for America.

62. ———. "Background to the Grenville Program, 1756-1763,"
    WMQ, 22 (1965), 93-104.

    The essay covers illicit trade, the Sugar Act, and the
    resulting colonial discontent.

63. ———. TRADE AND EMPIRE: THE BRITISH CUSTOMS SERVICE
    IN COLONIAL AMERICA, 1660-1775. Cambridge: Harvard
    University Press, 1967.

    The author explains that the British empire could not
    have been a true mercantile empire because the American
    colonies could never be forced to play the role which
    contemporary economic theory required. Barrow carefully
    examines the structure of British-American trade and com-
    merce and demonstrates why the relationship was doomed.
    This was the first definite monograph on the subject and
    though it sheds little new on colonial relations, the
    volume is excellent in covering English political forces,
    the Navigation Acts, the development of specialized bu-
    reaucracies, and mercantilistic thought. The bibliography
    is carefully annotated.

64. Beer, George L. BRITISH COLONIAL POLICY, 1754-1765. New
    York: Macmillan and Co., 1907.

    This work was probably the first detailed and systematic
    study of British thought on the topic. Beer tried to as-
    certain what colonial policy meant to officials formulating
    a program. Though the writing is ponderous, and the view-
    point almost entirely pro-English, this work is a well-
    reasoned, convincing argument about the benefits of eight-
    eenth-century imperialism.

65. Brooke, John. "Burke in the 1700's." S ATL Q, 68 (1959),
    548-555.

    The essay concerns Burke's professional correspondence
    which demonstrates the workings of a very fertile mind in
    politics.

66. Buel, Richard, Jr. "Democracy and the American Revolu-
    tion: A Frame of Reference." WMQ, 21 (1964), 165-190.

    The Americans were familiar with the contract theory of
    politics, the extension of the franchise, and the practice
    of representation.

67. Chafee, Zachariah, Jr. "Colonial Courts and the Common
    Law." MASS HIST SOC PROC, 68 (1944-47), 132-159.

    Examining four meanings of common law, the author notes
    that the colonists adapted it to a new environment.

68. Christie, Ian and Benjamin W. Labaree. EMPIRE OR INDE-
    PENDENCE, 1760-1887; A BRITISH AMERICAN DIALOGUE ON THE
    COMING OF THE AMERICAN REVOLUTION. New York: W.W. Norton
    and Co., 1976.

    Here is a very sophisticated analysis about the coming
    of the Revolution. The commentary on key legislation and
    the ensuing results is very perceptive. Labaree stresses
    ideology and Christie the taxation issue to show that the
    Revolution was not inevitable. This is a fully docu-
    mented account that is readable and perceptive.

69. Dion, Leon. "Natural Law and Manifest Destiny in the Era
    of the American Revolution." CAN J ECON POL SCI, 23
    (1959), 227-247.

    The British colonies were considered by European intel-
    lectuals as the promise of a new beginning for western
    civilization.

70. Ernst, Joseph. "A Genesis of the Currency Act of 1764:
    Virginia Paper Money and the Protection of British In-
    vestments." WMQ, 22 (1965), 33-94.

    The compromise between London merchants and Virginia
    planters over legal tender for private debts was a failure.

71. ————. "The Currency Act Repeal Movement: A Study of
    Imperial Politics and Revolutionary Crisis, 1764-1767."
    WMQ, 25 (1968), 177-211.

    The currency question became entangled in the dispute
    over parliamentary taxation.

72. Fergusson, James R. "Reason in Madness: The Political
    Thought of James Otis." WMQ, 36 (1979), 194-214.

    Four tracts written by Otis in 1764-65 show distinct
    political theories regarding the right to tax.

73. Fiore, Jordon D. "The Temple-Bernard Affair: A Royal
    Custom House Scandal in Essex County." ESSEX HIST INST
    COLL, 90 (1954), 58-63.

    Quarrels between Massachusetts Governor Bernard and the
    Surveyor-General of the Customs over bribes and the dis-
    position of court cases led to Bernard's downfall.

74. Gipson, Lawrence H. "Aspects of the Beginning of the American Revolution in Massachusetts Bay, 1760-1761." AMER ANTIQ SOC PROC, 67 (1957), 11-32.

    In a key general court decision, James Otis contended that Parliament was limited in its power of extending British regulations to the colonies.

75. ————. "The American Revolution as an Aftermath of the Great War for the Empire, 1754-1763." SOC SCI Q, 65 (1950), 86-104.

    This is a convenient summary of Gipson's vast research which demonstrates how a war can modify thought and institutions.

76. Greene, Jack P. THE QUEST FOR POWER THE LOWER HOUSES OF ASSEMBLY IN THE SOUTHERN ROYAL COLONIES, 1689-1776. Chapel Hill: University of North Carolina Press, 1963.

    Here is a superb study about the growing influence of assemblies in four colonies. Most of the book is devoted to examining the specific powers acquired by these houses and to determining the extent of their authority by 1763. The book offers fresh insights, is well reasoned, demonstrates an enviable command of archival sources, and it is lucidly organized. This is a key work that should be consulted by specialists.

77. ————. "Search for Identity: An Interpretation of the Meaning of Selected Patterns, of Social Response in Eighteenth-Century America." J SOC HIST, 3 (1970), 189-220.

    Greene examines the tensions arising between optimism about an American identity and the pervasive sense of frustration in the colonies.

78. ————. "The Social Origins of the American Revolution: An Evaluation and an Interpretation." POL SCI Q, 88 (1973), 1-22.

    The author doubts if historians can assign any "of the components of social strain ... " as factors in causing the war.

79. Harper, Lawrence A. "Mercantilism and the American Revolution." CAN HIST REV, 22 (1943), 1-15.

    England handled imperial programs well until 1764, but thereafter the government bungled.

80. ————. "The Effect of the Navigation Acts on the Thirteen
    Colonies." See entry 13, pp. 3-33.

    Constant changes in imperial regulations caused increas-
    ing friction.

81. Hickman, Emily. "Colonial Writs of Assistance." NEQ, 5
    (1932), 83-104.

    Here is a valuable explanation of the origins, use, and
    results of the writs that created additional colonial
    resistance.

82. Hughes, Edward. "The English Stamp Act Duties, 1664-1764."
    ENG HIST REV, 56 (1941), 234-264.

    This is an excellent discussion of the antecedents of the
    famous Stamp Act with lists of the duties on licences and
    documents.

83. Jacobson, David L. "John Dickinson's Fight Against Royal
    Government, 1764." WMQ, 19 (1963), 64-85.

    Here is a detailed examination of the Franklin-Galloway
    plan to replace Pennsylvania's proprietary system with a
    royal government.

84. Jellison, Richard M., and Jack Greene. "The Currency Act
    of 1764 in Imperial-Colonial Relations, 1764-1776."
    WMQ, 18 (1961), 465-518.

    Colonial grievances over the Act convinced Americans that
    London failed to comprehend imperial problems.

85. Johnson, Allen S. "The Passage of the Sugar Act." WMQ,
    16 (1959), 507-514.

    Then considered minor legislation, the Act was the most
    significant measure enacted by Parliament in 1764.

86. Johnson, Herbert A., and David Syrett. "Some Nice Quillets
    of the Customs Law: The New York Affair, 1763-1767."
    WMQ, 25 (1968), 432-451.

    This was a key legal matter involving a ship carrying
    European merchandise that had not cleared through an
    English port.

87. King, Joseph Edward. "Judicial Flotsam in Massachusetts
    Bay." NEQ, 27 (1959), 365-381.

    Here is good coverage of major legal cases handled by
    the Massachusetts-Bay Vice Admiralty District, a (jury-
    less) branch of the High Court of Admiralty.

88. Klein, Milton M. "Prelude to Revolution in New York: Jury
     Trial and Judicial Tenure." WMQ, 17 (1950), 439-462.

     The capable New York lawyers developed, in the Forsey case
     and quarrels with the Lieutenant-Governor, the constitu-
     tional grounds for revolution.

89. Liddle, William D. "'Virtue and Liberty': An Inquiry into
     the role of the Agrarian Myth in the Rhetoric of the
     American Revolutionary Era." S ATL Q, 17 (1978), 15-38.

     The colonists had an agrarian conception of their society
     and disliked British political corruption.

90. Lovejoy, David S. "Rights Imply Equality: The Case Against
     Admiralty Jurisdiction in America, 1764-1766." WMQ,
     16 (1959), 459-484.

     American jurists argued that courts exercised authority
     beyond that of their traditional English precedents.

91. Matthews, Lois K. "Benjamin Franklin's Plan for a Colonial
     Union, 1750-1775." AMER POL SCI REV, 8 (1914), 393-412.

     Here is a good summary of Franklin's Albany Plan and his
     concepts of a constitution.

92. Miller, Helen H. THE CASE OF LIBERTY. Chapel Hill: Uni-
     versity of North Carolina Press, 1965.

     This is a key work which is vital in understanding the
     major court cases involving personal freedoms during the
     era. Carefully researched, well organized and soundly
     argued, Miller's book is necessary reading. The chapters
     on the jury trial of Forsey vs. Cunningham (1764), and the
     McDougall Affair - which concerned New York's response to
     the Quartering Act in 1765-66 - are covered brilliantly.

93. Morgan, Edmund S. "Colonial Ideas of Parliamentary Power."
     WMQ, 7 (1950), 353-392.

     Morgan questions some historians' views of famous con-
     temporary documents on this topic and suggests new ap-
     proaches.

94. Morris, Richard B. "The Spacious Empire of Lawrence Henry
     Gipson." WMQ, 24 (1967), 169-189.

     This review is the best summation of Gipson's imperial
     school of historiography which demonstrates that British
     mercantilism was changed by the Seven Years War.

95. ————· "'Then and There the Child Independence Was Born,'"
     AMER HERITAGE, 15(2), (1962), 36-39, 82, 84.

James Otis of Boston was a fiery champion of rights of priv-
acy and a dedicated opponent of writs of assistance.

96. Nadelhaft, Jerome J. "Politics and the Judicial Tenure Fight
    in Colonial New Jersey." WMQ, 28 (1971), 46-63.

    This essay summarizes key court cases in the colony which
    marked the judiciary's efforts to free the courts from crown
    control.

97. Ramsom, Roger L. "British Policy and Colonial Growth: Some
    Implications of the Burden From the Navigation Acts." J ECON
    HIST, 28 (1968), 427-435.

    The author claims that Britian could have compromised in en-
    forcing the Navigation Acts and thereby could have averted a
    war.

98. Ripley, Randell B. "Adams, Burke, and Eighteenth Century Con-
    servatism." POL SCI Q, 80 (1965), 216-235.

    Both thinkers could be considered fathers of conservative
    political thought.

99. Rogers, Alan. EMPIRE AND LIBERTY: AMERICAN RESISTANCE TO
    BRITISH AUTHORITY, 1755-1763. Berkeley: University of
    California Press, 1974.

    British policies in the Seven Years War radicalized American
    colonists. Military necessity prevailed, and hence impressment,
    seizure, trade regulation, and subordination of colonial poli-
    tical institutions typified the era. The author examines the
    colonial response to Crown actions and considers the American
    experience as a political training ground for eventual rebel-
    lion. Rogers is especially astute in appreciating American
    political and economic attitudes and suggests that colonial
    discord was emerging, as demonstrated by the Albany Congress.

100. Schutz, John A. THOMAS POWNALL, A BRITISH DEFENDER OF AMERI-
     CAN LIBERTY: A STUDY OF ANGLO-AMERICAN RELATIONS IN THE
     EIGHTEENTH CENTURY. Glendale, California: Arthur H. Clark,
     1951.

     Pownall had a meteoric success as a pre-revolutionary
     royal governor and political theorist. He demonstrated
     imagination in handling land claims, Indian affairs, future
     colonization, and in military matters. But even with his
     experience as Governor of Massachusetts, his theories seem
     to have been overlooked by policy-makers in Whitehall. This
     is a useful study, but it fails to assess Pownall's actual
     influence in London.

101. Spector, Margaret Marion. THE AMERICAN DEPARTMENT OF THE
     BRITISH GOVERNMENT, 1768-1782. New York: Columbia Univer-
     sity Press, 1940.

     Spector examines the origins, organization, and functions

of the department which was responsible for administering
the colonies, and for conduct of wars in North America.
The author concentrates on the influence of significant
Under-Secretaries such as William Knox and John Pownall.
Based on original sources, thoroughly researched, this
volume is useful for comprehending how colonial policies
were formulated.

102.   Surrency, Erwin C. "The Courts in the American Colonies."
        AMER J LEGAL HIST, 11 (1967), 253-276.

        Though the courts varied in jurisdiction and procedures,
        they were generally similar in handling cases and in dis-
        pensing justice.

103.   Thomas, Robert Paul. "A Quantitative Approach to the Study
        of the Effects of British Imperial Policy Upon Colonial
        Welfare: Some Preliminary Findings." J ECON HIST, 25
        (1965), 615-638.

        The author concludes that the economic burdens of the
        Navigations Acts did not impose major hardships on the
        colonies.

104.   ————. "British Imperial Policy and the Economic Inter-
        pretation of the American Revolution." J ECON HIST, 28
        (1968), 436-440.

        With empirical evidence from the workings of the Navi-
        gation Acts, the author concludes that the colonists
        benefitted from membership in the empire.

105.   Waters, John J., and Schutz, John A. "Patterns of
        Massachusetts Colonial Politics: The Writs of Assistance
        and the Rivalry Between the Otis and Hutchinson Fami-
        lies." WMQ, 24 (1967), 543-567.

        Two prominent families clashed not over ideological
        abstractions but over the controversial issue of the Writs.

106.   Weir, Robert M. "North Carolina's Reaction to the Cur-
        rency Act of 1764." NC HIST REV, 40 (1963), 183-199.

        This imperial legislation had significant ramifications
        for Carolina's economy and increased its revolutionary
        attitudes.

107.   Wierner, Frederick B. "The Rhode Island Merchants and the
        Sugar Act." NEQ, 3 (1930), 465-500.

        Led by Newport, and by Stephen Hopkins, the colony
        erupted with protests in 1764 that set precedents for the
        future.

108. Willon, Gary M. "The New Economic History and the Burden of
      the Navigation Acts." ECON HIST REV, 24 (1971), 553-542.

      This is a hard, penetrating look, with statistical evidence,
      at the views of several historians who contend the Navigation
      Acts exploited the colonies.

109. Wolkins, George G. "Daniel McLean and Writs of Assistance."
      MASS HIST SOC PROC, 57 (1924-35), 5-84.

      This is a key article about the legality of the Writs which
      invoked the opinions of Bernard, Hutchinson, Otis, John Adams,
      and Sam Adams.

                    C. THE STAMP ACT CRISIS

110. Adair, Douglas. "The Stamp Act in Contemporary English
      Cartoons." WMQ, 10 (1953), 538-542.

      Here are eight contemporary plates suggesting amusing as-
      pects of the controversial legislation.

111. Anderson, George P. "A Note on Ebenezer McKintosh." COL SOC
      MASS PUB, 26 (1924-28), 348-381.

      The famous Haverhill shoemaker is described by Tory Peter
      Oliver in 1781.

112. ————. "Ebenzer McKintosh, Stamp Act Rioter and Patriot."
      COL SOC MASS PUB, 26 (1924-28), 15-64.

      McKintosh was a famous radical wanted by the British, ac-
      cording to legend, dead or alive.

113. Chaffin, Robert J. "The Declaratory Act of 1766: A Reap-
      praisal." HISTORIAN, 37 (1974), 5-23.

      Usually overlooked by historians, the purpose of the Act
      was to silence provincial assemblies on issues of Parlia-
      mentary jurisdiction.

114. Christie, Ian R. "The Cabinet During the Grenville Admin-
      istration, 1763-1765." ENG HIST REV, 73 (1958), 86-92.

      Here is a good perspective of a ministry based on the
      minutes of fourteen meetings.

115. Chroust, Anton-Herman. "The Lawyers of New Jersey and the
      Stamp Act." AMER J LEG HIST, 6 (1942), 286-297.

      This is a solid article about conflicting legal interpre-
      tations of the Act.

116. Connolly, James C. "The Stamp Act and New Jersey's Opposi-
      tion to It." NJ HIST SOC PROC, 9 (1924), 137-150.

      The demonstrations held at Perth Amboy and New Brunswick
      were significant.

117. Crane, Verner W. "Benjamin Franklin and The Stamp Act." COL
      SOC MASS PUB, 32 (1933-37), 56-77.

      By 1768 Franklin was a determined advocate of colonial
      autonomy.

118. D'Innocenzo, Michael, and John J. Turner, Jr. "The Rule of
      New York Newspapers in the Stamp Act Crisis, 1764-1766."
      NY HIST SOC Q, 51 (1967), 215-231, 345-365.

      The press defined and articulated the Americans' view of
      their role in the Empire and helped to mold public opinion.

119. Ellefson, C. Ashley. "The Stamp Act in Georgia." GA HIST Q,
      46 (1962), 1-19.

      The colony remained loyal during the crisis but future com-
      promise would be difficult due to increased belligerency in
      politics and less willingess for conciliation.

120. Engleman, F.L. "Cadwallader Colden and the New York Stamp Act
      Riots." WMQ, 10 (1953), 560-578.

      The Lieutenant-Governor had difficulty in enforcing the
      Act and never regained the confidence of Crown nor colony.

121. Ericson, Fred J. "The Contemporary British Opposition to the
      Stamp Act, 1764-1765." PAP MICH AC SC ART LET, (1943), 489-
      505.

      Rebuking traditional interpretations, Ericson claims that
      many British politicans opposed the Act.

122. Giddens, Paul H. "Maryland and the Stamp Act Controversy."
      MD HIST MAG, (1932), 79-98.

      This essay examines the problems of Governor Sharpe, the
      Assembly, and the difficulties of distributing the stamps.

123. Gipson, Lawrence Henry. "The Great Debate in the Committee of
      the Whole House of Commons on the Stamp Act, 1766, as Re-
      ported by Nathanel Ryder." PA MHB, 86 (1962), 10-41.

      According to this M.P., the military factor (too few
      troops), and not economic issues, was the key to the
      discussions.

124. Granger, Bruce I. "The Stamp Act in Satire." AMER Q, 8
      (1956), 388-384.

      Here is a refreshing and amusing view of the great con-
      troversy in poems, essays, and letters, all of which had
      an anti-ministerial tone.

125. Greene, Jack P. "'A Dress of Horror': Henry McCulloh's
      Objection to the Stamp Act." HUNT LIB Q, 26 (1962-63),
      253-262.

      McCulloh, who helped prepare the legislation, refuted
      the finished product and demonstrated deep insight into
      colonial resentment.

126. ————, ed. "'Not to be governed or taxed, but by ... our
      Representatives ...', Four Essays in Opposition to the
      Stamp Act by Landon Carter." VA MHB, 16 (1968), 259-300.

      Here is a detailed analysis of the complaints of an
      articulate Virginian.

127. ————. "William Knox's Explanation for the American Revo-
      lution." WMQ, 30 (1973), 293-306.

      Knox, an Under-Secretary of State, believed that a new
      constitutional arrangment would satisfy the Americans.

128. Haywood, C. Robert. "Economic Sanctions: Use of the Threat
      of Manufacturers by the Southern Colonies." JSH, 25
      (1959), 207-219.

      The Sons of Liberty planned economic sanctions by pro-
      ducing articles traditionally imported from England.

129. ————. "The Mind of North Carolina Opponents of the
      Stamp Act." NC HIST REV, 29 (1952), 317-343.

      Here is a deft examination of a crisis which crystalized
      ideas, grievances, and techniques related to imperial
      legislation.

130. Humphreys, R.A. "Lord Shelburne and British Colonial
      Policy, 1766-1768." ENG HIST REV, 50 (1935), 257-277.

      The Secretary of State disagreed with the Chatham admin-
      istration's policy for the colonies.

131. Johnson, Allen S. "British Politics and the Repeal of the
      Stamp Act." S ATL Q, 62 (1963), 169-188.

      The Rockingham administration was weak because it lacked
      a disciplined majority in Parliament and because of the
      eccentricities of George III.

132. Kerr, Wilfred B. "The Stamp Act and the Floridas, 1765–
      1766." MVHR, 21 (1935), 436–470.

      A new colony with a mixed population of settlers, East
      Florida demonstrated little opposition to the Act.

133. ————. "The Stamp Act in Nova Scotia." NEQ, 6 (1933),
      552–566.

      Virtually all classes and politicians supported the
      legislation.

134. ————. "The Stamp Act in Quebec." ENG HIST REV, 47
      (1932) 648–651.

      The British here regarded the tax payment as their duty
      and opposed radicalism.

135. Laprade, William T. "The Stamp Act in British Politics."
      AHR, 35 (1930), 735–757.

      The issue was extremely involved, it demonstrated the
      intense bickering by British politicans, and it failed
      to salvage an empire.

136. Lee, E. Lawrence. "Days of Defiance: Resistance to the
      Stamp Act in the Lower Cap Fear." NC HIST REV, 53, (1966),
      186–202.

      The demonstrations centered at Brunswick where Governor
      Tryon fumbled in handling the imperial legislation.

137. Lemisch, L. Jesse. "New York's Petition and Resolves of
      December 1765: Liberals vs. Radicals." NY HIST SOC Q,
      49 (1965), 315–326.

      The author notes the difficulties of labeling liberals or
      conservatives as such within the context of the debate on
      this issue.

138. McAnear, Beverly. "The Albany Stamp Act Riots." WMQ, 4
      (1947), 486–498.

      Henry Van Schank described the coercive measures used by
      the Sons of Liberty on Tories.

139. Machinton, Walter E. "The Stamp Act Crisis: Bristol and
      Virginia." VA MHB, 73 (1965), 145–155.

      Alarmed at declining profits, merchants in Bristol,
      England called for repeal of the Act.

140. Maier, Pauline. "Coming to Terms with Samuel Adams." AHR,
      81 (1946), 12-37.

      In his writings, Adams appears to be a more complex man
      then the stereotype radical who manipulated mobs.

141. Marshall, Peter. "The British Empire and the American
      Revolution." HUNT LIB Q, 27 (1964), 135-145.

      The writer notes a growing interest in the theory of an
      emerging American nation and calls on British historians
      to place imperial relationships in a fresh perspective.

142. Morgan Edmund S. "The Postponement of the Stamp Act."
      WMQ, 5 (1948), 311-341.

      Here is a detailed examination of how Ben Franklin and
      others tried to have the Grenville program modified.

143. ————, and Helen M. Morgan. THE STAMP ACT CRISIS: PRO-
      LOGUE TO REVOLUTION. Chapel Hill: University of North
      Carolina Press, 1953.

      Here is an excellent analysis of a familiar topic with
      fresh evidence and new insights. The authors examine
      Grenville's machinations, they show that the colonists
      were opposed not only to taxation without representation
      but to taxation in general, and that the Americans made no
      distinction between internal and external taxation. The
      Sons of Liberty were generally dominated by an elite and
      were not an expression of lower class discontent. The de-
      bate over the Act caused the colonists to regard Parliament
      with suspicion. This is an imaginative and carefully re-
      searched account of the crisis with memorable portraits
      of many key individuals. The Morgans have produced the
      best volume on the subject.

144. Newcomb, Benjamin H. "Effects of the Stamp Act on Colonial
      Pennsylvania Politics." WMQ, 23 (1966), 157-272.

      Typified by Quaker pacificism, the colony was conservative,
      but this attitude changed in 1774.

145. Richardson, E.P. "Stamp Act Cartoons in the Colonies."
      PA MHB, 96 (1972), 275-297.

      Here is an illustrated collection of cartoons and carica-
      tures drawn in England and America in response to the Act.

146. Ritcheson, Charles R. "The Preparation of the Stamp Act."
      WMQ, 10 (1953), 543-559.

      The Act was an essential part of Grenville's plan for
      devising a coherent imperial system, and it was not in-
      tended to subvert local government.

147. Sosin, Jack M. "A Postscript to the Stamp Act Crisis. George
      Grenville's Revenue Measures: A Drain on Colonial Specie?"
      AHR, 63 (1967-68), 918-923.

      Grenville intended to have money expended on the army to re-
      main in the colonies.

148. Stout, Neil R. "Captain Kennedy and the Stamp Act." NY HIST,
      45 (1964), 44-58.

      While enforcing the Act, Kennedy of the Royal Navy became
      deeply embroiled in the controversy and had to vindicate his
      actions in order to re-establish his career.

149. Sutherland, Lucy S. "Edmund Burke and the First Rockingham
      Ministry." ENG HIST REV, 47 (1932), 46-72.

      Here is a solid account of English political rivalries and
      problems involved in the passage of the Stamp Act.

150. Thomas, P.D.G. BRITISH POLITICS AND THE STAMP ACT CRISIS;
      THE FIRST PHASE OF THE AMERICAN REVOLUTION, 1763-1767.
      New York: Oxford University Press, 1967.

      In a solid and definitive work intended for specialists and
      graduate students, Thomas examines the colonial programs of
      Grenville, Rockingham, and the early Chatham Ministry. He
      shows how policy-making was the result of complex and intri-
      cate relations among King, Ministries, Parliaments, colonial
      agents, civil servants, and interest groups. The debate
      over the Stamp Act resulted in a united claim of Parlia-
      mentary sovereignty over the colonies. Somewhat ponderous,
      nevertheless, this is a very thoughtful and provocative
      monograph.

151. Thompson, Mack E. "Massachusetts and New York and the Stamp
      Act." WHQ, 26 (1969), 253-258.

      The colonial Stamp Act (1755-56) contributed to the prepa-
      ration of the Parliamentary Stamp Act.

152. Watson, D.H. "William Baker's Account of the Debate on the
      Repeal of the Stamp Act." WMQ, (1969), 259-265.

      This is one of the few surviving accounts of the lobbying
      efforts in Commons in response to the repeal.

153. Young, Henry J. "Agrarian Resistance to the Stamp Act in
      Pennsylvania." PA HIST, 34 (1967), 25-30.

      The province was stirred by the economic implications of the
      legislation which made the transition to a royal colony more
      difficult; German farmers hastened to become naturalized in
      order to avoid higher fees on documents.

D. THE TOWNSHEND ACTS AND AMERICAN RESISTANCE

154. Alden, John E. "John Mein; Scourge of Patriots." COL SOC
      MASS PUB, 34 (1937-42), 571-599.

      Mein, a Tory bookseller who denounced Whigs and riotors,
      was arrested by patriots and eventually fled to London.

155. Andrews, Charles McLean. "Boston Merchants and the Non-Impor-
      tation Movement." COL SOC MASS PROC, 19 (1916-17), 159-259.

      Here is a key article which demonstrates how an attempt to
      redress trade grievances became an instrument of political
      agitation.

156. Bailyn, Bernard. "The Ordeal of Thomas Hutchinson." AMER
      HERITAGE, 25 (3) (1974), 4-7, 88-96.

      America's most prominent Loyalist (a Chief Justice and
      Lieutenant-Governor of Massachusetts) was caught between his
      duty and his love for America.

157. Basye, Arthur H. "The Secretary of State for Colonies,
      1768-1780." AHR, 28 (1922), 13-23.

      Under the Earl of Hillsborough, the functions and juris-
      diction of the office were centralized.

158. Brooke, John. THE CHATHAM ADMINISTRATION, 1766-1768. New
      York: St. Martins Press, 1956.

      This is a difficult book to read, but specialists will ap-
      preciate the author's skill in compiling this remarkably de-
      tailed account of a ministry from July, 1766 to October,
      1768. Brooke is astute in portraying leading politicians
      and civil servants, and his analysis of William Pitt is lucid
      and scholarly. Brooke is almost unexcelled in explaining the
      motives of key figures in the milieu of London officialdom.

159. Brunhouse, Robert L. "The Effects of the Townshend Acts on
      Pennsylvania." PA MHB, 54 (1930), 353-373.

      Quaker merchants still dominated the scene and were not
      sympathetic to mob activities.

160. Bumsted, John M., and Charles E. Clarke. "New England's
      Tom Paine: John Allen and the Spirit of Liberty." WMQ,
      21 (1964), 560-570.

      Basing his writings on Scripture, Bumsted of Boston was an
      advocate of an American Parliament.

161.   Calhoon, Robert M., and Robert M. Weir. "The Scandalous
       History of Sir Egerton Leigh." WMQ, 26 (1969), 47-74.

       Leigh, an Attorney-General in South Carolina, prosecuted
       cases involving infractions of the Navigation and Stamp Acts
       and thereby disenchanted the colony.

162.   Chaffin, Robert J. "The Townshend Acts of 1767." WMQ, 27
       (1970), 90-121.

       Here is a keen analysis of why the Chancellor of the
       Exchequer devised this controversial revenue measure, and
       why he worked to strengthen the Customs administration in
       America.

163.   Champagne, Roger. "Family Politics Versus Constitutional
       Principle: The New York Assembly of 1768 and 1769." WMQ,
       20 (1963), 57-99.

       Both the Livingston and De Lancey factions exploited im-
       perial crises for political expediency.

164.   Channing, Edward. "The American Board of Commissioners of
       the Customs." MASS HIST SOC PROC, 43 (1916), 477-490.

       The establishment of this bureaucracy virtually terminated
       illicit colonial trade on a wide scale, inadvertently
       diverted much coastal commerce to land routes, and thereby
       caused friction over tax matters.

165.   Clark, Dora Mae. "The American Board of Customs, 1767-1783."
       AHR 45 (1939-40), 777-800.

       Clark demonstrated why the Board failed to tighten its ad-
       ministrative controls in the colonies.

166.   Dickerson, Oliver Morton, comp. BOSTON UNDER MILITARY RULE,
       1768-1769: AS REVEALED IN A JOURNAL OF THE TIMES. Boston:
       Chapman and Grimes, 1936.

       This is an expertly edited version of a contemporary news
       sheet   published simultaneously in Boston, New York, and
       Philadelphia. It informed the colonists of events, it
       warned inhabitants about military infractions of political
       traditions, and it reminded the British of the futility of
       their coercion. The volume is a model of research; it is
       replete with useful data and fresh interpretations.

167.   ————. "England's Most Fateful Decision (1767." NEQ, 22
       (1949), 388-394.

       The decision was to create the American Board of Customs
       Commission.

168. ———. "John Hancock: Notorious Smuggler or New Victim of
      British Revenue Racketeers?" MVHR, 32 (1940), 517-540.

      Hancock was not a smuggler but a great patriot who insisted
      upon his legal rights.

169. ———. "The Attempt to Extend British Customs Control Over
      Intercolonial Commerce by Land." S ATL Q, 50 (1941),
      361-368.

      British officialdom tried to regulate inland commerce and
      coastal shipping from Quebec to the Bahamas.

170. ———. "The Commissioners of Customs and the 'Boston
      Massacre'." NEQ, 27 (1954), 307-325.

      The Board operated directly under the Treasury and its
      headquarters in Boston was like an imperial sub-treasury
      where its agents aided troops in the fighting.

171. ———. THE NAVIGATION ACTS AND THE AMERICAN REVOLUTION.
      Philadelphia: University of Pennsylvania Press, 1951.

      Dickerson claims that the Acts were not a serious cause of
      complaint until the eve of the Revolution and that the
      economic restrictions raised few protests. Hence the Acts
      cannot be cited as a major cause of rebellion. Dickerson
      corrected many misconceptions about British administration,
      he explained the implementation of imperial rule, and he
      concentrated on key officials who formulated policy. This
      is one of the most significant books about the causes of the
      war. It is readable, thoroughly researched, and it shows
      impressive scholarship.

172. ———. "Use Made of the Revenue From the Tax on Tea." NEQ,
      31 (1958), 232-243.

      The money was used for the salaries of British officials in
      the colonies for patronage, not for colonial defense measures.

173. Frese, Joseph R. "Some Observations on the American Board
      of Customs Commissions." MASS HIST SOC PROC, 81 (1969),
      3-30.

      The Customs irritated many occupational groups with its
      fees, taxes, search warrants, and its use of the Royal Navy.

174. Gerlach, Larry R. "Customs and Contentions: John Hatton of
      Salen and Cohansey, 1764-1776." NJ HIST, 89 (1971), 69-72.

      Here is a good account of a smugglers' haven on the Delaware
      that complicated problems for the local Customs collector.

175. Greene, Jack R. "Bridge to Revolution, The Wilkes Fund
      Controversy in South Carolina, 1769-1775." JSH, 29 (1953),
      19-52.

The augment over support to the radical Members of Parliament led to an impasse in Carolina's Assembly.

176. Henderson, Patrick. "Small Pox and Patriotism, The Norfolk
      Riots, 1768-1769." VA MHB, 73 (1965), 413-424.

      The pro-inoculators and the anti-inoculators divided along
      political lines.

177. Humphreys, Robert A. "Lord Shelburne and a Projected Re-
      call of Colonial Governors in 1767." AHR, 37 (1932), 267-
      272.

      Shelburne tried to recall some obnoxious royal governors in
      order to placate the colonists, but he did not receive
      ministerial support.

178. Labaree, Benjamin Woods. THE BOSTON TEA PARTY. New York:
      Oxford University Press, 1964.

      This is the best work on the subject although it is ex-
      tremely detailed, and it is difficult to read. The author
      provides ample information about the event, the developments
      that set other forces into political motion, Parliament's at-
      titude toward the uproar, and Boston's leadership in the tur-
      moil. Then, Labaree concentrates on the closing of Boston
      Port to the first meeting of the Continental Congress in
      September, 1774. The monograph is a fresh, perceptive in-
      quiry into the economic context of the drift toward rebel-
      lion. Though the work lacks adequate descriptions, a sus-
      tained narrative, and revealing character studies, the
      scholarship is thorough.

179. Lord, Donald C., and Robert M. Calhoon. "The Removal of the
      Massachusetts General Court From Boston, 1769-1773." JAH,
      55 (1968-1969), 735-755.

      In a constitutional crisis, a court challenged the Crown's
      right to interfere in calling, proroguing, and dissolving an
      assembly.

180. Lovejoy, David S. "Rights Imply Equality: The Case Against
      Admiralty Jurisdiction in America, 1764-1776." WMQ, 16
      (1959), 459-482.

      Here is a detailed explanation of how John Hancock and
      John Adams viewed the corruption of Admiralty courts in com-
      mon law and in civil courts.

181. McClelland, Peter D. "The Cost to America of British Imperial
      Policy." AMER ECON REV, 59 (1969), 370-381.

      With quantitative data, the writer measured the costs of
      the Acts of Trade to demonstrate that some historians have
      used incorrect conceptual frameworks.

182. Miller, John C. "The Massachusetts Convention, 1768." NEQ,
      7 (1934), 445-484.

      The meeting was a precursor of future provincial congresses
      and a key event in the radicalization of politics.

183. Nash, George H., III. "From Radicalism to Revolution: The
      Political Career of Josiah Quincy Jr." AMER ANTIQ SOC PROC,
      79 (1969), 253-90.

      This is a good sketch of a Massachusetts lawyer's growing
      alienation from Britain.

184. Simpson, W.Q. "Lord Shelburne and North America. HIST TODAY,
      10 (1960), 52-63.

      Here is a sympathetic view of a visionary Secretary of State
      who was tolerant toward the colonists.

185. Smith, Glenn Curtis. "An Era of Non-Importation Associations,
      1768-1773." WMQ, 20 (1945), 84-98.

      Virginia's response to the Townshend Acts was signalled by
      Arthur Lee's letters in the VIRGINIA GAZETTE.

186. Sutherland, Lucy S. "Lord Shelburne and East India Company
      Politics, 1776-1769." ENG HIST REV, 49 (1934), 456-486.

      There are ample clues here about Parliamentary alignments
      and the relationship of the East India Company to politics.

187. Thomas, P.D.G. "Charles Townshend and American Taxation in
      1767. ENG HIST REV, 83 (1968), 33-51.

      This article modifies traditional views about the relation-
      ship between raising revenues and subverting the authority of
      American assemblies.

188. Upton, Leslie F.S., ed. "Proceedings of Ye Body Representing
      the Tea." WMQ, 22 (1967), 287-300.

      This is a fascinating account by an unknown contemporary
      of arguments in 1773 about the tea ships in Boston harbor.

189. Varga, Nicholas. "Robert Charles. New York Agent, 1748-1770."
      WMQ, 18 (1961), 211-235.

      Charles was unique because of his long tenure, and because
      he was appointed by the elected branch of New York's govern-
      ment.

190. Watson, Derek. "The Rockingham Whigs and the Townshend
      Duties." ENG HIST REV, 84 (1969), 561-565.

      This is a murky article that attempts to clarify the

problems confronting Rockingham in relation to other current
legislation, to opposition by political enemies, and to
American resistance.

191. Wolkins, George G. "The Seizure of John Hancock's Sloop
      LIBERTY." MASS HIST SOC PROC, 55 (1931-32), 239-284.

      Using many illuminating documents, the author explains the
      resulting uproar in New England over the incident.

192. Younger, Richard D. "Grand Juries and the American Revolu-
      tion." VA MHB, 63 (1965), 257-268.

      Here is a good summary of struggles between chief justices
      and grand juries, mainly in Massachusetts and South Carolina.

193. Zobel, Hiller B. THE BOSTON MASSACRE. New York: W.W. Norton,
      Inc., 1970.

      This is a very graphic account of the famous incident. The
      book is characterized by lively writing, detailed accounts
      of key events, and meticulous research into court records.
      Unfortunately, Zobel neglects to estimate the repercussions
      of the affair outside of Boston, and he fails to clarify the
      matter of a possible conspiracy. But the material about the
      witnesses, and the judicial proceedings is skillfully
      covered.

                    E. THE TRANS-APPALACHIAN FRONTIER

194. Abernethy, Thomas Perkins. WESTERN LANDS AND THE AMERICAN
      REVOLUTION. New York: Appleton Century Co., Inc., 1937.

      In a seminal work, Abernethy demonstrates how soldiers,
      Indian agents, Crown officals, planters, merchants, and land
      speculators were involved in exploiting unsettled domains.
      This study is exceptionally valuable for details about the
      formation and progress of numerous land companies based
      mainly in Virginia; it is crammed with information; and it
      has excellent maps and a fine bibliography. However, the
      narrative is ponderous, the coverage on Indian attitudes is
      weak, and the author tends to neglect the influence of western
      lands on American diplomacy.

195. Alden, John R. JOHN STUART AND THE SOUTHERN COLONIAL FRONTIER:
      A STUDY IN INDIAN RELATIONS, WAR TRADE, AND LAND PROBLEMS
      IN THE SOUTHERN WILDERNESS, 1754-1755. Ann Arbor: Univer-
      sity of Michigan Press, 1944.

      This is a required reading for information about the com-
      plexities of southern Indian relations within the British
      sphere of influence. Alden clarifies the importance of a
      minor but influential Crown agent who toiled to delineate

Indian boundary lines from the Ohio to North Carolina.
Though the author includes excessive detail about massacres,
wars, and treaties and neglects to fuse material about
northern Indian affairs into his account, he is particularly
gifted in portraying an inept British officialdom.

196. Allen, Ben, and Dennis T. Lawson. "The Wautagans and the
     'Dangerous Example'." TENN HIST Q, 26 (1967), 137-147.

     Ignoring British and Indian protests, immigrants settled
     on Cherokee lands founding the first trans-Appalachian set-
     tlements in Tennessee and North Carolina.

197. Alvord, Clarence W. "The British Ministry and the Treaty
     of Fort Stanwix." WIS STATE HIST SOC PROC, 56 (1908),
     165-183.

     This is a good summary of the ramifications of the Quebec
     Act and official efforts to determine a land policy from
     1763 to 1768.

198. ———. "The Daniel Boone Myth." J ILL HIST SOC, 19 (1926),
     16-30.

     Alvord notes that Boone was an agent of land speculators
     who swarmed over Kentucky and questions the romantic legends
     about him.

199. ———. "The Genesis of the Proclamation of 1763." MICH
     HIST COLL, 36 (1909), 20-52.

     The original proclamation, one of America's most important
     state papers of the era, is reproduced here with an analysis
     of its origins, and its relationship to land and Indian prob-
     lems.

200. ———. THE MISSISSIPPI VALLEY IN BRITISH POLITICS: A STUDY
     OF TRADE, LAND SPECULATION, AND EXPERIMENTS IN IMPERIALISM
     CULMINATING IN THE AMERICAN REVOLUTION. 2 vols. Glendale,
     California: Arthur H. Clark Co., 1917.

     Here is a magisterial monograph about the settlement of the
     trans-montane areas after 1763. The work is valuable due to
     the revealing data about pioneers, rival land companies, and
     British agents who governed the areas ineptly. This work is
     essential to comprehend the whites' development of the
     Mississippi Valley for it contains copious footnotes and
     abundant information about a wide range of individuals in-
     volved in the surge westward. Though dull reading, the book
     deliberately shifts one's attention from the traditional
     stress on the colonial seaboard to the interior.

201. Bailey, Kenneth P. THE OHIO COMPANY OF VIRGINIA AND THE
     WESTWARD MOVEMENT, 1748-1792. Glendale, California:
     Arthur H. Clark Co., 1939.

Formed in 1747, the Company was still fighting for its
claims in the 1790s. Although this is not a path-breaking
study, the material about the original land grant, the member-
ship, early explorations, and rivalries with Pennsylvania
traders is nicely organized. The book has a useful bibliography, and it is meticulously footnoted.

202. Billington, Ray Allen. "The Fort Stanwix Treaty of 1768."
      NY HIST, 25 (1944), 182-194.

      The treaty was poorly devised and executed, for it cheated
      the Indians, encouraged land speculators, and left huge gaps
      in demarkation lines.

203. Born, John D., Jr. "Charles Strachan in Mobile: The Frontier
      Ordeal of a Scottish Factor, 1765-1768." ALA HIST Q, 27
      (1766), 23-42.

      Merchants had innumerable problems at the British outpost,
      particularly in collecting debts.

204. ————. "John Fitzpatrick of Manchac: A Scottish Merchant in
      the Lower Mississippi Prior to the Revolution." J MISS HIST,
      32 (1970), 117-134.

      This is a good summary of the problems involving in trading
      in the Spanish Borderlands, West Florida, and the competition
      by American traders in the area.

205. Brand, Irene B. "Dunmore's War." W VA HIST, 40 (1978-79),
      28-46.

      The essay adds nothing to familiar material on the subject,
      but high-schoolers could appreciate it.

206. Brown, Douglas S. "The Aberville Canal Project: Its Rela-
      tionship to Anglo-French Commercial Rivalry in the Mis-
      sissippi Valley, 1763-1775." MVHR, 32 (1946), 491-516.

      Here is a good tale about economic rivalries in the
      Louisiana country.

207. Buck, Solon J. "The Story of the Grand Portage." MINN HIST,
      5 (1923), 14-27.

      The site was a yearly rendevous for a thousand fur traders.

208. Carter, Clarence E. GREAT BRITAIN AND THE ILLINOIS COUNTRY,
      1763-1774. Washington, DC: American Historical Associ-
      ation, 1910.

      The author concentrated on the British administration of
      French settlements in the area above the Ohio acquired in
      1763. Replete with documents and amplified by excellent foot-
      notes, this book is not clearly written, for there are

excessive gaps in the narrative. However, it is essential
to understand policy-making for the Old Northwest prior to the
Revolution.

209. Curry, Richard. "Lord Dunmore and the West: A Re-evaluation."
     W VA HIST, 19 (1928), 231-243.

     The Virginia governor violated cabinet directives and
     warred on the Shawnee in 1774.

210. ———. "Lord Dunmore: Tool and Land Jobbers or Realistic
     Champion of Colonial Rights? An Inquiry." W VA HIST, 24
     (1963), 289-295.

     Here is a detailed examination of the controversial Gover-
     nor's land and Indian policies.

211. Curtis, Thomas D. "Land Policy: Pre-Conditions for the Suc-
     cess of the American Revolution." AMER J OF ECON AND SOC,
     31 (1972), 209-233.

     After 1763, Britain's land policies brought many diversified
     groups into opposition to the Crown.

212. Downes, Randolph. COUNCIL FIRES ON THE UPPER OHIO. Pitts-
     burgh: University of Pittsburgh Press, 1940.

     Downes wrote with sympathy about the plight of Indian
     tribes - particularly the Shawnee and Delaware - effected by
     white encroachments on their lands. Here is a plausible,
     conscientious attempt to present the viewpoint of the so-
     called "noble savage." This volume contains a mass of docu-
     mentation about the frontier struggle to 1794.

213. ———. "Dunmore's War: An Interpretation." W VA HIST, 21
     (1934), 311-330.

     The Shawnee were brutally treated while the British kept
     the Iroquois and Delaware neutral.

214. Gates, Paul W. "The Role of the Land Speculator." PA MHB,
     66 (1942), 314-333.

     The author examines, but leaves unanswered, the question of
     whether land speculators hastened or hindered trans-montane
     settlement.

215. Grant, Charles S. "Pontiac's Rebellion and the British
     Troop Movements of 1763." MVHR, 40 (1953), 75-88.

     The Indian uprising had no perceptible influence on the
     disposition of 10,000 British troops sent to America.

216. Henderson, Archibald. "The Creative Force in American Ex-
      pansion: Henderson and Boone." AHR, 20 (1914), 86-107.

      There is little analysis and excessive romanticism here
      about Daniel Boone's role in Kentucky.

217. ————. "Pre-Revolutionary Revolts in the Old Southwest."
      MVHR, 17 (1930), 191-212.

      The quest for land, symbolized by the Transylvania Company,
      was a motive for rebellion in Virginia.

218. Humphreys, Robert A. "Lord Shelborne and British Colonial
      Policy, 1766-1768." ENG HIST REV, 50 (1935), 257-277.

      Humphrey reviews Shelborne's policies for the Mississippi,
      his business links in America, and the failure of his plans
      during the Stamp Act crisis.

219. ————. "Lord Shelborne and the Proclamation of 1763." ENG
      HIST REV, 49 (1943), 241-254.

      This is a key article which exmaines the legal, constitu-
      tional, and territorial arrangements devised by the Board
      of Trade for three new colonies in North America.

220. Hurt, N. Franklin. "Growth of Local Action During the British
      Military Rule at Detroit, 1760-1774." MICH HIST, 40 (1965),
      451-464.

      British commanders ineptly handled the French, the Indians,
      and the fur traders until civil government improved matters
      by 1767.

221. Huston, James H. "Benjamin Franklin and the West." WEST
      HIST Q, 4 (1973), 425-434.

      Franklin had a Frederick Jackson Turner view of the west.

222. ————. "The British Evacuation of Fort Pitt, 1772." W PA
      HIST MAG, 48 (1965), 317-39.

      In an effort to cut costs, the ministry withdrew troops
      from this vital post.

223. Jacobs, Wilbur K. "The Indian Frontier of 1763." W PA HIST
      MAG, 34-35 (1951), 185-198.

      Here is a good summary of the white settlement line and of
      British negotiations with the Indians.

224. James, Alfred P. GEORGE MERCER OF THE OHIO COMPANY: A STUDY
      IN FRUSTRATION. Pittsburgh: University of Pittsburgh
      Press, 1963.

Mercer was a major figure in the French and Indian War
and in the Ohio Company. But his involvement as an official
attempting to execute the Stamp Act of 1765 caused him endless "frustration" and reduced his influence with settlers.
Though the author made a commendable effort to portray Mercer,
the work is flawed by the lack of adequate evidence about the
man. Nevertheless, this is an important study.

225. Kerby, Robert J. "'The Other War in 1774': Dunmore's War."
      W VA HIST, 36 (1974), 1-16.

      The 2,000 man expedition shattered Indian power in the
      Ohio and permitted three colonies to prepare for revolution.

226. Lewis, George E. THE INDIANA COMPANY, 1763-1798: A STUDY IN
      EIGHTEENTH CENTURY FRONTIER LAND SPECULATION AND BUSINESS
      VENTURE. Glendale, California: Arthur H. Clark Co., 1941.

      Provided with a three million acre tract (in what is now
      West Virginia) in 1768 by the Six Nations, the Company tried
      in vain to have its claims ratified by the British government,
      and the Continental Congress during the Revolution-Confedera-
      tion eras. This is a very objective and thoughtful study
      that is thoughtfully presented. The Company merits credit
      for exploring and mapping a new area.

227. Marshall, Peter. "Imperial Policy and the Government of
      Detroit: Projects and Problems, 1760-1774." J IMP COM HIST,
      2 (1974), 153-189.

      Pittsburgh, the Cumberland Gap, the St. Lawrence and the
      Mohawk Rivers, as well as Detroit, were all pivotal centers.

228. ———. "Lord Hillsborough, Samuel Wharton and the Ohio
      Grant, 1769-1775." ENG HIST REV, 80 (1966), 717-739.

      Wharton of Philadelphia acquired a vast land claim in 1768,
      but the Secretary of State attempted to check land speculation.

229. ———. "Sir William Johnson and the Treaty of Fort Stanwix,
      1768." J AMER STUD, 1 (1967), 149-179.

      This is a definitive article in which the author contends
      that Johnson has been unfairly appraised by historians.

230. Mowat, Charles L. "The Southern Brigade: A Sidelight on the
      British Military Establishment in America, 1763-1775." JSH,
      10 (1944), 59-67.

      Mowat tersely demonstrates the far-ranging responsibilities
      of the British army on the southern frontiers and the loca-
      tions of regiments.

38   CAUSES OF THE WAR

231. Oaks, Robert F. "The Impact of British Western Policy on the
      Coming of the Revolution in Pennsylvania." PA MHB, 101
      (1977), 171-189.

      In a concise summary, Oaks examines the conflicting in-
      terests of the Quaker Assembly, trade interests, and fron-
      tiersmen.

232. Reed, Marjorie G. "The Quebec Fur-Traders and Western
      Policy, 1763-1774." CAN HIST REV, 6 (1925), 15-32.

      Three fur-trading companies dominated British commerce in
      the Mississippi Valley.

233. Rice, Otis K. THE ALLEGHENY FRONTIER: WEST VIRGINIA BEGIN-
      NINGS, 1730-1830. Lexington: University Press of Kentucky,
      1970.

      Chapters four and six are useful and colorful introductions
      to the subject.

234. Russell, Nelson V. THE BRITISH REGIME IN MICHIGAN AND THE
      OLD NORTHWEST, 1760-1798. Northfield, Minnesota: Carleton
      College, 1939.

      Though this work is entertaining on social-conditions
      in the era, and it contains much data for the beginner, the
      volume is full of errors and misinterpretations of familiar
      documents. The specialist can overlook this book but for
      the general reader it is a good introduction to the subject.

235. ———. "The Governmental Organization of Michigan, 1760-
      1787." MICH HIST MAG, 23 (1939), 93-104.

      Lord Shelburne deserves credit for astute appointments
      which contributed to firm imperial control.

236. Sosin, Jack M. "The British Indian Department and Dunmore's
      Wars." VA MHB, 74 (1966), 34-50.

      British agents did not conspire with Governor Dunmore; in-
      stead they attempted to prevent a Shawnee uprising on the
      Virigina frontier.

237. ———. "The French Settlements in British Policy for the
      North American Interior, 1760-1774." CAN HIST REV, 39
      (1958), 185-208.

      The Quebec Act was a sensible solution to complex problems
      involving French settlers.

238. ———. "The Yorke–Camden Opinion and American Land Specu-
      lators." PA MHB, 85 (1961), 38-49.

CAUSES OF THE WAR   39

A legal decision about the land rights of the East India
Company in 1767 was used by land speculators for the Illinois
Company to legalize their claims in 1775.

239. ———. WHITEHALL AND THE WILDERNESS: THE MIDDLE WEST IN
      BRITISH COLONIAL POLICY, 1760-1775. Lincoln, Nebraska:
      University of Nebraska Press, 1961.

      Written within the context of the "imperial" school, Sosin
      cogently demonstrates that the Stamp Act was levied to finance
      a vast program for guarding and developing the west rather
      than to defray the debt left by the Seven Years War. Thor-
      oughly researched, well organized, and clearly defined, this
      work tends to praise British officialdom. It is only
      periphally concerned with the nature of American discontent
      with land policies. However, it is an excellent work and
      should be consulted.

240. Thomas, William H.B., and Howard McNight Wilson. "The Bat-
      tle of Point Pleasant." VA CAV, 24 (1975), 100-107.

      Here is a lively account of the Shawnee war on the Virginia
      frontier.

241. Van Every, Dale. FORTH TO THE WILDERNESS: THE FIRST AMERICAN
      FRONTIER, 1754-1774. New York: William Morrow and Co.,
      1961.

      For undergraduates and general readers, this may be the
      best volume on the topic. In clear and vivid chapters, the
      author provides dramatic accounts of key battles and about
      the careers of Pontiac, John Stuart, Colonel Henry Bouquet,
      and Sir William Johnson. The maps are especially good.

242. Wainwright, Nicholas B. GEORGE CROGHAM: WILDERNESS DIPLOMAT.
      Chapel Hill: University of North Carolina Press, 1959.

      Here is a detailed account of a major frontier figure who
      is generally regarded as a scoundrel. The book provides
      much information about the penetrations of the trans-Allegheny
      frontier and about the hardships of pioneering life. Too
      ponderous for general readers, this work - replete with de-
      tails and documentary citations - would appeal to the
      specialist.

243. Webster, Eleanor M. "Insurrection at Fort Loudon in 1765:
      Rebellion or Preservation of Peace." W PA HIST MAG, 47
      (1964), 125-139.

      This is a dramatic account of a Scot-Irish raid on a wagon
      train laden with muskets and whiskey intended for the Indians.

244. Williams, Edwards G. "The Orderly Book of Colonel Henry
      Bouquet's Expedition Against the Ohio Indians, 1764," W PA
      HIST MAG, 42 (1959), 9-33, 179-224, 283-316.

Bouquet's journal has fascinating data about a march from
Pittsburgh to Coshocton in order to secure the release of
white captives.

F. THE IDEOLOGY OF REBELLION

245. Bailyn, Bernard. ORIGINS OF AMERICAN POLITICS. Cambridge:
      Harvard University Press, 1967.

      In a seminal work, Bailyn holds that politics in eighteenth-
      century America "reflected the paradox of executive power
      swollen in theory but shrunken in practice." He clearly
      perceives the nature of the rebellion. In a brilliant analy-
      sis of the documents, the author demonstrates his grasp of
      eighteenth-century political rhetoric. This is a sensitive
      and judicious analysis of the emergence of American political
      thought.

246. ―――――, ed. PAMPHLETS OF THE AMERICAN REVOLUTION, 1750-1776.
      Vol. 1, 1750-1765. Harvard University Press, 1965.

      This is a carefully edited volume that comprises part of a
      four volume series on the most influential pamphlet litera-
      ture of the war. The items were selected on the basis of
      importance in the growth of American political thought, and
      on the impact of their influence in the debate over con-
      stitutional issues. Each of the fourteen pamphlets covered
      here has a bibliographical section containing data about the
      author, the circumstances surrounding publication, and a
      critique of the essay. The work has been highly acclaimed.

247. ―――――. "Political Experience and Enlightened Ideas in
      Eighteenth-Century America." AHR, 67 (1962), 339-351.

      Though the Enlightenment was not the instrument of social
      change in America, the completion and nationalization of its
      political ideas were implicit in the Revolution.

248. Bridenbaugh. Carl. MITRE AND SCEPTRE: TRANSATLANTIC FAITHS.
      IDEAS, PERSONALITIES, AND POLITICS, 1689-1775. New York:
      Oxford University Press, 1962.

      The author claims religious disputes were a basic cause of
      the Revolution and were a foundation for American national-
      ism. Despairing over the lack of attention paid by historians
      to religious issues, Bridenbaugh concentrates on Anglican
      efforts to secure complete episcopal hegemony in the colonies.
      This is a fine book which clarifies some heretofore puzzling
      questions about the status of Dissenters in some colonies.
      Yet episcopacy was not a central issue of rebellion. Inde-
      pendence implied not only political freedom but relief from
      aggressive Anglicanism, particularly for middle-class New
      Englanders. The book is provocative but it is weak about pub-
      lic opinion, and it omits necessary perspectives for the re-
      ligious issue.

249. Buel, Richard Jr. "Democracy and the American Revolution: A
      Frame of Reference." WMQ, 21 (1964), 165-190.

      Buel shows how historians measure the significance of the
      Revolution in relationship to the development of American
      democracy.

250. Calhoon, Robert M., ed. "'A Sorrowful Spectator of These
      Tumultuous Times.' Robert Beverly Describes the Coming
      of the Revolution." VA MHB, 73 (1965), 41-55.

      In a revealing letter, a back country gentlemen describes
      his opposition to rebellion.

251. Calkin, Homer L. "Pamphlets and Public Opinion During the
      American Revolution." PA MHB, 64 (1940), 22-42.

      From Virginia northward, pamphlets played an enormous role
      in formulating and shaping public opinion.

252. Cone, Carl B. BURKE AND THE NATURE OF AMERICAN POLITICS. 2
      vols. Vol. 1, THE AGE OF THE AMERICAN REVOLUTION. Lexing-
      ton: University of Kentucky Press, 1957.

      Writer, philosopher, statesman, Burke was an intellectual
      giant of the era. Although this work is reliable in dis-
      cussing Burke's concept of empire, the awkward phraseology
      of many pages and the muddled view of British politics in-
      hibits one from grasping Burke's viewpoints. This is a
      pro-Whig view of history in which the biographer rarely faults
      Burke, provides little information about his activities, and
      offers excessive information about his future influence. Even
      with these qualifications, and the author's inability to sum-
      marize his findings, this is a sound study that enlarges
      one's knowledge of the era.

253. Howe, John R., comp. THE ROLE OF IDEOLOGY IN THE AMERICAN
      REVOLUTION. New York: Holt, Rhinehart, and Winston, 1970.

      This is an excellent collection of essays. It contains ex-
      cerpts from the work of Edumnd S. Morgan, Robert A. Humphreys,
      Caroline Robbins, Perry Miller, Peter Gay, Louis Hartz, Elisha
      Douglass, Robert Palmer, Gordon Wood, and Bernard Bailyn.

254. Kaestle, Carl F. "The Public Reaction to John Dickinson's
      'Farmer's Letters'." AMER ANTIQ SOC PROC, 78 (1968), 323-
      353.

      Written in response to the Townshend Acts, the essay may
      have reached 80,000 of 200,000 literate Americans.

255. Kammen, Michael. "The Meaning of Colonization in American
      Revolutionary Thought." J HIST IDEAS, 31 (1970), 337-358.

      Revolutionaries had a unique view of how the original

colonial settlements in America provided the background for
political liberty and for religious toleration.

256. Kenyon, Cecilia M. "Republicanism and Radicalism in the
      American Revolution: An Old-fashioned Interpretation."
      WMQ, 19 (1962), 151-183.

      Noting the nature of the Revolution which still perplexes
      historians, Kenyon concludes that the rebellion was both
      radical and conservative.

257. ———. "Where Paine Went Wrong." AMER POL SCI R, 45 (1951),
      1086-1099.

      Here is a brilliant survey of Tom Paine's political thought
      typified by his belief that rational and good men would re-
      form society.

258. Koch, Adrienne, ed. THE AMERICAN ENLIGHTENMENT: THE SHAPING
      OF THE AMERICAN EXPERIMENT AND A FREE SOCIETY. New York:
      George Braziller, 1965.

      This careful selection of seminal essays from the works of
      Franklin, John Adams, Jefferson, Madison and others demon-
      strates the scope of their literary abilities, the nature of
      their intellectual contributions, and the essence of enlight-
      ened thought. These men were both practical and philosophi-
      cal. The samples here of their ideas, and the summary of their
      lives provide the reader with a convenient reference.

259. Lokken, Roy N. "The Concept of Democracy in Colonial Politi-
      cal Thought." WMQ, 16 (1959), 568-580.

      This is a sound essay which examines the degree to which the
      seeds of American democracy existed prior to 1775.

260. Maier, Pauline. "John Wilkes and American Disillusionment with
      Britain." WMQ, 20 (1963), 343-395.

      The radical Englishman who evoked such enthusiasm in
      America failed to win Parliamentary support.

261. Morgan, Edmund S. "Colonial Ideas of Parliamentary Power."
      WMQ, 5 (1948), 312-341.

      Not until the early 1770s did the Americans advance to a
      radical position of denying Parliamentary supremacy.

262. ———. THE AMERICAN REVOLUTION: TWO CENTURIES OF INTERPRE-
      TATION. Englewood Cliffs, New Jersey: Prentice-Hall, Inc.,
      1965.

      This is a very useful booklet for general readers on the
      basic historiography of the Revolution. It contains essays by
      David Ramsay, Friedrich Gentz, George Bancroft, Charles Kendall

Adams, J. Franklin Jameson, Daniel J. Boorstin, Eric Robson, Lawrence Henry Gipson, and Edmund S. Morgan. Each exerpt is preceded by a brief explanatory essay, and the work contains a helpful bibliography.

263.   ————. "The Puritan Ethic and the American Revolution." WMQ, 34 (1967), 3-43.

The trend toward revolution was derived from an inherited set of values collectively termed the Puritan Ethic.

264.   Morris, Richard B. "Legalism versus Revolutionary Doctrine in New England." NEQ, 4 (1931), 195-215.

Revolutionary ideas "blossomed in the barren soil of the common law ... "

265.   Mullett, Charles F. "English Imperial Thinking, 1764-1783." POL SCI Q, 45 (1930), 548-579.

Though somewhat outdated, this is a solid article about the relationship between the British Empire and the Commonwealth of Nations.

266.   Penniman, Howard. "Thomas Paine. Democrat." AMER POL SCI REV, 37 (1943), 244-262.

Here is a valuable summary of Paine's ideas about deism, democracy, and popular sovereignty.

267.   Robbins, Caroline H. THE EIGHTEENTH-CENTURY COMMONWEALTH: STUDIES IN THE TRANSMISSION, DEVELOPMENT AND CIRCUMSTANCES OF ENGLISH THOUGHT FROM THE RESTORATION OF CHARLES II UNTIL THE WAR WITH THE THIRTEEN COLONIES. Cambridge: Harvard University Press, 1959.

This is a solid examination of English liberal political thought from 1660-1775. With skill and clarity, Robbins provides a wealth of material about an era when discussions about social change were frequently viewed as dangerous. Encyclopedic in its coverage of many relatively obscure men, this is fine intellectual history for the specialist.

268.   Rossiter, Clinton. "Richard Bland: The Whig in America." WMQ, 10 (1953), 33-79.

A member of three Virginia legislatures, Bland's ideas voiced in 1764-1766 about self-government influenced Jefferson and Madison.

269.   Sanborn, F.B. "The American Farmer. St. John de Crevecoeur and His Famous Letters, (1735-1813)." PA MHB, 30 (1906), 257-286.

Here is a good sketch of the noted writer, with a suggestion of his influence.

270. Savelle, Max. "Nationalism and Other Loyalities in the American Revolution." AHR, 67 (1962), 901-923.

The Revolution was the result of a slow intellectual and emotional growth.

271. Schlesinger, Arthur M. "Politics, Propaganda, and the Philadelphia Press." PA MHB, 60 (1936), 309-322.

Philadelphia newspapers excited resistance to the Stamp Act and shifted from provincial to imperial politics in their views.

272. Shalhope, Robert E. "Toward a Republican Synthesis: The Emergence of an Understanding of Republicanism in American Historiography." WMQ, 29 (1972), 49-80.

Contemporary views of republicanism provide historians with a technique to comprehend the era.

273. Stantis, Peter J. "British Views of the American Revolution: A Conflict Over Rights of Sovereignty." EARLY AMER LIT, 11 (1976), 191-201.

Here is a good sampling of the attitudes of Joseph Tucker, David Horn and Edmund Burke.

274. Stourzh, Gerald. "Reason and Power in Benjamin Franklin's Political Thought." AMER POL SCI REV, 47 (1953), 1092-1115.

Here is a fine synthesis which shows the duality and flexibility in Franklin's commentaries on politics.

275. Tate, Thad W. "The Social Contract in America, 1774-1789. Revolutionary Theory as a Conservative Instrument." WMQ, 22 (1965), 375-392.

Americans attempted to provide legitimacy to a revolutionary course of action.

276. Varg, Paul A. "The Advent of Nationalism, 1758-1776." AMER Q, 16 (1964), 169-181.

During the controversies with Britain, the colonies became conscious of their national identity as a chosen people.

277. Ver Steeg, Clarence L. "The American Revolution Considered as an Economic Movement." HUNT LIB Q, 20 (1957), 361-372.

This is an excellent introduction to the subject of colonial economic activities as a cause of rebellion.

278. Wallett, Frances G. "James Bowdoin, Patriot Propagandist."
      NEQ, 23 (1958), 320-338.

      While not a Sam Adams, Bowdoin of Boston contributed essays
      for Whig propaganda.

279. Wishy, Bernard. "John Locke and the Spirit of '76." POL
      SCI Q, 73 (1958), 413-425.

      The author stresses the influence of Locke's political
      theories on Jefferson and on the "Signers" of the Declara-
      tion of Independence.

                        G. THE FINAL CRISIS

280. Adair, Douglass, and John A. Schutz, eds. PETER OLIVER'S
      ORIGIN AND PROGRESS OF THE AMERICAN REVOLUTION: A TORY
      VIEW. San Marino, California: The Huntington Library, 1961.

      This contemporary account about the development of the
      Revolution in Massachusetts from 1760 to 1775 is fascinating
      reading. Oliver's factual information is generally reliable.
      He was especially caustic about zealots who instigated a
      rebellion for personal reasons - James Otis, Sam Adams, John
      Hancock, and Congregational preachers. Excellent for a
      glimpse of Tory attitudes, this work is well-edited and has
      fine annotations.

281. Adams, Randolph G. "New Light on the Boston Massacre."
      AMER ANTIQ SOC PROC, 47 (1937), 259-354.

      With ample documentation, Adams questions old legends about
      the famous incident.

282. Ammerman, David. IN THE COMMON CAUSE: AMERICAN REPONSE TO
      THE COERCIVE ACTS OF 1774. Charlottesville: The Univer-
      sity Press of Virginia, 1974.

      This work shows the importance of the Act as a warning to
      colonists, many of whom were forced to commit themselves
      to a new political cause. Unfortunately, much of the writing
      is vague, imprecise with statistics, and uncertain about the
      importance of crowd behavior. The book really suggests how
      much more research is necessary to examine this topic.

283. Andrews, Charles M. "The American Revolution: An Interpre-
      tation." AHR, 31, (1926), 219-232.

      The colonies were approaching maturity, and it was impos-
      sible for Americans to continue in subordinate political
      status.

284. Bailyn, Bernard. "Common Sense, Tom Paine's Brilliant Pamph-
      let." AMER HERITAGE, 25 (1), (1973), 91-93.

      This is a fine popular summary about "one of the most bril-
      liant phamphlets ever written in English."

285. Bargar, B.D. LORD DARTMOUTH AND THE AMERICAN REVOLUTION.
      Columbia: University of South Carolina Press, 1965.

      Dartmouth is described here as kindly, ineffective, and
      occupying a weak post, but at least he modified royal at-
      titudes toward the colonies. The volume is useful for
      insights into the ignorance of officialdom about America,
      and how they misunderstood the nature of the resistance.
      But the book offers little new information, it is weak in
      analysis , and it deals almost entirely on constitutional
      issues to the neglect of human errors.

286. ———. "Lord Dartmouth's Patronage, 1772-1775." WMQ, 15
      (1958), 191-200.

      As Secretary of State, Dartmouth controlled land grants,
      Treasury appointments, and religious preferments in the
      colonies.

287. Barrow, Thomas C. "The American Revolution as a Colonial War
      for Independence." WMQ, 25 (1768), 452-464.

      Noting the difficulty of comparing the American Revolution
      with the French Revolution, Barrow stresses the current de-
      bates and arguments about the origins of the American Rebel-
      lion.

288. Bowles, Francis Tiffany. "The Loyalty of Barnstable in the
      Revolution." COL SOC MASS PUB, 25 (1922-24), 265-348.

      The author examines the circumstances by which a Massachu-
      sets town failed to instruct its delegates to vote for in-
      dependence.

289. Boyd, Julian Parks. ANGLO-AMERICAN UNION, JOSEPH GALLOWAY'S
      PLAN TO PRESERVE THE BRITISH EMPIRE, 1774-1788. Philadel-
      phia: University of Pennsylvania Press, 1941.

      A close associate of Franklin, Galloway was more conserva-
      tive, believing that the conflict would be resolved by im-
      perial-constitutional measures. The author presents five
      Galloway plans - which read like constitutions - and ex-
      plains why they were unsatisfactory. Boyd demonstrates firm
      control of his material and clarifies aspects of the con-
      troversy.

290. Brown, Gerald Saxon. THE AMERICAN SECRETARY; THE COLONIAL
      POLICY OF LORD GEORGE GERMAIN, 1775-1778. Ann Arbor: Uni-
      versity of Michigan Press, 1963.

Germain had a long tenure as Secretary of State for the
American Department. Though he could be stubborn, inefficient,
and inflexible, Germain was decisive in formulating and ex-
ecuting policies to prosecute the war. Inasmuch as this account ends in 1778 when the Revolution became a European war,
it is difficult to judge Germain's work. The book is heavily
detailed, it is written for the specialist, and it enhances
our knowledge of the period. Brown's main contribution is to
present a fresh portrayal of Germain.

291. Brown, Richard D. "Massachusetts Towns Reply to the Boston
      Comittee of Correspondence." WMQ, 25 (1968), 22-39.

      The towns displayed a range of reactions which demonstrated
      that they were not dominated or manipulated by Boston.

292. ————. REVOLUTION POLITICS IN MASSACHUSETTS: THE BOSTON
      COMMITTEE OF CORRESPONDENCE AND THE TOWNS, 1772-1774.
      Cambridge: Harvard University Press, 1970.

      The core of this fine work is about how Boston's attempts
      to draw other towns in the colony into resistance against
      Governor Hutchinson and the British government. This is a
      detailed analytic study of the Boston committee's relationship
      with patriots, showing that Boston did not dominate the
      Massachusetts countryside. The material about the degree of
      collaboration involved in the preparation of phamplets is
      exceptionally good.

293. Brown, Weldon A. EMPIRE OR INDEPENDENCE: A STUDY IN THE
      FAILURE OF RECONCILIATION, 1774-1783. Baton Rouge:
      Louisiana State University Press, 1941.

      Here is a detailed examination of ministerial incompetence
      by Lord North and his supporters who failed to appreciate the
      American temperament. The British proposals of 1778 to end
      the war might have been accepted earlier, but by then it was
      too late. This monograph shows a detailed investigation of
      source materials, it illuminates the innumerable plans, de-
      bates, and correspondence relating to ending the war, and
      it demonstrates an incisive writing style.

294. Calhoon, Robert M. "'I Have Deduced Your Rights': Joseph
      Galloway's Concept of His Role, 1774-1775." PA HIST, 35
      (1968), 356-378.

      Galloway tried vainly to resolve the contradictions implicit
      in the doctrine of representation and subordination, and he
      remained a Loyalist.

295. Cecil, Robert. "The Famous Tax Included, Tea Was Still
      Cheaper Here." AMER HERITAGE, 12 (3) (1961), 8-11.

      This is a close examination of how British politicians viewed
      the turmoil resulting from new taxes imposed on the colonies.

296. Champagne, Roger. "New York and the Intolerable Act." NY
      HIST SOC Q, 45 (1961), 195-207.

      After a three year's absence, the result of the law was to
      bring radicals Isaac Sears, John Lamb, and Alexander McDougall
      back into politics.

297. Chapin, Bradley. "Colonial and Revolutionary Origins of the
      American Law of Treason." WMQ, 17 (1960), 3-21.

      The Revolution maintained the traditional procedures of the
      English law of treason with juries, rights of the defendant,
      and conviction.

298. ————. "The American Revolution as Lese Majesty." PA MHB
      79 (1955), 310-330.

      The British law of treason that applied to rebellious
      colonists from 1753 onwards failed in its application.

299. Corner, Betsy C., and Dorothy W. Singer. "Dr. John Fothergill,
      Peacemaker." AMER PHIL SOC PROC, 98 (1954), 11-22.

      The prominent London Quaker and physician was a pivotal
      figure in the trans-Atlantic world of intellectuals who
      sought reconciliation between Britain and the colonies.

300. Cuming, William P., and Hugh F. Rankin. THE FATE OF A NATION:
      THE AMERICAN REVOLUTION THROUGH CONTEMPORARY EYES. London:
      Phaidon Press, 1975.

      This is a very stimulating work replete with lively narra-
      tive and contemporary documents. The editors have skillfully
      selected materials from a wide range of diaries, journals,
      correspondence, cartoons, and broadsides. The maps, diagrams,
      and other illustrations are excellent. The work is suited for
      a general audience.

301. Currey, Cecil B. ROAD TO REVOLUTION: BENJAMIN FRANKLIN IN
      ENGLAND, 1765-1775. Garden City, New York: Doubleday and
      Co., 1968.

      The author revises the view that Franklin was a political
      moderate who attempted to preserve imperial unity. By 1766
      he was a "radical" and contended that Parliament had no
      authority to legislate for the colonies. No other individual,
      the author claims, was more responsible for producing the rift
      between the two countries. Though Currey ignores the evidence
      that conflicts with his thesis, this is a well-written book
      that merits praise.

302. Davidson, Philip. PROPAGANDA AND THE AMERICAN REVOLUTION,
      1763-1783. Chapel Hill: University of North Carolina
      Press, 1941.

      Here is the standard view about the importance of propaganda

on the eve of and during the war. The work has a comprehensive list of essayists and pamphleteers who influenced urban
crowds and committees of correspondence.

303. ——————. "Sons of Liberty and Stamp Men." NC HIST REV,
      9 (1932), 38-56.

      This is a good summary of how radical patriots disrupted
      the sale of stamps in North Carolina.

304. Donoughue, Bernard. BRITISH POLITICS AND THE AMERICAN REVO-
      LUTION: THE PATH TO WAR, 1773-1775. New York and London:
      St. Martin's Press, 1964.

      In a very detailed analysis about the expectations of
      British ministers and their advisors concerning policies for
      North America, the author provides some interesting nuances
      and sidelights, but he leaves the basic interpretations of
      the crisis unchanged. The study has excellent material about
      the Tea Party and its consequences, and the innumerable argu-
      ments advanced by Crown, Parliament and key individuals about
      handling the colonists. The result is a fascinating picture
      of how opinions hardened in the Lord North administration, and
      in the Chatham and Rockingham factions. This is a fully docu-
      mented and well-written account.

305. Duff, Stella, F. "The Case Against the King: The Virginia
      Gazette Indicts George III." WMQ, 6 (1949), 383-397.

      Editorials about the Stamp Act, the Townshend Acts and
      the Wilkes controversy were preparations for a vicious attack
      on the Crown.

306. Ferling, John. "Compromise or Conflict: The Rejection of the
      Galloway Alternative to Rebellion." PA HIST, 43 (1976),
      5-20.

      This is a key article which explains why the Continental Con-
      gress rejected Galloway's plan.

307. Gerlach, Don R. "A Note on the Quartering Act of 1774." NEQ,
      39 (1939), 80-88.

      Historians have viewed this statute too harshly, for it was
      not a gross violation of constitutional rights.

308. Gimbel, Richard. "The Resurgence of Thomas Paine." AMER
      ANTIQ SOC PROC, 69 (1939), 97-110.

      Here is a good summary of Paine's famous political tracts,
      COMMON SENSE and the AMERICAN CRISIS.

309. Granger, Bruce I. POLITICAL SATIRE IN THE AMERICAN REVOLUTION,
      1763-1783. Ithaca: Cornell University Press, 1960.

This is a very cogent and comprehensive study of the use
of satire in speeches, pamphlets, and newspapers. The author
carefully explains how such material was used in revolutionary
ideology.

310. Greene, Jack P. "The North Carolina House and the Power to
      Appoint Public Treasurers, 1711-1775." NC HIST REV., 40
      (1963), 37-53.

The Assembly gradually assumed a greater share of executive
duties in nominating and appointing officials, even beyond that
of the British House of Commons.

311. Gruber, Ira D. "The American Revolution as a Conspiracy:
      The British View." WMQ, 26 (1959), 360-372.

Not until the battle of Lexington did British politicans
view the rebellion as a deliberate conspiracy.

312. Gummere, Richard M. "Thomas Paine: Was He Really Anticlassi-
      cal?" AMER ANTIQ SOC PROC, 75 (1965), 253-267.

Paine used Greek and Latin classics as models for expressing
fresh themes on traditional political questions.

313. Guttridge, George H. "Lord Germain in Office, 1775-1782."
      AHR, 33 (1927), 23-43.

Anxious to retire from office, Germain supported his King
on coercing the colonists and refused to become a scapegoat
for failures in the war.

314. Hall, Hubert. "Chatham's Colonial Policy." AHR, 5 (1899-
      1900), 659-675.

This is a sympathetic examination of Chatham's efforts to
keep peace with the colonists until 1775.

315. Halliday, E.M. "Nature's Gods and the Founding Fathers."
      AMER HERITAGE, 14 (6), (1962), 4-7, 100-106.

Here is a very convenient summary of how Jefferson and
Madison championed the fight for separation of church and
state.

316. Hample, Judy. "The Textual and Cultural Authenticity of
      Patrick Henry's 'Liberty or Death' Speech." QJ SPEECH,
      63 (1977), 298-310.

The famous March, 1775, speech was revised by William Wirt
who embellished the language in order to inspire America.

317. Handlin, Oscar, and Mary F. Handlin. "James Burgh and Ameri-
      can Revolutionary Theory." MASS HIST SOC PROC, 72 (1961),
      38-57.

Burgh's POLITICAL DISQUISITIONS (1774) was a widely respected
work which justified resistance against tyranny; it influenced
Jefferson and John Adams.

318. Haw, James. "Maryland Politics On the Eve of Rebellion: The
      Provincial Controversy, 1770-1773," MD HIST MAG, 65 (1970),
      103-129.

      The debate over home rule was influenced by laws on tobacco,
      officials' fees, and ministers' salaries.

319. Hinkhouse, Frank J. PRELIMINARIES OF THE AMERICAN REVOLUTION
      AS SEEN IN THE ENGLISH PRESS 1763-1775. New York: Columbia
      University Press, 1926.

      This useful work examines how journalistic opinion was
      formed in an era when editorials were not used. Letters of
      opinion written by prominent men were printed in newspapers
      and periodicals, thereby expressing points of view about the
      colonies. The volume is not easy to read, but it contains
      many interesting contemporary samples.

320. Jensen, Merrill, ed. TRACTS OF THE AMERICAN REVOLUTION,
      1763-1775. Chicago: Bobbs-Merrill Co., 1967.

      Jensen has compiled a valuable collection of some 400
      political pamphlets published during the era. Many, particu-
      larly those that produced a rebuttal, are coupled together
      to provide lively literary debates on an issue. The selec-
      tions are judicious, the spelling is modernized, and the
      insightful, introductory commentary provides a thoughtful
      perspective.

321. Jones, Alice Hanson. WEALTH OF A NATION TO BE: THE AMERICAN
      COLONIES ON THE EVE OF THE REVOLUTION. New York: Columbia
      University Press, 1980.

      This is one of the best books available for economic data
      on the colonies. It covers a broad geographic area, probes
      every economic activity of the Americans, and it examines pat-
      terns of wealth. Using probate records and sampling techni-
      ques, Hanson generalizes about population growth. The work
      is packed with interesting data which have broad social
      ramifications. The 50 pages of notes, 55 pages of appendices,
      and 150 tables and charts testify to the author's thoroughness.

322. Jordon, Winthrop D. "Familial Politics: Thomas Paine and the
      Killing of the King, 1776." JAH, 60 (1973), 298-308.

      Here is a highly imaginative essay about the popularity of
      COMMON SENSE which suggests the subconscious rejection of
      parental authority and the ritual of destroying authoritative
      figures.

323. Kaestle, Carl F. "The Public Reaction to John Dickinson's 'Farmer's Letters'." AMER ANTIQ SOC PROC, 78 (1968), 323-359.

This is an excellent view of the influence of the twelve letters which appeared in nineteen newspapers to help solidify public opinion about taxation.

324. Ketchum, Richard M. "Men of the Revolution: Lord North." AMER HERITAGE, 23 (2), (1972), 18-19.

This is an excellent portrait of George III's leading minister grappling with colonial problems.

325. Knollenberg, Bernhard. "Did Sam Adams Provoke the Boston Tea Party and the Clash at Lexington? AMER ANTIQ SOC PROC, 70 (1960), 493-503.

There is no evidence that Adams was responsible.

326. ———. "John Dickinson vs. John Adams, 1774-1776. AMER PHIL SOC PROC, 107 (1963), 134-144.

Here is a summary of varying views about the ideology of rebellion at the Continental Congress.

327. Lewis, Anthony M. "Jefferson's Summary View as a Chart of Political Union." WMQ, 5 (1948), 35-41.

The author claims that Jefferson's views on a diffusion of political power have been improperly interpreted.

328. Library of Congress. THE DEVELOPMENT OF A REVOLUTIONARY MENTALITY, LIBRARY OF CONGRESS SYMPOSIA ON THE AMERICAN REVOLUTION, PAPERS PRESENTED AT THE FIRST SYMPOSIUM, MAY 5 AND 6, 1972. Washington: The Library of Congress, 1972.

Here are extremely perceptive articles by Henry Steele Commager on the American Enlightenment; Caroline Robbins on the republican tradition before 1776; Pauline Maier on the origins of the Republic; Richard L. Bushman on corruption in provincial politics; and Mary Beth Norton on the differences between Whigs and Tories. The commentaries by J.H. Plumb, Jack P. Greene, Edmund S. Morgan, and Esmond Wright are insightful.

329. Lockridge, Kenneth. "Land, Population and the Evolution of New England Society, 1630-1790." PAST AND PRESENT, 39 (1968), 62-80.

New England was overcrowded and becoming like western Europe with respect to hierarchies, numbers of poor, and size of farms.

330. McCurry, Allen J. "The North Government and the Outbreak of
      the American Revolution." HUNT LIB Q, 34 (1971), 141-157.

      This is a key article explaining how Lord North wanted to
      punish Massachusetts quickly as an example and hoped to pre-
      vent Parliamentary debate on American viewpoints.

331. Martin, James Kirby. MEN IN REBELLION; HIGHER GOVERNMENTAL
      LEADERS AND THE COMING OF THE AMERICAN REVOLUTION. New
      Brunswick: Rutgers University Press, 1973.

      Martin examines a structural crisis in the power of the
      provincial elite. In a very systematic inquiry, he studies
      500 high office-holders to determine why some men became
      rebels. Plural office holding, placemen, and unchecked
      tenure of appointments created political immobility and in-
      creased the tension by blocking advancement for the talented.
      Hence, the rebellion was not a class struggle but a struggle
      within a class which confirmed the power of a traditional
      political elite. Even though the author is unclear about the
      scope of this frustration - due to insufficient data - this
      is a very useful book, replete with charts, graphs, and ap-
      pendices.

332. Matthews, Albert. "The Solemn League and Covenant, 1774."
      COL SOC MASS PUB, 18 (1915-16), 103-122.

      The document sent by the Boston Committee of Correspondence
      to Massachusetts towns helped to create patriot sentiments
      concerning the Boston Port Bill.

333. Miller, E.J. "The Virginia Committee of Correspondence, 1769-
      1770." WMQ, 22 (1913), 1-19.

      The committee was the first official recognition of dif-
      ferences between English merchants and the Virginians.

334. Morgan, Edmund S. THE BIRTH OF THE REPUBLIC, 1763-1789.
      Chicago: The University of Chicago Press, 1956.

      The first eighty-seven pages of this compact book provide a
      succinct introduction to the subject. Morgan concisely pre-
      sents the major issues and swiftly interprets them. The war
      was a struggle to clarify issues. Morgan sees the triumph
      of principles as the result of victory.

335. Morris, Richard B. "Class Struggle and the American Revolu-
      tion." WMQ, 19 (1962), 3-29.

      Here is a good examination of how different classes were
      influenced by revolutionary ideology and why they had
      dissimilar goals.

336. ————. "John Jay and the New England Connection." MASS
      HIST SOC PROC, 80 (1968), 16-37.

      Morris explains how New Englanders regarded their famous
      statesman and what he thought of them.

337. Page, Elwin L. "The King's Powder, 1774." NEQ, 18 (1945)
      83-92.

      The essay probes the legends and folklore about the rebel
      seizure of arms and powder from Fort William and Mary at
      Portsmouth in December, 1774.

338. Pierce, Michael D. "The Independence Movement in Virginia,
      1775-1776." VA MHB, 80 (1972), 442-452.

      The factors leading to rebellion were constitutional issues,
      regional pride, and the harshness of Britain in punishing
      Massachusetts and Virginia.

339. Proctor, Donald J. "John Hancock: New Soundings On An Old
      Board." JAH, 64 (1977), 652-677.

      Calling for a reappraisal of Hancock's vital role in the
      revolution, Proctor calls for a new biography of the patriot.

340. Reid, John D. Jr. "Economic Burden: Spark to the American
      Revolution?" JAH, 38 (1978), 81-100.

      In an essay full of theoretical concepts, the author claims
      economic grievances motivated the masses.

341. Robbins, Caroline. "Rights and Grievance at Carpenters Hall,
      September 5-October 26, 1774." PA HIST, 43 (1976), 101-118.

      The First Continental Congress demonstrated unity and cour-
      age in face of diversity.

342. Robinson, Eric. "Lord North." HIST TODAY, 2 (1952), 532-538.

      North had enormous difficulties with the colonies, Parlia-
      ment, George III, and the British armed forces.

343. Rogers, George C. "The Charleston Tea Party. The Signi-
      ficance of December 3, 1773." SC HIST MAG, 75 (1974), 153-
      168.

      The Tea Act tended to fuse diverse segments of Carolinian
      society in mass protests.

344. Schlesinger, Arthur M. THE COLONIAL MERCHANTS AND THE AMERI-
      CAN REVOLUTION, 1763-1776. New York: Columbia University
      Press, 1918.

      In the 1760's, merchant leaders allied with radicals in

protesting imperial legislation, but soon disillusioned with
radical tactics, the businessmen tried to restrain such
activities. By 1776, some merchants remained loyal, but
others supported the Revolution for profit motives. This is
a classic work because of the lucid writing style, the degree
of research, and the emphasis on economic interpretations.
Widely acclaimed for decades, the work has been recently
criticized for impreciseness in classifying who were, and
what motivated radicals, and, especially for vagueness in
identifying what was an entrepreneur in colonial America.

345. Schutz, John A. "Representation, Taxation, and Tyranny in
      Revolutionary Massachusetts." PAC HIST REV, 43 (1974),
      151-170.

      Here is a neat summation of local government functions, and
      how assemblies were responsive to popular will.

346. Sheridan, Richard B. "The British Credit Crisis of 1772 and
      the American Colonies." J ECON HIST, 20 (1960), 161-186.

      Public and private finance impinged on each other from 1763
      to 1775; after 1772 the debtor-creditor relationship deteri-
      orated, especially in the tobacco colonies.

347. Sioussat, St. George L. "The Breakdown of the Royal Manage-
      ment of Lands in the Southern Provinces, 1773-1775." AGRIC
      HIST, 3 (1927), 67-88.

      The article summarizes official reports about Indian rights,
      land grants, the North Carolina frontier, and the expansion
      of Virginia.

348. Smith, Page. "David Ramsay and the Causes of the American
      Revolution." WMQ, 17 (1960), 51-77.

      Smith traces the influence of Ramsay's early book about the
      Revolution on three later historians who refined the Caro-
      linian's work.

349. Sosin, John M. AGENTS AND MERCHANTS: BRITISH COLONIAL POLICY
      AND THE ORIGINS OF THE AMERICAN REVOLUTION, 1763-1775.
      Lincoln: University of Nebraska Press, 1965.

      Based on a thorough examination of fresh archival sources,
      this monograph for specialists concentrates on the role of
      imperial administrators who shaped colonial policies below
      the ministerial level. The book reveals much about the in-
      formal sessions between officials and private interest groups.
      There were many lobbies from the colonies, but these concerts
      of agents and merchants did not act for the same reasons, for
      frequently they had divergent aims.

350. ————. "The Massachusetts Acts of 1774: Coercion or Pre-
      vention?" HUNT LIB Q, 26 (1962-63), 235-252.

Here is an excellent analysis of Lord Dartmouth's view of the Boston Tea Party and the ensuing debate about Parliamentary authority.

351. Steedman, Marguerite. "Charlestown's Forgotten Tea Party." GA REV, 21 (1967), 240-259.

Charlestown boycotted British tea but a compromise was reached with three importers.

352. Stone, Frederick D. "How the Landing of Tea Was Opposed in Philadelphia by Colonel William Bradford and Others in 1773." PA MHB, 15 (1891), 385-393.

The public response was to convince the tea ship-captains to depart and to return to England with cargoes unloaded.

353. Stout, Neil R. "Gaols and the Enforcement of British Colonial Policy, 1763-1775." AMER NEP, 27 (1967), 211-220.

This is a good summary of the Royal Navy's role in enforcing a tighter control of American shipping.

354. Ubbelohde, Carl. THE VICE-ADMIRALTY COURTS AND THE AMERICAN REVOLUTION. Chapel Hill: The University of North Carolina Press, 1960.

This is a fine study about the personnel, officialdom, and jurisdiction of the eleven "salt water" courts that functioned from Newfoundland to Florida. These highly unpopular courts which enforced the Stamp Act were juryless, were run by judges, and were unfair. The burden was on the accused, prosecutors were not subject to control by common law courts, and judges were paid from the proceeds of ship-seizures. These courts were a minor but not a significant cause of colonial irritation with Britain.

355. Valentine, Alan. LORD GEORGE GERMAIN. New York: Oxford University Press, 1962.

Here is a harsh portrait of the British Secretary of State for Colonies during the Revolution. The author distorts the picture by neglecting to credit Germain with dedication, devotion to his King, and by overlooking features of high officialdom in Britain. However, the author is correct in focusing much of the blame for Saratoga and Yorktown on Germain, and the analysis of his subject demonstrates some brilliant vignettes of political life. This is an essential book to appreciate the British conduct of the war.

356. ———. LORD NORTH. 2 vols. Norman: University of Oklahoma Press, 1967.

Demonstrating sound historical judgment on key issues, Valentine portrays North as a pleasant, ineffective State

Secretary. Yet the book has numerous factual errors, it
projects a weak compilation of recent scholarship, and omits
some essential sources. As biography, the book is uneven
for the author attempts to make North a symbol of the evils
of eighteenth-century English politics.

357. Van Alstyne, Richard W. "Parliamentary Supremacy Versus
     Independence: Notes and Documents." HUNT LIB Q, 26 (1963),
     201-233.

     The thoroughly documented essay covers the indecision of
     British politicans in 1775 over the American crisis because
     of factional strife in London.

358. Varga, Nicholas. "The New York Restraining Act." NY HIST,
     37 (1956), 233-258.

     The imperial Act of 1767 convinced many Americans that
     Parliamentary jurisdiction over the colonies had to be cur-
     tailed.

359. Watson, D.H. "Joseph Harrison and the Liberty Incident."
     WMQ, 20 (1963), 585-595.

     A Boston custom collector was rudely handled by a mob and
     was ostracized for seizing Hancock's ship.

360. Wells, Robert V. THE POPULATION OF THE BRITISH COLONIES IN
     AMERICA BEFORE 1776: A SURVEY OF CENSUS DATA. Princeton:
     Princeton Univeristy Press, 1975.

     Here is a thoughtfully conceived and well-executed monograph
     that merits high praise. The work is replete with fresh data
     about twenty-one colonies, the author notes the connections
     between demography and social history, and he provides use-
     ful data about population patterns and interpretations about
     sectional features. Bolstered by some ninety charts and
     tables, it shows that the colonies had a great diversity
     and complexity.

361. Wickersham, Cornelius Ward, and Gilbert H. Montague. THE
     OLIVE BRANCH: PETITIONS OF THE AMERICAN CONGRESS TO GEORGE
     III, 1775 AND LETTERS OF AMERICAN ENVOYS, AUGUST-SEPTEMBER
     1775. New York: New York Public Library, 1954.

     The authors compiled fascimiles of petitions sent two
     months after Lexington-Concord and three related letters by
     Arthur Lee and Richard Penn. The annotation is sound, and
     the story of the contest between Adams and Dickinson is
     concise.

362. Wickwire, Franklin B. BRITISH SUBMINISTERS AND COLONIAL
     AMERICA, 1763-1783. Princeton: Princeton University Press,
     1966.

This work is an astute study about the importance of
British civil servants in secondary posts. Wickwire assesses
the role of these subministers and undersecretaries of the
Treasury, Admiralty, American Department, Board of Trade, and
the Customs Board. Some of these men had great influence in
implementing policies that fomented the Revolution. For a
view about the machinery of officialdom, this monograph is
invaluable.

363. Winston, Alexander. "Firebrand of the Revolution." AMER
      HERITAGE, 18 (3), (1967), 60-64, 105-108.

      Sam Adams had a burning desire to promote independence
      from Britain.

364. Wolf, Edwin II. "Authorship of the 1774 Address to the King
      Restudied." WMQ, 22 (1965), 189-224.

      A close study of the Address prepared by five delegates
      in the Continental Congress in October, 1774 shows differences
      in the drafts.

365. Wood, Gordon S. "Rhetoric and Reality in the American Revolu-
      tion." WMQ, 23 (1966), 3-32.

      Wood summarizes five decades of historical interpretations
      and calls for a Tory view of the rebellion to compensate for
      Whig attitudes.

366. Wright, Esmond. FABRIC OF FREEDOM. New York: Hill and Wang,
      1978.

      Wright traces the emergence of American nationality as a
      slow and uncertain process emanating from thirteen separate
      revolutions. In addition to nationalism, the author con-
      centrates on emergent democracy as a simultaneous develop-
      ment. Witty, impartial, and particularly good on the men-
      tality of British politicans and generals, this volume is
      excellent for the period.

367. Zimmer, Anna Y. "The 'Paper War' in Maryland, 1772-1773: The
      Paca-Chase Political Philosophy Tested." MD HIST MAG, 71
      (1970), 177-193.

      Two lawyers, in a controversy with Anglican clergyman
      Jonathan Boucher, tested the politics of resistance in the
      MARYLAND GAZETTE.

H. THE DECLARATION OF INDEPENDENCE

368. Becker, Carl Lotus. THE DECLARATION OF INDEPENDENCE; A STUDY
      IN THE HISTORY OF POLITICAL IDEAS. New York: Harcourt, 1922.

      This is a fine testimonial to the document. Becker wrote
      a brilliant, penetrating analysis of the Declaration and of
      the ideas which contributed to its making. He covered the
      political philosophy of the colonials, the state of griev-
      ances, the historical antecedents, and the philosophy of
      the natural rights doctrine. The author provided details
      about the manner of the drafting, the literary qualities,
      the influence at home and overseas. Here is a key work on
      the subject.

369. ————. "The Election of Delegates from New York City to the
      Second Continental Congress." AHR, 9 (1903), 66-87.

      The conservative program disintegrated during elections,
      and the city lost its former majority of delegates from New
      York.

370. Beveridge, Albert J. "Sources of the Declaration of Independ-
      ence." PA MHB, 50 (1928), 289-315.

      Here is a thoughtful essay about origins and implications
      of the document.

371. Blakeless, John, and Catherine Blakeless. SIGNERS OF THE
      DECLARATION. Boston: Houghton Mifflin Co., 1969.

      The authors provide neat, terse summaries about each signer
      as well as a useful chronology of major events from 1760 to
      1776. The bibliography is helpful.

372. Boyd, Julian P., ed. DECLARATION OF INDEPENDENCE: THE EVOLU-
      TION OF THE TEXT AS SHOWN IN THE FACSIMILES OF VARIOUS
      DRAFTS BY ITS AUTHOR, THOMAS JEFFERSON. Princeton: Prince-
      ton University Press, 1945.

      The editor reproduced thirty pages of all versions of
      Jefferson's rough drafts with alterations and marginal emen-
      dations of his colleagues. Some perplexing questions of text
      are examined here. Clearly, he was the sole author of the
      phraseology, but the ideas were drawn from many sources.
      Boyd reproduced ten documents here, including all the known
      first drafts written by Jefferson. This is a gracefully
      written work that merits a wide audience.

373. ————. "The Disputed Authorship of the Declaration on the
      Causes and Necessity of Taking Up Arms." PA MHB, 74 (1950),
      51-73.

      Boyd compares the drafts by Jefferson and Dickinson to show
      variations in style and presentation.

374. Burnett, Edmund C. "The Name 'United States' of America."
      AHR, 3] (1925), 79-8]).

      This is a brief commentary on the origins of the famous
      phrase.

375. Donovan, Frank R. MR. JEFFERSON'S DECLARATION. New York:
      Dodd, Mead and Co., 1968.

      Here is a well-crafted narrative with broad appeal. It
      contains a copy of Jefferson's first draft of the Declaration
      and thoughtful commentaries about various factions in Con-
      gress. For an introduction to the topic, this work is a good
      place to start.

376. Dutcher, George M. "The Rise of Republican Government in the
      United States." POL SCI Q, 55 (1940), 199-216.

      The essay summarizes how the American government became
      republican in form and in character.

377. Fehrenbach, T.R. GREATNESS TO SPARE. Princeton, Toronto,
      London, Melbourne: D. Van Nostrand, Inc., 1962.

      This is a helpful summary of the Declaration of Independence
      apparently intended for a high school audience. It contains
      a simple summary of the event and brief sketches of the
      signers.

378. Ferris, Robert G., ed. SIGNERS OF THE DECLARATION. Washing-
      ton: Government Printing Office, 1973.

      This is a delightful synthesis of the event. Ferris pro-
      vides a concise compendium of the lives of the signers and
      information about the framing of the document. Furthermore,
      he includes lively sketches about numerous buildings that had
      links to the events.

379. Filby, P.W., ed. "The Dunlap Declaration of Independence."
      MD HIST MAG, 65 (1970), 68-70.

      Only 16 known copies remain of the original 200 that were
      printed.

380. Fisher, Sydney George. "The Twenty-Eight Charges Against the
      King in the Declaration of Independence." PA MHB, 21 (1907),
      256-303.

      The author concentrates on the second part of the document
      and stresses the implications.

381. Hawke, David. A TRANSACTION OF FREE MEN. THE BIRTH AND
      COURSE OF THE DECLARATION OF INDEPENDENCE. New York:
      Charles Scribner's Sons, 1964.

This may be the best book on the subject. Providing ana-
lytical insights into the philosophic sources of the Declaration, Hawke nimbly assembles the evidence to demonstrate that
the Revolution succeeded because of the men who made it. The
author traces the evolution of the document as it emerged
from Jefferson's mind in drafts and in debates. Hawke writes
with skill and clarity and is especially astute in capturing
the excitement of the deliberations.

382. Head, John M. A TIME TO REND: AN ESSAY ON THE DECISION FOR
      AMERICAN INDEPENDENCE. Madison: State Historical Society
      of Wisconsin, 1968.

      The author studies the Delegates' careers in the First and
      Second Continental Congress to July 3, 1776. He evaluates
      their backgrounds and experiences, concentrating on Adams,
      Dickerson, Jefferson, and Rutledge. Unfortunately, there are
      factual errors here and some erroneous interpretations.
      However, for a good view of the conflicts among Delegates
      that is written in an engaging style this book is helpful.

383. Howell, Wilbur Samuel. "The Declaration of Independence and
      Eighteenth-Century Logic." WMQ, 18 (1961), 463-484.

      This is a clearly-reasoned explanation of the logic and
      rhetoric of the document in relation to the ideas of con-
      temporary political philosophers.

384. Jones, Howard Mumford. "The Declaration of Independence.
      A Critique." AMER ANTIQ SOC PROC, 85 (1975), 55-72.

      Here is a thoughtful commentary about "one of the two most
      powerful public papers ever issued in the country, the other
      being the Federal Constitution."

385. Ketchum, Richard M. "Men of the Revolution - John Hancock."
      AMER HERITAGE, 26 (2), (1976) 64-65, 81-82.

      Hancock led the rest in signing the Declaration of Independ-
      ence.

386. ———. "Men of the Revolution - John Warren." AMER HERITAGE,
      22 (5), (1971), 20-21.

      This is a fine sketch of the patriotic Bostonian physician.

387. Lacy, Dan. THE MEANING OF THE AMERICAN REVOLUTION. New York:
      American Library, 1964.

      This is a highly analytical exploration of events that led
      to rebellion which covers familiar ground. But it demon-
      strates a firm command of the literature. The book is inform-
      ative, well written, and it contains terse interpretation of
      recent scholarship. Although the author created wooden
      figures here, and he overlooked imperial aspects, he concluded

62

with a solid final chapter on the significance of the Revolution to the world. Lacy sees the upheaval as a continuous process that is still underway.

388. Lengyel, Cornel. FOUR DAYS. THE STORY BEHIND THE DECLARATION OF INDEPENDENCE. Garden City, New York: Doubleday and Co., Inc., 1958.

This is a moving account intended for the general reader. There are ample details and some lively anecdotes about the Founding Fathers. The simplistic sentences and paragraph structure make it easy to read.

389. Lyman, Susan Elizabeth. "The Search for the Missing King." AMER HERITAGE 9 (5), (1958), 62-63.

What happened to the statue of George III which was toppled in New York City in 1776?

390. Maier, Pauline. OLD REVOLUTIONARIES: POLITICAL LIVES IN THE AGE OF SAMUEL ADAMS. New York: Alfred A. Knopf, 1980.

Here are character studies of Sam Adams, Isaac Sears, Thomas Young, Richard Henry Lee, and Charles Carroll. Especially incisive on Adams, Lee, and Carroll, the author shows the diverse motives of these revolutionaries who were not bound by class, ideology, or interest group. This is a provocative and rewarding study.

391. Malone, Dumas. STORY OF THE DECLARATION OF INDEPENDENCE. New York: Oxford University Press, 1954.

Here is a superb compilation of words and pictures that captures the essense of the key historic moment. The text is lucid and replete with information; the material which explains the motivations of the signers is excellent. The profusion of prints, paints, and photographs help make this work a visual delight.

392. Meigs, Cornella. THE VIOLENT MEN: A STUDY OF HUMAN RELATIONS IN THE FIRST AMERICAN CONGRESS. New York: Macmillan Publishing Co., 1949.

As Meigs defines it, the Delegates seemed like violent men. The book has good coverage on the contests between John Adams and Tom Paine, Joseph Galloway and his critics, and John Dickinson and his conscience. However, the work lacks vignettes that would suggest tension and drama, and military events are virtually ignored.

393. Michael, William H. THE DECLARATION OF INDEPENDENCE. Washington: Government Printing Office, 1904.

This volume contains portraits and biographical data of all fifty-six signers.

394. Morris, Richard B. "Meet Dr. Franklin." AMER HERITAGE, 23
      (1), (1971), 80-91.

      Morris neatly covers Franklin's role as a Delegate to Con-
      gress and his wide range of intellectual interests.

395. Morrison, Samuel Eliot. "Prelude to Independence: The Virginia
      Resolution of May 15, 1776." WMQ, 8 (1951), 483-495.

      Here is a summation of a meeting held in Williamsburg to
      decide if Virginia was to become an independent state.

396. Nettels, Curtis P. "A Link in the Chain of Events Leading to
      American Independence." WMQ, 3 (1946), 36-47.

      The term "United States" and not "United Colonies" was first
      used on June 24, 1776, in a document of the Continental Congress.

397. Robbins, Caroline. "Decision in '76: Reflections of the 56
      Signers." MASS HIST SOC PROC, 89 (1977), 72-87.

      Here is a useful summary about the similarities and dis-
      parities of the signers.

398. Schaar, John H. "' ... And the Pursuit of Happiness.'" VA
      Q REV, 46 (1970), 1-26.

      There were four views on the meaning of "happiness" by the
      Founding Fathers.

399. Tourtellot, Arthur Benson. "' ... We Mutually Pledge to Each
      Other Our Lives, Our Fortunes, and Our Sacred Honor.'"
      AMER HERITAGE, 4 (1), (1962), 36-41.

      The author briefly traces the gains and losses in the careers
      of some signers.

II

CAMPAIGNS AND BATTLES

A. GENERAL HISTORIES

400. Alden John R. A HISTORY OF THE AMERICAN REVOLUTION. New
      York: Alfred A. Knopf, 1969.

      Here is a broad, dependable survey for the college student.
      The author astutely comments on colorful personalities, mis-
      takes in strategy, the problems of the Loyalists, along with
      innumerable vignettes of heroes and villains. For a book
      with accuracy, careful scholarship, cogent interpretation,
      along with a lively writing style, this work, is difficult to
      supercede. The bibliographic essay is particularly helpful.

401. ————. THE AMERICAN REVOLUTION, 1775-1783. New York: Harper
      Brothers, 1954.

      This work is the best brief account of the war available.
      Although Alden highlights military campaigns, he also covers
      political and economic aspects of the struggle. Though tradi-
      tional in interpretation, the book is highly informative and
      imaginative. Well-organized, clearly written, and judicious
      in analysis, Alden's book merits a wide audience.

402. Apetheker, Herbert. THE AMERICAN REVOLUTION, 1763-1783. New
      York: International Publishers, 1960.

      Though not informative about military and naval operations,
      this careful analytical study deserves attention for its
      chapters on diplomacy, and on the impact of the war on civil-
      ians. The specialist may appreciate the author's appraisal of
      the social aspects of the Revolution.

403. Belcher, Henry. THE FIRST AMERICAN CIVIL WAR: FIRST PERIOD,
      1775-1778. 2 vols. London: Macmillan and Co., Ltd., 1911.

      More argumentative than historical, this entertaining work
      may appeal to general readers. Belcher took nearly half the
      book to cover the eve of the Revolution, but his interpretations
      of differences between the patriots and Loyalists are interest-
      ing. The rest of the work on military affairs is rambling
      and disorganized. However, it contains an adequate summary
      of British military activities in North America during the
      war.

404. Carrington, Henry B. BATTLES OF THE AMERICAN REVOLUTION,
      1775-1781. HISTORICAL AND MILITARY CRITICISMS, WITH
      TOPOGRAPHICAL ILLUSTRATIONS. New York: A.S. Barnes and Co.,
      1871.

      This work has excellent maps, a good index, and sweeping
      coverage of the major campaigns. The author provided infor-
      mation about strategy and tactics, but he virtually neglected
      the Loyalists, partisan warfare, the South, and ended his
      story with Yorktown. Nevertheless, this book is one of the
      best on the subject from the nineteenth-century.

405. Commager, Henry S., and Richard B. Morris, eds. THE SPIRIT
      OF 'SEVENTY-SIX: THE STORY OF THE AMERICAN REVOLUTION AS
      TOLD BY PARTICIPANTS. Indianapolis: Bobbs-Merrill Co., Inc.,
      1958.

      Here is an excellent, comprehensive summation of the war as
      revealed through accounts of contemporaries in the struggle.
      The selections are vivid, cover most aspects of the war, and
      they reveal much about patriotic attitudes. Each section is
      preceeded by a knowledgeable introductory essay. For in-
      sights into the social impact of war, this anthology is
      highly recommended.

406. Cullen, Joseph P. "The Concise Illustrated History of the
      American Revolution." AMER HIST ILL, 6 (2), (1972), 1-64.

      Cullen wrote a terse and colorful summary about the rebel-
      lion for a popular audience, particularly for high-schoolers.

407. Dann, John C., ed. THE REVOLUTION REMEMBERED. EYEWITNESS
      ACCOUNTS OF THE WAR FOR AMERICAN INDEPENDENCE. Chicago:
      The University of Chicago Press, 1979.

      By extracting material from the rarely used Revolutionary War
      pension applications held in the National Archives, Dann has
      produced a stirring and highly readable series of contemporary
      accounts that should appeal to a broad readership. Of some
      80,000 documents, he selected 79 to provide coverage for main
      theaters of the war. Each testimony is preceeded by a concise
      biographical sketch of a serviceman. With a nicely balanced
      array of material concerning the emotions and attitudes of
      participants at key moments in the fights, Dann has provided
      fresh perspectives about the struggle. This book is the best
      of its kind on the Revolution.

408. Dupuy, Richard E. and Trevor N. AN OUTLINE HISTORY OF THE
      AMERICAN REVOLUTION. New York: Harper and Row, 1975.

      This work may be helpful for readers seeking data about
      battles. However, the material is poorly arranged, the fighting
      seems remote from society, and there is little information
      about strategy. The authors display little comprehension of
      the European war underway, and their plodding writing style
      detracts from the book's value.

409. ————. THE COMPACT HISTORY OF THE REVOLUTIONARY WAR. New
      York: Hawthorne Books, 1963.

      This book is useful for information on weapons, tactics,
      and on Washington's military leadership. The authors move
      quickly to the essentials of a campaign in well-organized
      sections featured by simple sentences. The Dupuys view the
      war as an American success and not as a British failure.
      For youngsters, this book is recommended.

410. Flood, Charles Bracken. RISE AND FIGHT AGAIN: PERILOUS TIMES
      ALONG THE ROAD TO INDEPENDENCE. New York: Dodd, Mead and
      Co., 1976.

      Bracken writes a fast-paced narrative for a popular audience.
      He concentrates on how specific American failures (Quebec,
      Fort Washington, Penobscot, battles in the Carolinas) actually
      toughened patriot resistance. This is a tedious retelling of
      familiar events without any fresh interpretations. It may be
      helpful for undergraduates; history "buffs" may enjoy it.

411. Greene, Francis Vinton. THE REVOLUTIONARY WAR AND THE MILI-
      TARY POLICY OF THE UNITED STATES. New York: Charles
      Scribner's Sons, 1911.

      Though somewhat outdated, this is still a useful treatment.
      The narrative is smooth, the insights cogent, and the use of
      documents is evident. The maps are excellent. The book re-
      presents one of the first scholarly commentaries on the war
      written by an American military specialist.

412. Griffith, Samuel B., III. IN DEFENSE OF THE PUBLIC LIBERTY.
      Garden City, New York: Doubleday and Co., Inc., 1976.

      This is one of the poorest summaries of the war to emerge
      during the Bicentennial. The author used standard sources,
      footnoted poorly, and the events and actions he describes
      seem unrelated to American society and to the world overseas.
      Very quaint and old-fashioned in style, the volume demon-
      strates the writer's unfamiliarity with recent trends in
      scholarship and his inability to evaluate evidence critically.

413. Higginbotham, Don. "American Historians and the Military
      History of the American Revolution." AHR, 70 (1964), 18-
      34.

      The author urges historians to examine the impact of the
      war on society and to forgo the traditional drum and bugle
      narratives.

414. ————, ed. RECONSIDERATIONS ON THE REVOLUTIONARY WAR. West-
      port, Connecticut: Greenwood Press, 1978.

      Here are nine pertinent essays on military aspects of the

war, some of which will be cited in the following pages. The
articles represent some of the best examples of current interpretations on the war. The volume is valuable for its focus
on the impact of war on society.

415.   ———. THE WARS OF INDEPENDENCE: MILITARY ATTITUDES, POLICIES
       AND PRACTICES, 1763-1789. New York: The Macmillan Co.,
       1971.

       Rather than concentrating on battles and campaigns, the
       author emphasizes that the American army was a projection of
       its society, and that the interaction between warfare and
       the nation's civilian institutions had significant ramifica-
       tions for the future. Particularly useful are the discussions
       about the militia, strategy, the fine vignettes of person-
       alties, and an excellent bibliographic essay. That the
       struggle was a people's war for independence Higginbotham
       makes clear in the best general book on the subject. This
       book would be a good choice for college courses on the war.

416.   Ketchum, Richard M., ed. THE AMERICAN HERITAGE BOOK OF THE
       REVOLUTION. New York: American Heritage, 1958.

       This is a carefully-balanced and scholarly narrative that
       has attracted a wide audience. The book is rich with stirring
       commentaries and colorful pictures. Ketchum is adept in mak-
       ing the Revolution come alive, and he writes with skill and
       clarity.

417.   Lancaster, Bruce. FROM LEXINGTON TO LIBERTY; THE STORY OF THE
       AMERICAN REVOLUTION. Garden City, New York: Doubleday and
       Co., Inc., 1955.

       This is a full, rich narrative intended for a broad
       audience. It is very readable - the descriptions of battles
       are vivid, the commentaries on the hardships of the soldiers
       are dramatic, and some passages seem like pages from an ad-
       venture novel. Though the work provides no fresh evidence
       (and academics can thereby overlook it), the volume is sound,
       reliable, and, possibly, the best volume of its kind on the
       war.

418.   McDowell, Bart. THE REVOLUTIONARY WAR; AMERICA'S FIGHT FOR
       FREEDOM. Washington, D.C.: National Geographic Society,
       1967.

       Replete with fine maps, plates and reproductions, this book
       is a visual treat. Although the text is rather dull, the
       portraits and photographs add a new dimension to the war.

419.   Miller, John C. TRIUMPH OF FREEDOM, 1775-1783. Boston:
       Atlantic Monthly Press, 1948.

       Written with vigor and clarity, this volume contains a mass
       of information. Though limited in coverage about the west and

the sea-war, the book delves into almost all other aspects of the struggle, particularly political problems. Miller has a colorful writing style, and his perception of wartime experiences demonstrates a thorough command of the source material.

420. Mitchell, Broadus. THE PRICE OF INDEPENDENCE: A REAL VIEW OF THE REVOLUTION. New York: Oxford University Press, 1974.

Concentrating on social and economic aspects of the war to the neglect of politics, and the fighting, Mitchell fashioned a weak account of the war. His interpretations of some segments of the war are not reliable. It is unclear for what audience this hazy work was conceived.

421. Mitchell, Joseph Brody. DECISIVE BATTLES OF THE AMERICAN REVOLUTION. New York: G.P. Putnam's Sons, 1962.

For a quick readable reference about the basic facts of an engagement, this compact volume should be consulted. It is quite readable, and the author's ability to compress his material into terse chapters is commendable. But Mitchell only considers ten generals and provides few insights about the struggle.

422. Montross, Lynn. THE STORY OF THE CONTINENTAL ARMY, 1775-1783. New York: Barnes and Noble, 1967.

This work offers a detailed coverage of major battles with a minimum of interpretation for the reader. Apparently, little original research was done for this sketchy treatment of standard themes. The material about the French, seafights, Loyalists, and army command structure is thin. Yet, the work is adequate as an introduction for undergraduates.

423. Moore, Frank, comp. DIARY OF THE AMERICAN REVOLUTION, 1775-1781. FROM NEWSPAPERS AND OTHER ORIGINAL DOCUMENTS. 2 vols. 1860. Reprint. New York: Arno Press, 1969.

Moore compiled a large collection of items from diaries, journals, correspondence, and from newspapers to provide an intimate picture of the era. Unfortunately, the newspaper coverage is quite limited, and the material is poorly organized.

424. Peckham, Howard H. THE WAR FOR INDEPENDENCE, A MILITARY HISTORY. Chicago: University of Chicago Press, 1958.

This book is a brief, highly readable synthesis by a historian who comprehends the military mind of the eighteenth century. It is an excellent summary of major engagements that has attracted a large readership. The volume is satisfactory for college classes.

425. Rankin, Hugh F. THE AMERICAN REVOLUTION. New York. G.P. Putnam's Sons, 1964.

Here is a nicely written narrative that makes the struggle
comprehensible for the general reader. Rankin's familiarity
with the documents, and his adept use of source material to
enliven his account are commendable. This is an intimate
portrayal of military life for the general reader. The book
contains a glossary of eighteenth-century military terms and
a serviceable bibliography.

426. Robson, Eric. THE AMERICAN REVOLUTION IN ITS POLITICAL AND
      MILITARY ASPECTS. London: The Batchworth Press, 1955.

This is one of the most perceptive general histories of
the war. The author deftly places the Revolution within a
global and imperial context, and he supplements his fine
descriptions of campaigns with lucid commentaries about
British generals and their ministries in London. From this
gracefully written work, one can appreciate how close the
British came to winning the struggle. Robson's book is
highly commendable.

427. Scheer, George F., and Rankin, Hugh F. REBELS AND REDCOATS.
      Cleveland, Ohio: The World Publishing Co., 1967.

The authors have made extensive use of contemporary sources
and have blended them into a graceful narrative. The result
is a work of outstanding literary quality that shows the
folly, tragedies, and brutality of war along with the epics
and unintentional comedies. For a volume that conveys a vivid
sense of "being there" on the battlefield, this stimulating
study is exciting to read.

428. Smelser, Marshall. THE WINNING OF INDEPENDENCE. Chicago:
      Quadrangle Books, 1972.

Though Smelser covered familiar ground and presents little
information about the states' efforts, he wrote a lively narrative that credits Washington and Congress with victory.
British blunders were decisive and American generals receive
little criticism here. The story is isolated from social-
economic themes and the world of British politics. But it
is a helpful introduction for general readers.

429. Smith, Page. A NEW AGE BEGINS: A PEOPLE'S HISTORY OF THE
      AMERICAN REVOLUTION. 2 vols. New York: McGraw-Hill Book
      Co., 1976.

While Smith is incredibly slow to reach Lexington and Concord in his account, he thereafter moves at a stirring pace.
There are no new facts or fresh interpretations here, but the
author writes skillfully and demonstrates a firm grasp of
strategy and tactics. For a general audience needing a broad
coverage of the war, this may be the ideal volume to consult.

430. Trevelyan, George O. THE AMERICAN REVOLUTION. 4 vols.
      London and New York: Longman Green and Co., 1915.

      This is a classic work that was superbly written. Unfor-
      tunately, this famed English historian only reached the year
      1778 in his account. Yet Trevelyan's comprehension of the
      strategic and logistical problems confronting the British
      generals, his understanding of the American cause, and,
      especially his analysis of the complex political scene in
      London are excellent. Here is a unique study that should
      not be overlooked.

431. Wallace, Willard M. APPEAL TO ARMS - A MILITARY HISTORY OF
      THE AMERICAN REVOLUTION. New York: Harper and Row, 1951.

      This is a sound, reliable study that stresses tactics and
      maneuvers. It is very detailed, carefully researched, pre-
      sents numerous moving anecdotes, and it contains fine maps.
      For classes in military history, this may be the best intro-
      ductory study.

432. Ward, Christopher. THE WAR OF THE REVOLUTION. Edited by
      John Richard Alden. 2 vols. New York: Macmillan Pub-
      lishing Co., 1952.

      These volumes are generally regarded as the best coverage
      of the military aspects of the war. Not only is the treat-
      ment of major battles and campaigns related here with pre-
      cision and ample documentation, but the works contain chapters
      on relatively obscure fights, ambushes, and skirmishes that
      are usually overlooked by other writers.

                    B. THE WAR IN THE NORTH

                    1. Lexington and Concord

433. Alden, John R. "Why the March to Concord?" AHR, 49 (1944),
      446-454.

      The clue is a letter from the Earl of Dartmouth which led
      General Gage to issue the marching orders.

434. Barnes, Eric W. "All the King's Horses ... and All the King's
      Men.'" AMER HERITAGE, 11 (6), (1960), 56-59, 86-87.

      At Salem, Massachusetts in March, 1775, the first American
      blood was shed in a clash between patriots and British
      regulars.

435. Barton, John A. "Lexington: The End of a Myth." HIST TODAY,
      9 (1959), 382-391.

      This is a detailed analysis of who may have fired the first
      shot.

436.   Clark, Jonas. "Opening of the War of the Revolution, 19th of
       April 1775." In Richard M. Dorson, ed. AMERICAN REBELS:
       NARRATIVES OF THE PATRIOTS. New York: Pantheon Books, 1953,
       pp. 17-29.

       Clark was on the village green at Concord and witnessed the
       famous encounter. The book contains an absorbing anthology of
       similar material about other aspects of the war.

437.   Coburn, Frank Warren. THE BATTLE OF APRIL 19, 1775 IN LEX-
       INGTON, CONCORD, LINCOLN, ARLINGTON, CAMBRIDGE, SOMERVILLE,
       AND CHARLESTOWN, MASSACHUSETTS. Lexington, Massachusetts:
       Pvt. ptd., 1912.

       Here is a very detailed and generally reliable account of the
       fighting. Coburn was a dull writer but a meticulous researcher.

438.   Cullen, Joseph R. "At Concord and Lexington." AMER HIST
       ILLUS, 2 (3) (1967), 4-11, 52-56.

       This is a colorful summary of the events written for high-
       schoolers.

439.   Cullen, Maurice R., Jr. BATTLE ROAD: BIRTHPLACE OF THE AMERI-
       CAN REVOLUTION. Old Greenwich, Connecticut: Chatham Books,
       1970.

       Here is a small, carefully researched description of the
       battles, skirmishes, houses, taverns, bridges and other sites
       that became famous as a result of Lexington and Concord. As
       a guidebook this volume is very useful.

440.   Farnsworth, Amos. "Journal of Amos Farnsworth." MASS HIST SOC
       COLL PROC, 12 (1897), 98-107.

       This account about April 17, 1775 includes a roster of
       Colonel William Prescott's men.

441.   Forbes, Esther. PAUL REVERE AND THE WORLD HE LIVED IN. Boston:
       Houghton Mifflin Co., 1942.

       This is a fine biography that approximates a novel more than
       it does history. It is well-written, it captures the spirit
       of the era, and the chapters show the result of diligent re-
       search to recreate the era. Forbes does not engage in hero-
       worship, and her appraisal of this ingenious artisan is fair.
       Particularly good on recapturing the Bostonian milieu, the
       book is recommended for a wide popular audience.

442.   French, Allen. DAY OF LEXINGTON. THE NINETEENTH OF APRIL,
       1775. Boston: Little, Brown and Co., 1925.

       French wrote a dramatic, readable account of the skirmish
       that is replete with patriotic glory. He made a commendable
       effort to reconstruct the surrounding events, to be impartial

in his judgments, and, particularly, to raise doubts about some evidence and about gaps in the testimonials. Though moved by patriotic ardor, French was careful in his narrative to be reasonably objective. This is a solid work that should be consulted.

443.   ———. THE FIRST YEAR OF THE REVOLUTION. Boston: Houghton Mifflin Co., 1934.

This is a compelling account of 1775-76 with particular attention to events around Boston to the neglect of patriotic activities elsewhere. The author explored many collections of documents and carefully worked his material into a lengthy and excessively detailed monograph. Though difficult to read, the work is full of information, it demonstrates an objectivity about the opposing sides in the conflict, and the coverage of events has not yet been superceded, particularly the data on the siege of Boston. French castigates George III and his ministers for instigating the war. The material about the MARGARETTA and the burning of Falmouth is useful.

444.   Fowler, Albert E. "The British Are Coming." NE GALAXY, 11 (1970), 43-47.

Massachusetts villages near Concord were quickly aroused by the British march.

445.   Goold, Nathan. "Captain John Moulton's Company." MASS HIST SOC COLL PROC, 10 (1899), 300-308.

This unit was the first volunteer group to march from Maine at the news of fighting.

446.   Ludlum, David M. "The Weather of American Independence: The War Begins - I." WEATHERWISE, 26 (1973), 152-63.

Professor John Winthroy's diary of meterological conditions on that historic day indicates that weather conditions were excellent for fighting the British under clear skies.

447.   Martyn, Charles. THE LIFE AND TIMES OF ARTEMUS WARD, THE FIRST COMMANDER-IN-CHIEF OF THE AMERICAN REVOLUTION. New York: A. Ward, 1921.

Ward, as described in this sympathetic account, was partially to blame for the bungling and confusion in correlating intelligence about enemy movements and for failing to trap the retreating British columns. But he was the nation's first chief general and he served at Bunker Hill. This is a readable and judicious account.

448.   Massachusetts-Bay, Provincial Congress. A NARRATIVE OF THE EXCURSIONS AND RAVAGES OF THE KING'S TROOPS UNDER THE COMMAND OF GENERAL GAGE ON THE NINETEENTH OF APRIL, 1775.

1775. Reprint. New York: Arno Press, 1968.

This collection of documents provides a fine view of the
fury of patriotic witnesses to the killing and wounding of
their countrymen, and of the destruction of their property.
It has a vituperative flavor that suggests the propaganda
value of inflaming the patriot cause.

449.   Murdock, Harold. THE NINETEENTH OF APRIL 1775. Boston and
       New York: Houghton Mifflin Co., 1923.

Murdock sought to dispell some of the myths surrounding the
famous incident. Carefully sifting the evidence, he neatly
demolished some famous legends about the fighting and left
many questions unresolved.

450.   Seybolt, Robert Francis. "A Note on the Casualties of April
       19, and June 17, 1775." NEQ, 4 (1931), 525-528.

A note written by Aaron Wright of Cambridge provides a
contemporary estimate of killed and wounded.

451.   Stevens, James. "The Revolutionary Journal of James Stevens
       of Andover Massachusetts." ESSEX INST HIST COLL, 48 (1918),
       41-71.

A private in Captain Thomas Poor's regiment at Lexington,
Stevens wrote an invaluable description of events in April
1775.

452.   Tourtellot, Arthur B. WILLIAM DIAMOND'S DRUM: THE BEGINNING
       OF THE WAR OF THE AMERICAN REVOLUTION. New York: Doubleday
       and Co., 1959.

This is the best account about Lexington and Concord. The
author has carefully extracted from the documents and other
accounts a fascinating tale of what happened. The information
about the inhabitants of Concord and Lexington, the data on
the British forays, and the confusion in the patriotic ranks
is dramatic. Splendidly written for a broad audience, this
scholarly and readable study is well-recommended. It is the
best work on the subject.

453.   Troiani, Don. "Lexington and Concord." AMER HERITAGE, 25
       (3), (1974), 8-11.

Here is a standard but compelling account of the famous
skirmishes and of the British disasters on their march back
to Boston.

454.   Weisberger, Bernard. "Paul Revere: The Man, the Myth, and
       the Midnight Ride." AMER HERITAGE, 28 (2) (1977), 24-37.

Here is a fine account of Revere's famous ride, his fiasco
at Penobscot Bay, and his post-war career.

455. Wheller, Richard. "Voices of Lexington and Concord." AMER
      HERITAGE, 22 (3) (1971), 8-13, 98-103.

      This is a fine summary of events by American and British
      contemporaries who participated in these encounters.

456. Wright, Esmond. "An Artisan of Revolution: Paul Revere."
      HIST TODAY, 25 (1975), 401-409.

      For a dramatic summary of the famed Bostonian engraver
      and silversmith who sounded the alarm, this essay is highly
      recommended.

              2. Bunker Hill and the Siege of Boston

457. Adams, Charles Francis. "The Battle of Bunker Hill." AHR,
      1 (1896), 101-113.

      This is a well-written but undocumented essay about the
      fighting.

458. Alden, John Richard. GENERAL GAGE IN AMERICA. Baton Rouge:
      Louisiana State University Press, 1948.

      Alden is a meticulous researcher who is thoroughly familiar
      with the documents. Furthermore, he writes engrossing mono-
      graphs. Here is a detailed and sympathetic account about the
      British commander who had enormous political and military
      responsibility to suppress the rebellion. Alden astutely
      explains Gage's dilemma in trying to maintain peace, to heed
      the Crown's instructions, and to command an army trapped in
      Boston.

459. Belknap, Jeremy. "Journal of My Tour to the Camp; an American
      Chaplain at the Siege of Boston." MASS HIST SOC PROC, 4
      (1856-60), 77-86.

      This interesting commentary begins October 16, 1775 at
      Cambridge.

460. Bixby, Samuel. "Diary of Samuel Bixby." MASS HIST SOC PROC,
      14 (1875-76), 285-298.

      Bixby served on the line in late 1775 and provided some
      lively details about the fighting.

461. Carter, Clarence E., ed. THE CORRESPONDENCE OF GENERAL
      THOMAS GAGE WITH THE SECRETARIES OF STATE, 1763-1770. 2
      vols. New Haven: Yale University Press, 1931-33.

      Here is a valuable collection of letters to and from Gage
      with cabinet secretaries. The material shows the scope of
      responsibilities for commanding the British army in North
      America, for Gage supervised the military in the Great Lakes,
      the Floridas, as well as the seaboard colonies.

462. Cheever, William. "William Cheever's Diary, 1775-1776."
      MASS HIST SOC PROC, 48 (1928), 91-97.

      Here is a good commentary about skirmishing and about camp
      conditions at Boston.

463. Chidsey, Donald Barr. THE SIEGE OF BOSTON: AN ON-THE-SCENE
      BEGINNINGS OF THE AMERICAN REVOLUTION. New York: Crown
      Publishers, 1966.

      Chidsey wrote in an excitable, semi-journalistic fashion,
      but he failed to evaluate the evidence critically. He added
      not a fresh fact to old tales. But for high-schoolers, this
      work is respectable.

464. Connecticut Historical Society. "Orderly Books and Journals
      Kept By Connecticut Men While Taking Part in the Revolution,
      1775-1778." CONN HIST SOC COLL, 7 (1899), 1-320.

      This anthology is one of the best collections of documents
      on the early war years. Relevant to this section are "The
      Orderly Book of Captain William Coits Company at the Siege of
      Boston" (pp. 1-98), "Journal of Ensign Nathaniel Morgan, April
      21 to December 21, 1777" (pp. 99-110), and the "Journal of
      Simeon Lyman of Sharon, August 10 to December 28, 1775" (pp.
      111-136).

465. Drake, Samuel Adams. BUNKER HILL: THE STORY TOLD IN LETTERS
      FROM THE BATTLEFIELD BY BRITISH OFFICERS ENGAGED. Boston:
      Nichols and Hall, 1875.

      To appreciate the enemy's viewpoint of the carnage, this
      work is useful. Earl Percy's description of the fighting is
      vivid. The correspondence shows how surprised were the
      British at the fierce American resistance.

466. Elting, John R. THE BATTLE OF BUNKER'S HILL. Monmouth Beach,
      New Jersey: Philip Freneau Press, 1975.

      This brief volume has details on tactics, terrain, equipment,
      and organization. It suffers from a casual treatment of
      personalities, and from excessive and irrelevant detail. Yet
      Elting relates a rousing tale, defends the British decision
      to attack, and he provides excellent maps.

467. Fitch, Jabez, Jr., "A Journal from August 5 to December 13,
      1775 at the Siege of Boston." MASS HIST SOC PROC, 9 (1890-
      95), 41-91.

      Fitch, a Lieutenant in the 17th Connecticut regiment, wrote
      vividly about the investment of the city.

468. Fleming, Thomas J. NOW WE ARE ENEMIES, THE STORY OF BUNKER
      HILL. New York: St. Martin's Press, 1960.

This exciting study is the best volume about Bunker Hill. It is smoothly written and is packed with fascinating anecdotes. Fully researched and illustrated with excellent maps, the book provides a fair assessment of the American and British units, and, especially, the problems of the opposing commanders. The material about the Royal Navy and General Gage's staff is illuminating, and the passages about the fighting are graphic.

469. Flexner, James Thomas. "Providence Rides a Storm." AMER HERITAGE, 19 (3) (1967), 13-17, 98-99.

Washington had good luck at Dorchester Heights when Howe attacked March 5-6, 1776.

470. French, Allen. THE SIEGE OF BOSTON. New York: Macmillan and Co., 1911.

French wrote probably the most comprehensive study of the siege. The material about bombardments, gun emplacements, the skirmishes, and raids is enlightening. French tended to overlook the British viewpoint during the investment, and he wrote a dull narrative. Yet, the work is essential reading.

471. Frothingham, Richard, Jr. HISTORY OF THE SIEGE OF BOSTON, AND OF THE BATTLES OF LEXINGTON, CONCORD, AND BUNKER HILL. Boston: Charles C. Little and James Brown, 1851.

First published in 1849, this is an interesting example of writing with an excessively patriotic flavor. Though it is dated by recent research, the book is a solid and reliable treatment about the opening phases of the Revolution.

472. Goold, Nathan. "Colonel James Scamman's 30th Regiment of Foot." MASS HIST SOC COLL PROC, 10 (1899), 337-402.

Scamman's men were the first to arrive at Bunker Hill from Maine.

473. ————. "History of Colonel Edmund Phinney's 18th Continental Regiment ... " MAINE HIST SOC COLL PROC, 9 (1898), 45-106.

There is useful biographical data here about some officers who served at Bunker Hill and at Ticonderoga.

474. Hammond, Otis, G. ed., LETTERS AND PAPERS OF MAJOR-GENERAL JOHN SULLIVAN, CONTINENTAL ARMY. 3 vols. Concord, New Hampshire Historical Society, 1930-39.

Based on over 500 letters to and from Sullivan, this is an invaluable collection. Sullivan held an important command at Boston, was New Hampshire's top general, and quarrelled perennially with other generals, politicians, and subordinates.

78   CAMPAIGNS AND BATTLES

475. Haraszti, Zoltan. "Besieging Boston with a Dwindling Army;
      The Last Stages of the Siege of Boston." MORE BOOKS, 7
      (1932), 123-138, 219-228.

      Based on two orderly books of the Pennsylvania Rifles, this
      account has ample data about camp life as the fighting ebbed.

476. Hatch, Robert M. "New Hampshire at Bunker Hill." HIST NH,
      30 (1975), 215-220.

      This is an undocumented essay about the 1,200 New Hampshire
      men involved in the fight.

477. Heath, William. MEMOIR OF MAJOR-GENERAL WILLIAM HEATH, BY
      HIMSELF TO WHICH IS ADDED THE ACCOUNTS OF BUNKER HILL BY
      GENERALS DEARBORN, LEE, AND WILKINSON. Edited by Rufus
      Rockwell Wilson. New York: A. Wessels, 1904.

      Heath had an incredibly exaggerated view of his relatively
      minor view in the war, but he provided some administrative
      details. The information provided by other generals is more
      useful.

478. [Henshaw, William]. "Orderly Book (of General Artemus Ward's
      Regiment)." MASS HIST SOC PROC, 15 (1876-1877), 75-160.

      The account covers the fighting from May 15, 1775 to
      September 25, 1775; it is useful about medical affairs and
      the troops' welfare.

479. [Henshaw, William]. "The Orderly Books of Colonel William
      Henshaw, October 1, 1775 Though October 3, 1776." AMER
      ANTIQ SOC PROC, 57 (1947), 17-234.

      This is one of the best and most detailed orderly books
      extant about the siege for it contains officers' names not
      cited elsewhere, much data about medical problems and the
      aftermath of the fighting as well as service in New Jersey.

480. Hill, John B. "Bunker Hill." GRANITE MONTHLY, 1 (1877-78),
      267-269.

      Here is a brief memoir by Colonel Bancroft of New Hampshire
      about his unit's role.

481. Hutchinson, Israel. "Orderly Books." MASS HIST SOC PROC, 16
      (1878), 336-364.

      Hutchinson served in General Nathanael Greene's regiment at
      Winter Hill.

482. Johnson, Richard Brigham, ed. "The Journal of Samuel Hawes."
      NE HIST GEN REG, 130 (1974), 208-219.

      A Massachusetts soldier related his exciting experience at
      Lexington, Cambridge and Roxbury, 1775-1776.

483. Ketchum, Richard M. DECISIVE DAY: THE BATTLE OF BUNKER HILL.
      Garden City, New York: Doubleday and Co., 1974.

      Ketchum wrote the best account about the British attempt
      to storm the American defenses. The information about Gen-
      eral Gage's preparations, the uncertainties on both sides
      about respective strengths and points of attacks, and,
      especially, the bombardments of American lines are well
      handled. There are innumerable colorful vignettes here
      based on careful research. Although there are no fresh
      interpretations, this remains the finest description of the
      battle.

484. ————. "The Decisive Day Is Come." AMER HERITAGE, 12 (5)
      (1962) 80-93.

      This is a very gripping summary about the attack on Bunker
      Hill by the British.

485. Knollenberg, Bernhard. "Bunker Hill Reviewed: A Study in
      the Conflict of Historical Evidence." MASS HIST SOC PROC,
      72 (1959-60), 84-100.

      The author compares conflicting incidents about the fight
      by historians.

486. Kurtz, Henry I. "Bunker Hill, 1775: A Dear Bought Victory."
      HIST TODAY, 25 (1974), 610-617.

      The large casualty list of British troops and the tough
      American resistance depressed George III's generals.

487. ————. "The Battle of Bunker Hill." AMER HIST ILLUS, 2 (7)
      (1967), 5-11, 47-53.

      This is an absorbing story, well depicted in numerous
      plates, for the general reader.

488. ————. "Victory on Dorchester Heights." AMER HIST ILLUS,
      4 (2) (1969), 20-34.

      Washington's long siege of Boston almost failed until
      Colonel Henry Knox arrived in January, 1776, with heavy can-
      non from Ticonderoga.

489. Ludlum, David M. "The Weather of American Independence - 2.
      The Siege and Evacuation of Boston." WEATHERWISE, 27 (1974),
      162-168.

      Ludlum, a meterologist, provides interesting details about
      temperature readings during the winter of 1775-76.

490. Lyman, Simeon. "Journal of Simeon Lyman of Sharon, August
      10 to December 28, 1775: An American Private at the Siege
      of Boston." CONN HIST SOC COLL, 7 (1849), 111-136.

      Lyman wrote an enthralling account of his experience on the
      line.

491. Manders, Eric I. "Notes on Troop Units in the Cambridge
      Army, 1775-1776.' MILT COLL HIST, 23 (1971), 70-74.

      This is the best summary of units and their commanders in-
      volved in the campaign near Boston.

492. Mayo, Lawrence S. "Colonel John Stark at Winter Hill, 1775."
      MASS HIST SOC PROC, 57 (1923-24), 328-336.

      Due to Stark's unusual behavior while in command, he was
      not promoted to the rank of general by Congress.

493. Moody, Sidney C. '76. THE WORLD TURNED UPSIDE DOWN. New
      York: The Associated Press, 1975.

      This is a valuable comprehensive survey of the first war
      year. Though it possesses nothing new for specialists, it
      is a good introduction for undergraduates. The text is
      cogent, the descriptions vivid, the political events well
      covered, and the illustrations are handsome.

494. Murdock, Harold. BUNKER HILL: NOTES AND QUERIES ON A FAMOUS
      BATTLE. Boston: Houghton Mifflin Co., 1927.

      Murdock carefully investigated the documentary sources in
      order to compile a detailed essay on the fighting. This is
      a standard discussion of the British and American units in-
      volved at Bunker Hill.

495. Perry, Clair Williard. "Big Guns for Washington." AMER
      HERITAGE, 6 (3) (1955), 12-15, 102.

      Knox hauled cannon in a bitter winter some 300 miles from
      Ticonderoga to Cambridge in early 1776.

496. Powell, William S. "A Connecticut Soldier Under Washington:
      Elisha Bostwick's Memoirs of the First Years of the Revo-
      lution." WMQ, 6 (94-106), 1949.

      This is one of the most compelling tales written by a
      soldier who suffered and endured during the siege. Bostwick
      in December, 1776 heard Washington's commands for the
      Delaware crossing at Trenton.

497. Price, Richard. "The Price Letters." MASS HIST SOC PROC, 17
      (1903), 262-278.

      A Massachusetts clergyman wrote to many prominent Englishmen
      about Bunker Hill and the siege of Boston.

498. Sargeant, Winthrop, comp. and ed. "Letters of John Andrews,
      Esq. of Boston, 1772-1776." MASS HIST SOC PROC, 8 (1864-
      65), 316-412.

      This is one of the best contemporary descriptions of the
      British evacuation for Nova Scotia in March 1776.

499. Smith, Charles, ed. "Diary of Benjamin Boardman." MASS HIST
      SOC PROC, 7 (1891-92), 98-117.

      A chaplain in General Joseph Spencer's Second Connecticut
      regiment related a good story.

500. Storrs, Experience. "Diary of Experience Storrs." MASS HIST
      SOC PROC, 14 (1875-76), 84-87.

      Here is a useful portrayal of the daily routine of a company
      through excerpts from orderly books.

501. Wright, Aaron. "Revolutionary Journal of Aaron Wright, 1775."
      HIST MAG, 6 (1869), 208-212.

      Wright summarized one year's hard service in Boston in a
      few pages.

                3. The Capture of Fort Ticonderoga, 1775

502. [Allen, Ethan]. "The Capture of Fort Ticonderoga." VT HIST,
      24 (1956), 221-225.

      This is an extract from Allen's journal about his famous
      deed, written while he was in captivity.

503. Arnold, Benedict. "Regimental Memorandum Book Written While
      at Ticonderoga and Crown Point in 1775." PA MHB, 8 (1884),
      365-376.

      Arnold's notes (May 10-June 24, 1775) are particularly good
      about naval vessels on Lake Champlain.

504. Callahan, North. "Henry Knox, General Washington's General."
      NY HIST SOC Q, 44 (1960), 150-165.

      Here is the familiar story of Knox's role in transporting
      heavy artillery from Ticonderoga to Boston by January, 1776.

505. Cullen, Joseph P. "The Capture of Fort Ticonderoga." AMER
      HIST ILLUS, 4 (3) (1969), 18-26.

      Cullen wrote a brisk, popular tale about the capture of the
      fortress by Allen, Arnold, and the Green Mountain Boys.

506. Davis, Kenneth S. "'In the Name of the Great Jehovah and the
      Continental Congress.'" AMER HERITAGE, 14 (4) (1963), 65-77.

      Davis questions if Ethen Allen, the brawling giant of the
      Green Mountains, ever uttered the famous phrase.

507. Flick, Alexander C. "General Henry Knox's Ticonderoga
      Expedition." NY STATE HIST ASSOC QJ, 9 (1928), 119-135.

      This is a reliable account of Knox's remarkable haul of
      eighty cannon to Boston from Lake Champlain.

508. French, Allen. THE TAKING OF TICONDEROGA IN 1775: THE BRITISH
      STORY, A MILITARY STORY OF CAPTURE AND CAPTIVES. Cambridge:
      Harvard University Press, 1928.

      This is the best and most reliable discussion of the famous
      American surprise attack on the citadel held by forty-five
      British troops. French deftly describes the involvement of
      Connecticut in the expedition, the role of the Green Mountain
      Boys, and the rivalry between Allen and Arnold. The plight
      of the captured soldiers and their families is handled with
      sympathy.

509. Gillman, Daniel, G., ed. "Journal of Captain Edward Mott."
      CONN HIST SOC COLL, 1 (1860), 163-188.

      The lively memoir of this Connecticut officer contains some
      letters by Ethan Allen.

510. Holdern, James A., and Robert D. Bascom, eds. "The Ticon-
      deroga Expedition of 1775." NY STATE HIST ASSOC PROC, 9
      (1910), 303-381.

      Compiled uncritically from a melange of sources, this arti-
      cle has a roster of Allen's men and debunks the myths about
      Allen.

511. Knox, Henry. "Knox's Diary During His Ticonderoga Expedition."
      NE HIST GEN REG, 30 (1976), 321-322.

      Here are some interesting details about acquiring supplies
      and transportation for the famous haul of artillery from
      November 1775 to January 11, 1776.

512. Sabine, David B. "Ethan Allen and the Green Mountain Boys."
      AMER HIST ILLUS, 11 (9) (1977), 8-15.

      For a good romanticized account, this article is useful for
      general readers.

4. The Invasion of Canada

513. Barton, John A. "The Battle of Valcour Island." HIST TODAY,
      9 (1959), 791-797.

      This is the best article about Benedict Arnold's naval de-
      feat on Lake Champlain in October, 1776 by a British fleet
      under Sir Guy Carleton.

514. Bird, Harrison. ATTACK ON QUEBEC: THE AMERICAN INVASION OF
      CANADA, 1775. New York: Oxford University Press, 1968.

      Bird demonstrates some talent in this exciting narrative
      about the Arnold-Montgomery attempt to capture Quebec. The
      book is dependable on military matters, but is weak on analy-
      sis, character development, and on the attitudes of the
      Canadians toward the Americans. It adds little to standard
      accounts.

515. Brendenberg, Oscar F. "The American Champlain Fleet, 1775-
      1777." FORT TIC MUS BULL, 12 (1968), 249-263.

      The first two vessels were the LIBERTY and the ENTERPRISE.

516. ————. "The Royal Savage." FORT TIC MUS BULL, 12 (1956),
      128-149.

      In a carefully researched article, the author concentrated
      on Arnold's flagship.

517. Codman, John. ARNOLD'S EXPEDITION TO QUEBEC. New York:
      Macmillan and Co., 1902.

      Though dated by recent research, this is still one of the
      more reliable sources on Arnold's expedition through the
      Maine wilderness. It depicts the hardships encountered by
      the Americans, their difficulties on the St. Lawrence, and
      the failure to storm Quebec. Unfortunately, the narrative
      is not well documented.

518. Cohen, Sheldon S. CANADA PRESERVED. THE JOURNAL OF CAPTAIN
      THOMAS AINSLIE. New York: New York University Press, 1968.

      Ainslie was a careful observer in the British army at the
      siege of Quebec. The information here about British settlers
      rallying to Carleton, the arrival of Burgoyne's army from
      Ireland, and the defeat of the Americans is well covered. This
      is an astutely compiled narrative with ample clues about the
      developments.

519. Crist, Robert G., and Joseph P. Cullen. "Arnold's March to
      Quebec." AMER HIST ILLUS, 3 (7) (1968), 4-11, 43-4.

      This is a popular treatment of the famous epic based on
      standard sources; the illustrations are excellent.

520. Dearborn, Henry. REVOLUTIONARY WAR JOURNALS OF HENRY DEARBORN,
      1775-1783. Edited by Lloyd A. Brown and Howard A. Peckham,
      1939. Reprint. New York: Da Capo Press, 1971.

      Dearborn served eight years as an officer, participating in
      the invasion of Canada, and six other major campaigns. His
      journal is one of the few comprehensive accounts that cover
      much of the war in the north. This is a well-edited work
      that shows Dearborn was a keen, unemotional observer of
      events, and one who was involved in innumerable military
      operations. The material about Quebec is excellent.

521. Gates, Horatio. ORDERLY BOOK OF THE NORTHERN ARMY AT TICON-
      DEROGA AND MT. INDEPENDENCE FROM OCTOBER 17, 1776 TO
      JANUARY 8, 1777 ... Albany, New York: J. Munsell, 1859.

      As commander of these northern fortresses against Carleton's
      invasion, Gates wrote comprehensive orders of the day, court-
      martial proceedings, sanitary rules, and battle orders. These
      documents are indispensable to an understanding of the American
      difficulties in late 1776 on Lake Champlain.

522. Hatch, Robert McConnell. THRUST FOR CANADA: THE AMERICAN AT-
      TEMPT ON QUEBEC IN 1775-1776. Boston: Houghton Mifflin Co.,
      1979.

      This is the best work on the subject. It is concise,
      thoroughly documented, reflects new source materials, and has
      a bibliography of 300 titles. While there are few novel
      interpretations here, it is highly reliable regarding the
      near-success of the Americans, the hesitation by the French-
      Canadians to participate, the delay of the British in rein-
      forcing the province, and the numerous battles and skirmishes.
      Benedict Arnold for the Americans and Allen MacLean for the
      Canadians emerge as the heroes in this definitive account.

523. Henry, John Joseph. ACCOUNT OF ARNOLD'S CAMPAIGN AGAINST
      QUEBEC, AND OF THE HARDSHIPS AND SUFFERINGS OF THE BAND OF
      HEROES WHO TRAVERSED THE WILDERNESS OF MAINE ... Albany,
      New York: J. Munsell, 1877.

      Henry wrote a vivid tale of the march through the uncharted
      forests of Maine. His summary of hauling boats up churning
      rapids, of the near-starvation of the men, and of the topo-
      graphical aspects of the adventure is worth reading.

524. Higginson, Francis J. "Naval Operations During the Revolu-
      tionary War." NY STATE HIST ASSOC QJ, 4 (1923), 65-77.

      This is an adequate summary about the fighting on Lake
      Champlain in late 1776.

525. Hubbard, Timothy William. "Battle of Valcour Island: Benedict
      Arnold." AMER HERITAGE, 17 (2) (1966), 8-11, 87-91.

Here is a fine account of the three day naval encounter in
October, 1776 by which the ramshackle American fleet delayed
the British invasion.

526. Jones, Charles Henry. HISTORY OF THE CAMPAIGN FOR THE CON-
      QUEST OF CANADA IN 1776, FROM THE DEATH OF MONTGOMERY TO
      THE RETREAT OF THE BRITISH ARMY UNDER SIR GUY CARLETON.
      Philadelphia: Porter and Coates, 1882.

      This narrative may appear somewhat antiquarian. But it is
      a dependable treatment about the American defeat at Quebec,
      the retreat by the shattered army up the St. Lawrence, the
      fierce battles to renew the invasion attempt by the Americans,
      and the second phase of the retreat to Fort Ticonderoga where
      winter weather delayed a British assault.

527. Livingston, Henry. "Journal of Major Henry Livingston of the
      Third New York Continental Line, August to December, 1775."
      PA MHB, 22 (1898), 9-33.

      Livingston wrote a fine description of his service under
      Montgomery in New York and at Quebec.

528. Maclean, Allen. "Arnold's Strategy at Quebec." MILT COLL
      HIST, 29 (1977), 133-137.

      Here is a brief compilation of the American units involved
      in the investment.

529. Maguire, J. Robert, ed. "Dr. Robert Knox's Account of the
      Battle of Valcour, October 11-13, 1776." VT HIST, 46
      (1978), 141-150.

      A physician on Carleton's staff described the pursuit of
      Arnold's fleet.

530. Manders, Eric I. "Notes on Troop Units in the New York Gar-
      risons, 1775-1776." MILT COLL HIST, 25 (1973), 18-21.

      This is a helpful article, for it locates the American regi-
      ments stationed at every military post in the state.

531. Meigs, Return Jonathan. "Lt. Col. Return J. Meig's Journal
      of Arnold's Expedition Against Quebec." MASS HIST SOC COLL,
      2 (1886), 266-305.

      There is fascinating data here about the difficulties of
      besieging the city.

532. Melvin, James. THE JOURNAL OF JAMES MELVIN, PRIVATE SOLDIER
      IN ARNOLD'S EXPEDITION AGAINST QUEBEC IN THE YEAR 1775.
      Portland, Maine: Hubbard W. Bryant, 1902.

      Melvin graphically described the problems involved because
      of sickness, food shortages, and supply routes.

533.   Meredith, R. Brian. "Carleton, Montgomery and Arnold."
       DALHOUSIE REV, 7 (1928), 390-400.

       This is a good summary of how Carleton defended Quebec against
       the American attacks.

534.   Mills, Howard. "Benedict Arnold's March to Canada. MAG AMER
       HIST, 12 (1885), 143-154.

       Here is a good, romanticized version of the expedition.

535.   Morison, George. "An Account of the Assault on Quebec, 1775."
       PA MHB, 14 (1890), 434-439.

       Morison was a Pennsylvania rifleman in Colonel William
       Thompson's battalion.

536.   Morris, George F. "Major General Whitcomb; Ranger and Parti-
       san Leader in the Revolution." HIST NH, 11 (1955), 1-20.

       This is a very useful article for data about Ticonderoga
       and Quebec.

537.   Mowatt, Henry. "Captain Henry Mowatt's Account." MAG HIST,
       3(1910), 46-55.

       Mowatt was involved in the fighting on the St. Lawrence under
       Arnold's command.

538.   Nelson, Paul David. "Guy Carleton versus Benedict Arnold:
       The Campaign of 1776 in Canada and on Lake Champlain." NY
       HIST, 57 (1976), 339-366.

       For data on the culmination of the disastrous American re-
       treat to Lake Champlain, this article is worth consulting.

539.   Nichols, Francis. "Diary of Lieutenant Francis Nichols, of
       Colonel William Thompson's Battalion of Pennsylvania Rifle-
       men, January to September, 1776." PA MHB, 20 (1896), 504-511.

       Nichols participated in the Quebec assault; he was captured
       and imprisoned.

540.   Norton, Ichabod. ORDERLY BOOK OF CAPT. ICHABOD NORTON OF COL.
       MOTT'S REGIMENT OF CONN. TROOPS DESTINED FOR THE NORTHERN
       CAMPAIGN IN 1776 ... Fort Edward, New York: Keating and
       Barnard, 1898.

       This orderly book provides ample data about camp life,
       marching orders, discipline, and related details.

541.   Pearson, Michael. "The Siege of Quebec." AMER HERITAGE, 23
       (2) (1972), 8-15, 104-108.

       The degree of Canadian resistance is described here in an
       article replete with fine maps and illustrations.

542.   Ritzema, Rudolphus.   "Journal of Col. Rudolphus Ritzema,
       August 8, 1775, to March 30, 1776." MAG AMER HIST, 1 (1877),
       98-107.

       Ritzema wrote a solid account of the Canadian expedition
       mounted from upper New York.

543.   Roberts, Kenneth, ed.   MARCH TO QUEBEC. New York: Doubleday,
       Doran & Co., 1938.

       Roberts, the famous historical novelist, compiled ten jour-
       nals, diaries, and memoirs for this work. The accounts some-
       times overlap, contradict each other, but in general, this
       volume is the best single contemporary source written by the
       surprisingly literate men who followed Arnold through Maine.
       It is a valuable collection that provides a good perspective
       on the campaign.

544.   Salsig, Doyen, ed.   PAROLE: QUEBEC; COUNTERSIGN: TICONDEROGA.
       SECOND NEW JERSEY REGIMENTAL ORDERLY BOOK, 1776. London &
       Toronto: Associated University Press, 1980.

       This volume has good maps and plates, and the documentary
       portion of Captain Jonathan Phillips' journal adds some minor
       details. The editor attempted to link the material together
       with her own comments. Unfortunately, the editor's writing
       is weak, her knowledge of contemporary events shaky, and her
       appreciation of army life very scant.

545.   Smith, Justin H.   ARNOLD'S MARCH FROM CAMBRIDGE TO QUEBEC: A
       CRITICAL STUDY, TOGETHER WITH A REPRINT OF ARNOLD'S JOUR-
       NAL. New York: Knickenbocker Press, 1903.

       This classic work, based on very careful sifting of source
       material, is a very dependable source. Although the writing
       style is somewhat ponderous, the narrative is far more ac-
       curate than Codman's book. This is a reliable study for a
       traditional view of the campaign.

546.   ————.   OUR STRUGGLE FOR A FOURTEENTH COLONY: CANADA AND
       THE AMERICAN REVOLUTION. 2 vols. New York: G.P. Putnam's,
       1907.

       Here is a meticulously prepared study based on a wide range
       of materials. The writing is dull, the story ends in 1778,
       and Canadian viewpoints tend to be overlooked. However, the
       books are crammed with details about American generals and
       Congress.

547.   Synder, Charles M.   "With Benedict Arnold at Valcour Island:
       The Diary of Pascal De Angelis." VT HIST, 42 (1974), 195-
       200.

       A seaman on a row galley at Crown Point wrote one of the
       few surviving accounts of the fight.

88   CAMPAIGNS AND BATTLES

548. Stanley, George F.G. CANADA INVADED, 1775-1776. Toronto
      and Sarasota: George G. Harrapp Co., Ltd., 1967.

      The author wrote a lively summary of how the Canadian popu-
      lation reacted to the invasion. The material about Carleton's
      preparations to repell the Americans, the mustering of Loyalist
      regiments from the Maritimes, and the attitudes of the French
      settlers are well-treated. The value of this fine work is
      enhanced by excellent maps, and by lists of British, German,
      and Loyalist troop units involved in the campaign.

549. Stone, Edwin M. "Invasion of Canada in 1775; Including the
      Journal of Captain Simeon Thayer Describing the Perils and
      Sufferings of the Army under Colonel Benedict Arnold."
      RI HIST SOC COLL, 6 (1867), 1-104.

      Here is a stirring narrative about the famous march through
      Maine that describes the sufferings of the men.

550. Trumbull, Benjamin. "A Concise Journal or Minutes of the
      Principal Movements Toward St. John in 1775." CONN HIST SOC
      COLL, 7 (1899), 139-173.

      This is one of the few printed descriptions of Montgomery's
      siege of the British fortress on Lake Champlain.

551. Ware, Joseph. "Expedition Against Quebec." NE HIST GEN REG,
      6 (1852), 129-145.

      Ware fought with Arnold and left a compelling description
      of his experience as a prisoner of war.

552. Watson, W.C. "Arnold's Retreat After the Battle of Valcour."
      MAG AMER HIST, 6 (1881), 414-417.

      Here is a brief and reliable summary of how Arnold's seamen
      escaped the British fleet at night.

553. Wayne, Anthony. "Orderly Book Fourth Pennsylvania Battalion,
      Col. Anthony Wayne, 1776." PA MHB, 29 (1905), 470-478,
      30 (1906), 91-103, 206-219.

      This is a fine contemporary source of regimental life on
      the march from Manhattan to the Isle de Noix on Lake Champlain.

554. Wells, Bay. "Journal of Bay Wells of Farmington, May 1775-
      February, 1777. At the Northward and in Canada." CONN HIST
      SOC COLL, 7 (1899), 239-299.

      Wells left an interesting account of his march via Fort
      George and Fort Ticonderoga to the St. Lawrence; he also
      participated in the 1777 defense of Ticonderoga.

555. Wild, Ebenezer.   "The Journal of Ebenezer Wild (1776-
      1781) Who Served as Corporal, Sergeant, Ensign, and Lieu-
      tenant in the American Army of the Revolution." MASS HIST
      SOC PROC, 6 (1890), 78-160.

      Wild participated in the Canadian adventure as well as later
      campaigns, writing with insight into the soldiers' plight.

556. Williams, John. "Mount Independence in Time of War, 1776-
      1783." VT HIST, 35 (1967), 89-108.

      The American fortress opposite Ticonderoga helped to
      sustain the American lines in 1776, and it was again important
      in 1777.

557. Worthern, Samuel C. "Bedel's Rangers at the Siege of St.
      John's." GRANITE MONTHLY, 52 (1920), 448-451.

      New Hampshire troops led by Montgomery encountered a tough
      fight at the British outpost.

            5. The New York-New Jersey Campaigns

558. Adams, Charles Frances. "The Battle of Long Island."
      AHR, 1 (1896), 650-670.

      Washington's courage and character nearly compensated for
      his tactical errors in this crucial fight.

559. Anderson, Enoch. PERSONAL RECOLLECTIONS OF CAPTAIN ENOCH
      ANDERSON, AN OFFICER OF THE DELAWARE REGIMENT IN THE REVO-
      LUTIONARY WAR, 1896. Reprint. New York: Arno Press, 1971.

      Anderson fought in numerous battles. His description of
      the fighting around Manhattan is one of the best intimate
      glimpses of the struggle.

560. Balch, Thomas, ed. PAPERS RELATING CHIEFLY TO THE MARYLAND
      LINE DURING THE REVOLUTION. Philadelphia: T.K. and P.G.
      Collins, 1839.

      In addition to Daniel McCurtin's journal of the Boston siege,
      this collection contains a memoir of Lawrence Everheart at
      Manhattan, and correspondence to Annapolis by General William
      Smallwood, probably Maryland's best field commander.

561. Bangs, Edward, ed. JOURNAL OF LIEUTENANT ISAAC BANGS, APRIL
      1 TO JULY 29, 1776. 1890. Reprint. New York: Arno Press,
      1968.

      This is a brief account about the social life in a Massachu-
      setts regiment stationed near Manhattan.

562. Beatty, Joseph M., ed. "Beatty Letters, 1773-1776." NJ HIST,
      80 (1962), 233-235, 81 (1963), 21-46.

      Four brothers wrote very colorful letters about the
      fighting in New Jersey and Pennsylvania.

563. Beatty, William. "Journal of Captain William Beatty, 1776-
      1781." MD HIST MAG, 3 (1906), 104-119.

      Here is a fine account of the '76 campaign in New York with
      information about later marches in the Carolinas.

564. Bill, Alfred Hoyt. THE CAMPAIGN OF PRINCETON, 1776-1777.
      Princeton: Princeton University Press, 1948.

      This is the best book on the subject. It is compact, ex-
      citing, imaginative, and exciting to read. Bill clearly de-
      picts Washington's dilemma about a winter campaign and Corn-
      wallis's efforts to trap him. The descriptions of fighting
      are models of clarity.

565. Billias, George A. GENERAL JOHN GLOVER AND HIS MARBLEHEAD
      MARINERS. New York: Henry Holt and Co., 1960.

      Billias wrote a solid account about the importance of am-
      phibious operations in the war. This is a thorough and lively
      study of how Glover's whaleboats ferried Washington's army
      from Long Island to Manhattan in a daring maneuver. The
      Mariners were also vital in late December, 1776 for trans-
      porting the troops across the Delaware back to New Jersey
      for the Trenton attack.

566. ————. "Pelham Bay: A Forgotten Battle." NY HIST SOC Q,
      42 (1958), 26-38.

      John Glover's Massachusetts regiment performed admirably
      at a crucial fight in which the British attempted to encircle
      Washington's army in October, 1776.

567. ————. "Soldiers in a Longboat." AMER HERITAGE, 11 (2),
      (1960), 56-59, 89-94.

      The essay is a convenient summary about the Marblehead
      Mariners.

568. Bliven, Bruce, Jr. BATTLE FOR MANHATTAN. New York: Henry
      Holt and Co., 1956.

      Bliven compiled a colorful portrait of Manhattan before
      and during the invasion by General William Howe's army in
      August, 1776. There is ample information here about social
      life in the city, preparations for battle, vignettes of key
      personalities, and about the defeats of the Continental army.
      Although specialists would find little new here, it is a well-
      written account that merits a wide audience.

569. ————. UNDER THE GUNS: NEW YORK 1775-1776. New York: Harper
      and Row, 1972.

      Here Bliven retells a familiar story that tends to duplicate
      his previous book. Yet, this is a solid, popular account about
      American blunders in strategy, preparations, and in constructing
      defenses on Manhattan and Long Island. The citing of battle
      lines and fortresses with present-day street locations is very
      helpful. The chronology and action is somewhat difficult to
      follow, but the author has done his homework for this absorb-
      ing tale.

570. Bolton, Reginald P. "The Defense of the Croton River in the
      Revolution." NY HIST SOC Q, 8 (1924), 35-39.

      The author explains some bitter fighting on the Hudson River.

571. ————. "The Defense of the Hudson River." NY STATE HIST
      ASSOC QJ 12 (1931), 360-365.

      Bolton describes how the Americans positioned a great chain
      to block the Hudson in November, 1776, and how they used fire-
      ships against the British.

572. ————. "The Fighting Around New York City in 1776." NY STATE
      HIST ASSOC QJ, 8 (1927), 49-52.

      This is a helpful summary of the major military events in the
      Manhattan campaign.

573. Bowie, Lucy L. "Maryland Troops in the Battle of Harlem
      Heights." MD HIST MAG, 43 (1948), 1-21.

      On September 16, 1776, Maryland soldiers routed British
      regulars in what was probably the first "pitched battle" of
      the war on the seaboard.

574. Carr, William H., and Richard J. Koke. TWIN FORTS OF THE
      POPOLOPEN: FORTS CLINTON AND MONTGOMERY; NEW YORK, 1775-1777.
      Bear Mountain, New York: Bear Mountain Trailside Museum, 1937.

      These forts were vital for the Americans in holding the
      Hudson Highlands and for blocking British expeditions up
      the Hudson. The authors wrote a very careful study about
      the construction and the importance of these bastions that
      is nicely mapped and well-documented.

575. Catterall, Ralph T. "Traitor or Patriot? The Ambiguous
      Career of Charles Lee." VA CAV, 24 (1975), 164-177.

      General Lee, one of America's prominent and most contro-
      versial generals, may have negotiated secretly with British
      commanders for his own welfare.

576.   Cohen, Sheldon S. "The Death of Colonel Thomas Knowlton."
       CONN HIST SOC BULL, 30 (1965), 50-57.

       Knowlton's Connecticut Rangers played a prominent role at
       the battle of Harlem Heights.

577.   Collins, Varnum Lansing. A BRIEF NARRATIVE OF THE RAVAGES OF
       THE BRITISH AND HESSIANS AT PRINCETON IN 1776-1777. Prince-
       ton, New Jersey: The University Press, 1906.

       This is a classic account of the battle of Princeton as
       described by an astounded farmer as the fighting raged around
       William Clark's orchards. The information about the battle
       lines, the Hessian killing of the American General Hugh Mercer,
       and the "atrocities" committed by the enemy is unique.

578.   Cullen, Joseph P. "Battle for Long Island." AMER HIST ILLUS,
       5 (3) (1970), 4-11, 48.

       This is a dramatic rendition for a popular audience about
       the blunders of Washington's generals and the near-entrapment
       of the American army.

579.   Davis. W.W.H. "Washington on the West Bank of the Delaware,
       1776." PA MAG HIST BIOG, 4 (1880), 33-163.

       The essay provides some information about Washington's
       strategy and movements in the winter campaign.

580.   Devine, Francis E. "The Pennsylvania Flying Camp." PA HIST,
       46 (1979), 59-78.

       Composed of men raised from Delaware, Maryland and Pennsyl-
       vania to reinforce the defense of Manhattan, these troops bore
       the burden of defeat at Fort Washington on the Hudson.

581.   Diamant, Lincoln. "First Blood for the Infantry-1777." MILT
       AFF, 15 (1951), 16-24.

       The author stresses that not until the fighting around New
       York did Washington's troops actually engage in regular field
       combat with the British.

582.   Douglas, William. "Letters Written During the Revolutionary
       War by Colonel William Dayton to His Wife ... July 19, 1775,
       to December 5, 1776." NY HIST SOC Q BULL, 12 (1928-29), 149-
       154; 13 (1929-30), 37-40, 118-122, 157-162; 14 (1930-31), 38-
       42.

       An officer described the fighting around New York.

583.   Elbert, Samuel. "Orderly book of Captain Sharp Daleney,
       Third Battalion, Pennsylvania Militia, July 16-25, 1775."
       PA MHG, 32 (1908), 302-306.

       Daleney served near Trenton and Woodbridge, New Jersey, and
       he wrote detailed notes about guard duty.

584.   Emmett, Thomas A.   "The Battle of Harlem Heights." J IRISH
       AMER SOC, 10 (1911), 261-277.

       The battle site was near the Trinity Church cemetary and not,
       as usually believed, around present-day Columbia University.

585.   Fast, Howard.   THE CROSSING.   New York: William Morrow and
       Co., 1971.

       Fast is a master of the romantic historical novel, but he
       is meticulous in gathering facts. The narrative about Washing-
       ton's crossing the Delaware on Christmas Eve, 1776 to attack
       the Hessians at Trenton, the fight to retain Trenton against
       Cornwallis, and Washington's brilliant gamble at Princeton
       are covered in a vivid style. This is a good book for the
       general reader.

586.   Field, Thomas W.   THE BATTLE OF LONG ISLAND.   Brooklyn, New
       York: The Long Island Historical Society, 1867.

       Though somewhat outdated, this is a good reliable account.
       The work is fully documented, and it contains material about
       the fighting that is not elsewhere available.

587.   Fleming, Thomas I.   1776: THE YEAR OF ILLUSION.   New York:
       W.W. Norton and Co., 1975.

       This is the best book on the topic. The coverage of the
       British occupation of Long Island, the American defense of
       Manhattan and the subsequent retreat are handled in a crisp
       style. There are very moving descriptions here not only of
       military operations, the blunders of generals and admirals
       but a sensitive appreciation of Washington's uncertainties
       in the campaign. Although there is little novel in this
       account, the author's writing ability and his frequent human
       interest anecdotes provide a colorful aspect to the story.

588.   Gardiner, Asa Bird.   "The New York Continental Line in the
       Army of the Revolution." MAG AMER HIST, 7 (1881), 401-
       419.

       Here is an adequate summary about New York troops in 1776-
       77.

589.   Johnston, Henry P.   THE BATTLE OF HARLEM HEIGHTS, SEPTEMBER
       16, 1776, WITH A REVIEW OF THE EVENTS OF THE CAMPAIGN.
       1897. Reprint. New York: AMS Press, 1972.

       The importance of this fight in Manhattan may be overstated
       by the author. Yet Johnston wrote the fullest account of this
       unusual contest which helped to restore plummeting American
       morale. Now somewhat antiquarian, it is still a very reliable
       source and is crammed with data.

94   CAMPAIGNS AND BATTLES

590.   ————. THE CAMPAIGN OF 1776 AROUND NEW YORK AND BROOKLYN.
       1878. Reprint. New York :Da Capo Press, 1971.

       This is the most comprehensive work on this campaign cover-
       ing the battles of Long Island, of Manhattan, and the British
       seizure of lower New York. It contains fine maps, extracts
       from documents, and copious descriptions of terrain and troop
       movements. The material devoted to tactical problems en-
       countered by the Americans and the British-Hessians is valu-
       able. This work is a dull but still a dependable account.

591.   Katcher, Philip. "They Behaved Like Soldiers: The Third
       Virginia Regiment at Harlem Heights." VA CAL, 26 (1976),
       64-69.

       The Virginians fought a battle that Washington never in-
       tended to win but that was essential to improve morale.

592.   Keller, Allan. "The Battles for New York." AMER HIST ILLUS,
       6 (4) (1971), 4-11, 44-49.

       In discussing seven major engagements of this campaign, the
       author stresses the advantages the British had in strategy,
       manpower, and professionalism.

593.   ————. "Washington's Crossing: The Turning Point." AMER
       HIST ILLUS 6 (10) (1976), 14-24.

       Here is a good summary of the Trenton and Princeton battles
       written for a general audience.

594.   Ketchum, Richard M. THE WINTER SOLDIERS. Garden City, New
       York: Doubleday and Co., Inc., 1973.

       Ketchum compiled a very compelling account of the fighting
       in 1776 and early 1777. The author handles the maneuvers of
       armies and the plans of generals with skill, and he stresses
       how the American cause seemed doomed that crucial campaign
       year. Though it offers few fresh insights, this well-crafted
       work is a treat to read because Ketchum has judiciously
       studied the documents, and he writes in a crisp and dramatic
       manner. The maps are excellent. The book is highly recom-
       mended.

595.   Knight, Russell W., ed. GENERAL JOHN GLOVER'S LETTERBOOK.
       ESSEX INSTIT HIST COLL, 112 (1976), 1-55.

       This document has fascinating material about Glover's
       Marblehead Mariners at Long Island, Trenton and at Saratoga
       and invaluable data about regimental affairs.

596.   Lee, Charles. THE LEE PAPERS. 4 vols. New York Historical
       Society Collections. New York: The Society, 1872-1875.

       General Charles Lee was one of the most controversial com-
       manders in the American army. His correspondence, which

covers his activities in South Carolina and Manhattan in
1776, demonstrates some of the reasons. There are many letters here to and from Lee with many prominent personages of
the era which make this collection essential to understand
the campaign.

597. Loddell, Jared C., ed. "The Revolutionary War Journal of
      Sergeant Thomas McCarty, August 23, 1776-February 16, 1777."
      NJ HIST SOC PROC, 82 (1964), 29-46.

This member of the Eighth Virginia Regiment left colorful
details about marching, skirmishing, provisions, and sickness
during the campaign.

598. Lundin, Leonard. COCKPIT OF THE REVOLUTION: THE WAR FOR IN-
      DEPENDENCE IN NEW JERSEY. Princeton: Princeton University
      Press, 1940.

The author aptly describes the complex military operations
in the state from 1776 through 1778. The narrative is plausi-
ble and well-paced, the documentation impressive, and the
chapters are quite readable. However, for information about
Loyalists, sectional and religious differences, and local
history, one must consult other books.

599. Ludlum, David M. "The Weather of American Independence: The
      Battle of Long Island." WEATHERWISE, 28 (1975), 118-121,
      146-147.

This is a unique view of the fighting from a meteorologist's
examination of the records indicating that the weather was
windy, rainy, and stormy.

600. ———. "The Weather of American Independence: The Loss of
      New York City and New Jersey." WEATHERWISE, 28 (1978),
      172-175.

There are fascinating clues here about how the weather was
a major factor for both sides in the fighting.

601. ———. "The Weather of Independence - Trenton and Princeton."
      WEATHERWISE, 29 (1976), 74-77.

The wind direction, the temperature, and the amount of rain
and snow for a two week period suggest that weather conditions
were decisive in planning American military operations.

602. McMichael, James. "Diary of Lieutenant James McMichael of
      the Pennsylvania Line, 1776-78." PA MAG HIST BIOG, 16
      (1892), 129-159.

This Scot in a Pennsylvania regiment participated in
numerous engagements in the New York and other campaigns.

603. Manders, Eric J. THE BATTLE OF LONG ISLAND. Monmouth Beach,
      New Jersey: Philip Freneau Press, 1978.

      The author narrates in detail the British and American bat-
      tle plans, the disposition of troops, and many small engage-
      ments that are usually overlooked in similar accounts.
      Though Manders provides excellent maps and numerous extracts
      from documents, he has overlooked much current scholarship
      about the American and British forces. Nevertheless, this
      is a valuable contribution.

604. ————. "Notes on Troop Units in the Flying Camp, 1776."
      MILT COLL HIST, 26 (1974), 9-12.

      This is a useful roster of regiments from three states that
      were garrisoned in New Jersey.

605. ————. "Notes on Troop Units in the Northern Army, 1776."
      MILT COLL HIST, 27 (1975), 1-12, 113-117.

      Manders lists all the Continental and militia regiments
      stationed in upper New York.

606. Maryland Historical Society. "Battle of Long Island." MD
      HIST MAG, 14 (1919), 110-120.

      At a crucial moment on August 27, 1776, 400 Marylanders
      checked a British attack on Washington's retreating army.

607. Miers, Earl Schenck. CROSSROADS OF FREEDOM; THE AMERICAN
      REVOLUTION AND THE RISE OF A NEW NATION. New Brunswick:
      Rutgers University Press, 1971.

      This is a rousing, popular history about the war in the
      north for youngsters and a popular audience. Relying heavily
      on standard published journals, Miers illuminates the strug-
      gle with colorful anecdotes and accounts of forgotten heroes.
      Though only the battle of Monmouth in 1778 is covered in
      detail, there is some fine material here about raids and
      skirmishes that relate to local history.

608. Nice, John. "Extracts from the Diary of Captain John Nice
      of the Pennsylvania Line." PA MAG HIST BIOG, 16 (1892),
      399-411.

      Captain Nice wrote exciting details about the fighting and
      his own capture on Long Island.

609. Paltsits, Victor Hugo. "The Jeopardy of Washington, September
      15, 1776." NY HIST SOC Q, 32 (1948), 253-268.

      Some Continental regiments stampeded after the British
      made a surprise landing at Kip's Bay, Manhattan.

610.   Rau, Louise, ed. "Sergeant John Smith's Diary of 1776."
       MVHR, 20 (1933), 247-270.

       This Rhode Islander in the New York fighting left some
       terse comments about pay, quarters, and provisions.

611.   Reed, Joseph. "General Joseph Reed's Narrative of the Move-
       ments of the American Army in the Neighborhood of Trenton
       in the Winter of 1776-77." PA MHB, 8 (1884), 391-402.

       The memoir is invaluable for data about the maneuvers of
       Washington's troops along the Delaware.

612.   Rodney, Thomas. DIARY OF CAPTAIN THOMAS RODNEY, 1776-1777.
       Wilmington, Delaware: Historical Society of Delaware, 1888.

       Rodney, an officer in the Dover (Delaware) Light Infantry,
       witnessed some of the key engagements of the campaign. In
       very lucid prose, he described the stirring events at
       Trenton and Princeton.

613.   [Rodney, Thomas]. "One Night in December. Crossing of the
       Delaware in December, 1776 ." AMER HERITAGE, 28 (1) (1976),
       52-53.

       This is a well-illustrated excerpt from the Rodney diary
       concerning the attack on Trenton.

614.   Sanchez-Saavedra, E.M. "'All Fine Fellows and Well Armed,'
       The Culpepper Minute Battalion, 1775-1776." VA CAV, 24
       (1974), 4-12.

       Here is a lively story of Virginians battling the enemy
       in numerous encounters.

615.   Scheer, George F. "Why Washington Stood Up in the Boat."
       AMER HERITAGE, 16 (1) (1964), 17-19.

       Scheer explains the errors made by painter Emanuel Leutze
       in his "Washington Crossing the Delaware."

616.   Schmitt, Dale J. "The Capture of Colonel Moses Rawlings."
       MD HIST MAG, 71 (1976), 205-211.

       The account of Rawling's rifle battalion at Fort Lee and
       Fort Washington contains much detail on these fights.

617.   Smith, John. "Sergeant John Smith's Diary of 1776." MVHR,
       20 (1933), 247-270.

       This Rhode Islander wrote a fine account of his marches,
       sicknesses, and services under Washington.

618.   Smith, Samuel Stelle. THE BATTLE OF PRINCETON. Monmouth
       Beach, New Jersey: Philip Freneau Press, 1967.

The author provides good plotting of the maneuvers and
ample details on troop movements during the fight. The maps
are splendid. However, Smith adds nothing novel to a familiar
story, and his knowledge of Washington's planning and judgment is faulty.

619.   ———. THE BATTLE OF TRENTON. Monmouth Beach, New Jersey:
       Philip Freneau Press, 1965.

Smith carefully reenacts the drama of Washington's Delaware
crossing by use of contemporary source material, particularly
diaries and journals kept by American and Hessian soldiers.
The encounters are clearly described and are supplemented by
excellent maps and related illustrations. This small book
is the best one about tactics in the fight.

620.   Snow, Richard F. "Battles of the Revolution - Fort Washing-
       ton." AMER HERITAGE, 25 (4) (1974), 57-60.

The British victory on the Hudson was bloody and decisive.

621.   ———. "Battles of the Revolution - Stand-Off at White
       Plains." AMER HERITAGE, 24 (3), (1973), 41-44.

This is a brief but dependable account of a battle that is
often overlooked in the campaign histories.

622.   ———. "Battles of the Revolution - Trenton." AMER HERITAGE,
       24 (5) (1973), 69-72.

Here is a splendid tale prepared for a general readership.

623.   Stehle, Raymond. "Washington Crosses the Delaware." PA HIST,
       31 (1964), 269-294.

Stehle wrote a good essay about Emannuel Leutze, a German
immigrant and resident of Philadelphia, who painted the famous
event.

624.   Stevens, John A. "The Battle of Harlem Plains." MAG AMER
       HIST, 4 (1880), 351-375.

This article has excellent maps and ample detail on the
fighting.

625.   Stryker, William S. THE BATTLES OF TRENTON AND PRINCETON.
       Boston: Houghton Mifflin, 1898.

Stryker wrote the classic account of these battles. The
work is thoroughly documented, presents a well-balanced
picture of both sides, and it attempts to analyze the motives
of Washington and Cornwallis. Although more details about
the campaign have emerged in recent decades, Stryker's study
is still quite readable.

626. Swanson, Susan Cochran. "Colonel Glover's Stand at Pelham."
      AMER HIST ILLUS, 15 (2) (1975), 14-22.

      On October 18, 1776, 750 Massachusetts troops held off
      4,000 British to cover Washington's retreat.

627. Thompson, Ray. WASHINGTON ALONG THE DELAWARE: THE BATTLES
      OF TRENTON AND PRINCETON. Fort Washington, Pennsylvania:
      Bicentennial Press, 1971.

      This concise volume is an excellent guide book for touring
      the battle sites. Thompson has mastered the source material
      and writes well. The maps and illustrations provide a fine
      dimension to the work.

628. Tilghman, Tench. MEMOIRS OF LIEUT. COL. TENCH TILGHMAN,
      SECRETARY AND AIDE TO WASHINGTON ... 1876. Reprint.
      New York: Arno Press, 1970.

      There is some valuable material here about Tilghman's
      views of life in Albany, and the Iroquois. But the most
      useful portion of this memoir is his impressions of Washington
      and the information he offers about activities at staff head-
      quarters in 1776.

629. Trumbull, Benjamin. "Journal of the Campaign at New York,
      1776-1777." CONN HIST SOC COLL, 7 (1899), 177-218.

      A Connecticut clergyman left a poignant commentary of his
      campaign experiences.

630. Tyler, Lyon G. "The Old Virginia Line in the Middle States
      during the American Revolution." TYLER'S Q HIST GEN MAG,
      12 (1930), 1-42, 90-141, 283-289.

      Here is a solid summary of every major engagement fought
      by Virginia troops from Boston through New York and New Jersey.

631. Van Horne, William E. "Revolutionary War Letters of Reverend
      William Van Horne." W PA MAG HIST, 53 (1970), 105-138.

      A Baptist minister from Bucks County, Pennsylvania, serving
      as a chaplain on numerous campaigns, left his impressions of
      camp life.

632. Weller, Jac. "Guns of Destiny: Field Artillery in the Trenton-
      Princeton Campaign, 25 December 1776 to 3 January 1777."
      MILT AFF, 20 (1956), 1-15.

      The high percentage of cannon used may account for Washing-
      ton's victories in these battles.

633. Widmer, Kimble T. THE CHRISTMAS CROSSING: THE TEN DAYS OF
      TRENTON AND PRINCETON. Trenton: The New Jersey Historical
      Commission, 1978.

With a nice dramatic touch, Widmer wrote a terse summary
of the events that may be of interest to high-schoolers and
college undergraduates.

634. Young, William. "Journal of Sergeant William Young, Written
      during the Jersey Campaign of the Winter of 1776-1777."
      PA MAG HIST BIOG, 8 (1884), 255-278.

      This is the best, printed, contemporary description of the
      battles of Trenton and Princeton written by an American sol-
      dier.

                    6. Fort Ticonderoga, 1776-1777

635. Baldwin, Thomas W., ed. THE REVOLUTIONARY JOURNAL OF COLONEL
      JEDUTHAN BALDWIN, 1775-j778. Bangor, Maine: De Burians,
      1906.

      Baldwin was the chief engineering officer in the Northern
      Department, serving under Schuyler, Gates, and St. Clair. He
      was an observant diarist and his comments about the defenses
      of Ticonderoga, Mt. Independence, and West Point are especial-
      ly useful.

636. Hamilton, Edward P. "Was Washington to Blame for the Loss
      of Ticonderoga in 1777?" FORT TIC MUS BULL, 10 (1963), 65-
      74.

      Hamilton notes that tactical mistakes may have caused the
      unnecessary evacuation of the fortresses by General St. Clair.

637. Lacey, John. "Memoirs of Brigadier-General John Lacey of
      Pennsylvania." PA MHB, 25 (1901), 1-13, 191-207, 341-354,
      498-515; 26 (1902), 101-111, 265-270.

      Lacey wrote a stirring account about fighting at Ticonderoga
      and Lake George in late 1776, continuing his story through
      1777.

638. Murray, Eleanor M. "The Court Martial of General Arthur St.
      Clair." FORT TIC MUS BULL, 7 (1947), 3-20.

      This is a very weak summary of documents taken verbatim
      from a volume in the published New York Historical Society
      Collections concerning the loss of Ticonderoga.

639. Schuyler, Philip. "Proceedings of a General-Court Martial
      ... for the trial of Major General Schuyler, October 1,
      1778." NY HIST SOC COLL, 12 (1857), 5-211.

      These proceedings provide a good view of how a court martial
      of a field commander functioned. Schuyler was cleared of
      charges relating to negligence concerning the loss of Ticon-
      deroga in July, 1777.

7. Hubbardton

640. Dupuy, Richard Ernest. THE BATTLE OF HUBBARDTON: A CRITICAL
      ANALYSIS. Prepared for the State of Vermont Historical
      Sites Commission, Cornwall, New York: The Commission, 1960.

      This is a plodding account of one of the bloodiest engage-
      ments of the war. The Americans under Colonel Seth Warner
      and the British under General Simon Frazer fought the only
      action occurring on Vermont territory.

641. ————. "The Battle of Hubbardton." VT LIFE, 17 (1963), 2-5,
      56-57.

      Dupuy wrote a brief popular summary featuring the Second
      New Hampshire Regiment.

642. Smith, Milford K., Jr. "Victory in Defeat." VT HIST, 33
      (1965), 463-468.

      Although there is no fresh information or analysis here,
      this is a good account of the fight based on standard second-
      ary sources.

643. Tolsom, William R. "Battle of Hubbardton." VT HIST Q, 20
      (1952), 3-18.

      The fight on July 7, 1777 is poorly covered in this undoc-
      mented essay about the battle with the heaviest casualty
      rates on both sides for the entire war.

8. Oriskany

644. Allen, Freeman H. "St. Leger's Invasion and the Battle of
      Oriskany." NY STATE HIST ASSOC PROC, 12 (1913), 158-171.

      Allen wrote a readable summary without citing documents.

645. Flexner, James T. "How a Madman Helped Save the Colonies."
      AMER HERITAGE, 8 (2), (1956), 26-30, 101.

      The ravings of a Tory lunatic helped Benedict Arnold to
      dupe Colonel Barry St. Leger, who was besieging Fort Stanwix,
      that a large American force was nearby.

646. Luzader, John F. THE CONSTRUCTION AND MILITARY HISTORY OF
      FORT STANWIX. Washington, DC: Department of the Interior.
      National Park Service, 1969.

      This is a solid account of how an Oneida site became Fort
      Schuyler (Rome, New York) and later Fort Stanwix. The details
      about the fort's construction and defenses uncovered in
      archeological excavations, the nicely-paced narrative, the
      copious notes, and the excellent maps enhance the value of
      this volume.

647. Patterson, Gerard A. "The Battle of Oriskany." AMER HIST
      ILLUS 10 (4) (1976), 8-17.

      For a solid popular treatment of how an American force
      under General Nicholas Herkimer was ambushed, this article
      is helpful.

648. Scott, John A. FORT STANWIX (FORT SCHUYLER) AND ORISKANY.
      Rome, New York: Rome Senteniel Co., 1927.

      Here is a very helpful collection of letters, diaries, and
      testimonials about the British attempt to capture this key
      defense on the Mohawk River. The material about Colonel Barry
      St. Leger and the rescue of the fortress made by Benedict
      Arnold is nicely organized and well-written.

649. Stone, William L., annot. ORDERLY BOOK OF SIR JOHN JOHNSON
      DURING THE ORISKANY CAMPAIGN. Albany: J. Munsell's Sons,
      1882.

      Johnson wrote careful notes about logistics, camp sites,
      Indian allies, Loyalist partisans, and his plans to conquer
      the Mohawk Valley. This is a reliable book that should be
      further annotated for it is a valuable source.

650. Venables, Robert W., ed. "'General Harkemer's Battle': A
      Poetic Account of the Battle of Oriskany." NY HIST, 58
      (1977), 471-477.

      Written by an unknown participant in the fight, this poem
      contains data unavailable elsewhere.

651. Willett, William M., ed. A NARRATIVE OF THE MILITARY ACTIONS
      OF COLONEL MARINUS WILLET, TAKEN CHIEFLY FROM HIS OWN MANU-
      SCRIPT. 1831. Reprint. New York: Arno Press, 1967.

      Colonel Willet was commander at Fort Stanwix when it was
      besieged by St. Leger's Tories and Indians. His services
      here and in numerous Mohawk Valley fights in 1781-82 are
      adequately summarized.

                          9. Bennington

652. Arndt, Karl J.R. "New Hampshire and the Battle of Bennington:
      Colonel Baum's Mission and Bennington Defeat As Reported by
      a German Officer Under General Burgoyne's Command." HIST
      NH, 32 (1977), 198-217.

      This is a fine contemporary commentary which suggests why
      Bennington was a prelude to Burgoyne's defeat.

653. Barrons, June. "Seth Warner and the Battle of Bennington:
      Solving a Historical Puzzle." VT HIST, 39 (1971), 101-106.

The evidence shows that Warner's men arrived in time to
repulse German reinforcements, and that Warner played a vital
role in the fighting.

654. [Clark, Peter]. "Letters Relative to the Battle of Bennington." Edited by H.W.D. Bryand. NE HIST GEN REG, 14 (1860),
121-133.

Here are some good descriptions of the fighting written by
a New Hampshire soldier to his wife.

655. Coburn, Frank W. A HISTORY OF THE BATTLE OF BENNINGTON, VER-
MONT. Bennington, Vermont: Livingston Press, 1912.

This is a useful documentary source containing correspondence by the Vermont Council of Safety, information about
raising troops, numerous letters between officials in Vermont
and the Hampshire Grants, and lists of officers and casualties.
The anecdotal material is helpful. Unfortunately, the volume
lacks an index.

656. Foster, Herbert D., and Thomas W. Streeter. "Stark's Independent Command at Bennington." NY STATE HIST ASSOC PROC,
5 (1905), 24-95.

This is the most detailed account of Stark's role, and one
that is based on ample documentation.

657. Mann, Donald L. "Bennington: A Clash Between Patriot and
Loyalist." HIST NH, 32 (1979), 171-188.

The presence of 600 Loyalists in the fight pitted neighbors
against each other in a bitter struggle.

                         10. Saratoga

658. Adams, Charles F. "The Defective Strategy of the Revolution
Campaign of 1777." MASS HIST SOC PROC, 44 (1910-11), 14-
63.

Both sides made serious strategic errors, but the Americans
should have had their Yorktown that year.

659. Alexander, David E., ed. "Diary of Captain Benjamin Warren
on the Battlefield of Saratoga." JAH, 3 (1909), 201-
216.

Extracts from Warren's notations, from July 21 to October
16, 1777, show some interesting details about the fighting.

660. Atkinson, C.T., ed. "Some Evidence for the Burgoyne Expedition." J SOC ARMY HIST RES, 26 (1948), 132-142.

A specialist on the eighteenth-century cites some fresh documents to provide statistics on the campaign.

661.   Bird, Harrison. MARCH TO SARATOGA: GENERAL BURGOYNE AND THE
       AMERICAN CAMPAIGN, 1777. New York: Oxford University Press,
       1963.

       Though Bird overlooked many essential documents, he wrote
       a lively and informative account of Burgoyne's invasion. The
       author demonstrates why the general made some serious mis-
       calculations. But Bird neglected to evaluate supply and
       logistical matters. Nevertheless, this is a good introduction
       to the subject.

662.   Chidsey, Donald Barr. THE WAR IN THE NORTH; AN INFORMAL
       HISTORY OF THE AMERICAN REVOLUTION IN AND NEAR CANADA.
       New York: Crown Publishers, 1967.

       Based on standard books, this is a very poor summary of
       campaigns that were fought mainly in New York. It is unorigi-
       nal, very superficial and is frequently erroneous in inter-
       pretation.

663.   Clarke, Donald F., ed. FORT MONTGOMERY AND FORT CLINTON:
       SEVERAL CONTEMPORARY ACCOUNTS OF THE BATTLE.... Fort
       Montgomery, New York: Town of Highlands, 1952.

       This work is especially good on details of local history.
       There is much data here about the capture of these Hudson
       River fortresses in the Highlands by General Clinton in
       his efforts to assist Burgoyne.

664.   Clarke, John B. "Colonel John Brown's Expedition Against
       Ticonderoga and Diamond Island, 1777." NE HIST GEN REG,
       74 (1920), 284-293.

       Clarke's essay, based on correspondence between Brown and
       General Benjamin Lincoln, is one of the few treatments of
       this American victory.

665.   Cullen, Joseph P. "Saratoga." AMER HIST ILLUS, 10 (1) (1975),
       3-41.

       Cullen wrote one of the best articles about the battle for
       a popular audience.

666.   Cuneo, John R. THE BATTLE OF SARATOGA: THE TURN OF THE TIDE.
       New York: Macmillan Co., 1967.

       Cuneo writes with verve about the tactics, personalities,
       and the major incidents of the fighting. Though specialists
       will discover nothing new here either in information or analy-
       sis, this is a well-balanced and reliable treatment of the
       struggles at Bemis Heights and Freeman's Farm that deserves
       a wide audience.

667. Dearing, James A. "How an Irishman Turned the Tide at
      Saratoga." J IRISH AMER HIST SOC, 10 (1911), 109-113.

      Rifleman Timothy Murphy shot the British General Simon
      Fraser and thus helped to demoralize the enemy.

668. Elting, John R. THE BATTLE OF SARATOGA. Monmouth Beach, New
      Jersey: Philip Freneau Press, 1977.

      Elting compiled a fine study of the tactics, weapons, and
      logistics related to the fight, and he added some new source
      material. The maps are excellent. The author correctly
      faults Burgoyne's strategy, but he tends to overlook the
      political and administrative aspects of the British campaign.

669. Ford, Worthington C., ed. GENERAL ORDERS ISSUED BY MAJOR-
      GENERAL ISRAEL PUTNAM WHEN IN COMMAND OF THE HIGHLANDS IN
      THE SUMMER AND FALL OF 1777. Brooklyn, New York: Historical
      Printing Club, 1893.

      These documents offer a good insight into why Putnam was
      inept in guarding the Highland forts on the Hudson against
      attacks by British forces from Manhattan under General Henry
      Clinton. A court of inquiry investigating Putnam's conduct
      led to a major political controversy in Congress.

670. Fox, Dixon Ryan. "Burgoyne, Before and After Saratoga."
      NY HIST, 10 (1929), 128-137.

      This is a standard but readable account about Burgoyne after
      his surrender.

671. Furneaux, Rupert. THE BATTLE OF SARATOGA. New York: Stein
      and Day, 1971.

      Careless proof-reading and many minor errors spoil what is
      a lively summary for non-specialists. There are many lengthy
      quotations from eyewitness accounts that add an intimate touch
      to this nicely paced narrative. Furneaux offers fair ap-
      praisals of Burgoyne, Gates, Schuyler, and Arnold.

672. Gerlach, Don R. "After Saratoga: The General, His Lady, and
      'Gentleman Johnny' Burgoyne." NY HIST, 52 (1971), 5-30.

      General Philip Schuyler has been unjustly rated by most
      historians; he should be credited for his sacrifices, his
      handling of Indian affairs, and particularly, for his logisti-
      cal ability.

673. Gerlach, Don R. "Philip Schuyler and 'The Road to Glory':
      A Question of Loyalty and Competence." NY HIST SOC Q, 44
      (1965), 341-386.

      Gerlach notes Schuyler's egotism and political blunders but
      credits him with preparations for the victory at Saratoga.

106   CAMPAIGNS AND BATTLES

674. Hargreaves, Reginald. "Burgoyne and America's Destiny."
      AMER HERITAGE, 7 (4) (1976), 4-7, 83-85.

      Here is a solid account of the events leading to the British
      defeat at Saratoga which Hargreaves regards as the turning
      point of the war.

675. Hitchcock, Enos. "Diary of Enos Hitchcock, D.D., A Chaplain
      in the Revolutionary Army." William B. Weeden, ed., RI
      HIST SOC PUB, 7-8 (1910-11), 87-134, 147-194, 207-321.

      Hitchcock preached to the troops, visited the wounded,
      and left some interesting comments about Saratoga.

676. Howard, Thomas D. "Charlestown-'Number Four'." GRANITE
      MONTHLY, 28 (1900), 93-97.

      The fortress was a pivotal post for American troops in
      western New England.

677. Lossing, Benjamin J. PICTORIAL FIELD-BOOK OF THE REVOLUTION.
      2 vols. 1851-52. Reprint. Rutland, Vermont: Charles E.
      Tuttle, 1972.

      Lossing compiled a massive collection of material based on
      conversations with army veterans, and visits to former camp
      sites. The books have the only surviving descriptions of
      some buildings and encampments in New York. Even with gen-
      erally unrealiable source materials and bewildering chapter
      organizations, these volumes have details unavailable else-
      where.

678. Ludlum, David M. "The Weather of Independence: Burgoyne's
      Northern Campaign." WEATHERWISE, 29 (1976), 236-240.

      The meteorological evidence shows that the weather for the
      August fighting was excellent.

679. ———. "The Weather of Independence: Burgoyne's Northern
      Campaign (Continued)." WEATHERWISE, 29 (1976), 288-290.

      Heavy rain, and constant morning and evening mists were
      key factors in the weather at Saratoga.

680. Lutnick, Solomon. "The American Victory at Saratoga: A View
      from the British Press." NY HIST, 44 (1963), 103-127.

      This is a fine summary of the defeat as viewed by twelve
      British newspapers.

681. Luzader, John F. DECISION ON THE HUDSON. THE SARATOGA CAM-
      PAIGN OF 1777. Washington, DC: Department of the Interior.
      National Park Service, 1975.

      Here is a brief but highly perceptive treatment of Burgoyne's
      invasion. Luzader is extremely capable in describing the

logistical and environmental factors involved as well as
offering the reader excellent portrayals of the battle lines.
Well researched, this is a solid and very dependable account.
It contains excellent maps and other illustrations.

682.   ————. "The Arnold-Gates Controversy." W VA HIST, 27 (1966),
       75-84.

       Luzader summarizes the famous quarrel between Horatio Gates
       and his subordinate Benedict Arnold on the field of battle.

683.   Miller, H.M., and David A. Donath. "'The Road Not Taken':
       A Reassessment of Burgoyne's Campaign." FORT TIC MUS BULL,
       13 (1973), 272-286.

       If Burgoyne had followed a route further west around Lake
       George, he might have been victorious.

684.   Mills, Borden H. "Troop Units at the Battle of Saratoga."
       NY STATE HIST ASSOC Q J, 9 (1928), 136-158.

       For material about where each regiment was located, and
       its part in the fighting, this article is worth consulting.

685.   Nelson, Paul David. "Legacy of Controversy: Gates, Schuyler,
       and Arnold at Saratoga: 1777." MILT AFF, 37 (1973), 41-
       47.

       Both Schuyler and Arnold have been overrated because Gates
       clearly appreciated the necessity of a defensive action
       against Burgoyne.

686.   ————. "The Gates-Arnold Quarrel, September 1777." NY HIST
       SOC Q, 55 (1971), 235-252.

       Here is a fresh interpretation of the feud that involved
       sharp personality differences between the two generals.

687.   Nickerson, Hoffman. THE TURNING POINT OF THE REVOLUTION; OR
       BURGOYNE IN AMERICA. Boston: Houghton Mifflin, 1928.

       Although this work should be revised due to fresh evidence,
       this excellent study remains the best on Burgoyne's campaign.
       The writing style is rather ponderous, but the organization
       of the material, and the mastery of the documents attest to
       Nickerson's research skills. It has a useful appendix and a
       detailed bibliography.

688.   Percy, J. Earle, ed. "To Saratoga and Back, 1777." NEQ, 10
       (1937), 785-787.

       Joseph Pillsbury of Massachusetts described his service in
       the campaign.

689.   Sherwin, Harry E. "Old Number Four." NH PROFILES, 1 (1952),
       40-42.

       This is a brief summary about the importance of Fort Number
       4 in the Burgoyne campaign.

690.   [Snow, Richard E]. "Saratoga." AMER HERITAGE, 27 (1) (1975),
       29-30.

       Here is a neat and well-illustrated summary of the fighting.

691.   Squier, Ephraim. "Diary of Ephraim Squier, Sergeant in the
       Continental Line of the Continental Army." MAG AMER HIST,
       2 (1878), 685-694.

       Squier described his exciting experiences serving under
       Arnold at Saratoga.

692.   Squier, James Duane. "Old Number Four: Yesterday and Today."
       NE SOC STUD BULL, 16 (1959), 11-14.

       Located on the Connecticut River at Charlestown, New Hamp-
       shire, the fortress was an American mobilization center.

693.   Stone, William L. THE CAMPAIGN OF GEN. JOHN BURGOYNE, AND THE
       EXPEDITION OF LIEUT. COL. BARRY ST. LEGER. Albany, New York:
       J. Munsell, 1877.

       Though the work needs revisions, it is a solid account of
       the British invasion and the American reaction. The material
       is generally reliable although it is ponderous reading. The
       chapters on St. Leger are good.

694.   Sturtevant, Walter B. "John Brown's Raid - September, 1777."
       INF J, 36 (1934), 475-485.

       Brown made a successful attack on the British garrison at
       Mt. Defiance near Ticonderoga.

695.   Wild, Ebenezer. "The Journal of Ebenezer Wild (1776-1781)
       Who Served as Corporal, Sergeant, Ensign, and Lieutenant
       in the American Army of the Revolution." MASS HIST SOC PROC,
       6 (1890), 78-160.

       This is one of the best published journals about the fight-
       ing by a Massachusetts soldier who was in innumerable battles,
       including Freeman's Farm.

696.   Wood, Virginia Steele. "The Journal of Private Vaughan:
       Revolutionary Soldier, 1777-1780." DAR MAG, 113 (1979),
       110-144, 256-257, 320-331.

       A soldier in the Fifth Massachusetts commented on Bemis
       Heights, camp life, and the British surrender.

11. The British Invasion of Pennsylvania

697. Brownlow, Donald Grey. A DOCUMENTARY HISTORY OF THE BATTLE OF
      GERMANTOWN. Germantown, Pennsylvania: Germantown Histori-
      cal Society, 1955.

      Brownlow compiled a good selection of source material about
      Washington's last major battle in 1777 to recover Philadelphia.
      This volume provides clues about the errors in American
      fighting plans, and why the far-flung patriot regiments found
      it difficult to coordinate the attack.

698. _____. A DOCUMENTARY HISTORY OF THE PAOLI "MASSACRE."
      Philadelphia: Paoli Memorial Association, 1952.

      This small collection helps to explain why the British night
      attack on an American camp was successful. The American
      blunders and the flexibility of enemy tactics are mentioned
      here.

699. Buck, William J. "Washington's Encampment on the Neshaminy."
      PA MHB, 1 (1877), 275-284.

      An American army was garrisoned in Bucks County in August,
      1777.

700. Cooch, Edward W. THE BATTLE OF COOCH'S BRIDGE, 1777.
      Wilmington: W.N. Cann, Inc., 1940.

      This skirmish to repell the British march from the Head of
      the Elk (river) deserves a more balanced treatment than this
      weak account.

701. Cullen, Joseph P. "Brandywine Creek." AMER HIST ILLUS, 15
      (5) (1980), 8-13, 40-43.

      This is a colorful summary of the bitter contest that oc-
      curred twenty miles from Philadelphia.

702. _____. "General William Howe." AMER HIST ILLUS, 7 (12)
      (1972), 24-31.

      The author contends that Howe's character and personality
      were reflected by his strategic blunders in the invasion from
      the Chesapeake.

703. Ford, Worthington Chauncey, ed. DEFENSES OF PHILADELPHIA IN
      1777. 1897. Reprint. New York: Da Capo Press, 1971.

      Here are letters from Washington's generals about defending
      Philadelphia that indicate a wide variety of opinions. This
      material is particularly valuable in examining the decisions
      to fight at Brandywine, the preparations for Germantown, and
      the problems of logistics and morale. The correspondence
      clarifies why Valley Forge was selected as the water encamp-
      ment.

110 CAMPAIGNS AND BATTLES

704. Futhey, J. Smith. "The Massacre at Paoli." PA MHB, 1 (1877), 285-319.

    This is a standard account that provides the factual data.

705. Gifford, Edward S., Jr. THE AMERICAN REVOLUTION IN THE DELAWARE VALLEY. Philadelphia: Pennsylvania Society of the Sons of the Revolution, 1976.

    This is a dull, ponderous, poorly conceived book. The material is frequently inaccurate, the author merely revives standard information without revealing a new fact or interpretation, and his writing demonstrates a quaint bombastic tone. Gifford seems unaware of recent historical literature on the Revolution. This is an unreliable account that should be ignored by general readers.

706. Heth, William. "Orderly Book of Major William Heth of the Third Virginia Regiment, May 15-July 1, 1777." VA HIST SOC COLL, 11 (1892), 317-326.

    This is a good commentary about discipline and camp routine at Bound Brook, New Jersey.

707. Hoyt, Edward A., ed. "A Revolutionary Diary of Captain Paul Brigham: November 19, 1777-September 4, 1778." VT HIST, 34 (1966), 2-30.

    Brigham wrote some interesting comments about Peekskill, Germantown, Fort Mifflin, Valley Forge, as well as Monmouth.

708. Jackson, John W. THE PENNSYLVANIA NAVY 1775-1781, THE DEFENSE OF THE DELAWARE. New Brunswick: Rutgers University Press, 1974.

    Though this work could be cited under State Navies, it should be mentioned here because of the amphibious nature of the British conquest of the Delaware. Pennsylvania's motley collection of rafts, ships, and galleys receives little credit here. The real heroes were the military defenders of Fort Mifflin on Mud Island and other fortresses, along with the American engineers who constructed ship-obstacles in the river. Along with innumerable details, there are fine descriptions of fighting on the Delaware. Due to the placid manner of writing, to the lack of modern maps, and to the fact that one-third of the volume is devoted to notes and appendices, this study is for specialists.

709. Jordan, John W., ed. "Orderly Book of the Pennsylvania State Regiment of Foot, May 10 to August 16, 1777." PA MHB, 22 (1898), 57-70, 196-210, 301-320, 475-478.

    The manuscript covers Colonel Walter Stewart's orders to the Thirteenth Pennsylvania encamped along the Delaware.

710. Lambdin, Alfred C. "Battle of Germantown." PA MHB, 1 (1877),
      368-403.

      Here is a well-mapped, adequately documented article about
      the key fight for Philadelphia.

711. Lawrence, Alexander A., ed. "Journal of Major Raymond
      Demara." GA HIST Q, 52 (1968), 337-347.

      Demara carried dispatches from Georgia to New Jersey and
      witnessed skirmishing on the Delaware.

712. [Morris, Lewis]. "Letters to General Lewis Morris, 1775-
      1782." NY HIST SOC COLL, 7 (1875), 433-512.

      Morris was a relatively obscure commander, but this collec-
      tion has letters from Washington, von Steuben and many other
      prominent figures in 1777-78.

713. [Morton, Robert]. "The Diary of Robert Morton. Kept in
      Philadelphia While that City Was Occupied by the British
      Army in 1777." PA MHB, 1 (1877), 1-39.

      There are numerous anecdotes here by a patriot living under
      enemy occupation.

714. Muhlenberg, Major John Porter. "Orderly Book, 26 March-20
      December, 1777." PA MHB, 33 (1909, 257-278, 457-474; 34
      (1910), 21-40, 166-189, 336-360, 438-477; 35 (1911), 58-
      89, 156-188, 290-303.

      This document provides intimate views about service in New
      Jersey, and, especially about the welfare of troops.

715. Murphy, Orville T. "The Battle of Germantown and the Franco-
      American Alliance of 1778." PA MHB, 82 (1958), 55-64.

      Reports to Paris about the Continentals' performance in
      battle - two weeks before Burgoyne's defeat - were influential
      in the French decision to intervene.

716. Myers, T. Bailey, trans. "The Attack on Fort Mifflin, 1777.
      Two Unpublished Letters of the Baron D'Arendt." HIST MAG,
      1 (1872), 77-79.

      A French officer described the British assault with flair
      and accuracy.

717. [Paine, Thomas]. "Military Operations Near Philadelphia in
      the Campaign of 1777-1778, Described in a Letter from
      Thomas Paine to Dr. Franklin." PA MHB, 2 (1878), 283-296.

      Paine wrote Franklin a vivid commentary about the fighting
      on the Delaware and at Germantown.

718. Pancake, John S. 1777: THE YEAR OF THE HANGMAN. University,
      Alabama: The University of Alabama Press, 1977.

      This is a well-written interpretation of the 1777 campaign
      which is particularly good on linking the operations of Howe,
      Clinton, and Burgoyne. Pancake uses a lucid style to unfold
      a series of dramatic events that year. Unfortunately, his
      coverage of fighting in New Jersey is weak, and virtually no
      fresh material has been added to conventional accounts of the
      campaigns. For beginners, however, this work is recommended.

719. Pennypacker, Samuel W. "The High Water Mark of the British
      Invasion." PA MHB, 31 (1907), 393-405.

      The British under General Howe marched as far as Reading,
      Pennsylvania.

720. Pleasants, Henry, Jr. "Controversial Brandywine." GEN MAG
      HIST CHRON, 54 (1952), 121-126.

      Pleasants notes the errors committed by Washington, but
      especially by General Sullivan, in failing to detect a flank-
      ing attack by Cornwallis.

721. ———. "The Battle of Paoli." PA MHB, 72 (1948), 44-53.

      British troops under Major General Charles Grey surprised
      General Anthony Wayne's men in a night attack.

722. Reed, Elizabeth. "John Eager Howard, Colonel of the Second
      Maryland Regiment." MAG AMER HIST, 7 (1881), 276-282.

      This is a good sketch of a Marylander's service at German-
      town, Monmouth, and at Cowpens.

723. Reed, John F. CAMPAIGN TO VALLEY FORGE, JULY 1, 1777-DECEM-
      BER 19, 1777. Philadelphia: University of Pennsylvania
      Press, 1965.

      Reed wrote the best synthesis of the complicated maneuver-
      ing and numerous battles and skirmishes related to the Howe
      invasion. The author is particularly good in packing his
      account with details, with vivid anecdotes, and with pro-
      viding data on strategic and logistical matters. Solidly
      documented and illustrated with good maps, this volume is
      worth perusing.

724. Smith, Samuel S. THE BATTLE OF BRANDYWINE. Monmouth Beach,
      New Jersey: Philip Freneau Press, 1976.

      Smith compiled one of the best accounts of this almost
      incomprehensible battle that has been written. The author
      clearly knows his strategy and tactics, even though he tends
      to overlook logistical and personality factors. The maps,

bibliography, and appendices are excellent. The reader can
now appreciate why the desperate American attack failed.

725.   ————. FIGHT FOR THE DELAWARE 1777. Monmouth Beach, New
        Jersey: Philip Freneau Press, 1970.

        This is a dependable summary of the British efforts to break
        the American resistance on the river and land routes to
        Philadelphia. Although it is somewhat vague concerning
        naval affairs, the maps are excellent, and the quotations
        from source material are vivid.

726.   Snow, Richard F. "Battles of the Revolution – Brandywine."
        AMER HERITAGE, 24 (2) (1972), 12–16.

        This is the best brief treatment of this fierce conflict.

727.   Stryker, William S. THE FORTS ON THE DELAWARE IN THE REVOLU-
        TIONARY WAR. Trenton, New Jersey: J.L. Murphy, 1901.

        This brief summary about the location, construction and the
        fighting involved at the American defenses around Philadelphia
        is now outdated due to more recent evidence. Nevertheless,
        Stryker was a good writer, meticulous in assembling details,
        and he used manuscripts that are difficult to locate.

728.   Thompson, Ray. WASHINGTON ALONG THE DELAWARE. Fort Washing-
        ton, Pennsylvania: Bicentennial Press, 1971.

        Thompson wrote with skill, packs his brief chapters with
        colorful anecdotes, and, apparently, he familiarized himself
        thoroughly with the sites and terrain that he describes. This
        is a fine introductory account of the 1776-77 year.

729.   ————. WASHINGTON AT GERMANTOWN. Fort Washington, Pennsyl-
        vania: Bicentennial Press, 1971.

        Thompson has ample data here about Washington's decision to
        attack Howe's lines and the related tactical planning. How-
        ever, the author's probing of personalities, his familiarity
        with source material, and his knowledgeability about key
        sites make this the best summary of the bloody fight.

730.   ————. WASHINGTON AT WHITEMARSH. PRELUDE TO VALLEY FORGE.
        Fort Washington, Pennsylvania: Bicentennial Press, 1970.

        In a short but very colorful essay, Thompson wrote a fine
        study of the movements of the Continental army in Pennsyl-
        vania prior to the late December encampment. Though there is
        little here for specialists, the author's familiarity with the
        sites, buildings, and terrain provides a very useful back-
        ground for a general audience.

731. Wells, G. Harlan. "The British Campaign of 1777 in Maryland
     Prior to the Battle of Brandywine." MD HIST MAG, 30 (1938),
     3-13.

     This is a needed synthesis about Howe's activities in the
     Chesapeake and at the Head of the Elk.

732. Winsor, Justin, ed. "Col. John Eager Howard's Account of the
     Battle of Germantown." MD HIST Q, 4 (1939), 314-320.

     Howard, famous for his heroism, penned a graphic account
     of the American failure.

                          12. Valley Forge

733. Baker, Henry M. "General Enoch Poor." J AMER HIST, 15 (1921),
     117-132.

     Poor's men endured the hardship of the encampment.

734. Bicker, Col. Henry. "Order Book of the Second Pennsylvania
     Continental Line, Valley Forge, 28 March-27 May 1778."
     PA MHB, 35 (1911), 333-342, 466-496; 36 (1912), 30-59, 236-
     253, 329-345.

     There is data here about rations, hygiene, discipline, and
     guard duty.

735. Bill, Alfred H. "Drill Master at Valley Forge." AMER
     HERITAGE, 6 (4) (1955), 36-39, 100-101.

     Baron von Steuben is credited with forming a trained Ameri-
     can army out of raw recruits.

736. ————. VALLEY FORGE: THE MAKING OF AN ARMY. New York:
     Harper and Row, Publishers, Inc., 1952.

     Bill wrote a very vivid interpretation of the Continental
     struggle to survive the winter of 1777-78. Due to this inter-
     colonial experience, a truly national army - better equipped,
     provisioned and officered - emerged to fight at Monmouth.

737. Bodle, Wayne K., and Jacqueline Thibaut. VALLEY FORGE HISTO-
     RICAL REPORT. 3 vols. Washington, DC: US Department of
     the Interior. National Park Service, 1980.

     This series is unsurpassed in information about the encamp-
     ment. Volume one contains a very readable and exhaustively
     researched chronological account that presents much fresh in-
     formation. Volume two has information about clothing, the
     Commissary, and military stores. It also has a valuable
     glossary and excellent appendices. Volume three presents data
     about maps, tools, structures, artifacts, and related arche-
     ological evidence. This work renders outdated every other
     work written about Valley Forge. It is highly recommended.

738. Brenneman, Gloria E. "The Conway Cabal: Myth or Reality."
      PA HIST, 40 (1973), 169-177.

      Brenneman tried to solve the question of whether Washington's
      subordinates and political enemies actually tried to supplant
      him in early 1778.

739. Busch, Noel F. WINTER QUARTERS: GEORGE WASHINGTON AND THE
      CONTINENTAL ARMY AT VALLEY FORGE. New York: Liveright
      Pub. Corp., 1974.

      For the general reader, this highly dramatic summary that
      is based on familiar sources is the best introduction to the
      subject. It is well-written, replete with absorbing anecdotes
      about the site, and it contains details about key personali-
      ties. The author tends to exaggerate the degree of patriotic
      idealism and overlooks the harsh realities of desertion, dis-
      cipline, and similar matters.

740. [Cadwalader, John]. "Prelude to Valley Forge." PA MHB, 82
      (1958), 466-471.

      A Pennsylvania general wrote a good summary to Washington
      about the strategic situation on December 3, 1777.

741. Chidsey, Donald Barr. VALLEY FORGE. New York: Crown Pub-
      lishers, Inc. 1959.

      Intended for a popular audience, this volume incorporates
      all the errors and legends about Valley Forge that have
      long been discarded. The factual framework and organization
      are weak, the author's knowledge of logistics and related
      matters is poor, and his familiarity with the basic source
      materials is very limited.

742. Cullen, Joseph P. "Victory, Defeat, Valley Forge." AMER
      HIST ILLUS, 7 (1) (1972), 47-52.

      The American cause survived at Valley Forge in a severe
      test of stamina and privation.

743. David, Ebenezer. A RHODE ISLAND CHAPLAIN IN THE REVOLUTION:
      LETTERS TO NICHOLAS BROWN, 1775-1778. Edited by J.D. Black
      and W.G. Roelker. 1945. Reprint. Port Washington, New
      York: Kennikat Press, 1972.

      David's letters to home about the miserable conditions that
      the troops endured are graphic. His comments about visits
      to camp hopsitals are unique.

744. Ewing, Thomas, ed. GEORGE EWING, GENTLEMEN, A SOLDIER OF
      VALLEY FORGE [1754-1824]. Yonkers, New York: Priv. prt.,
      1928.

      Here is a good commentary by a keen observer at the canton-
      ment. Some of Ewing's descriptions are quite vivid.

745. Hand, Edward. "Orderly Book of Colonel Edward Hand, Valley
      Forge, January, 1778." PA MHB, 41 (1917), 198-223, 257-
      273, 458-567.

      This is an excellent view of the tribulations of a Penn-
      sylvania regiment.

746. Heydinger, Earl J. "The Schuylkill, Lifeline to Valley Forge."
      MONT CO HIST SOC BULL, 9 (1953-55), 159-170.

      The Schuylkill River provided fish, water, and a vital sup-
      ply route.

747. Lutes, Lillian C. "The Evacuation of Valley Forge." JAH, 7
      (1913), 1261-1271.

      This is one of the few essays which explains the timing of
      American troop movement as the British prepared to leave
      Philadelphia in 1778.

748. Luvaas, Jay. "Baron von Steuben: Washington's Drillmaster."
      AMER HIST ILLUS, 2 (1) (1967), 4-11, 55-58.

      Here is a dependable, well-illustrated summation about
      the famous Prussian at Valley Forge.

749. Porter, William A. "Prelude to Valley Forge." PA MHB, 82
      (1958), 466-471.

      Here is a useful account of the manuevering after Germantown
      by the opposing armies as the campaign closed in late Decem-
      ber, 1777.

750. Reed, John F. "Red Tape at Valley Forge." MANUSCRIPTS, 20
      (1968), 20-27.

      The Paymaster Department had incredible difficulties with
      administrative "paperwork."

751. ————. VALLEY FORGE: CRUCIBLE OF VICTORY. Monmouth Beach,
      New Jersey: Philip Freneau Press, 1969.

      Written in a very readable manner, this is probably the best
      account of encampment available for a wide audience. Though
      incomplete on topics relating to discipline, provisioning,
      some key figures, and, particularly on analysis, this work is
      reliable as an introduction to the saga of Valley Forge.

752. Sims, William Gilmore. THE ARMY CORRESPONDENCE OF COLONEL
      JOHN LAURENS IN THE YEAR 1777-78.... New York: Bradford
      Club, 1867.

      Laurens, a member of Washington's staff, wrote some intimate
      details about the hardships of Valley Forge. The material is
      colorful and well compiled by the famed novelist of the south.

753. Stoudt, John Joseph. ORDEAL AT VALLEY FORGE. A DAY-BY-DAY
      CHRONICLE FROM DECEMBER 17, 1777 TO JUNE 18, 1778, COMPILED
      FROM THE SOURCES. Philadelphia: University of Pennsylvania
      Press, 1963.

      This is a collection of documents about the construction of
      the encampment, the hardships encountered, the weather, disease
      and related subjects. Though there is a paucity of interpre-
      tation by the author, this work is a valuable study. By using
      a large variety of source materials, Stoudt has recreated life
      at Valley Forge in a manner unmatched by other authors.

754. Trussell, John B.B. BIRTHPLACE OF AN ARMY: A STUDY OF THE
      VALLEY FORGE ENCAMPMENT. Harrisburg: Pennsylvania Histori-
      cal and Museum Commission, 1976.

      Trussell repeats the familiar story that Valley Forge was
      the birthplace of the American army, ignoring the evidence
      that the Continentals did perform sometimes well, or poorly,
      before and after Valley Forge. Using standard books, with
      little research, analysis, or interpretation, the author has
      compiled a dull booklet for tourists.

755. Walker, Howell. "Washington Lives Again at Valley Forge."
      NAT GEOG MAG, 105 (1954), 187-202.

      This is a gracefully written article profusely illustrated,
      that offers a literary substitute for a visit to the encamp-
      ment.

756. Washington, George. ORDERLY BOOK OF GEN. GEORGE WASHINGTON,
      COMMANDER IN CHIEF OF THE AMERICAN ARMY, KEPT AT VALLEY
      FORGE, 18 MAY-11 JUNE, 1778. Boston: Wolffe and Co., 1896.

      This printed document is useful to comprehend Washington's
      preparations to evacuate the camp and to pursue the enemy
      withdrawing from the Delaware.

757. Weedon, George. VALLEY FORGE ORDERLY BOOK OF GENERAL GEORGE
      WEEDON OF THE CONTINENTAL ARMY UNDER COMMAND OF GENERAL
      GEORGE WASHINGTON, IN THE CAMPAIGN OF 1777-78. Dodd, Mead
      and Co., 1902.

      Here is ample detail available about fighting at Brandywine,
      Warren's Tavern, Germantown, and Whitemarsh. The orders re-
      layed to regiments from Washington provide valuable insight
      into his concern for the welfare of the rank and file.

758. Wilcox, William J. "The Comic Opera Battle that Made A
      General." PA HIST, 13 (1946), 265-273.

      As commander of troops at Barren Hill, Pennsylvania in May,
      1778, Lafayette made so many errors that he was nearly trap-
      ped by General Henry Clinton.

118   CAMPAIGNS AND BATTLES

13. Monmouth

759. Fleming, Thomas J. "The 'Military Crime' of Charles Lee."
      AMER HERITAGE, 19 (3) (1968), 12-15, 83-89.

      This is an investigation of Lee's court-martial for his re-
      treat at Monmouth and his attempts to be exonerated by Con-
      gress.

760. Johnston, Henry P. "Colonel Christian Febiger of the Virginia
      Line." MAG AMER HIST, 6 (1881), 188-203.

      This Danish immigrant fought in many campaigns, including
      Monmouth.

761. [Leutze, Emmanuel]. "Washington at Monmouth." AMER HERITAGE,
      16 (4) (1965), 14-17.

      The editors of the magazine comment on the significance of
      painter Leutze's rediscovered canvas of Washington attempting
      to rally his troops.

762. Lewis, Theodore B. "Was Washington Profane at Monmouth?"
      NJ HIST, 89 (1971), 149-162.

      Did Washington curse Major General Charles Lee for bungling
      the attack?

763. Mitchell, Broadus. "The Battle of Monmouth Through Alexander
      Hamilton's Eyes." NJ HIST SOC PROC, 73 (1955), 239-257.

      Hamilton was on the front line and wrote a good commentary
      about Lee's actions.

764. Smith, Samuel S. THE BATTLE OF MONMOUTH. Monmouth Beach,
      New Jersey: Philip Freneau Press, 1964.

      This is one of Smith's best books on the many Revolutionary
      war engagements that he has described. He has included fas-
      cinating extracts from diaries and correspondence written by
      soldiers on both sides, and his maps are quite helpful. The
      author comes close to making comprehensible a battle that is
      puzzling to comprehend because of the unique terrain and the
      disorganization of the American troops.

765. [Snow, Richard F.]. "The Battle of Monmouth." AMER HERITAGE,
      27 (5) (1976), 68-71.

      This is the best brief article on the fight compiled from
      memoirs of participants.

766. Stryker, William S. BATTLE OF MONMOUTH. Edited by William
      Starr Myers. Princeton: Princeton University Press, 1927.

      Stryker's familiarity with the source materials and his

knowledge of the troop movements are evidenced in this fine
study of the battle. This is the fullest account of the
fighting, and although it is difficult to read, the work remains the best treatment of the subject.

767. Thayer, Theodore George. WASHINGTON AND LEE AT MONMOUTH: THE
      MAKING OF A SCAPEGOAT. Port Washington, New York: Kennikat
      Press, 1976.

      In contrast to the traditional faulting of Lee for retreat-
      ing, the author claims that the field commander actually saved
      the American army, and that Washington should be blamed for
      blundering. There are excellent details here of the fighting,
      occurring on the hottest day in memory. Lee's barely con-
      cealed contempt for Washington made him an inevitable victim.
      The book has fine maps, a serviceable bibliography, and it
      is quite readable.

                     14. The Sieges of Newport

768. Almy, Mary. "Mrs. Almy's Journal. Siege of Newport, RI,
      August, 1778." NEWPORT HIST MAG, 1 (1880-81), 17-36.

      The lady wrote a clear and concise account, stressing the
      degree of rain and fog during the operations.

769. Amory, Thomas C. "Siege of Newport, RI in 1778." MASS HIST
      SOC PROC. 17 (1879), 163-184.

      Amory wrote a standard account without much perception, but
      the data is substantially correct.

770. [Angell, Israel]. DIARY OF COLONEL ISRAEL ANGELL, COMMANDING
      THE SECOND RHODE ISLAND CONTINENTAL REGIMENT DURING THE
      AMERICAN REVOLUTION, 1778-1781. Compiled by Edward Field.
      Providence, Rhode Island: Rhode Island Historical Society,
      1899.

      This is an essential source for following the complicated
      maneuvers of the American army under General Sullivan attack-
      ing the British-held port in Rhode Island. The information
      about attempts to cooperate with the French fleet under Ad-
      miral D'Estaing provides insights about why the collaboration
      failed.

771. Billias, George N. "General Glover's Role in the Battle of
      Rhode Island [Aug. 1778]," RI HIST, 36 (1959), 33-42.

      Glover was not involved as usual in amphibious operations,
      but he played a key role in repulsing the British at Quaker
      Hill during an American retreat.

772. Dearden, Paul F. THE RHODE ISLAND CAMPAIGN OF 1778: INAUS-
      PICIOUS DAWN OF ALLIANCE. Providence: Rhode Island Bicen-
      tennial Foundation, for the Rhode Island Publications Soci-
      ety, Providence, Rhode Island: The Society, 1980.

      Dearden has written the only recent account of the aborted
      attempt by General Sullivan and Admiral d'Estaing to dislodge
      6,000 redcoats under Sir Robert Pigot. Instead of faulting
      American strategy, French indecision, or the undependable
      American militia (as historians have usually done), Dearden
      stresses that although d'Estaing had virtually isolated
      Pigot's force, Sullivan, hampered by inadequate logistical
      support, was unable to attack promptly. When a British fleet
      sailed to Rhode Island from New York, d'Estaing had to prepare
      for a sea fight, and hence the American effort was doomed with-
      out naval support. This is a well-researched version of the
      expedition that lacks an analysis of events, and the inclusion
      of recent material published about Lafayette and d'Estaing.

773. ————. "The Siege of Newport: Inauspicious Dawn of Alliance."
      RI HIST, 29 (1970), 17-35.

      This is a summary of the campaign which explains why the
      attack failed, and why the Americans realized their need for
      French naval support.

774. Reed, Silvanus. "Orderly Book of Silvanus Reed." NH HIST
      SOC COLL, 9 (1889), 264-414.

      Reed served in numerous regiments after fighting at Bunker
      Hill; his information about Providence in June, 1778 is re-
      vealing.

775. Shipton, Nathaniel H. "General Joseph Palmer: Scapegoat for
      the Rhode Island Fiasco of October, 1777." NEQ, 39 (1966),
      498-512.

      Three New England states sent men on an ill-fated venture
      that led to two long political inquiries of this first attempt
      to capture Newport.

                          15. Stony Point

776. Gamble, Robert. "Orderly Book of Captain Robert Gamble of the
      Second Virginia Regiment Commanded by Colonel Christian
      Febiger, August 21-November 16, 1779." VA HIST SOC COLL,
      11 (1892), 219-272.

      There is a wealth of information here about preparations to
      attack the British fortress on the Hudson River.

777. Johnston, Henry P. THE STORMING OF STONY POINT ON THE HUDSON
      MIDNIGHT, JULY 15, 1779. 1900. Reprint. New York: Da Capo
      Press, 1971.

Johnston wrote a well-documented narrative of General
Anthony Wayne's quick capture of a key British bastion. The
incident is important because it demonstrated careful planning by the Americans and their capabilities in bayonet attacks. Furthermore, as the author stresses, the victory was a
great boost to patriot morale. There are some one hundred
pages of text and one hundred pages of documents in this
essential study.

778. Skarsky, I.W. THE REVOLUTION'S BOLDEST VENTURE: THE STORY OF
      GENERAL "MAD ANTHONY" WAYNE'S ASSAULT ON STONY POINT. Port
      Washington, New York: Kennikat Press, 1965.

      This is a dramatic popular treatment of Wayne's successful
      attack on the outpost. There is no new information here, and
      the book is poorly written.

                          16. Penobscot

779. Bellico, Russell. "The Great Penobscot Blunder." AMER HIST
      ILLUS, 13 (8) (1978), 4-9.

      Blunders by Commodore Dudley Saltonstall and Lieutenant
      Colonel Paul Revere led to the loss of an army at Castine
      (Maine) in mid-1779.

780. Bourne, Russell. "The Penobscot Fiasco." AMER HERITAGE, 25
      (6) (1974), 28-33, 100-101.

      Seven hundred British troops repulsed America's greatest
      amphibious operation (nineteen naval vessels and twenty-four
      transports) in the war.

781. Goold, Nathan. "Colonel Jonathan Mitchell's Cumberland County
      Regiment, Bagaduce Expedition." MAINE HIST SOC COLL PROC,
      10 (1899), 52-80, 143-174.

      Some reasons for the failure of the Penobscot adventure are
      cited here.

782. Kevitt, Chester B. GENERAL SOLOMON LOVELL AND THE PENOBSCOT
      EXPEDITION, 1779. Weymouth, Massachusetts: Weymouth Histor-
      ical Commission, 1976.

      Indecisive commanders, poorly trained men, and lack of army-
      navy cooperation contributed to Lovell's decisive defeat in
      the effort to capture the British port. This is an adequate
      summary of events, but it contains little fresh material.

783. Kidder, Frederic. MILITARY OPERATIONS IN MAINE AND NOVA SCOTIA
      DURING THE REVOLUTION ... WITH NOTES AND A MEMOIR OF COL.
      JOHN ALLEN. Albany, New York: J. Munsell, 1867.

122   CAMPAIGNS AND BATTLES

       This is a still useful summary of how New Englanders at-
    tempted to retain the Maine coast, and how they planned raids
    on the Maritimes.

784. Scott, Kenneth. "New Hampshire's Part in the Penobscot Ex-
      pedition." AMER NEP, 7 (1947), 200-212.

      The state contributed 18 ships and 1,000 men to the fiasco.

785. Shaw, Henry I., Jr. "Penobscot Assault-1779." MILT AFF, 17
      (1953), 83-94.

      This is the best article about the American assault at
      Bagaduce Peninsula (Maine) to capture a British garrison and
      to cut off an enemy timber supply.

786. Williamson, Joseph. "The British Occupation of the Penobscot
      During the Revolution." MAINE HIST SOC COLL PROC, 1 (1890),
      389-400.

      This narrative of how Loyalists from Massachusetts in 1776,
      aided by British troops, held Castine for four years.

                17. The Sullivan-Clinton Expedition

787. Barton, William. "Journal of Lieutenant William Barton of
      Maxwell's Brigade." NJ HIST SOC PROC, 2 (1846-47), 22-42.

      The journal, extending from June 8 to October 9, 1779,
      covers the salient points of the campaign.

788. Brady, William Young. "Brodhead's Trail Up the Allegheny,
      1779." W PA HIST MAG, 37 (1954), 19-31.

      Brodhead led a wing of the Sullivan expedition from Fort
      Pitt.

789. [Clinton, James]. "James Clinton's Expedition." NY HIST, 13
      (1932), 433-438.

      Here are some documents about the march from Canajoharie,
      New York to Tioga Point, Pennsylvania.

790. Conover, George S., comp. JOURNALS OF THE MILITARY EXPEDITION
      OF MAJOR GENERAL JOHN SULLIVAN AGAINST THE SIX NATIONS OF
      INDIANS IN 1779 WITH RECORDS OF CENTENNIAL CELEBRATIONS.
      New York: Benchmark Publishing Co., 1976.

      This is a reprint of a volume by Frederick Cook who pub-
      lished in 1887 a volumnious set of diaries, memoirs, and jour-
      nals written by thirty soldiers on the expedition. It remains
      the single best compilation of documents for the episode, for
      the volume contains personal views about military life, the
      unknown wilderness, and glimpses of Indian life.

791. Davis, Andrew McFarland. "Sullivan Expedition Against the
      Indians of N.Y., 1779 ... " MASS HIST SOC PROC, 2 (1886),
      436-478.

      The article contains the journal of William McKendry which
      covers the entire campaign.

792. Dotz, Lockwood R. "The Massacre at Groveland." NY STATE HIST
      ASSOC Q J, 11 (1930), 132-140.

      On September 13, 1779, a small detachment under Lieutenant
      Thomas Boyd was ambushed by Indians.

793. Edson, Obed. "Brodhead's Expedition Against the Indians of
      the Upper Allegheny, 1777." MAG AMER HIST, 3 (1879), 649-
      675.

      Here is an adequate summary about a generally overlooked
      military operation in this campaign.

794. Flick, Alexander C. "New Sources on the Sullivan-Clinton
      Campaign in 1779." NY STATE HIST ASSOC Q J, 10 (1929),
      185-294, 266-315.

      Flick claimed that the expedition was planned by Washington
      as part of his diplomacy to control the upper frontier; less
      important to him was the defeat of the Iroquois.

795. Griffin, William E. "The New Hampshire Brigade in the Sulli-
      van Campaign." GRANITE MONTHLY, 42 (1910), 229-241.

      There are ample details here about New Hampshire's interest
      in the expedition.

796. Halsey, Edward D. "Diary of Dr. Jabez Campbell, Surgeon in
      Spencer's Regiment." NY HIST SOC PROC, 3 (1872-1874), 117-
      136.

      Campbell was one of the few medical men on the march, cover-
      ing May 23 to October 2, 1779 in his account.

797. Hart, Charles Henry. "Colonel Robert Lettis Hooper." PA MHB,
      36 (1916), 60-91.

      Hooper is credited for supervising the provisioning of
      Sullivan's men.

798. [Hubly, Adam, Jr.]. "Adam Hubly, Jr., Lt. Col. Cmdt., 11th
      Pennsylvania Regt. His Journal Commencing at Wyoming,
      July 30, 1779." PA MHB, 33 (1907), 129-146, 279-300.

      Hubly's account begins at Easton, Pennsylvania and provides
      data about the line of march into the Finger Lakes of New York.

799. Lauber, Almon W., ed. ORDERLY BOOKS OF THE FOURTH NEW YORK
     REGIMENT, 1778-1780, THE SECOND NEW YORK REGIMENT, 1780-83
     BY SAMUEL TALLMADGE AND OTHERS, WITH DIARIES OF SAMUEL
     TALLMADGE, AND JOHN BARR, 1778-1782. 1932. Reprint.
     Louisville, Kentucky: Lost Cause Press, 1958.

     About half of this material concerns the march into Iroquois
     lands. These documents provide insights about camp conditions,
     impressions of Indian villages, and some terse commentaries
     about the conduct of the campaign.

800. McAdams, Donald R. "The Sullivan Expedition: Success or
     Failure." NY HIST SOC Q, 54 (1970), 53-81.

     The expedition which supposedly broke the Iroquois Con-
     federacy was a failure because the Indians lost few warriors,
     and they continued to pillage the frontier until late 1781.

801. New York Division of Archives and History. THE SULLIVAN-
     CLINTON CAMPAIGN IN 1777. CHRONOLOGY AND SELECTED DOCU-
     MENTS. Albany: University of the State of New York, 1929.

     Washington and Congress committed many troops to this ex-
     pedition. The correspondence here by Sullivan, Clinton, and
     Brodhead is the best single source for information about the
     penetration of the Finger Lakes area.

802. [Norris, James]. "Major Norris' Journal of the Sullivan Ex-
     pedition. June to October, 1779." BUFF HIST SOC PUB,
     1 (1870), 217-252.

     A New Hampshire soldier left an interesting commentary about
     his experiences.

803. Parker, Robert. "Journal of Robert Parker of the Second Con-
     tinental Artillery, 1779." PA MHB, 27 (1905), 404-420;
     28 (1908), 12-25.

     Parker served at Brandywine and Germantown but his remarks
     about fighting the Iroquois are especially incisive.

804. Rogers, William D. "The Journals of a Brigade Chaplain in
     the Campaign of 1777 Against the Six Nations Under the Com-
     mand of Major-General John Sullivan." RI HIST TRACTS, 7
     (1879), 1-136.

     This is one of the best contemporary discourses about vari-
     ous encampments and the Indian fighting by a Pennsylvanian
     in General Edward Hand's brigade.

805. Russell, E.L. "The Lost Story of the Brodhead Expedition."
     NY STATE HIST ASSOC Q J, 11 (1930), 252-263.

     The author used Seneca and Cayugha legends to document this
     account.

806.   Stone, Rufus B. "Brodhead's Raid on the Seneca: The Story
       of the Little Known Expedition in 1779 from Fort Pitt to
       Destroy the Indian Villages on the Upper Allegheny." W PA
       HIST MAG, 7 (1924), 88-101.

           Stone wrote a terse, dependable account of the march into
       Indian country.

807.   Vail, R.W.G., ed. "Diary of Obediah Gore, Jr. in the Sulli-
       van-Clinton Campaign of 1779." NY PUB LIB BULL, 33 (1929),
       711-742.

           The former Wyoming Valley blacksmith showed a remarkable
       degree of literacy in these passages.

808.   ————. "The Western Campaign of 1779." NY HIST SOC Q, 41
       (1957), 35-69.

           Sergeant Moses Sproule of New Jersey wrote a picturesque
       account of Indian fights in his diary.

           18.   The Stalemate in the North, 1778-1783

809.   Angelakos, Peter. "The Army at Middlebrook, 1778-1779." NJ
       HIST SOC PROC, 70 (1952), 97-120.

           Middlebrook, New Jersey was a large encampment which quar-
       tered many brigades.

810.   Bartenstein, Fred, Jr. "New Jersey Brigade Encampment in the
       Winter of 1779-1780." NJ HIST, (1968), 135-137.

           This is a good account of a recent archeological search for
       a campsite near Basking Ridge and the Passiac River, New
       Jersey.

811.   Bill, Alfred H. NEW JERSEY AND THE REVOLUTIONARY WAR. New
       York: D. Van Nostrand Co., Inc., 1964.

           Here is a very readable account about the impact of the war
       on New Jersey. It is especially pertinent in stressing the
       state's strategic importance after Monmouth, and how fre-
       quently it was the scene of raids and ambushes by both sides
       in the struggle.

812.   Bradford, S. Sydney. "Hunger Menaces the Revolution, Decem-
       ber, 1779-January 1780." MD HIST MAG, 61 (1966), 1-23.

           Severe shortages of food nearly broke Continental morale at
       Morristown until Maryland and New Jersey provided grain and
       cattle in the worst winter for Washington's army.

813. Brown, Richard C. "How Washington Dealt with the Crisis of
      1780." HIST TEACHER, 5 (1971), 44-54.

      Here is a discussion for high-schoolers of Benedict Arnold's
      plot to surrender West Point to the British, and how Washing-
      ton deftly handled the matter.

814. Buel, Richard, Jr. "Time: Friend or Foe of the Revolution."
      See 414, pp. 124-133.

      Due to a shattered economy, grain shortages, and currency
      depreciation, time was running out for the American cause by
      1780.

815. Burns, Brian. "Carleton in the Valley, or the Year of the
      Burning. Major Christopher Carleton and the Northern In-
      vasion of 1780." FORT TIC MUS BULL, 13 (1980), 398-411.

      A British raid in the Lake Champlain area caused a great
      destruction of crops, property, and army supplies.

816. Cullen, Joseph P. "I Have Almost Ceased to Hope." AMER HIST
      ILLUS, 14 (9) (1980), 30-35.

      Cullen describes how close to mutiny were Washington's men
      at Morristown because of food shortages and a brutal winter
      (1779-80).

817. Culver, Francis B. "Last Blood of the Revolution." MD HIST
      MAG, 5 (1910), 329-337.

      Captain William Wilmot of Maryland apparently was the last
      American to be killed in the war.

818. Fleming, Thomas. "Springfield - The Reason Why." NJ HIST,
      92 (1974), 211-224.

      The bloody battle at Springfield, New Jersey in 1780 was a
      decisive test of American morale.

819. ————. THE FORGOTTEN VICTORY: THE BATTLE FOR NEW JERSEY,
      1780. New York: Readers' Digest, 1973.

      In June, 1780 the British burned and plundered during raids
      on the Watchung Mountains near Morristown. Though the Ameri-
      can militia fought well and the actions then seemed decisive,
      the incident is now almost forgotten. Fleming has extracted
      a surprising amount of material from the documents, and he
      relates his story with verve and drama. This very readable
      account is especially good in describing local surroundings
      and colorful incidents.

820. Fox, Dixon Ryan. "Washington at Temple Hill." NY HIST, 13
      (1932), 284-291.

This essay covers Washington's cantonment at New Windsor,
near Newburgh, New York.

821. Goodrich, Chauncey. "Invasion of New Haven By the British
      Troops, July 5, 1779." NEW HAVEN COL HIST SOC PAP, 2
      (1877), 37-92.

      A victim of the raid on Connecticut described his experi-
      ences in graphic terms.

822. Harris, William W. BATTLE OF GROTON HEIGHTS: A COLLECTION OF
      NARRATIVES, OFFICIAL REPORTS, RECORDS, ETC. OF THE STORM-
      ING OF FORT GRISWOLD ... ON THE SIXTH OF SEPTEMBER, 1781.
      Revised and enlarged by Charles Allyn. New London, Con-
      necticut: Charles Allyn, 1882.

      Here is a miscellaneous collection of memoirs, correspond-
      ence, and journals about the British raid on Connecticut that
      took a bloody toll of patriots. The work is difficult to
      follow, and it lacks a central theme.

823. Hinnett, Dorothy Humphreys, and Frances Riker Duncombe. THE
      BURNING OF BEDFORD, 1779. Bedford, New York: Bedford His-
      torical Society, 1974.

      The author compiled a nice piece of local history about a
      little known raid. British cavalry under Tarleton devestated
      the village. This is a well-documented and graphically il-
      lustrated account.

824. Hornow, William M., Jr. "The Obstruction of the Hudson River
      during the Revolution." AMER COLL, 2 (1926), 436-445.

      The Sterling Ironworks constructed a great chain in 1778 to
      block the upper Hudson River from use by the Royal Navy.

825. [Johnson, Jeremiah]. "Recollections of Incidents of the Rev-
      olution." Edited by Thomas W. Field. J OF LONG ISLAND
      HIST, 12 (1976), 4-21, 22-48.

      General Johnson of King's County, New York reflected on the
      hardships of living under British occupation and his term on
      a prison ship off Manhattan.

826. Kemp, Franklin W. 'A NEST OF REBEL PIRATES'; THE ACCOUNT OF
      AN ATTACK BY THE BRITISH FORCES ON THE PRIVATEER STRONGHOLD
      AT LITTLE EGG HARBOR ON OCTOBER 6, 1778 ... Egg Harbor
      City, New Jersey: Laureate Press, 1966.

      This is a lively summary of an obscure incident. Though
      not skillfully written, the work demonstrates what can be
      done in local history. Information about the amphibious
      raids on the New Jersey and New York shorelines has been dif-
      ficult to find in print.

827. Kyte, George. "A Projected British Attack Upon Philadelphia
      in 1781." PA MHB, 76 (1952), 379-393.

      That General Clinton in New York still contemplated such a
      raid is evidence that it was still possible for the British
      to win the war.

828. Livermore, Daniel. "Orderly Book of Captain David Livermore's
      Company, Continental Army, 1780." NH HIST SOC COLL, 9
      (1889), 200-244.

      The company clerk kept good notes about a New Hampshire
      unit stationed at Orangetown, New Jersey.

829. Loddell, Jared C., ed. "Action at Hopperstown, April 15,
      1780." NJ HIST, 80 (1962), 261-266.

      This is a vivid summary by an officer in the Queen's Ameri-
      can Rangers of fighting in Bergen County, New Jersey.

830. ———. "Hooperstown, April 16, 1780: A Note." NJ HIST, 88
      (1970), 43-48.

      The author describes British forays from Manhattan into New
      Jersey that culminated in the fierce fight at Springfield.

831. ———. "Paramus in the War of the Revolution." NJ HIST SOC
      PROC, 78 (1960), 162-177.

      At the junction of three supply routes, Paramus was raided
      continually by the British from 1777 to 1779.

832. ———. "Two Forgotten Battles in the Revolutionary War."
      NJ HIST, 85 (1967), 225-234.

      Here is an useful undocumented sketch of two bitter skir-
      mishes involving over 1,000 British troops in Middlesex
      County, New Jersey in January, 1779.

833. Mansinne, Andrew, Jr. "The West Point Chain." AMER HIST
      ILLUS, 1 (3) (1966), 23-26.

      The strategic upper Hudson River was blocked by a five
      hundred yard iron chain which the British were unable to
      break.

834. McLellan, Hugh. "Captain Job Wright's Company of Willett's
      Levies at Ballston in 1782." NY HIST, 50 (1969), 454-462.

      The documents reveal that the troops at this New York post
      were often undisciplined.

835. Palmer, Dave R. THE RIVER AND THE ROCK: THE HISTORY OF
      FORTRESS WEST POINT, 1775-1783. New York: Greenwood Pub-
      lishing Co., 1969.

This big and handsomely printed book is crammed with data about the forts and redoubts at West Point. The author repeats the old tales about the suffering of the troops, the treason of Arnold, and attacks in the Hudson by the Royal Navy, but seldom has a writer done so with such thoroughness, and with such fine cartography. But strategy, tactics, and related political matters are confusing to follow here, and the author seems unfamiliar with much essential source material. His obsession with the strategic importance of the fortress mars what could have been a good popular treatment.

836. Powell, Walter L. "The Strange Death of Colonel William Ledyard. CONN HIST SOC BULL, 40 (1975), 61-64.

One half of the American defenders of Fort Griswold, Connecticut were killed in September, 1781, and its commander was bayoneted while surrendering to the British.

837. Scott, Kenneth. "Major General Sullivan and Colonel Stephen Holland." NEQ, 18 (1945), 303-324.

Tory Holland from New Hampshire tried to tempt Sullivan to desert when the American cause was supposedly fading, 1781-83.

838. Shelley, Fred. "Ebenezer Hazard's Diary: New Jersey During the Revolution." NJ HIST, 90 (1972), 169-180.

This document offers valuable insight into garrison duty at several Jersey posts.

839. Smith, Samuel Stelle. WINTER AT MORRISTOWN, 1779-1780. THE DARKEST HOUR. Monmouth Beach, New Jersey: Philip Freneau Press, 1979.

This work is excellent for details about American and enemy troop units and their locations in New Jersey. It has good maps, concise summaries of encampments, and readable prose. Unfortunately, the volume has excessive sections and chapters, and the footnotes are difficult to comprehend. The information about raids and fighting in the area is colorful, but the material about Morristown is inadequate.

840. [Snow, Richard F.]. "Battle of the Revolution. Fort Griswold." AMER HERITAGE, 24 (6) (1973), 69-72.

Benedict Arnold led a British force to hit the Groton, Connecticut area in the last major fight in the north by regular forces (September 6, 1781).

841. Stowe, Gerald C., and Jac Weller. "Revolutionary West Point: The Key to the Continent." MILT AFF, 19 (1958), 81-98.

Good maps and fine topographical data demonstrate why the fortress was the center of the Hudson Highlands' defenses and the pivot of Washington's strategy.

130   CAMPAIGNS AND BATTLES

842. Tallmedge, Samuel, and others. ORDERLY BOOKS OF THE FOURTH
      NEW YORK REGIMENT, 1778-1789, THE SECOND NEW YORK REGIMENT,
      1780-1783. Albany, New York: University of the State of
      New York, 1932.

      These documents include the diaries of Samuel Tallmadge and
      John Burr and provide a good view of regimental camp life.

843. Thayer, Theodore G. "The War in New Jersey: Battles, Alarums,
      and the Men of the Revolution." NJ HIST SOC PROC, 71 (1953),
      83-110.

      With a small population and only one large town (1,500
      residents of Elizabethtown), the war had a decided impact on
      rural New Jersey.

844. Thomas, William S. "Revolutionary Camps of the Hudson High-
      lands." Q J NYS HIST ASSOC, 2 (1921), 1-45.

      The lists list innumerable cantonments along the Hudson
      that were used by Continentals and militia.

845. Todd, Charles B. "The Massacre of Fort Griswold." MAG AMER
      HIST, 7 (1881), 161-175.

      This is a vivid summary about the British raid near New
      London, Connecticut in September, 1781.

846. Weig, Melvin J. MORRISTOWN, A MILITARY CAPITAL OF THE AMERI-
      CAN REVOLUTION. Washington, DC: Department of the Interior.
      National Park Service, 1950.

      Although this work needs to be revised, it remains the best
      summary of Morristown. The author provides abundant data
      about the selection of the site, its surrounding resources,
      the routes to the encampment, and descriptions of social life
      at the post. The material about Washington's staff and the
      training of troops is thoughtful.

                        C. THE WAR IN THE SOUTH

                     1. Campaigns From 1775 to 1779

847. Alden, John Richard. THE SOUTH IN THE REVOLUTION, 1762-1789.
      VOL. 3 OF THE HISTORY OF THE SOUTH. Edited by Weldon C.
      Stephenson and E. Merton Coulter. Baton Rouge: Louisiana
      State University Press, 1957.

      For students and general readers this work is a good intro-
      duction to the topic. Vivid and well-written, the volume has
      concise descriptions of major battles in the south, and it is
      particularly helpful in describing the partisan units under
      Marion, Pickens, and Summter. However, it is less dependable
      about Loyalist activities and British strategy.

848.   Ashmore, Otis, and Charles H. Olmstead. "The Battles of
       Kettle Creek and Brier Creek." GA HIST Q, 10 (1926), 85-
       125.

       This is a reliable account of how Lt. Colonel Archibald
       Campbell's British force smashed American resistance in
       Georgia.

849.   Azoy, A.C. Mariano. "Palmetto Fort, Palmetto Flag." AMER
       HERITAGE, 6 (6) (1955), 60-64, 99.

       The patriots at Sullivan's Island in Charleston harbor re-
       pulsed a fierce British bombardment in 1776.

850.   Barnwell, Joseph W. "Bernard Elliott's Recruiting Journal,
       1775." SC HIST MAG, 18 (1916), 95-100.

       A South Carolina officer wrote an amusing tale of his re-
       cruiting efforts.

851.   ———, ed. "Letters of John Rutledge." SC HIST MAG, 17,
       (1916), 131-146; 18 (1917), 43-49, 59-69, 131-142, 155-167.

       This is a valuable commentary on the war which covers the
       defeats at Charleston, Camden, partisan warfare, and service
       on the Santee River.

852.   Bullen, Ripley P. "Fort Tonyn and the Campaign of 1778."
       FLA HIST Q, 29 (1951), 253-260.

       The British outpost on Amelia Island, twenty-five miles up
       St. Mary's River, was a pivotal position to check American
       invasions of East Florida.

853.   Cann, Marvin L. "Prelude to War: The First Battle of Ninety
       Six, November 19-21, 1775." SC HIST MAG, 75 (1976), 197-
       214.

       The Tory victory inaugurated the war in South Carolina and
       prodded the state's provincial congress into action.

854.   Cashin, Edward J., Jr. "Augusta's Revolution of 1779."
       RICHMOND CO HIST, 7 (1975), 5-14.

       Here is a helpful commentary on the effects of the British
       invasion of Georgia effecting Richmond, Wilkes, and Burke
       counties.

855.   Cavanagh, John C. "American Military Leadership in the
       Southern Campaign: Benjamin Lincoln." In W. Roberts
       Higgins, ed. THE REVOLUTIONARY WAR IN THE SOUTH, POWER,
       CONFLICT AND LEADERSHIP: ESSAYS IN HONOR OF JOHN RICHARD
       ALDEN. Durham: Duke University Press, 1979, pp. 101-131.

       General Lincoln was a sound organizer but a weak strategist
       who lost an American army at Charleston.

856. Coker, C.F.W. "Journal of John Graham, South Carolina Militia,
      1779." MILT COLL HIST, 19 (1967), 36-47.

857. Cowen, Bob. "The Siege of Savannah." MILT COLL HIST, 27
      (1975), 52-59.

      A French captain left a vivid account of events, September
      13-October 20, 1779.

858. Cox, William E. "Brigadier General John Ashe's Defeat in the
      Battle of Brier Creek." GA HIST Q, 57 (1973), 295-302.

      Southern militia and Continentals were mauled near Augusta,
      Georgia because of inept planning and poor discipline.

859. Cullen, Joseph P. "Moore's Creek Bridge." AMER HIST ILLUS,
      4 (7) (1970), 10-15.

      This bloody fight between partisan forces in North Carolina
      early in the war ended in a signal American triumph.

860. Davis, Robert S., and Kenneth H. Thomas, Jr. KETTLE CREEK:
      THE BATTLE OF THE CANE BRAKES, WILKES COUNTY, GEORGIA.
      Atlanta: State of Georgia. The Department of Archives and
      History, 1975.

      The authors have compiled a fascinating study about a rela-
      tively obscure fight near Augusta. Their narrative is well-
      paced and nicely organized. It is crammed with details about
      the British penetration of the "back-country," the reactions
      of local citizenry, rosters of soldiers, and why the Loyalists
      were defeated. How the writers authenticated the battle sites
      is particularly interesting.

861. Drayton, John. MEMOIRS OF THE AMERICAN REVOLUTION. FROM THE
      COMMENCEMENT TO THE YEAR 1776 ... 2 vols. Charleston: A.E.
      Miller, 1821.

      This is a good eye-witness account of some military develop-
      ments in the south, particularly South Carolina in the early
      war years. The details cited here are generally unavailable
      elsewhere, but the emphasis is heavily political.

862. Elbert, Samuel. "Order Book of Samuel Elbert, Colonel and
      Brigadier General in the Continental Army, October 1776 to
      November 1778." GA HIST SOC COLL, 5 (1902), 5-191.

      This document provides clues about marches, camp sites, and,
      especially, about fighting at Savannah.

863. Farley, M. Foster. "The Battle of Sullivan's Island." HIST
      TODAY, 26 (1976), 83-91.

      Here is a solid description of why the British were repulsed
      at Charleston in June, 1776.

864. Gates, Horatio. "The Southern Campaign, 1780. Gates at
      Camden ... " MAG AMER HIST, 5 (1880), 241-320.

      There are numerous documents here from Gates's correspond-
      ence relating to his march to the Carolinas and the disposi-
      tion of troops before his defeat at Camden.

865. Gibbes, R.W., ed. REMINISCENCES, DOCUMENTARY HISTORY OF THE
      AMERICAN REVOLUTION ...   3 vols. New York: D. Appleton
      and Co., 1857.

      Gibbes complied a wealth of information from contemporary
      materials, much of which has disappeared. Here are innumer-
      able diaries, journals, letters, proclamations and related
      sources that offer much information about the struggle in the
      south. The descriptions of minor actions are invaluable.

866. Greene, Jerome A. NINETY SIX: A HISTORICAL NARRATIVE. Denver,
      Colorado: Denver Service Center Branch of Historical Pre-
      servation. Southeast/Southwest Team. Department of the
      Interior. National Park Service, 1979.

      This important South Carolina town was a focus of British
      hegemony in the backcountry. Greene compiled a solid histori-
      cal-archeological account about the construction of the fort,
      life at the post, and the aborted siege of Ninety Six by
      Nathanael Greene in May-June, 1781. Well-organized and nicely
      written, this study merits a wide audience.

867. Grimke, John Fauchereaud. "Journal of My Campaign to the
      Southward, May 9th to July 14th, 1778." SC HIST GEN MAG,
      12 (1911), 118-134, 160-69, 190-206.

      This is the best contemporary account of the Georgia-South
      Carolina expedition led by General Robert Howe to capture
      Fort Tonyn in British Florida.

868. ———. "Order Book of Fauchereaud Grimke, August 1778 to May
      1780." SC HIST GEN MAG, 13 (1912), 42-55, 89-103, 148-155,
      205-212; 14 (1913), 44-57, 98-111, 160-170, 219-224; 15
      (1915), 41-59, 82-90, 124-132, 166-170; 16 (1915), 39-48,
      85-85, 123-128, 178-183; 17 (1916), 26-33, 82-86, 116-120,
      167-174; 18 (1917), 78-84, 149-153, 175-179; 19 (1918), 101-
      104, 181-188.

      Colonel Grimke of the South Carolina artillery wrote detailed
      accounts of the frustrated American efforts to invade East
      Florida.

869. Hilborn, Nat, and Sam Hilborn. "A Show of Strength at Sul-
      livan's Island." SC HIST ILLUS, 1 (1970), 11-19, 57-60.

      This is a standard account of how Carolinians defended
      Charleston from a British assault in 1776 that was written
      for a general audience.

870. Hough, Franklin B., ed. THE SIEGE OF SAVANNAH BY THE COM-
      BINED AMERICAN AND FRENCH FORCES UNDER THE COMMAND OF GEN.
      LINCOLN AND THE COUNT D'ESTAING IN THE AUTUMN OF 1779.
      Albany, New York: J. Munsell, 1866.

      This work represents a collection of documents written by
      Lincoln, d'Estaing and their staff officers. The correspond-
      ence demonstrates the environmental and tactical problems that
      the American-French forces encountered in attempting to re-
      take Savannah. There is much material here that is difficult
      to locate in other works on the topic. But the book lacks
      a theme, and it is poorly organized.

871. Jackson, Harvey H. "The Battle of the Riceboats. Georgia
      Joins the Revolution." GA HIST Q, 58 (1974), 229-243.

      A British raid on Savannah to capture twenty merchant ships
      laden with rice was checked.

872. Kennedy, Benjamin, ed. and trans. MUSKETS, CANNON BALLS AND
      BOMBS: NINE NARRATIVES OF THE SIEGE OF SAVANNAH IN 1779.
      Savannah, Georgia: The Beehive Press, 1974.

      This is a well-edited collection of memoirs and journals by
      some of the officers on both sides of the fighting. The best
      is by Antoine Francois Terence O'Connor, a French engineer.
      Comments by d'Estaing, members of his staff, and a journal by
      General Augustin Prevost of the British defenders provide ad-
      ditional clues about this bitter contest.

873. Kurtz, Henry I. "The Battle of Sullivan's Island." AMER.
      HIST ILLUS, 3 (3) (1968), 18-26.

      Carolinians defended Charleston from a British attack in
      June, 1776 and held the port for four more years.

874. Kyte, George W. "The British Invasion of South Carolina in
      1780." HISTORIAN, 14 (1952), 149-172.

      Kyte documents the British strategy for the invasion and
      why it was doomed to fail by 1782.

875. Landers, H.L. THE BATTLE OF CAMDEN, SOUTH CAROLINA, AUGUST
      16, 1780. Washington, DC: Government Printing Office, 1929.

      Here is a reliable summary about Gates's preparations for,
      and his defeat, at Camden. Landers was quite familiar with
      the terrain and battle sites. Although his account is un-
      imaginative, it is reliable on strategy, tactics, weapons,
      and the units involved.

876. Lawrence, Alexander A. "General Robert Howe and the British
      Capture of Savannah in 1778." GA HIST Q, 36 (1952), 303-
      327.

Although outnumbered, Howe ineptly defended the city, and,
consequently, was subject to a court-martial.

877. ———. STORM OVER SAVANNAH: THE STORY OF COUNT D'ESTAING AND
      THE SIEGE OF THE TOWN IN 1779. Athens: University of
      Georgia Press, 1951.

      Lawrence wrote the best account of the heroic but aborted
      French-American effort to recapture British-held Savannah.
      The descriptions of the fighting are vivid, the explanation
      of the careful British defense preparations is thorough, and
      the reasons why the Allies terminated their investment are
      clearly explained.

878. Lee, Henry. MEMOIRS OF THE WAR IN THE SOUTHERN DEPARTMENT OF
      THE UNITED STATES. 1812. Reprint. With revisions and a
      biography of the author by Robert E. Lee. New York:
      University Publishing Co., 1869.

      This is one of the best contemporary sources about campaigns
      in the south. Lee was a daring soldier, witnessed much
      fighting, and he wrote some colorful passages about clashes
      with the British.

879. Moore, Frank, ed. "Siege of Savannah 1779: General Orders of
      the Count D'Estaing for the Attack by the Allied Forces 8th
      and 9th October." MAG AMER HIST, 2 (1878), 548-551.

      There are hints here about the Anglo-French battle plans
      for the assault.

880. Moultrie, William. MEMOIRS OF THE AMERICAN REVOLUTION ...
      2 vols. 1802. Reprint. New York: Arno Press Co., 1966.

      Moultrie was a key figure in defending Charleston against
      General Howe's assault in 1776. He was a keen observer of
      events and was quite familiar with developments in Georgia,
      North and South Carolina. Though generally dependable as
      a primary source, the work is naturally flawed by a limited
      perspective and by an inevitable sense of righteousness for
      the American cause.

881. Naisawald, L. Van Loan. "Major General Robert Howe's Activi-
      ties in South Carolina and Georgia, 1776-1779." GA HIST Q,
      35 (1951), 23-30.

      The author is unable to clarify why such an untalented sol-
      dier was the south's top commander until 1779.

882. ———. "Robert Howe's Operations in Virginia, 1775-1776."
      VA MHB, 60 (1952), 437-443.

      North Carolina sent two regiments under Howe to assist
      Virginians against Lord Dunmore's forces.

883. Nelson, Paul David. "Horatio Gates in the Southern Depart-
      ment, 1780: Serious Errors and a Costly Defeat." NC HIST
      REV, 50 (1973), 256-272.

      Gates was unprepared for battle and made inept plans for
      the contest at Camden.

884. ————. "Major General Horatio Gates as a Military Leader:
      The Southern Experience." See 855, pp. 132-158.

      This is the best article about Gates' ineptness as a com-
      mander in the south.

885. Rankin, Hugh F. "The Moore's Creek Campaign, 1776." NC HIST
      REV, 30 (1953), 23-60.

      Here is a detailed discussion of a major Tory defeat, and
      how it shook the complacency of Loyalists in the Carolinas.

886. Reeves, Enos. "Extracts from the Letterbook of Lieutenant
      Enos Reeves of the Pennsylvania Line." PA MHB, 20 (1896),
      302-314, 456-472; 21 (1897), 72-83, 235-256, 376-391, 466-
      476.

      Reeves served in many campaigns; his comments about march-
      ing orders, court-martials, and regimental movements in
      Virginia and the Carolinas are pertinent.

887. Russell, Peter. "The Siege of Charleston: Journal of Peter
      Russell, December 25, 1779 to May 2, 1780." AHR, 4 (1899),
      478-501.

      Extant memoirs about the American defense of Charleston are
      so rare this essay is especially useful.

888. Searcy, Martha Condray. "The Georgia-Florida Campaigns in
      the American Revolution, 1776, 1777, and 1778." Ph.D.
      dissertation, Tulane University, 1979.

      This is a fine synthesis of the vicious partisan warfare
      that devastated settlements between the St. Johns and Altahama
      Rivers. The author has diligently researched this virtually
      overlooked subject by concentrating on climate, topography,
      qualities of leadership in Georgia, and in Florida, and the
      interaction with the Creek tribes. Neither the better organ-
      ized British forces under General Prevost and Governor Tonyn,
      nor the factionalized Georgians with inferior leadership, were
      able to crack the other side's defenses and communications.

889. Serf, Col. Christian. "Plan of the Battle Near Camden." MAG
      AMER HIST, 5 (1880), 275-278.

      Here is a battleplan extracted from the von Steuben Papers.

890. South Carolina Line. "An Order Book of the 1st Regt., SC
      Line, Continental Establishment." SC HIST MAG, 7 (1905),
      75-80, 130-142, 194-203; 8 (1906), 12-28, 69-87.

      There is interesting data here about garrison duty at Fort
      Moultrie, December, 1777 to June, 1778.

891. Stevens, John Austin. "The Southern Campaign 1780: Gates
      at Camden." MAG AMER HIST, 5 (1880), 241-281, 425-446.

      Here is a somewhat dated but generally reliable commentary
      about the American defeat.

892. Stubblefield, George. "Order Book of the Company of Captain
      George Stubblefield, Fifth Virginia Regiment, from March 3,
      1777 to July 10, 1776 ... " VA HIST SOC COLL, 6 (1887),
      41-191.

      Stubblefield's clerk wrote a good account of activities on
      a march from Williamburg to Norfolk.

893. Tarter, Brent, ed. "The Orderly Book of the Second Virginia
      Regiment, Setpember 27, 1775-April 15, 1776." VA MHB, 85
      (1977), 156-183, 302-336.

      This is a useful document which includes orders of Colonel
      Patrick Henry and Colonel William Woodford.

894. Webber, Mabel L. "Revolutionary Letters." SC HIST MAG, 38
      (1937), 1-10, 75-80, 107.

      There are valuable clues here about Lincoln's encampment
      at Perrysburg in January, 1779 and the fighting at Charleston.

895. Weller, Jac. "The Irregular War in the South." MILT AFF, 24
      (1960), 124-136.

      With little aid from the north, the Southerners won the
      war in the deep south by using unorthodox tactics.

896. Wolff, Bernard Preston. "The Death of General Casimir
      Pulaski." GA HIST Q, 52 (1962), 222-223.

      The gallant Polish count was mortally wounded at the siege
      of Savannah.

                2. Greene's Campaign in the Carolinas

897. Agniel, Lucien. THE LATE AFFAIR HAS ALMOST BROKE MY HEART,
      THE AMERICAN REVOLUTION IN THE SOUTH, 1780-1781. Old Green-
      wich, Connecticut: The Chatham Press, 1972.

      Replete with factual errors and gross misinterpretations,
      this work is an undependeable survey of the late war years.

Written in a supposedly journalistic manner, the book provides little background data, few maps, and contains confusing information about localities. Undergraduates should
be wary of this narrative.

898.   Balt, Richard John. "The Maryland Continentals, 1780-1781."
       Ph.D. dissertation, Tulane University, 1974.

       Although, ordinarily, this item would be cited under the
       topic of unit organizations, it deserves to be mentioned here
       because the author concentrates far more on the contributions
       made by the dependable Maryland regiments. These troops
       were involved in operations from Virginia to the Carolinas
       and often represented the major regular force under Gates
       and Greene. This is a nicely paced and thoroughly researched
       study that contains some excellent chapters on conditions
       about the rank and file in the south.

899.   Bartholomees, James Boone, Jr. "'Fight or Flee': The Combat
       Performance of the North Carolina Militia in the Campaign
       in the Cowpens-Guilford Courthouse Campaign, January to
       March, 1781. Ph.D. dissertation, Duke University, 1978.

       A solid piece of research based on fresh source materials
       on local governments, this dissertation merits praise. The
       author concentrates on determining in what battle situations
       the militia were dependable, and when they were not. He is
       explicit in explaining how the militia supplemented the regu-
       lars at Guilford, the tactics used against Cornwallis, and
       why Morgan was more successful with the militia at Cowpens.

900.   Cann, Marvin L. "War in the Backcountry: The Siege of Ninety
       Six, May 22-June 19, 1781." SC HIST MAG, 72 (1971), 1-14.

       This important Loyalist post repulsed Greene's attack; later
       its garrison evacuated it for Charleston.

901.   Carpenter, Hugh. KING'S MOUNTAIN - AN EPIC OF THE REVOLUTION;
       WITH HISTORICAL AND BIOGRAPHICAL SKETCHES AND ILLUSTRATIONS.
       Knoxville, Tennessee: Prv. ptd., 1936.

       Based on standard sources, Carpenter adds little in his
       sketch of the epic fight to familiar interpretations. His
       knowledge of the topography, however, is apparent.

902.   Cashin, Edward J. "Nathanael Greene's Campaign for Georgia
       in 1781." GA HIST Q, 61 (1977), 43-58.

       Greene not only conducted warfare in the interior, and sent
       Wayne to besiege Savannah, but he also tried to restore civil
       government and to reconcile the defeated Loyalists.

903.   Chidsey, Donald B. THE WAR IN THE SOUTH, THE CAROLINAS AND
       GEORGIA IN THE AMERICAN REVOLUTION, AN INFORMAL HISTORY.
       New York: Crown Publishers, 1969.

Chidsey wrote a highly romanticized version about the hardships experienced by Greene's command and the partisan corps.
Because it contains numerous mistakes, and displays the
author's unfamiliarity with basic source material, the volume
should be treated with caution.

904. Coleman, George P., Jr. "The Southern Campaign, 1781." MAG
      AMER HIST, 7 (1881), 136-146.

      Here is an old, but generally reliable, summary of the
      year's fighting.

905. Conrad, Dennis Michael. "Nathanael Greene and the Southern
      Campaign, 1780-1783." Ph.D. dissertation, Duke University,
      1979.

      This is the best treatment of Greene's campaign. There are
      ample descriptions of his contest with Cornwallis, his rounds
      of losses, his tactics of wearing down the enemy war machine
      in the wilderness, and his relations with the often unmanage-
      able American partisans and uncooperative state governments.
      Conrad's main contribution, however, is explaining how Greene
      made his command more like the Continental army, how he
      established Congressional authority in the war-weary south,
      and how he increased his own prerogatives. The material here
      about Greene's effort to rebuild shattered state governments
      and to end Loyalist fighting is valuable.

906. Crowson, E.T. "Colonel William Campbell and the Battle of
      King's Mountain." VA CAL, 30 (1980), 23-27.

      This is a popular account of how American frontiersmen de-
      feated a Loyalist force at a major fight in South Carolina
      (October 1780); it is well-illustrated.

907. Davis, Burke. THE COWPENS-GUILFORD COURTHOUSE CAMPAIGN.
      Philadelphia; J.B. Lippincott, Co., 1962.

      Davis knows the standard source material well and weaves
      together an exciting account of Daniel Morgan's famous fight
      against Banastre Tarleton's Legion at Cowpens, and the maul-
      ing battle between Greene and Cornwallis at Guilford. Though
      this is a good general account, the author added not a fresh
      fact or novel interpretation to a familiar story.

908. De Peyster, J. Watts. "The Affair at King's Mountain." MAG
      AMER HIST, 5 (1880), 491-424.

      Here is an old but reliable account of a bloody fight.

909. Draper, Lyman Copeland. KING'S MOUNTAIN AND ITS HEROES:
      HISTORY OF THE BATTLE OF KING'S MOUNTAIN, OCTOBER 7, 1780
      AND THE EVENTS WHICH LED TO IT. Cincinnati: P.G. Thomson,
      1881.

      This classic work on the fighting west of Charlotte has not
      been surpassed. The amount of documentation by American and
      British participants is invaluable.

910.   Farley, M. Foster. "'The Old Wagoner' and the 'Green Dra-
        goon'." HIST TODAY, 25 (1975), 190-195.

        This is a lively summary of Daniel Morgan's victory over
        Banastre Tarleton at Cowpens on January 17, 1781.

911.   Frink, Madge C., comp. "A Day to Remember: October 7, 1780
        (King's Mountain)." DAR MAG, 124 (1980), 996-999.

        Here are some pertinent extracts from Draper's seminal work
        on the subject.

912.   Griffin, Willie Lew. "The Battle of Eutaw Springs." SC HIST
        ILLUS, 1 (3) (1970), 24-27.

        The British won a tactical victory over Greene, but it re-
        presented their last stand in South Carolina's interior.

913.   Hamilton, J.G. de Roulhac. "King's Mountain: Letters of
        Colonel Isaac Shelby." JSH, 4 (1938), 367-377.

        Shelby's letters written in 1814, constitute one of the
        best sources about the fighting by his Mountain Men.

914.   Hatch, Charles E. THE BATTLE OF GUILFORD COURT HOUSE.
        Washington, DC: Department of the Interior. National Park
        Service, 1971.

        This is the most reliable study of the famous battle. Hatch
        is thoroughly familiar with the terrain, major sites, and the
        battle lines. He includes many colorful incidents in the nar-
        rative, and his pages on exchanges of prisoners and care of
        the wounded are excellent.

915.   Kyte, George W. "Francis Marion as an Intelligence Officer."
        SC HIST MAG, 77 (1976), 215-226.

        Marion emerges here as an excellent interpreter
        of enemy movements in South Carolina for 1781-82.

916.   ———. "General Wayne Marches South, 1781." PA HIST, 30
        (1963), 301-315.

        This is a standard account of how well the Pennsylvania line
        performed in continuous actions throughout Virginia, and in
        the Carolinas.

917.   ———. "Strategic Blunder: Cornwallis Abandons the Caro-
        linas." HISTORIAN, 22 (1960), 129-144.

        When Cornwallis marched to the Carolina coast after Guil-
        ford, and then to Yorktown, he erred in assuming his posts
        in South Carolina and Georgia were safe.

918.   ————. "Victory in the South: An Appraisal of General
        Greene's Strategy in the Carolinas." NC HIST REV, 37 (1960),
        321-347.

        Defeated in every engagement in the south, Greene emerged
        as a top strategist by breaking the power of two British
        armies.

919.   Lee, Henry. THE CAMPAIGN OF 1781 IN THE CAROLINAS TO WHICH
        IS ADDED AN APPENDIX OF ORIGINAL DOCUMENTS, RELATING TO
        THE HISTORY OF THE REVOLUTION. Philadelphia: E. Littell,
        1824.

        This is one of the best contemporary sources of Greene's
        campaign. Lee describes battle scenes with clarity, and
        added interesting vignettes about the contest with Cornwallis.

920.   MacKenzie, George C., and Robert W. Young. KING'S MOUNTAIN
        NATIONAL MILITARY PARK, SOUTH CAROLINA. Washington, DC:
        Department of the Interior. National Park Service, 1955.

        Here is a solid summary of the fighting written by histori-
        ans of the Park. There are numerous fascinating sidelights
        mentioned in this useful work, and it contains fine maps and
        illustrations.

921.   Mahlen, Michael D. "The Battle of Cowpens." MILT REV, 51
        (1971), 56-63.

        Except for the stress on tactics, this is a standard ac-
        count.

922.   Messick, Hank. KING'S MOUNTAIN: THE EPIC OF THE BLUE RIDGE
        "MOUNTAIN MEN" IN THE AMERICAN REVOLUTION. New York: Little,
        Brown, and Co., 1976.

        This book is adequate for high schoolers but it contains
        innumerable errors, reveals ignorance of familiar sources,
        and its value is dubious. The American victory did not end
        the war in the Carolinas, as the author claims.

923.   Montross, Lynn. "America's Most Imitated Battle." AMER
        HERITAGE. 7 (3) (1956), 34-37, 100-102.

        With his militia at Cowpens, in January, 1781, Daniel Morgan
        inflicted a smashing defeat on a British force and thereby in-
        stigated a novel battle tactic.

924.   Pierce, William. "Southern Campaign of General Greene, 1781-
        2; Letters of William Pierce to St. George Tucker." MAG
        AMER HIST, 7 (1881), 431-445.

        The letters contain some information about Greene's logis-
        tical problems.

925.   Rankin, Hugh F. "Cowpens: Prelude to Yorktown." NC HIST REV,
       31 (1954), 333-369.

       Cowpens was the first major victory in the south over
       British regulars and wrecked Cornwallis's plan for conquering
       the Carolinas.

926.   ————. GREENE AND CORNWALLIS: THE CAMPAIGN IN THE CAROLINAS.
       Raleigh, North Carolina: The Division of Natural Resources.
       Department of History and Archives, 1976.

       This is an abbreviated version for a general audience of
       Rankin's work on the North Carolina campaign.

927.   ————. THE NORTH CAROLINA CONTINENTALS. Chapel Hill: The
       University of North Carolina Press, 1971.

       Rankin wrote one of the best histories of a state unit.
       This is a meticulously researched study of the many battles,
       skirmishes, raids, marches, and the sufferings of these troops
       with particular attention to the southern theater. The author
       deftly illustrates the complex field maneuvers, the difficulty
       of provisioning these units on campaigns, and the training
       and discipline of these fine fighters.

928.   Reid, Courtland T. GUILFORD COURTHOUSE NATIONAL MILITARY PARK,
       NORTH CAROLINA. Washington, DC: Department of the Interior.
       National Park Service, 1959.

       Here is a handsomely illustrated and carefully mapped ac-
       count of the bloody engagement between Greene and Cornwallis.
       This is one of the best summaries of the fight.

929.   Roberts, Kenneth. THE BATTLE OF COWPENS: THE GREAT MORALE
       BUILDER. Garden City, New York: Doubleday and Co., Inc.,
       1958.

       From a reknown story-teller, this relatively unimaginative
       work is a disappointment. Roberts delved into the sources
       but seemed unable to present a fresh perspective on a familiar
       event. However, his descriptions of Morgan and Greene are
       enthralling.

930.   Robinson, Blackwell P. THE REVOLUTIONARY WAR SKETCHES OF
       BLACKWELL P. ROBINSON. Raleigh, North Carolina: The Divi-
       sion of Natural Resource. Department of Archives and His-
       tory, 1976.

       This is a nicely edited version of Robinson's account of
       what he witnessed in the barbaric partisan warfare in the
       Carolina Piedmont prior to Yorktown. Clearly, the war in the
       south was somewhat different from that in the north.

931. Rutledge, Archibald. "The Battle of King's Mountain." AMER
     HIST ILLUS 1 (1) (1966), 22-30.

     British Major Patrick Fergusson and his Loyalist legion
     were overwhelmed by Tennessee and Carolina irregulars in the
     fight that broke British hopes of holding the backcountry.

932. Scheer, George F. "Some Events of the American Revolution in
     South Carolina as Recorded by Rev. James Jenkins." SC HIST
     ASSOC PROC, 2 (1945), 23-34.

     This is a terse but exciting eyewitness account of fighting
     near the Pee Dee River by Marion's men.

933. ————. "The Elusive Swamp Fox." AMER HERITAGE. 9 (3)
     (1958), 40-47, 111.

     Scheer investigates the legends about Francis Marion and
     finds them substantially correct.

934. Schenck, David. NORTH CAROLINA, 1780-1781; BEING A HISTORY OF
     THE INVASION OF THE CAROLINAS BY THE BRITISH ARMY UNDER LORD
     CORNWALLIS IN 1780-81. Raleigh, North Carolina: Edwards and
     Broughton, 1887.

     Here is an unsurpassed account of political and military
     events. Many of the chapters were based on material no
     longer available. Schenck wrote informative passages about
     Loyalists, the impact of the war on Carolina, and about
     partisan activities.

935. Seymour, William. "A Journal of the Southern Expedition."
     PA MHB, 7 (1883), 286-295, 377-394.

     Seymour wrote cogently about his service with DeKalb and
     with Gates; the description of the race to the Dan River under
     Greene is one of the best contemporary accounts.

936. Snow, Richard F. "Eutaw Springs." AMER HERITAGE, 26 (5)
     (1975), 53-56.

     Due to his commanders' errors, Greene lost the last big
     fight in the deep south (September 8, 1781).

937. ————. "Guilford Court House." AMER HERITAGE, 24 (4)
     (1973), 17-20.

     This is a good sample of eyewitness accounts in Greene's
     fight against Cornwallis.

938. Tilden, John Bell. "Extracts From the Journal of Lieutenant
     John Bell Tilden, Second Pennsylvania Line, 1781-1782."
     PA MHB, 19 (1895), 208-233.

     Tilden, who served under von Steuben in Virginia, wrote some
     perceptive commentaries about the Carolina campaigns.

939. Treacy, N.F. PRELUDE TO YORKTOWN: THE SOUTHERN CAMPAIGN OF
      NATHANAEL GREENE, 1780-81. Chapel Hill: University of
      North Carolina Press, 1963.

      This is a well-balanced treatment of a campaign that is
      ordinarily difficult to comprehend because of its scope, the
      environmental factors, and the innumerable supply centers
      used by Greene and Cornwallis. Treacy wrote in a readable
      style, did some investigation of the documents, and provided
      the reader with information to explain this contest. While
      scholars will find little new here, this is a good intro-
      duction to the subject for college students.

940. Tucker, St. George. "The Southern Campaign, 1781. From
      Guilford Court House to the Siege of York." Edited by
      George W. Coleman, Jr. MAG AMER HIST, 7 (1881), 36-46.

      This is a small set of letters describing in vivid terms
      the difficulties that Greene's men encountered on the march.

941. Weigley, Russell. THE PARTISAN WAR: THE SOUTH CAROLINA CAM-
      PAIGN OF 1780-1782. Charleston: University of South Caro-
      lina Press, 1970.

      Weighley wrote a clear, concise summary about the bewilder-
      ing fighting in the Carolinas that is one of the best on the
      topic. Particularly good on the strategic and environmental
      factors involved, the book, however, is quite weak on the
      lack of southern state support to Greene. Weigley's knowledge
      about the partisanship aspects of the war is also hazy.

942. Williams, Samuel C. "General Richard Winn's Notes, 1780."
      SC HIST MAG, 43 (1942), 201-212; 44 (1943), 1-10.

      Beginning with the loss of Charleston, Winn wrote a good
      summary of the effects of Britisher Tarleton's advance to
      December, 1780.

                            3. Yorktown

943. Adams, Randolph G. "A View of Cornwallis's Surrender at
      Yorktown." AHR, 37 (1931-32), 25-49.

      This is a useful summary of why the British lost in Virginia.

944. Butler, Richard. "General Richard Butler's Journal of the
      Siege of Yorktown." HIST MAG, 8 (1864), 102-112.

      Dating from September 1 to October 25, 1781, this memoir is
      a vivid description of the fighting.

945. Carrington, Henry B. "Lafayette's Virginia Campaign." MAG
      AMER HIST, 6 (1881), 341-352.

Though weak on source material, this is a satisfactory
introduction to Lafayette's contest with Cornwallis.

946.   Chidsey, Donald B.   VICTORY AT YORKTOWN.   New York: Crown
       Publishers, 1962.

Here is a highly romanticized account about the siege which
deviates frequently from the documented evidence about key
events.   Intended to be a popular treatment, this work is not
reliable either in fact or in interpretation.

947.   Davis, Burke.   THE CAMPAIGN THAT WON AMERICA - THE STORY OF
       YORKTOWN.   New York: Dial Press, 1970.

Though there is nothing novel here either in evidence or
in synthesis, this work is recommended as an adequate introduction for a wide audience.   Davis wrote an exciting narrative, he attempted to explain the strategic factors involved,
and he gave ample credit to the French forces under Rochambeau
and De Grasse.

948.   Davis, John.   "The Yorktown Campaign: Journal of Capt. John
       Davis of the Revolutionary Line."   PA MHB, 5 (1881), 290-
       311.

Wounded in the fighting, Davis compiled a colorful summary
of his observations.

949.   Dayton, Elias.   "'The Drum Beats to Arms ... ' Two Letters
       from Yorktown and a Missing Map."   PRINCETON U LIB CHRON,
       31 (1970), 209-213.

Colonel Dayton of the Second New Jersey regiment described
the surrender of Cornwallis.

950.   Eckenrode, H.J.   THE STORY OF THE CAMPAIGN AND SIEGE OF YORK-
       TOWN.   Washington: Government Printing Office, 1931.

Here is a solid account of the fighting on the Virginia Tidewater.   Though the author gave less attention to the French
forces than later writers, this study is a reliable narrative.
But it is related in a ponderous manner.

951.   Fleming, Thomas J.   BEAT THE LAST DRUM: THE SIEGE OF YORKTOWN,
       1781.   New York: St. Martin's Press, 1963.

This is the best synthesis of the land and sea fighting on
the Virginia coast.   It is carefully researched, and it provides thrilling portraits of battle scenes.   Fleming is a skil-
led writer who has mastered the source material.   He is especially careful about stressing the importance of the French
participation at Yorktown, and about handling the clashes of
personalities.   The book is highly recommended for its style
and authenticity.

952. Hammes, Doris D. "The Road to Glory and Great Possessions."
     VA CAL, 19 (1969), 12-19.

     Baron von Steuben had great difficulties in waging war
     against Cornwallis in 1780-1781, and he received little aid
     from Virginia politicians.

953. Handlin, Oscar. "Independence at Yorktown; Chance or Destiny?"
     ATL. MONTHLY, 194 (1954), 27-32.

     This is a spirited summary of the event stressing the great
     American-French gamble and the sheer luck involved in the
     victory.

954. Hatch, Charles E., Jr. "The Affair Near James Island (or
     'The Battle of Green Springs'), July 6, 1781." VA MHB, 53
     (1945), 172-196.

     Hatch wrote a good summary of how Wayne and Lafayette were
     nearly trapped by Cornwallis as he marched toward the Virginia
     coast.

955. ————. YORKTOWN AND THE SIEGE OF 1781. Washington, DC:
     Government Printing Office. National Park Service, 1957.

     Hatch compiled a fine summary of events that led to the
     American triumph. This small book is replete with excellent
     maps of the contests on land and sea, and it contains the best
     bibliography on the subject.

956. Hollowell, M. Edgar, Jr. "The Point of Fork Arsenal." MILT
     COLL HIST, 28 (1970), 11-13.

     Forty-five miles from Richmond, the American arsenal was a
     major supplier of equipment for the campaign.

957. [Hudson, John]. "'Such Has Been the Flow ... '" AMER HIST
     ILLUS, 16 (6) 1980), 18-23.

     Hudson, a soldier at Yorktown, wrote a poignant memoir about
     the siege of Yorktown.

958. Johnston, Henry P. THE YORKTOWN CAMPAIGN AND THE SURRENDER OF
     CORNWALLIS, 1781. New York: Harper and Brothers, 1881.

     Though outdated, this is a good example of traditional his-
     torical writing which suggests the patriotic ardor related to
     the war. The maps are excellent. The material about the sea
     fights and the French army is adequate. This is a reliable
     and readable account.

959. Keller, Allan. "The Long March to Triumph." AMER HIST ILLUS,
     13 (4) (1978), 4-9, 44-47.

     Rochambeau's French army marched from Rhode Island to
     Virginia in order to trap Cornwallis.

960. Landers, Howard E. Lee. VIRGINIA CAMPAIGN AND THE BLOCKADE
      AND SIEGE OF YORKTOWN, 1781, INCLUDING A BRIEF NARRATIVE OF
      THE FRENCH PARTICIPATION PRIOR TO THE SOUTHERN CAMPAIGN.
      Washington, DC: Government Printing Office, 1931.

      Landers was so meticulous in studying the archival material
      that virtually little has been added (except details about
      the navies) to this scholarly account. The background to the
      entrapment of Cornwallis is well told, and the maneuvers of
      the French and British fleets are aptly described. The study
      is a Congressional document: U.S. Congress, 71st Cong., 3rd
      Sess. Senate Doc. 273.

961. Larrabee, Harold A. "A Near Thing at Yorktown." AMER HERITAGE,
      12 (6) (1961), 8–64.

      Here is a well written and superbly illustrated summary of
      the sea fights off the Virginia coast.

962. ———. DECISION AT THE CHESAPEAKE. New York: Clarkson N.
      Putter, 1964.

      Larrabee is one of the few popular writers who appreciated
      the significance of the French and British fleet positions as
      the military operations at Yorktown proceeded. He makes clear
      why the Royal Navy, straining to provide adequate seapower at
      crucial areas, was unable to rescue the British army. With
      meticulous attention to weather conditions, position of squad-
      rons, and the tricky maneuvering leading to the battle of the
      Chesapeake Bay, Larrabee clarifies why Admiral Thomas Graves
      was unable to defeat De Grasse, why it was virtually a stale-
      mate, and how the action virtually terminated Cornwallis's
      opportunities for a rescue.

963. Lutnick, Solomon M. "The Defeat at Yorktown: A View from
      the British Press." VA MHB, 72 (1964), 471–478.

      Lutnick described the reaction in England to the American
      victory.

964. MacMaster, Richard K., ed. "News of the Yorktown Campaign:
      The Journal of Dr. Robert Honeyman, April 17–November 25,
      1781." VA MHB, 79 (1971), 387–426.

      A Virginia physician wrote to his friends about the siege.

965. Riley, Edward M. "Yorktown during the Revolution." VA MHB,
      57 (1949), 22–43, 176–188, 274–285.

      There are ample details here about the social, economic and
      political life of this key port.

966. Selby, John. THE ROAD TO YORKTOWN. London: Hamish Hamilton,
      1976.

      This work is adequate for high school readers.

967. Thayer, Theodore G. YORKTOWN: CAMPAIGN OF STRATEGIC OPTIONS.
      Philadelphia: J.B. Lippincott, Co., 1975.

      Although this volume purports to emphasize the strategy in-
      volved at Yorktown, it merely echoes familiar themes without
      providing fresh evidence. The land fighting is adequately
      covered in contrast to the author's unfamiliarity with the
      implications of sea power. Thayer tends to overlook the
      decisive role of the French fleet, and, in particular, he
      fails to link the siege to the fighting in the lower south.

968. Tucker, St. George. "St. George Tucker's Journal of the Siege
      of Yorktown, 1781." Edited by Edward M. Riley. WMQ, 5
      (1946), 375-395.

      Here is a carefully edited essay of an important eye-witness
      account of events.

969. [Wayne, Anthony]. "Anthony Wayne at Green Spring, 1781: His
      Account of the Action." MAG AMER HIST, 15 (1886), 201-202.

      Wayne tended to overlook his near defeat by Cornwallis in
      Virginia.

970. Wright, John W. "Notes on the Siege of Yorktown in 1781 with
      Special Reference to the Conduct of a Siege in the Eight-
      eenth Century." WMQ, 12 (1931), 229-249.

      This is the best essay on the siege for readers desiring
      data about warfare during the Age of Enlightenment.

                          4. Post-Yorktown

971. Barnwell, Joseph W. "The Evacuation of Charleston by the
      British in 1782." SC HIST MAG, 11 (1910), 1-26.

      This is a useful description about how the British relin-
      quished their last garrison in the Carolinas.

972. [Gray, Robert]. "Colonel Robert Gray's Observations on the
      War in the Carolinas." SC HIST MAG, 11 (1910), 139-159.

      A Loyalist in a provincial corps commented in early 1782
      about the errors of British strategists.

973. Kyte, George W. "General Greene's Plan for the Capture of
      Charleston, 1781-1782." SC HIST MAG, 62 (1961), 96-106.

      Greene would have used French sea power if Rodney had not
      defeated De Grasse in the West Indies.

974. McKinney, Francis F. "The Integrity of Nathanael Greene."
      RI HIST, 28 (1969), 57-61.

> Greene helped to restore civil government in the south and
> helped some Loyalists recover their property.

975. Mitchell, Robert G., ed. THE WAYNE-GREENE CORRESPONDENCE,
      1782. In Howard H. Peckham, SOURCES OF AMERICAN INDEPEND-
      ENCE. SELECTED MANUSCRIPTS FROM THE COLLECTION OF THE
      WILLIAM H. CLEMENTS LIBRARY. 2 vols. The University of
      Chicago Press, 1978. Vol. 2, pp. 361-426.

      That the campaign to drive the British from their last
      major outposts in the deep south was an ardous one is mani-
      fest in this fascinating documentation between the two
      generals.

976. Sanders, Jennings B. "After Yorktown, What?" SOC STUD, 56
      (1965), 9-17.

      The author urges historians to study the complex military
      activities in the south that transpired after Yorktown.

                    D. WAR ON THE FRONTIERS

                  1. The Northwestern Frontier

977. Alexander, David E., ed. "Diary of Captain Benjamin Warren
      at the Massacre of Cherry Valley." J AMER HST, 3 (1909),
      377-384.

      A Massachusetts officer commented about the famous atrocity
      committed by Indians.

978. Alvord, Clarence W. CAHOKIA RECORDS, 1778-1790. Vol. 2.
      Illinois Historical Society Collections. Springfield,
      Illinois: The Society, 1897.

      The material on pages 1-153 is pertinent to the Revolution
      in the Illinois country and in the upper Mississippi. There
      is a fine and long introductory essay; the volume is filled
      with documents in English and in French; the bibliography
      and index are excellent.

979. ————. KASKAKIA RECORDS, 1778-1790. Vol. 5. Illinois
      Historical Society Collections. Springfield, Illinois: The
      Society, 1907.

      Alvord compiled a massive collection of proclamations,
      treaties and correspondence concerning the American conquests
      in the Old Northwest. The material here about trade, Indian
      relations, French settlers, and George Rogers Clark is in-
      valuable.

980. ————. "Virginia and the West: An Interpretation." MVHR,
      3 (1916), 19-38.

This is a fine synthesis about the state's massive terri-
torial claims beyond the Appalachians and the background to
the expedition by George Rogers Clark.

981. Angle, Paul M. "George Rogers Clark: Illinois and the Revo-
      lution." CHIC HIST, 4 (1975), 4-13.

      Here is a version for high-schoolers about Clark's career
      and his influence in the Northwest.

982. Appel, John C. "Colonel Daniel Brodhead and the Lure of
      Detroit." PA HIST, 38 (1971), 265-282.

      Brodhead made several efforts from Fort Pitt from 1778 to
      1781 to capture the British stronghold.

983. Bailey, Kenneth P. THE OHIO COMPANY OF VIRGINIA AND WEST-
      WARD MOVEMENT. Gendale, California, A.H. Clark, 1939.

      The Company, founded in 1749, struggled to 1790's to legalize
      its land claims with the British and United States govern-
      ments. Though this narrative is basically a retelling of an
      old story, and the author overlooked pertinent manuscript
      material, it is generally authoritative and well compiled.
      The chapters about the membership of the company, the explor-
      ations, the rivalries with other speculators, and the efforts
      to secure Virginia's support are informative.

984. Ballard, Edward, ed. "Attack on Cherry Valley." HIST MAG,
      5 (1869), 276-277.

      Here is a contemporary description of one of the most
      famous Indian massacres of the war.

985. ———. "Letters of General Stark and Others Relating to
      Operations in Cherry Valley in 1778." HIST MAG, 10 (1866),
      172-176.

      Stark's units tried in vain to protect the American settle-
      ments on the frontier.

986. Barnhart, John D. "A New Evaluation of Henry Hamilton and
      George Rogers Clark." MVHR, 37 (1951), 643-652.

      Britisher Hamilton at Vincennes was not a "hair-buyer,"
      nor was he cruel to American settlers.

987. ———. HENRY HAMILTON AND GEORGE ROGERS CLARK IN THE AMERI-
      CAN REVOLUTION WITH THE UNPUBLISHED JOURNAL OF LIEUT.
      GENERAL HENRY HAMILTON. Crawfordville, Indiana: K.E.
      Banta, 1951.

      Here is a summary of the contest in the Old Northwest be-
      tween Clark and the British. The author is an expert on the

strategy involved, Indian affairs, the attitudes of the
French settlers, and the local topography. Hamilton's journal
is very revealing.

988. ――――. VALLEY OF DEMOCRACY. THE FRONTIER VERSUS THE PLANTA-
      TION IN THE OHIO VALLEY, 1775-1818. Bloomington: University
      of Indiana Press, 1953.

      Barnhart applies the thesis of Frederick Jackson Turner that
      the frontier was the cutting edge of democracy. Though the
      author concentrates on the struggle between farmers and planters,
      and on western constitutions in the post-war era, this volume
      is helpful in explaining early American penetration of the
      Ohio country.

989. Batchellor, Albert S. "The Ranger Service in the Upper Valley
      of the Connecticut and the most Northerly Regiment of New
      Hampshire Militia in the Period of the Revolution." MAG HIST,
      6 (1907), 187-205, 249-268.

      Here is a well-documented essay about the topography, limits
      of white settlements, and Ranger duties in the Hampshire
      Grants area.

990. Bellinger, L.F. "The Unknown Battle of German Flats, 1783, and
      George Washington's Possible Connection With It." NY HIST,
      13 (1932), 129-141.

      A band of Tories and Indians attempted to capture Washington
      when he visited the village on the Mohawk.

991. Bertin, Eugene P. "Frontier Forts on the Susquehanna." NOW
      AND THEN, 14 (1965), 376-393.

      The American outposts in the river valley were devastated from
      1777 to 1779 by Indian-Tory raids.

992. Bourne, Clara L. "Massacre at Wyoming July 3, 1778." AMER
      MONTHLY, 6 (1895), 665-673.

      Indians virtually destroyed the frontier village.

993. Boyd, Julian R., and Robert J. Taylor, eds. THE SUSQUEHANNAH
      PAPERS. 11 vols. New Haven: Yale University Press, 1935-
      1971.

      Volumes six through nine of this superbly edited collection
      are pertinent to the war era. There is a mass of documenta-
      tion here, preceeded by lucid introductory essays and detailed
      annotation about the Connecticut land company that operated
      in the Wyoming Valley of Northeastern Pennsylvania. Clearly,
      the 300 settlers here perceived the war quite differently
      than inhabitants of the seaboard. The significance of the
      Company was in bitter and often bloody disputes between Con-
      necticut settlers and Pennsylvania pioneers as the debates,
      initiated in the late colonial era continued in the Continen-
      tal Congress. The editor(s) provide cogent explanations for

"the trial at Trenton" in 1782 involving the rival land
claims, and the quest for solutions by politicians. Many
Delegates were men of limited vision, the settlers were a
quarrelsome group who resented legal restraints, and the behavior of many participants in decades of disputes was often
unedifying to the nation. These volumes represent the epit-
ome of fine historical writing, meticulous scholarship, and
judicious analysis.

994.   Burgess, Charles E. "John Rice Jones, Citizen of Many Ter-
       ritories." J ILL STATE HIST ASSOC, 61 (1968), 58-82.

       Jones attempted to establish settlements at Kaskakia,
       Louisville, and Vincennes.

995.   Bushnell, David. "The Virginia Frontier in History - 1778."
       VA MHB, 33 (1915), 113-133, 256-268, 337-351; 24 (1916),
       44-55, 168-179.

       Successive American commanders at Fort Pitt encountered
       innumerable problems with Indians.

996.   Cantlidge, Anna M. "Colonel John Floyd: Reluctant Adven-
       turer." KENT HIST SOC REG, 66 (1968), 317-366.

       Floyd was a surveyor, militia officer and Indian fighter
       with Daniel Boone.

997.   Caruso, John Anthony. THE APPALACHIAN FRONTIER: AMERICA'S
       FIRST SURGE WESTWARD. New York: Bobbs-Merrill Co., 1959.

       The volume is a useful compendium of information for under-
       graduates on the aftermath of the French and Indian War, the
       early settlements in Kentucky and Tennessee, the rivalries
       of land speculators, and hardships of pioneering families.
       Caruso is gifted in depicting the terror of the wilderness,
       and there are good narratives here extracted from the memoirs
       of many adventurers. The maps are very useful.

998.   ————. THE GREAT LAKES FRONTIER: AN EPIC OF THE OLD NORTH-
       WEST. Indianapolis: Bobbs-Merrill Co., 1961.

       This is a sweeping account for general readers about the
       American surge in Ohio, Indiana, Illinois, Michigan and
       Wisconsin. Though many chapters pre-date and post-date the
       war era, the volume is particularly valuable in documenting
       Indian wars, pioneer life, sectional rivalries, and the
       blunders and accomplishments of the pioneers. Caruso care-
       fully documented this study.

999.   Chaput, Donald. "Treason or Loyalty? Frontier French in the
       American Revolution." J MICH STATE HIST SOC, 71 (1968),
       242-251.

Some promiment French ex-army officers, expelled from
Canada after 1763, were British agents in the Illinois country.

1000.   Clark, Thomas D.   "Boonesborough – Outpost   of the American
        Westward Movement." KTY HIST SOC REG, 72 (1974), 391-397.

        Richard Henderson and Daniel Boone merit credit for fund-
        ing the settlement.

1001.   ———. FRONTIER AMERICA. New York: Charles Scribner's
        Sons, 1959.

        For a broad audience this book is well-recommended. It is
        an engrossing narrative of major political, economic, and
        social trends in the late eighteenth-century surge westward.
        Clark depicts the heroes, villains as well as the ugly and
        unglamorous aspects of pioneering. Full of vivid quotations
        and lavish illustrations, here is an exciting work. The chap-
        ter on frontier culture is imaginative.

1002.   Connelly, Thomas Lawrence. "Indian Warfare on the Tennessee
        Frontier, 1776-1794: Strategy and Tactics." E TENN HIST
        SOC PUB, 36 (1965), 3-22.

        The author claims that some tribes (Shawnee, Cherokee,
        Chickamagua, Creeks) learned to modify their battle plans
        against the whites.

1003.   Curtis, Thomas D. "Land Policy: Pre-Conditions for the Suc-
        cess of the American Revolution." AMER J ECON SOC, 31
        (1972), 209-223.

        The thesis is that the British change of land-policies
        brought divergent interest groups into opposition as a factor
        in continuing the rebellion.

1004.   Derleth, August. VINCENNES: PORTAL TO THE WEST. Englewood
        Cliffs, New Jersey: Prentice-Hall, Inc., 1968.

        After 1763, this outpost on the Wabash River was re-named
        Fort Sackville. This is a compact study of how the French,
        English, Americans and Indians struggled to gain control of
        an area that would comprise five states. The details on
        George Rogers Clark and the marches to central Ohio, Vincennes,
        and Detroit are vivid. The excessive documentation and
        copious footnotes may awe the general reader, but this vol-
        ume is well-worth consulting.

1005.   Donnelly, Ralph W. "George Rogers Clark's Row Galley Miami:
        Virginia Marines in the Ohio Valley, 1782." VA CAV, 27
        (1968), 114-117.

        Clark controlled Fort Nelson (Louisville), and the Miami
        River in Ohio with some boats.

1006.   Downes, Randolph C. "Cherokee American Relations in the
        Upper Tennessee Valley, 1776-1791." E TENN HIS SOC PUB, 8
        (1936), 35-53.

        The Cherokees assumed the British would win but were re-
        peatedly defeated by the Americans.

1007.   ———. "Indian War on the Upper Ohio, 1779-1782." W PA
        HIST MAG, 17 (1934), 93-115.

        The Northwest territory was still full of hostile tribes
        by the war's end.

1008.   Eckert, Allan W. "The Bloody Year in Ohio 1782." See
        1063, pp. 244-268.

        An American massacre of Delaware Indians caused four other
        tribes to retaliate.

1009.———. THE WILDERNESS WAR. A NARRATIVE. Boston: Little,
        Brown, and Co., 1978.

        Eckert wrote a semi-fictional account of warfare in frontier
        New York - the Sullivan Expedition, the Cherry Valley Massacre,
        and the Indian raids in the Mohawk Valley. The volume is good
        for general readers because of the information on the Iroquois,
        the vivid descriptions of fighting, and on geographic factors.
        Unfortunately, the author used only published sources and
        overlooked much of the excellent manuscript material in the
        Draper Manuscript Collection. The volume is very uneven in
        its coverage of the Old Northwest territory.

1010.   Edson, Obed. "Brodhead's Expedition Against the Indians of
        the Upper Allegheny, 1779." MAG AMER HIST, 3 (1879), 647-
        671.

        There is an excellent bibliography in this essay about the
        adventures of a wing of the Sullivan expedition.

1011.   Edward, Brother C. "The Wyoming Valley Massacre, July 3,
        1778 in Pennsylvania." AMER HIST ILLUS, 13 (8) (1968),
        32-40.

        John Butler's Tory-Indian raid was one of the bloddiest of
        the war.

1012.   Evans, William A., ed. DETROIT TO FORT SACKVILLE, 1778-1779.
        THE JOURNAL OF NORMAN MACLEOD. Detroit: Wayne State Uni-
        versity Press, 1978.

        Macleod left a fascinating account of his service as a
        British officer in the Northwest. This is a finely edited
        account about obscure tribes, forgotten military posts, and
        exciting incidents with the Indians.

1013.   Fall, Ralph Emmett. "Captain Samuel Brady (1756-1795), Chief
        of the Rangers and His Kin." W VA HIST, 29 (1968), 203-
        223.

        The Brady family of Pennsylvania was famous for Indian
        fighting.

1014.   Farrell, David. "Settlement Along the Detroit Frontier,
        1760-1796." MICH HIST, 52 (1968), 87-107.

        This essay provides detailed information about the French
        and the British land tenure system in the area.

1015.   Fee, Walter R. "Colonel George Morgan at Fort Pitt." W PA
        HIST MAG, 11 (1928), 217-224.

        Fort Pitt was vital to the defense of Pennsylvania and a
        base of operations against the Indians.

1016.   [Fletcher, Ebenezer]. "The Trial of Ebenezer Fletcher."
        AMER HIST ILLUS, 15 (5) (1970), 25-31.

        Fletcher wrote a dramatic memoir about his boyhood adven-
        tures as an Indian captive.

1017.   Forroy, Richard Reuben. "Edward Hand: His Role in the Ameri-
        can Revolution." Ph.D. dissertation, Duke University, 1976.

        Famous for his role as commander of rifle regiments early
        in the war, Hand led a brigade under Sullivan against the
        Iroquois. He was less successful in leading an expedition
        from Fort Pitt into the Ohio country. Forroy has done his
        research, but there is not enough material here to enliven
        what could have been a solid biography of a frontier soldier.

1018.   Gerlach, Don R. "Philip Schuyler and the New York Frontier
        in 1781." NY HIST SOC Q, 53 (1969), 148-181.

        After being replaced by Gates as commander before Saratoga,
        Schuyler remained in Albany where he kept some Indian tribes
        neutral.

1019.   Gibb, Harky L. "Colonel Guy Johnson, Superintendant-General
        of Indian Affairs, 1774-1782." PAP MICH AC SC AR LT, 37
        (1943), 596-613.

        Here is a sympathetic account of a prominent Loyalist of-
        ficial who was instrumental in organizing Indian raids on
        American settlements.

1020.   Goodnough, David. THE CHERRY VALLEY MASSACRE, NOVEMBER 11,
        1778; THE FRONTIER ATROCITY THAT SHOCKED A YOUNG NATION.
        New York: Franklin Watts, 1968.

        A Loyalist-Indian raid destroyed Fort Alden, an outpost

which guarded the Cherry Valley approach to the Mohawk Valley.
This is a brief account that would appeal to youngsters.

1021.   Graham, Louis E.   "Fort McIntosh."   WEST PA HIST MAG, 15
        (1932), 93-119.

        The author documents the importance of the post as crucial
        to the defense of the western frontier.

1022.   Hagy, James W.   "The Frontier at Castle's Woods, 1769-1786."
        VA MHB, 75 (1967), 410-428.

        This post, where Daniel Boone once lived, was the first
        permanent settlement in Russell County, Virginia.

1023.   [Hand, Edward].   "Correspondence of General Edward Hand of
        the Continental Line, 1779-1781."   PA MHB, 33 (1909), 353-
        360.

        Some reasons why Hand, an able field commander, was less
        successful at Fort Pitt are alluded to in these letters.

1024.   Harrison, Lowell H.   "George Rogers Clark and the Conquest
        of Illinois."   AMER HIST ILLUS, 11 (10) (1977), 4-7, 44-48.

        This essay is a summary of the author's book written for a
        general audience.

1025.   ———.   GEORGE ROGERS CLARK AND THE WAR IN THE WEST.   Lexing-
        ton, Kentucky: University Press of Kentucky, 1976.

        Although there are some errors in the text and maps, this
        work is a generally well-balanced treatment of Clark's ex-
        ploits. It incorporates much recent research on the Revolu-
        tion in the Northwest. Particularly good on Clark's per-
        sonality and motives, it is weak about aspects of the war in
        the Ohio and Illinois country, especially about strategy. Yet
        Harrison's unromanticized account is one of the best of many
        studies on this topic. For undergraduates, this work is
        recommended.

1026.   Havighurst, Walter.   "A Sword for George Rogers Clark."   AMER
        HERITAGE, 13 (6) (1982), 56-64.

        With the aid of French settlers, Clark captured Kaskakia,
        Cahokia, and Vincennes in 1778-79.

1027.   Henderson, Archibald.   "The Creative Forces in American Ex-
        pansion: Henderson and Boone."   AHR, 24 (1914), 86-107.

        Here is a romanticized summary, with little analysis, about
        how frontier expansion in Kentucky represented American
        creativity.

1028.   Horsman, Reginald. "Great Britian and the Illinois Country
        in the Era of the American Revolution." J ILL STATE HIST
        SOC, 69 (1976), 100-109.

        For a good perspective of how London and Quebec viewed this
        area for trade and expansion, this is a terse summary of
        developments.

1029.   Hough, Franklin B., ed. THE NORTHERN INVASION OF OCTOBER,
        1780: A SERIES OF PAPERS RELATING TO THE EXPEDITION FROM
        CANADA UNDER SIR JOHN JOHNSON AND OTHERS AGAINST THE
        FRONTIER OF NEW YORK. New York: n.p., 1866.

        This collection of correspondence covers the British-Loy-
        alist-Indian attacks from Canada on the New York frontier in
        1780. Well-documented here is material that is now relatively
        difficult to locate. The raids were in retaliation for the
        Sullivan expedition of 1779 at the Iroquois Confederacy.

1030.   Hutson, James H. "Benjamin Franklin and the West." WEST HIST
        Q, 4 (1973), 425-434.

        Like Frederick Jackson Turner, Franklin perceived that the
        abundance of free land in the west was the decisive factor
        in creating a distinctly American society.

1031.   James, James A. "An Appraisal of the Contributions of George
        Rogers Clark to the History of the West." MVHR, 7 (1930),
        98-115.

        James wrote a fine appraisal of Clark's role in one of the
        best articles on the subject.

1032.   ————, ed. GEORGE ROGERS CLARK PAPERS, 1771-1781, 1781-84.
        Vols. 8 and 19. Illinois State Historical Collections.
        Springfield, Illinois: The Society, 1912, 1924.

        Both volumes have solid and lengthy introductions about
        Clark's role in the northwest. The volumes are packed with
        intriguing documents, provide much information about Ameri-
        can activities in the area, and are superbly edited. This is
        an essential collection that should be consulted.

1033.   ————. "Pittsburgh, a Key to the West During the American
        Revolution." OHIO ARCH HIST Q, 22 (1913), 64-79.

        Here is a solid treatment about Colonel George Morgan, a
        British Indian agent, and why Pittsburgh was the American base
        for advance into the Northwest.

1034.   ————. "The Northwest: Gift or Conquest?" IND MAG HIST, 30
        (1934), 1-15.

        Clark's raid on the Shawnee in November, 1782 was the last
        major fight in the area, and his conquests helped the United
        States acquire the Northwest Territory.

1035. ————. "To What Extent Was George Rogers Clark in Military
       Control of the Northwest at the Close of the American Revo-
       lution?" AMER HIST ASSOC ANN REP, 1 (1917), 313-329.

       The American grip along the Great Lakes and the Upper Mis-
       sissippi was still tenuous by the end of the war.

1036. Jordan, John W., ed. "Adam Hubly, Jr., Lt. Col. Commdt.
       with Penna Regt., His Journal Commencing at Wyoming, July
       30, 1777." PA MHB, 33 (1909), 126-146, 279-302, 409-422.

       Jordan compiled a lively narrative about Hubly's adventures
       in Indian fighting.

1037. Kenny, James F., ed. "Walter Butler's Journal of an Expedi-
       tion Along the Northern Shores of Lake Ontario, 1779."
       CAN HIST REV, 1 (1920), 381-391.

       The article focuses on an exchange of prisoners after the
       Cherry Valley Massacre.

1038. Ketchum, Richard M. "Men of the Revolution VI - George Rogers
       Clark." AMER HERITAGE, 25 (1) (1973), 32-33, 78.

       Ketchum wrote a colorful essay which nicely summarizes
       Clark's accomplishments in the Illinois country.

1039. Kincaid, Robert L. WILDERNESS ROAD. Indianapolis: Bobbs-
       Merrill Co., 1947.

       Kincaid wrote a colorful tale about how a mere trail through
       the Cumberland Gap became a major road of penetration to the
       west. Although there is excessive material here on Indian
       skirmishes, pioneer marches, and American encampments, the
       volume is useful for comprehending the economic exploitation
       of east Tennessee. Written with a thorough knowledge of the
       area and its people, this journalistic narrative is good
       reading.

1040. Lambert, Joseph I. "Clark's Conquest of the Northwest." IND
       MAG HIST, 36 (1940), 337-354.

       This is an article that high-schoolers could appreciate.

1041. Laub, C. Herbert. "The Problem of Armed Invasion of the North-
       west During the American Revolution." VA MHB, 42 (1934),
       18-37, 132-144.

       Virginia attempted to capture Detroit, the center of British
       influence in the Ohio Valley.

1042. Lenoir, William. "Journal of the Cherokee Expedition. 1776."
       Edited by J.C. de Rodhac Hamilton, JSH, 6 (1940), 247-259.

       Lieutenant Lenoir of North Carolina related the destruction
       of the Cherokee in August, 1776.

1043. Lewis, Anthony Marc. "Jefferson and Virginia's Pioneers, 1774-1781." MVHR, 34 (1948), 551-588.

Jefferson defied land monopolists and aided frontiersmen to obtain property.

1044. Lewis, George E. THE INDIANA COMPANY, 1763-1778. Glendale, California: A.H. Clark Co., 1941.

The tract consisted of three million acres in present-day West Virginia. The Company tried to have its claim ratified by Britain and then by the United States in a long, and ineffective lobbying effort. This is a careful, thoughtful, and thoroughly-researched monograph which shows the greed and rivalries of land speculators in the early Republic.

1045. MacDonald, Kenneth R., Jr. "The Battle of Point Pleasant: First Battle of the Revolution." W VA HIST, 36 (1974), 40-49.

The fight at the junction of the Ohio and Kanawah Rivers with Indians was not part of the revolution, but it was an isolated frontier incident.

1046. McGinn, Robert, and Larry Vades. "Michael Cresap and the Cresap Rifles." W VA HIST, 39 (1978), 341-347.

Formed by Maryland, the rifles represented the first official American military unit to serve west of the Alleghenies.

1047. Massay, F.G. "Fort Henry in the American Revolution." W VA HIST, 24 (1962-63), 248-257.

The outpost (now Wheeling, West Virginia) was vital in repelling Indian attacks.

1048. Mechan, Thomas A. "Jean Baptiste Point du Sable, the First Chicagoan." J ILL STATE HIST SOC, 56 (1963), 439-453.

The first permanent settler at Chicago was a black fur trader.

1049. Morris, Richard B. "The West in Peace Negotiations." See 1063, pp. 269-304.

Morris demonstrates that the acquisitions of the Northwest was secondary to the greater problem of devising a boundary line between the United States and Canada.

1050. O'Donnell, James H., Jr. "The Virginia Expedition Against the Overhill Cherokees, 1776." E TENN HIS SOC PUB, 39 (1967), 13-25.

A 4,000 man army from Virginia virtually destroyed the Cherokee in an awesome warning to other tribes in the south.

1051.   Orrill, Lawrence A.   "General Edward Hand." W PA HM, 25
        (1942), 99-112.

        Hand was a prominent leader of Continental riflemen but
        he was relatively unsuccessful in defending outposts on the
        Pennsylvania frontier.

1052.   Pease, Theodore C.   "1780 - The Revolution at Crisis in the
        West." ILL STATE HIST SOC, 23 (1931), 644-681.

        The British made elaborate plans to recover their former
        outposts in the Northwest, but they were checked by George
        Rogers Clark.

1053.   Pieper, Thomas I., and James B. Gidney. FORT LAURENS, 1778-
        1779: THE REVOLUTIONARY WAR IN OHIO. Kent, Ohio: Kent
        State University Press, 1976.

        This work is a carefully researched account of a frontier
        post (now Zoan, Ohio) commanded by Americans McIntosh and
        Brodhead. Here the patriots attempted to protect settlers
        from Indian attacks, and to mount expeditions to Detroit and
        to Sandusky. In a well-paced narrative, the authors stress
        the difficulties confronting the military in the trans-
        Appalachian West. The maps are excellent.

1054.   Proceedings of an Indiana American Revolution Bicentennial
        Symposium. THE FRENCH, THE INDIANS, AND GEORGE ROGERS
        CLARK IN THE ILLINOIS COUNTRY (HELD AT VINCENNES UNIVER-
        SITY, VINCENNES, INDIANA, MAY 14-15, 1976). Indianapolis:
        Indiana Historical Society, 1977.

        John F. McDermott wrote about the social cultural patterns
        of French settlers, pp. 3-33; George C. Chalon summarized the
        Indian situation in the Ohio country, pp. 33-45; George M.
        Weller noted the importance of Detroit in the war, pp. 46-66;
        John H. Long, in the best essay in the collection, commented
        about the cartography of Clark's campaigns, pp. 67-91; and
        Dwight L. Smith noted that American control of the Northwest
        actually began in 1790.

1055.   Quaife, Milo M.   "The Ohio Campaign of 1782." MVHR, 17 (1931),
        515-529.

        Slaughter by both whites and Indians typified Colonel
        Crawford's expedition to Sandusky on Lake Erie.

1056.   Randall, James G.   "George Rogers Clark's Services of Supply."
        MVHR, 8 (1921), 250-263.

        Here is a detailed analysis of the logistical and trans-
        portation problems which delayed American expeditions in the
        Northwest.

1057. Reibel, Daniel B. "The British Navy on the Upper Great Lakes,
       1760-1789." NIAGARA FRONTIER, 20 (1973), 66-75.

       Beginning with a vessel built at Detroit in 1761, the
       British easily dominated the rivers and lakes during the war
       with thirty-five small craft.

1058. Rice, Otis K. THE ALLEGHENY FRONTIER: WEST VIRGINIA BEGIN-
       NINGS, 1730-1830. Lexington: University Press of Kentucky,
       1970.

       Chapters four and six contain thoughtful commentaries about
       early explorations, pioneer settlements, Indian problems, and
       land speculation. This is a very readable and scholarly ac-
       count.

1059. ————. "The Ohio Valley in the American Revoluiton."
       See 1063, pp. 5-13.

       This is a fine summary about the trans-montane settlements
       at Pittsburgh, Wheeling, and Point Pleasant.

1060. Rosenthal, Gustave, ed. "Journal of a Volunteer Expedition
       to Sandusky." PA MHB, 18 (1894), 129-157, 293-328.

       This is an excellent memoir by Major John Rose, a Russian
       nobleman, who wrote a lively sketch about marches into
       northern Ohio.

1061. Siebert, Wilbur H. "Kentucky's Struggle with Its Loyalist
       Proprietors." MVHR, 7 (1920), 113-126.

       The author summarizes the problems involved with Tory
       speculators, the settling of Louisville, and the clearing
       of land titles.

1062. Skaggs, David C., Jr. "Between the Lakes and the Bluegrass:
       An Overview of the Revolution in the Old Northwest." NW
       OHIO Q, 48 (1976), 89-101.

       This is a very readable and thoughtful summary that covers
       much geographic territory.

1063. ————. "THE OLD NORTHWEST IN THE AMERICAN REVOLUTION, AN
       ANTHOLOGY. Madison, Wisconsin: The State Historical Society
       of Wisconsin, 1977.

       This is a convenient summary of recent scholarship con-
       cerning the impact of the Revolution in the area. It contains
       thirteen essays on the war, and eight on the post-war era.
       Some of the articles are new, some are reprints of published
       articles; others are extracts from major works about the
       frontier. Although not footnoted nor indexed, the book has
       fine maps and a lengthy bibliography. Skaggs's collection is
       excellent for general readers or for a college audience.

1064.   Sosin, Jack M. THE REVOLUTIONARY FRONTIER, 1763-1783. New
        York: Holt, Rinehart and Winston, 1976.

        Here is the best synthesis about the effects of the war in
        the west. Bridging the gaps between the colonial, revolu-
        tionary, and Federal periods, the work stresses the uneven
        advances made by white settlers into the wilderness before
        1775, and the complex interactions among Indians, pioneers,
        land speculators, and imperial officials. The author deftly
        covers numerous Indian wars, the Spanish and British intri-
        gues to dominate the Mississippi, and he is particlarly
        astute in citing relatively obscure individuals and incidents
        of the era. The discussions about the settlement of Kentucky
        and Tennessee are well covered. The maps and vast bibliog-
        raphy are excellent.

1065.   Stealey, John Edward III. "French Lick and the Cumberland
        Compact." TENN HIST Q, 22 (1963), 323-334.

        The article covers the settlement of today's Nashville.

1066.   ————"George Clendinen and the Great Kanawha Valley Frontier:
        A Case Study of the Frontier Development of Virginia." W
        VA HIST, 37 (1966), 276-296.

        An Indian fighter and member of the Virginia Assembly,
        Clendinen was successful in promoting his land schemes.

1067.   Stone, Lyle M. FORT MICHILIMACKINAC, 1715-1781; AN ARCHAE-
        OLOGY PERSPECTIVE ON THE REVOLUTIONARY FRONTIER. East
        Lansing: Michigan State University Press, 1974.

        The fortress, Britain's major bastion in Michigan's Upper
        Peninsula, was a center for fur trade and for Indian diplo-
        macy. Stone wrote a very perceptive interpretation about
        the excavations underway there for years. This is a fine
        example of the blending of history and archaeology in
        order to recreate the significance of an important outpost.

1068.   Sutton, Robert M. "George Rogers Clark and the Campaign in
        the West: The Five Major Documents." IND MAG HIST, 76
        (1980), 334-345.

        This summary about what an authority considers dependable
        source material about Clark is worth consulting.

1069.   Swiggett, Howard. WAR OUT OF NIAGARA: WALTER BUTLER AND THE
        TORY RAIDERS. New York: Columbia University Press, 1933.

        Apparently intended for a popular audience, this work has
        been criticized for its careless scholarship and distortion
        of facts in order to rehabilitate the bloody Butlers and to
        discredit Mohawk Joseph Brant. The author shows little
        knowledge of ethnology or of Indian history. The book is
        almost fiction.

1070.   Talbert, Charles G. "A Roof for Kentucky." FILSON CLUB Q,
        29 (1955), 145-165.

        Kentucky settlers were protected by a chain of forts on
        the Ohio, Kanawha, and Kentucky Rivers.

1071.   Thwaites, Rueban Gold, and Louise Phelps Kellogg. FRONTIER
        DEFENSE ON THE UPPER OHIO, 1777-1778. Madison: Wisconsin
        Historical Society, 1912.

        This is an indispensable collection of correspondence,
        mainly by American army commanders and pioneer leaders, about
        the brutal warfare in the Ohio country. The collection is
        well-edited; the material reveals insights about local con-
        ditions that are not elsewhere available. The brief narrative
        is adequate enough to tie these documents together. This is
        an essential source about Indian fighting, and British-Tory
        raids. The 100 documents were compiled from the Draper
        Manuscript Collection and cover the west from the Ohio to
        Kentucky.

1072.   ————. THE REVOLUTION ON THE UPPER OHIO, 1775-1777. Madi-
        son: Wisconsin Historical Society, 1908.

        Here is an excellent collection of over forty documents
        about the difficulties and privations of the American fron-
        tiersmen in repelling Indian-Tory raids. The material is
        invaluable, and it contains much correspondence now dif-
        ficult to trace.

1073.   Turner, Frederick Jackson. "Western State-Making In the Revolu-
        tionary Era." AHR, 1 (1895), 70-87, 251-259.

        This is a classic essay about how a new nation, blessed
        with an abundance of free land, handled conflicting claims
        from the states, and how the East checked "the crude, bois-
        terous west.... "

1074.   Underwood, Wynn. "Indian and Tory Raids on the Otter Valley,
        1777-1782." VT Q, 15-16 (1947), 195-221.

        After the fall of Ticonderoga, Indian war parties devastated
        American settlements on the eastern shore of Lake Champlain.

1075.   Van Every, Dale. A COMPANY OF HEROES: THE AMERICAN FRONTIER,
        1775-1783. New York: William Morrow Co., 1962.

        This book is excellent for information about white trap-
        pers, traders, settlers, and soldiers who penetrated the
        northwest. It is a fine summation of an American success
        story - Clark's brilliant sweep over the Illinois country
        and the recapture of Vincennes. The book is carefully re-
        searched; it carries a sustained dramatic pace; and it incor-
        porates recent findings. For information about the French,
        Spanish, and the southern frontier, however, one must look
        elsewhere.

1076. Venables, Robert W. "Tryon County 1775-1783: A Frontier in
       Revolution." Ph.D. dissertation, Vanderbuilt University,
       1967.

       Venables examines the motives of whites and Indians of this
       frontier New York area in selecting sides in the war. Because
       the Iroquois supported the British, many neutral settlers
       were driven into the patriotic ranks. Others became patriots
       in opposition to the local hegemony of Sir William Johnson
       and his family. This is a useful examination of frontier war-
       fare in a locale that has received relatively little attention
       by historians in the past decades.

1077. Waller, George M. AMERICAN REVOLUTION IN THE WEST. Chicago:
       Nelson Hall Inc., 1976.

       This very readable and well-organized book that tends to con-
       centrate on the brutality of frontier fighting to the neglect
       of political and diplomatic activities. The degree to which
       dramatic incidents are emphasized make this work interesting
       for a high school or undergraduate audience. The illustra-
       tions enhance the book's usefulness.

1078. ————. "George Rogers Clark and the American Revolution in
       the West." IND MAG HIST, 72 (1976), 1-20.

       Clark adroitly handled the French, the Indians, waged guer-
       rilla warfare and pinned down large numbers of British regu-
       lars.

1079. Wattington, Patricia. "Discontent in Frontier Kentucky."
       KENT HIS SOC REG, 65 (1967), 77-93.

       Embittered over Virginia's land and Indian policies, some
       Kentuckians remained Loyalists; others supported the Revolu-
       tion, anticipating that Congress would support aspirations
       for statehood.

1080. Williams Edward G., ed. "A Revolutionary Journal and Orderly
       Book of General Lachlan McIntosh's Expedition, 1778." W PA
       HIST MAG, 43 (1960), 1-17, 159-177, 267-288.

       Robert McCready's memoir offers lucid insights about ex-
       peditions from Fort Pitt.

1081. ————. FORT PITT AND THE REVOLUTION ON THE WESTERN FRONTIER.
       Pittsburgh: Historical Society of Western Pennsylvania, 1968.

       This is a worthwhidle study that is crammed with documentation.
       It stresses the problems that four successive American com-
       manders encountered at Fort Pitt, the importance of the bas-
       tion as a counterpart to George Rogers Clark's expedition, and
       the post's link to other outposts. However, the author ap-
       pears uncertain about British strategy, and he exaggerates the
       importance of the fortress which could have toppled without
       causing a catastrophe to the patriotic cause.

1082. ————. "The Journal of Richard Butler, 1775.
       Continental Congress Envoy to the Western Indians." W PA
       HIST MAG, 47 (1964), 31-46, 141-156.

       This Indian Agent for the Middle Department wrote a grip-
       ping account of his discussions with potential tribal allies.

1083. Williams, Richmond D. "Col. Thomas Hartley's Expedition of
       1778." NOW AND THEN, 12 (1957-60), 258-260.

       Hartley described Indian fighting on Pennsylvania's frontier.

1084. Williams, Samuel Cole. TENNESSEE DURING THE REVOLUTIONARY
       WAR. Nashville: The Tennessee Historical Commission, 1944.

       This is still the most dependable work on the topic. The
       author wrote with verve and carefully documented his chapters.
       The material about the wars with the Cherokee, settlements on
       the Cumberland River, boundary problems with the Carolinians,
       the role of the Mountain Men in southern campaigns is clearly
       explained. However, there are some errors of fact and inter-
       pretations; hence the work needs to be revised.

1085. Wolf, George. "The Big Runaway of 1778." WYOMING HIST GEN
       SOC PROC COLL, 23 (1970), 3-19.

       News about the Wyoming Valley Massacre caused many set-
       tlers along the Susquehanna to panic and to seek protection
       at Fort Augusta near Sunbury, Pennsylvania.

1086. ————. "The Politics of Fair Play." PA HIST, 32 (1965),
       8-24.

       One hundred families at Lock Haven and Williamsport, Penn-
       sylvania developed a unique political device known as the
       Fair Play System.

1087. Woolworth, Nancy L. "Grand Portage in the Revolutionary War."
       MINN HIST, 44 (1975), 198-208.

       The British sent troops from Michigan to the North Shore of
       Lake Superior in 1778 to protect the vital fur trade.

                        2. The Southwestern Frontier

1088. Abbey, Kathryn T. "Efforts of Spain to Maintain Sources of
       Information in the British Colonies Before 1779." MVHR,
       15 (1926), 56-68.

       Madrid had an elaborate system of gathering intelligence
       about British military and naval strengths in North America.

1089. ————. "Spanish Projects for the Reconstruction of Florida
       during the American Revolution." HISP AMER HIST REV, 9
       (1929), 265-285.

Anxious to recover the lost colony, Spanish officials pondered numerous schemes to invade with the aid of Americans, Indians, and Spanish Floridians.

1090. Bannon, John Francis. "The Spaniards and the Illinois Country, 1762-1800." J ILL STATE HIST SOC, 69 (1976), 110-118.

The author's meticulous research about Spanish aims and outposts in the Northwest as well as his fine writing make this a key article.

1091. Beekman, Eric. "Jose de Ezpeleta: Alabama's First Spanish Commandant During the American Revolution." ALA REV, 29 (1976), 249-260.

Ezpeleta commanded at Mobile after Galvez captured it in 1781.

1092. ————. "'Yo Solo' Not 'Solo': Juan Antonio de Riano." FLA HIST Q, 58 (1979), 174-84.

The Spanish officer's key role in the fighting in March, 1781, at Pensacola Bay merits more attention.

1093. Boyd, Mark F., and Jose Navarro Latorre. "Spanish Interest in British Florida and the Progress of the American Revolution." FLA HIST Q, 32 (1953), 92-130.

Here is a good account of how Madrid viewed a weak British-held colony, especially after Spain entered the war.

1094. Caughey, John. BERNARDO DE GALVEZ IN LOUISIANA, 1776-1783. Berkeley: University of California Press, 1934.

Galvez, Spain's astute governor in Louisiana, tactfully tried to assist the Americans before Spain entered the war, adroitly handled Indian problems and encouraged the trade and commerce of New Orleans. Galvez next led his troops to victories over the British on the Mississippi, Mobile, and Pensacola. This is an extremely well-researched biography that contains much data about Spain's administration of the Louisiana country, and the diplomatic repercussions in Madrid about the Revolution.

1095. ————. "The Natchez Rebellion of 1781 and Its Aftermath." LA HIST Q, 16 (1933), 57-83.

The Spanish under Galvez easily crushed a British effort to recover this outpost.

1096. ————. "Willing's Expedition Down the Mississippi, 1778." LA HIST Q, 15 (1932), 5-36.

The British blunted an American expedition to capture Natchez and other Mississippi outposts, and they reinforced their west Florida garrisons.

1097. Coker, William S., Jack D.L. Holmes, Samuel Proctor, and J.
Leitch Wright, Jr. "Research in the Spanish Borderlands."
LAT AMER RES REV, 7 (1972), 3-94.

This is an excellent discussion about the historiography of
the area with ample references to the role of Spain in the
Revolution.

1098. Corbitt, D.C. "James Colbert and the Spanish Claim of the
East Bank of the Mississippi." MVHR, 24 (1938), 457-482.

The essay covers the complications that arouse due to the
uncertainties of Spanish-British claims, and to the value
of the trade in the area.

1099. Din, Gilbert C. "Early Spanish Colonization Efforts in
Louisiana." LA STUD, 11 (1972), 31-49.

Governor Antonio de Ulloa established numerous outposts
and augmented Spain's grip on the Illinois country and the
fringes of West Florida.

1100. ———. "Protecting the 'Barrera': Spain's Defenses in
Louisiana, 1763-1779." LA HIST, 19 (1978), 183-211.

Three Spanish governors deserve praise for making Louisiana
a barrier to Texas and New Spain, and for mobilizing an army
for the invasion of Florida in 1779.

1101. ———. "Spain's Immigration Policy and Effects on Louisiana
During the American Revolution." LA STUD, 14 (1975), 241-
257.

Due to French settlements on the lower Mississippi, and to
the British threat from West Florida, Spanish officials made
energetic efforts to populate the area with dependable subjects.

1102. [Galvez, Bernardo de]. "Diary of Operations Against Pensacola,
1781." LA HIST Q, 1 (1917), 44-84.

Here is a transcript about the Spanish siege of the British-
held village.

1103. Gold, Robert L. "Governor Bernardo de Galvez and Spanish
Episonage in Pensacola, 1777." See 1120, pp. 87-99.

Galvez obtained detailed information about British troop
strengths in West Florida.

1104. Haarman, Albert W. "The Siege of Pensacola: An Order of
Battle." FLA HIST Q, 44 (1966), 193-199.

Spain had 8,000 men against Britain's 2,000 troops at the
investment; both armies were composed of mixed ethnic and
nationality groups.

1105.   ———. "The Spanish Conquest of British West Florida,
         1779-1781." FLA HIST Q, 39 (1960), 107-134.

         This is a good summary of Galvez's military achievements in
         capturing British fortresses in three campaigns.

1106.   Haynes, Robert V. "Historians and the Mississippi Territory."
         J MISS HIST, 29 (1967), 412-418.

         The article summarizes the work of six specialists who wrote
         about the area from 1846 to 1925.

1107.   ———. "James Willing and the Planters of Natchez: The
         American Revolution Comes to the Southwest." J MISS HIST,
         37 (1975), 1-42.

         Here is a fine essay about an American expedition in 1778
         which, though temporarily disrupting British trade on the
         Mississippi, failed to open up the route for American mili-
         tary supplies (via New Orleans) and forced the British to
         strengthen West Florida.

1108.   ———. THE NATCHEZ DISTRICT AND THE AMERICAN REVOLUTION.
         Jackson, Mississippi: University Press of Mississippi, 1976.

         This very readable work is the most comprehensive treatment
         of the war in the lower Mississippi Valley which was deeply
         divided in national allegiances. The Willing expedition from
         Fort Pitt to Natchez was a bungled affair, aroused support
         for the British by settlers in the area, and Willing was
         neutralized in efforts to use New Orleans as a supply base.
         Haynes then adroitly covers the topic with fresh archival ma-
         terial with emphasis on the Galvez campaign from 1779 to 1781.
         This is a lucid summary of Spain's role.

1109.   Holmes, Jack D.L. "Alabama's Bloodiest Day of the American
         Revolution: Counter-attack at the Village, January 7, 1781."
         ALA REV, 29 (1976), 208-219.

         A furious British-Indian attack on a Mobile River outpost
         failed and led to the subsequent fall of Pensacola.

1110.   ———. HONOR AND FIDELITY, THE LOUISIANA INFANTRY REGIMENT
         AND THE LOUISIANA MILITIA COMPANIES. Birmingham, Alabama:
         Pvt. ptd., 1965.

         Here is a valuable account of military units whose contri-
         butions to the war have been generally overlooked. The author
         writes with the authority of one familiar with Spanish archi-
         val sources in New Orleans. He demonstrates the importance of
         these regiments in Spain's conquest of the Floridas. The
         information about 1,500 men will be useful for genealogists.

1111.   ————. "Interpretations and Trends in the Study of the
         Spanish Borderlands in the Old Southwest." SOUTHWEST HIST
         Q, 74 (1974), 464-465.

         This is a convenient summary which cites recent work about
         the Revolution's impact on the area.

1112.   ————. "Juan de la Villebeuvre: Spain's Commandant of
         Natchez during the American Revolution." J MISS HIST, 37
         (1975), 97-127.

         Villebeuvre had the difficult task of defending Natchez
         while Galvez conquered Florida.

1113.   ————. "Some Irish Officers in Spanish Louisiana." IRISH
         SWORD, 6 (1965), 234-247.

         This is a fine summary of Irish Catholics who fought with
         Spain during the war in the southwest.

1114.   ————. "Three Early Memphis Commandants: Beauregard, Deville
         Degoutin, and Folch." W TENN HIST SOC PAP, 18 (1964), 4-38.

         These Spanish officers served at Chickasaw Bluffs, a vital
         outpost during the Revolution.

1115.   James, James Alton. "Spanish Influence in the West during
         the American Revolution." MVHR, 4 (1917), 193-208.

         Spain's desire to control the entire Mississippi Valley was
         a major factor in the Franco-Spanish Alliance of April, 1779.

1116.   Kinnaird, Lawrence, ed. SPAIN IN THE MISSISSIPPI VALLEY,
         1764-1794. American Historical Association Annual Report
         for 1945. Vols. 2-4. Washington, DC: The American Histori-
         cal Association, 1946-1949.

         This is an immense collection of correspondence and other
         official documents that contains one of the best primary
         sources in English about Spanish expansion in the area. The
         material was collected from innumerable archives, and the
         work is essential to comprehend the scope of the topic.

1117.   ———— "The Spanish Expedition Against Fort St. Joseph in
         1781: A New Interpretation." MVHR, 19 (1932), 173-191,
         207-221.

         The purpose of the raid (at Niles, Michigan) was to elimi-
         nate British influence there and to impress Indian allies.

1118.   ————. "The Western Fringe of Revolution." WEST HIST Q, 7
         (1976), 253-270.

         Kinnaird urges historians to pay more attention to Spain's
         role in the west, and to men like Clark, Galvez, O'Reilly,
         and Pollock.

1119. McDermott, John Francis. "The Battle of St. Louis, 26 May
       1780." MISSOURI HIST SOC BULL, 36 (1980), 131-151.

       British Colonel Henry Hamilton's attack on the Spanish
       outpost was repulsed in a bitter engagement.

1120. ———. "The Myth of the Imbecile Governor: Captain Fernando
       de Leyba and the Defense of St. Louis in 1780." In John
       Francis McDermott, ed. THE SPANISH IN MISSISSIPPI. Urbana:
       The University of Illinois Press, 1974, pp. 315-405.

       This is a stirring account about a brave officer who de-
       fended his garrison against British-Indian assaults.

1121. [Miranda, Francisco de]. "Miranda's Diary of the Siege of
       Pensacola, 1781." Trans. by Donald E. Worcester. FLA
       HIST Q, 29 (1951), 163-196.

       One of the future liberators of Latin America took an active
       role in the fighting.

1122. Murphy, W.S. "The Irish Brigade of Spain at the Capture of
       Pensacola, 1781." FLA HIST Q, 38 (1960), 216-225.

       An Irish Catholic contingent played a vital role under
       Galvez.

1123. Nachbin, Jac. "Spain's Report of the British in Louisiana."
       LA HIST Q, 15 (1932), 486-491.

       Galvez reported to his superiors in Havanna and Madrid
       about Spanish victories on the Mississippi in 1779.

1124. Nasatir, Abraham P. "The Anglo-Spanish Frontier during the
       American Revolution, 1778-1783." J ILL STATE HIST SOC, 21
       (1928), 291-358.

       Here is a fine summary of the British-Spanish struggle to
       control the Upper Mississippi trade, which centered at St.
       Louis, and to win Indian alliances.

1125. ———. "The Shifting Borderlands." PAC HIST REV, 34 (1965),
       1-20.

       Spain wanted the Illinois country in order to dominate the
       fur trade.

1126. O'Neil, Charles Edward. "The State of Studies on Spanish
       Colonial Louisiana." See 1120, pp. 16-25.

       This is a useful summary of current research underway in
       the historiography of the area.

1127. Rea, Robert R. "Assault on the Mississippi - The Loftus
       Expedition, 1764." ALA REV, 26 (1973), 173-193.

       Major Arthur Loftus failed to open up the Illinois country
       or the Ohio River to British influence.

1128. Rickey, Don, Jr. "The British-Indian Attack on St. Louis,
       May 20, 1780." MISSOURI HIST REV, 55 (1960), 35-45.

       The British thrust from Michigan was repulsed and the
       Spanish retaliated with two attacks.

1129. Ropes, James E. "The Revolutionary War on the Fourth
       Chickasaw Bluffs." W TENN HIST SOC PROC, 29 (1975), 5-24.

       The present site of Memphis was a pivotal point for access
       to the Mississippi.

1130. Scamuzza, V.M. "Galveztown, a Spanish Settlement of Colonial
       Louisiana." LA HIST Q, 13 (1930), 533-609.

       The village was located on the Amite River near Bayou
       Manchac in 1776 to check British penetration of the area.

1131. Scott, Kenneth, ed. "Britain Loses Natchez, 1779: An Unpub-
       lished Letter." J MISS HIST, 26 (1964), 45-46.

       Over sixty settlers praised the British commander for his
       defense of the town against the Spanish.

1132. Sequera, Pearl Mary, trans. and ed. "The Capture of the Bluff
       of Baton Rouge." LA HIST Q, 17 (1976), 40-48.

       This is a fine rendition about the bitter Spanish-English
       fight to seize this key junction point.

1133. Tregle, Joseph G. "British Spy Along the Mississippi:
       Thomas Hutchins and the Defense of New Orleans, 1773."
       LA HIST Q, 18 (1977), 313-327.

       Long before the war, Britain was contemplating an assault
       on the Spanish port.

1134. Young, Carol F. "A Study of Some Developing Interpretations
       of History of Revolutionary Tennessee (1776-1781)." E TENN
       HIST SOC PUB, 25 (1953), 24-34.

       This is a convenient summary of the work of specialists on
       the Tennessee frontier which shows a variety of viewpoints
       about the war in the area.

III

THE AMERICAN ARMY

A. STRATEGY

1135. Millis, Walter, ed. AMERICAN MILITARY THOUGHT. Indianapolis:
Bobbs-Merrill Co., 1969.

Chapter one, entitled "The Formative Period to 1815," has
a perceptive commentary on the evolution of the American
military mind as a result of the Revolution.

1136. Morton, Louis. "Origins of American Military Policy." MILT
AFF, 22 (1975), 75-90.

This is a good attempt to formulate the concepts that shaped
the development of strategic thought in the early Republic.

1137. Palmer, Dave R. "General George Washington: Grand Strategist
or Mere Fabian." PARAMETERS, 4 (1974), 1-16.

Did Washington have a plan to win the war, or was he stal-
ling for time in order to wear down the enemy?

1138. ————. THE WAY OF THE FOX: AMERICAN STRATEGY IN THE WAR FOR
AMERICA, 1775-1783. Westport, Connecticut: Greenwood Press,
1975.

Palmer is critical of historians for mis-understanding or
over-simplifying Washington's strategy. The author champions
Washington's abilities both on the offensive and defensive.
But this material is very weak on the political, economic
and diplomatic aspects of this subject. Yet the work is a
satisfactory introduction to the topic, and it should be consulted.

1139. Rothenberg, Gunther E. "Steuben, Washington and the Question
of 'Revolutionary war'." IND MILT HIST J, 3 (1978), 5-11.

This is an excellent commentary of how European officers
with Washington viewed the strategic implications of the war.

1140. Weigley, Russell F. "American Strategy: A Call for A Critical
Strategic History." See 414, pp. 32-53.

Weigley notes the unprofessional nature of the Continental
forces and urges a broad strategy study.

1141.   ———. THE AMERICAN WAR OF WAR; A HISTORY OF THE UNITED
         STATES MILITARY STRATEGY AND POLICY. New York: Macmillan
         Publishing Co., 1973.

         Weigley is an authority on American military history.
         Pages 1-40 in this volume provide a neat summary about the
         unique strategic aspects of the war waged by the patriots.
         The material about the significance of Greene's southern
         campaigns is useful.

                          B.   THE OFFICERS

1142.   Billias, George A., ed.   GEORGE WASHINGTON'S GENERALS.   New
         York: Morrow, 1964.

         Experts summarize the military careers of Lee, Schuyler,
         Gates, Green, Sullivan, Arnold, Lincoln, Lafayette, Knox,
         Wayne, and Morgan.   In general, the essays are lively and
         well-written with serviceable footnotes and bibliographies.

1143.   Boynton, Edward C., comp.   GENERAL ORDERS OF GEORGE WASHING-
         TON, COMMANDER-IN-CHIEF OF THE ARMY OF THE REVOLUTION, IS-
         SUED AT NEWBURGH ON THE HUDSON, 1782-1783.   1909.   Reprint.
         Harrison, New York: Harbor Hill Books, 1973.

         This is a collection of Washington's orders on a variety
         of topics effecting strategy, dicipline, and the troops'
         welfare during the last two years of the war.

1144.   Catterall, Ralph T.   "Traitor or Patriot?   The Ambiguous
         Career of Charles Lee."   VA CAV, 24 (1975), 164-177.

         The controversial Continental general dabbled in intrigue.

1145.   Gratz, Simon.   "The Generals of the Continental Line in the
         Revolutionary War."   PA MHB, 27 (1903), 385-403.

         Gratz compiled a list of all the generals, citing their
         rank and date of appointments.

1146.   Heitman, Francis B.   HISTORICAL REGISTER OF OFFICERS OF THE
         CONTINENTAL ARMY DURING THE WAR OF THE REVOLUTION, APRIL
         1775 TO DECEMBER, 1783.   1893.   Reprint.   Washington, DC:
         Rare Book Publishing Co., 1914.

         This is a standard reference work which provides the names
         of most officers in the Continental army along with detailed
         lists of general field officers by unit and by state.   Al-
         though it is incomplete and overlooks some line regiments,
         the work is an indispensable source for data about American
         officers.

1147.   Higginbotham, Don.   "Military Leadership in the American Rev-
         olution."   In LEADERSHIP IN THE AMERICAN REVOLUTION.   3RD

SYMPOSIUM ON THE AMERICAN REVOLUTION. Washington, DC:
Library of Congress, pp. 91-112.

An expert commented on the characteristics of successful
American generals - their traits, experience, and contributions to the war.

1148.   Kaplan, Sidney. "Pay, Pensions and Power. Economic Griev-
        ances of the Massachusetts Officers of the Revolution."
        BOSTON PUB LIB Q, 3 (1951), 15-34, 127-142.

        This is an excellent discussion of the material rewards
        that Continental officers expected from Congress and their
        states - pay increases, land bounties, and pensions.

1149.   Knight, Russell, W. "General Glover Battles a 'Temporal
        Cause'. " ESSEX INSTIT HIST COLL, 101 (1965), 115-120.

        Glover's efforts to recover his fortunes at Marblehead after
        the war were generally successful.

1150.   Knollenberg, Bernhard. WASHINGTON AND THE REVOLUTION. A
        REAPPRAISAL: GATES, CONWAY, AND THE CONTINENTAL CONGRESS.
        New York: Macmillan Co., 1940.

        The attempt to remove Washington from command in 1777
        has long fascinated historians. The 'Conway Cabal' included
        generals and politicians who had varying motives for partici-
        pation in the supposed plot. Knollenberg made a meticulous
        study of the evidence and wrote a compelling narrative about
        the rivalries between generals and delegates.

1151.   Kohn, Richard H. "American Generals of the Revolution: Sub-
        ordination and Restraint." See 414, pp. 104-123.

        Kohn argues that the fear of a military "take-over," the
        suspicions by politicans of a standing army, and the aliena-
        tion of many ranking Continental officers by the war's end
        were all factors.

1152.   ———. "The Coup D'Etat that Failed." NY HIST SOC BULL,
        12 (1975), 30-36.

        Washington thwarted the Newburgh Conspiracy of 1783 which
        centered around Horatio Gates.

1153.   ———. "The Inside History of the Newburgh Conspiracy:
        America and the Coup d'Etat." WMQ, 27 (1970), 187-220.

        Gates and his supporters apparently let the news circulate
        to prod Congress into redressing officers' grievances in an
        effort to subvert the political framework.

1154.   Lawrence, Alexander A. "General Lachlan McIntosh (1727-1806)
        and his Suspension from Continental Command During the

Revolution." GA HIST Q, 38 (1954), 101-141.

McIntosh quarrelled with Georgia's Governor George Walton, killed Button Gwinett in a duel, was dismissed for military ineptness in 1780, but he was eventually vindicated by Congress.

1155. Lieber, G. Norman. "Martial Law During the Revolution." MAG AMER HIST, 1 (1877), 538-541.

This is a provocative and well documented essay on an overlooked topic.

1156. Mahon, John K. "Pennsylvania and the Beginnings of the Regular Army." PA HIST, 21 (1954), 33-44.

Due to Indian problems in the west, the Quaker State took the lead in recruiting for a peacetime army in 1783-84.

1157. Miller, Randall M. "The Founding of a Father: John Adams and the Appointment of George Washington As Commander-in-Chief of the Continental Army." MD HISTORIAN, 4 (1973), 13-23.

Adams selected Washington for political reasons in order to satisfy the north and the south.

1158. Nelson, Paul David. "Horatio Gates at Newburgh, 1783: A Misunderstood Role [with a rebuttal by Richard H. Kohn]." WMQ, 29 (1972), 143-158.

Nelson doubts that Gates planned a coup, even considering the grievances of his fellow officers; but Kohn claims that Gates was implicated in such a plot and violated the Articles of War.

1159. ———. "Citizen Soldiers or Regulars: The Views of American General Officer's on the Military Establishment, 1775-1781." MILT AFF, 43 (1973), 126-132.

Ranking officers preferred regulars because the militia were frequently unreliable.

1160. Rossie, Jonathan Gregory. THE POLITICS OF COMMAND IN THE AMERICAN REVOLUTION. Syracuse, New York: Syracuse University Press, 1975.

This is an interesting attempt to clarify the complicated political relationships of Continental army commanders. It examines the questions of rank, precedent, areas of jurisdiction, regional pride, Congressional attitudes, and the endless bickering and quarreling of many top American generals. While useful on the Gates-Schuyler rivalry, the work is weak on other major feuds, tends to overlook the south, and it never really provides a clear thesis.

1161.   Rossman, Kenneth. "Conway and the Conway Cabal." S ATL Q,
        41 (1948), 32-38.

        Rossman made a commendable effort to clarify the puzzle of
        why Conway, Gates, Rush, and others attempted to displace
        Washington.

1162.   Ryan, Dennis P., ed. A SALUTE TO COURAGE: THE AMERICAN REVO-
        LUTION AS SEEN THROUGH WARTIME WRITINGS OF OFFICERS OF THE
        CONTINENTAL ARMY AND NAVY. New York: Columbia University
        Press, 1975.

        Samples from more than 175 letters, diaries, and journals
        are represented here in this rich collection of unofficial
        documents written by line officers. Though some of the ma-
        terial came from famous generals, most of the correspondence
        here was written by lesser-known officers of all ranks who
        usually described battles, privations, and their views of
        the war. Some information here has been previously published,
        but there are many items that have not been printed. This is
        a useful and well-organized collection.

1163.   Skeen, C. Edward. "The Newburgh Campaign Reconsidered." WMQ,
        31 (1974), 273-298.

        Skeen believes that any attempted coup by officers has been
        highly exaggerated. Replying to the criticism, Richard H.
        Kohn claims that the discontented officers at Newburgh and
        elsewhere planned to march on Congress.

1164.   Spalding, Oliver L., Jr. "The Military Studies of George
        Washington." AHR, 29 (1924), 674-680.

        The author explains that Washington was quite familiar with
        the latest books by European authorities about the art of war.

1165.   Tallmadge, Benjamin. MEMOIR OF COL. BENJAMIN TALLMADGE, 1858.
        Reprint. New York: Arno Press, 1968.

        Tallmadge's commentary about his responsibility for guard-
        ing the British spy Major John Andre is worthwhile.

1166.   Tilghman, Trench. MEMOIR OF LIEUT. COL. TRENCH TILGHMAN,
        SECRETARY AND AID TO WASHINGTON. TOGETHER WITH AN APPENDIX
        CONTAINING REVOLUTIONARY JOURNALS AND LETTERS HITHERTO UN-
        PUBLISHED. Albany: J. Munsell, 1876.

        This is one of the best sources for a view of command func-
        tions at Washington's headquarters.

1167.   Van Domclen, John E. "Hugh Henry Brackenridge and the Order
        of Cincinnati." WEST PA HIST MAG, 47 (1964), 47-53.

        Here is useful data about the society formed by officers of
        the Continental army and navy at the war's end.

1168. Vivian, Jean H. "Military Land Bounties during the Revolu-
       tion and Confederation periods." MD HIST MAG, 61 (1966),
       231-256.

       The author examines the fulfillment of Congressional pledges
       regarding land tracts to the military, and how these promises
       were complicated by conflicting state claims.

1169. Wade, Herbert Treatdwell, and Robert Alexander Lively, eds.
       THIS GLORIOUS CAUSE; THE ADVENTURES OF TWO COMPANY OFFICERS
       IN WASHINGTON'S ARMY. Princeton: Princeton University
       Press, 1958.

       The letters of Joseph Hodgkins and Nathaniel Wade of
       Ipswich, Massachusetts about army life - particularly Bunker
       Hill, Princeton, Valley Forge - are interwoven with the
       editors' narrative. Hodgkins was a prolific letter-writer
       and provided his wife Sarah with intimate portrayals of his
       sacrifices. There are innumerable glimpses of a war-torn
       society; there is a focus on the determination of these of-
       ficers to win the struggle; and there is a sense of patriotism
       here that is authentic. The book is superbly edited and may
       be the best of its kind in print.

1170. Ward, Harry M. THE DEPARTMENT OF WAR, 1781-1795. Pittsburgh:
       University of Pittsburgh Press, 1982.

       Ward compiled a useful monograph about the founding of the
       War Department which occurred after numerous experiments with
       military administration by Congress. The material about the
       fledging bureaucracy and the work of capable General Benjamin
       Lincoln is valuable. Unfortunately, the writing is ponderous,
       and there are some factual errors. However, the index, an-
       notations, and the appendix are excellent.

1171. Washington, George. ORDERLY BOOK OF GEN. GEORGE WASHINGTON,
       COMMANDER-IN-CHIEF OF THE AMERICAN ARMY, KEPT AT VALLEY
       FORGE, 18 MAY - 11 JUNE, 1778. Boston: Wolffe and Co.,
       1898.

       This document is particularly useful for comprehending
       Washington's preparations to evacuate the camp and for a pur-
       suit of the British withdrawing from the Delaware.

1172. Wells, Thomas L. "An Inquiry into the Registration of Quar-
       termaster Nathanael Greene in 1780." RI HIST, 24 (1965),
       41-48.

       Greene had an impossible task and quit because of unfair
       Congressional criticisms.

1173. Wright, John W. "Some Notes on the Continental Army." WMQ,
       11 (1931), 81-105, 185-209; 12 (1932), 79-104; 13 (1933),
       85-95.

This remains the best brief synthesis about the organization, command structure, and components of the Continental
army. The material about the characteristics of muskets,
rifles, and cannon is invaluable.

1174. Wright, Robert Kenneth J. "Organization and Doctrine in the
       Continental Army, 1774 to 1784." Ph.D. dissertation, The
       College of William and Mary, 1980.

       Rather than stress traditional battles and tactics, the
       author concentrates on intellectual and institutional history
       in this provocative study. Wright shows how the army func-
       tioned on the command level and on lower echelons and he
       demonstrates how the eighteenth-century attitude toward war
       was modified by the American experience. The book is excel-
       lent for showing Washington's key role, shifts in regimental
       organization, the adoption of French weapons, and for an ex-
       amination of contemporary theories of warfare.

                        C. THE CONTINENTAL LINE

1175. Alexander, Arthur J. "Exemptions from Military Service in
       the Old Dominion During the War of the Revolution." VA MHB,
       53 (1943), 163-171.

       Exemptions (from ages 16 to 50) existed for blacks, mulat-
       toes, Indians, skilled artisans, professionals, Quakers, and
       Mennonites.

1176. Applegate, Howard. "Constitutions Like Iron: The Life of the
       American Revolutionary War Soldier in the Middle Department,
       1775-1783." Ph.D. dissertation, Syracuse University, 1966.

       Though this study needs to be re-written and its footnotes
       arranged in a coherent manner, it represents the best inves-
       tigation about the rank and file in five states. There is
       abundant information about recruiting, training, discipline,
       rations, pay and pensions, standards of morality, amusements
       of the troops, and vignettes of camp life. The author notes
       that the factors of patriotism, economic reasons, and unit
       pride may explain why fifteen units from these states cam-
       paigned to the war's end.

1177. Bolton, Charles Knowles. THE PRIVATE SOLDIER UNDER WASHING-
       TON. New York: Charles Scribner's Sons, 1902.

       This is the pioneering work on a subject long neglected by
       historians. It records many facets of a soldier's life, but
       without much detail. For a brief summary of this topic, the
       work is adequate, but the reader seeking a better documented
       and analytical account will search elsewhere.

1178. Bowman, Allen. THE MORALE OF THE AMERICAN REVOLUTIONARY ARMY.
       Washington, DC: American Council on Public Affairs, 1943.

The author investigated a difficult topic that needs more
research. Bowman wrote interesting chapters on recruiting,
pay and rations, clothing and shelter, medical care, the
prevalence of women with the army, and touched on recreational
activities and propaganda efforts. This is a suggestive and
thoughtful monograph.

1179. Bray, Robert C., and Paul E. Bushnell, eds. DIARY OF A COM-
        MON SOLDIER IN THE REVOLUTION, 1775-1782: AN ANNOTATED EDI-
        TION OF THE MONTHLY JOURNAL OF JEREMIAH GREENMAN. De Kalb,
        Illinois: Northern University Press, 1978.

        This is one of the best accounts of its type in print. Not
        only did Rhode Islander Greenman rise from the ranks to become
        an officer, but he served in many campaigns until his capture
        in 1780. Rarely did a serviceman leave a memoir with such
        detail and for such a lengthy chronological span. The editors
        researched meticulously, they annotated skillfully, and they
        wrote a neat biographical sketch. The revision of the manu-
        script is quite readable and often fascinating. This book
        merits a broad audience.

1180. Cook, Fred J. "Allen McLane: Unknown Hero of the Revolution."
        AMER HERITAGE, 7 (6) (1956), 74-77, 118-119.

        McLane of Philadelphia was a dashing cavalryman who per-
        formed successful intelligence missions for Washington.

1181. ————. "Francisco the Incredible." AMER HERITAGE, 10 (6)
        (1959), 22-25, 92-95.

        The legendary Peter Francisco of Virginia could carry a
        half-ton cannon, and with his broadsword he was a small army
        in action.

1182. ————. WHAT MANNER OF MEN: FORGOTTEN HEROES OF THE AMERICAN
        REVOLUTION. New York: William Morrow and Co., 1959.

        Cook reviews the exploits of some heroic men such as Allen
        McLane, Timothy Murphy, Marinus Willet, Peter Francisco, John
        Peck Rathburn, and some remarkable women warriors.

1183. Cullen, Joseph P. "The Continental Soldier." AMER HIST
        ILLUS, 2 (4) (1967), 20-25.

        Written for a general audience, this is a lively summary of
        life in the ranks of Washington's army.

1184. Daniel, J.R.V. "The Giant of Virginia." VA CAV, 1 (2) (1951),
        36-39.

        Peter Francisco was virtually a one-man army in combat.

1185. Hillard, Elias Brewster. "Last Survivors of the Revolution."
        AMER HERITAGE, 9 (3) (1958), 28-33.

In 1864, the last six surviving veterans of the Revolutionary War reminisced.

1186. Honeyman, A. Van Doren. "The Pension Laws Concerning Revolutionary Soldiers." NJ HIST SOC PROC, 6 (1921), 116-118.

This is too brief an essay for this important topic but it is suggestive for future research.

1187. Leach, Frederic B. "The Man Whose Praise We Sing." AMER HERITAGE, 16 (3) (1965), 62-63, 97.

Nicholas Stoner of Fulton County, New York was a legendary fighter in several northern campaigns.

1188. Ledbetter, Bonnie S. "Sports and Games of the American Revolution." J SPORT HIST, 6 (1949), 25-40.

Amusements were ball games, cock-fights, horse racing, sledding and swimming.

1189. Lender, Mark E. "The Enlisted Line: The Continental Soldiers of New Jersey." Ph.D. dissertation, Rutgers University, 1975.

This is a good sociological examination of the Jersey troops. Here is abundant material about recruiting, discipline, morale, and relations with officers. Some novel viewpoints are that patriotism frequently was not a motive in enlisting, that the regiments were often composed of misfits, British deserters and lower classes. Yet, a man sometimes viewed army service as an opportunity to improve his social status in post-war society.

1190. ————. "The Mind of the Rank and File: Patriotism and Motivation in the Continental Line." In William C. Wright, ed. NEW JERSEY IN THE REVOLUTION, III. PAPERS PRESENTED AT THE SEVENTH ANNUAL NEW JERSEY HISTORY SYMPOSIUM, DECEMBER 6, 1975. Trenton: New Jersey Historical Commission, pp. 21-34.

A need for economic improvement and a vague sense of patriotism were motives for enlisting, not hatred for the British.

1191. ————. "The Social Structures of the New Jersey Brigade: The Continental Line As An American Standing Army." In Peter Karsten, ed. THE MILITARY IN AMERICA FROM THE COLONIAL ERA TO THE PRESENT. New York Free Press, 1980, pp. 27-44.

The Jersey troops represented lower classes, a situation which wealthy Whigs feared.

1192. McDonald, Hugh. "A Teen-Ager in the Revolution." AMER HIST ILLUS, 1 (2) (1966), 25-34.

Fourteen year old McDonald had an adventurous time as a
soldier serving from North Carolina to Pennsylvania.

1193.   Martin, Joseph Plumb. PRIVATE YANKEE DOODLE: BEING A NAR-
        RATIVE OF SOME OF THE ADVENTURES, DANGERS AND SUFFERINGS
        OF A REVOLUTIONARY SOLDIER. Edited by George F. Scheer,
        Boston: Little, Brown, and Co., 1962.

        Martin enlisted at the age of fourteen and served for seven
        years. He wrote a highly literate and entertaining story of
        his experiences in several Continental regiments, in the
        Light Infantry, and the Corps of Sappers and Miners. This
        thoughtfully edited work is one of the best of its kind and
        it is one of the few lengthy narratives extant that was writ-
        ten by an enlisted man.

1194.   ――――. "Private Yankee Doodle." AMER HERITAGE, 13 (3)
        (1962), 37-40.

        The article is a condensation of the author's book writ-
        ten for a popular audience.

1195.   Middlekauf, Robert. "Why Men Fought in the American Revolu-
        tion." HUNT LIT Q, 43 (1980), 135-142.

        This essay suggests that militia were less dependable than
        Continentals whose discipline and long comradeship sustained
        them.

1196.   Morrisey, Charles T., ed. "Action in Vermont During the
        Revolution: Dan Kent's Narrative." VT HIST, 39 (1971), 107-
        112.

        In a pension claim filed in 1832, Kent wrote an exciting
        tale about Ticonderoga, Bennington, and Indian fighting.

1197.   Papenfuse, Edward C., and Gregory A. Stiverson. "General
        Smallwood's Recruits: The Peacetime Career of the Revolu-
        tionary War Private." WMQ, 30 (1973), 117-132.

        A recruiting roster provides data about the birthplaces,
        households, property, and class backgrounds for some Maryland
        troops.

1198.   Quaife, Milo M., ed. "A Boy Soldier Under Washington: The
        Memoir of Daniel Granger." MVHR, 16 (1930), 538-560.

        Written at the age of eighty-six, Granger reminisced about
        Burgoyne's surrender and about Arnold's treason at West Point.

1199.   Royster, Charles. A REVOLUTIONARY PEOPLE AT WAR; THE CON-
        TINENTAL ARMY AND AMERICAN CHARACTER, 1775-1783.   Chapel
        Hill: University of North Carolina, 1979.

        The author attempts to examine the relationship of American

character and the military demands of the war by probing evidence about emotions, attitudes and the conduct of the Continentals. He contends, in well-documented but murky prose, that national character of the troops created one aspect of wartime allegiance. This work is not traditional military history. It is a social and psychological history of the ideals and aspirations developing in the ranks during the war. The book's value is to stress the patriotism of the troops, their willingness to endure hardships, and their growing pride and professionalism.

1200. Sellers, John P. "The Common Soldier in the American Revolution." In MILITARY HISTORY OF THE AMERICAN REVOLUTION: PROCEEDINGS OF THE 6TH MILITARY HISTORY SYMPOSIUM, USAF ACADEMY. Stanley J. Underdal, ed. Washington, DC: United States Air Force and United States Air Force Academy, 1976, pp. 151-161.

Sellers commented briefly about the soldier's ages, their bounties, post-war migrations, and a need for a thorough investigation of the rank and file.

1201. Stadelman, Bonnie S.S. "The Amusements of the American Soldier During the Revolution." Ph.D. dissertation, Tulane University, 1969.

In a unique contribution, Stadelman concentrates on the recreational activities of the troops. The topics cover dancing, sports, singing, sightseeing, theatre, gambling, and plundering, all described in an amusing manner. Officers and men had the same amusements; the recreation frequently related to patriotic themes; and the army provided no organized recreation.

1202. Symmes, Rebecca P. A CITIZEN-SOLDIER IN THE AMERICAN REVOLUTION: THE DIARY OF BENJAMIN GILBERT IN MASSACHUSETTS AND NEW YORK. Cooperstown, New York: New York State Historical Association, 1978.

Gilbert penned a lively account of eight years of service from fifer to officer. Most of the material here is about regimental social life. His tale cannot rival the color and romance of many similar accounts, but it is helpful for an insight into how soldiers viewed the war.

1203. Wilbur, C. Keith. PICTURE BOOK OF THE CONTINENTAL SOLDIER. Harrisburg: Stackpole Books, 1976.

This is a profusely illustrated book with copious descriptions about persons, uniforms, and accoutrements of American troops. It is a handsome volume recommended not for its prose but for its visual material.

1204. Wright, John W. "The Corps of Light Infantry in the Continental Army." AHR, 31 (1926), 454-461.

This relatively new unit in warfare performed well at Stony
Point and at Yorktown; it represented an elite corps of men
from many states.

D. THE MILITIA

1205. Alexander, Arthur J. "Pennsylvania's Revolutionary Militia."
       PA MHB, 69 (1945), 15-25.

       The author notes the difficulties one state had in filling
       militia quotas due to exemptions, religious views, inept re-
       cruitment, and the use of proxies.

1206. ———. "Service by Substitute in the Militia of Lancaster
       and Northhampton Counties (Pennsylvania) During the War of
       the Revolution." MILT AFF, 9 (1945), 278-282.

       Alexander points out that over forty-three per cent of
       militiamen called for service failed to appear and employed
       substitutes to do their fighting.

1207. Anderson, John R. "Militia Law in Revolutionary New Jersey."
       NJ HIST SOC PROC, 7C (1958), 280-299; 77 (1959), 16-21.

       New Jersey learned-by closer supervising, by tightening the
       laws on substitutes, and by payments in lieu of service-to
       improve her militia by 1781.

1208. Boucher, Ronald L. "The Colonial Militia of a Social Insti-
       tution: Salem, Massachusetts, 1764-1775." MILT AFF, 37
       (1973), 125-129.

       The author demonstrates the importance of the militia as
       a local institution, how towns were taxed for their support,
       and how Loyalist officers were replaced.

1209. Bowers, Ray L., Jr. "The American Revolution. A State in In-
       surgency." MILT REV, 46 (1966), 67-42.

       Placing the popular uprising of 1775 within the context of
       recent global insurgencies, the author notes that the ground-
       swell of the Revolution was difficult to sustain.

1210. Cole, David. "South Carolina Militia System." SC HIST ASSOC
       PROC, 55 (1954), 14-21.

       Though there is little information here about the Revolu-
       tion, the essay covers the organization and functions of the
       Carolina militia.

1211. Cress, Lawrence Delbert. "Radical Whiggery on the Role and
       the Militia: Ideological Roots of the American Revolutionary
       Militia." J HIST IDEAS, 40 (1979), 43-60.

Cress stresses Whig ideology about standing armies as in-
struments of tyranny; hence such concepts shaped the arguments for state militia and the need for a constitutional
balance in control of the military.

1212.   Edwards, William Walker. "Morgan and his Rifleman." WMQ,
        23 (1914), 73-108.

        This is a good article which demonstrates the performance
        of militia in Canada, on the Hudson, and in the Carolinas.

1213.   Fergusson, Clyde R. "Functions of the Partisan - Militia
        During the American Revolution: An Interpretation."
        See 855, pp. 239-258.

        The southern militia long had a variety of functions; they
        were virtually equivalent to Continentals in experience and
        were essential in defeating the British.

1214.   Galvin, John R. "A New Look at the Minutemen." MILT REV,
        47 (1967), 80-88.

        This is a helpful sketch of the famous Massachusetts Minute-
        men, but it fails to distinguish them from the typical militia
        of the province.

1215.   Globbal, Luther. "The Militia in North Carolina in Colonial
        and Revolutionary Times." TRINITY COLL HIST PAP, 13 (1939),
        135-51.

        Here is an excellent survey about pay, rations, and the
        organization of the Carolina militia.

1216.   Goldenberg, Joseph A., Eddie D. Nelson, and Rita N. Fletcher.
        "Revolutionary Ranks: An Analysis of the Chesterfield Sup-
        plement." VA MHB, 87 (1979), 182-189.

        Here is a useful statistical analysis of the age, occupation,
        and wealth of 917 militiamen from a 1780 muster roll.

1217.   Gross, Robert A. THE MINUTEMEN AND THEIR WORLD. New York:
        Hill and Wang, 1976.

        In a detailed, quantitative examination of the wealth, prop-
        erty, local government, and social status of the patriots at
        Lexington and Concord, Gross has contributed one of the most
        valuable books recently published on the war. The book sug-
        gests why these men decided to fight, even though the docu-
        mentary evidence about Lexington and Concord is murky. There
        is ample evidence here about these communities, but the ex-
        planations for the human actions of the Minutemen remain elu-
        sive.

1218.   Hayes, John T. "The Connecticut Light House, 1776-1783."
        MILT COLL HIST, 22 (1970), 109-112.

Composed of farmers and merchants, this unit served well
in northern campaigns.

1219. Higginbotham, Don. "The American Militia: A Traditional In-
       stitution With Revolutionary Responsibilities." See
       414, pp. 83-103.

       In the best article on the subject, and one with an exten-
       sive bibliography, the author notes that the militia fought
       best on home-ground, they had a favorable "image," and that
       they were involved in ferocious civil war against Loyalist
       units.

1220. Hobbard, Jake T. "Americans as Guerrilla Fighters: Robert
       Rogers and his Rangers." AMER HERITAGE, 22 (5) (1971), 81-
       86.

       This is a good account of the famous Ranger unit from the
       French and Indian Wars whose survivors served at Bunker Hill
       and Bennington while the famous Rogers joined the British,
       became an alcoholic, and died debt-ridden in London.

1221. Jameson, Hugh. "Equipment for the Militia of the Middle
       States, 1775-1781." J MILT INSTIT, 3 (1939), 26-38.

       Here is a summary about the lack of preparation by politi-
       cians for the militia of the Middle States, described by the
       author as "hasty, unsystematic, and wholly inadequate."

1222. ————. "Subsistence for Middle States Militia, 1776-1781."
       MILT AFF, 30 (1966), 121-134.

       The author contends that both Congress and the states
       victimized the militia by failing to arm, and to provision
       them.

1223. Leach, Edward. ARMS FOR EMPIRE: A MILITARY HISTORY OF THE
       BRITISH COLONIES IN NORTH AMERICA, 1607-1763. New York:
       Macmillan Publishing Co., 1973.

       Chapter one contains a good summary about the development
       of the colonial militia through the French and Indian Wars.

1224. Lockhard, E. Kidd. "Some Problems of the Draft in Revolu-
       tionary Virginia." W VA HIST, 37 (1976), 201-210.

       Virginia tried to raise men by money, conscription, and
       land bounties; but due to the fear of Indian raids and to
       the necessity of harvesting food, men were reluctant to serve.

1225. McBridge, John P. "The Virginia War Effort, 1775-1783. Man-
       power, Political and Practice." Ph.D. dissertation, Uni-
       versity of Virginia, 1977.

       This study is a fine description of the difficulties

encountered by a southern state in meeting its quotas of
Continentals, militia, and the problems involved in acquiring weapons, uniforms, gunpowder, and provisions.

1226. Morton, Louis. "The Origins of American Military Policy."
       MILT AFF, 22 (1958), 75-82.

       Congressional and state politicans regarded the militia
       as essential to support American regulars.

1227. Murphy, Orville T. "The American Revolutionary Army and the
       Concept of Levee in Masse." MILT AFF, 23 (1959), 13-20.

       Murphy notes the impact of French enlightened thought on
       the example of American militia as soldier-citizens as a
       portent for patriot troops in the French Revolution.

1228. Nelson, Paul David. "Citizen Soldiers as Regulars: The Views
       of American General Officers on the Military Establishment,
       1775-1781." MILT AFF, 43 (1979), 126-132.

       In an analysis of how generals viewed a patriotic army of
       long-term or short-term enlistees, Nelson stresses a com-
       promise reached in 1783.

1229. Pancake, John. "American Militia in the War of Independence."
       HIST TODAY, 22 (1972), 793-798.

       While the British ministries underestimated the abilities
       of the American militia, British generals learned to appreci-
       ate the power of the patriot volunteers in pitched battles.

1230. Pugh, Robert C. "The Revolutionary Militia in the Southern
       Campaign," WMQ, 14 (1957), 154-175.

       This is a key article which refutes the traditional assump-
       tions about the supposed inferiority of the militia by analyz-
       ing their use by Gates at Camden and Morgan at Cowpens.

1231. Quarles, Benjamin. "The Colonial Militia and Negro Manpower."
       MVHR, 45 (1958-59), 643-652.

       Despite colonial laws, blacks enlisted in the militia, but,
       generally they were excluded until 1775. The need for man-
       power during the war caused emotional debates on this issue
       in Congress and in some states.

1232. Radabaugh, Jack S. "The Militia as a Social Outlet in Colo-
       nial Massachusetts." SOC STUD, 49 (1958), 106-109.

       Prior to the war, the militia had numerous social functions
       in addition to its military duties.

1233. Reid, Brian Holden. "A Survey of Militia in 18th Century
       America." ARMY Q DEF REV, 10 (1980), 48-55.

       This is a helpful general sketch of the topic.

THE AMERICAN ARMY

1234. Rosswurn, Steven. "Arms, Culture and Class: The Philadelphia
       Militia and the 'Lower Orders' in the American Revolution,
       1763 to 1783." Ph.D. dissertation, Northern Illinois Uni-
       versity, 1979.

       In a good analysis of Philadelphia crowd life, the author
       asserts that membership in the militia by members of the
       lower class hastened the growth of political consciousness
       in their ranks. Due to this factor and their deeds at bat-
       tles like Princeton, the radicals in the militia promoted
       republican ideology to its limits. This is a thoughtful,
       well-researched study with very pertinent appendices.

1235. Schaeffer, Paul N. "Pennsylvania's Draft Laws During the
       Revolution." BERKS CNTY HIST REV, 6 (1910), 2-4.

       One of the first articles on this topic, this essay needs
       to be revised.

1236. Scisco, Louis D. "The Evolution of Colonial Militia in Mary-
       land." MD HIST MAG, 35 (1940), 166-177.

       The author concentrates on the pre-1775 militia, but the
       discussion of the command structure is useful.

1237. Shy, John W. "A New Look at the Colonial Militia." WMQ, 20
       (1963), 175-185.

       With the decline of Indian warfare by the early 1770s, the
       militia had more social than military functions.

1238. ————. "The American Revolution: The Military Revolution
       Considered as a Revolutionary War." See 19, pp. 121-125.

       Militia units were instrumental in a leveling of class dif-
       ferences in the army and provided social mobility for ambi-
       tious men.

1239. ————. A PEOPLE NUMEROUS AND ARMED: REFLECTIONS ON THE
       MILITARY STRUGGLE FOR INDEPENDENCE. New York: Oxford
       University Press, 1976.

       This is a collection of essays previously published by
       the author. Though the chapters are unconnected, and it
       is difficult to follow Shy's murky prose, there are some
       penetrating observations. The militia was vital in
       pacification; the degree of British violence caused
       varying patriot reactions; and the militia was essential in
       supporting the Continentals in numerous functions.

1240. Smith, Jonathan. "How Massachusetts Raised Her Troops in the
       Revolution." MASS HIST SOC PROC, 55 (1923), 345-370.

Even with drafts, bounties, substitutes, and short-term
enlistments, Massachusetts by 1783 could field only some
4,400 troops and not the required 8,350.

1241. Stuart, Reginald. "War, Society, and the 'New' Military
History of the United States." CAN REV AMER STUD, 8 (1977),
1-10.

Stuart notes that since 1945, military historians have
stressed interpretations of the war from a civilian perspective with increasing attention focused on civil-military
relations.

1242. Vermeule, Cornelius. "Service of the New Jersey Militia in
the Revolutionary War." NJ HIST SOC PROC, 9 (1924), 234-
248.

This is a fine article detailing the numbers of men raised,
how they were mustered, and where they served; about 16,000
men came from New Jersey.

1243. Weller, Jac. "Irregular But Effective: Partisan Weapons and
Tactics in the American Revolution, Southern Theatre."
MILT AFF, 21 (1957), 118-131.

Warfare in the south, explains Weller, was quite different
from that in the north, due to the nature of guerrilla warfare waged by both sides.

1244. Wheeler, E. Milton. "Development and Organization of the
North Carolina Militia." NCHR, 61 (1964), 307-323.

Here is data about pay, rank, training, and exemptions.

E. THE CAVALRY

1245. Armand, Charles Tuffin, Marquis de la Rouerie. "Letters of
Col. Armand." Vol. 4-5. NY HIST SOC COLL FOR 1878, (1879),
287-356.

Known as Colonel Armand, the Marquis impressed Washington
with his ardor, and he succeeded Pulaski as commander.
Armand's letters are vivid and detailed about efforts to raise
a cavalry regiment.

1246. Dounes, William F. "Logistical Support of the Continental
Light Dragoons." MILT COLL HIST, 24 (1982), 101-106.

The Light Dragoons were rarely used effectively by Washington due in part to equipment shortages.

1247. Gerson, Noel B. LIGHT-HORSE HARRY: A BIOGRAPHY OF WASHINGTON'S
GREAT CAVALRYMAN, GENERAL HENRY LEE. Garden City, New York:
Doubleday and Co., Inc. 1966.

Lee was daring and romantic as a horseman and always in the thick of battle. This is a somewhat overblown biography with more attention to the man and his heroics than necessary. Occasionally, the author elaborates on the importance of the cavalry, particularly in the southern campaigns.

1248. Gordon, William W. "Count Casimir Pulaski." GA HIST Q, 13 (1929), 198-227.

Here is a sketch of the gallant Polish Count who was killed at the siege of Savannah.

1249. Graham, A.S., and M.V. Woodhull. "Anthony Walton White, Brigadier in the Continental Army." MAG HIST, 1 (1905), 40-44; 2 (1905), 394-402.

White was not a famous officer but the data here about his activities with armed horsemen in Virginia and in the Carolinas is helpful.

1250. Haarman, Albert W. "General Armand and His Partisan Corps, 1777-1783." MILT COLL HIST, 12 (1980), 97-102.

Though uniforms receive more attention here, this is a dependable summary of cavalry fighting in the north.

1251. Hall, Charles S. BENJAMIN TALLMADGE: REVOLUTIONARY SOLDIER AND AMERICAN BUSINESSMAN. New York: Columbia University Press, 1943.

Now almost forgotten, this Connecticut cavalryman performed brilliantly in battle. Unfortunately, though, in this excellent monograph that presents a big chunk of Americana, the author stresses his hero's career as a Delegate and Congressman.

1252. Hayes, John T. CONNECTICUT'S REVOLUTIONARY CAVALRY: SHELDON'S HORSE. Chester, Connecticut: Pequot Press, 1975.

Though not a famous unit, Sheldon's troops performed invaluable service as fighters, guards, scouts and messengers. This is a good, reliable account.

1253. Moylan, Stephen. "Selections from the Correspondence of Col. Stephen Moylan of the Continental Line." PA MHB, 37 (1913), 341-380.

There are only a few colorful letters from Moylan, a Colonel of Dragoons and a leading cavalryman; the article suggests the difficulties in outfitting horsemen.

1254. Spencer, Richard Henry. "Pulaski's Legion." MD HIST MAG, 13 (1918), 214-226.

The essay is basically a roll of officers and men, many of whom were recruited in Maryland.

1255. Stutesman, John H., Jr. "Colonel Armand and Washington's
      Cavalry." NY HIST SOC Q, 45 (1961), 5-42.

      This is a fine article about Washington's use of cavalry
      and the fighting in New York's "Neutral Ground" and at Camden.

1256. Washington, Ella Bassett. "William Washington, Lieut-Col.
      Third Light Dragoons, Continental Army." MAG AMER HIST, 9
      (1883), 94-107.

      Washington was a gallant horseman who fought at Trenton and
      at Guilford Court House.

1257. Whitbridge, Arnold. "The Marquis De La Rouerie, Brigadier
      General in the Continental Army." MASS HIST SOC PROC, 79
      (1967), 47-63.

      Known as Colonel Armand, the French horseman impressed
      Washington with his ability.

                        F. THE ARTILLERY

1258. Abernathy, Thomas J. "Crane's R.I. Company of Artillery-
      1775." RI HIST, 29 (1970), 46-51.

      Major John Crane's thirty-five men served at Bunker Hill.

1259. Callahan, North. HENRY KNOX: GENERAL WASHINGTON'S GENERAL.
      New York: Rhinehart and Co., 1958.

      This is an exciting biography of Washington's artilleryman.
      Knox hauled cannon from Ticonderoga to Boston, planned and
      sited fortifications, handled artillery at Trenton, and he
      took the leading role in the creation of American artillery
      power. Here is a compelling and thoughtful study of a signif-
      icant military figure.

1260. Leake, Isaac Q. MEMOIR OF THE LIFE AND TIMES OF GENERAL JOHN
      LAMB. Albany, New York: J. Munsell, 1850.

      Lamb was an artillery captain on the Canadian expedition and
      a colonel in the Second Continental Artillery by early 1777.
      He was commander at West Point during Arnold's treason. At
      Yorktown, Lamb won the praise of Henry Knox, Washington's
      key artilleryman. This is a dated but useful biography of
      a capable officer and an active politician.

1261. Lee, William, ed. "Record of the Services of Constant Free-
      man, Captain of Artillery in the Continental Army." MAG
      AMER HIST, 2 (1878), 249-360.

      Lee was at Boston as a New Hampshire artilleryman and com-
      mander of a unit in the Northern Department.

1262. Meyer, Mary K., ed. "Captain John Fulford's Company: February
       13, 1776 to May 21, 1777." MD HIST MAG, 69 (1974), 93-97.

       This is a useful essay which shows a muster roll that in-
       dicates the civilian occupations of these troops.

1263. Nead, Benjamin M. "A Sketch of General Thomas Proctor." PA
       MHB, 4 (1880), 454-470.

       The article is helpful by citing the types of equipment used
       by Proctor's regiment which participated in many northern
       campaigns.

1264. Peterson, Harold L. ROUND SHOT AND RAMMERS. Harrisburg,
       Pennsylvania: Stackpole Books, 1969.

       Peterson is an expert on the subject of weaponry. This work
       is a fine summary of the various types of cannon, their mis-
       siles, and the attempted standardization of artillery during
       the war. The author notes the wide variety of American-made
       and foreign-made artillery used by the Continentals. The
       illustrations are quite helpful.

1265. Pleasants, Henry J. "Contraband From Lorient." MILT AFF, 7
       (1943), 123-132.

       That French weapons and ammunition were vital to the patri-
       ots before the French Alliance of 1778 is clear.

1266. Pope, Dudley. GUNS FROM THE INVENTION OF GUNPOWDER TO THE
       20TH CENTURY. New York: Delacorte Press, 1965.

       Pope is an expert on European artillery. His knowledge of
       its use on land, and, particularly, in sea battles is exten-
       sive. Though only the material here related to weaponry of
       the British and French armies in the eighteenth-century is
       relevant here, this is the best book for background informa-
       tion about cannon, mortars, and howitzers used in the revolu-
       tion.

1267. Stevens, John Austin. "Ebenezer Stevens, Lieutenant Colonel
       of Artillery in the Continental Army." MAG AMER HIST, 1
       (1877), 588-610.

       Stevens was a key figure at Boston, Ticonderoga, and Saratoga.

1268. Wallace, Lee A., Jr. "The Battery at Hoods: An Ambitious
       Fortification Failed to Protect Richmond in the Revolution."
       VA CAV, 23 (1973), 38-47.

       Virginian artillerymen were unable to repulse British Gen-
       eral Simcoe's raid on Richmond in 1781.

1269. Weller, Jac. "The Artillery of the American Revolution."
       MILT COLL HIST, 8 (1956), 61-65, 97-101.

Weller's expertise in heavy weapons is apparent in this neat summary.

1270. ———. "Revolutionary War Artillery in the South." GA HIST Q, 46 (1962), 250-273, 376-387.

The use of artillery in many accounts may have accounted for fifty percent of the casualties.

1271. Wilbur, C. Keith. "Artillery in the Revolution." AMER HIST illus, 4 (3) (1969), 27-30.

One learns in this enlightening article how to load and fire cannons, mortars, and howitzers.

1272. Zabrecki, David. "Tadeusz Kosciuszko: Father of Military Tactics." FIELD ART J, July-August, 1980, pp. 58-60.

The famous Polish artilleryman taught the Americans the European techniques of directing bombardments.

G. THE ENGINEERS

1273. Bedini, Silvio. THINKERS AND TINKERS: EARLY AMERICAN MEN OF SCIENCE. New York: Charles Scribers' Sons, 1975.

Here is the best survey about the work of innumerable colonial scientists like David Rittenhouse the astronomer and Andrew Ellicot the surveyor. Franklin does not dominate the scene here which is full of obscure men who cultivated the application of science to technology. The chapers about the scope of contemporary mathematical knowledge and about instrument-makers are insightful. Though brief in analysis, the book contains much data about the contemporary state of engineering.

1274. Buell, Rowena, ed. THE MEMOIRS OF RUFUS PUTNAM AND CERTAIN OFFICIAL PAPERS AND CORRESPONDENCE. Boston: Houghton, Mifflin, and Co., 1903.

Putnam was instrumental in preparing the defenses at Bunker Hill. Always regarded as a hero, (but not as a capable field general by Washington), one of Putnam's major contributions was to supervise the building of fortresses and defense works along the Hudson and in the Highlands. His comments on these activities are interesting.

1275. Froneck, Thomas. "Kosciusko." AMER HERITAGE, 26 (4) (1975), 4-11, 78-81.

Kosciusko, a Polish military engineer, performed brilliant service for the Americans, particularly by constructing the defense works at Saratoga.

1276. Haiman, Miecislaus. KOSCIUSKO IN THE AMERICAN REVOLUTION.
       New York: Polish Institute of Arts and Sciences in America,
       1943.

       The famous Polish engineer merits a far better book than
       this. However, the author used sources in three languages,
       attempted to explain the state of engineering in the eight-
       eenth-century, and wrote a dependable but plodding story.
       Kosciusko deserves praise for his defense-works at Saratoga
       and for designing the fortress at West Point. He was Poland's
       most famous participant in the Revolution.

1277. Kite, Elizabeth S. BRIGADIER-GENERAL LOUIS LEBEQUE DUPORTAIL:
       COMMANDANT OF ENGINEERS IN THE CONTINENTAL ARMY, 1777-1783.
       Baltimore: The Johns Hopkins Press, 1933.

       Though Kite deserves praise for extracting material from a
       wide range of sources, her account of the famed French en-
       gineer is inadequate. The reader is rarely certain what were
       Duportail's specific contributions. Furthermore, there is
       relatively no information here about the state of engineering
       science in the era.

1278. Palmer, David R. "Fortress West Point: 19th Century Concept
       in an 18th Century War." MILT ENG, 68 (1976), 171-174.

       Palmer, who has studied the fortress for years, notes the
       traditional and innovative features in the construction of
       the bastion.

1279. Whitbridge, Arnold. "Kosciusko, Polish Champion of American
       Independence." HISTORY TODAY, 25 (1975), 453-461.

       Whitbridge wrote a lively summary of Kosciusko's career in
       America and in Europe during the Polish Revolts of the 1790's.

                        H.   THE CARTOGRAPHERS.

1280. Adams, Randolph G. BRITISH HEADQUARTERS MAPS AND SKETCHES
       USED BY SIR HENRY CLINTON WHILE IN COMMAND OF THE BRITISH
       FORCES OPERATING IN NORTH AMERICA.... Ann Arbor, Michigan:
       William L. Clements Library, 1928.

       Adams compiled an invaluable collection of cartographic
       material from the Clinton Papers in the William L. Clements
       Library. The charts and sketches provide a unique insight
       into the state of map-making in the late eighteenth century.

1281. Cappon, Lester, ed., and others. ATLAS OF EARLY AMERICAN
       HISTORY. THE REVOLUTIONARY ERA, 1760-90. Princeton:
       Princeton University Press, Newberry Library, and the
       Institute of Early American History and Culture, 1976.

This is the best collection of maps available on the war.
Here are about 286 maps, mostly in color and pastels that are
skillfully drawn. One can find population patterns, city
sizes, the geographic circulation of newspapers, and the
religious and ethnic patterns. The maps on the military aspects are excellent, especially those for the overseas areas.
This handsomely reproduced volume also has full textual commentaries.

1282.   ————. "Geographers and Map-Makers, British and American
         From About 1750 to 1789." AMER ANTIQ SOC PROC, 81 (1971),
         243-271.

         Noting the inexactness of contemporary geography, Cappon
         cites eight famous American cartographers, notes the British
         were actively mapping North America after 1763, and that
         Washington used fifty men for chart-making.

1283.   ————. "Revolutionary War Mapmakers." PROLOGUE, 9 (1977),
         171-177.

         Here is a convenient summary about the level of map-making
         in the American, French, British, and Hessian forces involving
         over 300 cartographers.

1284.   Carrington, Henry B. BATTLE MAPS AND CHARTS OF THE AMERICAN
         REVOLUTION WITH EXPLANATORY NOTES AND SCHOOL HISTORY REFER-
         ENCES. With an introduction by George A. Billias. New
         York: Arno Press, 1974.

         The author drew, or had drawn, from his many works on the
         Revolution some of the best maps about battles and campaigns.
         This volume is a compilation of maps extracted from his other
         books, with some additional ones, and explanations about where
         to locate other cartographic material.

1285.   Clark, David Sanders. INDEX TO MAPS OF THE AMERICAN REVOLU-
         TION IN BOOKS AND PERIODICALS ILLUSTRATING THE REVOLUTIONARY
         WAR AND OTHER EVENTS OF THE PERIOD 1763-1789. Westport,
         Connecticut: Greenwood Press, 1972.

         Here is an excellent reference guide to hundreds of printed
         maps. The three sections include basic map references, a sub-
         ject and name index, and a list of publishers. Maps are cited
         by subject, date, size, mapmaker, engraver and publisher. Most
         of the maps concern military operations but the selection of
         maps for social-economic matters is comprehensive. From
         hundreds of books, one can find here a map of virtually any
         combat activity.

1286.   Cummings, Hubertis M. "The Villefranche Maps for the Defense
         of the Delaware." PA MHB, 84 (1960), 424-434.

         The Chevalier de Villefranche of the French engineer corps
         was an expert cartographer, and his map was instrumental in
         siting American defenses.

1287. Greenwood, W. Bart, comp. THE AMERICAN REVOLUTION, 1775-1783:
       AN ATLAS OF 18TH CENTURY MAPS AND CHARTS: THEATRES OF OPERA-
       TION. Washington, DC: Department of the Navy, Naval History
       Division, 1972.

       This excellent collection shows what maps were available to
       American and British commanders in twenty areas where navies
       were involved. The index of some 10,000 places is invaluable.
       The essay by Louis De Vorsey on colonial cartography is very
       helpful.

1288. Guthorn, Peter J. "A Hessian Map from the American Revolu-
       tion: Its Origin and Purpose." Q J LIB CONG, 33 (1976),
       219-231.

       An American authority explains the importance of the map,
       presumably drawn by Lt. Charles Auguste de Gironcourt.

1289. ————. AMERICAN MAPS AND MAP MAKERS OF THE AMERICAN REVOLU-
       TION. Monmouth Beach, New Jersey: Philip Freneau Press, 1966.

       This is a brief but valuable guide to the science of cartog-
       raphy in the American army. There are clues here about con-
       temporary map-makers that are not available elsewhere.

1290. ————. BRITISH MAPS OF THE AMERICAN REVOLUTION. Monmouth
       Beach, New Jersey: Philip Freneau Press, 1972.

       Here is a fine explanation about the importance of plotting
       and charting military naval maneuvers for the British forces.
       Because of their technical contributions, cartographers were
       enjoying increased status.

1291. ————. "The Role of New Jersey in British Strategy As
       Demonstrated in Maps." In William C. Wright, ed. NEW JERSEY
       IN THE AMERICAN REVOLUTION II. Trenton: New Jersey Histori-
       cal Commission, 1973, pp. 53-68.

       Guthorn notes the amazing amount of geographic data that the
       British accumulated about raids, villages, and American out-
       posts in New Jersey.

1292. Harley, John Brian, Barbara Bartz Petchenik, and Lawrence M.
       Towner. MAPPING THE AMERICAN REVOLUTION. Chicago: The
       Newberry Library, 1978.

       Here are some fifty-six major maps, twenty-eight plates, a
       full bibliography, a detailed index in this attractive volume.
       These contemporary maps of the war are classified by function,
       and technical differences along with details about the back-
       ground of mapmakers. This is a fine work and should be con-
       sulted.

1293. Heusser, Albert H. GEORGE WASHINGTON'S MAP MAKER; A BIOGRAPHY
       OF ROBERT ERSKINE. Edited, with an introduction by Herbert
       G. Schmidt. New Brunswick, New Jersey: Rutgers University
       Press, 1976.

Until a better one is available, this work will have to
suffice on the Geographer and Surveyor-General of the Continental army. It is poorly researched, ignores numerous
sources, and it leaves puzzling gaps in Erskine's career. The
material on the defense of the Delaware, however, is good.

1294. Holmes, Jack D.L. "Jose De Evia and His Activities in Mobile,
       1780-1784." ALA HIST, 34 (1972), 105-112.

       De Evia was probably the greatest Spanish explorer and car-
       tographer of the Gulf of Mexico area in the eighteenth century.

1295. ————. "Maps, Plans, and Charts of Louisiana in Spanish
       and Cuban Archives: A Checklist." LA STUD, 2 (1963), 183-
       203; 4 (1965), 200-221.

       Holmes cites some 250 items in this useful essay.

1296. McLaughlin, Patrick. "The American Revolution in Maps." AMER
       ARCH, 37 (1974), 43-49.

       Six recent publications about late colonial cartography are
       reviewed in this convenient summary.

1297. Marshal, Douglas W., and Howard H. Peckham. CAMPAIGNS OF THE
       AMERICAN REVOLUTION: AN ATLAS OF MANUSCRIPT MAPS. Ann
       Arbor, Michigan and Maplewood, New Jersey: University of
       Michigan Press and Hammond, Inc., 1976.

       One half of these maps from the William L. Clements Library
       have never been published before.

1298. Nebenzahl, Kenneth, and Don Higginbotham. ATLAS OF THE AMERI-
       CAN REVOLUTION. Chicago: Rand McNally and Co., 1974.

       This may be the most valuable collection of maps on the
       Revolution that has been published. The details of the major
       theatres of war are impressive, the coverage of the land cam-
       paigns is admirable, and there is ample information about
       activities on the several western frontiers. Here is a
       lavishly illustrated work with an excellent appendix that
       should be consulted.

1299. Rice, Howard C., Jr. "Rochambeau's Army in New Jersey: The
       Cartographic Records." See 1291, pp. 71-82.

       This is a good summary of the routes and campsites that the
       French army used in marching to and from the Delaware.

1300. Ristow, Walter W. "The Maps of the American Revolution: A
       Preliminary Survey." Q J LIB CONG, 28 (1971), 196-215.

       This article neatly summarizes the revival of interest in
       the subject, sites the importance of maps to armies and navies,
       and notes the location of major map collections.

I. THE MEDICAL MEN

1301. Angelakos, Peter. "The Army at Middlebrook, 1778-79." NJ
       HIST PROC, 70 (1952), 97-120.

       This is a good sketch of disease problems at a relatively
       unknown military encampment in New Jersey.

1302. Applegate, Howard Lewis. "The Medical Administrators of the
       American Revolutionary War." MILT AFF, 25 (1961), 1-10.

       Here are brief sketches about the Director-Generals -
       Church, Morgan, Shippen and Cochran.

1303. Beck, Herbert M. "The Military Hospitals at Lititz, 1777-78."
       HIST PAP LAN CTY HIST SOC, 23 (1919), 5-14.

       Lititz played a prominent role as a haven for American
       casualties during the British invasion of Pennsylvania.

1304. Bell, Whitfield, Jr. JOHN MORGAN. CONTINENTAL DOCTOR.
       Philadelphia: University of Pennsylvania Press, 1965-

       Morgan was the most prominent physician in late colonial
       America and the second Director-General of the army. Although
       this work needs revisions, it is a readable account of the dif-
       ficulties that confronted army medical personnel from 1775
       through 1777.

1305. Blake, John B. "Diseases and Medical Practice in Colonial
       America." INTER REC MED, 171 (1958), 350-362.

       This is a thoughtful and incisive summary about the state of
       medical practice in the northern colonies.

1306. Blanco, Richard L. PHYSICIAN OF THE AMERICAN REVOLUTION.
       JONATHAN POTTS. New York: Garland Publishing, Inc., 1979.

       Potts was a capable administrator of army hospitals. This
       study summarizes the state of military medicine in the north-
       ern campaigns from 1775 through 1779.

1307. Blanton, Wyndham B. MEDICINE IN VIRGINIA IN THE EIGHTEENTH
       CENTURY. Richmond, Virginia: Garrett, and Massie, 1931.

       Blanton's massive work on colonial medicine in Virginia has
       not been superceded. There are excellent descriptions here
       of surgery, apothecary shops, and hospitals during the south-
       ern campaigns. This is a very readable and well-documented
       study.

1308. Block, Harry. "Medical Conditions at Valley Forge." NY STATE
       MED J, 70 (1970), 3010-3012.

       Here is a suggestive essay which touches on medical care at
       the encampment.

1309. Cash, Philip. "The Canadian Military Campaign of 1775-1776.
       Medical Problems and Effects of Disease." JAMA, 235 (1976),
       52-56.

       This is an excellent discussion of the effects of smallpox
       and other diseases on the disastrous American invasion of
       Canada.

1310. ———. MEDICAL MEN AT THE SIEGE OF BOSTON, APRIL 1775-APRIL
       1776. Philadelphia: American Philosophical Society, 1973.

       In a series of vivid, incisive chapters, Cash wrote the
       best medical history of a Revolutionary war campaign. There
       is excellent material here about the treatment of casualties
       at Lexington and Concord, the state of health of the Conti-
       nental army at Boston, and the problems of organization for
       the army medical department. Cash is one of the few writers
       to treat the impact of ecological and logistical conditions
       in relation to the health of troops.

1311. Corner, George W. THE AUTOBIOGRAPHY OF BENJAMIN RUSH. Prince-
       ton: Princeton University Press, 1948.

       One of the most prominent physicians in America, and one of
       the nation's prolific writers on numerous subjects, Rush served
       briefly as a ranking medical officer. His comments about army
       hospitals and about his feud with Dr. William Shippen, Jr.
       provide colorful background.

1312. Cowen, David L. A BIBLIOGRAPHY ON THE HISTORY OF COLONIAL
       AND REVOLUTIONARY MEDICINE AND PHARMACY. Madison, Wisconsin:
       American Institute of the History of Pharmacy, 1976.

       Though the references to medicine are too limited in scope,
       this is the best introduction to articles about the pharma-
       cology of the era.

1313. ———. MEDICINE IN REVOLUTIONARY NEW JERSEY. Trenton: New
       Jersey Historical Commission, 1975.

       Here is a very useful summary about the state of medicine
       during the war in one state. Well organized and soundly writ-
       ten, the booklet is the best introduction to the subject for
       college students.

1314. Davis, David B. "Medicine in the Canadian Campaign of the
       Revolutionary War: The Journal of Doctor Samuel Fisk
       Merrick." BULL HIST MED, 44 (1970), 461-473.

       Merrick left a vivid account of the plight of army doctors
       attempting to check the ravages of smallpox on the St. Lawrence.

1315. Duffey, John. EPIDEMICS IN COLONIAL AMERICA. Baton Rouge:
       Louisiana State University Press, 1953.

Written by a major historian, this book provides much data
and insight into the nature of pestilence in the colonies.
The coverage by diseases and by geographic area is especially
valuable.

1316. Duncan, Louis G. MEDICAL MEN IN THE AMERICAN REVOLUTION, 1775-
       1783. Carlisle, Pennsylvania: Medical Field Service School,
       1931.

       This work is the starting point for investigations into
       military medicine during the war. It has excellent chapter
       organization, reads easily, covers a vast amount of material,
       and it contains data unavailable elsewhere. Though the docu-
       mentation is weak, the volume is one of few studies about
       medical care in southern campaigns.

1317. Estes, J. Worth. "Medical Letters from the Siege of Boston."
       J HIST MED ALLIED SCI, 31 (1951), 271-291.

       Dr. Hall Jackson's comments about care for the troops are
       invaluable.

1318. Gibson, James E. BODO OTTO AND THE MEDICAL BACKGROUND OF THE
       AMERICAN REVOLUTION. Springfield, Ohio: Charles C. Thomas,
       1937.

       Otto was a minor medical officer who served in the Middle
       States at numerous hospitals. There is some valuable data
       in this work, but the material is so disorganized and so
       devoid of analysis that the study is marred. Without cita-
       tions to footnotes, or a commentary on source material, this
       book has limited value.

1319. ————. "The Role of Disease in the 70,000 Casualties in the
       American Revolutionary Army." TRANS SOC COLL PHYS PHIL,
       17 (1941), 121-127.

       Disease took a greater toll of troops than the musket balls
       and bayonets.

1320. Gill, Harold, Jr. THE APOTHECARY IN COLONIAL VIRGINIA.
       Williamsburg: University Press of Virginia, 1972.

       This compact volume is quite readable and contains revealing
       photographs. The study reveals much about the work and tools
       of colonial druggists.

1321. Gilman, Malcolm C. "Military Surgery in the American Revolu-
       tion." J MED SOC NJ, 57 (1960), 492-496.

       Gilman writes about surgeons performing amputations on the
       battlefield.

1322. Griffenhagen, George D. "Drug Supplies in the American Revolu-
       tion." NAT MUS BULL, 225 (1951), 110-133.

This is a very valuable essay about the importation and manu-
facture of drugs for the army. Unfortunately, the story ends
in 1778 when the drug shortage became worse.

1323. Guerra, Francisco. AMERICAN MEDICAL BIBLIOGRAPHY. New York:
       Lathrop C. Harper, Inc., 1962.

       Guerra produced an excellent reference tool. The book cites
       innumerable books and articles written by colonial physicians
       in North America. The listing of references to medical and
       pharmaceutical matters cited in newspapers is invaluable.

1324. Jones, Gordon W. "Medicine in Virginia in Revolutionary
       Times." J HIST MED ALLIED SCI, 31 (1976), 250-270.

       Covering more than medical aspects of Virginia, this essay
       is the best article for background information.

1325. Jordan, John W. "Continental Hospital Returns." PA MHB, 23
       (1899), 35-50, 210-233.

       This is a list of American casualties quartered at several
       Pennsylvania hospitals which shows the type of diseases pre-
       valent in the army.

1326. ———. "The Military Hospitals at Bethlehem and Lititz
       During the Revolution." PA MHB, 20 (1896), 137-157.

       Jordan described the impact of the war on two towns used to
       quarter sick soldiers.

1327. Kebler, Lyman F. "Andrew Craigie, The First Apothecary Gen-
       eral of the United States." J AMER PHAR ASSOC, 17 (1926),
       63-74, 157-178.

       Though data on Craigie is limited, there is some information
       here about the procurement of drugs.

1328. Kennedy, Samuel. "Letters of Dr. Samuel Kennedy to His Wife
       in 1776." PA MHB, 8 (1885), 111-116.

       Kennedy wrote some touching descriptions about an army
       doctor's life.

1329. King, Lester S. THE MEDICAL WORLD OF EIGHTEENTH CENTURY.
       Chicago: University of Chicago Press, 1958.

       King wrote the best work on the theoretical background to
       medical concepts of western Europe in the Age of Enlightenment.
       He cogently elaborated on the dominant physiological concepts
       of the era in elegant prose, and he demonstrated how these
       ideas influenced the practice of medicine.

1330. Klebs, Arnold C. "The Historic Evolution of Variolation."
       BULL JOHNS HOPKINS HOSP, 24 (1913), 69-83.

This a reliable introduction about inoculation procedures
used to ward off smallpox.

1331. Middleton, William S. "Medicine at Valley Forge." ANN MED
       HIST, 3 (1941), 481-486.

       This essay covers medical care at the famous encampment,
       but with little analysis.

1332. Norwood, William. "Medicine in the Era of the American Revo-
       lution." INTER REC MED, 171 (1958), 391-407.

       Here is a good general account about military medicine that
       laymen can appreciate.

1333. Owen William A., ed. THE MEDICAL DEPARTMENT OF THE UNITED
       STATES ARMY DURING THE PERIOD OF THE REVOLUTION. THE LEG-
       ISLATIVE AND ADMINISTRATIVE HISTORY, 1776-1786. New York:
       Paul B. Hoeber, 1920.

       Though this work is dull reading, it is essential to compre-
       hend the organizational changes in the medical department. The
       author cited Congressional actions on the matter, pay scales,
       and changes in hospital regulations.

1334. Saffron, Morris H. SURGEON TO WASHINGTON, DR. JOHN COCHRAN
       (1730-1807). New York: Columbia University Press, 1977.

       This may be one of the oddest books written in the Bicenten-
       nial era. Supposedly a biography of a key medical figure,
       it is a very poorly written and inadequately researched col-
       lection of genealogy, correspondence, and a letterbook.

1335. Shryrock, Richard H. "Eighteenth Century Medicine in America."
       AMER ANTIQ SOC PROC, 59 (1949), 275-292.

       Though there is little data here about the army, Shryock re-
       veals how little the medical profession actually knew about
       medicine.

1336. Temkin, Owsei. "The Role of Surgery in the Rise of Modern
       Medical Thought." BULL HIST MED, 25 (1951), 248-259.

       This is a key article which helps to explain why surgical
       practices of the era may seem so rudimentary.

1337. Thacher, James. A MILITARY JOURNAL DURING THE AMERICAN REVO-
       LUTIONARY WAR, FROM 1775 to 1783. Boston: Cottons and
       Barnard, 1827.

       Dr. Thacher served in numerous campaigns in the north and at
       Yorktown. His journal is virtually the only lengthy chrono-
       logical account by an army medical man. Unfortunately, though
       some vivid material is covered here, the author seemed far
       more interested in military than in medical matters.

1338. Thursfield, Hugh. "Smallpox in the War of Independence."
       ANN MED HIST, 4 (1932), 312-318.

       The coverage here is limited to the north, but it is a use-
       ful essay.

1339. Toner, Joseph M. THE MEDICAL MEN OF THE REVOLUTION WITH A
       BRIEF HISTORY OF THE MEDICAL DEPARTMENT OF THE CONTINENTAL
       ARMY. Philadelphia: Collins, 1876.

       With a grasp of the material that has been difficult to
       match, Toner wrote the most comprehensive study of army
       medical care. He wrote well, organized his data carefully,
       and included some graphic descriptions. Toner was one of the
       few medical historians to mention conditions in southern
       campaigns.

1340. Torres-Reyes, Ricardo. 1779-80 ENCAMPMENT. A STUDY OF MEDI-
       CAL SERVICES. Washington, DC: National Parks Service, 1971.

       This is one of the best treatments available about medicine
       at a major cantonment. The author included some excellent
       material about the level of surgery and preventive medicine,
       and he listed some interesting statistical data about the
       incidence of disease.

1341. Waldo, Albigence. "Valley Forge, 1777-78. Diary of Surgeon
       Albigence Waldo, of the Continental Line." PA MHB, 21 (1897),
       299-323.

       Though the authenticity of this document is dubious, it
       provides an imaginative picture of a doctor's life during a
       famous winter.

1342. Wangensteen, Owen H., Jacqueline Smith, and Sarah D.
       Wangensteen. "Some Highlights in the History of Amputation
       Reflecting Lessons in Wound Healing." BULL HIST MED, 41
       (1967), 97-131.

       This is a key article which traces the evolution of opera-
       tive surgery over several centuries.

                        J. SUPPLY AND LOGISTICS

1343. Anspack, Peter. DAY BOOK OF PETER ANSPACK, PAYMASTER TO THE
       QUARTERMASTER GENERAL'S DEPARTMENT, SEPTEMBER 10, 1781 TO
       MAY 17, 1782. Foreward by Nellie Waldenmaier. Washington,
       DC: National Genealogical Society, 1941.

       Anspack wrote detailed notes and correspondence about ra-
       tions, provisions, and payments to suppliers. His letters
       reveal much about the functioning of the support services.

1344.   Aylett, William. "Correspondence of Colonel William Aylett,
        Commissary General of Virginia." TYLER'S Q HIST GEN MAG, 1
        (1919-20), 57-110, 145-161.

        Aylett had responsibilities for provisioning Virginia's
        troops as revealed in his letters.

1345.   Biever, Dale E. "Ordinance at Hopewell Furnace." MILT COLL
        HIST, 23 (1971), 113-118.

        Mark Bird's iron foundry near Reading, Pennsylvania pro-
        duced musketballs and cannonballs.

1346.   Coleman, Elizabeth Dabney. "Guns for Independence." VA CAV,
        13 (1963), 40-47.

        Virginia had a state factory at Fredericksburg that pro-
        duced muskets and bayonets.

1347.   Condit, William Ward. "Christopher Ludwick, the Patriotic
        Gingerbread Baker." PA MHB, 81 (1957), 365-390.

        Ludwick, a German immigrant and Superintendent of Bakers,
        supervised the ovens at Morristown, Skippack, Valley Forge,
        and Yorktown.

1348.   Dounes, William F. "Logistical Support of the Continental
        Light Dragoons." MILT COLL HIST, 24 (1972), 101-106.

        This is a detailed account of the problems involved in sup-
        plying four regiments with special equipment.

1349.   Greene, Nathanael. "Letters of Nathanael Greene to Colonel
        Jeremiah Wadsworth." PA MHB, 22 (1898), 211-216.

        There are some clues here about the Commissary General of
        Purchases regarding supplies.

1350.   Hart, Charles H. "Colonel Robert Lettis Hooper, Deputy
        Quarter-Master General in the Continental Army and Vice
        President of NJ." PA MHB, 35 (1912), 60-91.

        Hooper supervised the purchase of foodstuffs and the opera-
        tions of mills in Pennsylvania.

1351.   Hatch, Louis Clinton. THE ADMINISTRATION OF THE AMERICAN
        REVOLUTIONARY ARMY. New York: Longmans Green, 1904.

        Hatch made a pioneering effort to unravel the complexities
        of logistics for the war. Though the result is dull reading,
        it is essential to grasp the essentials of the support serv-
        ices. Pages 86-123 on logistics are valuable.

1352.   Hutson, James A. "The Logistics of Arnold's March to Quebec."
        MILT AFF, 32 (1968), 110-124.

This is an excellent summary about the calculations for
boats, tools, weapons and provisions that were made for the
famous expedition through Maine.

1353. ————. THE SINEWS OF WAR: ARMY LOGISTICS, 1775-1953. Wash-
       ington, DC: Office of the Chief of Military History, 1966,
       pp. 3-74.

       This is a useful summary of how the army obtained provisions
       from the states, and the wagons, bridges, roads, and store-
       houses it built. Clearly, this is still a relatively unre-
       searched area of the war, but Hutson made a start.

1354. Johnson, Keach. "The Genesis of the Baltimore Ironworks."
       JSH, 19 (1953), 157-179.

       The foundry began by producing weapons and chains for the
       army.

1355. Johnson, Victor L. "Robert Morris and the Provisioning of
       American Army During the Campaign of 1781." PA MHB, 5 (1938),
       7-20.

       Congress granted Morris, the Superintendent of Finance, the
       authority to contract for all army supplies and for the means
       of transporting these supplies to the troops.

1356. ————. THE ADMINISTRATION OF THE AMERICAN COMMISSARIAT DUR-
       ING THE REVOLUTIONARY WAR. Philadelphia: University of
       Pennsylvania Press, 1941.

       From 1775 to 1781, the Commissary directed by four men in
       succession - Joseph Trumbull, William Buchanan, Jeremiah
       Wadsworth, Ephraim Blaine - directed the provisioning of the
       troops with varying degrees of success. This is a dull but
       essential book for information about that department's dif-
       ficulties and why the system sometimes collapsed.

1357. Joslin, Joseph, Jr. "Journal of Joseph Joslin, Jr. of South
       Killingly: A Teamster in the Continental Service, March '77-
       August '78." CONN HIST SOC COLL, 7 (1899), 297-369.

       This is a rare account by a wagoner who hauled supplies in
       Connecticut.

1358. Leonard, Eugenie A. "Paper as a Critical Commodity during the
       American Revolution." PA MHB, 74 (1950), 488-489.

       Despite Congressional and state efforts, the fifty-three
       American paper mills were perennially short of raw material
       and a labor force.

1359. Metzger, Charles K. "'The New Army Shall be Clothed in Uni-
       forms': Washington Prescribes Military War." MID-AMER, 53
       (1971), 78-93.

Shortages of cloth, the vague uniform regulations, and difficulties with state officials all delayed the systematic uni-
forming of the troops.

1360.   Nelson, William. "Beginnings of the Iron Industry in New
        Jersey." PA MHB, 35 (1911), 228-243.

        The forges tried to cast cannon and cannon-balls, but they
        were successful only in making iron fittings during the war.

1361.   Reynolds, Donald E. "Ammunition Supply in Revolutionary Vir-
        ginia." VA MHB, 73 (1965), 56-77.

        This essay contains a valuable explanation about gunpowder
        manufacture and explains why Virginia was the only supplier
        of lead for the southern armies after trying to obtain am-
        munition overseas.

1362.   Risch, Erna. QUARTERMASTER SUPPORT OF THE ARMY: A HISTORY OF
        THE CORPS, 1775-1939. Washington, DC: Office of the Quarter-
        master General, 1966.

        On pages 1-73, Risch summarizes the problems of provisioning
        the army, maintaining supply routes, and locating sources of
        food, raw materials, containers, and transport.

1363.   Robbins, Peggy. "Washington's Baker-General." EARLY AM LIFE,
        8 (1977), 56-57, 82-85.

        Christopher Ludwick, a Philadelphia Lutheran, provided
        Washington's army with bread for seven years.

1364.   Salay, David L. "The Production of Gunpowder in Pennsylvania
        During the American Revolution." PA MHB, 99 (1975), 422-
        442.

        The British wrecked or confiscated the state powder mills,
        and throughout the war, domestic production of gunpowder was
        much less than that imported from Europe.

1365.   ————. "The Production of War Material in New Jersey." See
        1291, pp. 7-20.

        The state tried to produce a variety of war material, but
        its success was primarily in iron castings.

1366.   Smith, C.C. "Scarcity of Salt in the Revolutionary War."
        MASS HIST SOC PROC, 15 (1856-57), 221-227.

        The northern states tried various means to produce salt or
        to import the commodity which was as crucial as gunpowder.

1367.   Stapleton, Darwin H. "General Daniel Roberdeau and the Mine
        Expedition, 1778-1779." PA HIST, 28 (1971), 361-371.

The Sinking Spring deposit in Pennsylvania produced only one
ton of lead; the mining terminated due to its small output,
Indian raids, and the arrival of French munitions.

1368. Stephenson, Orlando W. "The Supply of Gunpowder in 1776."
       AHR, 30 (1925), 271-281.

       Virtually all the gunpowder of the American army by late
       1777 came from the West Indies with French aid.

1369. Svejda, George. QUARTERING, DISCIPLINING, AND SUPPLYING THE
       ARMY AT MORRISTOWN, 1779-1780. Washington, DC: Department
       of the Interior. National Parks Service, 1970.

       This is a fine account of how Washington's army fared at the
       New Jersey encampment. Svejda carefully studied the terrain
       and routes to the camp. The result is a summary about con-
       struction of huts, the efforts to obtain supplies, and, par-
       ticularly, how local natural resources were used to sustain
       the army.

1370. Weiss, Jacob. THE LETTERBOOK OF JACOB WEISS, DEPUTY QUARTER-
       MASTER GENERAL OF THE REVOLUTION. Edited by Melville J.
       Boyer. Alberton, Pennsylvania: Lehigh County Historical
       Society, 1952.

       The 267 letters from and to Weiss provide a unique insight
       into the problems of supplying the army 1778 to 1781.

                         K. SMALL ARMS

1371. Brown, M.L. FIREARMS IN COLONIAL AMERICA, THE IMPACT OF
       HISTORY AND TECHNOLOGY, 1472-1772. Washington, DC: Smith-
       sonian Institute Press, 1980.

       This is the best book on the subject. Brown clearly demon-
       strates the influence of fire-arms manufacturing on colonial
       technology and industrialization. The volume has detailed
       coverage about rifles, pistols, muskets, swords, gunpowder,
       cannonshot, metallurgy, gunsmiths, armorers, and related sub-
       jects. The study is a pleasure to read, and the illustrations
       are excellent. It contains ten detailed maps, a serviceable
       index and a comprehensive bibliography. Chapter seven on the
       Revolution is especially pertinent.

1372. Gill, Harold B., Jr. THE GUNSMITH IN COLONIAL VIRGINIA.
       Williamsburg, Virginia: Colonial Williamsburg Foundation,
       1974.

       Here is a specialized work that has ample information about
       small arms in the Revolution. Writing in clear prose that
       demonstrates diligent research, Gill wrote about the level of
       handgun technology for one colony, but the examples given here
       could be duplicated elsewhere. The reader becomes acquainted
       with the tools, the technology, and the inventory of a gun-
       smith's shop as well as types of pistols and muskets.

1373. Held, Robert. THE AGE OF FIREARMS. New York: Harper and
       Row, 1957.

       Most of this well-written and profusely illustrated volume
       is outside the chronology era of the Revolution. However,
       chapter eight has an excellent discussion about firearms of
       the Continentals and their opponents.

1374. Moore, Warren. WEAPONS OF THE AMERICAN REVOLUTION ... AND
       ACCOUTREMENTS. New York. Funk and Wagnalls, 1967.

       Moore wrote a very useful survey of the various types of
       weapons - pistols, muskets, edged blades - that is complete
       with data about designs, models, degree of effectiveness and
       related topics. The material on a solider's accoutrements
       such as canteens, knapsacks, and footwear is imaginative.

1375. Neuman, George C. THE HISTORY OF WEAPONS OF THE AMERICAN
       REVOLUTION. New York: Harper and Row, 1967.

       An expert on the subject, Neuman compiled a lavishly il-
       lustrated volume about cannon, fire-arms, and edged weapons
       used in the war. For the undergraduate, this is the best
       introductory volume for it is packed with illustrations.

1376. Peterson, Harold L. ARMS AND ARMOR IN COLONIAL AMERICA, 1526-
       1783. Harrisburg: Stackpole Books, 1956.

       Approximately the last two-thirds of the definitive work
       are relevant to the Revolution. Besides the expert discus-
       sions of infantry weapons, this volume contains useful material
       about pikes, cannon, and the swords, armor, and helmets worn
       by horsemen.

1377. ————. "Lock, Stock and Barrel." AMER HIST ILLUS, 2 (4)
       (1968), 27-47.

       This essay is a good one for high-schoolers for it shows
       the importance of the Brown Bess musket.

1378. ————. THE BOOK OF THE CONTINENTAL SOLDIER; BEING A COMPLETE
       ACCOUNT OF THE UNIFORMS, WEAPONS AND EQUIPMENT WITH WHICH
       HE LIVED AND FOUGHT. Harrisburg: Stackpole Books, 1968.

       Peterson, probably the expert on this subject, compiled a
       lively account about the dress, weapons, and accoutrements
       of the Continental Line. This work is the most comprehensive
       survey of the topic, and it is admirably illustrated.

1379. Reichman, Felix. "The Pennsylvania Rifle: A Social Interpre-
       tation of Changing Military Techniques." PA MHB, 69 (1945),
       3-14.

       Of European origin, the rifle was perfected by gunsmiths in
       Berks and Lancaster Counties, Pennsylvania, and it enabled the
       infantry to devise new tactics for battle.

1380. Wittlinger, Carlton O. "The Samll Arms Industry of Lancaster
       County, 1710-1840." PA HIST, 24 (1957), 121-136.

       The manufacture of muskets and rifles, instigated by German
       immigrants, was a highly significant factor in arming Penn-
       sylvania's troops.

1381. Wright, John W. "The Rifle in the American Revolution." AHR,
       29 (1924), 293-299.

       In a key article, the author explains why the musket was
       more durable than the rifle which took longer to load and
       which lacked a bayonet.

1382. York, Neil L. "Pennsylvania Rifle: Revolutionary Weapon in a
       Conventional War." PA MHB, 100 (1979), 302-324.

       Due to limitations on American technology, and to the type
       of training required for the rifle, the weapon was generally
       limited in use by Americans except in some fights in the north,
       and by southern militia.

                            L. DISCIPLINE

1383. Alexander, Anthony J. "A Footnote on Deserters from the
       Virginia Forces During the American Revolution." VA MHB,
       55 (1947), 137-146.

       Some 655 enlisted men deserted the state's forces but few
       non-commissioned officers did so.

1384. ————. "A Footnote on Massachusetts' Deserters Who Went to
       Sea During the American Revolution." AMER NEP, 10 (1950),
       43-53.

       This fascinating article explains why prize money and a
       greater personal freedom on shipboard appealed to some 1,200
       army deserters.

1385. ————. "Desertion and Its Punishment in Revolutionary
       Virginia." WMQ, 3 (1946), 383-397.

       The high desertion rate (perhaps fifty per cent) was not
       solved by legislation nor by stringent military measures.

1386. Berlin, Robert Harry. "The Administration of Military Justice
       in the Continental Army During the American Revolution,
       1775-1783." Ph.D. dissertation, the Univeristy of Califor-
       nia, Santa Barbara, 1976.

       The author examines an ironic aspect of the war. Soldiers
       fought for independence yet they sacrificed degrees of free-
       dom as servicemen. The author presents fully documented in-
       formation about many topics: the problems of maintaining

discipline in the ranks, the functions of court-martials as
independent judicial units which often imposed varying penal-
ties on offenders, the increased use of flogging and execution
as punishments, the court trials of general officers, and
information about the army's first advocate-generals (William
Tudor, John Laurens, Thomas Edwards). Even with inconsisten-
cies in judicial decisions on innumerable cases, the writer
contends that the flexibility of the system was partially
responsible for the success of the disciplinary code.

1387. Bernath, Stuart L. "George Washington and the Genesis of
       American Military Discipline." MID-AMER, 49 (1967), 83-100.

       Washington deserves great credit for his astute handling of
       individual cases.

1388. Bradford, S. Sydney. "Discipline in the Morristown Winter
       Encampment." NJ HIST SOC PROC, 80 (1962), 1-29.

       This is a good study about the difficult task of imposing
       discipline; the death penalty was sometimes imposed.

1389. Bowman, Larry. "The Court-Martial of Captain Richard Lippin-
       cott." NJ HIST, 89 (1971), 25-36.

       In retaliation for an enemy atrocity, Washington ordered the
       trial of a captured British officer.

1390. Fleming, Charles J. "The 'Military Crime' of Charles Lee."
       AMER HERITAGE, 19 (3) (1968), 12-15, 83-89.

       For misconduct in battle at Monmouth, General Lee was sub-
       ject to a court-martial.

1391. Furlong, Patrick J. "A Sermon for the Mutinous Troops of the
       Connecticut Line, 1782." NEQ, 43 (1970), 621-631.

       This is a rare clue about a chaplain's appeal to soldiers
       to remain on duty.

1392. Gragg, Larry. "Mutiny in Washington's Army." AMER HIST ILLUS,
       11 (6) (1976), 34-45.

       Here is a terse and reliable summary of the reasons why
       Pennsylvania and New Jersey Continentals stationed in New
       Jersey mutinied in 1781.

1393. Lutz, Paul V. "Rebellion Among the Rebels." MANUSCRIPTS, 19
       (1967), 10-16.

       The Pennsylvania line mutinied in January 1, 1781 over unful-
       filled promises; a compromise was devised by Washington and
       Congress which improved morale.

1394.   Maurer, Maurer. "Military Justice Under General Washington."
        MILT AFF, 28 (1964), 8-16.

        Washington was firm but fair in dispensing punishments.

1395.   Steuben, von Baron. REGULATIONS FOR THE ORDER AND DISCIPLINE
        OF THE TROOPS OF THE UNITED STATES. Philadelphia: Styner
        and Cist, 1779.

        Derived from von Steuben's Prussian experience, here are
        the basic rules for drill formations, the manual of arms, line
        of march, selecting camp sites, regulation of company admin-
        istration, hygienic matters and many other aspects which dem-
        onstrate clearly that the Continentals followed European pre-
        cedents in bayonet and musketry drills, and in dispensing
        military justice.

1396.   Thomas, David. "How Washington Dealt with Discontent." S ATL
        Q, 32 (1933), 63-73.

        This is a summary of how Washington handled officer dis-
        content over back-pay related to the Newburgh Address in 1783.

1397.   Van Doren, Carl. MUTINY IN JANUARY. New York: Viking Press,
        1943.

        Though mutiny was more common than Van Doren realized when
        he wrote this work, nevertheless it remains the seminal treat-
        ment of the January, 1781 mass discontent expressed by the
        Pennsylvania and New Jersey line. The author depicts the
        misery of the rank and file, the soldiers' self-governing
        committees, and their patience as the negotiations proceeded
        with generals and with Congress. That this incident was a
        critical factor in the army's history is well explained. The
        author deftly notes why the British were unable to take ad-
        vantage of this crisis. Carefully researched and dramatically
        written, this remains the best work on the topic.

                     M. EPISONAGE AND PROPAGANDA

1398.   Bakeless, John. TURNCOATS, TRAITORS AND HEROES. Philadelphia
        and New York: J.B. Lippincott, 1959.

        A lively and exciting account of thirty American and British
        spies who supplied army commanders with intelligence informa-
        tion, this narrative is the best popular account of espionage
        conducted in the Middle States by both sides in the war.

1399.   ———. "Spies in the Revolution." AMER HIST ILLUS, 6 (3)
        (1971), 36-45.

        The article summarizes the author's book on the subject for
        a general audience.

1400. Berger, Carl. BROADSIDES AND BAYONETS: THE PROPAGANDA WAR OF THE AMERICAN REVOLUTION. San Rafael, California: Presidio Press, 1977.

This is a poor description about British and American efforts to use propaganda. The author does not define his topic, he ignores contemporary satirical literature and newspaper commentaries, and he is unfamiliar with current research in this area. The book is a dull retelling of standard tales - bribery, kidnapping, assassination attempts, and efforts to cause desertions.

1401. Brown, Richard C. "Three Forgotten Heroes. John Andre Encounters Yankee Doodle." AMER HERITAGE, 16 (5) (1975), 25-29.

This is the true story of three American farmers who captured the artful spy.

1402. Burnett, Edmund C. "Ciphers of the American Revolution." AHR, 22 (1917), 329-334.

The author noted how codes were used in diplomatic correspondence and in the acquisition of intelligence data.

1403. Butterfield, Lyman H. "Psychological Warfare in 1776: The Jefferson-Franklin Plan To Cause Hessian Desertions." AMER PHIL SOC PROC, 94 (1950), 221-241.

Congress attempted to encourage German troops in General Howe's command to desert.

1404. Byrne, Leonard. "Nathan Hale: A Testament to Courage." NEW ENG GALAXY, 16 (1975), 13-22.

Here is a summary of Hale's career and his execution by the British.

1405. Cook, Fred J. "Allen McLane, Unknown Hero of the Revolution." AMER HERITAGE, 7 (3) (1956), 74-77, 118-119.

Here is a brief summary of a daring American scout who acquired information about enemy movements for Washington.

1406. Crary, Catherine S. "The Tory and the Spy: The Double Life of James Rivington." WMQ, 16 (1959), 61-72.

The author contends that Rivington, supposedly a notorious Loyalist publisher in New York, was actually a spy for Washington.

1407. Cummings, Light. "Spanish Espionage in the South During the American Revolution." SOUTHERN STUDIES, 19 (1980), 39-49.

This is a good account of the high priority that Madrid gave to intelligence gathering by agents scattered from Cuba to New Orleans.

1408. Decker, Malcolm. TEN DAYS OF INFAMY: AN ILLUSTRATED MEMOIR
       OF THE ARNOLD ANDRE CONSPIRACY. New York: Arno Press, 1969.

       This book is a useful compilation of familiar material about
       Benedict Arnold's treason at West Point and the involvement
       of British secret agents. The maps and illustrations are
       particularly good.

1409. Falkner, Leonard. "A Spy For Washington." AMER HERITAGE, 8
       (5) (1975), 57-59.

       John Honeyman's efforts to dupe the British along the Dela-
       ware helped make Washington's surprise attack on Trenton into
       a victory.

1410. ———. "Capture of the Barefoot General." AMER HERITAGE,
       11 (5) (1960), 28-31, 98-100.

       British General Richard Prescott was captured in his bedroom
       at Newport, Rhode Island in 1779.

1411. Flexner, James T. THE TRAITOR AND THE SPY: BENEDICT ARNOLD
       AND JOHN ANDRE. New York: Harcourt and Brace, 1953.

       In a carefully researched account, the author wrote the
       best coverage of the famous plot to turn over West Point,
       Washington himself, and an entire garrison to a British ex-
       pedition. There are fascinating dimensions here about the
       leading participants in the treasonous attempt. The bibliog-
       raphy, illustrations are excellent, and the narrative pace
       is absorbing.

1412. Ford, Corey. A PECULIAR SERVICE. Boston: Little, Brown and
       Company, 1965.

       Here is a thoroughly documented version of the activities
       of the American secret service operating around New York City.
       The account of the more famous spies, as well as lesser-
       known agents, reads like fiction. The study has not been
       surpassed in its coverage.

1413. French, Allen. GENERAL GAGE'S INFORMERS, BENJAMIN THOMPSON
       AS LOYALIST AND THE TREACHERY OF BENJAMIN CHURCH, JR. Ann
       Arbor: University of Michigan Press, 1932.

       French wrote a solid account of the complex intelligence
       network that provided the British with information about
       patriot military preparations in 1775 and early 1776. Thomp-
       son, a famous scientist, later joined the British army. Dr.
       Church, head of the American army medical department, was
       captured, imprisoned, and exiled by his countrymen.

1414. Furlong, Patrick J. "An Execution Sermon for Major John
       Andre." NY HIST, 51 (1970), 63-69.

A sermon about the hanging of the British spy at Tappan, New
Jersey was never delivered.

1415. Haimes, Herbert. "The Execution of Major Andre." ENG HIST
       REV, 5 (1890), 31-40.

       In an emotional tirade, the author blames Washington for
       the "illegal" execution.

1416. Heinisch, B.A., and Heinisch, H.K. "Major Andre." J GEN ED,
       28 (1976), 237-264.

       Here is a good summary of the literature, plays, paintings,
       and sculpture related to Andre's execution.

1417. Johnson, Henry P. "The Secret Service of the Revolution."
       MAG AMER HIST, 7 (1882), 95-105.

       Though outdated, the essay is one of the first scholarly
       efforts to unravel the roles of Washington's secret agents.

1418. Lawson, John L. "The 'Remarkable Mystery' of James Rivington,
       'Spy.'" JOURN Q, 35 (1958), 317-323, 394.

       Why the Tory editor was unpunished after the war is un-
       clear; perhaps the reason is that former Loyalist journalists
       were generally treated leniently in the new Republic.

1419. Maguire, J. Robert. "The British Secret Service and the At-
       tempt to Kidnap Jacob Bayley of Newberry, Vermont, 1782."
       VT HIST, 44 (1976), 141-167.

       Bayley was a target for opposing British General Haldimand's
       effort to recapture (later-day) Vermont.

1420. Mulligan, Luciel M. "Hercules Mulligan, Secret Agent." DAR
       MAG, 105 (1971), 232-235, 320.

       Mulligan maintained an extensive espionage operation because
       British officers patronized his New York shop.

1421. O'Dea, Anna, and Samuel A. Pleasants. "The Case of John
       Honeyman: Mute Evidence." NJ HIST SOC, 88 (1966), 174-181.

       Honeyman was a valuable spy for Washington along the Dela-
       ware in late 1776.

1422. Pemberton, Ian C. "The British Secret Service in the Champ-
       lain Valley During the Haldimand Negotiations." VT, 44
       (1976), 129-140.

       British agents spread false rumors about American disasters
       and attempted to kidnap patriot leaders.

1423. Pennypacker, Morton, GENERAL WASHINGTON'S SPIES ON LONG ISLAND
       AND IN NEW YORK. Brooklyn, New York: Long Island Historical
       Society, 1939.

       This is a detailed, reliable account about espionage. It
       contains many fascinating letters about spy activities written
       by Washington's staff to agents in the field. The study pro-
       vides a fresh perspective to familiar tales.

1424. —————. "The Two Spies: Nathan Hale and Robert Townshend."
       NY HIST ASSOC Q J, 12 (1931), 122-128.

       Here is a brief account of the men who were linked to Hale's
       espionage on Manhattan.

1425. Philbrick, Norman. TRUMPETS SOUNDING, PROPAGANDA PLAYS OF THE
       AMERICAN REVOLUTION. New York: Benjamin Blon, Inc., 1972.

       The author provides good summaries and commentaries on seven
       American plays such as "The Battle of Brooklyn, A Farce of Two
       Acts" (1776).

1426. Pickering, James H. "Enoch Crosby, Secret Agent of the Neutral
       Ground: His Own Story." NY HIST, 47 (1966), 61-73.

       Crosby, the presumed source of James Fenimore Cooper's THE
       SPY (1821), operated in Duchess and Westchester Counties, New
       York.

1427. Royster, Charles. "The 'Nature of Treason': Revolutionary
       Virtue and American Reaction to Benedict Arnold." WMQ, 36
       (1979), 163-193.

       War-weary America was shocked at Arnold's treason, an event
       related to "public virtue" and the quest for a stronger central
       government.

1428. Scheer, George F. "The Sergeant Major's Strange Mission."
       AMER HERITAGE, 8 (6) (1975), 26-29.

       The Americans plotted to capture traitor Benedict Arnold
       from his British sanctuary in Manhattan.

1429. Seed, Geoffrey. "A British Spy in Philadelphia: 1775-1775
       [Gilbert Barkly]." PA MHB, 85 (1961, 3-37.

       Supposedly a patriot, this Scot wrote to London officials
       about American military preparations.

1430. Seymour, G.D. "The Last Days and Valiant Death of Nathan Hale."
       AMER HERITAGE, 15 (4) (1964), 50-51.

       Here is a terse summary of the patriot's execution.

1431.   Shelton, William Henry. "What Was the Mission of Nathan Hale?"
        JAH, 9 (1915), 259-289.

        Hale may have been ordered to commit arson in British-held
        territory.

1432.   Sizer, Theodore. "The Perfect Pendant: Major Andre and Colonel
        Trumbull." NY HIST SOC Q, 35 (1954), 400-404.

        The famous painter had an interesting link to the British
        spy.

1433.   Smith Joshua Hett. AN AUTHENTIC NARRATIVE OF THE CAUSES WHICH
        LED TO THE CAPTURE OF MAJOR ANDRE. 1808. Reprint. New
        York: Arno Press, 1967.

        Smith was the last survivor who participated in the Arnold-
        Andre conspiracy for West Point. He published a memoir full
        of intrigue about the plans to capture the American fortress.
        Here is an interesting eye-witness account that should be con-
        sulted.

1434.   Stone, William L. "Schuyler's Faithful Spy: An Incident in the
        Burgoyne Campaign." MAG AMER HIST, 2 (1878), 414-419.

        Moses Harris, a British messenger, actually served in the
        American cause.

1435.   Stout, Neil R. "The Spies Who Went Out in the Cold." AMER
        HERITAGE, 23 (2) (1972), 52-55, 100-102.

        Two British officers attempted to map troop routes for
        General Gage in early 1776.

1436.   Thompson, Ray. "The Spy Who Went Out in the Cold." GREATER
        PHIL, 57 (1966), 30-32, 35-36, 38, 40, 42, 44.

        Lydia Darragh of Philadelphia performed valuable secret
        service work for Washington.

1437.   Tregle, Joseph G. "British Spy Along the Mississippi: Thomas
        Hutchins and the Defense of New Orleans, 1773." LA HISTORY,
        9 (1767), 313-327.

        Hutchins, a cartographer and explorer, provided General Gage
        with information about the Spanish defenses at New Orleans.

1438.   Van Doran, Carl. SECRET HISTORY OF THE AMERICAN REVOLUTION:
        AN ACCOUNT OF THE CONSPIRACIES OF BENEDICT ARNOLD AND NUMER-
        OUS OTHERS, DRAWN FROM THE SECRET SERVICE PAPERS OF THE
        BRITISH HEADQUARTERS IN NORTH AMERICA. New York: The Viking
        Press, Inc., 1941.

        Van Doran was a meticulous researcher who wove documentary
        material into intriguing stories. This book is a well-balanced

and highly readable account of the Arnold-Andre plot as well
as other lesser-known British espionage schemes during the war.

1439.   Walker, Warren S.   "The Prototype of Harvey Birch." NY HIST,
        37 (1956), 399-413.

        James Fenimore Cooper's hero in THE SPY was a real secret
        agent named "Samuel Culper," a pseudonym actually used by two
        American spies.

1440.   Wallace, Willard M.   TRAITOROUS HERO: THE LIFE AND FORTUNES OF
        BENEDICT ARNOLD. New York: Harper and Row, 1941.

        Here is a very lively and sympathetic account of Arnold, his
        wife, Peggy Shippen and Major Andre. Interwoven in the narra-
        tive is a penetrating analysis of why Arnold betrayed his
        country and why he served the British on expeditions to Vir-
        ginia. This is probably the most balanced biography of Arnold.

1441.   Wilcox, C.De.W.   "The Ethics of Major Andre's Mission." NY
        STATE HIST ASSOC PROC, 15 (1916), 126-137.

        This is a very intriguing commentary on the military neces-
        sity of terming Andre a spy.

                        N.   BLACK TROOPS

1442.   Adrien, Claude. "The Forgotten Heroes of Savannah." AMERICAS,
        30 (11-12) (1978), 55-57.

        This article covers the epic of the Haitian Black Legion
        which aided the Americans and the French at their aborted
        siege of Savannah in 1779.

1443.   Barnett, Paul.   "The Black Continentals." NEGRO HIST BULL,
        33 (1970), 6-10.

        Here is a readable treatment of a black regiment serving
        under Colonel Christopher Greene.

1444.   Boatner, Mark M., III.   "The Negro in the Revolution." AMER
        HIST ILLUS, 4 (2) (1969), 36-44.

        Some 5,000 blacks served on the American side, and an un-
        known number for the British. Many slaves wanted to join the
        patriot cause, but most colonists feared a slave insurrection.

1445.   Brown, Wallace. "Negroes and the American Revolution." HIST
        TODAY, 14 (1964), 556-563.

        Brown provides a convenient analysis of blacks used by the
        Americans and the British in the armed forces and as laborers
        during the war.

1446.   Bull, Lisa A. "The Negro." HIST J OF WEST MASS, Supplement,
        (1976), 67-74.

        The author explains that the prime motivation of blacks
        who served in integrated and segregated military units was
        to gain freedom.

1447.   Conlon, Noel P. "Rhode Island Negroes in the Revolution: A
        Bibliography." RI HIST, 29 (1970), 52-53.

        Here are some forty citations about Rhode Island blacks dur-
        ing the war.

1448.   Cresto, Kathleen M. "The Negro: Symbol and Participant of the
        American Revolution." NEGRO HIST BULL, 39 (1976), 628-631.

        This summary is useful for high-schoolers.

1449.   Davis, Burke. BLACK HEROES OF THE AMERICAN REVOLUTION. New
        York: Harcourt, Brace, Jovanovich, 1976.

        Written for high school students, this readable work provides
        an easily comprehensible summary of some famous black soldiers,
        army messengers, and other black patriots.

1450.   Farley, M. Foster. "The South Carolina Negro in the American-
        Revolution, 1775-1783." SC HIST MAG, 79 (1978), 75-80.

        Carolina slaves were used by both sides as soldiers, sailors,
        and laborers.

1451.   Foner, Philip S. BLACKS IN THE AMERICAN REVOLUTION. Westport,
        Connecticut: Greenwood Press, 1976.

        Though there is little new presented here, either in infor-
        mation or interpretations, this book could be helpful in class-
        rooms. There is background material about pre-war abolition
        movements, the role of black regiments on both sides of the
        fighting, and the post-war termination of the slave trade in
        the north. Three useful appendices are attached to what are
        basically one hundred pages of text that appeared in Foner's
        previous work on colonial blacks.

1452.   Gough, Robert J. "Black Men and the Early New Jersey Militia."
        NJ HIST, 88 (1970), 227-338.

        Excluding blacks from the pre-war colonial militia, New Jersey
        permitted freed blacks to serve in mixed regiments in 1777; but
        the status of black soldiers remained uncertain until 1792.

1453.   Greene, Lorenzo J. "Some Observations on the Black Regiment
        of Rhode Island in the American Revolution." J NEGRO HIST,
        37 (1952), 142-172.

In a valuable essay, Greene tabulates the names of 168 men raised for a Rhode Island regiment in February, 1778. Slaves were permitted to join and their masters were compensated.

1454. Hargrove, W.B. "The Negro Soldier in the American Revolution." J NEGRO HIST, 1 (1916), 110-137.

Hargrove examines the debate in Congress about permitting freedmen to enlist in eighteen regiments, and how the states handled the matter.

1455. Jackson, Luther P. "Virginia Negro Soldiers and Seamen in the American Revolution." J NEGRO HIST, 27 (1942), 247-267.

In a sweeping summary, Jackson focuses on the debate about using freedmen or slaves as soldiers. Masters used slaves as substitutes for their own service; perhaps 500 Virginia blacks were in uniform during the war.

1456. Kaplan, Sidney. THE BLACK PRESENCE IN THE ERA OF THE AMERICAN REVOLUTION, 1770-1800. Greenwich, Connecticut: New York Graphic Society, 1973.

Though without footnotes or a bibliography, this handsomely illustrated volume may be useful for undergraduates. Kaplan notes that blacks were involved in virtually every major campaign, and that some were Loyalists. The visual material is excellent.

1457. McConnell, Richard C. NEGRO TROOPS OF ANTEBELLUM LOUISIANA, A HISTORY OF THE BATTALION OF MEN OF FREE COLOR. Baton Rouge: Louisiana State University Press, 1968.

Pages fifteen to twenty-two contain data about black militia who fought under the Spanish led by Galvez at Mobile and Pensacola.

1458. Maslowski, Pete. "National Policy Toward the Use of Black Troops in the Revolution." SC HIST MAG, 73 (1972), 1-17.

Despite the efforts of Henry and John Laurens to draft blacks into the services, the South Carolina and Georgia legislators opposed this approach. Yet Benjamin Lincoln and Nathanael Greene had black troops in their commands.

1459. Moore, George H. "Historical Notes on the Employment of Negroes in the American Army of the Revolution." MAG OF HIST, 1 (1907),

This is an early attempt to analyze the number of blacks used as regulars, militia, and as laborers for the Continentals.

1460. Nell, William C. THE COLORED PATRIOTS OF THE AMERICAN REVOLUTION. 1855. Reprint. New York: Arno Press, 1968.

This is one of the first scholarly works to document the contributions of blacks in the patriotic cause. Harriet Beecher
Stowe and Wendell Phillips, the famed abolitionists, wrote
introductions to this book.

1461. Porter, Dorothy B. "The Black Role During the Revolution."
        SMITHSONIAN, 4 (1973), 52-57.

        This essay feebly summarizes the role of prominent American
        black males in the 1700-1800 era.

1462. Quarles, Benjamin. "Crispus Attucks." AMER HIST ILLUS, 5 (4)
        (1970), 38-42.

        Here is a convenient summary about a black hero of the
        Revolution killed in the Boston Massacre.

1463. ————. THE NEGRO IN THE AMERICAN REVOLUTION. Chapel Hill:
        University of North Carolina Press, 1961.

        This fine study is the first comprehensive treatment of this
        topic. Although it is now outdated by current scholarship,
        it clearly indicates how important the participation of blacks
        was for both sides in the war. The book is particularly use-
        ful in explaining why some states were unable to fill their
        regimental quotas with black slaves or freedmen. The material
        about the colonial status of blacks is excellent.

1464. Rider, Sidney S. "Historical Inquiry Concerning the Attempt
        to Raise a Regiment of Slaves By Rhode Island During the
        War of the American Revolution." RI HIST TRACTS, 10 (1880),
        1-86.

        Rider wrote a good account of slaves who enlisted in Contin-
        ental regiments, with comments about their owners and their
        market value.

1465. Walker, James St.G. "Blacks as American Loyalists: The Slave
        War for Independence." HIST REFLECTIONS, 2 (1975), 51-67.

        Under Dunmore and Clinton, the British recruited black troops
        who were not pro-British but were "pro-black," hoping that
        military service would lead to freedom. This is a very thought-
        ful article and perhaps the best on the subject.

1466. White, David O. CONNECTICUT'S BLACK SOLDIERS, 1775-1783.
        Chester, Connecticut: Pequot Press, 1973.

        This is a pedestrian account about the status of slavery in
        Connecticut. But the tabulation of some 290 black soldiers
        from the state is useful for the author has determined the
        towns the blacks served, their service, and if they were pen-
        sioned.

O. PRISONERS OF WAR

1467. Alexander, John K. "American Privateersmen in the Mill Pri-
       son during 1777-1782, An Evaluation." AMER NEP, 10 (1930),
       43-51.

       Alexander carefully examines the documentary evidence to
       determine the numbers confined and conditions of internment in
       the famous English prison.

1468. ————. "American Privateersmen in the Mill Prison, 1777-1782.
       An Evaluation." ESSEX INST HIST COLL, 102 (1966), 318-340.

       Expanding his thesis, Alexander notes that researchers must
       compare conditions in six other prisons, examine British source
       material, and they should avoid the trap of plagiarism evident
       in three contemporary accounts.

1469. ————. "Fortin Prison During the American Revolution: A Case
       Study of British Prisoner of War Policy and the American
       Prisoners' Response to that Policy." ESSEX INST HIST COLL,
       103 (1967), 365-389.

       Alexander presents a balanced picture concerning the 1,200
       American seamen held at Fortin in a detailed examination of
       diaries and journals. The treatment of inmates was harsh but
       not barbaric.

1470. ————. "Jonathan Carpenter and the American Revolution: The
       Journal of an American Prisoner of War and Vermont Indian
       Fighter." VT HIST, 36 (1968), 74-90.

       Captured on the privateer REPRISAL in 1777, Carpenter was
       confined at Fortin Prison and eventually was exchanged.

1471. Ammerman, Richard H. "Treatment of American Prisoners During
       the Revolution." NJ HIST, 78 (1960), 257-275.

       The author claims that captives were cruelly treated by the
       British and that one-third perished in confinement. Prisons
       in New York harbor were particularly notorious.

1472. Anderson, Olive. "American Escapees from British Naval Pri-
       sons During the War of Independence." MM, 41 (1955), 238-
       240.

       Many American captives escaped due to their determination,
       lax security, and English public support.

1473. ————. "The Impact of the Disposal of Prisoners of War in
       Distant Waters, 1689-1783." MM, 45 (1959), 243-249.

       Anderson shows that not until the Revolutionary War did the
       Royal Navy make "efficient efforts" to recover its own seamen
       captured by British enemies.

1474. ————. "The Treatment of Prisoners of War in Britain During
       the War of Independence." BULL INST HIST RES, 28 (1955), 63-
       83.

       The author contends that British treatment of captive Ameri-
       can seamen was fairly humane due to the Ministry's desire for
       comparable treatment of its troops.

1475. Applegate, Howard Lewis. "American Privateersmen in the Mill
       Prison, 1777-1782." ESSEX INST HIST COLL, 97 (1961), 303-
       320.

       Applegate claims that American prisoners were inhumanely
       treated, but he fails to compare Mill with other prisons and
       has accepted some dubious contemporary evidence about the
       625 inmates.

1476. Banks, James Lennox, ed. DAVID SPROAT AND NAVAL PRISONERS IN
       THE WAR OF THE REVOLUTION. New York: The Knickenbocker
       Press, 1909.

       This book is a satisfactory account of the problems encoun-
       tered by the British Commissary General of Naval Prisoners in
       New York from 1776 to 1782. The material about the ship-hulks
       used as prisons is especially vivid.

1477. Boden, William Hammond, ed. "Diary of William Widger of
       Marblehead. Kept at Mill Prison, England, 1781." ESSEX
       INST HIST COLL, 73 (1937), 311-347; 74 (1938), 22-48, 142-
       158.

       This is a diary kept by a captured American privateersman
       that is particularly good in describing conditions under con-
       finement.

1478. Boudinet, Elias. JOURNAL OF HISTORICAL RECOLLECTIONS OF AMERI-
       CAN EVENTS DURING THE REVOLUTIONARY WAR. Philadelphia:
       Frederick Bourguin, 1894.

       Boudinet was appointed by the Continental Congress to be Com-
       missary General of Prisons. Serving from June, 1777 to April,
       1778, Boudinet had the responsibility not only for supervising
       the treatment of British-Hessian captives, but for ameliorating
       the conditions of Americans held on prison ships in New York.
       This is a fascinating account of his duties.

1479. Bowden, Mary Weatherspoon. "In Search of Freneau's Prison
       Ships." EARLY AMER LIT,14 (1979), 174-198.

       Bowden analyzes four versions of poet Philip Freneau's "The
       British Prison Ship," and she suggests that he may have been
       help captive in New York.

1480. Bowman, Larry. CAPTIVE AMERICANS: PRISONERS DURING THE AMERI-
       CAN REVOLUTION. Athens, Ohio: Ohio University Press, 1976.

This is the best account of the ordeals suffered by captured
American soliders, seamen, and civilians at British prisons
in America and England from 1775-1782. Bowman did a fine job
of fusing materials from often incomplete diaries and journals.
He shows the lack of a comprehensive policy for dealing with
prisoners by both sides, particularly in the frequently frustrated prisoner of war exchanges. Surveying prison conditions
at Quebec, Halifax, New York Charleston, Savannah, and St.
Augustine, Bowman has compiled a thoughtful and provocative
commentary.

1481.   ————. "The New Jersey Prisoner Exchange Conference, 1778-
         1780." NJ HIST, 97 (1979), 149-158.

         The article covers the negotiations at Perth Amboy that
         served as a model for the future repatriation of captives at
         the war's end.

1482.   ————. "The Pennsylvania Prisoner Exchange Conference, 1777-
         8." PA HIST, 45 (1978), 257-269.

         An attempted exchange of prisoners failed because the Brit-
         ish refused to recognize the American republic.

1483.   Bushnell, Charles I., ed. THE ADVENTURES OF CHRISTOPHER
         HAWKINS. 1864. Reprint. Arno Press, 1968.

         A young Rhode Islander was incarcerated on a British ship
         off Manhattan. Even though his memoir was written decades
         later, his account of his imprisonment and his escape is
         thrilling reading.

1484.   Cohen, Shelden S. "Thomas Wren: Ministering Angel of Fortin
         Prison." PA MHB, 103 (1979), 279-301.

         An English clergyman tried to improve conditions for Ameri-
         can captives and negotiated for exchanges of prisoners.

1485.   Cutler, Samuel. "Journal of Samuel Cutler." NE HIST GEN REG,
         32, (1878), 43-44, 184-188, 305-308, 395-398.

         Imprisoned at Mill Prison near Plymouth, England, Cutler
         commented about the ravages of smallpox.

1486.   Cutler, William R., ed. "A Yankee Privateersman in Prison in
         England, 1777-1779." NE HIST GEN REG, 30 (1876), 174-177,
         343-352.

         This is a well-documented memoir of the miseries of prison
         life.

1487.   ————. "American Prisoners at Fortin Prison, 1777-1783."
         NE HIST GEN REG, 33 (1879), 36-41.

Here is a detailed account of conditions at the infamous
British prison.

1488. Dandridge, Danske, ed. AMERICAN PRISONERS OF THE REVOLUTION.
       1911. Reprint. Baltimore: Genealogical Publishing Co.,
       1967.

       The editor compiled an anthology of contemporary accounts
       by American patriots held at British prisons in New York.
       The prisonship JERSEY which held 8,000 men over the years
       is adequately described. But Dandridge virtually ignored
       prisons at Charleston and elsewhere in the south.

1489. Evan, Mary T. "Letters of Dr. John McKinley to His Wife
       While Prisoner of War, 1777-1778." PA MHB, 34 (1910),
       9-20.

       Captured at Brandywine, McKinley of Delaware wrote touching
       letters home.

1490. Fletcher, Ebenezer. "The Trials of Ebenezer Fletcher." AMER
       HIST ILLUS, 5 (2) (1970), 25-31.

       Fletcher was captured at Hubbardton, Vermont and described
       his tribulations as a prisoner.

1491. Ford, Worthington Chauncey, ed. "British and American Pris-
       oners of War, 1778." PA MHB, 17 (1893), 125-174, 316-324.

       Colonel Samuel Webb of Connecticut supervised an exchange
       of captive officers.

1492. Green, John. "American Prisoners in Mill Prison, Plymouth,
       England, in 1782." SC HIST GEN MAG, 10 (1909), 110-124.

       This is a dated but interesting commentary about patriot
       seamen held captive.

1493. Greene, Albert G., ed. RECOLLECTIONS OF THE JERSEY PRISON
       SHIP ... FROM THE ORIGINAL MANUSCRIPTS OF THE LATE THOMAS
       DRING ... 1829. Reprint. New York: Corinth Books, 1961.

       This standard collection contains accounts about the misery
       and inhumane treatment of American prisoners on prison hulks
       in Wallabout Bay, New York. Many authors who later wrote
       on this topic relied upon this work.

1494. Huguenin, Charles A. "Ethan Allen, Parolee on Long Island,
       January-August, 1777." VT HIST, 25 (1957), 103-125.

       Captured at Montreal, Allen was confined for seven
       months, but he was paroled and exchanged.

1495. Jenrich, Charles H. "The Old JERSEY Prison Ship." USNIP, 89
       (1963), 168-171.

       The author adds nothing new to a familiar story of horrors
       on the JERSEY, but the article is a convenient summary of how
       thousands of men died.

1496. Jorden, Helen, ed. "Colonel Elias Boudinet in New York City,
       February, 1778." PA MHB, 24 (1900, 453-466.

       Here is the diary of the American Commissary of Prisons
       during his investigation of Yankee captives held in New York.

1497. Laurens, Henry. "Narrative of His Capture, of His Confinement
       in the Tower of London, etc., 1780, 1781, 1782." SC HIST
       SOC COLL, 1 (1857), 18-83.

       Laurens wrote a good account of his captivity in England
       from 1780 to 1782.

1498. Leach, John. "A Journal During his Confinement by the British
       Gaol in 1775." NE HIST GEN REG, 19 (1865), 255-263.

       This is a lively account of how an American prisoner viewed
       his confinement.

1499. Lemisch, Jesse. "Listening to the 'Inarticulate': William
       Widger's Dream and the Loyalties of American Revolutionary
       Seamen in British Prisons." J SOC HIST, 3 (1969), 1-27.

       In a very enlightening article, Lemisch demonstrates that
       between 10,000 and 20,000 American seamen suffered in British
       prisons, but they managed to retain a strong patriotic identity
       by rejecting service in the Royal Navy and by forming their
       own self-governing society in captivity.

1500. McCaw, Walter D. "Captain John Harris in the Virginia Navy:
       A Prisoner of War in England, 1777-1779." VA MHB, 22 (1914),
       160-172.

       This is an interesting but prosiac account of a sea cap-
       tain's term in prison.

1501. Northern, Irene. "The Great Escapes: American Prisoners in
       Mill Prison." NE GALAXY, 18 (1976), 57-64.

       The author analyzes the ingenius escape methods devised by
       a privateer crew in 1780.

1502. Parramore, Thomas C. "The Great Escape from Fortin Goal:
       An Incident of the Revolution." NC HIST REV, 45 (1968),
       349-356.

       This is a thrilling account of the escape by the entire crew
       of the brig FAIR AMERICA.

1503. Portersfield, Sergeant Charles. "Diary of a Prisoner of War
       at Quebec, 1776." VA MHB, 9 (1901), 144-152.

       Here is a very brief but valuable account of confinement
       by an American soldier captured during the American invasion
       of Canada.

1504. Prelinger, Catherine M. "Benjamin Franklin and the American
       Prisoners of War in England During the American Revolution."
       WMQ, 32 (1975), 281-294.

       As a peace commissioner of France, Franklin worked for the
       amelioration of American captives in Britain and for a recip-
       rocal exchange of prisoners, but his efforts were frustrated
       by British obstinacy.

1505. Reck, W. Emerson. "Living Death on the Old Jersey." AMER
       HIST ILLUS, 11 (3) (1976), 18-23.

       The infamous JERSEY prison-ship caused the death - due to
       disease and starvation - of some 7,000 patriots.

1506. Roddis, Louis H. "The New York Prison Ships in the American
       Revolution." USNIP, 61 (1935), 331-336.

       Roddis reviews a familiar story, but his account is valuable
       because of his extensive knowledge of sanitary practices and
       disease problems abroad sailing vessels.

1507. Sabine, William H.W., ed. THE NEW YORK DAIRY OF LIEUTENANT
       JABEZ FITCH OF THE SEVENTEENTH (CONNECTICUT) REGIMENT FROM
       AUGUST 22, 1776 TO DECEMBER 15, 1777. 1854. Reprint. New
       York: Arno Press, 1971.

       Basing his narrative on a critical evaluation of Fitch's
       memoir, the author compiled a solid account about the British
       prison ships anchored off Manhattan and Brooklyn. The intro-
       duction is dependable, and the observations about conditions
       seem accurate.

1508. Sterling, David L., ed. "American Prisoners of War in New
       York: A Report by Elias Boudinet." WMQ, 13 (1956), 376-393.

       This is the text of Boudinet's comments to the American
       Board of War regarding his February, 1778, inspection of
       patriots confined in New York prison with suggestions about
       improving the deplorable conditions.

1509. Tourtellot, Arthur B. "Rebels, Turn Out Your Dead." AMER
       HERITAGE, 21 (5) (1970), 16-17, 90-93.

       Tourtellot wrote a very graphic description about the
       horrors of prison life on the JERSEY in the East River, New
       York.

1510.   Turner, Eunice H. "American Prisoners of War in Great Britain,
        1777-1783." MM, 45 (1959), 200-206.

        Though American prisoners were treated fairly decently at
        eight prisons in England, British magistrates made serious
        mistakes in handling them. This is a fully documented article
        that merits attention.

1511.   West, Charles E. "Prison Ships in the American Revolution."
        JAH, 5 (1911), 121-128.

        This is a weak and undocumented essay on the topic, but it
        is interesting as an example of how emotional the issue was
        to Americans, even on the eve of World War One.

1512.   [Widger, William]. "The Diary of William Widger of Marblehead
        Kept at Mill Prison, England, 1781." ESSEX INST HIST COLL,
        73 (1973), 311-347; 74 (1938), 22-48, 142-158.

        Captured on the brig PHOENIX, Widger spent eighteen months
        as a captive, leaving intimate details about food, disease,
        and his inmates.

                              P. SONGS

1513.   Camus, Raoul F. MILITARY MUSIC OF THE AMERICAN REVOLUTION.
        Chapel Hill: The University of North Carolina Press, 1976.

        American military music evolved from three major influences
        - the British army, the colonial militia, and the American
        environment. Though band music had only a peripheral part in
        the Revolution, the music from fife, drum, horns, and bands
        furnished inspiration to combat troops. The research in this
        work is impressive for the author demonstrates the importance
        of field and band music in the major campaigns, he supplies
        innumerable examples of soldiers' songs and ballads and he
        lists fife tutors, drum manuals, and many examples of regi-
        mental band music. The material on British regimental bands
        from 1775-1783 is especially pertinent.

1514.   Carey, George. "Songs of Jack Tar in the Darbies." J AMER
        FOLKLORE, 85 (1972), 167-180.

        The author extracted several eighteenth-century sea chants
        from the memoir of an American prisoner of war.

1515.   Hazen, Margaret Hindle. "Songs of Revolutionary America." NE
        HIST GEN REG, 130 (1976), 179-195.

        Analyzing fourteen songs, Hazen notes that Franklin and
        other famous patriots wrote tunes.

1516.   Hudson, Arthur Palmer. "Songs of the North Carolina Regu-
        lators." WMQ, 4 (1947), 470-485.

This is a perceptive commentary about pre-1775 songs that
had implications for the folklore of the Revolution.

1517. Lemay, J.A. "The American Origins of 'Yankee Doodle'." WMQ,
       33 (1976), 435-464.

       Originating in the 1740's, this famed song from New England
       had many stanzas and quatrains.

1518. Moore, Frank, ed. SONGS AND BALLADS OF THE AMERICAN REVOLU-
       TION, WITH NOTES AND ILLUSTRATIONS. New York: D. Appleton,
       1856.

       Here are examples of the most famous songs sung by soldiers
       in the north - the "War Song" of 1776, songs about Saratoga,
       General Sullivan, Nathan Hale, and other significant events
       and personalities.

1519. Platt, Charles D. BALLADS OF NEW JERSEY IN THE REVOLUTION.
       Port Washington, New York: Kennikat Press, 1972.

       This is the best summary of songs, tunes, and ballads sung
       by soldiers from one state.

1520. Schlesinger, Arthur M. "A Note on Songs as Patriot Propa-
       ganda, 1765-1775." WMQ, 11 (1954), 78-88.

       Folk ballads were martial, narrative, or hortatory.

1521. Stone, William L., comp. BALLADS AND POEMS RELATED TO THE
       BURGOYNE CAMPAIGN. 1893. Reprint. Port Washington, New
       York: Kennikat Press, 1970.

       An expert on campaigns in the north, Stone collected a mass
       of songs and poems about Burgoyne, Gates, Arnold, Jane McCrea
       and other personalities.

                          Q. UNIT HISTORIES

1522. Berg, Fred A. ENCYCLOPEDIA OF CONTINENTAL ARMY UNITS: BAT-
       TALIONS, REGIMENTS, AND INDEPENDENT CORPS. Harrisburg:
       Stackpole Books, 1972.

       This is an indispensable source of information. Berg pro-
       vides capsule histories of every Continental unit; even the
       most obscure ones are cited here. The data covers chronology,
       commanders, organization, staff functions, and peculiarities
       of unit structures.

1523. Billias, George A. GENERAL JOHN GLOVER AND HIS MARBLEHEAD
       MARINERS. New York: Henney Holt Co., 1960.

       Glover headed a regiment that pioneered an amphibious opera-
       tion. Its role in evacuating troops from Manhattan in the

autumn of 1776, and over the Delaware in the winter of 1776
was crucial. The men also performed well as infantry at
Saratoga. This is a well-written, spirited account of
remarkable troops.

1524. Linn, John Blair, and William H. Egle, eds. PENNSYLVANIA IN
       THE WAR OF THE REVOLUTION, BATTALIONS AND LINE, 1775-1783.
       Pennsylvania Archives, 2nd Ser., Vol. 2. Harrisburg,
       Pennsylvania: Busch, 1896.

       This is one of the best descriptions written in the nine-
       teenth century of a state's military units. Though there are
       some errors in nomenclature, and some companies are over-
       looked, the volume is generally reliable.

1525. Sanchez-Saavedra, E.M., comp. A GUIDE TO VIRGINIA MILITARY
       ORGANIZATIONS IN THE AMERICAN REVOLUTION, 1774-1787. Rich-
       mond, Virginia State Library, 1978.

       This is a model of its kind. There are detailed chapters on
       Continental infantry, the Virginia militia, partisan corps,
       artillery, dragoons as well as the Virginia state navy, and
       Loyalist organizations. The officers and services of each
       regiment are cited with ample footnotes and appendices.

1526. Trusell, John B.B., Jr. THE PENNSYLVANIA LINE: REGIMENTAL
       ORGANIZATIONS AND OPERATIONS, 1776-1783. Harrisburg: Penn-
       sylvania Historical and Museum Commission, 1977.

       This is a ponderous, ineptly-organized, and poorly-written
       attempt to identify Pennsylvania military units. It is often
       repetitious (some facts are cited three times), and the author
       seems unfamiliar with recent historical trends.

1527. Ward, Christopher Longstreth. THE DELAWARE CONTINENTALS,
       1776-1783. Wilmington, Delaware: The Historical Society
       of Delaware, 1941.

       This is a well-written account that encompasses more than
       a narrative about a particular unit. The Delaware line was
       justifiably regarded by American officers as superior in
       efficiency and dependability. The author provided a fine ac-
       count of strategy and tactics, colorful descriptions, and some
       good characterizations of a regiment that fought from 1775 to
       1783, ending with only 100 out of the original 700 men.

1528. White, J. Todd, and Charles H. Lesser, eds. FIGHTERS FOR IN-
       DEPENDENCE A GUIDE TO SOURCES OF BIOGRAPHICAL INFORMATION
       ON SOLDIERS AND SAILORS OF THE AMERICAN REVOLUTION. Chicago:
       The University of Chicago Press, 1977.

       Here is the most dependable and scholarly genealogical guide
       available about servicemen in the Revolution. There are 876
       separate entries here divided into four categories: military
       and related records, compiled lists of names and biographical

information, and a general category of 500 items entitled
"Diaries, Journals, Memoirs and Autobiographies". The volume
contains ample clues for genealogists but especially for
historians. The bibliography contains a listing of published
unit histories that omits only a handful of articles and books.
The introductory material about pension and bounty land claims
is pertinent. One chapter lists nearly 300 entries related
to manuscript collections.

R. CASUALTIES

1529. Lesser, Charles H., ed. THE SINEWS OF INDEPENDENCE: MONTHLY
       STRENGTH REPORTS OF THE CONTINENTAL ARMY. Chicago: Univer-
       sity of Chicago Press, 1976.

       This work is the most thorough investigation of the number,
       condition, and location of units in the Continental army.
       Some ninety monthly statistical reports from 1775 through
       1784 have been compiled for analysis. These are reports of men
       who were sick, on furlough, or on special duties. There is
       abundant information here about desertions, discharges, and
       mortality rates. Lesser compiled an indispensable work and
       one of the most valuable contributions from the Bicentennial
       era.

1530. Peckham, Howard H., ed. THE TOLL OF INDEPENDENCE, ENGAGE-
       MENTS AND BATTLE CASUALTIES OF THE AMERICAN REVOLUTION.
       Chicago: The University of Chicago Press, 1974.

       Here is an excellent summary which lists killed, wounded,
       captured, missing, and deserted soldiers and seamen for every
       battle and skirmish of the war (although privateering actions
       are omitted). It is an unsurpassed chronological guide to
       each action listing the date, place, and nomenclature of the
       event. The author concludes that the Revolution was second
       only to the Civil War (for all major wars fought by the United
       States) in deaths relative to population, and that twelve and
       one-half per cent of the servicemen were casualties.

1531. Peterson, Clarence S. KNOWN MILITARY DEAD DURING THE AMERICAN
       REVOLUTIONARY WAR, 1775-1783. Baltimore: Genealogical Pub-
       lishing Co., 1959.

       One can identify in this volume veterans by name, rank, date
       of enlistment and date and place of death. Some 9,500 names
       are mentioned.

1532. Vermeule, Cornelius C. "Numbers of Soldiers in the Revolution."
       NJ HIST SOC PROC, 7 (1922), 223-227.

       The author claims nearly 47,000 men were Continentals.

IV. THE AMERICAN NAVY

A. THE CONTINENTAL NAVY

1533.   Albion, Robert G. NAVAL AND MARITIME HISTORY: AN ANNOTATED
        BIBLIOGRAPHY. 4th ed., rev. and expanded. Mystic, Con-
        necticut: Munson Institute of American Maritime History,
        1972.

        This is an excellent reference work for maritime lore. It
        contains detailed chapters listing books, dissertations and
        government documents on a variety of topics - references,
        merchant marine, warships, captains and crews, maritime sci-
        ence, and exploration, commerce and shipping, navies by topic
        and chronology, and special sections. Unfortunately, material
        about the Revolution is widely scattered here, and citations
        for periodicals are overlooked.

1534.   Allen, Gardner. THE NAVAL HISTORY OF THE AMERICAN REVOLUTION.
        2 vols. Boston: Hougton Mifflin, 1913.

        Allen wrote one of the first solid treatments about the
        naval side of the war that remained a standard source for
        decades. The author summarized operations in the Atlantic,
        the Caribbean, Lake Champlain, and in European waters. Be-
        cause of its stilted prose style, the mass of details, and
        the author's tendency to exaggerate the importance of minor
        events, the book is difficult to read. Yet the work is
        soundly executed, the information about innumerable topics
        like naval prisons, the Penobscot expedition, and the excel-
        lent use of documentary material make this an essential tool
        for the specialist.

1535.   Barnes, John S., ed. FANNING'S NARRATIVE: BEING THE MEMOIR
        OF NATHANIEL FANNING, AN OFFICER OF THE REVOLUTIONARY NAVY,
        1778-1782. Vol. 2. Publications of the Naval Historical
        Society, New York: The Society, 1912.

        This is good material about how John Paul Jones was viewed
        by a subordinate. Here is a thrilling saga that is one of the
        best of its kind in print.

1536.   Barton, John A. "The Battle of Valcour Island, 1776: Benedict
        Arnold's Defense." HIST TODAY, 9 (1959), 791-799.

        This is an excellent discussion of how Arnold's fleet bought
        time for the American cause.

1537.   [Biddle, Nicholas]. "Letters of Captain Nicholas Biddle."
        Edited by William B. Clark. PA MHB, 74 (1950), 348-405.

        Much of this correspondence concerns the RANDOLPH, an ill-
        fated frigate.

1538.   Bird, Harrison. NAVIES IN THE MOUNTAINS: THE BATTLES ON THE
        WATERS OF LAKE CHAMPLAIN AND LAKE GEORGE, 1609-1814. New
        York: Oxford University Press, 1962.

        Although most of this book covers material prior to and
        after the Revolution, the material here about naval operations
        on these lakes from 1775-1777 is pertinent. Bird has mastered
        the documents, writes with zest, and concentrates on the ex-
        peditions under Carleton, Arnold, and Burgoyne.

1539.   Bolander, Louis H. "Arnold's Retreat from Valcour Island."
        USNIP, 55 (1929), 1060-1062.

        This is a terse but accurate account of how Arnold's fleet
        managed to escape.

1540.   [Bon Homme Richard]. THE LOG OF THE BON HOMME RICHARD.
        Mystic, Connecticut: Marine Historical Association, 1936.

        This is a brief but colorful document about John Paul
        Jones's famous ship.

1541.   Bonnel, Ulane Zeeck. "The Debree Papers at Nantes." QJ LIB
        CONG, 28 (1971), 253-259.

        Nantes, the French port, had a crucial role in provisioning
        American vessels.

1542.   Brewington, Marion V. "American Naval Guns, 1775-1785."
        AMER NEP, 3 (1943), 11-18, 148-158.

        Here is a technical account about manufacturing, types,
        ammunition, and range of the cannon.

1543.   ————. "The Battle of Delaware Bay, 1782." USNIP, 65
        (1939), 231-240.

        This is a weak article about a minor naval clash.

1544.   ————. "The Designs of Our First Frigate." AMER NEP, 8
        (1948), 11-25.

        John Humphreys of Philadelphia designed and built ten of
        the first thirteen frigates, among them was the RALEIGH built
        at Portsmouth, New Hampshire.

1545.   ————. "Washington's Boats at the Delaware Crossing." AMER
        NEP, 2 (1942), 167-170.

For the attack on Trenton, Washington used the familiar
Durham cargo boats.

1546.   Chadwick, French E.   "Sea Power: The Decisive Factor in Our
        Struggle for Independence."   In THE ANNUAL REPORT OF THE
        AMERICAN HISTORICAL ASSOCIATION, 1915.   Washington, DC:
        Government Printing Office, 1916, pp. 171-189.

        Although Chadwick overestimates the importance of the Ameri-
        can navy, he gives ample credit to the French fleet.

1547.   Chapelle, Howard I.   "The Design of the American Frigates of
        the Revolution and Joshua Humphreys."   AMER NEP, 9 (1949),
        161-168.

        Chapelle notes that Congress established three classes of
        frigates and doubts that Humphreys deserves so much credit
        as a ship architect.

1548.   ————.   HISTORY OF THE AMERICAN SAILING NAVY.   New York:
        W.W. Norton and Co., 1949.

        The first chapters are packed with data about the design
        and building of the first United States naval vessels.   The
        information here is replete with details about designs, costs,
        materials, dimensions, and biographical information about many
        Continental warships.

1549.   Clark, Thomas.   NAVAL HISTORY OF THE UNITED STATES, FROM THE
        COMMENCEMENT OF THE REVOLUTIONARY WAR TO THE PRESENT TIME.
        2 vols.   2nd. ed.   Philadelphia: M. Carey, 1814.

        This work represents one of the first successful efforts to
        write a naval history of the period.   Clark's work is a de-
        pendable source because he obtained much of his information
        from participants in key naval engagements.

1550.   Clark, William B.   "American Naval Policy, 1775-1776."   AMER
        NEP, 1 (1941), 1-16.

        Here is a well-documented account of how the Founding
        Fathers learned to appreciate the value of sea power in the
        first year of the war.

1551.   ————.   GEORGE WASHINGTON'S NAVY: BEING AN ACCOUNT OF HIS
        EXCELLENCY'S FLEET IN NEW ENGLAND WATERS.   Baton Rouge:
        Louisiana State University Press, 1960.

        That Washington early recognized the importance of sea
        power is apparent in this stirring narrative by a prominent
        naval historian.   His small fleet of schooners operated on
        numerous hit-and-run raids to disrupt British convoys for
        Boston, Halifax, and New York.   This is a solid study that is
        well-recommended.

1552.   ———. "James Josiah, Master Mariner." PA MHB, 79 (1955),
         452-484.

         Josiah of Philadelphia served on a galley on the Delaware,
         and on two Continental vessels.

1553.   ——— and William James Morgan, eds. NAVAL DOCUMENTS OF THE
         AMERICAN REVOLUTION. 8 vols. Naval Department of the Navy,
         Naval Historical Center, Washington, DC: GPO, 1965- .

         This massive collection of source materials has presently
         reached the date May 31, 1777 and covers, as does no other
         comparable documentary collection on the navy, a wealth of
         information about operations in American and European theaters.
         The manuscripts have been collected from widely scattered
         depositories and from private collections in the United States
         and abroad. Foreign language documents have been translated.
         Each volume contains about 1,500 items on every phase of mari-
         time activity. The maps, index, bibliographies are excellent.
         This is the indispensable source for naval history in the
         Revolution, for it contains innumerable committee reports,
         ships' logs, journals, account books, cargo manifests, crew
         lists, newspaper extracts, diaries and journals.

1554.   ———. THE FIRST SARATOGA, BEING THE SAGA OF JOHN YOUNG AND
         HIS SLOOP-OF-WAR. Baton Rouge: Louisiana State University
         Press, 1953.

         From a wide variety of sources, the author compiled a lively
         account of a ship that raided British commerce and that dis-
         appeared in a Caribbean storm. Clark demonstrates that Cap-
         tain Young was a vigorous commander and strategist, and that
         this forgotten hero merits attention.

1555.   ———, ed. "The Letters of Captain Nicholas Biddle." PA
         MHB, 74 (1950), 348-405.

         The 36 gun frigate Randolph was destroyed by a 64 gun Brit-
         ish ship-of-the-line as revealed in a fascinating document.

1556.   Coggins, Jack. SHIPS AND SEAMEN OF THE AMERICAN REVOLUTION:
         VESSELS, CREWS, WEAPONS, GEAR, NAVAL TACTICS, AND ACTIONS
         OF THE WAR FOR INDEPENDENCE. Harrisburg: Stackpole Books,
         1969.

         For the non-specialist who wants a dependable introduction
         to the subject, this is worth consulting. The author pro-
         vides very readable commentaries about ship design, con-
         struction, masts and sails, armament, ship fittings and re-
         lated topics. Furthermore, he explains signalling, tactics
         at sea, and some major combat operations in this attractively
         illustrated volume.

1557. Collins, J. Richard. "The HANNAH-NAUTILUS Affair." ESSEX
       INST HIST COLL, 104 (1968), 34-41.

       The first naval engagement of the war occurred on October
       10, 1775.

1558. [Conyngham, Gustavus]. LETTERS AND PAPERS RELATING TO THE
       CRUISES OF GUSTAVUS CONYNGHAM, A CAPTAIN OF THE CONTINENTAL
       NAVY, 1777-1779. Edited by Robert W. Neeser. Publications
       of the Naval History Society, vol. 6. New York: The Society,
       1915.

       A fifty-three page introduction provides a perspective for
       this interesting collection of documents. The material is
       mostly about Conyngham and not written by him, but the let-
       ters from diplomats, politicians, naval agents, and prisoners
       of war is invaluable. Conyngham was the terror of British
       shipping and his actions caused a steep increase in cargo
       insurance rates.

1559. Conyngham, Gustavus. "Narrative of Captain Gustavus
       Conyngham, U.S.N. While in Command of the 'Surprise' and
       'Revenge,' 1777-1779." PA MHB, 22 (1899), 479-488.

       Conyngham captured British ships in the North Atlantic as
       described in letters to his father.

1560. Crown Publishers. THE VISUAL ENCYCLOPEDIA OF NAUTICAL TERMS
       UNDER SAIL. New York: Crown Publishers, Inc., 1978.

       This book is a visual treat. There are twenty sections on
       such topics as anchor, capstan, and windlass; ballast and
       stowage; ship types; boats, calls, and commands; sailing and
       seamanship; signalling; fishing and whaling; and wind and
       weather. The volume contains innumerable maps, drawings, and
       photographs.

1561. Department of the Navy. DICTIONARY OF AMERICAN NAVAL FIGHTING
       SHIPS. 6 vols. Department of the Navy, History Division,
       Washington, DC: GPO, 1959.

       This is an excellent source for the entries in volume one
       contain a wealth of data about the early navy.

1562. Dowdell, Vincent S. "The Birth of the American Navy." USNIP,
       81 (1955), 1251-1257.

       The activities of the HANNAH in September 5, 1775 led to
       the formation of a Congressional naval committee.

1563. Eller, Ernest M. "Sea Power and the American Revolution."
       USNIP, 62 (1936), 777-789.

       The author provides a global sweep to the effect of maritime
       affairs on the war.

1564. Faibisy, John Dewar. "Penobscot, 1777: The Eye of a Hurri-
       cane." MAINE HIST SOC Q, 19 (1979), 91-117.

       In June-August, 1779 the British gave the United States its
       most severe naval defeat off Maine's coast, but the Royal
       Navy was unable to control the surrounding waters.

1565. Foster, Joseph. "The Continental Frigate RALEIGH." GRANITE
       MONTHLY, 60 (1928), 558-566.

       The RALEIGH was the first man-of-war built in New Hampshire.

1566. Fowler, William M. Jr. "Disaster in Penobscot Bay." NAVAL
       WAR COLL REV, 31 (1979), 75-80.

       This is an incisive summary of the greatest naval defeat in-
       flicted on the Americans in the war.

1567. ————. "James Nicholson and the Continental Frigate VIR-
       GINIA." AMER NEP, 34 (1973), 135-141.

       Virginia had great difficulties in outfitting and manning
       its contribution of ships to the navy.

1568. ————. REBELS UNDER SAIL: THE AMERICAN NAVY DURING THE
       REVOLUTION. New York: Charles Scribner's Sons, 1976.

       Here is the best single volume about the Continental Navy.
       The author's sparse writing style, grasp of detail, con-
       centration on maritime affairs and administrative matters
       show his mastery of the subject. Fowler stresses the ex-
       ploits of some commanders, avoids romanticizing, and he notes
       the many inept captains in the navy. The sectional rivalries
       in Congress, problems in budgeting and ship-building, and the
       colorful vignettes make this the best and most readable study
       to date. The bibliography and annotations are especially use-
       ful.

1569. ————. "The NEW YORK Frigate." AMER NEP, 38 (1978), 15-27.

       Construction delays prevented the completion of the vessel
       which was destroyed before its capture by the enemy.

1570. ————. "The Non-Volunteer Navy." USNIP, 100 (1974), 74-78.

       The Continental Navy impressed hundreds of Americans into
       service causing furious debates in Congress.

1571. ————. "William Ellery: An American Lord of Admirality."
       AMER NEP, 31 (1971), 232-252.

       Ellery, a Rhode Island Delegate, was the key figure on the
       Congressional Naval Board for nearly two years; but he was
       hampered by financing in constructing naval vessels.

1572. Frothingham, Thomas G. "The Sequences that Led to Yorktown."
       USNIP, 57 (1931), 1326-1330.

       This is a useful but highly oversimplified version of the
       naval maneuvering off Virginia.

1573. Gaines, William H. "The Battle of the Barges." VA CAL, 4
       (1954), 33-37.

       In late 1782, off the Eastern Shore of Maryland occurred
       the last naval fight of the war.

1574. Gilligan, Arthur E. "The Battle of Valcour Island." USNIP,
       92 (1967), 157-160.

       This is a good sketch about the significance of Arnold's
       fight.

1575. Hale, Richard Jr. "New Light on the Naval Side of Yorktown."
       MASS HIST SOC PROC, 71 (1957), 124-132.

       Here is a fine explanation of the tactics used by de Grasse
       and the mistakes in signalling among the British admirals.

1576. Halliday, Mark. "An Agreeable Voyage." AMER HERITAGE, 21
       (4) (1970), 8-11, 70-76.

       John Paul Jones's incredible achievements within 48 hours
       in British waters are neatly summarized here.

1577. Hanks, Carla U. "A Cruise for Gunpowder." USNIP, 65, (1939),
       324-327.

       This is a weak summary of an American raid in the Bahamas.

1578. Hayes, Frederic H. "John Adams and American Sea Power." AMER
       NEP, 15 (1965), 35-45.

       Adams emerges as the champion of American naval strength in
       Congress.

1579. Jones, John Paul. MEMOIRS OF REAR-ADMIRAL PAUL JONES, COM-
       PILED FROM HIS ORIGINAL JOURNALS AND CORRESPONDENCE. 1830.
       Reprint New York: Da Capo, 1972.

       Here in Jones's own words is the panorama of his incredible
       career. Partly autobiographical, partly self-reassurance,
       Jones is portrayed here as an adventurer, a braggart, a
       ceaseless opportunist. His reminiscences about the war at
       sea are invaluable. An anonymous compiler collected the
       material and interspersed the narrative with additional docu-
       ments which add dimensions to the tale.

1580. Keller, Allan. "The American Revolution at Sea." AMER HIST
       ILLUS, 8 (4) (1973), 4-11, 43-46.

       This essay swiftly encapsulates the glories and the trage-
       dies of the Continental navy.

1581. Kemp, Peter, ed. THE OXFORD COMPANION TO SHIPS AND THE SEA.
       London, New York, Melbourne: Oxford University Press, 1972.

       This is a superb reference book which covers the rich
       language of the sea. In descriptions ranging from a para-
       graph to one or two pages, the editor provides the definitions
       and derivations of hundreds of words and phrases related to
       maritime lore. This big volume is not only excellent for
       locating technical terms, but also for the many line drawings
       of knots, splices, rigging, implements of seamanship, navi-
       gational devices, and sketches of battles.

1582. Kleber, Louis C. "Jones Raids Britain." HIST TODAY, 19
       (1969), 277-283.

       The RANGER'S landing on the English coast in April, 1778,
       had little material effect, but the event shook British
       public opinion.

1583. Larrabee, Harold A. "A Near Thing at Yorktown." AMER HERIT-
       AGE, 12 (10) (1961), 56-64, 69-73.

       The author summarizes the battle of the Virginia Capes.

1584. Lloyd, Malcolm. "The Taking of the Bahamas by the Con-
       tinental Navy in 1776." PA MHB, 49 (1925), 349-366.

       British officials in the West Indies were astounded at this
       American audacity.

1585. MacClay, Edgar S. "A Sea Fight Long Forgot." MAG HIST, 11
       (1910), 150-154.

       One Continental vessel fought off several British ships on
       September 9, 1780, off the French coast.

1586. ————. "How Our Infant Navy Strangled a War Horror." USNIP,
       45 (1919), 2041-48.

       The American ship LEE captured the NANCY and its fifty
       'town-burning machines' destined for Tories.

1587. McCusker, John Jr.   "The American Invasion of Nassau in
       the Bahamas." AMER NEP, 25 (1965), 189-217.

       This is the best account of Commodore Esek Hopkin's ambi-
       tious raid on New Providence with eight American vessels, an
       event that astounded the British and forced the Admiralty to
       detach ships from the Mediterranean to the West Indies.

1588. ————. "The Continental Ship ALFRED." NAUT RES J, 13 (1965),
       37-68.

       This is a technical discussion about the dimensions and ton-
       nage of the navy's pride in 1776.

1589. Mahan, Alfred T. "John Paul Jones in the Revolution."
       SCRIBNER'S MAG, 24 (1898), 22-36, 204-219.

       This is a superb essay by America's famed naval historian.

1590. ————. MAJOR OPERATIONS OF THE NAVIES IN THE WAR OF INDE-
       PENDENCE. Boston: Little, Brown and Co., 1913.

       This is a masterly synthesis of a historian who championed
       American seapower. Although the data about the Continental
       navy is sparse, there is ample information here about the move-
       ments of the British, French, and Spanish navies. This is a
       remarkable study that is worth consulting.

1591. [Matthewman, Luke]. "Narrative of Lieut. Luke Matthewman of
       the Revolutionary Navy." MAG AMER HIST, 2 (1874), 174-185.

       This officer of the LEXINGTON brig wrote a good portrayal
       of conditions at sea.

1592. Mayhew, Dean R. "The Bagaduce Blunder. Commodore Saltonstall
       and the Penobscot Expedition." MM, 61 (1975), 27-30.

       A New England expedition to destroy a Loyalist base in Maine
       ended as a fiasco for the British easily repelled the patriots.

1593. Melville, Phillips. "Eleven Guns for the 'Grand Union.'"
       AMER HERITAGE, 9 (6) (1958), 58-64.

       The Governor of Dutch St. Eustatius risked dismissal by
       ordering the first salute to an American ship, the ANDREA
       DORIA, on November, 1776.

1594. ————· "LEXINGTON - Brigantine of War, 1776-1777." USNIP,
       86 (1960), 51-57.

       The merchantman WILD DUCK became a Continental naval vessel
       in French waters in 1776.

1595. Miles, A.H. "Sea Power and the Yorktown Campaign." USNIP,
       53 (1927), 1169-1184.

       This is a fine summary with excellent maps about the naval
       implications of the campaign.

1596. Millar, John Fitzhugh. AMERICAN SHIPS OF THE COLONIAL AND
       REVOLUTIONARY PERIODS. New York: W.W. Norton Co., 1979.

       Here is a brief but dependable summary of the evolution of

ship design and ship building in the eighteenth-century. The author describes about 150 vessels from the TURTLE submarine to the 74 gun AMERICA. The text is full of drawing, tables of dimensions and reproductions of extant paintings which make it an excellent reference work.

1597.   Miller, Nathan. SEA OF GLORY; THE CONTINENTAL NAVY FIGHTS
        FOR INDEPENDENCE, 1775-1783. New York: D. McKay Co., 1978.

        This is an adequate book for the general reader. The author relied almost entirely on standard sources, he ignored recent published material, and his maps, organization, and bibliography are weak. Written in a journalistic fashion, and with some distortions of the facts, nevertheless it is a readable introduction to the subject.

1598.   Morgan, William J. "The Stormy Career of Captain Hector
        McNeill, Continental Navy." MILT AFF, 16 (1954), 119-122.

        McNeill, the third ranking American naval officer and commanding the frigate BOSTON, was reprimanded unfairly for negligence.

1599.   Morris, Richard B. "The Revolution's CAINE Mutiny." AMER
        HERITAGE, 11 (3) (1960), 10-13, 88-91.

        The crew of a frigate mutinied against its French captain in August, 1779.

1600.   Morrison, Samuel E. "The Battle that Set Us Free." SAT EVE
        POST, 229 (July, 1963), 32-33, 56-57, 59.

        A master historian described the battle of the Chesapeake.

1601.   Nielson, John M. "Penobscot: From the Jaws of Victory - Our
        Navy's Worst Defeat." AMER NEP, 37 (1977), 288-305.

        This is the best article about the American amphibious failure on the Maine coast that demonstrated incredible blunders by commodores and generals commanding 3,600 men.

1602.   Ogden, Mark. "Where was Our Navy Born?" DAR MAG, 114 (1980),
        646-68.

        Marblehead (Mass.), Whitehall (N.Y.), and Philadelphia (Pa.) all deserve the credit.

1603.   Paullin, Charles O. "The Administration of the Continental
        Navy of the American Revolution." USNIP, 31 (1905), 625-675.

        Though outdated, this is a sweeping and convenient summary of how the navy was directed.

1604. ————, ed. OUT-LETTERS OF THE CONTINENTAL MARINE COMMITTEE
       AND BOARD OF ADMIRALTY, AUGUST, 1776-SEPTEMBER, 1780. Vols.
       4 and 5. Publications of the Naval Historical Society. New
       York: The Society, 1914.

       These letters from the American equivalent of the British
       Admiralty are an invaluable reference source for the special-
       ist. The instructions to naval captains were extracted from
       over 500 letters written by the Marine Committee held by the
       Library of Congress. A glance at the excellent index reveals
       the wide scope of the topics covered in this invaluable col-
       lection.

1605. Perry, James M. "Disaster on the Delaware." USNIP, 88 (1962),
       84-92.

       Perry describes the factors involving the failure of the
       Americans - using batteries, fortresses, various small craft
       and obstacles placed in the river - to prevent the Royal
       Navy from mastering the Delaware by November 21, 1777.

1606. Potter, Gail M. "The LEXINGTON of the Seas." NE GALAXY, 10
       (1969), 50-57.

       The MARGARETTA "Affair" in June 1775 was the first naval
       fight of the U.S. navy.

1607. Powers, Stephen Tallichet. "Robert Morris and the Courts -
       Martial of Captain Samuel Nicolson and John Manley of the
       Continental Navy." MILT AFF, 44 (1980), 13-17.

       The navy was close to collapse by early 1783, and the un-
       official Secretary of the Navy was Morris.

1608. Rankin, Hugh F. "The Naval Flag of the American Revolution."
       WMQ, 11 (1954), 339-353.

       Although the navy did not have a distinct flag until June
       14, 1777, John Paul Jones hoisted the Grand Union Flag on
       December 3, 1775.

1609. Rathbun, Frank H. "Rathbun's Raid on Nassau." USNIP, 96
       (1970), 40-47.

       The expedition to the Bahamas captured two fortresses and
       three prizes, but financially, the voyage was a failure.

1610. Rider, Hope S. VALOUR FORE AND AFT: BEING THE ADVENTURES OF
       THE CONTINENTAL SLOOP PROVIDENCE, 1775-1777, FORMERLY FLAG-
       SHIP KATY OF RHODE ISLAND'S NAVY. Annapolis: Naval Insti-
       tute Press, 1977.

       A lucky ship under four captains (such as Whipple and Jones),
       the vessel captured many prizes. This is a handsome volume,
       copiously illustrated with fine plates. But the author ignores
       essential American and British documents, provides little new

information, and leaves unanswered many questions. Yet the
book is adequate for navy "buffs."

1611.   Roland, Alex. "Bushnell's Submarine: American Original or
         European Import?" TECH CULT, 18 (1977), 157-174.

         The American craft was not original, for its design was
         copied from European publications.

1612.   Salisbury, William. "John Paul Jones and His Ships: the Need
         for More Research." AMER NEP, 28 (1968), 195-205.

         Here are excellent descriptions of the RANGER and BONHOMME
         RICHARD.

1613.   Sanders, Harry. "The First American Submarine." USNIP, 62
         (1936), 1743-1745.

         David Bushnell's TURTLE attacked HMS EAGLE off Manhattan in
         1776.

1614.   Shafroth, John F. "The Strategy of the Yorktown Campaign,
         1781." USNIP, 57 (1931), 721-736.

         Although not documented, this is a good account of the event.

1615.   Smith, Charles R. "And Take What We Pleased." BY VALOUR AND
         ARMS, 3 (1977), 6-13.

         This article summarizes Rathbun's raid on Nassau in 1778.

1616.   Smith, David B. "The Capture of the WASHINGTON." MM, 20
         (1934), 420-425.

         On December 13, 1775 an American brig was captured with a
         document which revealed American strategic plans.

1617.   Smith, D.E. Huger. "Commodore Alexander Gillon of the Frigate
         SOUTH CAROLINA." SC HIST GEN MAG, 9 (1908), 189-219.

         This is a hard-luck story about an inept and unfortunate
         skipper and his captured ship.

1618.   Smith, Philip C.F., and Russell W. Knight. "In Troubled
         Waters; The Elusive Schooner HANNAH." AMER NEP, 30 (1970),
         86-116.

         In a superb essay, the author probes the legends and the
         known facts about this American vessel that harrassed British
         shipping in 1775-76.

1619.   Smith, Philip Chadwick Foster. "Captain Samuel Tucker (1747-
         1833), Continental Navy." ESSEX INSTIT HIST COLL, 112
         (1976), 155-268.

One of the most active and successful naval officers in
the war, Tucker captured forty-two enemy ships but encountered
difficulties in securing backpay from Congress.

1620.   ————. FIRED BY MANLEY ZEAL: A NAVAL FIASCO OF THE REVOLU-
         TION. Salem, Massachusetts: Peabody Museum of Salem, 1977.

         This is a brisk, authoritative narrative about a fight be-
         tween two American and two British ships in July, 1777. In
         an inquiry over the comedy of errors, Captain John Manley was
         acquitted and Captain Hector McNeill court-martialed. Smith
         writes with style and elan in this very worthwhile account.

1621.   Stokes, Durward T., ed. "The Narrative of John Kilby." MD
         HIST MAG, 67 (1972), 21-53.

         Kilby, a gunner with Jones, wrote a vivid description of the
         fight with the SERAPIS.

1622.   Stone, Richard G., Jr. "'The SOUTH CAROLINA We've Lost':
         The Bizarre Saga of Alexander Gillon and his Frigate."
         AMER NEP, 39 (1979), 159-72.

         Gillon ineptly handled the purchasing and refitting of a
         Dutch ship which was captured by the British in December, 1782.

1623.   Storch, Neil T. "Convoys for Our Envoys." USNIP, 101 (1979),
         78-81.

         Six Continental vessels had the task of transporting Ameri-
         can envoys to Europe.

1624.   Tilley, John A. "The Development of American Revolutionary
         Naval Policy April 1775-July, 1776." NAUT RES J, 25 (1979),
         69-78, 119-126, 195-199.

         Here is a thoughtful examination of how Congress and
         Washington formed naval policy early in the war.

1625.   Trevett, John. "Journal of Lieut. John Trevett, 1775-1780."
         RI HIST MAG, 6 (1886), 73-74, 103-110, 195-210, 271-278.

         Trevett served on the CATEA under Abraham Whipple and later
         became a captain.

1626.   U.S. Naval Institute. "The Birth of a Navy." USNIP, 101
         (1975), 18-65.

         This article has the best summary about the origins of the
         Continental navy.

1627.   Warner, Oliver. "The Action off Flamborough Head." AMER
         HERITAGE, 14 (5) (1963), 42-49, 105.

This is a stirring narrative about John Paul Jones' BONHOMME
RICHARD in action against HMS SERAPIS off England in September,
1779.

1628. ———. "Paul Jones in Battle." HIST TODAY, 15 (1965), 613–
       618.

A prominent British naval historian sketches Jones's life,
career, his naval tactics, and his post-war service for
Russia.

B. STATE NAVIES

1629. Allard, Dean C. "The Potomac Navy of 1776." VA MHB, 84
       (1976), 411–430.

The five small vessels were important in amphibious operations and in protecting the Tidewater.

1630. Allen, Gardner W. "State Navies and Privateers in the Revolu-
       tion." MASS HIST SOC PROC, 46 (1913), 171–191.

This is a good general summary that stresses the maritime
contributions during the war of the northern states.

1631. Berkeley, Edmund, Jr. "The Naval Office in Virginia, 1776–
       1789." AMER NEP, 33 (1973), 20–33.

Virginia established seven naval districts similar to the
traditional British control of imports and exports.

1632. Brewington, Marion V. "The State Ship GENERAL GREENE." PA
       MHB, 60 (1936), 229–241.

The ship took many prizes, and helped to reopen trade on
the Delaware in 1779.

1633. Campbell, Randolph B. "The Case of the 'Three Friends': An
       Incident in Maritime Regulation During the Revolutionary
       War." VA MHB, 74 (1966), 190–224.

Virginia and North Carolina feuded over the jurisdiction of
a captured prize in February, 1782.

1634. Cohen, Sheldon S. "Captain Robert Niles, Connecticut State
       Navy." AMER NEP, 40 (1979), 190–208.

Niles played a vital role for his state in defending ports,
intercepting enemy shipping, and transporting provisions from
the West Indies.

1635. Copeland, Peter F., and Marko Zlalich. "The HERO Galley,
       Virginia State Navy, 1776-1778." MILT COLL HIST, 16 (1962),
       114-116.

       A ninety foot galley patrolled the Tidewater for three years.

1636. Gaines, William H. "The Battle of the Barges."   VA CAV, 4
       (1954), 33-37.

       The 1782 fight in the Chesapeake Bay demonstrated the value
       of Virginia's small naval craft.

1637. Jackson, John W. THE PENNSYLVANIA NAVY, 1775-1781; THE DE-
       FENSE OF THE DELAWARE. New Brunswick, New Jersey: Rutgers
       University Press, 1974.

       This is the first full account of a state navy's activities
       against General William Howe's invasion of Pennsylvania in
       1778. It is a vivid account of the incredible task that the
       Americans faced of building forts, batteries, obstacles, and
       a fleet on the Delaware. The material on Pennsylvania's
       State Navy, the performances of ship captains, and the fiascos
       of politicians are fully explained. Though the writing style
       is uninspiring and the endless accumulation of excessive de-
       tail is tedious, this is a good summary.

1638. Middlebrook, Louis F. HISTORY OF MARITIME CONNECTICUT DURING
       THE AMERICAN REVOLUTION, 1775-1783. 2 vols. Salem, Massa-
       chusetts: The Essex Institute, 1925.

       This is an excellent reference work for the specialist. It
       contains data about some 300 privateers and state naval ves-
       sels. The author meticulously compiled documents about the
       records of these ships from ships' logs, journals, and memoirs.
       The book is crammed with information about sea-faring. Volume
       one covers Connecticut's state navy; volume two treats Con-
       necticut's privateers.

1639. ————. THE FRIGATE 'SOUTH CAROLINA'; A FAMOUS REVOLUTIONARY
       WAR SHIP. Salem, Massachusetts: Essex Institute, 1929.

       Built at Amersterdam in 1777, purchased in France by South
       Carolina, the vessel sailed in August, 1781 for America. The
       luckless Captain Alexander Gillon, who had already bungled the
       outfitting, was unable to prevent British ship from capturing
       the expensive vessel.

1640. Mouzon, Harold A. "DEFENSE: A Vessel of the Navy of South
       Carolina." AMER NEP, 13 (1953), 28-50.

       Probably the first southern state naval vessel to sail
       (November 11, 1775) the DEFENSE protected cargoes of gun-
       powder and had an interesting history in Carolina waters
       until 1778.

1641. Neafie, John. "Captain Peter Nafey and His Whaleboat Crew in the Revolution." NJ HIST SOC PROC, 13 (1928), 421-424.

Several hundred men from New Jersey participated in raids on British shipping off Manhattan.

1642. ———. "The Ship PROSPER." SC HIST MAG, 59 (1958), 1-10.

The South Carolina vessel lacked stability; it was unseaworthy and never sailed.

1643. Owen, Hamilton. "Maryland's First Warship." MD HIST MAG, 38 (1943), 199-204.

The schooner DEFENSE saw little action but it protected Baltimore.

1644. Paullin, Charles O. "The Administration of the Massachusetts and Virginia Navies of the American Revolution." USNIP, 32 (1906), 131-164.

This is a good comparison of how two state navies were administered.

1645. Scheina, Robert L. "A Matter of Definition: A N.J. Navy, 1777-1783." AMER NEP, 39 (1979), 209-217.

New Jersey had sixteen gunboats and whaleboats to harass British shipping around New York.

1646. Scott, Kenneth. "New Hampshire's Part in the Penobscot Expedition." AMER NEP, 7 (1947), 200-215.

Portsmouth provided several vessels, particularly the brig HAMPDEN, for the famous fiasco in Maine.

1647. Stewart, Robert A. THE HISTORY OF VIRGINIA'S NAVY OF THE REVOLUTION. Richmond: Mitchel and Hotchkiss, 1934.

This is a convenient account of the various maritime craft used by the state in the war. It is a well-documented account of statistics about ships and rosters of crews.

1648. Still, William N., Jr. NORTH CAROLINA'S REVOLUTIONARY WAR NAVY. Raleigh, North Carolina: Department of Cultural Resources, 1976.

This is a well-documented booklet. The state's navy consisted of five brigs and galleys. The fleet was generally unsuccessful and virtually non-existent by 1781.

1649. Zlalich, Marko, and Copeland, Pete F. "The Virginia State Navy, 1776-1780." MILT COLL HIST, 20 (2) (1968), 150-52.

This article covers the difficulties in trying to standardize the uniforms for the state navy.

C. PRIVATEERS

1650. Allen, Gardner, W. "Massachusetts Privateers of the Revolu-
       tion." MASS HIST SOC COLL, v. 77. Boston: The Society,
       1927.

       This is one of the best books on the subject. After a sixty-
       page introduction, the author cites commissions, letters of
       marque, bonds for voyages, distribution of prize money, and
       a detailed listing of ships by date, type, guns, officers,
       and owners. The bibliographic references and sources of
       locations for the work are invaluable.

1651. Bell, Charles H. "The Privateer General Sullivan, Records
       of the Proprietors." NE HIST GEN REG, 23 (1869), 47-53,
       183-185, 289-292.

       The famous ship from Portsmouth, New Hampshire sailed with
       great expectations of capturing prizes.

1652. Bryant, Samuel W. "Details of the Late Yankee Victory off
       Labrador - 1782." AMER NEP, 29 (1969), 211-223.

       Captured American privateers escaped confinement while on
       the enemy brig Prince Edward in September, 1782.

1653. Carey, George C., ed. A SAILOR'S SONGBAG: AN AMERICAN REBEL
       IN AN ENGLISH PRISON, 1777-1779. Amherst, Massachusetts:
       The University of Massachusetts Press, 1976.

       After a good introduction about Yankee sea chants, the
       author presents some sixty songs or poems collected by a
       privateersman languishing in Fortin Prison. There are clues
       here about patriotism, the Revolution, and a working class
       consciousness that offer valuable insights about seamen.

1654. Cary, John. "Contrary Wind at Sea and Contrary Times at Home
       - The Sea Logs of Francis Boardman." ESSEX INST HIST COLL,
       101 (1965), 3-26.

       Boardman's memoir provides a good glimpse of sea lore.

1655. Chidsey, Donald B. THE AMERICAN PRIVATEERS. New York: Dodd,
       Mead and Co., 1962.

       This work is a satisfactory introduction to the subject for
       the general reader. The author relates familiar tales from
       standard sources. The elements of romance in his narrative
       would appeal to high-schoolers and undergraduates.

1656. Clark, William B. BEN FRANKLIN'S PRIVATEERS: A NAVAL EPIC OF
       THE AMERICAN REVOLUTION. Baton Rouge: Louisiana State
       University Press, 1956.

Early in the war, Franklin commissioned three French-owned
ships to raid enemy commerce around the British Isles and to
capture British seamen to be exchanged for American prisoners.
Although only some 100 Yankees were paroled, the ships took
114 prizes in a year. Due to violations of neutrality in
France, Franklin terminated the operation. This is a fine
story related in a straight forward style that reads almost
like a historical novel.

1657.   ————. "That Mischievous HOLKER: The Story of a Privateer."
         PA MHB, 79 (1955), 27-63.

         The 16 gun brig captured 70 prizes in 4 years.

1658.   Collins, James F. "Whale Boat Warfare on Long Island Sound."
         NY HIST, 15 (1944), 195-201.

         Loyalists made numerous raids in 1777-78 that degenerated
         into piracy.

1659.   Davies, Wallace E. "Privateering Around Long Island During
         the Revolution." NY HIST, 20 (1939), 283-292.

         Refugees from both sides raided from New York, New Jersey,
         and Connecticut; the opportunities for Americans was particu-
         larly profitable.

1660.   Dowdell, Vincent J. "Captain Mugford and the Powder Ship."
         USNIP, 82 (1956), 1358-1359.

         On April 6, 1776, Mugford's schooner FRANKLIN fought a bit-
         ter duel with the British transport HOPE.

1661.   Faibisy, John Dewar. "Privateers and Prize Cases: The Impact
         Upon Nova Scotia, 1775-1783." PROLOGUE, 11 (1979), 185-199.

         Nova Scotia might have joined the Revolution, but the colony
         was alienated by the piratical actions of American privateers.

1662.   Farmham, Charles W. "Crew List of the Privateer Independence
         1776." RI HIST, 26 (1906), 125-128.

         Here is a roster of the owners, officers, and seamen of an
         armed sloop.

1663.   Howe, Octavious T. "Beverly Privateers in the American Revo-
         lution." COL SOC MASS PUB, 24 (1934), 318-435.

         This is an excellent article which cites tonnage, crew
         lists, types of vessels, and ownership.

1664.   Howland, Henry R. "A British Privateer in the American Revo-
         lution." AHR, 7 (1902), 285-303.

         The VENGEANCE cruised off the Georgia coast in 1779.

1665. Jones, Peter E. "'Grant Us Commissions To Make Reprisals Upon
       Our Enemies Shipping'." RIH, 34 (1975), 105-119.

       Jones wrote a perceptive essay about American efforts to
       break the British blockade of Narragansett Bay, letters of
       marque, types of vessels, and the prizes captured by Rhode
       Islanders.

1666. Johnston, Ruth Y. "American Privateers in French Ports,
       1776-1778." PA MHB, 53 (1929), 352-374.

       This is an adequate summary of French aid to American
       privateers.

1667. Lincoln, Charles H. "American Revolutionary Naval Service.
       New Hampshire Privateers." NE GEN REC, 5 (1908), 161-170.

       Here is a partial list of New Hampshire's privateers in
       the Revolution.

1668. MacClay, Edgar. A HISTORY OF AMERICAN PRIVATEERING. New York:
       D. Appleton Co., 1899.

       This work is still a reliable introduction of the subject
       for students. The prose is clear; the narrative full of
       lively incidents, and the tone is one of high adventure. The
       maps and plates, however, now seem outdated.

1669. Malo, Henri. "American Privateers at Dunkerque." USNIP, 37
       (1911), 933-993.

       This is a fine article about the haven the Americans found
       at a French port for safety, acquiring supplies, and selling
       their prizes.

1670. Martin, Asa E. "American Privateers and the West Indian Trade,
       1776-1777." AHR, 39 (1934), 700-706.

       Nine Connecticut ships had profitable runs to St. Eustatius.

1671. Meserve, John B. "A Privateersman of the Revolution."
       GRANITE MONTHLY, 59 (1927), 135-143.

       Captain William Collins Meserve sailed the GENERAL LINCOLN,
       a sixty-ton schooner.

1672. Morgan, William James. "American Privateering in America's
       War for Independence, 1775-1783." AMER NEP, 36 (1976),
       79-87.

       Privateers returned with essential commodities to American
       ports; Congress should have concentrated more on encouraging
       privateering than in building a navy.

1673. Morison, Samuel E. "Remarks in Communicating Joseph Bartlett's
       Log of the PILGRIM, 1781-1782." MASS HIST SOC PUB, 25
       (1924), 94-124.

       Here is a vivid account of the successful voyages of a
       Beverly, Massachusetts privateer.

1674. Morse, Sidney G. "New England Privateers in the Revolution."
       Ph.D. dissertation, Harvard University, 1941.

       Here is a carefully researched study based on fresh source
       material. It delves into the careers of many privateering
       skippers, and it provides ample data about their ships, crews,
       financing, and voyages. The work is well-written, and the
       author skillfully portrayed the dangers of this trade with
       copious extracts from documents written by seamen.

1675. ————. "State or Continental Privateers." AHR, 52 (1946),
       68-73.

       Though most privateers were commissioned by Congress, the
       states issued commissions, had naval boards, and prize-courts.

1676. ————. "The Yankee Privateersmen of 1776." NEQ, 17 (1944),
       71-86.

       Here is a solid article which depicts the colorful life at
       sea of privateer crews.

1677. Nichols, G.E.E. "Nova Scotia Privateers." NOVA SCOTIA HIST
       SOC PROC, 13 (1908), 111-152.

       This is an excellent summary about the importance of Halifax
       and Yarmouth as bases for privateers from the Maritimes which
       raided New England waters.

1678. Norris, John M. "Benedict Arnold's Plan for Privateering,
       1782." WMQ, 13 (1956), 94-96.

       Arnold requested subsidies from Lord Shelburne to construct
       a frigate in order to raid the American coast.

1679. Paine, Ralph D. PRIVATEERS OF '76. Philadelphia: Penn Pub-
       lishing Co., 1923.

       This work concentrates mainly on mariners from Salem,
       Massachusetts. It is a romantic sea-story closer to a novel
       than to history. Paine relates the adventures of young Stephen
       Cleghorn, a young privateersman, who was captured, imprisoned
       and escaped. Youngsters would enjoy this portrait of sea lore.

1680. ————. THE SHIPS AND SAILORS OF OLD SALEM; THE RECORD OF A
       BRILLIANT ERA IN AMERICAN ACHIEVEMENT. New York: Outing
       Publishing Co., 1909.

This is a useful reference work which contains copious
descriptions of New England privateers. The selections from
numerous ships-logs, memoirs, and journals add a sense of
authenticity to the narrative.

1681. Philips, James Duncan. "Salem Revolutionary Privateers Con-
        demned at Jamaica." ESSEX INST HIST COLL, 76 (1940), 46-
        54.

        The article is based on the proceedings of a British Vice-
        Admiralty court at Jamaica which impounded eighteen captured
        Salem ships.

1682. Rand, Edwin Holmes. "Maine Privateers in the Revolution."
        NEQ, 11 (1938), 826-834.

        The essay covers lists of ships, crews, owners, vessels,
        guns, and home ports.

1683. Rogers, Bertram M.H. "The Privateering Voyages of the TARTAR
        of Bristol." MM, 17 (1931), 236-243.

        The TARTAR was a heavily armed vessel that captured many
        American prizes.

1684. Siebert, Wilbur H. "Privateers in Florida Waters and North-
        wards in the Revolution." FLA HIST Q, 22 (1943), 62-73.

        Privateering was common by both sides in the waters from
        Charleston to St. Augustine.

1685. Steiner, Bernard C. "Maryland Privateers in the Revolution."
        MD HIST MAG, 3 (1906), 99-103.

        About 220 Maryland vessels are identified here; some of the
        owners are cited.

1686. Wilbur, C. Keith. PICTURE BOOK OF THE REVOLUTION'S PRIVATEERS.
        Harrisburgh: Stackpole Books, 1973.

        Here is a good book for high-schoolers and undergraduates.
        There is information about how ships were constructed, manned,
        and handled at sea. The details about masts and rigging is
        interesting, and the illustrations are good. However, the
        text is poorly written.

                          D. THE MARINES

1687. Fagan, Louis S. "Samuel Nicholas, First Officer of American
        Marines." MARINE CORPS GAZ, 18 (1933), 5-15.

        Nicholas of Philadelphia was commissioned November 10, 1775
        when Congress authorized two battalions of Marines.

1688. Hardy, Joseph. "Private Journal On Board the CONFEDERACY
       Frigate Kept by Captain Joseph Hardy in Command of Marines."
       In James L. Howard, SETH HARDING, MARINER: A NAVAL PICTURE
       OF THE REVOLUTION, pp. 213-277. New Haven: Yale University
       Press, 1930.

       Hardy sailed on a stormy passage with envoys to Europe in
       October 1779 and described how the ship was repaired and re-
       fitted in French Martinque in March, 1780. After further duty
       the CONFEDERACY was captured in the West Indies, and Hardy
       was imprisoned in Ireland. He escaped to France and wrote
       a valuable commentary about the duties of a Marine officer.

1689. Jennison, William. "Extracts from the Journal of William
       Jenison Jr., Lieutenant of Marines in the Continental Navy."
       PA MHB, 15 (1891), 101-8.

       Jennison served on the frigate WARREN while under construc-
       tion (1776) and then on the frigate BOSTON on several exciting
       cruises (1777-79).

1690. McClellan, Edwin M. "American Marines in the Revolution."
       USNIP, 49 (1923), 957-963.

       This is a good summary of the functions that the Marines
       performed in the war.

1691. ———. "Marine Officers of the Revolution." DAR MAG, 55
       (1921), 303-312; 56 (1922), 23-33, 560-568.

       About 130 officers and some 2,000 enlisted men served in
       the Marines.

1692. ———. "The First American Flag to Fly Over Foreign Soil."
       MARINE CORPS GAZ, 18 (1933), 3-5.

       After capturing fortresses on Nassau (March 3, 1776), the
       Marines hoisted the American flag.

1693. Smith, Charles R. MARINES IN THE REVOLUTION. A HISTORY OF
       THE CONTINENTAL MARINES IN THE AMERICAN REVOLUTION, 1775-
       1783. Washington: History and Museum Division Headquarters,
       U.S. Marine Corps, 1975.

       In fourteen well-organized chapters, Smith wrote an excel-
       lent history of the Marines. There is ample information here
       about the duties and deeds of the Corps on sea and land, in-
       cluding adventures on the Mississippi, amphibious operations,
       and with Washington at Trenton and Princeton. The narrative
       is brisk; the documentation scholarly, and the hundred il-
       lustrations are a treat. The book's value is enhanced by
       valuable appendices listing several journals, information
       about muster and pay, and biographical sketches of famous
       Marine officers. This work should be regarded as the defini-
       tive text.

1694. [Trevett, John]. "Journal of John Trevett, 1775-1780." RI
       HIST MAG, 6 (1886), 72-74; 7 (1887), 194-199, 271-278.

       Trevett wrote the best memoir extant of an Marine officer,
       serving on the brig ANDREA DORIA, the sloop PROVIDENCE, and
       the frigate TRUMBULL.

1695. Tyson, Carolyn A., and Roland P. Gill. AN ANNOTATED BIBLIOG-
       RAPHY OF MARINES IN THE AMERICAN REVOLUTION. Washington,
       DC: US Marine Corps Headquarters, History Division, 1972.

       This very complete bibliography summarizes books and arti-
       cles about the Corps in a seventy-two page essay.

                            E. NAVAL MEDICINE

1696. Drowne, Solomon. "Life on a Privateer, 1780." In THE BUILD-
       ING OF THE REPUBLIC, 1689-1783. Vol. 2 of Albert B. Hart,
       ed. AMERICAN HISTORY AS TOLD BY CONTEMPORARIES. 5 vols.
       New York: Macmillan Co., 1897-1929, pp. 497-498.

       Drowne, a Rhode Island physician, served on the privateer
       HOPE.

1697. Gray, Ernest. "Naval Hygiene in the Eighteenth Century."
       DURHAM UJ, 4 (1943), 98-101.

       This is a brief sketch about the problems of scurvy, sani-
       tation, and ventilation aboard ships.

1698. [Green, Ezra]. DIARY OF EZRA GREEN, M.D. SURGEON ON BOARD THE
       CONTINENTAL SHIP OF WAR RANGER UNDER JOHN PAUL JONES, FROM
       NOVEMBER 1, 1777 TO SEPTEMBER 27, 1778 ...   Edited by
       George H. Preble, Boston: D. Clapp, 1875.

       Green was one of the few American naval surgeons who de-
       scribed his experiences in trying to heal the sick and wounded.
       There are only hints here of the difficulties he encountered.

1699. Gordon, Maurice Bear. NAVAL AND MARITIME MEDICINE DURING THE
       AMERICAN REVOLUTION. Ventnor, New Jersey: Ventnor Pub-
       lishers, 1978.

       This book represents an effort to acquaint the layman with
       the rudiments of medicine at sea. Though the author cites
       some scattered data about the background, functions, medica-
       tions, and tools of naval doctors, he has produced a poorly
       organized volume from standard sources. A reader would be
       baffled by Gordon's explanation of contemporary medical
       theories, and by the lack of information about the lists of
       drugs and instruments cited. The volume is profusely il-
       lustrated but many are poorly reproduced.

1700. Keevil, John J. MEDICINE AND THE NAVY, 1220-1290. 4 vols.
       Edinburgh: E. and S. Livingston, 1957-1963. Volume 3 on
       the 18th century was completed by Christopher Lloyd and Jack
       L.S. Coulter after Keevil's death.

       This is the best work in English on naval medicine in the
       Royal Navy. As much of the material covered in this fasci-
       nating work about hygiene, rations, fevers, drugs, operating
       procedures, and surgeons' duties could relate to the Con-
       tinental navy, this volume has particular value. The chapters
       about James Lind and his efforts to cure scurvy are very use-
       ful.

1701. Lloyd, Chirstopher, comp. THE HEALTH OF SEAMEN: SELECTIONS
       FROM THE WORKS OF DR. JAMES LIND, SIR GILBERT BLANE, AND
       DR. THOMAS TROTTER. Publications of the Naval Records
       Society, vol. 107. London: The Society, 1965.

       Lloyd has compiled summaries written by Lind of his ex-
       periments with citrus fruit at sea in order to ward off
       scurvy, the most prevalent of sea diseases. Blane served
       with Rodney in the West Indies and commented about water
       supply, sanitation, ventilation and rations.

1702. Parker, William M. "Rodney and His Naval Physician." ARMY Q,
       62 (1941), 150-165.

       Dr. Gilbert Blane was Rodney's Physician to the Fleet in the
       later part of the war and wrote an illuminating account of the
       battle of the Saintes.

1703. Roddis, Louis. "A Partial List of Medical Men in the Maritime
       Service of the Colonies during the American Revolution."
       MILT SURG, 79 (1963), 357-58.

       Though far from complete - because of the paucity of data
       about medical men on state navies - this roster is at least
       a start.

1704. Rosen, George. "Occupational Diseases of English Seamen During
       the 17th and 18th Centuries." BULL HIST MED, 7 (1935), 751-
       758.

       Not only dietary deficiencies, but respiratory ailments and
       numerous sprains, fractures and wounds were part of a sailor's
       life.

1705. Syrett, David. "Living Conditions on the Navy Board's Trans-
       ports During the American War, 1775-1783." MM, 58 (1969),
       87-94.

       Life at sea for the British troops EN ROUTE to the Americas
       was hellish.

V. THE FRENCH FORCES

A. THE FRENCH ARMY

1706. Alexander, Dennis W. "The Forgotten French." AMER HIST ILLUS,
        16 (6) (1981), 10-16.

        The author notes how much the American victory at Yorktown
        depended on French military and naval support.

1707. Annon. "Letters of a French Officer, Written at Easton,
        Pennsylvania in 1777-1778." PA MHB, 35 (1911),
        90-102.

        These documents apparently were forwarded to Paris on a
        Boston ship captured by the Royal Navy; they provide a good
        view of social life in the Continental army.

1708. Bakshian, Aram. "Foreign Adventurers in the American Revolu-
        tion." HIST TODAY, 21 (1971), 187-197.

        This is a good summary of European military professionals
        who served in the American cause - Charles Lee, Lafayette,
        von Steuben, Kosciusko, Duportail, and other dignitaries.

1709. Balch, Thomas. THE FRENCH IN AMERICA DURING THE WAR OF IN-
        DEPENDENCE OF THE UNITED STATES, 1777-1783, 2 vols.
        Philadelphia: Porter and Coates, 1891-1895.

        Volume one is the famous work that Balch first published in
        French (1872). It provides a detailed account of French
        military and naval operations in North America from 1778-1783.
        Considering the unavailability of much source material when
        Balch wrote, this is a remarkable work and an indispensable
        source about the French alliance. Volume two is a register
        of French army and naval officers on duty in America.

1710. Bishop, Morris. "A French Volunteer." AMER HERITAGE, 17 (5)
        (1966), 46-49, 103-108.

        The author provides a lively sketch of the adventures of
        Denis-Jean Debouchet who served at Saratoga, Morristown, and
        at Newport.

1711. Blanchard, Claude. THE JOURNAL OF CLAUDE BLANCHARD, COMMIS-
        SARY OF THE FRENCH AUXILIARY ARMY SENT TO THE UNITED STATES
        DURING THE AMERICAN REVOLUTION, 1780-1783. Trans. by Thomas
        Balch. Albany: J. Munsell, 1876.

Blanchard wrote a thoughtful and informative account of his
duties and observations on the FANTASQUE with Admiral de
Ternay to Rhode Island in 1780. He continued his journal
with the squadron of Admiral Detouches to the Chesapeake in
1781. This is one of the best contemporary accounts of the
French forces.

1712. Bonsal, Stephen. WHEN THE FRENCH WERE HERE; A NARRATIVE OF
        THE SOJOURN OF THE FRENCH FORCES IN AMERICA AND THEIR
        CONTRIBUTION TO THE YORKTOWN CAMPAIGN, DRAWN FROM UNPUB-
        LISHED REPORTS AND LETTERS OF PARTICIPANTS IN THE NATIONAL
        ARCHIVES OF FRANCE AND THE ARCHIVE MS. DIVISION OF THE
        LIBRARY OF CONGRESS. Garden City, New Jersey: Doubleday,
        Doran and Co., 1945.

        This is a valuable collection of journals, memoirs and
        correspondence about the French expedition to Newport (Rhode
        Island), to Savannah, the West Indies, and to Yorktown. It
        contains a vast amount of information about military and
        naval manuevers that is not conveniently available elsehwere.

1713. [Clermont-Crevecoeur, Comte Jean-Francois-Louis de]. "The
        Observant French Lieutenant." AMER HERITAGE, 23 (6) (1972),
        62-64.

        A French artillery officer was a fascinated observer of
        America, particularly its women.

1714. Closen, Ludwig Baron von. REVOLUTIONARY JOURNAL, 1780-1783.
        Translated and edited by Evelyn M. Acomb. Chapel Hill:
        University of North Carolina Press, 1958.

        Von Closen was aide-de-camp to Rochambeau. He wrote
        perceptive comments about garrison duty in Rhode Island,
        the link with the Continental army outside of New York, and
        the famous march to Yorktown. This work is an indispensable
        source, and it is extremely well-footnoted.

1715. Colomb, Pierre. "Memoirs of a Revolutionary Soldier." COL-
        LECTOR, 63 (1950), 198-201, 223-225, 247-249.

        Colomb, a French officer who served in the southern cam-
        paigns, was imprisoned on a British vessel.

1716. Cromot du Bourg, Marie Francois Joseph Maxime, Comte de.
        "Diary of a French Officer, 1781." MAG AMER HIST, 4 (1880),
        205-14, 293-308, 376-385, 441-452; 7 (1881), 283-295.

        Written by Rochambeau's aide, this account has perceptive
        material about the sailing of the expedition from Brest to
        Newport. There are interesting insights here about the ad-
        justment of French troops to American society. The maps are

excellent, and the passages about the march to the Elk River, Maryland and to Yorktown are colorful.

1717.   D'Auberteuil, Hillard. "List of French Officers Who Served in the American Army with Commissions From Congress Prior to the Treaties Made Between France and the United States of America." MAG AMER HIST, 3 (1879), 364-369.

There are scores of virtually unknown French volunteers on this list.

1718.   D'Estaing, Comte. "General Orders at the Siege of Savannah." MAG AMER HIST, 1 (1877), 548-551.

The French admiral acted as a military commander as these directives indicate.

1719.   Deux Ponts, Guillaume, Comte de. MY CAMPAIGN IN AMERICA: A JOURNAL, 1780-1781. Translated with notes by Samuel Abbot Green. Boston: J.K. Wiggin and William Parsons Lunt, 1868.

Although Deux Ponts was not a gifted writer, his comments about life at Newport and Yorktown, particularly during the final siege, are valuable. The information about staff operations is helpful.

1720.   Du Coudry, Comte de. "Du Coudry's 'Observations on the Forts Intended for the Defense of the Two Passages of the Delaware', July 1777." PA MHB, 24 (1960), 343-347.

As an engineer, De Coudry made penetrating comments about the state of the American preparations to defend the Delaware from British attacks.

1721.   Echeverria, Durand, and Orville T. Murphy. "The American Revolutionary Army: A French Estimate in 1777." MILT AFF, 27 (1963), 153-162.

Probably composed by a French artillery officer (Louis de Recicourt de Garnot), this is an excellent commentary about the strengths and weaknesses of the American forces as perceived by a professional European soldier, particularly matters of morale and discipline.

1722.   Forbes, Allen. "Marches and Camp Sites of the French Army in New England during the Revolutionary War." MASS HIST SOC PROC, 58 (1925), 267-285; 67 (1941-44), 152-167.

This is a rather amusing and very detailed commentary about the march of Rochambeau's army from Rhode Island to Virginia. The information on the aftermath of Yorktown and the maps are dependable.

1723.   Gallatin, Gabriel Gaspard, Baron de. JOURNAL OF THE SIEGE OF YORKTOWN. UNPUBLISHED JOURNAL OF THE SIEGE OF YORKTOWN

IN 1781, OPERATED BY THE GENERAL STAFF OF THE FRENCH ARMY,
AS RECORDED IN THE HAND OF GASPARD DE GALLATIN. 71st Cong.,
3rd sess., Sen. Doc. no 322. Washington, DC: GPO, 1931.

Here is an excellent source of information about the land
operations against Cornwallis on the Virginia coast. It contains data about unit locations, battle lines, daily events
in the fighting, and about cooperative measures performed with
the American forces.

1724.   ———. "With Rochambeau at Newport, the Narrative of Baron
        Gaspard de Gallatin." Translated by Warrington Dawson,
        FRANCO-AMER REV, 1 (1937), 330-340.

        Here is a charming account of the landing at Newport by the
        French expedition, the Baron's impression of Indians, descrip-
        tions of actions at sea, and a trip to Peekskill, New York.

1725.   Gottschalk, Louis. "The Attitude of European Officers in the
        Revolutionary Army Toward General George Washington." J ILL
        STATE HIST SOC, 32 (1939), 20-30.

        Among the view of many foreign officers cited here, only
        Duportail, Lafayette, and von Steuben praised Washington as
        a commander.

1726.   Idzerda, Stanley J., ed. LAFAYETTE IN THE AGE OF THE AMERICAN
        REVOLUTION. SELECTED LETTERS AND PAPERS, 1776-1790. Ithaca,
        New York: Cornell University Press, 1977- . 3 vols. to
        date.

        This projected six-volume series contains the correspondence
        of the romantic, young French nobleman to his wife, Washing-
        ton, John Adams, Henry Laurens and scores of contemporary
        dignitaries in the French-American alliance. There are many
        new letters in this collection as well as valuable commen-
        taries about Lafayette by third parties. This is an invaluable
        and revealing commentary about the famous soldier who bridged
        two worlds, and who had a key role in promoting Bourbon inter-
        vention in the war. Volume 3 carries the story to December,
        1781 after Lafayette's gallant Virginia campaign. Although
        reviewers have lamented the lack of biographical data, descrip-
        tive information, and, laconic footnotes, these volumes meet
        the highest standards of editing and scholarship. The ap-
        pendices of French text add another dimension to this excel-
        lent work.

1727.   Jones, Charles C., Jr., trans. and ed. SIEGE OF SAVANNAH IN
        1779. AS DESCRIBED IN TWO CONTEMPORARY JOURNALS OF FRENCH
        OFFICERS IN THE FLEET OF COUNT D'ESTAING. Albany, New York:
        J. Munsell, 1874.

        One account of the aborted assault on Savannah was by
        d'Estaing himself. The other, which provides a slightly dif-
        ferent view of the problems, was written by an anonymous staff
        officer.

1728. Kennett, Lee, ed. and trans. "A French Report on St. Augustine
       in the 1770's." FLA HIST Q, 44 (1965), 133-35.

       Written by an unknown French officer sometime in 1778-79,
       this document suggests how to storm the British fortress.

1729. ————. THE FRENCH FORCES IN AMERICA, 1780-1783. Westport,
       Connecticut: Greenwood Press, 1977.

       There are many strengths and some weaknesses in this book.
       Most of the material concerns the French army; there is very
       little on the navy. The author barely mentions d'Estaing's
       fiascos in 1777-78 on the American coast, and there is little
       here about the decisive Battle of the Capes and the siege of
       Yorktown. However, while not a definitive work, this book
       demonstrates that the French forces were not the best units
       that France had available, that d'Estaing, Ternay, and Barras
       were difficult allies for the Americans, and that Rochambeau
       was a fine and cooperative soldier for Washington. It is the
       best brief summary of the French military available, and it is
       quite readable.

1730. ————. THE FRENCH ARMIES IN THE SEVEN YEARS WARS: A STUDY
       OF MILITARY ORGANIZATION AND ADMINISTRATION. Durham, North
       Carolina: Duke University Press, 1957.

       This is the best study in English of how the Bourbon army
       of France functioned. It is deftly written, well-organized,
       and it contains a wealth of information about army units, some
       of which later served with the Yankees. The bibliography and
       footnotes are extensive.

1731. Leighton, Robert ed. "Meyronnet de Saint-Marc's Journal of
       the Operations of the French Army under d'Estaing at the
       Siege of Savannah, 1779." NY HIST SOC Q, 36 (1952), 255-
       287.

       This is a very colorful and valuable description of the
       aborted siege of Savannah by the American-French forces under
       General Benjamin Lincoln and d'Estaing.

1732. Lopez, Claude A. "Benjamin Franklin, Lafayette, and the
       LAFAYETTE." AMER PHIL SOC PROC, 108 (1964), 181-223.

       Franklin and Lafayette secured a ship to transport military
       supplies to America.

1733. Magallon, de la Morliere, Louis Antoine, Chevalier de. "A
       French Account of the Siege of Charleston, 1780." Edited
       by Richard K. Murdoch. SC HIST MAG, 67 (1961), 138-154.

       Morliere's journal from February 21 to May 12, 1780 provides
       a vivid description of the siege and suggests why Lincoln was
       defeated.

1734. Morgan, Marshall. "Alexander Berthier's Journal of the
       American Campaign: The Rhode Island Sections." RI HIST,
       24 (1965), 77-88.

       This essay is a translation of a portion of Berthier's
       memoir which describes conditions at Newport with particular
       attention to the dangers poised by the Royal Navy.

1735. Murdock, Richard K. "A Note on 'A French Account of the Siege
       of Charleston, 1780'." SC HIST MAG, 67 (1966), 138-154;
       68 (1968), 57-83.

       Murdock amplifies a contemporary description of the battle with
       some additional data about the British attack on the city.

1736. Murphy, Orville T. "The French Professional Soldier's Opinion
       of the American Militia in the War of the Revolution." MILT
       AFFAIRS, 32 (1969), 191-198.

       While highly critical of the American forces, especially the
       militia, this perceptive report was not a decisive factor in
       the French court's desire for an American military alliance.

1737. Murphy, W.S. "The Irish Brigade of France at the Siege of
       Savannah, 1779." IRISH SWORD, 2 (1955), 95-102.

       Along with biographical data about some Irishmen serving
       France, this commentary has useful summaries about the tactics
       used by the brigade in fighting.

1738. Prelinger, Catherine M. "Less Lucky Than Lafayette: A Note
       on the French Applications to Benjamin Franklin for Com-
       missions in the American Army, 1776-1783." PROC WEST SOC
       FR HIST, 4 (1976), 263-271.

       In 1776 Franklin received 321 applications for service in
       America; he supported those candidates with influential
       sponsors.

1739. Quimby, Robert S. THE BACKGROUND OF NAPOLEONIC WARFARE: THE
       THEORY OF MILITARY TACTICS IN EIGHTEENTH CENTURY FRANCE.
       New York: Columbia University Press, 1957.

       Although this fine monograph concentrates on theories of
       warfare that evolved during the French Revolution, it is clear
       that long before 1789 military specialists were discussing new
       uses of the column and line in battle and the role of the
       artillery and irregular corps. Whether the French theorists
       were influenced by the performance of the Bourbon army in
       America during the Revolution, however, is not clear.

1740. Rice, Howard C. Jr., and Anne S.K. Brown, trans, and eds.
       THE AMERICAN CAMPAIGNS OF ROCHAMBEAU'S ARMY, 1780, 1781,
       1782, 1783. 2 vols. Princeton, Providence: Princeton
       University Press, 1972.

This is the best single source on the French military
campaigns. Volume one contains the superbly edited journals
of the Comte de Clearmont-Crevecoeur, J.-B.-A. de Verger,
and Louis-Alexandre Berthier. Volume two, with splendid maps,
illustrations and much topographical data about the line of
marches, covers the itineraries by land and sea of the French
army on the march from Providence to Yorktown.

1741. Ricketts, Rowland, Jr. "The French in Lebanon, 1780-1781."
       CONN HIST SOC BULL, 26 (1971), 42-58.

       About 200 French troops were stationed in a Connecticut
       village used to protect Newport and to collect provisions.

1742. Stember, Sal. "EN EVANT with our French Allies to Yorktown
       Victory." SMITHSONIAN, 8 (1977), 64-70.

       This is a lucid description for the general reader of the
       march and camp sites of the march of Rochambeau's 4,000
       troops from Newport, past Manhattan, and onto Williamsburg,
       Virginia in 108 days.

1743. Stevens, John A. "The French in Rhode Island." MAG AMER HIST,
       3 (1879), 385-436.

       While somewhat outdated, this is a well-documented and use-
       ful general account of the French presence at Newport during
       the war citing the quarters of French officers.

1744. Stone, Edward Martin. OUR FRENCH ALLIES ... IN THE GREAT
       WAR OF THE AMERICAN REVOLUTION FROM 1778 TO 1782 ...
       Providence, Rhode Island: Providence Press, 1884.

       This is a voluminous and detailed treatment of both military
       and naval operations at Rhode Island. There is material here
       about social life, the march to Yorktown and innumerable docu-
       ments relating to Lafayette, Rochambeau, D'Estaing, De Ternay,
       Barras, and De Grasse.

1745. Whitbridge, Arnold. "La Fayette Goes to America." HIST TODAY,
       20 (1970), 527-533.

       Here is the tale of the ardent young nobleman sailing from
       Bordeaux to join the American cause in April, 1777.

1746. ———. "Two Aristocrats in Rochambeau's Army." VA Q R, 40
       (1964), 114-121.

       The essayist notes that the relatively forgotten Chevalier
       de Chastellux and the Duc de Lauzen made significant contri-
       butions to the American cause.

1747. ———. "Washington's French Volunteers." HIST TODAY, 24
       (1924), 593-603.

       LaFayette had some eighty French officers with him,
       particularly Baron de Kalb.

1748. Woodridge, George. "Rochambeau: Two Hundred Years Later."
       NEWPORT HIST, 53 (1980), 5-21.

       This is a summary of the French general's command in 1780-81.

1749. Wright, Esmond. "Lafayette: Hero of Two Worlds." HIST TODAY,
       7 (1957), 653-661.

       The author provides a fine summary of Lafayette's back-
       ground, his role in the Revolution, and as a symbol of Franco-
       American friendship.

                            B. THE FRENCH NAVY

1750. Anderson, R.C. "French Masts and Spars in 1780." MM, 45
       (1980), 224-226.

       The huge MAJESTEAUX built at Toulon in 1780 had 110 guns.

1751. Borome, Joseph A. "Dominica During the French Occupation,
       1778-1784." ENG HIST REV, 84 (1969), 36-58.

       This is a good discussion of how the French ruled a captured
       West Indian island.

1752. Boudriot, Jean. "The French Fleet During the War of Independ-
       ence." Translated by H. Bartlett Wells.   NAUT RES J, 25
       (1969), 79-86.

       The French navy experienced a remarkable regeneration in the
       1770's.

1753. Bowles, Francis T. "America's Debt to De Grasse." MASS HIST
       SOC PROC, 60 (1927), 235-250.

       Here is an undocumented essay about the famous French admi-
       ral that high school students could appreciate.

1754. Brown, Gerald S. "The Anglo-French Naval Crisis, 1778: A
       Study of Conflict in the North Cabinet." WMQ, 13 (1956),
       3-25.

       The Revolution became a global war when France entered the
       war; the Battle of Ushant caused a crisis in the British
       government.

1755. Cavaliero, Raymond. "Admiral Suffren in the Indies." HIST
       TODAY, 20 (1970), 472-481.

       Suffren, the French Nelson, fought five relatively indecisive
       battles in eighteen months off the coast of India.

1756. Chenevix, Trench R.B. "An Eighteenth Century Invasion Alarm."
       HIST TODAY, 6 (1956), 457-465.

A French-Spanish expedition against the British Channel
fleet was thwarted by winds, the weather, and by the superior
tactics of the Royal Navy.

1757. Dillon, Philip R. "The Strange Case of Admiral de Grasse, For-
        gotten by France and America." PA MHB, 51 (1927), 193-206.

        The author claimed that the famous sailor has been over-
        looked by historians.

1758. Dull, Jonathan R. THE FRENCH NAVY AND AMERICAN INDEPENDENCE:
        A STUDY OF ARMS AND DIPLOMACY, 1774-1787. Princeton:
        Princeton University Press, 1975.

        Dull wrote the most comprehensive study of French naval
        power. It is crammed with penetrating insights about the
        rise of the French navy after the Seven Years War, information
        about budgets and shipbuilding, biographical data about numer-
        ous dignitaries, and it is full of valuable statistical data.
        Though the volume is tedious reading, it provides a fine
        picture of French squadrons operating in North America, the
        West Indies, the Mediterranean, and India. Clearly, the
        French navy was the decisive factor in defeating the British.
        Based on exhaustive research, this work is recommended for
        specialists.

1759. Knox, Dudley W. "D'Estaing's Fleet Revealed." USNIP, 61
        (1935), 153-188.

        A French artist made six drawings of the fleet in action in
        1778.

1760. Lewis, Charles L. ADMIRAL DE GRASSE AND AMERICAN INDEPENDENCE.
        Annapolis: U.S. Naval Institute, 1945.

        Though difficult to read, this detailed treatment provides
        a fine perspective of De Grasse, the symbol of French naval
        power. Though the narrative lacks color and drama, it is a
        thoughtful presentation of the admiral who checked the British
        fleet at the Virginia Capes. The maps of the sea-fights are
        excellent.

1761. McGuffie, Tom W. THE SIEGE OF GIBRALTAR, 1779-1783.
        Philadelphia: Dufour, 1965.

        This is an admirable and very readable account of the French-
        Spanish attempts to capture the British bastion. McGuffie
        wrote an excellent summary about the complex blockade opera-
        tions, the Royal Navy's yearly provisioning of the fortress,
        conditions at Gibraltar during the siege, and other actions
        in the Mediterranean. The study is a fine counterbalance to
        the typical emphasis placed on North America by American
        historians. The author demonstrated that Spain entered the
        war mainly to recover Gibraltar, that the French had to con-
        tribute ships and men, and that the siege took a heavier toll
        of men than any other campaign in the Revolution.

1762. Moran, Charles. "D'Estaing, an Early Exponent of Amphibious
       Warfare." MILT AFF, 9 (1945), 314-332.

       This solider-sailor experimented in landing troops for
       battles in the West Indies during the war.

1763. ————. "Suffren, the Apostle of Action." USNIP, 64 (1938),
       315-325.

       Here is a good summary about Suffren's activities off Rhode
       Island and in the Indian Ocean.

1764. Patterson, Alfred T. THE OTHER ARMADA: THE FRANCO-SPANISH
       ATTEMPT TO INVADE BRITAIN IN 1779. Manchester, England:
       Manchester University Press, 1960.

       Patterson wrote a heavily documented account about the huge
       fleet that was destined to land troops for an invasion of
       England. The author explained the intricacies of diplomacy
       between France and Spain, the importance of Gibraltar to
       Madrid, and the difficulties of this doomed maritime collabo-
       ration. As the author stresses, the British held the Channel
       and outmaneuvered the poorly-captained and disease-wracked
       enemy vessels. This work is highly recommended for specialists
       and graduate students.

1765. Scott, H.M. "The Importance of Bourbon Naval Reconstruction
       to the Strategy of Choiseul After the Seven Years War."
       INTER HIST REV, 1 (1979), 17-35.

       Anxious for revenge after her defeat by the British, France
       concentrated on regenerating her navy.

1766. Sherman, Constance A., ed. and trans. "Journal of the 1781,
       1782, and 1783 Campaigns on the Royal Ship HERCULES." NY
       HIST SOC Q, 61 (1977), 7-48.

       A French officer left a fine narrative about the 74-gun ves-
       sel at Yorktown and the West Indies.

1767. Syrett, David. "D'Estaing's Decision to Steer for Antiqua,
       20 November, 1779." MM, 61 (1975), 155-162.

       Instead of sailing to the Indies, D'Estaing should have
       attacked a British convoy from New York.

1768. Taylor, A.H. "The French Fleet in the Channel." MM, 24
       (1938), 275-288.

       Admiral Sir Charles Hardy's ships managed to elude a French
       fleet.

1769. Tournquist, Carl G. THE NAVAL CAMPAIGN OF COUNT DE GRASSE
       DURING THE AMERICAN REVOLUTION, 1781-1783. Translated by
       Amandus Johnson. Philadelphia: The Swedish Colonial Society,
       1942.

Tourquist was a Swedish naval officer who volunteered for
French service. He was on De Grasse's staff aboard the
VALIANT and wrote an absorbing account of his life at sea and
the engagements he witnessed.

1770. Yeager, Henry J., trans. "The French Fleet at Newport, 1780-
81." RI HIST, 30 (1971), 87-93.

The article covers a portion of the memoir of Chevalier de
Villebresme who sailed with Ternay, Destouches, and Barras.

VI. THE BRITISH ARMY

A. BACKGROUND

1771. Atkinson, C.T. "British Forces in North America, 1774-1781:
Their Distribution and Strength." JSAHR, 16 (1937), 3-23;
19 (1940), 163-166; 20 (1941), 190-192.

This is a convenient summary of the disposition of British
regiments, along with provincial units and German auxiliaries,
during the war.

1772. Barnett, Correlli. BRITAIN AND HER ARMY, 1509-1970. New
York: William Morrow and Co., 1970.

Though a small portion of this concise, and well-written
summary covers the Revolution, it provides a fine portrayal
of the customs and traditions of George III's army.

1773. Beers, Henry P. "British Commanders in Chief in North America,
1754-1783." MILT AFFAIRS, 13 (1949), 79-84.

Here is a useful list of thirteen commanders in this era and
the location of their personal papers.

1774. Clode, Charles M. THE MILITARY FACES OF THE CROWN: THEIR AD-
MINISTRATION AND GOVERMENT. 2 vols. London: John Murray,
1869.

This work is still the best source for the administration
of the eighteenth-century army. The chapters are difficult
to read, yet the information about the operations of the War
Office, the various Secretaries of State, recruitment policies,
budgetary matters, relations with the Cabinet, Parliament, the
Crown as well as other branches of government is useful. The
material about appointments, promotions, military justice, and
traditions of the army is invaluable.

1775. Curtis, Edward E. THE ORGANIZATION OF THE BRITISH ARMY IN THE
AMERICAN REVOLUTION. New Haven: Yale University Press, 1926.

Until recently, this was the best general source of information on the army. It has detailed chapters about the components of the army, the combat units, the auxiliary forces
along with data about commissions, recruiting, and regimental
strengths. Written in a crisp, coherent style, this work is
worth consulting to comprehend the British war machine.

267

1776. Davies, R.G., ed. DOCUMENTS OF THE AMERICAN REVOLUTION, 1770-
       1783. (Colonial Office Series), 21 vols. Dublin: Irish
       University Press, 1979.

       These summarized transcripts of Colonial Office manuscripts
       in the Public Record Office, London, provide an enormous
       amount of information about British military activities. Much
       concerns correspondence between British generals and Crown
       officials but the documents cover such a range of administra-
       tive detail that this series is an invaluable source for a
       comprehension of the British war administration. The index
       is excellent.

1777. Fortescue, J.W. A HISTORY OF THE BRITISH ARMY. 13 vols.
       London: Macmillan and Co., 1935.

       Fortescue wrote the classic and still unsurpassed history of
       the army covering the 1660-1918 era. Volume 3 covers the
       Revolution in incredible detail and with deep insight that
       has been difficult to match. To understand the mentality of
       British generals, this is the work to ponder.

1778. Fuller, J.F.C. BRITISH LIGHT INFANTRY IN THE EIGHTEENTH
       CENTURY. London: Hutchinson and Co., 1925.

       Written by one of England's top military historians, this
       is a solid account which demonstrates how the standard regi-
       mental line was adapted to environmental conditions in Europe,
       India, and America. By Bunker Hill, the British were not
       novices in the use of light companies which were used for
       many purposes. This volume is remarkable for demonstrating
       how theories about tactics were implemented in the field,
       particularly in a manual used during the French Revolutionary
       era.

1779. MacLennon, Alastair. "Highland Regiments in North America,
       1756-1783." FORT TIC MUS BULL, 12 (1966), 119-127.

       This is a useful list of Scottish regiments, their com-
       manders, and their battle records in North America.

1780. Marshall, Douglas, W. "The British Engineers in America,
       1775-1783." JSAHR, 51 (1973), 155-163.

       Here is a valuable account of a professional corps – in-
       volved in building bridges, redoubts, and fortresses – which
       had an anamalous position in the army.

1781. Paret, Peter. "Colonial Experience and European Military
       Reform at the End of the Eighteenth Century." BULL INST
       HIST RES, 37 (1964), 47-59.

       Here is a thoughtful article demonstrating that the British
       army did modify its tactics and formations on the basis of
       overseas experiences.

1782.   Pearson, Michael. THOSE DAMNED REBELS, THE AMERICAN REVOLU-
        TION AS SEEN THROUGH BRITISH EYES. New York: G.P. Putnam's
        Sons, 1972.

        This is a rather naive and one-sided view of the war that
        has numerous mistakes in the narrative. Except for recap-
        turing the spirit of hostility by British toward Americans
        in an unintentionally amusing manner, the author has not
        compiled a coherent description of the British military.

1783.   Robson, Eric. "British Light Infantry in the Mid-Eighteenth
        Century, the Effect of American Conditions." ARMY Q, 63
        (1952), 200-222.

        Every regiment ususally had a light company that was gen-
        erally armed with rifles.

1784.   ————. "The Armed Forces and the Art of War." In THE OLD
        REGIME, 1713-1740. Edited by J.O. Lindsay. Cambridge:
        Cambridge University Press, 1957, pp. 163-190.

        Robson wrote a brilliant summation about the relatively
        static nature of warfare in an era when the military stressed
        the importance of disciplined troops, armed with muskets and
        bayonets.

1785.   ————. "The Raising of a Regiment in the War of American
        Independence." JSAHR, 27 (1949), 107-115.

        This is a valuable perspective on how men were recruited for
        service, and how economic conditions influenced enlistments.

1786.   Rogers, H.C.B. THE BRITISH ARMY OF THE EIGHTEENTH CENTURY.
        London: Allen & Unwin, 1977.

        The author attempts to eradicate the typical view that the
        British regiments were composed of society's misfits who were
        brutally disciplined by aristocratic officers. The book is
        useful for information about recruiting, training, and ad-
        ministration from the 1750s thru the Revolution. High school
        students and undergraduates might enjoy this work.

1787.   Russell, Peter E. "Redcoats in the Wilderness: British Of-
        ficers and Irregular Warfare in Europe and America, 1740-
        1760." WMQ, 35 (1978), 629-652.

        British officers experienced in fighting the Scots during
        the 1740's applied guerrilla methods in the French and Indian
        War.

1788.   Savory, Reginald. HIS BRITANNIC MAJESTY'S ARMY IN GERMANY
        DURING THE SEVEN YEARS' WAR. Oxford: Clarendon Press, 1976.

        This is meticulously researched volume for specialists.
        It provides excellent coverage of the major campaigns in the

270

Germanies, Lowlands, and in Portugal. There is much information here about the organization and administration of the British army that pertains to the American Revolution.

1789. Shy, John. TOWARD LEXINGTON: THE ROLE OF THE BRITISH ARMY IN THE COMING OF THE REVOLUTION. Princeton: Princeton University Press, 1965.

This is a sophisticated treatment of an important theme – the institutional impact of the British army on a civilian population. Shy demonstrates that the army had a multitude of functions, that it was commanded by men of varying abilities, that many British officers had land and mercantile interests in America, that some of them married into American families, and that the army was deeply influenced by politics. The material on how the army was distributed on the continent, and how it was used to maintain order is quite perceptive. The writing style is turgid and plodding but the data is rewarding.

1790. Stedman, Charles. THE HISTORY OF THE ORIGINS, PROGRESS, AND TERMINATION OF THE AMERICAN WAR. 2 vols. London: John Murray, 1794.

Stedman served under Generals Howe, Clinton, and Cornwallis. He provided a unique and reasonably impartial account of the phases of the war that he witnessed. This is a valuable contemporary source about decisions made at headquarters.

1791. Young, Peter and J.P. Lawford, ed. HISTORY OF THE BRITISH ARMY. New York: G.P. Putnams' Sons, 1970.

Chapter nine on the Revolution is a concise and well-illustrated summary of George III's army. This is basically an outline history written in simple terms about men and conditions of war by numerous experts. The book is useful for undergraduates.

B. STRATEGY

1792. Fyers, Evan W.H. "General Sir William Howe's Operations in Pennsylvania, 1777." JSAHR, 8 (1929), 228-241.

The author examines the reasons for Howe's strategy in aiming at Philadelphia, a campaign that may have cost him the war.

1793. Gee, Olive. "The British War Office in the Later Years of the American War of Independence." J MOD HIST, 26 (1954),

Under Charles Jenkinson, Secretary of War (1778-82), and General Jeffrey Amherst, the War Office demonstrated an unusual degree of efficiency.

1794.   Gruber, Ira D.   "British Southern Strategy."   See   414,
        pp. 205-238.

        The British plans reconquering the south were doomed long
        before Yorktown because of the lack of Loyalist support.

1795.   ————.   "British Strategy: The Theory and Practice of
        Eighteenth-Century Warfare."   See 855, pp. 14-31.

        This is a good summary of the military doctrine held by
        professional soldiers and why it was a factor in the British
        defeat.

1796.   ————.   "Lord Howe and Lord George Germain: British Poli-
        tics and the Winning of American Independence."   WMQ, 22
        (1965), 225-243.

        General Howe and the Colonial Secretary quarreled about
        strategy; not until Howe was recalled in 1777, did Britain
        really face the realities of the war.

1797.   Kyte, George W.   "Plans for the Reconquest of the Rebellious
        Colonies in America, 1775-1783."   HISTORIAN, 10 (1948), 101-
        117.

        Lord Germain pondered numerous schemes to win the war in-
        cluding one to use the Chesapeake as a base of operations.

1798.   Mackesey, Piers.   "British Strategy in the War of American
        Independence."   YALE REV, 52 (1963), 539-557.

        Noting how often the Americans were defeated, Mackesey notes
        that victory came by attrition, by inept British generalship,
        the dependence on the navy, and the entry of France and Spain
        into the war.

1799.   ————.   "The Redcoat Revived."   In William L. Fowler Jr., ed.
        PERSPECTIVES ON THE AMERICAN REVOLUTION.   Boston: North-
        eastern University Press, 1979, pp. 82-98.

        By the 1780's the British had overcome earlier administrative
        intertia in military affairs and deficiencies in generalship
        that had impeded victory.   They were winning in the south;
        the American allies were close to peace but Parliament by
        late 1781 lost the determination to continue the struggle.
        This is a perceptive study.

1800.   ————.   THE WAR FOR AMERICA, 1775-1783.   Cambridge, Massachu-
        setts: Cambridge University Press, 1965.

        This masterly work is the best study of the British military
        and naval strategy of the war.   Based on vast documentation,
        the author demonstrates the administrative machinery of the
        armed forces, the problems of conducting a large war overseas,
        the difficulties in mobilizing armies, acquiring provisions,

and in preparing fleets. Macksey has a remarkable grasp of
military and maritime operations underway simultaneously in
numerous theaters of war, and he astutely notes how British
politics and personalities were factors in decision-making.
This is much detail on relatively unknown operations, much
information on the impact of the French-Spanish-Dutch navies
on hampering the British war effort, and the squabbles of
generals, admirals and cabinets. With the war a global one,
a Yorktown was inevitable as Britain could no longer stretch
her limited resources to protect her colonies. Nothing
written by an American historian can match the scope of this
work.

1801.   Skaggs, David Curtis. "Lexington to Cuddalore: British
        Strategy." MILT REV, 56 (1976), 41-55.

        For a concise summary of the war in North America, the
        Caribbean, Europe, and India, this essay is useful.

1802.   Willcox, William B. "British Strategy in America, 1778."
        J MOD HIST, 19 (1947), 97-121.

        The British rarely systematically studied their strategic
        options; instead they improvisioned, counted on luck, and
        consequently, contending with the French navy after 1778,
        British planning became more vulnerable to failures.

1803.   ———. "Too Many Cooks: British Planning Before Saratoga."
        J BRIT STUD, 2 (1962), 56-90.

        Burgoyne's campaign of 1777 was doomed because of the
        intellectual limitations of generals, lack of logistical sup-
        port, and the clashes of personalities.

1804.   Van Alstyne, Richard W. "Great Britain, the War for Indepen-
        dence, and the 'Gathering Storm' in Europe, 1775-1778."
        HUNT LIB Q, 27 (1964), 311-346.

        The British were well informed of European aid to the
        Americans, and by late 1777 the war had assumed global pro-
        portions as France prepared to fight.

                C.   CAMPAIGNS AND BATTLES: THE NORTH

1805.   Ainslie, Thomas. CANADA PRESERVED; THE JOURNAL OF CAPTAIN
        THOMAS AINSLIE. Edited by Sheldon S. Cohen. New York:
        New York University Press, 1969.

        Ainslie, Collector of Customs for Quebec, aptly describes
        the American threat to Canada, December, 1775 to May, 1776.
        Unfortunately, though this is a handsome volume and Ainslee's
        Anglophobe views are interesting, the work is poorly edited,
        and it ignores many recent studies about the American invasion.

1806. Allaire, Anthony. DIARY OF LIEUT. ANTHONY ALLAIRE. 1881.
       Reprint. New York: Arno Press, 1968.

       The diary was originally published by Lyman C. Draper. The
       value of the document is its view of fighting in the Carolina
       backcountry with Major Patrick Fergusson's Loyalist corps.

1807. Anbury, Thomas. TRAVELS THROUGH THE INTERIOR PART OF AMERICA.
       1923. Reprint. New York: Arno Press, 1969.

       Published in 1789, in London this is a detailed account of
       the Burgoyne expedition in Canada, at Saratoga, and of a
       captive army. There are numerous insights here about French-
       Canadian mores and customs in Quebec. Unfortunately, about
       half the book was plagiarized from such sources as the ANNUAL
       REGISTER.

1808. Anderson, Troyer Steele. THE COMMAND OF THE HOWE BROTHERS
       DURING THE AMERICAN REVOLUTION. New York: Oxford Univer-
       sity Press, 1936.

       Though based on limited documentary evidence, this is a
       well-written account of the famous team of general and ad-
       miral who were frustrated in their efforts to defeat Washing-
       ton in 1776-77. It is a carefully reasoned study that is
       worth consulting.

1809. Andre, John. MAJOR ANDRE'S JOURNAL. Edited by Henry Cabot
       Lodge. 1903. Reprint. New York: Arno Press, 1968.

       Andre, a ranking staff officer, wrote fine descriptions of
       operations from New York under Generals Howe and Clinton,
       June, 1777 to November, 1778.

1810. Balderston, Marion. "Lord Howe Clears the Delaware." PA MHB,
       96 (1972), 326-345.

       The seemingly foolish error of invading Pennsylvania in 1777
       via the Chesapeake and not by the Delaware was committed by
       Admiral Howe, not General Howe.

1811. Bamford, William. "Bamford's Diary: Diary of the Revolution-
       ary Days of a British Officer." MD HIST MAG, 27 (1932),
       240-259, 296-314.

       Captain Bamford abbreviated his written observations, but
       his comments about service in 1776 at Boston, Halifax, Staten
       Island, and Manhattan are worthwhile.

1812. Barker, John. THE BRITISH IN BOSTON, BEING THE DIARY OF
       LIEUTENANT JOHN BARKER OF THE KING'S OWN REGIMENT FROM
       NOVEMBER 15, 1774 TO MAY 31, 1776. With notes by Elizabeth
       Ellery Davis. Cambridge: Harvard University Press, 1924.

       Barker wrote a detailed memoir of his service in Boston. He commented on military units, criticized the pay and rations, grumbled about the weather, and sat on courts-martial.

1813. Barnes, Eric W. "All the King's Horses ... And All the King's Men." AMER HERITAGE, 11 (6) (1960), 56-59, 86-87.

British troops at Salem, Massachusetts in February, 1775 caused the shedding of American blood two months before Lexington and Concord.

1814. Baxter, James P., ed. THE BRITISH INVASION FROM THE NORTH – THE CAMPAIGN OF GENERAL CARLETON AND BURGOYNE FROM CANADA, 1776-1776, WITH THE JOURNAL OF WILLIAM DIGBY. 1867. Reprint. New York: De Capo Press, 1942.

This is a perceptive narrative of the British effort to dislodge the Americans from the St. Lawrence, the capture of Fort Ticonderoga, and the battle of Saratoga. The work is improperly edited but the authenticity of events as described by Lieutenant Digby of the 53rd Grenadiers rings true.

1815. Bird, Harrison. MARCH TO SARATOGA: GENERAL BURGOYNE AND THE AMERICAN CAMPAIGN. New York: Oxford University Press, 1963.

Though Bird did little original research on this topic, he compiled a very readable and exciting account of Burgoyne's difficulties. This work is the best popular account of the June to October, 1777 campaign.

1816. Bolton, Charles Knowles, ed. LETTERS OF HUGH PERCY, FROM BOSTON AND NEW YORK, 1774-1776. Boston: Charles L. Goodspeed, 1902.

Percy, a top field commander, wrote lucidly about his fighting experiences. His comments about the march back from Lexington and Concord, and the British attack on Bunker Hill provide a good insight.

1817. Bradford, S. Sydney, ed. "Lord Francis Napier's Journal of the Burgoyne Campaign." MD HIST MAG, 17 (1962), 285-333.

Napier, a Second Lieutenant in the 31st Infantry blames Lord Germain, and particularly, Burgoyne for underestimating the logistical difficulties on the march to the Hudson.

1818. British Army. "Assessment of Damages Done By the British Troops During the Occupation of Philadelphia, 1777-1778." PA MHB, 25 (1901), 323-335, 544-559.

Here is a detailed listing of damages to American property in Philadelphia.

1819. ———. "British, Hessian, and Provisional Troops at Paulus Hook, 18th-19th August, 1779." JSAHR, 45 (1967), 177-183.

This summary of troops stationed at the outpost in New
Jersey corrects previous descriptions about the units garrisoned there.

1820. ————. "Journal of the Most Remarkable Occurrences in Quebec,
       1775-1776." NY HIST SOC COLL, 13 (1880), 173-236.

       An unknown officer of the British garrison wrote a fine
       description of the siege of Quebec, disease, privations,
       and the defeat of the Americans on the St. Lawrence.

1821. Burgoyne, John. A STUDY OF THE EXPEDITION FROM CANADA, AS
       LAID BEFORE THE HOUSE OF COMMONS. London, 1780. Reprint.
       New York: Arno Press, 1969.

       Here is Burgoyne's own testimony before Parliament. He
       tried to defend his conduct of the campaign by blaming faulty
       communications, topographical difficulties, personality clashes
       with ministers, and inept coordination with General Howe.
       It includes revealing correspondence, war plans, and detailed
       maps.

1822. ————. ORDERLY BOOK OF LT. GEN. JOHN BURGOYNE. Edited by
       E.B. O'Callaghan. New York: J. Munsell, 1860.

       This is an authentic reproduction of Burgoyne's orders from
       his preparations at Quebec to his defeat at Saratoga. There
       is abundant information here about Indian relations, the
       sailing of his fleet, the movements of the troops to
       Ticonderoga, and the march to the Hudson. The material about
       Councils of War held with staff reveals valuable data.

1823. Burns, Brian. "Massacre or Muster? Burgoyne's Indians and
       Militia at Bennington." VT HIST, 45 (1977), 133-144.

       In a good summary of Burgoyne's warning to American set-
       tlers and his control over Indian allies, the author denies
       any link between the murder of Jane McCrea and the mobiliza-
       tion of western New England militia to the Hudson by July 1777.

1824. Burt, A.L. "The Quarrel Between Germain and Carleton: An
       Invented Story." CAN HIST REV, 11 (1938), 202-230.

       The grudge developed as a result of Germain's combat per-
       formance at Minden, and because of Carleton's ill-temper, and
       the patronage over civil and military appointments in Canada.

1825. Carter, Clarence E., ed. THE CORRESPONDENCE OF GENERAL THOMAS
       GAGE WITH THE SECRETARIES OF STATE, 1763-1775. 2 vols. New
       Haven, Connecticut: Yale University Press, 1931-1933.

       Head-quartered in Manhattan until 1773 as commander-in-chief
       and later in Boston, Gage had a fine vantage point to gather
       information from subordinates stationed throughout the colonies.
       His comments to the ministers about events in New York, espe-
       cially about the Stamp Act, are illuminating.

1826.   Clark, Jane.   "Responsibility for the Failure of the Burgoyne
        Campaign." AHR, 35 (1930), 542-559.

        Burgoyne merits only part of the blame for communication de-
        lays. The independent commands of Howe and Carleton were
        also factors.

1827.   ———. "The Command of the Canadian Army for the Campaign
        of 1777." CAN HIST REV. 10 (1729), 129-135.

        This is a key article about a famous jurisdictional dis-
        pute, involving Howe and Clinton, that had major ramifications
        for Burgoyne at Saratoga.

1828.   Clinton, Sir Henry. PROCEEDINGS OF A BOARD OF GENERAL OF-
        FICERS OF THE BRITISH ARMY AT NEW YORK, 1781. Vol. 49.
        New York Historical Society Collections. New York: The
        Society, 1916.

        Convened by Sir Henry Clinton when he assumed command of
        British forces in the rebellious colonies, the Board com-
        piled muster rolls of troops, lists of civilians within the
        British occupied area, and names of vessels in and around
        New York City.

1829.   ———. THE AMERICAN REBELLION. SIR HENRY CLINTON'S NAR-
        RATIVE OF HIS CAMPAIGNS, 1775-1782. Edited by William B.
        Willcox. New Haven, Connecticut: Yale University Press,
        1954.

        This is one of the best sources about the British military
        in America for it contains an intimate description of how
        Clinton formulated his strategy and his relationships with
        his superiors and subordinates. Written in an attempt to
        redeem his military leadership, Clinton was quite blunt in
        his appraisal of mistakes made by others. Here is a fine,
        readable edition of Clinton's correspondence with additional
        letters and memorandums. The volume contains an appendix of
        original documents.

1830.   ———. THE SIEGE OF CHARLESTON BY THE BRITISH FLEET AND
        ARMY UNDER THE COMMAND OF ADMIRAL ARBUTHNOT AND SIR HENRY
        CLINTON WHICH TERMINATED WITH THE SURRENDER OF THAT PLACE
        ON THE 12TH OF MAY, 1780. Albany, New York: J. Munsell,
        1867.

        Here is an invaluable set of documents which illustrates
        the measures taken for the expedition to the Carolinas, the
        progress of the siege, and the degree to which the British
        army and navy cooperated. For a valuable insight into the
        nature of a remarkably successful British victory, this cor-
        respondence is worth consulting.

1831. Cullen, Joseph P. "General William Howe." AMER HIST ILLUS,
       7 (12) (1972), 24-31.

       Features of Howe's character and personality were reflected
       in his strategic blunders during his invasion of Pennsylvania.

1832. Damon, Allan L. "The Melancholy Case of Captain Asgill."
       AMER HERITAGE, 21 (2) (1979), 92-96.

       Asgill, a captured British officer, was nearly hung by
       Washington in reprisal for a British massacre in New Jersey
       in 1782; he was only saved by French intercession.

1833. Danford, Jacob. "Quebec Under Siege, 1775-1776: The 'Memo-
       randums' of Jacob Danford." Edited by John F. Roche, CAN
       HIST REV, 50 (1969), 68-85.

       An artilleryman at the successful defense of Quebec from
       the Arnold-Montgomery assault in December, 1775, Danford
       wrote a very revealing account.

1834. DeFonblanque, Edward Barrington. POLITICAL AND MILITARY
       EPISODES IN THE LATTER HALF OF THE EIGHTEENTH CENTURY, DE-
       RIVED FROM THE LIFE AND CORRESPONDENCE OF THE RIGHT HON
       [ARABLE] JOHN BURGOYNE. 1876. Reprint. New York: Gregg
       Press, 1972.

       This is a lengthy polemic mainly about Burgoyne's career
       in North America. Using Burgoyne's official correspondence
       and family letters, the author made the classic defense of
       the British defeat at Saratoga by blaming inept fellow
       generals, topographical conditions in New York and Canada,
       and poor administration from London.

1835. Eaton, H.R. "Lieutenant-General Patrick Sinclair. An Ac-
       count of His Military Career." JSAHR, 56 (1978), 122-142,
       215-232; 57 (1979), 45-55.

       Here is a fine summary about fighting in the Great Lakes
       area as viewed by a perceptive commander.

1836. Falkner, Leonard. "Capture of the Barefoot General." AMER
       HERITAGE, 11 (5) (1960), 29-31, 98-100.

       American Colonel William Barton made an audacious capture
       of the despotic British general in Newport, Richard Prescott.

1837. Felter, Frank Whitson. "Who Were the Foreign Mercenaries of
       the Declaration of Independence." PA MHB, 104 (1980), 508-
       513.

       The Founding Fathers were enraged at the Scot Highlanders
       garrisoned at Boston, (not the Hessians who arrived in North
       America in late 1776) in their famous condemnation.

1838. Fleming, Thomas J. "The Engima of General Howe." AMER
        HERITAGE, 15 (2) (1964), 6-11.

        Although Howe repeatedly defeated Washington, he was un-
        able to crush the rebellion due to his personality traits and
        to political differences with the ministry.

1839. Glover, Michael. GENERAL BURGOYNE IN CANADA AND AMERICA:
        SCAPEGOAT FOR A SYSTEM. New York: Antheneum, 1976.

        The author vainly attempts to vindicate Burgoyne by placing
        the blame on innumerable generals, politicians, and ministers.
        Glover neglected to examine familiar documents, he offers no
        new evidence, and he adds nothing to a standard story. The
        maps are poor and the footnoting weak. This may be the
        poorest book written about Burgoyne in decades.

1840. Graham, Samuel. "An English Officer's Account of His Ser-
        vices in America, 1779-1781: Memoirs of Lt.-General
        Samuel Graham." HIST MAG, 9 (1865), 241-249, 267-274, 301-
        308.

        As an officer in the 76th Highlanders at New York in
        1780, Graham wrote a valuable account of service under
        Clinton and the expedition to Yorktown.

1841. Gruber, Ira D. THE HOWE BROTHERS AND THE AMERICAN REVOLUTION.
        New York: Antheneum, 1972.

        The author examines the puzzle of why General Sir William
        Howe and Admiral Lord Richard Howe - with all the military
        and naval power at their disposal - were unable to inflict
        decisive defeats on the Americans. This is a fascinating
        account of strategic mistakes, failures of peace negotiations,
        factions in the British Ministry, the lack of logistical sup-
        port to the armed forces in America, and the Howe brothers'
        own personalities. Brilliantly researched and nicely writ-
        ten, this is one of the best monographs on the reasons for
        the British indecisiveness that led to Saratoga and to the
        stalemate in the north.

1842. [Hadden, James M.]. HADDEN'S JOURNAL AND ORDERLY BOOKS. A
        JOURNAL KEPT IN CANADA AND UPON BURGOYNE'S CAMPAIGN IN 1776
        AND 1777 ... WITH AN EXPLANATORY CHAPTER AND NOTES BY
        HORATIO ROGERS. Albany: J. Munsell, 1884.

        This Royal Artillery officer wrote a good terse commentary
        on the Burgoyne expedition that provides abundant data about
        the campaign not ordinarily available elsewhere. It includes
        orders issued by Generals Carleton, Burgoyne, and Phillips.

1843. Hargreaves, Reginald. "Burgoyne and American Destiny."
        AMER HERITAGE, 7 (4) (1956), 4-7, 83-85.

        The writer exaggerates the impact of Burgoyne's defeat at
        Saratoga because the British could still have won the war.

1844. ————. "The Man Who Didn't Shoot Washington." AMER
       HERITAGE, 7 (1) (1955), 62-65.

       Chivalrous Major Patrick Fergusson, a British rifle expert,
       refused to shoot "at a sitting bird" at Brandywine.

1845. Haslewood, William. "Journal of a British Officer During the
       American Revolution." MVHR, 7 (1920), 51-58.

       A Captain in the 63rd British Infantry on duty at Boston,
       on the Hudson, and in Philadelphia wrote excellent impres-
       sions of his experiences.

1846. Howe, William. GENERAL WILLIAM HOWE'S ORDERLY BOOK AT
       CHARLESTON, BOSTON, AND HALIFAX JUNE 17, 1775 to 26 MAY
       1776; TO WHICH IS ADDED THE OFFICIAL ABRIDGEMENT OF GENERAL
       HOWE'S CORRESPONDENCE WITH THE ENGLISH GOVERNMENT DURING
       THE SIEGE OF BOSTON. Edited by Benjamin Franklin Stevens,
       London, 1890. Reprint. Port Washington, New York: Ira
       J. Friedman, 1970.

       This is an invaluable set of documents which provides many
       clues about the conduct of operations in the Carolinas and
       New England. The material about the exodus of the British
       army and the Massachusetts Loyalists to the Maritimes is
       especially useful. The name and subject indexes are quite
       serviceable.

1847. Hughes, Thomas. A JOURNAL OF THOMAS HUGHES, 1778-1784.
       Cambridge: Cambridge University Press, 1947.

       As an Ensign in the 53rd Regiment, Hughes witnessed combat
       on the Canadian front in 1776. He served with Burgoyne
       in 1777, was captured at Ticonderoga, and he spent the next
       two years as a prisoner on parole in New England. His journal
       is replete with shrewd observations and commentaries about
       American social life.

1848. Jackman, Sidney, ed. WITH BURGOYNE FROM QUEBEC: AN ACCOUNT
       OF THE LIFE AT QUEBEC AND OF THE FAMOUS BATTLE AT SARATOGA.
       New York: St. Martins' Press, 1963.

       The editor used Thomas Anbury's famous memoir as the basis
       for a good perspective of Burgoyne's army. The plagiarized
       portions in the original version have been deleted, and copious
       headnotes and footnotes have been added.

1849. Jackson, John W. WITH THE BRITISH ARMY IN PHILADELPHIA, 1777-
       1778. San Rafael, California: Presidio Press, 1979.

       The result of copious research, this work is a well-paced
       and entertaining account of why the British were unable to
       cling to eastern Pennsylvania. The details on the battles
       for the Delaware and Schuylkill are good. The author's com-
       ments about the deterioration of Loyalist support, the aliena-
       tion of a neutral populace demonstrate why such factors eroded
       military strength.

1850.   Jones, G. "An Early Amphibious Operations: Danbury, 1777."
        JSAHR, 46 (1968), 129-131.

        A document reproduced here demonstrates that the British
        could easily mount forays some twenty miles inland.

1851.   Kemble, Stephen. COLONEL STEPHEN KEMBLE'S JOURNAL AND
        BRITISH ARMY ORDERS, 1775-1778, 1780-81. 2 vols. New
        York Historical Society Collections. New York: The
        Society, 1883-1884.

        Here is one of the best sources of information about the
        war in the north. It contains the Kemble Journals and
        Order Books, General Howe's General Orders, General Clinton's
        General Orders, Orders by Major-General Daniel Jones,
        Kemble's Orders and Journals for 1780-81, as well as miscel-
        laneous correspondence.

1852.   Ketchum, Richard M. "Men of the Revolution - Cornwallis."
        AMER HERITAGE, 24 (5) (1973), 56-56.

        Here is a neat sketch of the famous British commander who
        nearly won the war in the south.

1853.   ————. "Men of the Revolution - Frederick Mackenzie."
        AMER HERITAGE, 26 (6) (1976), 16-17, 74-75.

        Major Mackenzie's voluminous diary provides an important
        source for a view of campaigns in New England and New York
        by the Royal Welsh Fusiliers.

1854.   ————. "Men of the Revolution - The Howe Brothers." AMER
        HERITAGE, 25 (3) (1974), 12-14.

        General William Howe and Admiral Richard Howe were in command
        of the British forces in North America during 1776-77.

1855.   ————. "New War Letters of Banastre Tarleton." NY HIST
        SOC Q, 51 (1967), 61-81.

        Tarleton, the dashing cavalry commander, described opera-
        tions around New York City.

1856.   Klein, Milton M. "An Experiment that Failed: General James
        Robertson and Civil Government in British New York, 1779-
        1783." NY HIST, 61 (1980), 228-254.

        The British effort was doomed because of counterinsurgency,
        inability to pacify the countryside, and because of mistaken
        premises about Loyalist strength.

1857.   Koke, Richard J. "Forcing the Hudson River Passage, October
        9, 1781." PA MHB, 76 (1952), 379-393.

        Clinton had a clever plan to destroy American supplies in
        mid-1781, but he was impeded by Cornwallis's Virginia campaign.

1858. Lansing, Amy E. "Baum's Raid." NY STATE HIST ASSOC Q J, 9
      (1928), 45-56.

      This is a brief treatment about the harassment of Baum's
      Hessians and Tories preceding the battle of Bennington by
      American militia in Vermont.

1859. Luethy, Ivor C.E. "General Sir Frederick Haldimand: A Swiss-
      Governor-General of Canada (1777-1786)." CAN ETHNIC STUD,
      3 (1971), 63-75.

      Haldimand, one of Britain's best military administrators in
      North America, had a remarkable record of dealing with Indians,
      Loyalists, and with American forces.

1860. Luykx, John M. "Fighting for Food: British Foraging Opera-
      tions at St. George's Island." MD HIST MAG, 71 (1976), 212-
      219.

      This is an excellent summary of why Lord Dunmore's expedition
      in the Chesapeake Bay during 1776 was blunted by Virginia
      and Maryland patriots.

1861. Lydenberg, Henry Miller, ed. ARCHIBALD ROBERTSON, LIEUTENANT-
      GENERAL ROYAL ENGINEERS. HIS DIARIES AND SKETCHES IN
      AMERICA, 1762-1780. BULL NY PUB LIB, 37 (1930), 18-32.

      Few British engineering officers left publishable manu-
      scripts of their experiences in America. This extensive
      memoir of five connected diaries has excellent insights and
      fine drawings. Robertson served from Boston to Yorktown.

1862. McDevitt, Robert. CONNECTICUT ATTACKED: A BRITISH VIEWPOINT,
      TRYON'S RAID ON DANBURY. Chester, Connecticut: Pequot
      Press, 1973.

      Former royal Governor William Tryon was involved in re-
      peated efforts to retaliate at weak enemy sectors. This is
      a good examination of Tryon's famous raid which caused much
      devastation of American property, led to vociferous American
      protests and did little to help Loyalists in the area.

1863. Mackenzie, Frederick. DIARY OF FREDERICK MACKENZIE, GIVING
      A DAILY NARRATIVE OF HIS MILITARY SERVICE AS AN OFFICER OF
      THE REGIMENT OF ROYAL WELSH FUSILIERS DURING THE YEARS 1775-
      1781 IN MASSACHUSETTS, RHODE ISLAND AND NEW YORK. 2 vols.
      Cambridge, Massachusetts: Harvard University Press, 1930.

      Mackenzie penned a vivid and detailed account of operations
      in key areas. His descriptions of fighting around Manhattan,
      and the defense off Newport, Rhode Island are insightful.
      As Deputy-Adjutant General in New York in 1781, he had a
      good perspective of a losing cause.

1864. Millar, John F., ed. "A British Account of the Siege of
       Rhode Island, 1778." RI HIST, 38 (1979), 79-85.

       John Peter Reina, a Midshipman on the frigate JUNO, left
       a lively memoir of the aborted American attack.

1865. Montresor, John. THE MONTRESOR JOURNALS. Edited by G.D.
       Scull. Vol. 14. New York Historical Society Collections.
       New York: The Society, 1881.

       Montresor was Chief of Engineers in Howe's army and wrote
       the best surviving account of the British invasion of
       Pennsylvania. His vivid and detailed remarks about the
       battle of Brandywine and the clearing of the Delaware pro-
       vide ample clues. He also witnessed Stamp Act disturbances
       in New York City and Albany.

1866. Moomaw, W.H. "The Denouncement of General Howe's Campaign
       of 1777." ENG HIST REV, 79 (1964), 498-512.

       Traditionally blamed for urging Howe not to sail up the
       Delaware, Captain Sir Andrew Snape Hammond of the Royal Navy
       actually advised Howe not to land on the Chesapeake.

1867. Nickerson, Hoffman. THE TURNING POINT OF THE REVOLUTION, OR
       BURGOYNE IN AMERICA. 2 vols. Reprint. Port Washington,
       New York: Kennikat Press, 1967.

       This is the best work on the Burgoyne campaign, and it is
       relied on heavily by writers of the topic. Though it is
       cumbersome reading, the volume has a mass of detail, excel-
       lent maps, and information difficult to obtain elsewhere. The
       author's mastery of documents, his careful use of anecdotes,
       and his thorough research make this volume still unsurpassed
       in its coverage of the invasion.

1868. Pattison, James. OFFICIAL LETTERS OF MAJOR GENERAL JAMES
       PATTISON. Vol. 8. New York Historical Society Collections.
       New York: The Society, 1875.

       Pattison was the commandant of British-held New York from
       July 15, 1779 to August 13, 1780. His letters are somewhat
       dull to read, but there are flashes here about the workings
       of a headquarters that give invaluable clues about staff
       operations.

1869. Pell, Joshua, Jr. "Diary of Joshua Pell, Junior : An Officer
       in the British Army in America, 1776-1777." BULL FORT TIC
       MUS, 1 (1929), 2-14.

       Pell served in Burgoyne's army until Saratoga.

1870. Pennypacker, Samuel W. "The High Water Mark of the British
       Invasion." PA MHB, 31 (1907), 393-405.

       Howe's army stopped at Phoenixville, Pennsylvania at French
       Creek on September 21, 1777.

1871. Ritchie, Carson I.A. "A New York Diary of the Revolutionary
       War." NY HIST SOC Q, 50 (1966), 221-280, 441-446.

       The diary, covering the June, 1778 to December, 1779 period,
       provides intimate glimpses of the war in New York but its
       authorship (perhaps General James Pattison of the Royal Artil-
       lery) is uncertain.

1872. Schaukirk, Ewald G. "Occupation of New York City by the
       British." PA MHB, 10 (1886), 418-445.

       Though somewhat outdated, this essay is a perceptive ac-
       count of how the British and Hessians garrisoned their first
       major conquest in the colonies during the war.

1873. Serle, Ambrose. THE AMERICAN JOURNAL OF AMBROSE SERLE.
       Edited by Edward H. Tatum, Jr. 1940. Reprint. New York:
       Arno Press, 1969.

       Serle served as Howe's secretary in New York and Philadel-
       phia. This well-edited account covers the Loyalist views of
       the rebellion, and their proposals for ending the war. The
       material about Serle's efforts to make the NEW YORK GAZETTE
       into an instrument of British propaganda is enlightening.

1874. Stanley, George F.G., ed. FOR WANT OF A HORSE: BEING A JOUR-
       NAL OF THE CAMPAIGN AGAINST THE AMERICANS IN 1776 AND 1777
       CONDUCTED FROM CANADA BY AN OFFICER WHO SERVED WITH LIEU-
       TENANT GENERAL BURGOYNE. Sackville, New Brunswick: The
       Tribune Press, 1961.

       This is the journal of a staff officer with Carleton in
       1776 and Burgoyne in 1777. It contains little new infor-
       mation or fresh interpretations.

1875. Snobel, Robert. FOR WANT OF A NAIL, IF BURGOYNE HAD WON AT
       SARATOGA. New York: Macmillan, and Co., 1978.

       The author speculates that the war would have ended if the
       British had been victorious in 1777. But his account is
       sheer fantasy and full of conjured events in the realm of
       "might have been" history. The work cannot be taken seri-
       ously by a popular audience.

1876. Snoddy, Oliver. "The Volunteers of Ireland." IRISH SWORD,
       7 (1965), 147-159.

       Clinton and Cornwallis had several hundred Irish troops
       from 1778 to 1782.

1877. Tucker, Louis L. "'To My Inexpressible Astonishment': Admi-
       ral Sir George Collier's Observations on the Battle of
       Long Island." NY HIST Q, 48 (1964), 293-305.

       Collier was amazed that Howe did not destroy the beaten
       American forces in August, 1776.

1878. Upham, George B. "Burgoyne's Great Mistake." NEQ, 3 (1930),
       657-680.

       Here is the standard emphasis on Lord Germain's neglect in
       instructing Howe in Philadelphia to assist Burgoyne as he
       advanced to the upper Hudson River.

1879. Vivian, Frances. "A Defense of Sir William Howe with a New
       Interpretation of His Action in New Jersey, June, 1777."
       JSAHR, 44 (1966), 69-83.

       As a result of the Seven Years War, Howe was instrumental
       in providing a light infantry company to every regiment.

1880. ————. "The Capture and Death of Major Andre." HIST TODAY,
       7 (1957), 813-819.

       This is a popular treatment of Andre's mission, arrest,
       and execution in September, 1780.

1881. Washington, Ida and Paul A. Washington. CARLETON'S RAID.
       Canaan, New Hampshire: Phoenix Press, 1977.

       In October, 1778 Major Christopher Carleton raided the
       Lake Champlain area, captured Americans, and destroyed pro-
       visions for 12,000 Continentals. This is a clear and concise
       account of an obscure aspect of the war that has been well
       researched and nicely mapped.

1882. Wierner, Frederick B. "The Military Occupation of Philadel-
       phia in 1777-1778." AMER PHIL SOC PROC, 111 (1967), 310-
       313.

       This article summarizes the attempts by the British to
       restore civil government to eastern Pennsylvania.

            D. CAMPAIGNS AND BATTLES: THE SOUTH

1883. Adams, Randolph G. "Arnold's Expedition to Richmond, 1781."
       WMQ, 12 (1932), 181-190.

       Arnold's invasion by British toops and ships was ineptly
       opposed by Virginia's state navy.

1884. Ashmore, Otis, ed. "Account of the [1779] Siege of Savannah,
       from a British Source." GA HIST SOC COLL, 5 (1901), 129-
       139.

       This is a simple contemporary account taken from the ROYAL
       GEORGIA GAZETTE, November 18, 1779.

1885. Barnwell, Joseph W. "The Evacuation of Charleston by the
       British in 1782." SC HIST GEN MAG, 11 (1910), 1-26.

There is little of value in this essay based on standard
works except lengthy quotations about the event from two
Loyalist newspapers.

1886. Bass, Robert D. "The Last Campaign of Major Patrick
       Fergusson." SC HIST ASSOC PROC, 5 (1968), 16-28.

This is a general discussion of the battle of King's
Mountain in 1780 and the annihilation of Fergusson's Loyalist
corps.

1887. Buker, George E., and Richard Apley Martin. "Governor Tonyn's
       Brown-Water Navy: East Florida During the American Revolu-
       tion, 1775-1778." FLA HIST Q, 58 (1979), 58-71.

British Governor Patrick Tonyn held the St. John's River
with a flotilla of gallies and schooners.

1888. Bulger, William T., ed. "Sir Henry Clinton's Journal of the
       Siege of Charleston, 1780." SC HIST MAG, 66 (1965), 147-
       174.

There are invaluable details in this April-May, 1780 memoir
about Clinton's staff, the navy, and the progress of the siege.

1889. ————. "The British Expedition to Charleston, 1779-80." Ph.
       D. dissertation, University of Michigan, 1957.

Using the Clinton Papers at the William L. Clements Library,
Bulger compiled a dry but informative account of the successful siege. The author summarizes the reason for the
invasion, the strategy involved, the anticipated Loyalist
rising, and the reasons for the British victory. The material
about the difficulties that confronted the British army and
navy is the best part of this work.

1890. Campbell, Colin, ed. THE JOURNAL OF LIEUTENANT COLONEL
       ARCHIBALD CAMPBELL DURING THE INVASION OF GEORGIA IN 1778-
       1779. Augusta, Georgia: Richmond County Historical Society,
       1980.

Here is a detailed narrative by one of Britain's finest
soldiers in the southern campaigns. He describes his preparations, routes, degree of patriot opposition, comments on the
Loyalists, and adds innumerable data about expeditions to the
back country. This is a very valuable memoir.

1891. Cornwallis, Charles C. AN ANSWER TO THAT PART OF THE NAR-
       RATIVE OF LT. GENERAL SIR HENRY CLINTON, K.B. WHICH RE-
       LATES TO THE CONDUCT OF LT. GENERAL EARL CORNWALLIS DURING
       THE CAMPAIGN IN NORTH AMERICA IN THE YEAR 1781. London:
       J. Debrett, 1783.

This is a fascinating work which contains material related
to the Earl's attempt to refute the changes of inept leadership during events leading to and during the siege of

Yorktown. He claimed that he was inadequately supported,
blamed Clinton and the admirals for ignoring his warnings,
and Cornwallis admitted to only a small portion of the defeat.

1892.   ————. CORRESPONDENCE OF CHARLES, 1ST MARQUIS CORNWALLIS.
Edited by Charles Ross. 3 vols. London: John Murray, 1859.

Cornwallis served in northern and southern campaigns. He
was a gifted field commander with great political influence
in London. His letters provide an excellent perspective on
the dilemma he faced due to disagreements over strategy,
shortage of troops, and logistical problems. His letters
about his quarrels with Clinton and about his marches in
the Carolinas to Yorktown are revealing.

1893.   Davis, Robert S., Jr. "The British Invasion of Georgia in
1778." ATLANTA HIST J, 24 (1980), 5-25.

This is the best summary about how General Augustin Prevost
from Florida and Lt. Colonel Archibald Campbell from New York
swept over the state to conquer Savahanna.

1894.   Farmer, Robert. "The Siege of Pensacola in 1781: Robert
Farmer's Journal of the Siege of Pensacola." HIST MAG, 4
(1860), 160-172.

Lieutenant Farmer described the Spanish siege of the
British-held fortress in detail.

1895.   Furlong, Patrick J. "Civilian-Military Conflict and the
Restoration of the Royal Province of Georgia, 1778-1782."
JSH, 38 (1972), 415-442.

Both Lieutenant-Colonel Archibald Campbell and Governor Sir
James Wright had great difficulties in reconquering Georgia,
partly due to Lord Germain and to General Henry Clinton.

1896.   Hawes, Lila, M. "Minute Book, Savannah Board of Police, 1779."
GA HIST Q, 45 (1961), 245-257.

Until civil government was restored in occupied Georgia,
British officers supervised licensing, management of
estates, and sequestered American property.

1897.   Hough, Franklin Benjamin, ed. THE SIEGE OF CHARLESTON, BY
THE BRITISH FLEET AND ARMY UNDER THE COMMAND OF ADMIRAL
ARBUTHNOT AND SIR HENRY CLINTON WHICH TERMINATED WITH THE
SURRENDER OF THAT PLACE ON THE 12TH OF MAY, 1780. Albany:
J. Munsell, 1867.

This is a dull prosaic treatment. But it is one of the
few volumes on this key event. The volume contains useful
excerpts from contemporary correspondence.

1898.   Jones, Eldon. "The British Withdrawal from the South." See
        855, pp. 259-285.

        This is an excellent article about how Carleton supervised
        the complex evacuation procedures from Charleston, Savannah
        and in East Florida at the war's end.

1899.   Kepner, Frances Reece. "A British View of the Siege of
        Charleston, 1776." JSH, 11 (1945), 93-103.

        James Simpson, a Carolinian Loyalist, explained to Lord
        Germain why the Royal Navy was unable to crush the American
        defenses in the harbor.

1900.   Kyte, George W. "British Invasion of South Carolina in 1780."
        HISTORIAN, 14 (1952), 149-172.

        This is a standard and relatively unimaginative story of a
        familiar theme.

1901.   ———. "Strategic Blunder: Lord Cornwallis Abandons the
        Carolinas, 1781." HISTORIAN, 22 (1960), 129-144.

        Cornwallis disregarded his security links on his march to
        Yorktown leaving scattered British forces in the Carolinas
        and Georgia under Lord Rawdon's command.

1902.   McCowen, George Smith, Jr. THE BRITISH OCCUPATION OF CHARLES-
        TON, 1780-1782. Columbia, South Carolina: University of
        South Carolina Press, 1972.

        This is a solid study, based on much original research, of
        how the British restored order in a reconquered city. The
        author covers topics such as loyalty oaths, sequestration of
        estates, the problems of inflation, trade, and slavery as
        well as how civil control was gradually reasserted. Though
        this work would have limited appeal to the general reader,
        it helps to fill a void on this topic for scholars.

1903.   Moomaw, William H. "The British Leave Colonial Virginia,"
        VA MHB, 66 (1958), 147-160.

        Lord Dunmore had to evacuate British forces in 1775-76; he
        was later unable to mount an offensive from the Chesapeake.

1904.   Newsome, A.R., ed. "A British Orderly Book, 1780-1781." NC
        HIST REV, 9 (1932), 57-58, 163-186, 273-298, 366-392.

        There are numerous unexplained abbreviations and contempor-
        ary references in this detailed orderly book written for
        Major-General Alexander Leslie in the Carolinas.

1905.   Nunis, Doyce, B., Jr., ed. "Colonel Archibald Campbell's
        March from Savannah to Augusta, 1779." GA HIST Q, 45
        (1961), 275-286.

The description of roads, trails and the topography is
quite useful; Campbell was a resourceful soldier.

1906. O'Hara, Charles. "Letters of Charles O'Hara to the Duke of
       Grafton." Edited by George C. Rogers. SC HIST MAG, 65
       (1964), 158-60.

       Brigadier General O'Hara's six letters here (1780-81) in-
       dicated that the Americans were unconquerable.

1907. Osborn, George. "Major General John Campbell in British West
       Florida." FLA HIST Q, 27 (1949), 317-337.

       Without men, money, or ships it was inevitable that Campbell
       would lose Mobile and Pensacola to the Spanish.

1908. Patten, David. "Fergusson and his Rifle." HIST TODAY, 28
       (1978), 446-454.

       Major Patrick Fergusson invented the flint-lock, breech-
       loading rifle.

1909. Robertson, Heard. "The Second British Occupation of Augusta."
       GA HIST Q, 58 (1941), 422-446.

       The conquest of Georgia seemed secured when it was captured
       by the British, but holding Augusta was doomed against an
       American counter-offensive.

1910. Robson, Eric. "The Expedition to the Southern Colonies, 1775-
       1776." ENG HIST REV, 66 (1951), 535-560.

       The Clinton expedition to assist Loyalists in the Cape Fear
       area and to capture Charleston was a fiasco.

1911. Russell, Peter. "The Siege of Charleston: The Journal of
       Captain Peter Russell, December 25, 1779 to May 2, 1780."
       AHR, 4 (1890), 478-501.

       An officer in the 64th Regiment wrote about his adventures
       with the British fleet from New York to the Carolina coast
       in colorful prose.

1912. Selby, John. THE ROAD TO YORKTOWN. New York: St. Martin's
       Press, 1976.

       Though adequately written, this tale adds nothing to the
       familiar story of Cornwallis's defeat. Ths work is very weak
       in footnotes and in bibliography. The same story has been
       handled far better by many other writers.

1913. Shy, John. "British Strategy for Pacifying the Southern
       Colonies, 1778-1781." Crowe, Jeffrey, and Larry E. Tise, eds.
       THE SOUTHERN EXPERIENCE IN THE AMERICAN REVOLUTION. Chapel
       Hill: The University of North Carolina Press, 1978, pp.155-173.

       The emphasis on using Loyalist troops was to free British
       regulars for the impossible task of pacification.

1914. Smith, W. Calvin. "Mermaids Riding Alligators: Divided Com-
       mand on the Southern Frontier, 1776-1778." FLA HIST Q, 54
       (1976), 443-464.

       Governor Patrick Tonyn of East Florida and General Augustine
       Prevost quarrelled over numerous issues, including control of
       the (Loyalist) East Florida Rangers.

1915. Stevens, Benjamin Franklin, ed. THE CAMPAIGN IN VIRGINIA,
       1781. REPRINT OF SIX RARE PAMPHLETS ON THE CLINTON-
       CORNWALLIS CONTROVERSY. 2 vols. London: n.p., 1888.

       Both Cornwallis and Clinton attempted to rally political
       support in London after the war in order to shift the blame
       for Yorktown on the other. As polemical pamphlet literature
       was typical of such controversies, this collection contains
       excerpts from the generals' correspondence and other docu-
       ments that is now difficult to locate. To appreciate the
       Yorktown campaign, these volumes are worth consulting.

1916. Stoessen, Alexander L. "The British Occupation of Charleston,
       1780-82." SC HIST MAG, 63 (1962), 71-82.

       The article summarizes the treatment of American prisoners,
       the exiles of some to St. Augustine, the question of booty,
       and the eventual evacuation some fourteen months after York-
       town.

1917. Tarleton, Banastre. A HISTORY OF THE CAMPAIGNS OF 1780 AND
       1781 IN THE SOUTHERN PROVINCES OF NORTH AMERICA. London:
       T. Cadell, 1787.

       Tarleton was the famous leader of a cavalry regiment. His
       descriptions of the fighting in the Carolina backcountry
       are about bloody partisan warfare. Tarleton vindicates him-
       self from errors such as Cowpens, blames his superiors for
       failures with southern campaigns and remained almost un-
       emotional in describing numerous engagements.

1918. Waring, Joseph Ioor, ed. "Lt. John Wilson's Journal of the
       Siege of Charleston." SC HIST MAG, 66 (1965), 173-182.

       Wilson, an engineer, left a unique account about erecting
       gun batteries and building retrenchments.

1919. Willcox, William B. "The British Road to Yorktown: A Study
       in Divided Command." AHR, 52 (1946), 1-35.

       Willcox blames Howe for lack of foresight and Cornwallis
       who underestimated the ramifications of sea power.

1920. Wyllis, John Cook, ed. "New Documentary Light on Tarleton's
       Raid: Letters of Newman Brockenbough and Peter Lyons."
       VA MHB, 74 (1966), 452-461.

Here are two letters extracted from the VIRGINIA GAZETTE
about the British raid on Charlottesville in June, 1781.

E. LOGISTICS

1921. Baker, Norman. GOVERNMENT AND CONTRACTORS: THE BRITISH
TREASURY AND WAR SUPPLIES, 1775-1783. London: Athlone,
1971.

Although this may be a dull subject about men of limited
vision involved in a gigantic enterprise of trying to provide
supplies, provisions and weapons for armies overseas, this
is an excellent work that carefully delineates the difficulties encountered by British officials in attempting to
coordinate the war effort in England and Ireland. The
Treasury Office was the chief administration unit which es-
timated the army's needs, placed contracts and acquired shipping space. This account is carefully researched and is
replete with fascinating anecdotes about corruption, Parliamentary "influence" on contracts, and the inertia of officialdom, factors which help to explain why the British
generals failed to receive enough logistical support in North
America.

1922. Biddulph, Violet. ed. "Letters of Robert Biddulph." AHR, 29
(1923), 87-109.

Biddulph, a contracting agent for a London firm, remarked
on supply problems in New York and in Charleston with some
insight.

1923. Bowler, R. Arthur. LOGISTICS AND THE FAILURE OF THE BRITISH
ARMY IN AMERICA, 1775-1783. Princeton, New Jersey:
Princeton University Press, 1975.

This is a ponderous account about why the British were
poorly provisioned during the war. The army was seldom provided enough food, fuel, forage, housing and transport,
partly because of administrative malfunctioning at home, but
also because of difficulties of acquiring these items in North
America, particularly when British armies were generally
restrained in operations to major ports. The book is valuable for data about peculation, sources of supply, and
forays to find food but it is weak about campaigns in the
south and overlooks the problems of disease in the army.
Yet, even with these limitations it is worth reading.

1924. ———. "Sir Henry Clinton and Army Profiteers: A Neglected
Aspect of the Clinton-Cornwallis Controversy." WMQ, 31
(1974), 111-122.

This is a good account about corruption in army officialdom in North America.

1925. ————. "The American Revolution and British Army Reforms."
       JSAHR, 68 (1980), 66-77.

       By the war's end, some improvements transpired in pro-
       visioning the army.

1926. Rainsford, Commissary. "Commissary Rainsford's Journal of
       Transactions, Etc., 1776-1777." NY HIST SOC COLL, 12
       (1879), 315-348.

       John Rainsford wrote a unique story about the mobilization
       and transportation of German troops to North America.

                    F. THE OFFICER CORPS

1927. Balderston, Marion and David Syrett, eds. THE LAST WAR:
       LETTERS FROM BRITISH OFFICERS DURING THE AMERICAN REVOLU-
       TION. New York: Horizon Press, 1975.

       Here are some 200 personal letters from British army and
       naval officers which show their concern with patronage (and
       not patriotism), their contempt for the American colonists,
       and their belief in British invincibility. This is a ran-
       domly selected and disjointed book that is adequate for
       undergraduates.

1928. Bruce, Anthony. THE PURCHASE SYSTEM IN THE BRITISH ARMY,
       1660-1871. Royal Historical Society Studies in History
       Series, number 20, London: The Society, 1980.

       Though incredibly dull for a seemingly fascinating subject,
       this small work offers an examination of how the infamous
       purchase-of-commissions system worked and suggests why
       talented militarists often held low ranks because of their
       impecunious condition.

1929. Gilbert, Arthur N. "Law and Honour Among Eighteenth Century
       British Army Officers." HIST J, 19 (1976), 75-87.

       In an imaginative article, Gilbert suggests the customs,
       mores, and attitudes about class pride typical of British
       officers.

1930. Hayes, James. "Scottish Officers in the British Army."
       SCOTTISH HIST REV, 37 (1958), 23-33.

       After the Jacobite uprising in 1745, many impecunious young
       Scots won promotion and prestige by serving in the army of
       George III.

1931. Katcher, Philip. "Officers and Other Ranks in the War of
       American Independence." JSAHR, 54 (1966), 171-175.

       The ratio of officers to men was normally one to eighteen,
       but in North America it was one to twenty.

1932. Robson, Eric, ed. LETTERS FROM AMERICA, 1773 TO 1780: BEING
       THE LETTERS OF A SCOTS OFFICER, SIR JOHN MURRAY, TO HIS
       HOME DURING THE WAR OF INDEPENDENCE. Manchester, England:
       Manchester University Press, 1951.

       Murray participated in the '76 attack on Charleston and
       in the Long Island campaign, and finished the war in the
       West Indies. While highly critical of his superiors at
       first, he became more disgusted with the Americans and their
       methods of fighting. This meticulously edited account pro-
       vides an excellent view by an articulate officer.

1933. ———. "Purchase and Promotion in the British Army in the
       Eighteenth Century." HISTORY, 36 (1961), 57-72.

       This is a lucid summary of how the aristocracy and gentry
       were able to buy successive commissions in regiments to the
       detriment of sometimes more capable middle-class officers.

G. THE ENLISTED MEN

1934. Bradford, S. Sydney. "The Common Foot Soldier—From the
       Journal of Thomas Sullivan, 49th Regiment of Foot." MD
       HIST MAG, 52 (1967), 219-253.

       As few good journals were written by British enlisted men,
       this account of service in the northern fighting, Sullivan's
       advance through the ranks, and his desertion to marry an
       American woman in 1778 is fascinating.

1935. Burns, R.E. "Ireland and British Military Preparations for
       War in 1775." CITHARA, 2 (1963), 42-61.

       Cork was a major military supply base, and Irish man power
       was recruited for the expeditions to America.

1936. Frey, Sylvia P. "British Military Justice during the Ameri-
       can Revolution." EIGHTEENTH CENTURY: THEORY AND INTER-
       PRETATION, 20 (1979), 24-38.

       Desertion and destruction of property were the most com-
       mon crimes before general court-martials which ordered
       fifty per cent of the offenders flogged.

1937. ———. "Courts and Cats: British Military Justice in the
       Eighteenth Century." MILT AFFAIRS, 43 (1979), 5-11.

       Punishments such as flogging and branding were typical of
       European armies.

1938. ———. THE BRITISH SOLDIER IN NORTH AMERICA. A SOCIAL
       HISTORY OF MILITARY LIFE IN THE REVOLUTIONARY PERIOD.
       Austin, Texas: University of Texas Press, 1980.

       This is a definitive account about the British rank and

file. Frey has compiled a thoroughly researched, well documented, readable and often fascinating narrative about the
recruitment, training, pay, provisions, discipline, and
experiences of ordinary British troops. The sections on the
social background, medical conditions and the barbarity of
punishments, and the welfare of the troops are especially
good. This monograph easily surpasses anything else written
on the subject.

1939. Gilbert, Arthur N. "An Analysis of Some Eighteenth Century
       Army Recruiting Records." JSAHR, 54 (1976),
       38-47.

       There are clues here about the physical, geographic, and
       occupational characteristics of troops in some regiments.

1940. ———. "Military Recruitment in the Eighteenth Century."
       JSAHR, 57 (1979), 34-44.

       This is a good analysis of how the vagaries of the economy,
       the fame of regiments, and the personalities of regimental
       commanders could influence recruiting.

1941. ———. "Why Men Deserted from the Eighteenth Century
       British Army." ARMED FORCES AND SOC, 6 (1980), 553-557.

       The article summarizes the standards of pay, rations, and
       discipline to suggest the need for a much broader study of
       desertion rates.

1942. Hargreaves, Reginald. THE BLOODYBACKS - THE BRITISH SERVICE-
       MAN IN NORTH AMERICA AND THE CARIBBEAN, 1655-1783. New
       York: Walker, 1968.

       Although the author has done little original research on
       this subject and relies almost entirely on standard published
       works, this is a good readable treatment about the misery and
       the bravery of British regiments serving in American waters.
       It is worthwhile for the general reader.

1943. Lamb, Roger. AN ORIGINAL AND AUTHENTIC JOURNAL OF OCCUR-
       RENCES DURING THE LATE AMERICAN WAR. 1809. Reprint.
       New York: Arno Press, 1968.

       This is probably the best written and most engaging memoir
       about Burgoyne's campaign written by a very literate British
       sergeant in the Royal Welsh Fusiliers. His descriptions of
       the siege of Ticonderoga, the battles of Hubbardton, and
       Saratoga are excellent.

1944. Rawle, William B. "Plundering by the British Army during the
       American Revolution." PA MHB, 25 (1901), 114-117.

       The Hessians, not the English, were known, according to a
       contemporary source, for their "meaness, rapacity and brutal-
       ity."

1945. Rea, Robert R. "Military Deserters from British West
       Florida." LA HIST, 9 (1968), 123-138.

       Large numbers of British troops deserted from Pensacola
       and Mobile to find haven in Louisiana.

                         H. PRISONERS OF WAR

1946. Beroth, Janet. "The Convention at Saratoga." NY STATE HIST
       ASSOC Q J, 8 (1927), 257-280.

       The essay covers the terms of the British capitulation and
       how infractions occurred on both sides.

1947. Bowie, Lucy Leigh. "German Prisoners in the American Revolu-
       tion." MD HIST MAG, 40 (1945), 185-200.

       Here is a convenient summary about prison regulations with
       emphasis on the 2,000 Hessian captives held in Maryland,
       Virginia, and Pennsylvania.

1948. Bowman, Larry. "The Court-Martial of Captain Richard Lip-
       pincott." NJ HIST, 89 (1971), 23-36.

       A captured British officer was nearly hanged for an atrocity
       committed by British troops in New Jersey.

1949. Campbell, Colin. "The 71st Highlanders in Massachusetts,
       1776-1780." NE HIST GEN REG, 112 (1958), 200-213, 265-
       275; 113 (1959), 3-14, 84-94.

       Some members of this famous regiment deserted while in
       captivity, and some married American women.

1950. Chilton, Harriet A. "A Journal of the Yorktown Prisoners to
       Winchester, Virginia and Frederick, Maryland." DAR MAG,
       114 (1980), 200-203.

       Captured Hessians were marched 240 miles under close guard.

1951. Clark, Jane. "The Convention Troops and the Perfidy of Sir
       William Howe." AMER HIST ILLUS, 37 (4) (1932), 121-122.

       By indicating his suspicion of the exchange agreement for
       Burgoyne's captured soldiers, Howe provided Congress with
       excuses to ignore provisions of the cartel concerning
       prisoners.

1952. Dabney, William Minor. AFTER SARATOGA: THE STORY OF THE CON-
       VENTION ARMY. Albuquerque: University of New Mexico Press,
       1954.

       Here is a scholarly account about the tribulations of
       British-Hessian troops captured at Saratoga. Due to distrust,

bickering, and mutual violations of the surrender terms,
Congress and the Lord North Ministry were unable to agree on
how and where to repatriate Burgoyne's army. As a conse-
quence, the troops were interned in several states for the
war's duration.

1953. Dixon, Martha Williamson. "The American Management of the
       Revolutionary War Prisoners, 1775-1783. Ph.D. disserta-
       tion, University of Utah, 1977.

       The theme concerns the difficulty that Congress had in
       devising a policy to handle captured troops, a problem
       compounded by the nature of the war (a revolution against
       the Crown), a lack of funds and the attitudes of state
       governments. Hence, supervision of prisoners remained under
       local controls, and states even made their own cartel ar-
       rangements with the British. This study demonstrates insuf-
       ficient research, unfamiliarity with European prisoner ar-
       rangements, a haphazard organization of chapters, and a
       bewildering chronology.

1954. Fleming, Thomas. "Burgoyne's Wandering Army." AMER HERITAGE,
       24 (11) (1972), 10-15, 89-93.

       This is an excellent summary about 6,000 British troops
       held captive for five years.

1955. Haffner, Gerald O. "A British Prisoner of War in the Ameri-
       can Revolution: The Experience of Jacob Schlieffelin. From
       Vincennes to Williamsburg, 1779-1780." VA MHB, 86 (1978),
       17-25.

       A captured British officer was harshly treated by George
       Rogers Clark in reprisal for enemy treatment of American
       prisoners.

1956. ————. "Captain Charles Asgill: An Anglo-American Incident,
       1782." HIST TODAY, 7 (1975), 329-334.

       A captured British officer was nearly executed for an
       atrocity, but European officialdom managed to change the
       views of Congress on the matter.

1957. Lingley, Charles R. "The Treatment of Burgoyne's Troops Un-
       der the Saratoga Convention." POL SCI Q, 22 (1907), 440-
       459.

       The author blames both sides for violating the agreement.

1958. Richards, Henry M.M. "The Pennsylvania-Germans and the
       British Military Prisons of the Revolutionary War." PAP
       GER SOC PROC, 32 (1934), 5-33.

       Due to ethnic affiliations, German-Americans in many Penn-
       sylvania villages tried to ease the plight of captive Hessian
       troops.

1959. Wall, Alexander J. "The Story of the Convention Army."
       NY HIST SOC Q BULL, (1927-28), 67-97.

       The essay is a detailed account about Burgoyne's troops
       after Saratoga.

1960. White, Herbert Humphrey. "British Prisoners of War in
       Hartford During the Revolution [1775-1777]." CONN HIST
       SOC BULL, 19 (1954), 65-81.

       This is a weak summary of how a town responded to a unique
       situation regarding captives.

1961. Wroth, K., ed. "Vengeance. The Court-Martial of Captain
       Richard Lippincott." See 975, pp. 499-511.

       This is the best account of the famous trial of a captured
       Britisher charged with instigating a massacre of Americans.

VII. THE GERMAN TROOPS

1962. Atwood, Rodney. MERCENARIES FROM HESSEN-KESSEL IN THE
AMERICAN REVOLUTION. Cambridge, London, New York:
Cambridge University Press, 1980.

This is the best study available in English about German
troops in the Revolution. The author notes the transition
in eighteenth-century Europe from feudal levies to hiring
alien troops, and then to a national conscript army. With
documentation gathered from innumerable sources, Atwood notes
that European princes viewed the hiring-out of their troops
like a form of subsidy money for an alliance. This work is
a superb summary of the recruiting, training, discipline,
organization, and transportation of one of the six German
corps hired by Britain. It is highly readable, demonstrates
the superiority of Hessian troops in battle, covers the debate over the morality of subsidy treaties in German diplomacy, and it cites many works generally unfamiliar to American readers. The appendices which show the battles and garrison service of Hessian units are valuable.

1963. Baurmeister, Carl L. REVOLUTION IN AMERICA: CONFIDENTIAL
LETTERS AND JOURNALS 1776-1784. Edited and translated by
Bernard A. Uhlendorf. New Brunswick, New Jersey: Rutgers
University Press, 1957.

In a fine account of fighting in the Middle States from
1776-78, and of garrison duty in New York to 1783, Major
General Baurmeister wrote an engaging and exciting account
of his experiences in a Hessian regiment to Baron von
Jungken of Hesse-Cassel.

1964. Copeland, Peter F., and Haarman, Albert W. "The Provisional
Companies of Hesse-Cassel During the Revolutionary War."
MILT COLL HIST, 18 (1958), 11-13.

The authors trace the activities of German light infantry
regiments that fought in New York, Newport, and Philadelphia.

1965. Doehla, Johann Conrad. "The Doehla Journal." Translated
by Robert J. Tilden. WMQ, 22 (1944), 229-274.

Here is a penetrating commentary by a Hessian soldier who
fought in the Virginia campaigns of 1780-81.

1966. Elking, Max von. THE GERMAN ALLIED TROOPS IN THE NORTH
AMERICAN WAR OF INDEPENDENCE, 1776-1783. Translated by
J.G. Rosengarten. 1893. Reprint. Baltimore: Genealogical
Publishing Co., 1969.

Although this work displays meticulous research in German
archives and a soldier's eye for combat details, the editor
was uncritical of his source material, and, apparently, unfamiliar with the available American literature.

1967. Ewald, Johann. "A Hessian Visits the Victors." AMER HERI-
       TAGE, 30 (5) (1979), 97-103.

       A German soldier noted how raw provincial Americans with-
       stood British and German professional troops.

1968. ————. DIARY OF THE AMERICAN WAR: A HESSIAN JOURNAL. Trans-
       lated and edited by Joseph P. Tustin. New Haven: Yale
       University Press, 1979.

       This is a well-edited documentary of a German captain's
       experience in the war. He was a professional soldier who
       made significant comments about combat in the six northern
       campaigns. Reluctantly, he came to admire the fighting
       abilities of the American enemy. His account of the
       Brandywine battle is good, and his thirty maps included here
       are invaluable. The book has over 900 footnotes.

1969. Fann, Willard R. "On the Infantryman's Age in Eighteenth
       Century Prussia." MILT AFF, 41 (1977), 165-170.

       Here is a concise summation of why the musket and bayonet
       were dominant weapons in that era.

1970. Gradisch, Stephen F. "The German Mercenaries in North
       America During the American Revolution: A Case Study."
       CAN J HIST, 4 (1969), 23-46.

       The author compiled a convenient statistical study about
       some German units in the northern campaigns; many Hessians
       protected Canada and many remained as settlers after the war.

1971. Greene, George Washington. THE GERMAN ELEMENT IN THE WAR OF
       AMERICAN INDEPENDENCE. New York: Hurd and Houghton, 1876.

       Greene wrote three essays about the German participation in
       the war. Two concern von Steuben and John Kalb who fought
       with the Americans. The material about the German mercenaries
       serving Britain was carefully researched and is quite read-
       able.

1972. Haarman, Albert W. and Donald W. Holst. "Contemporary Ob-
       servations on the Hesse-Cassel Troops Sent to North America,
       1776-1781." JSAHR, 54 (1976), 130-133.

       The views expressed here by Colonel William Faucitt of the
       British army sent to Germany for mustering troops are valu-
       able.

1973.   ————. "Notes on the Brunswick Troops - In British Service
        During the War of Independence." JSAHR, 48 (1970), 140-143.

        Here are fascinating details concerning the 4,300 troops
        furnished Britain by Karl I, Duke of Brunswick.

1974.   ————. "The Anspach-Bayreuth Troops in North America, 1777-
        1783." MILT COLL HIST, 19 (1967), 48-49.

        The article summarizes the organization, and the equipment
        provided by the Margrave of Brandenberg for service of his
        troops in North America.

1975.   ————. "The Army of Brunswick and the Corps in North
        America, 1776-1777." MILT COLL HIST, 16 (1964), 76-78.

        Here is a detailed list of Brunswickers who served in
        North America.

1976.   ————. "The Hessian-Hanau Free Corps of Light Infantry,
        1780-83." MILT COLL HIST, 15 (1963), 46-52.

        The article describes a diplomatic agreement between
        Britain and a German prince (January 1781) for the use of a
        light infantry corps in New York.

1977.   ————. "The 3rd Waldeck Regiment in British Service, 1776-
        1783." JSAHR, 48 (1980), 182-185.

        This item concerns a treaty signed by the Elector of
        Waldeck for the hiring of his infantry and artillery for
        British service.

1978.   Hinrich, Johann. "Extracts From the Letterbook of Captain
        Hinrich's Hessian Jaeger Corps, 1778-1780." PA MHB, 22
        (1898), 137-170.

        Hinrich described America well in addition to the fighting
        he witnessed in the Middle Colonies.

1979.   Holmes, Jack D.L. "German Troops in Alabama During the Ameri-
        can Revolution: The Battle of January 7, 1781." ALA HIST
        Q, 38 (1946), 5-9.

        This is a fine account of the tough 3rd Waldeck Regiment
        which fought from 1778-81 in Florida, Alabama, and Louisiana.

1980.   Huth, Hans. "Letters from A Hessian Mercenary." PA MHB, 62
        (1938), 488-501.

        Huth has carefully edited the impressions of Colonel Carl
        Emil Curt von Donop who fought under General Howe and was
        killed at the Delaware in 1777.

1981. Kipping, Ernst. THE HESSIAN VIEW OF AMERICA, 1776-1783.
       Monmouth Beach, New Jersey: Philip Freneau Press, 1973.

       In a valuable description of recruiting, transport, and
       the morale of German troops, Kipping compiled seventeen
       Hessian views about America, the war, and their comments
       about blacks, Indians, and German-American communities. He
       notes that some 6,000 German troops out of 50,000 elected to
       remain here after the war. The book has excellent appendices
       on regimental organization, names of officers, men captured
       at Trenton, and related information not available elsewhere.

1982. Krafft, John Charles Philip von. THE JOURNAL OF LIEUTENANT
       JOHN CHARLES PHILIP VON KRAFFT OF THE REGIMENT VON BOSE,
       1776-1784. Edited and translated by T.D. Edsall. Vol. 15.
       New York Historical Society Collections. New York: The
       Society, 1882, pp. 1-202.

       Krafft began as a corporal in von Donop's Regiment in 1781
       and became a Lieutenant in the von Bose Regiment by 1782.
       His journal begins in Germany in 1778 and ends in 1784. It
       is an excellent source for a professional soldier's view of
       the war.

1983. Lowell, Edward J. THE HESSIANS AND OTHER GERMAN AUXILIARIES
       OF GREAT BRITAIN IN THE REVOLUTIONARY WAR. 1884. Reprint.
       Port Washington, New York: Kennikat Press, 1970.

       Lowell was one of the first English-speaking historians
       to study the hiring of German troops. Although this is a
       commendable pioneering effort to describe the practice, the
       author denounces the German princes for their traffic in
       the blood of their subjects. Unfortunately, Lowell seemed
       unaware of the European practice of employing alien troops
       and that payments for German troops was often expended on
       schools, hospitals, and humanitarian projects in the Ger-
       manies.

1984. Muenchhausen, Fredrich Ernst von. "At General Howe's Side,
       1777-1778. Translated by Ernst Kipp and annotated by
       Samuel Stelle Smith. Monmouth Beach, New Jersey: Philip
       Freneau Press, 1974.

       This is a valuable and thoroughly documented diary (Novem-
       ber, 1776 to May, 1778) by the adjutant for all German units
       in North America, and the aide-de-camp to General Howe. As
       relatively few of Howe's papers are extant, this perceptive
       account provides much data on the functioning of his army.

1985. ————. "The Battle of Germantown Described by a Hessian
       Officer." PA MHB, 16 (1892), 197-201.

       Here are brief but vivid comments about the battle by a
       German Captain who served under Generals Howe and Clinton.

THE GERMAN TROOPS 301

1986. Pettingill, Ray W., ed. LETTERS FROM AMERICA, 1776-1779: BEING LETTERS OF BRUNSWICK, HESSIAN, AND WALDECK OFFICERS WITH THE BRITISH ARMY DURING THE AMERICAN REVOLUTION. Boston: Houghton, Mifflin, 1924.

Here are dozens of intimate letters written home by a score of officers from German regiments. Their stamina, courage, discouragements, and concerns about their future provide a valuable commentary about how soldiers viewed the war.

1987. Popp, Stephen. "Popp's Journal, 1777-1783." J.C. Rosengarten, ed. PA MHB, 26 (1902), 25-41, 245-254.

A Bayreuth soldier, Popp provided a remarkable tale of his enlistment, the voyage to America, the fighting he witnessed, and his return to Germany along with some remarkable maps.

1988. Ray, Frederick E., and Elting, John. "The Brunswick Infantry Regiment Von Rhetz." MILT COLL HIST, 17 (1965), 45-51.

This essay concerns the dress and rations of the Duke of Brunswick's contingent in North America, 1776-78.

1989. Riedesel, Friederike, Charlotte Louisa. LETTERS AND JOURNALS RELATING TO THE WAR OF THE AMERICAN REVOLUTION, AND THE CAPTURE OF THE GERMAN TROOPS AT SARATOGA. Translated by William L. Stone. Albany, New York: Joel Munsell, 1867.

Baroness Riedesel, who accompanied her husband with her children to Canada and through the Burgoyne campaigns, was a perceptive observer. She related much about staff activities, social life, the horrors of the battlefield, and her confinement at Albany. This is a fascinating commentary.

1990. Rosengarten, Joseph C. "A Defense of the Hessians." PA MAG HIST BIOG, 23 (1899), 157-183.

Published in Cassel (1879) by an unknown writer, this essay sympathizes with German princes who hired out troops; it also covers the views of German historians' views on this controversial issue.

1991. ———. trans. "The Battle of Germantown Described By A Hessian Officer." PA MHB, 16 (1892), 197-201.

Better disciplined and experienced Hessian troops were instrumental in the British victory.

1992. ———. "The German Soldiers in Newport, 1776-1779, and the Siege of 1778." RI HIST MAG, 7 (1886-87), 81-118.

This is an adequate summary about Hessian regiments defending the base against French-American attacks.

1993. Schmidt, H.D. "The Hessian Mercenaries: The Career of a Political Cliche." HISTORY, 43 (1948), 207-215.

Here is a useful commentary about how patriot Americans
viewed the use of Hessian troops in the war, how the theme
became a propaganda device to arouse fervor, and how it
attracted French sympathy.

1994.   Seume, J.G.   "Memoirs of a Hessian Conscript: J.G. Seume's
        Reluctant Voyage to America."   Translated by Margaret
        Woefful.   WMQ, 5 (1948), 553-570.

        Seume, a conscripted student from the University of
        Leipzig, wrote a very amusing and touching account of his
        adventures in the army, particularly his Atlantic voyage.

1995.   Shaaber, Andrew.   "The Hessian Camp at Reading, Pennsylvania,
        1781-1783."   BERKS CNTY HIST SOC TRANS, 3 (1982), 23-46.

        Reading was a major prison encampment for German prisoners
        who were treated decently.

1996.   Sherman, Constance D.   "Captain Diemar's Regiment of Hessians
        on Long Island."   J LONG ISLAND HIST, 5 (1965), 1-16.

        This is a useful description of the equipment and duties
        of 180 Brunswickers who served under General Clinton (1779-
        81).

1997.   Stokesbury, James L.   "Hessians in the American Revolution."
        AM HIST ILLUS, 11 (8) (1976), 5-7, 39-42.

        Written for a high-school audience, this article stresses
        the role of Hessians in the war.

1998.   Stone, William L., ed.   JOURNAL OF CAPTAIN GEORGE PAUSCH,
        CHIEF OF THE HANAU ARTILLERY, DURING THE BURGOYNE CAMPAIGN.
        1886.   Reprint.   New York: Arno Press, 1970.

        Pausch left an interesting commentary about his services.
        He mentions preparations for the campaign in Canada, naval
        actions on Lake Champlain, the fight at Bennington, and
        conditions at Saratoga.

1999.   Stutesman, John H., Jr.   "New Jersey's Foreign Legion."
        NJ HIST, 85 (1967), 66-71.

        This is an interesting account of how Baron Nicholas
        Dietrich von Ottendorf, a friend of America, was authorized
        by General Washington to recruit German indentured servants
        in the Middle States for service in the Continental army.

2000.   Tharp, Louise Hall.   "New England Under Observation."   NE
        GALAXY, 6 (1964), 3-9.

        This is an amusing account of how German troops viewed
        New Englanders.

2001. Uhlendorf, Bernard A., ed. THE SIEGE OF CHARLESTON; WITH
       AN ACCOUNT OF THE PROVINCE OF SOUTH CAROLINA. TRANSLATED
       FROM THE VON JUNGKENN PAPERS IN THE WILLIAM L. CLEMENTS
       LIBRARY. Ann Arbor, Michigan: University of Michigan
       Press, 1938.

       This is a carefully researched account of General Clinton's
       successful attack on Charleston. Colonel von Jungkenn was
       a very perceptive officer and his descriptions of the siege
       are invaluable.

2002. Von Papet, Frederick J. "The Brunswick Contingent in America,
       1776-1783." PA MHB, 15 (1891), 218-224.

       Based on a two volume diary of Lieutenant Frederick Julius
       von Papet of the Von Rhetz Regiment's voyage from Stade to
       America, the material here provides some information.

2003. Wiederhold, Andreas. "Colonel Rall at Trenton." PA MHB, 22
       (1898), 462-67.

       Captain Wiederhold of the Knyphausen Regiment was very
       dubious of Colonel Rall's military abilities which accounted,
       in part, for the American victory at Trenton.

2004. ————. "The Capture of Fort Washington Described by Andreas
       Wiederhold of the Hessian Regiment Knyphausen." PA MHB,
       23 (1899), 95-97.

       Here is a fine account of a key victory by a participant
       in the action.

2005. Wildenmuth, Larry. "Hessians and the Citizens of Berks
       County." HIST REV BERKS CTY, 35 (1970), 46-49, 66-75.

       Reading, Pennsylvania, housed 1,000 Hessian prisoners who
       caused little trouble, but the local American population
       complained bitterly about their presence and the costs of
       provisioning them.

VIII. THE LOYALIST TROOPS

2006. Bass, Robert D. "The South Carolina Regiment; A Forgotten
Loyalist Regiment." SC HIST ASSOC PROC, 10 (1977), 64-71.

Under Major John Harrison, sixty-three men fought against
Marion and Sumter in partisan warfare.

2007. Callahan, North. ROYAL RAIDERS: THE TORIES OF THE AMERICAN
REVOLUTION. Indianapolis and New York: Bobbs-Merrill,
1963.

This is an adequate, though a romanticized account for
the general reader with some information about Loyalist political and military efforts. New York and Georgia figure
heavily in this account.

2008. Chidsey, Donald Barr. THE LOYALISTS: THE STORY OF THOSE
AMERICANS WHO FOUGHT AGAINST INDEPENDENCE. New York:
Crown, 1973.

Written in a journalistic fashion, this work is a useful
summary about the 50,000 Americans who fought on the British
side. The emphasis on the class and regional cross-section
of their regiments, and the sketches of leading Tory politicians is useful.

2009. Cleggett, David A.H., ed. "Hector McAlester's Plans for the
Subjugation of Virginia, 1780." VA MHB, 82 (1974), 75-83.

This essay covers the scheme of a Norfolk merchant who
suggested methods for a British conquest of the ports of
Jamestown, Yorktown, and Gloucester.

2010. Cruikshank, Ernest A. "The King's Royal Regiment of New York."
ONTARIO HIST SOC PAP, 27 (1931), 193-324.

This is an excellent discussion of a Loyalist regiment that
was active in Tryon Country, New York and one that served
under St. Leger and the Johnson family.

2011. Cuneo, John R. "The Early Days of the Queen's Rangers,
August, 1776-February, 1777." MILT AFF, 22 (1958), 65-74.

Founded by Major Robert Rogers during the French and Indian
War, this famous unit was poorly handled by the British.

2012. Davis, Robert Scott, Jr. "The Loyalist Trials at Ninety Six
in 1779." SC HIST MAG, (1979), 172-181.

This is a fine article about the officially sanctioned
execution of five Loyalists captured after the Battle of
Kettle Creek.

2013. Fergusson, Clyde R. "Carolina and Georgia Patriot and Loyal-
        ist Militia in Action, 1778-1783." See 1913, pp. 174-199.

British military strategy was doomed because patriot
militia suppressed political dissent, maintained social
stability, and performed well in combat.

2014. Holmes, Jack D.L. "Robert Ross's Plan for an English In-
        vasion of Louisiana in 1782." LA HIST, 5 (1964), 161-177.

This essay summarizes two letters from a New Orleans merchant to Lord Dunmore for a proposed expedition into Spanish
territory.

2015. Honeyman, A. Van Doren. "Concerning the New Jersey Loyalists
        in the Revolution." NJ HIST SOC PROC, 51 (1933), 117-133.

Here is a nicely balanced view of the military contributions of Jersey Tories to the British cause.

2016. Jarvis, Stephen. "An American Experience in the British
        Army: Manuscript of Col. Stephen Jarvis ... Revealing the
        Life of a Loyalist." JAH, 1 (1907), 727-740.

Here is a vivid account of the campaign of Charleston
and a Loyalist's experience as a prisoner of war.

2017. Katcher, Philip. "Loyalist Militia in the War of Indepen-
        dence." JSAHR, 54 (1976), 136-141.

Here is a list of the Provincial Corps and Loyalist
militia units, involving over 25,000 Americans who served
in the British army during the war.

2018. Klingle, Philip. "Soldiers of Kings." J LONG ISLAND HIST,
        12 (1976), 22-35.

Of three Loyalists regiments recruited in Kings County,
New York, only one saw action in the south against Marion,
Sumter, and Greene.

2019. Klyberg, Albert T. "The Armed Loyalists As Seen by American
        Historians." NJ HIST SOC PROC, 82 (1964), 101-108.

This is a useful summary of the historiography about the
United Empire Loyalists and the bitterness with which they
have been regarded by American historians.

2020. McDonald, Alexander. "Letter-Book of Captain Alexander
      McDonald of the Royal Highland Emmigrants, 1777-1779."
      COLL NY HIST SOC, 15 (1882), 203-498.

      McDonald was active in a regiment recruited in the Mari-
      times. Although virtually no battle engagements are cited
      here, his letters to Generals Massey, Gage, and Howe are
      illuminating about garrison duty at Halifax.

2021. Miller, Randall M. "A Backcountry Loyalist Plan to Retake
      Georgia and the Carolinas, 1778." SC HIST MAG, 75 (1974),
      207-214.

      In a thoroughly researched article, Miller studies the
      scheme of Moses Kirkland to use slave rebellions and Indian
      raids to assist an anticipated invasion of the south by a
      British expedition under Clinton.

2022. Nye, W.S. "Aftermath of Moore's Creek, Plight of the Tories."
      AMER HIST ILLUS, 4 (9) (1970), 17-19.

      This account is based on a memorial by Alexander Morrison
      of Cumberland County, North Carolina.

2023. Olson, Gary D. "Loyalists and the American Revolution: Thomas
      Brown and the South Carolina Backcountry, 1775-1776." SC
      HIST MAG, 68 (1967), 201-219; 69 (1968), 44-56.

      Brown tried to overcome the isolation of fellow Loyalists
      by integrating their efforts, and by using the Creeks and
      Cherokees for raids on the frontier.

2024. ———. "Thomas Brown, Loyalist Partisan, and the Revolu-
      tionary War in Georgia, 1777-1782." GA HIST Q, 54 (1970),
      1-19, 183-208.

      With the aid of Governor Patrick Tonyn of East Florida,
      this fiery Tory organized Brown's Rangers which terrorized
      the Georgia frontier, participated in the fighting at
      Charleston and Savannah, and on the Florida border.

2025. Robertson, Heard. "Notes on the Muster Rolls of the King's
      Rangers." RICHMOND CNTY HIST, 4 (1972), 5-15.

      Robertson comments on the activities of a Tory legion in
      Florida and the Carolinas, and how it twice captured Augusta.

2026. Siebert, Wilbur H. "Loyalist Troops of New England." NEQ,
      4 (1931), 108-147.

      Here is a now outdated but convenient summary of five
      Loyalist units mainly from Massachusetts and New Hampshire.

2027. ———. "The Loyalists and the Six Nations in the Niagara
      Peninsula." ROYAL SOC CAN TRANS, 9 (1915), 79-128.

This is a familiar story about the importance of Fort
Niagara as a rendevous for the Iroquois. The material, however on the post-war settlement of Loyalists is valuable.

2028. Smith, Paul H. LOYALISTS AND REDCOATS: A STUDY IN BRITISH
       REVOLUTIONARY POLICY. Chapel Hill: University of North
       Carolina Press, 1964.

       This is a key work which considers the role of Loyalists in
       British strategy. Unfortunately for the Tories, the British
       generals generally overlooked their value as sympathizers,
       partisans, and as troops attached to regulars. Consequently,
       the British failed to coordinate military operations with
       Loyalist uprisings, as in North Carolina in 1776. Loyalist
       troops were treated as inferior soldiers, and by 1778
       Toryism was ebbing. The scope of this well-crafted book
       is limited to the thirteen colonies. One-half of the volume
       is devoted to warfare in the south, 1780-81.

2029. Stone, William L., ed. "Sir John Johnson's Orderly Book
       During the Campaign From La Prairie to Fort Stanwix." MAG
       AMER HIST, 6 (1881), 204-216, 283-296.

       This essay covers Tory-Indian raids in the Mohawk Valley
       during 1777.

2030. Tebbenhoff, Edward H. "The Associated Loyalists: An Aspect
       of Militant Loyalism." NY HIST SOC Q, 63 (1979), 115-144.

       In a nicely written essay, the author demonstrates how the
       British under Clinton and Carleton tempered some Loyalists
       in what might have been brutal partisan warfare.

2031. Underwood, Wynn. "Indian and Tory Raids on the Otter Valley,
       1777-1782." VT Q, 15 (1947), 195-221.

       There are excellent details here about a relatively unknown
       series of bloody episodes on the Vermont side of Lake
       Champlain.

2032. Villers, David H. "The British Army and the Connecticut
       Loyalists During the War of Independence, 1775-1783." CONN
       HIST SOC, 43 (1978), 65-80.

       Out of 2,500 Tories in Connecticut, about 1,000 served the
       British in foraging, harassing patriots, skirmishing, and
       stealing cattle; but they received little assistance from
       the British command in New York.

IX. THE BRITISH NAVY

2033. Adams, Scarritt. "The Loss of the Royal George, 1782." HIST
       TODAY, 9 (1959), 837-840.

       A 100 gun ship, anchored in Portsmouth, sunk by leaking.

2034. Albion, Robert G. FORESTS AND SEA-POWER, THE TIMBER PROBLEM
       OF THE ROYAL NAVY, 1652-1862. Cambridge, Massachusetts:
       Harvard University Press, 1926.

       This is a very valuable account about the Navy's supplies
       of masts, spars, and hulls in an era when relatively few
       changes occurred in ship architecture. The material here
       about the Navy's difficulties in acquiring ship's stores
       during the Revolution is revealing.

2035. Anderson, Olive. "The Establishment of British Naval
       Supremacy at Sea and the Exchange of Naval Prisoners of
       War, 1779-1788." ENG HIST REV, 75 (1960), 77-89.

       The author examines the complicated negotiations with the
       French concerning prisoner exchanges.

2036. Ballard, George A. "Hughes and Suffren." MM, 13 (1927),
       348-356.

       This is a fine summary of five sea fights in the Indian
       Ocean between these admirals.

2037. ———. "The Last Battlefleet Struggle in the Bay of
       Bengal." MM, 13 (1927), 124-144.

       Nine naval fights occurred off the Carnatic coast during
       the war; the last one, on June 20, 1783, had no impact on
       peace negotiations.

2038. Barham, Charles M. LETTERS AND PAPERS OF CHARLES LORD BARHAM,
       ADMIRAL OF THE RED SQUADRON, 1758-1813. Edited by John K.
       Laughton. 3 vols. Publications of the Naval Records
       Society. Nos. 32, 38, 39. London: The Society, 1907-1911.

       Volume 1 contains ample documentation about Burham's ser-
       vice in the North Atlantic, West Indies, and the North Sea.
       Volume 2 to p. 157 has material that is related to the
       Revolution.

2039. Barnett, Richard C. "The View from Below Decks: The British
       Navy, 1777-1781." AMER NEP, 37 (1978), 92-100.

John Stradley, an armorer's mate on the HMS GRAFTON, wrote a
lively diary of events at sea.

2040.   Barrington, Samuel. THE BARRINGTON PAPERS. SELECTED FROM
        THE LETTERS AND PAPERS OF ADMIRAL THE HON. SAMUEL BARRINGTON.
        Edited by David Bonner-Smith. 2 vols. Publications of
        Naval Records Society. Nos. 71, 81. London: The Society,
        1937.

        Volume two is particularly valuable for operations against
        the French in the Caribbean. It covers the capture of St.
        Lucia, and Vice-Admiral Byron's assumption of command. There
        is a fine introduction to the letters, and the volumes are
        well-indexed.

2041.   Barritt, M.K. "The Navy and the Clyde in the American War,
        1777-1783." MM, 55 (1969), 33-42.

        As the tobacco importing trade ended, Scot privateers
        raided French and American sea lanes.

2042.   Beatson, Robert. NAVAL AND MILITARY MEMOIRS OF GREAT BRITAIN
        FROM 1727 TO 1783. 6 vols. 2nd ed. London: Longman,
        Hurst, Rees, and Orme, 1904.

        Volumes four through six cover the Revolution. This is a
        dated but still dependable source. The amount of detail
        here about squadrons, commanders, fire power, sailing tactics,
        sea fights and related matters is almost overwhelming. Much
        of the data is now difficult to locate.

2043.   Biographical Memoirs. "Biographical Memoirs of Arthur Philip,
        Esq." NAVAL CHRONICLE, 27 (1912), 1-9.

        The NAVAL CHRONICLE, published from 1799 to 1818, contains
        some sixty-four concise and well-written biographical sketches
        about British naval commanders in the war.

2044.   Bonner-Smith, David. "Byron in the Leeward Islands, 1779."
        MM, 30 (1944), 38-48, 81-92.

        In a poorly written but well-documented article, the author
        stresses the difficulties of communications from London to
        admirals overseas.

2045.   ———. "The Case of the SARTINE." MM, 21 (1935), 305-322.

        The essay concerns the seamanship of Captain Roddom Home
        off Cape St. Vincent in 1780.

2046.   Bradford, Gersham. "Nelson in Boston Bay." AMER NEP, 11
        (1951), 239-244.

        Horatio Nelson was a young officer during the Revolution.

2047. Breen, K.C. "The [British] Navy and the Yorktown Campaign,
       1781." Ph.D. dissertation, University of London, 1966.

       This is a thorough study of why the Royal Navy was unable
       to protect Cornwallis. Blunders by the Admiralty, inadequate
       intelligence about French fleets, the inability of Clinton
       in New York and Cornwallis in Virginia to cooperate are part
       of this fascinating account. In a nicely-paced narrative,
       the author places the blame on Rodney for failing to send
       enough ships from the Caribbean, and on tactical errors by
       Graves and Hood in letting de Grasse slip by with artillery
       for Washington.

2048. Breen, Kenneth. "Graves and Hood at the Chesapeake." MM,
       67 (1980), 57-65.

       Graves and Hood are blamed for incompetence at the battle
       of the Capes.

2049. Broomfield, J.H. "Lord Sandwich at the Admiralty Board:
       Politics and the British Navy, 1771-1778." MM, 51 (1954),
       7-17.

       Sandwich was not inept or corrupt but one of the best First
       Lords of the century.

2050. ———. "The Keppel-Palliser Affair, 1778-1779." MM, 47
       (1961), 195-207.

       For their failures to trap a French fleet off Ushant, the
       two admirals quarreled and divided the officers in hostile
       groups for years after a Gilbert and Sullivan court-martial.

2051. Calderhead, William L. "British Naval Failure at Long Island:
       A Lost Opportunity in the American Revolution." NY HIST,
       57 (1976), 321-338.

       The Royal Navy was impeded in capturing Washington's re-
       treating army because of American galleys, fireboats, and
       underwater obstacles.

2052. Callender, Geoffrey A.K. "With the Grand Fleet in 1780."
       MM, 9 (1923), 258-270, 290-304.

       Admiral Francis Geary rates praise for his seamanship at
       Spithead in May, 1780.

2053. Carlton, William R. "New England Masts and the King's Navy."
       NEQ, 12 (1939), 4-18.

       This is a very informative essay about the cutting and
       transporting of white pine to Portsmouth, New Hampshire.

2054. Chenevix, Trench B.B. "National Service Two Centuries Ago:
       The Press Gang." HIST TODAY, 6 (1936), 37-44.

THE BRITISH NAVY

Here is a worthwhile description about the impressment of potential shiphands.

2055. Clowes, William L. THE ROYAL NAVY: A HISTORY FROM THE EARLI-
EST TIMES TO THE PRESENT. 7 vols. London: Sampson, Low,
Marston, 1897-1903.

In volume 3, pages 358-568, Alfred T. Mahan contributed an
essay about the Revolution in what has been an essential
reference work about the British navy.

2056. [Collier, George Sir]. "'To My Inexpressible Astonishment':
Sir George Collier's Observations on the Battle of Long
Island." NY HIST SOC Q, 48 (1964), 293-305.

Collier was amazed that the Royal Navy failed to trap the
Americans.

2057. Comtois, George. "The British Navy in the Delaware, 1775 to
1777." AMER NEP, 40 (1980), 7-22.

Why the British took so long to attack the American defenses is clarified in this well-documented essay.

2058. Cresswell, John. BRITISH ADMIRALS OF THE 18TH CENTURY:
TACTICS IN BATTLE. London: Allen and Unwin, 1972.

This is a very handy reference to the rules for sea warfare
and how the Royal Navy attempted to adhere to these regulations. The material on the Battles of the Chesapeake Capes
and the Saintes is pertinent.

2059. Cundall, H.M. "Admiral Lord Rodney in Jamaica." MM, 24
(1938), 289-292.

Why Rodney remained at Jamaica and de Grasse at Martinque
in April, 1782 is clarified here.

2060. Dodwell, Henry H. "The Carnatic, 1761-1784." In THE CAM-
BRIDGE HISTORY OF INDIA. 6 vols. Cambridge: Cambridge
University Press, 1922-1934. Vol. 5, 273-293.

Here is a good account of the strategic significance of
the fighting in the Indian Ocean between Hughes and Suffren.

2061. Forester, Cecil Scott. "The Battle of the Saintes." AMER
HERITAGE, 9 (4) (1958), 4-9, 108.

No United States ships were involved in the most important
naval encounter of the war - Rodney against de Grasse in the
West Indies.

2062. Goold, William. "The Burning of Falmouth (New Portland),
Maine, By a British Soldier, in 1775." NE HIST GEN REG,
27 (1873), 256-266.

This is a rare eye-witness account that explains the
patriotic reaction to the incident.

2063. Graves, Thomas. GRAVES PAPERS AND THE OTHER DOCUMENTS RE-
       LATING TO THE NAVAL OPERATIONS OF THE YORKTOWN CAMPAIGN.
       Edited by French E. Chadwick. Publications of the Naval
       Records Society, No. 7. London: The Society, 1916.

       Graves commanded the British fleet at Yorktown. His papers
       reveal the difficulties he had with the weather off the
       Virginia Capes in trying to coordinate his ship movements,
       and the difficulties in ascertaining the presence of the
       French fleets.

2064. Hood, Samuel Viscount. LETTERS WRITTEN BY SIR SAMUEL
       HOOD (VISCOUNT HOOD) IN 1781-2-3. ILLUSTRATED BY EXTRACTS
       FROM LOGS AND PUBLIC RECORDS. Edited by David Hannay.
       Publications of the Naval Records Society. No. 3. London:
       The Society, 1895.

       Hood commanded the rear squadron of the British fleet under
       Graves at the battle of the Virginia Capes. There are some
       excellent descriptions of sea-fights here.

2065. James, William M. THE BRITISH NAVY IN ADVERSITY: A STUDY
       OF THE WAR OF AMERICAN INDEPENDENCE. London: Longmans,
       Green, 1926.

       This is a solid study about naval operations on many
       oceans. It emphasizes the logistical difficulties en-
       countered by the Royal Navy in attempting to protect commerce,
       to provide troops and supply transport, and to mount amphib-
       ious activities in several parts of the world simultaneously.
       The British navy not only fought American naval and privateer
       vessels, but it also had to contend with the French, Spanish,
       and Dutch navies.

2066. Keith, George Elphinstone, Lord. THE KEITH PAPERS: SELECTED
       FROM THE LETTERS AND PAPERS OF ADMIRAL VISCOUNT KEITH.
       Edited by W.G. Perrin and Christopher Lloyd. 3 vols.
       Naval Records Society Publications. Nos. 62, 90, 96.
       London: Naval Records Society, 1927-1964.

       Volume one, pp. 23-176, contains information about opera-
       tions off East Florida, the capture of Charleston, and convoy
       duty.

2067. Kershaw, Gordon E. "John Wentworth vs. Kennebeck Proprietors:
       The Formation of a Royal Mast Policy, 1769-1778." AMER
       NEP, 32 (1973), 95-119.

       Wentworth was the Royal Governor of New Hampshire and also
       Surveyor-General of the King's Woods which provided white
       pine for masts.

2068. Koke, Richard J. "Forcing the Hudson River Passage, October
       9, 1776." NY HIST SOC Q, 36 (1954), 458–466.

       The Royal Navy tried to penetrate the American fortresses
       and river obstacles on the Hudson.

2069. ———. "The Struggle for the Hudson: The British Naval
       Expedition under Captain Hyde Parker and Captain James
       Williams, July 12–August 18, 1776." NY HIST SOC Q, 40
       (1956), 114–175.

       This is the best treatment of British naval operations
       along the Hudson in the effort to cut off Washington's army
       from escaping.

2070. Knight, R.J.B. "Pilfering and Theft from the Dockyards at
       the Time of the American War of Independence." MM, 61
       (195), 215–225.

       The loss of timber and ships' stores was costly to the
       Royal Navy and damaged its efficiency.

2071. ———. "The Introduction of Copper Sheathing into the Royal
       Navy, 1779–1786." MM, 59 (1973), 299–310.

       The use of metalled hulls warded off the seaworm from ship
       planking and prevented the formation of excessive barnacles
       below the water line.

2072. Lloyd, Christopher. "Armed Forces and the Art of War: Part
       I, Navies." In A. Goodwin, ed. THE AMERICAN AND FRENCH
       REVOLUTIONS, 1763–1793. Vol. 7 of The Cambridge Modern
       History. Cambridge: Cambridge University Press, 1957.

       This is an expert summation of the Royal Navy's role during
       the Revolution written by a famed naval historian.

2073. Lloyd, Christopher. "The [British] Navy in the Eighteenth
       Century." In A GUIDE TO THE SOURCES OF BRITISH MILITARY
       HISTORY. Edited by Robin Higham. Berkeley: University
       of California Press, 1971, pp. 152–176.

       This is a useful annotated bibliography for the Revolu-
       tionary era.

2074. Maps, James. "The Battle of Ushant – and After." USNIP,
       90 (1964), 80–87.

       This is an adequate summary of the first major sea fight
       in the war between the British and French forces.

2075. Marcus, Geoffrey J. HEART OF OAK: A SURVEY OF BRITISH SEA
       POWER IN THE GEORGIAN ERA. New York: Oxford University
       Press, 1975.

       This is an excellent survey which covers the 1750–1815 era.

The chapters on the American Revolution are well-written,
full of information, and provide much information about the
seemingly impossible task that Britain faced in her overseas
empire. The book is carefully researched, and the author
obviously knows his ships and seamen.

2076. Mason, George C. "The British Fleet in Rhode Island." RI
       HIST SOC COLL, 7 (1885), 299-325.

       Here is a good summary about the stations the navy used in
       Rhode Island before the war and the increased quarreling with
       the local citizenry.

2077. Maurer, Maurer. "Coppered Bottoms for the Royal Navy: A
       Factor in the Maritime War of 1778-1783." MILT AFF, 14
       (1950), 57-61.

       By late 1781, most of the British fleet had copper-bottomed
       hulls; by eliminating the encumbrances of barnacles and
       marine borers, the speed and maneuverability was increased.

2078. Radall, Thomas H. HALIFAX, WARDEN OF THE NORTH. London:
       Dent, 1948.

       Halifax, Nova Scotia was the prime naval base for the Royal
       Navy in North America. This book provides an excellent per-
       spective of naval affairs in the Maritimes.

2079. Reibel, Dorothy B. "The British Navy on the Upper Great
       Lakes, 1760-1785." NIAG FRONT, 20 (1973), 66-75.

       With a handful of small craft, the British maintained
       complete control of the Great Lakes in the war.

2080. Richmond, Herbert W. "The Hughes-Suffren Campaigns." MM,
       13 (1927), 219-237.

       Richmond praises Hughes as the true hero in the fighting
       in the Indian Ocean with the French.

2081. Rodney, George Lord. LETTER BOOKS AND ORDER BOOKS OF GEORGE,
       LORD RODNEY, ADMIRAL OF THE WHITE SQUADRON, 1780-1782. 2
       vols. The New York Historical Society Collections. Vols.
       65, 66. New York: The Society, 1932.

       Rodney was probably the most important admiral in the Royal
       Navy during the Revolution with respect to successful voyages
       against the French. Although his remarkable work at Gibraltar
       is not covered here, there are hundreds of letters to and from
       Rodney concerning his North Atlantic and his Caribbean opera-
       tions. How Rodney handled the disposition of his squadrons
       in the West Indies made a crucial difference at the Battle
       of the Virginia Capes.

2082. Sands, John Ogilby. "Sea Power at Yorktown: The Archeology
       of the Captive Fleet." Ph.D. dissertation, George Washing-
       ton University, 1980.

       Here is an excellent analysis of the role of sea power in
       the Yorktown campaign. The author describes the strategic
       background, logistical problems, and the tactical consequences.
       A major point that emerges is the difficulties of the British
       in a unique situation when its Navy, short of vessels, was
       unable to extricate Cornwallis. A second point covers
       Cornwallis's 60 odd craft which enabled him to control the
       York River and to prevent a French amphibious landing. The
       descriptions of the ships wrecked and recently examined by
       marine archeologists is fascinating.

2083. Sandwich, John Montagu, 4th Earl of. THE PRIVATE PAPERS OF
       THE JOHN, EARL OF SANDWICH, FIRST LORD OF THE ADMIRALTY,
       1771-1782. Edited by G.R. Barnes and H.J. Owen. 4 vols.
       Publications of the Naval Records Society. Nos. 69, 71,
       75, 78. London: The Society, 1932-38.

       This collection may provide the best coverage of a British
       admiral from the 1771-82 years. The material on the opening
       phase of the war in North America is refreshing in Volume
       one. Volume two covers cruises in home waters and the famous
       court-martial involving Admiral Keppel. Volumes three and
       four survey operations with the Western Squadron, and maneu-
       vers in North America and in the Caribbean.

2084. Sherman, Constance D. "An Account of the Scuttling of His
       Majesty's Armed Sloop LIBERTY." AMER NEP, 20 (1980), 243-
       249.

       The British ship, famous for seizing illicit imports to
       Rhode Island, was seized by colonists in Newport and destroyed.

2085. Spencer, Frank. "Lord Sandwich, Russian Masts and American
       Independence." MM, 44 (1958), 116-127.

       This is a good commentary about the importance of Russian
       timber for French ships and Britain's difficulties with the
       Declaration of Armed Neutrality in March, 1780.

2086. Stout, Neil R. "Manning the Royal Navy in North America,
       1763-1775." AMER NEP, 23 (1963), 174-185.

       Hundreds of Americans were impressed from New York, Rhode
       Island and Massachusetts due to large desertion rates from
       British fleets.

2087. ————. THE ROYAL NAVY IN AMERICA, 1760-1775. A STUDY OF
       THE ENFORCEMENT OF BRITISH COLONIAL POLICY IN THE ERA OF
       THE AMERICAN REVOLUTION. Annapolis: Naval Institute Press,
       1973.

       This is a fine study of how the British Navy attempted to

enforce imperial legislation in North America before the war.
This is a valuable book for it demonstrates how the ineptness
of Admiral John Montagu angered patriots; it stresses the
difficulties the commanders had in enforcing the Townshend
Acts, and it notes that the length and contours of the
American coast made patrolling with insufficient ships a
difficult task. This is an essential book in understanding
how maritime matters were a factor in revolt.

2088. Syrett, David. "HMS Armed Ship Vigilant, 1777-1780." MM,
       64 (1978), 57-62.

       A transport was converted into a fire-support vessel and
       performed well at Mud Island in the Delaware in late 1777.

2089. ———. SHIPPING AND THE AMERICAN WAR, 1775-1783: A STUDY
       IN BRITISH TRANSPORT ORGANIZATION. New York: Oxford
       University Press, 1970.

       Here is a valuable account of how complicated were the
       procedures involving the leasing of British merchant vessels
       for supply ships and troop transports. Though it is dull
       reading, the work is solidly documented, has detailed dis-
       cussions of the Navy Board, contractual measures, and some
       vivid passages about the complexities in shipping men and
       supplies overseas. For a good study of the mechanism of
       naval logistics, this is an essential book.

2090. ———. "The Disruption of HMS Flora's Convoy, 1776." MM,
       56 (1976), 423-448.

       Due to a variety of factors, six out of the thirty-three
       British merchant ships were captured by Americans in the
       North Atlantic.

2091. ———. "The Fleet that Failed." USNIP, 101 (1975), 66-77.

       Regardless of the British navy's power, experience, and
       strategic advantages, the tasks imposed were too great con-
       sidering the many oceans involved and the number of enemy
       squadrons; there were not enough ships and men for the job.

2092. ———. "The Methodology of British Amphibious Operations
       during the Seven Years' and American War." MM, 58 (1972),
       269-280

       This is a good survey of the landing craft and special
       equipment needed which gave the British great flexibility in
       their landing operations.

2093. Tilley, John Andrew. "The Royal Navy in North America, 1774-
       1781: A Study in Command." Ph.D. dissertation, The Ohio
       State University, 1980.

       The author notes the difficulties that the Navy had in
       crushing American resistance that was compounded when France

318 THE BRITISH NAVY

and Spain entered the struggle which became a global war
fought in the classic traditions of the age of sail. Concentrating on the American theatre, Tilly stresses the sea
actions, the personalities of admirals, and their relationships to British generals. He faults the Admiralty for corruption, inept administration, the lack of a coherent scheme
for simultaneously crushing a rebellion and fighting a
traditional naval war, and for permitting the French navy
to take the initiative.

2094. Usher, Roland G. "Royal Navy Impressment During the Ameri-
        can Revolution." MVHR, (1951), 673-688.

        Some 150 press gangs operated on land and sea to seize
        over 116,000 men but only 43,000 were actually pressed.

2095. Whiteley, W.H. "The British Navy and the Siege of Quebec,
        1775-1776." CAN HIST REV, 61 (1980), 13-27.

        The naval contribution to the defense of the city was con-
        siderable, and the Admiralty acted promptly in dispatching
        a relief expedition up the St. Lawrence.

2096. Willcox, William B. "Admiral Rodney Warns of Invasion, 1776-
        1777." AMER NEP, 4 (1944), 193-198.

        Rodney notified the Admiralty of potential French landings
        long before the Franco-American Alliance.

2097. ———. "Arbuthnot, Gambier, and Graves: 'Old Women.'" In
        George A. Billias, editor. GEORGE WASHINGTON'S OPPONENTS:
        BRITISH GENERALS AND ADMIRALS IN THE AMERICAN REVOLUTION.
        New York: Morrow and Co., 1969, pp. 260-290.

        Here are three incisive portraits of incompetent admirals
        who had ample opportunities to attack the Americans and
        French.

2098. ———. "British Strategy in America, 1778." J MOD HIST,
        19 (1947), 97-121.

        After Yorktown, the admirals planned bolder sweeps of
        American waters and generals in North America.

2099. ———. "Rhode Island in British Strategy, 1780-81." J
        MOD HIST, 17 (1945), 304-331.

        Admiral Arbuthnot and General Clinton were unable to cooper-
        ate in efforts to attack the French squadron in Newport.

2100. ———. "The Battle of Porto Praya, 1781." AMER NEP, 5
        (1945), 64-78.

        Suffren defeated Commodore Johnstone in a fierce fight off
        the Cape Verde Islands, took Capetown, and sailed on to the
        Indian Ocean.

2101.   ———. "The British Road to Yorktown: A Study in Divided
         Command." AHR, 19 (1947), 97-121.

         This article provides ample clues about the quarrels of
         British admirals and generals in North America.

2102.   Yerxa, Donald A. "The Burning of Falmouth, 1775: A Case
         Study in British Imperial Pacification." MAINE HIST Q,
         14 (1975), 119-160.

         The October, 1775 bombardment by five British ships only
         helped to stiffen American resistance.

2103.   ———. "Vice Admiral Graves and the North American Squadron,
         1774-1776." MM, 62 (1976), 371-385.

         Graves had insufficient ships, increasing duties and was
         impeded by strategic planning in London.

X. DIPLOMACY OF THE AMERICAN REVOLUTION

2104. Abarca, Ramon E. "Classical Diplomacy and the Bourbon
       'Revanche' Strategy 1763-1770." REV POL, 32 (1970), 313-
       37.

       This is a thoughtful discussion of France's desire for
       revenge due to losses in the Seven Years War.

2105. Abernethy, Thomas P. "Commercial Activities of Silas
       Deane in France." AHR, 39 (1934), 477-485.

       Diplomat Deane was a war profiteer whose secret business
       operations remain a mystery.

2106. Alden, Dauril. "The Marquis of Pompal and the American
       Revolution." AMERICAS, 17 (1960), 369-382.

       No friend of the Revolution, Portugal's strong man tried
       to gain advantages between Spain and Britain; Portuguese
       shipping was hurt by American privateers.

2107. Auger, Helen. "Benjamin Franklin and the French Alliance."
       AMER HERITAGE, 7 (3) (1956), 65-88.

       Here is a refreshing essay on Franklin's diplomatic
       activities in Paris.

2108. ————. THE SECRET WAR OF INDEPENDENCE. New York: Duell,
       Sloane, and Pearce, 1955.

       In a thorough study through a maze of documents, Auger wrote
       a fine account of the material and diplomatic assistance
       rendered by European powers before the Franco-American Alli-
       ance of 1778. The work is especially good on matters con-
       cerning secret loans, undercover shipments, aid to privateers,
       and the difficulties confronting Continental agents in
       European capitals and in the West Indies in their quest for
       diplomatic support.

2109. Bamford, Paul W. "France and the American Market in Naval
       Timber and Masts, 1776-1786." J ECON HIST, 12 (1952), 21-
       34.

       France desired American timber for her fleet, and this
       factor had diplomatic ramifications.

2110. Barton, H.A. "Sweden and the War of American Independence."
       WMQ, 23 (1966), 408-430.

The Swedes were allied to France, were quasi-supporters of
the Revolution, resented British maritime strength, wanted
opportunities to trade with America, and they joined the
League of Armed Neutrality in 1780.

2111. Beirne, Frank F. "Mission to Canada: 1776." MD HIST MAG,
       60 (1950), 404-420.

       The author compiled a lucid narrative about the frustrated
       American diplomatic efforts in Quebec in order to unite
       Canadians with the American Revolutionary effort. The key
       obstacle was the pro-British attitude of the French Bishop of
       Quebec.

2112. Bemis, Samuel Flagg. "British Secret Service and the Franco-
       American Alliance." AHR, 29 (1924), 474-495.

       A famed historian wrote the fascinating essay about Dr.
       Edward Brancroft, William Eden, and Paul Wentworth who
       spied on American agents in Paris.

2113. ————. "Canada and the Peace Settlement of 1782-1783." CAN
       HIST REV, 14 (1933), 265-284.

       Very useful in comprehending the tricky questions about
       fisheries and boundaries at the French and Spanish courts,
       this article notes John Jay's key role in the negotiations.

2114. ————. THE DIPLOMACY OF THE AMERICAN REVOLUTION. New York:
       D. Appleton-Century Co., 1935.

       Bemis, the dean of early American foreign policy, wrote a
       pioneering work on the reasons why, against great obstacles,
       American diplomats were successful in gaining allies, material
       support, and a successful peace treaty in 1783. Although
       somewhat moralistic and now outdated, this is a highly read-
       able and thoroughly documented account that should be con-
       sulted.

2115. Bolkovitinov, Nicholai N. RUSSIA AND THE AMERICAN REVOLUTION.
       Translated and edited by C. Jay Smith. Tallahassee: The
       Diplomat Press, 1967.

       A famed Russian historian wrote an incisive study of early
       American-Russian relations. The book demonstrates the sur-
       prising number of contacts of various types between the two
       nations. It contains ample data on trade and commerce; and
       it shows the establishment of early cultural and scientific
       links between America and Russia.

2116. Boyd, Julian P. "Silas Deane: Death By A Kindly Teacher of
       Treason." WMQ, 16 (1957), 165-187.

       Boyd notes Deane's treasonous activities, his links to Dr.
       Edward Bancroft (a double agent), and Deane's mysterious death
       by poison.

2117. Brown, Margaret L. "William Bingham, Agent of the Con-
       tinental Congress in Martinique." PA MHB, 61 (1937), 54-
       87.

       In a crisp essay, Brown reviews the profitable diplomatic
       career of an agent who acquired weapons in the West Indies
       and reported on enemy fleet maneuvers.

2118. Brown, Marvin L., Jr. "American Independence Through
       Prussian Eyes: A Neutral View of the Negotiations of 1782-
       1782." HISTORIAN, 18 (1955-56), 189-201.

       Frederick the Great viewed the war as a British matter and
       doubted if the American republic could endure.

2119. Burnett, Edmund C. "Notes on American Negotiations for
       Commercial Treaties." AHR, 16 (1910-11), 579-587.

       This is a good summary of American trade discussions with
       Austria, Prussia, Sweden, and the United Provinces.

2120. Buron, Edmund. "Statistics on Franco-American Trade, 1778-
       1806." J ECON BUS HIST, 4 (1932), 571-586.

       The article shows how the French modified their practice
       of restricting trade within their Caribbean colonies in
       order to assist the American cause.

2121. Calkin, Homer L. "American Influence in Ireland, 1760-1800."
       PA MHB, 71 (1947), 103-120.

       Calkin notes the differences and similarities of America
       and Ireland as British possessions, that Ireland was hurt
       economically by the war, and that its leaders were split
       into many factions.

2122. Clark, Dora M. "British Opinion of Franco-American Relations,
       1775-1795." WMQ, 4 (1947), 305-316.

       The writer notes that Britain favored reconciliation with
       America after 1781 to damage the French threat in Europe.

2123. Caughey, John W. "The Panis Mission to Pensacola, 1772."
       HISP AMER HIST REV, 10 (1930), 480-489.

       As an episode in Anglo-Spanish rivalry on the Gulf coast,
       Madrid sent Captain Jacinto Panis as a spy for future mili-
       tary expeditions.

2124. Chinard, Gilbert, ed. THE TREATIES OF 1778, AND ALLIED DOCU-
       MENTS. Baltimore: Johns Hopkins University Press, 1928.

       Here is a superb study of the events leading to the Franco-
       American Alliance and the commitment of French to the Ameri-
       can cause. The work is quite readable, packed with informa-
       tion and source material, and it provides valuable insights
       into American foreign policy of the era.

2125.   Corwin, Edward S. FRENCH POLICY AND THE AMERICAN ALLIANCE
        OF 1778. Princeton: Princeton University Press, 1916.

        This is a solid pioneering study of the Franco-American
        Alliance. It is traditional diplomatic history with the
        emphasis on correspondence and policy-making by dignitaries
        in the two nations. Although it minimizes the importance of
        French seapower (in the light of recent interpretations) and
        the French link to Spain in the war, it is a scholarly and
        dependable introduction to the study.

2126.   ————. "The French Objective in the American Revolution."
        AHR, 21 (1915), 35-61.

        This is an excellent discussion of how Bourbon attitudes
        were based solely on traditional balance of power concepts
        and not on sympathy for the patriotic endeavors.

2127.   Cowing, Cedric B., ed. THE AMERICAN REVOLUTION: ITS MEANING
        TO ASIANS AND AMERICANS. Honolulu: The East-West Center,
        1977.

        Written by scholars from the United States and nine Asian
        nations, these essays probe the question whether the American
        experience had relevance to older, more stable societies in
        the East. The Revolution had some effect in trade, stimu-
        lating some discussions about political ideals and about
        the relationship between public authority and private free-
        dom.

2128.   Crosby, Alfred W., Jr. "The Beginnings of Trade Between the
        United States and Russia." AMER NEP, 21 (1961), 207-215.

        Traditional exchanges of Russian naval stores for American
        agricultural products were checked by Britain to 1775, but
        direct trade with St. Petersburg began actively in 1783.

2129.   Douglas, Elisha P. "German Intellectuals and the American
        Revolution." WMQ, 17 (1960), 200-218.

        In a thoughtful article covering the ideas of some ten in-
        fluential German thinkers, Douglas notes their views on
        mercenaries, Loyalism, and armed rebellion.

2130.   Dull, Jonathan R. "Franklin in France: A Reappraisal." WEST
        SOC FR HIST, 4 (1976), 256-282.

        Dull concludes that Franklin in Europe from 1776-82 per-
        formed a masterful task in diplomacy.

2131.   Dupuy, R. Ernest, Gay Hammerman, and Grace P. Hayes. THE AMERI-
        CAN REVOLUTION: A GLOBAL WAR. New York: David McKay Co.,
        1977.

        One familiar with the war and diplomacy of the Revolution
        would quickly recognize that there is not a single new fact

or fresh interpretation in this work complied from familiar
sources. General readers might benefit from it as a highly
simplistic introduction to the era, but the work should be
used with caution.

2132. Duyvermann, J.P. "An Historic Friendship." HALVE MAEN,
        40 (1965), 11-12.

        Jean Luzac, influential editor of the GAZETTE DE LEYDE,
        assisted   John Quincy Adams in Europe and championed the
        American cause in The Netherlands.

2133. Einhorn, Nathan R. "The Reception of the British Peace Offer
        of 1778." PA HIST, 16 (1949), 191-214.

        Poorly documented and rambling, this essay attempts to
        explain why Congress rejected Britain's Carlisle Commission.

2134. Fagerstrom, D.I. "Scottish Opinion and the American Revolu-
        tion." WMQ, 11 (1954), 252-275.

        The author stresses the great interest in Scot cities about
        the rebellion overseas due to the tobacco trade, political
        factors at home, and the flowering of enlightened thought.

2135. Fernandez-Show, Carlos M. "Spain's Aid in the Independence
        of the United States." INTER-AMER REV BIB, 26 (1976),
        456-508.

        This is the best article in English about Spain's signifi-
        cant role in aiding the Americans, long before 1779. The
        essay mentions numerous battles Spanish troops fought in
        North America against Britain and the amount of material aid
        to the United States.

2136. Gilbert, Felix. "The New Diplomacy of the Eighteenth Century."
        WORLD POL, 4 (1951), 19-24.

        This is a penetrating summary of what the word "alliance"
        meant to European politicians.

2137. Golden, Frank A. "Catherine II and the American Revolution."
        AHR, 21 (1915), 92-96.

        The Tsarina viewed the revolution in terms of power only,
        and she joined the League of Armed Neutrality against Britain.
        But she was cautious about helping or recognizing the republic.

2138. Griffiths, David M. "American Commercial Diplomacy in Russia,
        1780 to 1783." WMQ, 27 (1970), 279-410.

        This is an excellent discussion of the American mission of
        Francis Dane to St. Petersburg frustrated by British intrigue,
        trade conditions, Catherine's fear of rebellion, and the need
        for a Russian-Austrian alliance against the Turks.

2139.   ————. "An American Contribution to the Armed Neutrality
         of 1780." RUSS REV, 30 (1971), 164-172.

         This article demonstrates the influence of American
         privateering off Norway as a crucial factor in the re-
         generation of Russian maritime power on the Baltic.

2140.   ————. "Nikita Panin, Russian Diplomacy, and the Other
         Revolution." SLAVIC REV, 28 (1969), 1-24.

         This is a solid article which examines Russian attitudes
         toward the revolution in great detail.

2141.   Gunther, Hans Karl. "Frederick the Great, the Bavarian War
         of Succession and the American War of Independence."
         DUQUESNE REV, 16 (1971), 59-74.

         While favorable to the American cause and anti-British,
         Frederick was involved in a European war (1778-79) and
         was unable to expand Prussia's commercial links to the
         republic.

2142.   Harris, Robert D. "French Finances and the American War,
         1777-1783." J MOD HIST, 48 (1970), 233-258.

         Here is a key article about the cause and effect relation-
         ship to the French Revolution. While noting the huge loans
         France made to America, Harris doubts if these credits were
         a major factor in precipitating the French financial crisis
         by 1788.

2143.   Haworth, P.L. "Frederick the Great and the American Revolu-
         tion." AHR, 9 (1904), 460-478.

         Frederick displayed little concern over the American strug-
         gle. He hated England and only wanted to expand Prussian com-
         merical ties to the new republic.

2144.   Hoffman, Philip C. "Australia's Debt to the American Revolu-
         tion." HISTORIAN, 17 (1955), 143-156.

         Tory exiles, along with convicts from Britain, colonized
         New South Wales before France penetrated the area.

2145.   Hunninghen, Benjamin. "Dutch-American Relations During the
         Revolution." NY HIST SOC Q, 37 (1953), 170-184.

         In a concise summary, the essayist notes the interlocking
         themes of Dutch idealism and investment opportunities in
         America as well as the work of John Quincy Adams negotiating
         with the Netherlands.

2146.   Hutson, James H. "Early American Diplomacy: A Reappraisal."
         Q J LIB CONG, 33 (1976), 183-198.

Hutson stresses that American diplomats were not idealistic, not particularly concerned with mercantile aspirations, but that they applied contemporary concepts of European politics in their negotiations.

2147. ————. "Intellectual Foundation of Early American Diplomacy." DIP HIST, 1 (1977), 1-15.

This is a well-reasoned essay about how Congress overestimated the importance of American trade, and how wary it was of being a French client-state.

2148. ————. JOHN ADAMS AND THE DIPLOMACY OF THE AMERICAN REVOLUTION. Lexington: University Press of Kentucky, 1980.

In one of the best studies of early foreign policy, Hutson shows how Adams's views were not uniquely American or revolutionary but were conventional for the eighteenth-century. This is a very insightful volume about how American diplomats considered the shifting balance of power, the need to preserve independence after the war, and their fears of becoming too dependent upon France.

2149. ————. "The Partition Treaty and the Declaration of Independence." JAR, 58 (1972), 877-890.

Numerous American leaders were convinced in 1776 that Britain planned to partition the colonies with France and Spain in return for military and naval aid.

2150. Irvine, Dallas D. "The Newfoundland Fishery: A French Objective in the War of American Independence." CAN HIST REV, 15 (1932), 268-284.

The peace negotiations in Europe pivoted not only around Spain's desire to recover Gibraltar but also about France's intentions to recover a sphere of influence near the St. Lawrence.

2151. Jameson, J. Franklin. "St. Eustatius in the American Revolution." AHR, 8 (1903), 683-708.

This influential article focused on the key role of the Dutch colony in the Caribbean which as a free port played an important role in providing essential commodities to the Americans.

2152. Kaplan, Lawrence S. THE AMERICAN REVOLUTION AND "A CANDID WORLD." Kent, Ohio: Kent State University Press, 1977.

There are five essays here that offer fresh perspectives on American diplomacy. James H. Hutson appraises the aims and achievements of Congress (pp. 40-68); William C. Stincombe concentrates on the role of John Adams in treaty-making (pp. 69-84); David M. Griffiths notes the role of Catherine the Great concerning Britain (pp. 85-110); Gregory L. Lint places

the Revolution within the context of international law (pp.
111-133); and Lawrence S. Kaplan studies Franco-American
relations from 1775 to 1801 (pp. 134-160). These are stimulating essays, each amplified by a full bibliography.

2153. Ketchum, Ralph L. "France and American Politics, 1763-
       1793." POL SCI Q, 78 (1963), 198-223.

       Here is the conventional view that the French alliance was
       the deciding factor in the American victory.

2154. Kirk, Grayson. "The United States in the Family of Nations."
       AMER PHIL SOC PROC, 100 (1956), 289-295.

       Kirk sketches a familiar story about Franklin's diplomatic
       achievements in Europe.

2155. Kite, Elizabeth S. "French 'Secret Aid'; Precursor to the
       Franco-American Alliance, 1776-1777." FRANCO-AMER REV, 1
       (1948), 143-152.

       The author credits Silas Deanne and Beaumarchais with ship-
       ping clandestine material which helped the Americans at
       Saratoga.

2156. Johnson, Amandus. "The American-Swedish Treaty of 1783."
       AMER SCAND REV, 46 (1958), 152-156.

       Gustavus III of Sweden proposed to Franklin a remarkably
       modern commercial agreement which was not ratified for thirty-
       three years.

2157. Klein, Milton M. "Failure of a Mission: the Drummond Peace
       Proposal of 1775." HUNT LIB Q, 35 (1972), 343-351.

       Lord Drummond's unofficial efforts for peace were doomed
       because Congress insisted on concessions.

2158. Klingelhofer, Herbert E. "Matthew Ridley's Diary During the
       Peace Negotiations of 1782." WMQ, 20 (1963), 95-133.

       The comments by Maryland's Ridley in Paris provide some
       fascinating details about the peacemakers.

2159. Klotz, Edwin F. "An American Patriot in Spain: 1781." SOC
       STUD, 57 (1960), 124-126.

       This is a brief sketch about diplomat John Trumbull of
       Connecticut.

2160. Lass, William E. "How the Forty-Ninth Parallel Became the
       International Boundary." MINN HIST, 44 (1975), 209-219.

       Here is an excellent discussion of how the negotiators, rely-
       ing on mistaken cartography, sought to close a boundary gap
       by relying on imaginary river routes.

2161. Lewis, James A. "Las Damas de la Havana, El Precursor, and
       Francisco de Saavadra: A Note on Spanish Participation
       in the Battle of Yorktown." AMERICAS, 37 (1980), 83-99.

       Twenty-eight wealthy Cubans led by Governor Saavadra loaned
       money to De Grasse's expedition; the author is dubious of
       the role of Miranda and the legend of Cuban women donating
       their jewels.

2162. Library of Congress. SYMPOSIA ON THE AMERICAN REVOLUTION, 4th,
       1975. THE IMPACT OF THE AMERICAN REVOLUTION ABROAD.
       Washington: Library of Congress, 1976.

       This collection of articles by prominent scholars concerns
       the influence of the Revolution in France, Holland, Britain,
       Russia, Ireland, Germany, Spain, Latin America, and Japan.
       While it is difficult to trace dominant themes to unify these
       essays, the material is refreshing, generally well-written,
       and global in scope. The main impact of the war on Britain,
       and the major international importance of the Revolution was
       that it was the only successful example of a modern patriotic
       rebellion.

2163. Libiszowska, Zofia. "Polish Opinion of the American Revolu-
       tion." POL AMER STUD, 34 (1977), 5-15.

       This is a thoughtful commentary about the pro-American
       views of educated Poles who were interested in American
       political theory.

2164. Lint, Gregg L. "John Adams on the Drafting of the Treaty
       Plan of 1776." DIP HIST, 2 (1978), 313-320.

       Adams's influencial role is stressed in this key essay.

2165. Liss, Peggy K. "The Significance of the American Revolution
       for United States-Spanish American Relations.". ORBIS, 20
       (1978), 147-159.

       This is a weak article which suggests the impact that the
       American revolution had on intellectuals in Latin America.

2166. McCadden, Helen M. "Juan de Miralles and the American
       Revolution." AMERICAS, 29 (1973), 359-375.

       This Havana-based secret agent channeled material aid to
       America, and he labored for Spanish participation in the
       war in return for the Floridas.

2167. Meng, John J. "A Foot-note to Secret Aid in the American
       Revolution." AHR, 43 (1938), 791-795.

       Meng credits Caron de Beaumarchais of Paris with adminis-
       tering the clandestine flow of material to America in 1776-
       77.

2168. ———. "French Diplomacy in Philadelphia: 1778-1779."
       CATH HIST REV, 24 (1938), 39-57.

       This is a good summary of French envoys dealing with the
       new republic.

2169. Meistrich, Herbert A. "Lord Drummond and Reconciliation."
       NJ HIST SOC PROC, 81 (1963), 256-277.

       Why the Drummond mission failed to reach a compromise
       with Congress is carefully explained in this incisive essay.

2170. Morris, Richard B. "The Jay Papers ... Mission to Spain."
       AMER HERITAGE, 19 (2) (1968), 8-21, 85-96.

       This is a fine summary of Jay's aborted effort at Madrid
       to win financial aid and diplomatic recognition.

2171. ———. THE PEACEMAKERS: THE GREAT POWERS AND AMERICAN
       INDEPENDENCE. New York: Harper and Row, 1965.

       This is the best account of American negotiations in Europe
       from 1778-83. Based on a fresh source of material from
       innumerable archives, the book provides a thoughtful analysis
       of the Power's reaction to the Revolution. Written with
       drama, humor and insight, this monograph provides excellent
       appraisals of the major and minor diplomats involved with
       particular attention to the author's hero, John Jay.
       Clearly, Spain was no sincere friend of the Republic, and
       France was quite willing to frustrate American territorial
       aspirations.

2172. Morton, Brian. "Vergennes, Beaumarchais and Roderique
       Hortalez et Cie." WEST SOC FR HIST, 3 (1975), 156-262.

       Morton provides the details here about the 'dummy' cor-
       poration of Beaumarchais that funneled secret aid to America.

2173. Murphy, Orville T. "Charles Gravier de Vergennes: Profile
       of an Old Regime Diplomat." POL SCI Q, 83 (1968), 400-416.

       This is a useful profile of the French Secretary of State
       for Foreign Affairs which shows him influenced by balance
       of power concepts.

2174. ———. "The Battle of Germantown and the Franco-American
       Alliance of 1778." PA MHB, 82 (1958), 55-64.

       Although defeated in the battle, the Americans performed
       so well against British troops that the fight was a major
       factor in convincing the French that Washington could win.

2175. ———. "The Comte de Vergennes, the Newfoundland Fisheries,
       and the Peace Negotiations of 1783: A Reconsideration."
       CAN HIST REV, 46 (1965), 35-46.

Here is an interesting sidelight of how France attempted
to hold off the Americans from sharing this valuable
area with the British after the war.

2176. O'Connel, Maurice R. "The American Revolution and Ireland."
        EIRE-IRELAND, 11 (1970), 3-12.

Though American revolutionary ideology was not decisive
in late eighteenth-century Irish history, it was influential
in the thought of nineteenth-century Irish political leaders.

2177. Plumb, J.H. "The French Connection." AMER HERITAGE, 26 (4)
        (1974), 26-57, 86-87.

In a masterly summary, Plumb reminds us that though
Franklin and LaFayette symbolize the link, there were in-
numerable Frenchmen – anxious for revenge after the Seven
Years War – fighting with the Americans.

2178. Rabb, Reginald E. "The Role of William Eden in the Peace
        Commission of 1778." HISTORIAN, 20 (1958), 153-170.

The mission of the future Baron Auckland to Congress was
doomed as British concessions were too late, particularly
after Burgoyne was defeated.

2179. Rakove, Jack N. "French Diplomacy and American Politics: The
        First Crisis." MID-AMERICA, 60 (1978), 27-35.

This is a simplistic account about the formation of American diplomatic concepts which provided in the Constitution
broad presidential prerogatives in diplomacy.

2180. Rinehard, Robert. "Denmark Gets the News of '76." SCANDA
        REV, 64 (1976), 5-14.

Here is a fine account of the Danish reaction which
stressed possible British trade reprisals, threats to the
Virgin Islands, and to shipping problems in the Baltic.

2181. Roslund-Mercurio, Carol. "Sweden and the American Revolu-
        tion." SCANDA REV, 64 (1976), 45-51.

This is a good study of Swedish reactions based on British
seizure of ships, and the reasons why Sweden joined the
League of Armed Neutrality and negotiated with the United
States in 1782.

2182. Saul, Norman. "The Beginnings of American-Russian Trade,
        1763-1766." WMQ, 26 (1969), 596-600.

Due to a boom in shipbuilding, Boston took the lead in
acquiring naval stores from Russia.

2183. Schoenbrun, David. TRIUMPH IN PARIS: THE EXPLOITS OF
       BENJAMIN FRANKLIN. New York: Harper and Row, 1976.

       Although there is little new in this account, it is
       extremely well written and highly entertaining. Schoenbrun
       is especially good on portraits of French society, court
       intrique, and Franklin's activities. The book's innumerable
       anecdotes about the era provide verve and color lacking in
       similar accounts.

2184. Sokol, Irene M. "The American Revolution and Poland: A
       Bibliographic Essay." POLISH REV, 12 (1967), 3-17.

       American influence on Polish thought was limited after two
       partition treaties by European powers, and because Polish
       newspapers were few.

2185. Starbuck, James C. "Ben Franklin and Isle Royle." MICH
       HIST, 46 (1962), 157-166.

       The author refutes the story that Franklin wanted the is-
       land because of its supposed copper deposits; the actual
       reason is that the area was an easily identifiable boundary,
       due to a cartographer's error.

2186. Stille, Charles J. "Beaumarchais and the 'lost million':
       A Chapter in the Secret History of the American Revolution."
       PA MHB, 11 (1887), 1-36.

       This is a detailed account of French expenditures for the
       American cause with stress on the unpublicized sums handled
       by Beaumarchais.

2187. Stincombe, William C. THE AMERICAN REVOLUTION AND THE FRENCH
       ALLIANCE. Syracuse, New York: Syracuse University Press,
       1969.

       Though there are no significant interpretative changes
       here, the author adds an abundance of detail to earlier
       studies on this topic. He adroitly covers privateering,
       secret aid, diplomatic maneuvers, and the decisions for the
       French intervention in American waters. Nicely written,
       thoroughly documented, this is a very readable book that
       merits a wide readership.

2188. Stock, Leo F. "The Irish Parliament and the American Revolu-
       TION." US CATH HIST SOC REV, 30 (1939), 11-29.

       There were many shades of opinion due to the dominance of
       the Anglo-Irish.

2189. Stover, John F. "French-American Trade During the Confedera-
       tion, 1781-1789." NC HIST REV, 35 (1958), 399-414.

       Though both nations hoped to augment their wartime - stimulated
       commerce, Congress was ineffectual in negotiating adequate
       commercial treaties.

2190. Streeter, Floyd B. "The Diplomatic Career of William
       Carmichael." MD HIST MAG, 8 (1913), 119-146.

       This dedicated patriot, assigned to Berlin and Paris,
       did a satisfactory job.

2191. Thomson, Buchan Parker. SPAIN: FORGOTTEN ALLY OF THE AMERI-
       CAN REVOLUTION. North Quincy, Massachusetts: Christopher,
       1976.

       Though a book in English about Spain's involvement in the
       Revolution is badly needed, this work cannot be recommended.
       Not only was the author unable to comprehend Spain's role
       in America and in Europe, but the volume is replete with fac-
       tual errors, grammatical mistakes, and incredible misinter-
       pretations of events. It appears to have been based entirely
       on three books published in the 1930s and little from
       Spanish archives.

2192. Tolles, Frederick B. "Franklin and the Pulteney Mission
       (1778): An Episode in the Secret History of the American
       Revolution." HUNT LIB Q, 17 (1953), 37-58.

       This article concerns the "peace feelers" from London to
       Paris which offered America a dominion status under the
       British crown.

2193. Toth, Charles W. "Anglo-American Diplomacy and the British
       West Indies, 1783-1789." AMERICAS, 32 (1976), 418-436.

       This article notes that from 1776-1789, the Indies provided
       a lucrative market for American shipping which was closed to
       the United States in 1783.

2194. United States. Department of State. THE REVOLUTIONARY DIP-
       LOMATIC CORRESPONDENCE OF THE UNITED STATES. Edited by
       Francis Wharton. 6 vols. Washington: Government Printing
       Office, 1889.

       This collection of documents is the basic source for dip-
       lomatic historians. Although this material is being re-
       vised for publication, Wharton's work is adequately edited
       and is crammed with information about the evolution of Ameri-
       can foreign policy during the war. Unfortunately, the docu-
       ments lack adequate explanatory introductions.

2195. Van Alstyne, Richard W. EMPIRE AND INDEPENDENCE: THE INTER-
       NATIONAL HISTORY OF THE AMERICAN REVOLUTION. New York:
       John Wiley and Sons, 1966.

       The author minimizes the importance of Saratoga in diplomacy
       and concentration on the implications of naval warfare by
       Britain against France and Spain. France had to pursue a
       broad maritime war, contends Van Alstyne, because of her
       Caribbean colonies, interests in India, and her desire to

assist the Americans. The factor of French seapower, and to
a lesser degree that of Spain and Holland, was decisive in
the war.

2196. ————. "Great Britain, the War for Independence, and the
Gathering Storm in Europe, 1775-1778." HUNT LIB Q, 27
(1964), 311-345.

This is a very useful summary of how British leaders viewed
the potential coalition of enemies against them and how they
feared the dismemberment of the empire.

2197. Van Oosten, F.C. "Some Notes Concerning the Dutch West
Indies During the American Revolutionary War." AMER NEP,
36 (1976), 155-169.

This is an excellent summary about the Dutch policy of
attempting neutrality, of trading with the Americans, and
repelling raids from the British. Of the six Dutch colonies,
St. Eustatius was the key one.

2198. Van Tyne, Claude F. "Influences Which Determined the French
Government to Make A Treaty with America, 1778." AHR, 21
(1916), 528-541.

Here is a solid essay which clearly explains why France
accepted the risks of warfare with Britain.

2199. Vigness, David M. "Don Hugo O'Conor and New Spain's
Northeastern Frontier, 1764-1776." J WEST, 6 (1967), 27-
40.

Here is a well-documented summary about Spain's major
figure in Texas and the Louisiana Territory until the
Revolution.

2200. Wead, Eunice. "British Public Opinion of the Peace With
America, 1782." AHR, 34 (1929), 513-531.

The press was not a guide or shaper of public views but
only mirrored public opinion which was well-informed on the
failures in North America.

2201. Whitbridge, Arnold. "Beaumarchais and the American Revolution." HIST TODAY, 17 (1967), 98-105.

The author compresses the lively career of the talented
musician, playwright, financier, and champion of America
into a neat essay.

2202. York, Neil L. "Clandestine Aid and the American Revolutionary War Effort: A Re-Examination." MILT AFF, 43 (1977)
26-30.

York notes that the shortages of weapons and gunpowder in

the American army in 1777 were partly overcome by imports
from Europe, and that much of this material came from other
sources than the trading company of Beaumarchais.

2203. Young, Philip. "The Netherlands and the United States."
       HALVE MAEN, 40 (1966), 7-8, 14.

This article concerns the achievements of John Adams
in convincing Dutch bankers to fund the American Revolution,
and in securing diplomatic recognition from the United
Provinces.

XI. THE IMPACT OF WAR ON SOCIETY

A. THE DEVELOPMENT OF A NATIONAL GOVERNMENT

2204. Adams, Willi Paul. THE FIRST AMERICAN CONSTITUTIONS:
REPUBLICAN IDEOLOGY AND THE MAKING OF THE STATE CONSTITU-
TIONS IN THE REVOLUTIONARY ERA. Translated by Rita and
Robert Kimberg. Chapel Hill: The University of North
Carolina Press, 1980.

In this solid and penetrating study, Adams claims that the
best source of information about the political thought of
the Founding Fathers is the state constitutions made in the
1776-80 era. In spirited prose, he argues that such
principles as the separation of powers, the system of checks
and balances, the independence of the judiciary, and the
consent of the governed are found in these documents. This
is a provocative account for the serious student.

2205. Batchelder, Robert F. "The Counterfeiting of Colonial Paper
Money as Seen Through the Letters of Signer of the Declaration of Independence, Josiah Bartlett." MANUSCRIPTS, 31
(1979), 207-211.

A Congressional delegate feared that the British counterfeiting of American paper currency would upset the patriot
economy.

2206. Becker, Robert A. REVOLUTION, REFORM AND THE POLITICS OF
AMERICAN TAXATION, 1763-83. Baton Rouge: Louisiana State
University Press, 1980.

Here is an excellent account about the practice of colonial
states regarding internal sources of revenue. The stress
here is less on familiar rhetoric but on the actual modes of
tax measures. Becker contends that by using tax legislation
as a model, one can perceive that the Revolution was fought as
a conflict of competing sectional and economic groups. This
is a profound study that is cleverly written.

2207. Bevan, Edith R. "The Continental Congress in Baltimore,
December 20, 1776 to February 27, 1777." MD HIST MAG, 42
(1947), 21-28.

Driven from Philadelphia, the Delegates spent ten miserable
weeks in the drab town.

2208. Burnett, Edmund C., ed. LETTERS TO MEMBERS OF THE CONTINEN-
TAL CONGRESS, 8 vols. Washington: Government Printing
Office, 1921-1926.

These volumes which cover the 1774-1789 era contain letters from constitutents to Delegates. The correspondence
covers a broad scope of problems that confronted Congress.
The series is well-footnoted, adequately indexed, and the
prefaced in each volume provide a useful perspective.

2209.   Coleman, John M. "How 'Continental' Was the Continental
        Congress." HIST TODAY, 18 (1968), 540-550.

        Congress actually had no intention of incorporating
        French Canada into the American republic.

2210.   Collier, Christopher. "Inside the American Revolution: A
        Silas Deane Diary Fragment." CONN HIST SOC BULL, 29 (1964),
        86-96.

        Deane was a diligent Delegate, but he was distrusted by
        politicians from his state.

2211.   ————. "Silas Deane Reports on the Continental Congress:
        A Diary Fragment: October 1-6, 1774."   CONN HIST SOC
        BULL, 29 (1964), 1-8.

        This article provides clues about the debate on the Con-
        tinental Association.

2212.   Cometti, Elizabeth. "Civil Servants of the Revolutionary
        Period." PA MHB, 75 (1951), 159-167.

        Here is an excellent summary of the functions of a bureauc-
        racy that was overworked and underpaid, and yet it main-
        tained a keen sense of duty.

2213.   Dabney, William M. "Drayton and Laurens in the Continental
        Congress." SC HIST MAG, 60 (1959), 41-82.

        Together in Congress for eighteen months, the two patri-
        cians diverged on many pertinent political issues.

2214.   Deane, Silas. "Correspondence of Silas Deane, Delegate to
        the First and Second Congresses at Philadelphia, 1774-
        1776." CONN HIST SOC COLL, 2 (1870), 127-368.

        Deane's letters with some twenty colleagues are full of
        gossip about contemporary affairs.

2215.   Dutcher, George M. "Rise of Republican Government in the
        United States." POL SCI Q, 55 (1940), 199-216.

        The author demonstrates why the nation became permanently
        committed to the theory and practice of a republican form
        of government.

2216.   Ferguson, E. James. "Business, Government, and Congressional
        Investigation in the Revolution." WMQ, 16 (1959), 293-316.

In 1778, Congress began to investigate profiteering, supposedly committed by Morris, Deane, Bingham, Arnold, Greene, and Wadsworth.

2217. ———. "The Nationalists of 1781-1783 and the Economic Interpretation of the Constitution." JAH, (1969), 241-261.

In a provocative revision of the economic interpretation of the Constitution, Ferguson demonstrates the Nationalist's views on the taxing power, the nation's debt, and the development of a centralized government to encourage capitalistic growth.

2218. ———. THE POWER OF THE PURSE: A HISTORY OF AMERICAN PUBLIC FINANCE, 1776-1790. Chapel Hill: University of North Carolina Press, 1961.

This is the best treatment of the financial problems of the era with ample quantitative data and details about the cost of war. The tables on income and expenditures, state payments for military services, the holdings of government securities, and the depreciation of Continental currency are invaluable. Though somewhat vague about the achievement of Robert Morris, about agrarian versus mercantile-capitalist interests, and about rivalries between various business groups, the monograph is a solid, scholarly contribution that should be read by specialists. The author's command of the literature, and his knowledge of source material are impressive.

2219. Garver, Frank H. "The Transition from the Continental Congress to the Congress of the Confederation." PAC HIST REV, 1 (1932), 221-234.

Garver viewed the Second Continental Congress as the Congress of the Confederation.

2220. Gerlach, Larry R. "A Delegation of Steady Habits: the Connecticut Congress, 1774-1789." CONN HIST SOC BULL, 31 (1966), 65-75; 32 (1967), 33-39.

Led by Roger Sherman, the Delegates adroitly handled issues of trade, finance, and currency.

2221. Harlow, Ralph V. "Aspects of Revolutionary Finance." AHR, 35 (1929), 46-68.

The author uses the conversion rate of $3.33 to £1 in order to demonstrate the paper money policies of Congress and the states.

2222. Harmon, George D. "The Proposed Amendments to the Articles of Confederation." S ATL Q, 24 (1925), 298-314.

There were fifty amendments proposed which all were re-
jected because of state claims, sectional rivalries, and
western lands.

2223. Henderson, H. James. "Congressional Factionalism and the
       Attempt to Recall Benjamin Franklin." WMQ, 27 (1970),
       246-267.

       The Lee-Deane controversy about removing Franklin from
       his European mission is a good example of a North-South
       alignment in voting.

2224. ————. "Constitutionalists and Republicans in the Con-
       tinental Congress, 1778-1786." PA HIST, 36 (1969), 119-
       144.

       A study of the Pennsylvania Delegates shows a shift to a
       more conservative stance by 1780, along with most southerners.

2225. ————. PARTY POLITICS IN THE CONTINENTAL CONGRESS. New
       York: McGraw-Hill Book Co., 1974.

       Henderson offers a revisionist approach that challenges
       the viewpoints of Nationalist and Progressive historians in
       this excellent work that should modify interpretations of
       the Confederation era. Party politics did not take the
       typical eighteenth-century form of factionalism but instead
       were sectional coalitions. Typically, New England contended
       with the South on key issues with the Middle States shifting
       in voting on legislation. Henderson delineates three eras
       of political organization and clearly identifies the leaders
       and the rivalries. The study is a commendable blend of docu-
       mentary evidence with quantitative examinations of congres-
       sional voting patterns to show that the main issue was
       federalism versus state's rights. The partisan alignments
       of this era prefigured the composition and program of the
       American party system   claims the author with compelling
       evidence.

2226. Hunt, Agnes. PROVINCIAL COMMITTEES OF SAFETY OF THE AMERI-
       CAN REVOLUTION. Cleveland: Winn and Judson, 1904.

       Though in need of revision due to recent studies, this
       pioneering study is well worth consulting. It provides a
       good analysis of the broad functions of the Committees in
       gathering information, defining policies, and supervising
       recruiting, propaganda, and the Loyalist problen.

2227. Jensen, Merrill. THE ARTICLES OF CONFEDERATION: INTERPRE-
       TATION OF THE SOCIAL CONSTITUTIONAL HISTORY OF THE AMERI-
       CAN REVOLUTION. Madison: University of Wisconsin Press,
       1940.

       This is a pioneering study about the framing and ratifica-
       tion of the first constitution of the United States with
       respect to the thinkers who wrote and approved it. Major

themes here are the number of accomplishments achieved by
Congress during and immediately after the war, and the relative strengths and not weaknesses of the Confederation.
Though astute on land problems, Jensen clouded the issues
of how issues related to property and representative democracy were transferred from the states to the national arena,
and these factors were responsible for the Articles. Nevertheless, this is a provocative monograph that has merited
wide attention from scholars.

2228.   ———. "The Cession of the Old Northwest." MVHR, 23 (1936–
         37), 27–48.

         Here is a fine discussion of state claims to frontier
         territory that were resolved after the war with Virginia's
         concessions as the key.

2229.   ———. "The Creation of the National Domain, 1781–84."
         MVHR, 26 (1939), 323–342.

         Jensen reviews the states' cession of western lands,
         particularly the pivotal argument between Virginia and
         Maryland.

2230.   ———. THE NEW NATION: A HISTORY OF THE UNITED STATES
         DURING THE CONFEDERATION. New York: Alfred A. Knopf, 1950.

         Jensen questions many traditional assumptions about the
         supposed weaknesses of the new nation. The era was not
         characterized by corruption, disintegration, pessimism,
         and bankruptcies, but it was featured by relative prosperity
         and optimism. Written clearly and replete with fresh data,
         this monograph is a dazzling rebuttal of the classic inter-
         pretation of the pre–1787 era as one of stagnation.

2231.   Lint, Gregg L. "The American Revolution and the Law of
         Nations, 1776–1789." DIP HIST, 1 (1977), 20–34.

         This is a good discussion of how Congress used, modified
         or extended international law concepts by using the Treaty
         Plan of 1776.

2232.   Lutz, Paul V. "Land Grants for Service in the Revolution."
         NY HIST SOC Q, 48 (1964), 221–235.

         Congress and the states were generous to enlistees and to
         veterans with provisions for cash, lands, pension bills,
         and depreciation certificates.

2233.   MacMillan, Margaret B. THE WAR GOVERNORS IN THE AMERICAN
         REVOLUTION. New York: Columbia University Press, 1943.

         Although the author did not have sufficient documentary
         material about several energetic state governors in the war,
         this is a convenient summary of their crucial roles.
         Trumbull of Connecticut and Clinton of New York rate high.

2234. McDonald, Forrest. E PLURIBUS UNUM: THE AMERICAN REPUBLIC,
       1776-1790. Boston: Houghton Mifflin, 1965.

       Here is a fine summary of the critical years when the
       government seemed barely able to continue. This is a highly
       literate work that provides a fresh and exciting re-creation
       of some fourteen crucial years of early national politics.
       McDonald stresses selfishness, sectional interests, and the
       lack of personal principle instead of emphasizing that many
       politicians may have had idealism and patriotism as their
       goals. The author's seventy pages of footnotes and references
       demonstrate a commendable grasp of the sources and of detail.
       The material on how the Revolution was consolidated, state
       by state (particularly in the south) is invaluable.

2235. McLoughlin, William C. "Isaac Backus and the Separation of
       Church and State in America." AHR, 73 (1968), 1392-1413.

       A prominent Baptist preacher and writer, Backus opposed
       laws that required compulsory church attendance on the Sab-
       bath.

2236. Main, Jackson Turner. POLITICAL PARTIES BEFORE THE CONSTI-
       TUTION. Chapel Hill: The University of North Carolina
       Press, 1973.

       This is a major work for graduate students and specialists.
       Main sees a trend toward democracy in the composition of the
       colonial assemblies and the state legislatures which demon-
       strated a gradual decline of wealthy representatives. He
       provides evidence of a two party system in effect by 1776.
       Using quantitative methods to handle the aggregate data,
       the author, in dry prose, provides greater precision to what
       have been questionable assertions about the nature of poli-
       tical behavior.

2237. ———.   THE SOVEREIGN STATES, 1775-1783. New York: New
       Viewpoints, 1973.

       This insightful synthesis has several organizational com-
       ponents. Four chapters summarize the colonial social struc-
       ture on the eve of war and the ideological political dif-
       ferences. Then Main traces the details about the individual
       state constitutions, concluding with an analysis about the
       degree of change, particularly with respect to the Loyalists
       and the economy. The constitutions represented a consensus
       with the democratic impulse liberated, but with full real-
       ization of democracy far in the future. Though weak in
       studying economic developments during the war, and hazy
       about the distinctions between Whig and Tory, this is an
       important work with prudent commentaries.

2238. ———.   THE UPPER HOUSE IN REVOLUTIONARY AMERICA, 1763-
       1788. Madison, Wisconsin: University of Wisconsin Press,
       1967.

By an astute analysis of the composition of the provincial governors' councils which tended to become state senates, the author demonstrates a democratizing trend of the Revolution. Main has compiled an impressive quantity of data from genealogies, tax and probate records, and local histories to determine the social-economic characteristics of some 1,100 senators and councillors and the relationship of the upper to the lower houses. He concludes that the war blunted aristocratic control of most senates and increased the degree of political factionalism. Although nebulous about classifying the middle class and the poor, Maine makes a major contribution in this volume.

2239. Marshall, Peter. "Radicals, Conservatives and the American Revolution." PAST AND PRESENT, 23 (1962), 44-56.

After surveying recent findings, the writer claims that a further investigation of the Confederation is required to determine if a real revolution occurred.

2240. Martin, James Kirby. THE HUMAN DIMENSION OF NATION MAKING: ESSAYS ON COLONIAL AND REVOLUTIONARY AMERICA. Madison: State Historical Society of Wisconsin, 1976.

Thirteen specialists contributed essays to this volume consisting of short, detailed studies of politics in specific areas. There appears to be no central theme and the topics vary considerably in scope but the contributors demonstrate a common reliance on data, an insistence on facts, and a tendency to avoid theorizing. The best essays are by John P. Kaminski, "Democracy Run Riot" (about Rhode Island), Jackson Turner Main, "The Distribution of Property in Colonial Connecticut," and Joseph L. Davis, "Sectional Reinterpretation of the Revolution."

2241. Monroe, John A. "Nonresident Representation in the Continental Congress: The Delaware Delegation of 1782." WMQ, 9 (1952), 166-190.

Delaware Delegates had difficulties in attending Congress so plural representation from Pennsylvania (such as Samuel Wharton) was common until 1782.

2242. Morris, Richard B. "The Confederation Period and the American Historian." WMQ, 13 (1956), 139-156.

This is excellent historiography about the attitudes of Federalists and anti-Federalists as viewed by ten major historians.

2243. Nevins, Allen. THE AMERICAN STATES DURING AND AFTER THE REVOLUTION, 1775-1789. New York: Macmillan and Co., 1924.

This famous work represented an effort to trace the political and economic development of each state during and after

the war. It is a fine example of "local history," but Nevins
sought an integrated pattern in the Progressive tradition of
historiography. Though it must be supplemented by more recent monographs, it is gracefully crafted, provocative, and
indispensable to students.

2244. Nichols, Marie A. "The Evolution of the Articles of Con-
        federation, 1775-1781." S ATL Q, 2 (1964), 307-340.

        This is a convenient summary about the plans devised by
        Franklin and Dickinson for a union of the provinces pre-
        sented to Congress in July, 1776.

2245. Oaks, Robert F. "Philadelphia Merchants and the First Con-
        tinental Congress." PA HIST, 40 (1973), 145-188.

        Few Quakers were involved in the influential merchant
        membership of Philadelphia "radicals."

2246. Pavlovsky, Arnold M. "'Between Hawk and Buzzard': Congress
        as Perceived by its Members, 1775-1783." PA MHB, 101
        (1977), 349-364.

        Delegates were frustrated by arduous duties, low pay,
        tedious debates, absenteeism, and mutual distrust.

2247. Rakove, Jack N. THE BEGINNINGS OF NATIONAL POLITICS: AN
        INTERPRETATIVE HISTORY OF THE CONTINENTAL CONGRESS. New
        York: Alfred A. Knopf, 1979.

        This is a solid study that merits examination. Differing
        with other specialists about the nature of political align-
        ments in Congress during the Revolution and about how the
        war was administered, Rakove concentrates on the mechanism
        of policy-making and the formation of bureaucratic controls.
        No single group controlled or distributed national offices.
        Instead of a revolutionary cadre manipulating legislation,
        practical politicans adjusted to the exigencies of war.
        Here is a fine book that merits study.

2248. Ryan, Frank W., Jr. "The Role of South Carolina in the First
        Continental Congress." SC HIST MAG, 60 (1959), 147-163.

        This is a good summary of five Delegates - Henry Middleton,
        Christopher Gadsden, Thomas Lynch, John Rutledge, and Edward
        Rutledge.

2249. Sanders, Jennings B. THE EVOLUTION OF EXECUTIVE DEPARTMENTS
        OF THE CONTINENTAL CONGRESS, 1774-1789. New York: Oxford
        University Press, 1935.

        Here is a fine study of administrative history. The
        author demonstrates how the executive departments evolved,
        and how these agencies operated individually and jointly.
        There are some penetrating insights here and abundant clues
        about the nature of Congressional elections and organization
        during the war years.

2250. Smith, Paul H. and others, eds. LETTERS OF DELEGATES TO
      CONGRESS, 1774-1789. 6 vols. Washington: Government
      Printing Office, 1976 - .

      Supplanting Burnett's earlier study these volumes, which
      carry the account through December, 1776 (with future
      volumes underway), contain a detailed chronology of Congres-
      sional activities. There are abundant letters - sometimes
      four to six for one day - written by Delegates to families,
      friends, and associates. These volumes provide fascinating
      clues about the thoughts of the Founding Fathers on current
      events. The correspondence requires close reading, but the
      amount of information is enormous. The material is superbly
      indexed, and the detailed footnotes are extremely useful.
      Here is ample material about how the nation's politicians
      directed the war effort. This is a key work, and it should be
      consulted.

2251. Tate, Thad W. "The Social Contract in America, 1774-1787."
      WMQ, 22 (1965), 375-391.

      The social contract theory, used to justify rebellion, was
      actually a conservative doctrine which discouraged radical
      thought.

2252. Taylor, Robert J. "Trial at Trenton." WMQ, 26 (1969), 521-
      547.

      This is a key article about the quarrel between Pennsylvania
      and Connecticut over the Susquehanna Company which demon-
      strates the legal machinery of two states, problems of land
      cessions and property claims, Indian rights, and the formation
      of a public land policy.

2253. United States Continental Congress. JOURNALS OF THE CONTIN-
      ENTAL CONGRESS, 1774-1789. Edited by Worthington C. Ford
      and others. 34 vols. Washington: Government Printing
      Office, 1904-1937.

      This collection of original records is an indispensable
      source of information. It provides a dependable chronology
      of events, information about debates, details about pro-
      cedures, composition of committees, and the passage of
      legislation. The index is particularly valuable.

2254. Van Tyne, Claude H. "Sovereignty in the American Revolu-
      tion: an Historical Study." AHR, 12 (1907), 529-549.

      Van Tyne suggest that "a dawn of the idea of a national
      state" emerged during the war.

2255. Vivian, James F. and Jean H. Vivian. "Congressional Indian
      Policy During the War for Independence: The Northern
      Department." MD HIST MAG, 53 (1968), 241-274.

Considering that the security of the frontier was vital,
Congress made alliances with certain tribes, but it shifted
and modified its policies leaving Indian allies with only
token assistance by 1783.

2256. Vivian, Jean H. "Military Land Bounties During the Revolution and Confederation Periods." MD HIST MAG, 61 (1966),
231-256.

This is an excellent summary of how Congress handled
demands for land by military veterans, Indian tribes, and
land companies.

2257. Wilmerding, Lucius, Jr. "The United States Lottery." NY
HIST SOC Q, 47 (1963), 5-39.

To solve its fiscal problems, Congress in 1776 tried to
attract the savings of the lower classes; but the plan was
a failure and it was liquidated in 1782.

2258. Wood, Gordon S. THE CREATION OF THE AMERICAN REPUBLIC,
1776-1787. Chapel Hill: The University of North Carolina
Press, 1969.

In a seminal work, Wood demonstrates how American politics
developed in the state conventions to the adoptions of the
federal constitutions. The Founding Fathers altered pre-
vailing political theory to adopt a new form of government
that provided for numerous checks upon excessive authority.
This monograph is one of the most insightful books recently
written on the Revolution. Though he writes in a ponderous
style, Wood demonstrates through his meticulous research an
enviable comprehension of early constitutional law and
incipient party politics. Stressing the inherent radicalism
of the Revolution, Wood's volume fills a former gap in a
long neglect of constitutional thought after 1776 to 1783.
The study is likewise valuable for its refreshing insights
into pre-1776 ideology, its comments on state constitutions,
its viewpoints about legislation, and, especially on the
"Critical Period" of the Confederation.

2259. Wright, Benjamin F. CONSENSUS AND CONTINUITY, 1776-1789.
Boston: Boston University Press, 1958.

The author shows the links between the political theory
of 1776 and that of 1787 in the formation of the national
union. Such concepts emerged from the colonial heritage of
self-government, from the early debates in 1775-76, and from
a basic consensus on political arrangements. To Wright, conflicts over economic questions mirrored sectional rather than
class differences. His contribution is to question the
familiar economic determination usually associated with the
framing of the Constitutions and to stress that when differences existed, there was a general willingness by leading
politicians to compromise. Wright's book is provocative,
stimulating, and it deserves careful study.

B. THE STATES

1. New Hampshire

2260. Adams, Charles T. MATTHEW THORNTON OF NEW HAMPSHIRE: A PATRIOT
OF THE AMERICAN REVOLUTION. Philadelphia: Dando Printing
and Publishing Company, 1903.

This is a compact narrative about one of the signers of
the Declaration of Independence and one of the state's foremost politicians.

2261. Akers, Charles W. "Honorary Lieutenant Governor: John Temple
and the American Revolution." HIST NH, 30 (1975), 79-99.

Temple was appointed by the crown during the war but never
held the office.

2262. Aldrich, Edgar. "The Affair of the Cedars and the Service
of Col. Timothy Bedel in the War of the Revolution." NH HIST
SOC PAP, 3 (1891), 194-231.

Bedel's regiment was badly defeated by the British on the
St. Lawrence in 1776.

2263. Amory, Thomas C. THE MILITARY SERVICES AND PUBLIC LIFE OF
MAJOR-GENERAL JOHN SULLIVAN OF THE AMERICAN REVOLUTIONARY
ARMY. 1888. Reprint. New York: Kennikat Press, 1968.

Sullivan was New Hampshire's most important general but his
combat achievements were debatable. This volume is really
a vindication of Sullivan's conduct and not an actual biography. However, it contains useful insights into the state's
politics.

2264. Anderson, Leon W. MAJOR JOHN STARK, HERO OF BUNKER HILL AND
BENNINGTON, 1778-1826. Concord, New Hampshire: Evans
Printing Co., 1972.

This is a brief sketch of Stark's colorful career that is
quite readable.

2265. Andersen, Karen E. "A Return to Legitimacy: New Hampshire's
Constitution of 1776." HIST NH, 31 (1976), 155-163.

Representatives from 162 towns met at Exeter in December,
1775 to legitimize the new government, and to make New
Hampshire the first "independent" colony of the thirteen.

2266. Aykroyd, Elizabeth Rhoades. "Notes on the Raids on Fort
William and Mary." HIST NH, 32 (1977), 144-147.

This article contains depositions about the raid led by
Pierce Long and John Landon with men from New Castle and
Portsmouth.

2267. Bail, Hamilton Vaughn. "A Letter to Lord Germain About Vermont." VT HIST, 34 (1966), 226-234.

Loyalist Joshua Locke sought a land title guarantee and to make the Hamphire Grants an independent province with a large extension of its boundaries.

2268. Baker, Henry M. "General Enoch Poor." JAH, 15 (1921), 117-132.

An Exeter soldier, Poor fought at Bunker Hill, in Canada, and at Saratoga.

2269. Bascom, R.O. "Fort Edward." MAG HIST, 17 (1913), 142-152.

This is a good summary of the post's importance in the northern campaign, 1776-1777.

2270. Beane, Samuel C. "General Enoch Poor." NH HIST SOC PROC, 3 (1899), 435-472.

Although this article is not documented, it is the best account of Poor's contributions in several campaigns.

2271. Belknap, Jeremy. THE HISTORY OF NEW HAMPSHIRE. WITH A NEW INTRODUCTION BY JOHN KIRTLAND WRIGHT. 2 vols. New York and London: Johnson Reprint Corporation, 1970.

This is a reprint of a three volume edition published in 1812. Belknap was the state's famed historian. Although carelessly documented, the work is useful because of the coverage of events, its long notes, a good introduction, and a rich bibliography.

2272. Bell, Charles H. "Exeter in 1776." GRANITE MONTHLY, 3 (1879-80), 410-424.

This is a good account of the capital during a crucial year.

2273. Bittinger, J.Q. "Colonel Charles Johnston." GRANITE MONTHLY, 15 (1893), 185-196.

A citizen of Haverhill, Johnston led a militia regiment at Bennington.

2274. Blake, Amos J. "General James Reed." NH HIST SOC PROC, 1 (1875), 109-115.

A minor figure at the siege of Boston and at Ticonderoga, Reed was a wealthy proprietor of land tracts.

2275. Bouton, Nathaniel and others, eds. DOCUMENTS AND RECORDS RELATING TO THE PROVINCE, TOWNS, AND STATE OF NEW HAMPSHIRE. 40 vols. Concord, Nashua, and Manchester, New Hampshire: 1867-1943.

Though poorly organized and edited, these volumes still provide the single best source of data about eighteenth-century
politics in New Hampshire. Here are replicas of letters, town
charters, legislative proceedings, petitions, and a variety
of miscellaneous documents. For the Revolutionary era, volumes seven, eight, fourteen through sixteen, twenty and
thirty should be consulted.

2276. Brown, Sanborn, C., and Kenneth Scott. "Count Rumford: Inter-
       national Informer." NEQ, 21 (1948), 34-49.

       A famous scientist with Tory connections, Rumford was ap-
       pointed to lucrative official posts by the Crown and provided
       the British with military information about New England regi-
       ments.

2277. Butters, Avery J. "New Hampshire History and the Public Ca-
       reer of Meshech Weare, 1713-1786." Ph.D. dissertation.
       Fordham University, 1961.

       Here is an adequate narrative of politics in the state during
       the era. Weare was one of New Hampshire's foremost patriots,
       he was deeply involved in the war effort, and he dominated
       numerous state committees. His biography provides a good in-
       sight into a state attempting to prosecute the war on several
       fronts.

2278. Caswell, Fred M. "John Stark, Originator of N.H. State Motto:
       'Live Free or Die'." HIST NH, 1 (1945), 1-6.

       This is a very weak summary of a famous hero.

2279. Cathers, Darryl J. "Power to the People: The Revolutionary
       Structure Behind the Attacks on Fort William and Mary, 1774."
       HIST NH, 29 (1974), 261-280.

       The storming of the British garrison by a crowd in Portsmouth
       demonstrated the network of political cooperation among
       Hampshire towns and the formation of the "Friends of Liberty."

2280. Chase, Frederick. A HISTORY OF DARTMOUTH COLLEGE AND THE TOWN
       OF HANOVER, NEW HAMPSHIRE. Edited by John K. Lord. 2 vols.
       Cambridge, Massachusetts: John Wilson and Son University
       Press, 1891.

       Pages 318-421 in volume one cover the 1774-82 era and the
       influence of the war on the college; pages 422-527 treat the
       institution's role in state politics.

2281. Chase, Theodore. "The Attack on Fort William and Mary." HIST
       NH, 18 (1963), 20-37.

       This is a good summary of the famous incident in Portsmouth
       on December 14, 1774 involving two hundred patriots.

2282.   Clement, John. "Vermont in the Making: A Review." VT HIST
        SOC PROC, 7 (1939), 178-184.

        Clement raises many incisive questions about how historians
        have described Vermont's early political life.

2283.   Clough, Ovando D. "The Vermont Grants, New Hampshire's In-
        terest in Them." GRANITE STATE, 5 (1908), 23-28, 114-119,
        185-190, 245-251.

        The transition from Grants to statehood was politically
        turbulent.

2284.   ————. "The War of the Grants; Or, Along the Political High-
        way to Vermont." THE VERMONTER, 13 (1908), 47-53, 81-88.

        This essay has data about how New Hampshire's Provincial Con-
        gress handled demands for a new state formed from lands in the
        Grants and the Connecticut River Valley.

2285.   Clough, William O. "Colonel Alexander Scammell." GRANITE
        MONTHLY, 14 (1892), 262-275.

        Scammell, active in several major campaigns, merits a far
        better article than this one.

2286.   Collier, Christopher. "Roger Sherman and the New Hampshire
        Grants." VT HIST, 30 (1962), 211-219.

        Sherman was instrumental in settling a disputed land claim
        west of the Connecticut River that helped to check a separatist
        movement.

2287.   Commissioners' Convention. "Revolutionary War Records of
        Commissioner's Convention - December, 1776, January, 1778,
        and 1780." NH HIST SOC COLL, 9 (1889), 245-271, 272-303.

        These documents provide information about a regional war
        effort in recruiting, hounding Tories, controlling prices, and
        related activities.

2288.   Daniell, Jere. EXPERIMENT IN REPUBLICANISM: NEW HAMPSHIRE
        POLITICS AND THE AMERICAN REVOLUTION, 1741-1794. Cambridge,
        Massachusetts: Harvard University Press, 1970.

        Here is an excellent and comprehensive account of issues in
        the state during the war. After summaries of the Wentworth
        rule and the militia, the author probes the machinery of local
        government which did little before the war. This is the best
        analysis of the state's constitution and its relationship to
        the federal union.

2289.   ————. "Lady Wentworth's Last Days in New Hampshire." HIST
        NH, 23 (1968), 14-30.

Here is a good sketch of the collapse of royal government
under Governor John Wentworth.

2290. ———. "Politics in New Hampshire Under Governor Benning
Wentworth, 1741-1767." WMQ, 23 (1966), 76-105.

Though Wentworth, his family and friends completely dominated Hampshire politics and even quashed elections, the
colony remained stable and the Assembly thanked him in 1767.

2291. Downs, Deborah. "The New Hampshire Constitution of 1776:
Weathervane of Conservatism." HIST NH, 31 (1976), 164-175.

The constitution was a practical and not a theoretical document; it provided for a temporary state government, and it
satisfied moderates and conservatives.

2292. Foster, Herbert D., and Thomas W. Streeter. "Stark's Independent Command at Bennington." GRANITE STATE MAG,
6 (1910-11), 5-20, 57-72.

Stark led the Hampshire militia at the fierce fight in 1777.

2293. Foster, Joseph. "William Whipple, Signer of the Declaration
of Independence." GRANITE MONTHLY, 43 (1911), 205-219.

Whipple of Portsmouth was a general at Saratoga and a delegate to Congress.

2294. Gemmill, John R. "The Problem of Power: New Hampshire's
Government During the Revolution." HIST NH, 22 (1967), 27-
38.

The provisional government drafted four constitutions, re-
organized the provincial assembly, and administered 9,000
loyalty oaths.

2295. Hadley, Eldridge Drew. "The Revolt of New Hampshire; A
Royal Government Vanishes - Popular Government Evolves."
GRANITE MONTHLY, 43 (1911), 277-283.

This is a satisfactory account of a regional rebellion,
town by town.

2296. Hale, Richard Walden. "Some Account of Benjamin Thompson,
Count Rumford." NEQ, 1 (1928), 505-531.

An officer in the New Hampshire militia, Thompson became a
Loyalist artilleryman, a physicist, a London intellectual,
and Prime Minister of Bavaria.

2297. Hendricks, Nathaniel. "A New Look at the Ratification of the
Vermont Constitution of 1777." VT HIST, 34 (1966), 136-140.

The article surveys plebiscites, town meetings, and the ratification procedures by which Vermont attempted to create a new
state.

2298. ———. "The Experiment in Vermont Constitutional Govern-
       ment." VT HIST, 34 (1966), 63-65.

       Delegates met at Windsor from seven towns to create a
       Republic of Vermont in 1777.

2299. Jones, Matt B. VERMONT IN THE MAKING, 1750-1777. Cambridge,
       Massachusetts: Harvard University Press, 1939.

       This is a carefully compiled work written with skill. It
       offers a detailed account of the complex feud over the
       Hampshire land grants which involved New Hampshire, New York,
       land speculators, and disgruntled settlers who threatened
       to deal with Great Britain during the war in order to achieve
       autonomy.

2300. Kalinoski, Sarah V. "Sequestration, Confiscation, and the
       'Tory' in the Vermont Revolution." VT HIST, 45 (1977), 230-
       246.

       The sale of Loyalist property was ineptly administered, but
       it encouraged immigration and eliminated opposition for an
       independent Vermont.

2301. Kaplan, Sidney. "The History of New Hampshire, Jeremy Belknap
       as Literary Craftsman." WMQ, 21 (1964), 18-39.

       A patriot parson, Belknap's three volume history merits
       praise for its use of witnesses, first hand accounts, and its
       documentation.

2302. Kidder, Frederic. HISTORY OF THE FIRST N.H. REGIMENT IN THE
       WAR OF THE REVOLUTION. Albany, New York: Joel Munsell,
       1868.

       This narrative covers the fourteen companies who enrolled
       in 1775 to serve at Boston, in Canada, and Trenton. It in-
       cludes lists of officers and men, various letters and other
       documents, and the Journal of Lieutenant Thomas Blake, the
       Paymaster.

2303. Kirsch, George B. "Clerical Dismissals in Colonial and Revo-
       lutionary New Hampshire." CHURCH HIST, 49 (1980), 160-177.

       This is a fascinating article which explains why clergymen
       were dismissed by their congregations in order to restore
       harmony, and why few were reinstated during the war.

2304. ———. "Jeremy Belknap and the Coming of the Revolution."
       HIST NH, 29 (1974), 151-172.

       The famous historian was cautious about rebellion in his
       sermons until the news of Lexington and Concord converted
       him into an ardent patriot.

2305. Knipe, William A. "The Mast Trade in New Hampshire." AMER
       NEP, 23 (1962), 67-70.

       Here is a thoughful analysis of a specialized industry
       which flourished in the area from 1670-1789.

2306. Lacy, Harriet S. "Ephraim Roberts - Memorandum Book: 1771-
       1776." HIST NH, 24 (1969), 20-33.

       Roberts, a resident of Alton, wrote an interesting account
       of local events.

2307. Lettieri, Ronald and Charles Wetherell. "The New Hampshire
       Committees of Safety and Revolutionary Republicanism, 1775-
       1784." HIST NH, 35 (1980). 241-283.

       The authors comment on membership, attendance, sessions,
       and scope of activities that the Committees performed.

2308. Linscott, Elizabeth. "Ethan Allen: Soldier, Creator, Author."
       NE GALAXY, 19 (1977), 45-56.

       Vermont's hero captured Ticonderoga, was imprisoned in
       Canada and in England; he was a leader in Vermont's independ-
       ence movement and wrote philosophical tracts.

2309. Little, Arthur. "William Whipple, the 'Signer'." MAG HIST,
       9 (1909), 257-268.

       Whipple of Portsmouth was a signer of the Declaration of
       Independence.

2310. Looney, John F. "Benny Wentworth's Land Grant Policy: A
       Reappraisal." HIST NH, 23 (1768), 3-13.

       Pre-war Governor Wentworth deserves praise for promoting the
       settlement of western New Hampshire.

2311. Martin, James Kirby. "A Model of the Revolution: The Birth
       and Death of the Wentworth Oligarchy in New Hampshire,
       1771-1776." J SOC HIST, 4 (1970), 41-60.

       The structure of this entrenched political elite collapsed
       before 1775 under the pressure of socially mobile officials
       who challenged the oligarchy.

2312. Mayo, Lawrence S. JOHN LANGDON OF NEW HAMPSHIRE. Concord,
       New Hampshire: Rumford Press, 1937.

       Langdon of Portsmouth was a prominent politician in New
       Hampshire before and after the Revolution. Familiar with many
       of the famous personages of America, Langdon later became
       governor of the state. This work is interesting, but it is
       not the definitive work on the subject.

2313.   ———. JOHN WENTWORTH: GOVERNOR OF NEW HAMPSHIRE, 1767–
        1775. Cambridge, Massachusetts: Harvard University Press,
        1921.

        This is a dependable biography of the last royal governor
        of New Hampshire. Based on a wide range of source material,
        including Wentworth's letters, it provides a suitable per-
        spective of the pre-Revolution days.

2314.   Murdock, Richard K. "A French Report on Vermont, (October)
        1778." VT HIST, 34 (1968), 217–225.

        An agent of Vergennes commented on the area's future, land
        claims, and the debate on its sovereignty.

2315.   New Hampshire Committee of Safety. "Record of the Committees
        of Safety." NH HIST SOC COLL, 7 (1863), 1–40.

        This compilation of documents is one of the best sources of
        a committee's work for it contains the daily minutes of six
        long meetings.

2316.   Newton, Earle W. "Green Mountain Rebels." VT LIFE, 1 (1948),
        24–37.

        Here is a popular account of John Stark's militia at
        Bennington.

2317.   Page, Elwin L. "Josiah Bartlett and the Federation." HIST
        NH, 3 (1947), 1–6.

        Bartlett was a physician from Kingston who served at
        Bennington and was active in state politics.

2318.   ———. "What Happened to the King's Powder?" HIST NH, 19
        (1964), 29–33.

        The mystery is unraveled as the author notes that the
        ninety-eight stolen barrels of gunpowder were sold within five
        months.

2319.   Patten, Matthew. THE DIARY OF MATTHEW PATTEN OF BEDFORD, N.H.
        Concord, New Hampshire: Rumford Printing Co., 1903.

        An Irish immigrant who became an American citizen, Patten
        represented Bedford and Merrimack in the General Court of
        the state and later served on the Council during the war.
        His diary offers an unique view of the turmoil from the per-
        spective of a farmer.

2320.   Russell, Alfred. "Colonel David Webster." GRANITE MONTHLY,
        20 (1901), 93–106.

        Webster of the Eleventh New Hampshire Regiment fought at
        Bunker Hill, Ticonderoga, and Bennington.

2321.   Ryan, Walter A. "A Note on a Founding Father: Newport's
        Benjamin Giles, Twice a Rebel." HIST NH, 32 (1977), 18-27.

        Giles held many public offices during the war, and his
        leadership in local affairs was significant.

2322.   Safford, Moses A. "General William Whipple." MAINE HIST
        SOC COLL, 6 (1895), 337-357.

        Whipple of Portsmouth represented the town at Exeter, was
        involved in land speculation, and he commanded a militia
        brigade.

2323.   Saltonstall, William G. PORTS OF PISCATAQUA. SOUNDINGS IN
        THE MARITIME HISTORY OF PORTSMOUTH ... Cambridge,
        Massachusetts: Harvard University Press, 1941.

        Chapters seven and eight have useful data about the state's
        maritime contribution to the war. Portsmouth and nearby
        towns built three vessels for the Continental navy, and they
        manned numerous privateers which raided British commercial
        shipping.

2324.   Scales, John. "General Joseph Cilley." GRANITE STATE MAG,
        5 (1908), 233-240; 6 (1910-11), 73-80, 117-124, 145-160,
        281-284; 7 (1919), 89-95.

        Cilley was a leader in the raid on Fort William and com-
        manded a regiment through most of the war.

2325.   ————. "Colonel Jonathan Wentworth." GRANITE MONTHLY, 36
        (1904), 108-114.

        Wentworth of Dover served at Bunker Hill, the siege of
        Boston, in the Canadian invasion, at Saratoga, Newport, and
        West Point.

2326.   ————. "Colonel Stephen Evans." GRANITE MONTHLY, 35 (1903),
        245-253.

        Evans was active in provincial politics, helped provision
        the militia, and he fought at Bennington and Saratoga.

2327.   Shaeffer, John N. "A Comparison of the First Constitutions
        of Vermont and Pennsylvania." VT HIST, 45 (1974), 33-43.

        There is a good account here of the Hampshire Grants ques-
        tion, and the efforts of its citizenry to form an independent
        state during the war.

2328.   Sherwin, Harry E. "New Hampshire Helps Begin the U.S. Navy."
        HIST NH, 9 (1953), 1-20.

        John Langdon of Portsmouth financed the building of several
        naval vessels, notably the RANGER and the RALEIGH.

2329.   Smith, Jonathan. "How New Hampshire Raised Her Armies For
        the Revolution." GRANITE MONTHLY, 54 (1922), 7-18.

        The article summarizes the methods used to muster men by
        bounties, and town quotas.

2330.   ————. PETERBOROUGH, NEW HAMPSHIRE IN THE AMERICAN REVOLU-
        TION. Peterborough, New Hampshire: Peterborough Historical
        Society, 1913.

        This work is an early examination of how one town adjusted
        to the war. It contains lists of men who served in the armed
        forces, anecdotes about the area, and an adequate explanation
        of social-economic conditions.

2331.   Squires, J. Duane. "New Hampshire, in the War for Independ-
        ence." NH PROFILES, 20 (1971), 24-25, 58-60.

        Here are some obscure but interesting events that occurred
        during the war in the state.

2332.   ————. THE GRANITE STATE OF THE UNITED STATES: A HISTORY
        OF N.H. FROM 1623 TO THE PRESENT. 4 vols. New York:
        American Historical Co., 1958.

        Volume one contains a compact summary of the era for a
        popular audience. In chapter six there is a good account of
        the events leading to independence. In chapter seven, there
        is a fine coverage of the state's problems under the impact
        of war. The notes on source material are valuable.

2333.   Upton, Richard F. REVOLUTIONARY NEW HAMPSHIRE: AN ACCOUNT OF
        THE SOCIAL AND POLITICAL FORCES UNDERLYING THE TRANSITION
        FROM ROYAL PROVINCE TO AMERICAN COMMONWEALTH, WITH A NEW
        INTRODUCTION BY THE AUTHOR. 1936. Reprint. New York:
        Octagon Press, 1971.

        This is one of the standard works on the state. The author
        provides information about provincial committees, the
        machinery of the new government, the role of New Hampshire
        in Congress, and details about its contribution to the army,
        navy, as well as to privateering. The bibliography on
        materials published since 1936 to 1970 is useful.

2334.   Walker, Joseph B. "Three Important Acts of New Hampshire at
        the Beginning of the War of the Revolution." GRANITE MONTH-
        LY, 38 (1906), 147-153, 178-181.

        Here is a summary of the colony's military preparedness,
        the Association Test, and the state's Declaration of Independ-
        ence.

2335.   Webber, Laurence E. "Powder for the Revolution: The Story of
        New Hampshire's First Powder Mill." NEW HAMPSHIRE PROFILES,
        12 (1972), 36-39.
        The gunpowder mill was at Exeter.

2336. Wilderson, Paul. "The Raid on Fort William and Mary: Some
       New Evidence." HIST NH, 30 (1975), 178-202.

       This article reveals fresh information about the incident
       as revealed in Governor Wentworth's report about the role
       of John Langdon as leader of the mob.

2337. Worthern, Samuel Copp. "Colonel Pierce Long's Regiment ...
       GRANITE MONTHLY, 57 (1925), 262-266.

       This Portsmouth regiment served at Ticonderoga and at
       Skenesboro.

                        2. Massachusetts

2338. Anderson, Charles M. "The Boston Merchants and the Non-
       Importation Movement." COL SOC MASS PUB, 19 (1916-17), 155-
       259.

       This is a key article which demonstrates that the movement
       originally designed to obtain redress of grievances culminated
       as "an instrument in the hands of political agitators and
       radicals ..."

2339. Bailey, Jacob. "Letters from Rev. Jacob Bailey in 1775, De-
       scribing the Destruction of Falmouth, Maine." MAINE HIST
       SOC COLL, 5 (1857), 437-450.

       Here is a good contemporary description of the British naval
       raid in October, 1775.

2340. Billias, George A. "Beverly's Seacoast Defenses During
       the Revolutionary War." ESSEX INST HIST COLL, 94 (1948),
       119-131.

       Because Beverly contributed so many men and ships to
       privateering and to Washington's navy, its coastal defenses
       were weakened by 1779.

2341. Breen, Timothy H. "John Adams' Fight Against Innovation in
       the New England Constitution: 1776." NEQ, 40 (1967), 501-
       520.

       Breen notes Adams's commitment to the political concepts of
       the colonial founders of the Bay Colony, his respect for
       tradition, and his defense of republican government.

2342. Brown, Robert E. "Democracy in Colonial Massachusetts."
       NEQ, 25 (1952), 291-313.

       With ample statistical data about voter participation, Brown
       claims that the Bay Colony was "very close to a full demo-
       cracy ..." by 1775, and, thereby, he doubts the probability
       of class conflict.

2343.   ———. MIDDLE-CLASS DEMOCRACY AND THE REVOLUTION IN MASSA-
         CHUSETTS, 1691-1780. Ithaca, New York: Cornell University
         Press, 1955.

         In a meticulously researched work, Brown makes a sweeping
         assault on traditional views about the degree of democracy
         in the colony and state. He shows that a widespread franchise,
         and an equitable representation of classes and regions ex-
         isted; and that Massachusetts was already a middle-class
         democracy. Hence, the Revolution was fought to preserve the
         existing social order.

2344.   ———. "Restrictions of Representation in Colonial Massa-
         chusetts." MVHR, 40 (1953), 463-476.

         The author contends that back county farmers and not the
         seaboard aristocracy held control of the legislature.

2345.   Bumsted, John M. "Doctor Douglas' Summary: Polemic for Re-
         form." NEQ, 37 (1965), 242-250.

         The famous Boston doctor and historian wrote a frequently
         overlooked phamplet about the means to reconcile freedom and
         order.

2346.   Churchill, Edwin A. "The Historiography of the Margaretta
         Affair, or, How Not to let the Facts Interfere with a Good
         Story." MAINE HIST SOC Q, 15 (1975), 60-74.

         This is a well-documented essay about the burning of the
         MARGARETTA in 1775.

2347.   Clarfield, Gerard H. "The Short Unhappy Civil Administration
         of Thomas Gage." ESSEX INSTIT HIST COLL, 109 (1973), 138-
         151.

         This is a provocative discussion about General Gage's un-
         successful handling of the Bay Colony's problems in 1774-75.

2348.   Colgrove, Kenneth. "New England Town Mandates: Instructions
         to the Deputies in Colonial Legislatures." PUB COL SOC
         MASS, 21 (1920), 411-449.

         The author discusses the mechanisms of initiative, referen-
         dum, and recall in town meetings.

2349.   Cook, Edward M., Jr. "Social Behaviour and Changing Values
         in Dedham, Massachusetts, 1700 to 1775." WMQ, 27 (1970),
         545-580.

         Here is a model study of a town which shows growing politi-
         cal and judicial flexibility, along with shifting patterns in
         social attitudes and increasing evidence of dissent.

2350. Coughlin, Sister Magdalen. "The Entrance of the Massachusetts
       Merchant into the Pacific." S CAL Q, 48 (1966), 327-352.

       With the loss of West Indian trade, Congress sought com-
       merce in the Far East; the first Yankee ship was the EMPRESS
       OF CHINA which sailed from Boston in 1784.

2351. Dwight, Timothy. "The Story of General Wadsworth." MAINE
       HIST SOC Q, 15 (1976), 226-256.

       The Maine general was captured and imprisoned by the British
       in 1781 but eventually he escaped.

2352. Edmonds, John H. "How Massachusetts Received the Declaration
       of Independence." AMER ANTIQ SOC, 35 (1926), 227-252.

       The article covers the transmission of the news about the
       great event in Boston.

2353. Emerson, Everett. "Salem Voices in Revolutionary Days."
       ESSEX INSTIT HIST COLL, 112 (1976), 290-305.

       The author examines a wide sampling of articles in the
       ESSEX GAZETTE from 1764-83 which indicated a variety of poli-
       tical opinions.

2354. Hale, Richard W., Jr. "The American Revolution in Western
       Massachusetts." NE HIST GEN REG, 129 (1975), 325-34.

       This essay concerns the rivalry between three western
       counties and five seacoast counties that emerged in town
       meeting disputes and in efforts to draft a state constitution.

2355. Hammett, Theodore M. "Revolutionary Ideology in Massachusetts:
       Thomas Allen's Vindication of the Berkshire Constitution-
       alists, 1778." WMQ, 33 (1976), 514-527.

       Allen, a Pittsfield Congregationalist pastor, led the move-
       ment to close county courts in order to dramatize demands for
       political reforms during the war.

2356. Handlin, Oscar and Mary F. Handlin. "Radicals and Conserva-
       tives in Massachusetts after Independence." NEQ, 17 (1944),
       343-355.

       The Handlins question if revolutionary parties continued
       into the post-war era, and they doubt the typical two party
       system approach to this problem, noting that newcomers gained
       by buying state-confiscated property.

2357. ————. "Revolutionary Economic Policy in Massachusetts."
       WMQ, 4 (1947), 3-26.

       The state's involvement in mustering troops, collecting
       taxes, collecting provisions, and experimenting in price con-
       trols had significant ramifications for the future.

360 THE IMPACT OF WAR ON SOCIETY

2358. Harlow, Ralph V. "Economic Conditions in Massachusetts
During the American Revolution." With remarks by Samuel
E. Morison. COL SOC MASS PUB, 20 (1920), 163-193.

Under the economic influence of inflation, speculation,
privateering, and commodity shortages, the merchants prospered and the farmers suffered until their positions were
reversed by 1780.

2359. Henretta, James A. "Economic Development and Social Structure
in Colonial Boston." WMQ, 22 (1965), 75-92.

Here is a thoughtful statistical analysis showing how Boston
from 1750 to 1775 underwent a transformation from a landed
gentry to a maritime-dominated society.

2360. Kaplan, Sidney. "Veteran Officers and Politics in Massachusetts." WMQ, 9 (1952), 29-59.

Kaplan notes that many Continental officers were in politics, members of the Society of the Cincinnati involved in
Masonry, and in land speculation schemes.

2361. Knight, Russell W. "Fire, Smoke, and Elbridge Gerry." ESSEX
INSTIT HIST COLL, 106 (1970), 32-45.

The appearance in December, 1775 of three British naval
vessels off Marblehead panicked the community.

2362. Longley, R.S. "Mob Activities in Revolutionary Massachusetts."
NEQ, 6 (1933), 98-130.

From Stamp Act turmoil onward, radicals cultivated mobs to
augment social unrest and to destroy Tory property.

2363. Lord, Donald C., and Robert M. Calhoon. "The Removal of the
Massachusetts General Court from Boston, 1769-1772." JAH,
55 (1969), 735-755.

This essay concerns the bitter argument between Governor
Bernard and the General Court over the legality of removing
the court from Boston to Cambridge.

2364. McKindy, Charles Robert. "A Bar Divided. The Lawyers of
Massachusetts and the American Revolution." AMER J LEGAL
HIST, 16 (1972), 205-214.

This is a good discussion of the divergent views of Tory
and rebel lawyers in 1775-1776.

2365. Matthews, Albert. "Joyce Junior Chairman of the Committee
for Tarring and Feathering in Boston Before and During the
Revolutionary War." COLL SOC MASS PUB, 8 (1906), 90-104.

Joyce, who was widely quoted in British newspapers, rallied
patriots to the cause.

2366. ———. "Joyce Junior Once More." MASS HIST SOC COLL, 11
      (1910), 280-294.

      Matthews traced the lively career of this patriot who
      hounded Tories.

2367. Morris, Richard J. "Wealth Distribution in Salem, Massachu-
      setts, 1759-1799: The Impact of Revolution and Independence."
      ESSEX INSTIT HIST COLL, 114 (1978), 87-102.

      Morris stresses that wealth tended to be concentrated in a
      few hands, but that this acquisition of power was not con-
      tinuous nor clearly defined, and that re-distribution of Tory
      property was not a factor.

2368. Morrison, Samuel E. "The Commerce of Boston on the Eve of
      Revolution." AMER ANTIQ SOC, 32 (1923), 24-51.

      This is a very detailed analysis by commodity and by area
      of export.

2369. Newcomer, Lee Nathaniel. "Yankee Rebels of Inland Massachu-
      setts." WMQ, 9 (1952), 156-165.

      While weak on details, this is a suggestive article about
      the duties of provincial officials, and about the power of
      towns in three western counties.

2370. Nichols, Charles L. "Samuel Seabury--A Boston Merchant in
      the Revolution." AMER ANT SOC, 35 (1926), 46-63.

      Though poorly edited, this essay helps to re-create the
      excitement of 1775.

2371. Norton, William B. "Paper Currency in Massachusetts During
      the Revolution." NEQ, 7 (1934), 43-49.

      This is a solid discussion of how the state handled finan-
      cial crises by the issuance of bills of credit and treasury
      notes.

2372. Patterson, Stephen E. POLITICAL PARTIES IN REVOLUTIONARY
      MASSACHUSETTS. Madison, Wisconsin: University of Wisconsin
      Press, 1973.

      Though not a definitive work because of its vagueness con-
      cerning party and sectional alignments, it is a good dis-
      cussion about organized contests at the town and legislative
      levels. It is particularly insightful about describing the
      numerous divisions at the local assembly levels, and about
      explaining the rhetoric of the Revolution. The comments
      about the arguments between the coastal counties and the
      western counties are plausible and imaginative.

2373. Philip, Edward Hake. "Salem, Timothy Pickering, and the American Revolution." ESSEX INSTIT HIST COLL, 111 (1975), 65-78.

Salem's most famous patriot was on the Committee of Safety, at Lexington and Concord, and was the state's Quartermaster General.

2374. Phillips, James Duncan. "Why Colonel Leslie Came to Salem." ESSEX INSTIT HIST COLL, 90 (1954), 313-316.

Leslie's expedition on February 20, 1775 could have been an early Lexington and Concord.

2375. Pole, J.R. "Suffrage and Representation in Massachusetts: A Statistical Note." WMQ, 14 (1957), 560-592.

In one of the best essays on this topic, Pole presents seven pages of tables to show voting patterns; in many towns by 1780 over eighty per cent of white adult males had the franchise.

2376. Pope, Charles. "Machias in the Revolution." MAINE HIST SOC PROC, 6 (1895), 121-138.

The article covers the mission of the British ship MARGARETTA sent to procure timber for the army in May, 1775.

2377. Rogers, George V. "Springtime in Boston, 1775." NE GALAXY, 16 (4) (1975), 49-57.

This is a good discussion on the reaction in the metropolis to the news of Lexington and Concord.

2378. Sargeant, John. "Letters of John Andrew." MASS HIST SOC PROC, 8 (1864-65), 316-412.

This correspondence provides a fine insight about the war from a civilian's viewpoint.

2379. Scott, Kenneth. "Price Control in New England During the Revolution." NEQ, 19 (1946), 453-473.

The efforts were regarded as temporary palliatives and were inadequate due to inflation, the "black market," and to the lack of centralized control for foodstuffs and basic commodities.

2380. Shipton, Clifford K. "Peleg Wadsworth." MAINE HIST Q, 15 (1976), 211-226.

This is a good sketch of a Maine soldier who had a prosperous post-war life as a merchant and landowner in Portland.

2381. Syrett, David. "Town-Meeting Politics in Massachusetts,
       1776-1786." WMQ, 21 (1964), 352-366.

       Though a vague democracy was emerging, the meetings were
       poorly attended and were dominated by a minority or by offi-
       cials willing to break the rules of procedures.

2382. Taylor, George Rogers. "Nantucket Oil Merchants and the
       American Revolution." MASS REV, 18 (1977), 561-606.

       Nantucket whalers were relatively unaffected by the war
       and traded regularly with the Loyalist Maritime Provinces.

2383. Taylor, Robert J. "Construction of the Massachusetts Con-
       stitution." AMER ANTIQ SOC PROC, 90 (1980), 317-346.

       The "oldest written organic law still in operation ..."
       has only 113 amendments; it was approved by two-thirds of
       free males over 21, and John Adams deserves credit for his
       visionary work.

2384. Thorpe, James A. "Colonial Suffrage in Massachusetts."
       ESSEX INSTIT HIST COLL, 106 (1970), 169-181.

       Although many enfranchised males did not vote, suffrage
       was broad at the town and provincial levels to make democracy
       prevail.

2385. Van Ness, James S., ed. "The Diary of Rev. Joseph Perry
       Written During the Siege of Boston, February 16 to March
       28, 1776." BOSTONIAN SOC PROC, 18 (1963), 18-56.

       A chaplain in the Continental army wrote some lucid com-
       ments about the investment of the city.

2386. Warden, G.B. "Inequality and Instability in Eighteenth-Cen-
       tury Boston: A Reappraisal." J INTERDISP HIST, 6 (1976),
       585-620.

       Noting that quantitative methods do not make literary
       evidence obsolete, Warden doubts that the increasing degree
       of social inequality was responsible for the evolvement of
       revolutionary ideology.

2387. Yerxa, Donald A. "The Burning of Falmouth 1775: A Case
       Study of British Imperial Pacification." MAINE HIST SOC Q,
       14 (1975), 119-161.

       In the best study of the topic, Yerxa demonstrates that the
       British raid did not intimidate but infuriated the inhabitants
       into opposition.

2388. Zornow, William F. "Massachusetts Tariff Policies, 1775-1789."
       ESSEX INSTIT HIST COLL, 90 (1954), 194-215.

Using tariffs for revenue, protection, regulation, and
retaliation, Massachusetts varied in policies from the
national norms until 1789.

2389. Zuckerman, Michael D. "The Social Context of Democracy in
       Massachusetts." WMQ, 25 (1968), 523-544.

       Doubting that claims of middle-class democracy in provincial
       Massachusetts can be sustained from electoral eligibility
       rolls, nevertheless, the writer notes that local politics in
       small towns may have been democratic.

                              3. Rhode Island

2390. Angell, Walter F. "Rhode Island's Declaration of Independ-
       ence." RI HIST SOC COLL, 19 (1926), 65-80.

       Here is the reproduction of the original document, May 4,
       1776.

2391. Bartlett, John Russell, ed. RECORDS OF THE COLONY OF RHODE
       ISLAND AND PROVIDENCE PLANTATIONS, IN NEW ENGLAND. 10 vols.
       1856. Reprint. New York: AMS Press, 1908.

       Volumes seven, eight and nine are crammed with information
       about politicians as well as military and wartime affairs.

2392. Bryant, Samuel W. "HMS Gaspee: The Court-Martial." RI HIST,
       25 (1966), 65-72.

       The article covers the burning of the vessel by patriots,
       the trial of its commander, and it reveals much about admi-
       ralty judicial machinery.

2393. ———. "Rhode Island Justice - 1772 Vintage." RI HIST, 26
       (1967), 65-71.

       The captain of the GASPEE was tried for illegal seizures
       of rum and sugar which he claimed as smuggled goods.

2394. Chudacoff, Nancy Fisher. "The Revolution and the Town:
       Providence, 1775-1783." RI HIST, 35 (1976), 71-89.

       This is an excellent essay about the influence of naval and
       military activity at the port with a conclusion that the war
       had no lasting impact on the area.

2395. Cohen, Joel A. "Democracy in Revolutionary Rhode Island: A
       Statistical Analysis." RI HIST, 29 (1970), 3-16.

       In a fine study of the relationship between wealth and
       office holding (1775-84), Cohen explains that a broad franchise
       existed.

2396. ————. "Lexington and Concord: Rhode Island Reacts." RI
       HIST, 26 (1967), 97-102.

       The colony was quick to respond with a re-organization of
       officialdom, and with the raising of militia.

2397. ————. "Molasses to Muskets - Rhode Island, 1763-1775."
       RI HIST, 34 (1975), 99-103.

       As the colony's trade economy was based on maritime acti-
       vity, it feared the impact of imperial legislation and any
       tampering with its charter.

2398. Coleman, Peter J. "The Insolvent Debtor in Rhode Island,
       1745-1808." WMQ, 22 (1965), 413-434.

       This is a detailed examination of insolvency petitions,
       and of the state's pioneering debtor relief and bankruptcy
       laws.

2399. Conley, Patrick J. "Revolution's Impact on Rhode Island."
       RI HIST, 34 (1975), 120-128.

       Although Newport declined in economic importance, the slave
       trade was banned, and emancipation enacted; due to lack of
       social upheaval, the war had little impact on the state's
       post-war politics.

2400. Conlon, Noel P. "Rhode Island Negroes in the Revolution:
       A Bibliography." RI HIST, 29 (1970), 52-53.

       There are references here to blacks in the armed forces
       and at the siege of Newport.

2401. Cooke, Nicholas. "Revolutionary Correspondence of Governor
       Nicholas Cooke, 1775-1781." AMER ANTIQ SOC PROC, 36 (1926),
       231-353.

       Cooke handled problems relating to finance, shipping, and
       state mobilization.

2402. DeVaro, Lawrence J., Jr. "The Gaspee Affair as Conspiracy."
       RI HIST, 32 (1973), 107-121.

       In the best article on this topic, the author notes that
       the British regarded the event as an effort to subvert the
       constitution, and that Americans were convinced that a
       vindictive Ministry was punishing them with repressive
       legislation.

2403. Fowler, William M., Jr. WILLIAM ELLERY: A RHODE ISLAND
       POLITICIAN AND LORD OF THE ADMIRALTY. Metuchen, New
       Jersey: Scarecrow Press, 1973.

       Ellery performed well in Congress, championed his con-
       stituency, and he was the most prominent member of the Marine

Committee which supervised naval affairs. Unable to overcome
Congressional indifferences and impeded by material difficulties, Ellery lamented the near-collapse of the Continental
Navy by 1781. Although written like a thesis, the study is
concise and rescues a dedicated Rhode Islander from obscurity.

2404. Gerlach, Larry R. "Charles Dudley and the Customs Quandary in
       Pre-Revolutionary Rhode Island." RI HIST, 30 (1971),
       53-59.

Dudley, Collection of Customs, suffered for his Loyalism
and was instrumental in the investigation of the Gaspee incident.

2405. Kaplan, Marilyn. "The Jewish Merchants of Newport, 1740-
       1790." RI JEW HIST SOC, 7 (1975), 12-29.

This is mainly a discussion of Aaron Lopez, the slave trade,
and the decline of Newport commerce.

2406. Leslie, William B. "The Gaspee Affair: A Study of Its Con-
       stitutional Significance." MVHR, 39 (1952), 233-256.

The article shows the incident underlying the sharp conflict
of law and jurisdiction which led to a theory of two mutually
exclusive legal fields encompassing the same area.

2407. Losben, Andrea Finkelstein. "Newport Jews and the American
       Revolution." RI JEW HIST NOTES, 7 (1976), 258-276.

Here is a good discussion of the Jewish community's war
support including the names of those who fought in battle;
the point is there was no official Jewish position about the
war any more than there was a Baptist or Congregationalist
official attitude toward the war.

2408. Lovejoy, David S. "Henry Merchant and the Mistress of the
       World." WMQ, 12 (1955), 375-378.

Merchant was an attorney general and colonial agent who
wrote a colorful account of his residence in London.

2409. ————. RHODE ISLAND POLITICS AND THE AMERICAN REVOLUTION,
       1760-1776. Providence, Rhode Island: Brown University Press,
       1958.

This is the best volume on the subject. It provides a compact summary of the rhetoric of revolution, convention meetings,
the Gaspee affair, and committees of safety. The account of
the rivalry between the Samuel Ward and Stephen Hopkins fac-
tions is lively. Rhode Island had no major class or ideological grievances, but it revolted to protect her politically
mature governmental system.

2410. ————. "Rights Imply Equality: The Case Against Admiralty
       Jurisdiction in America, 1764-1776." WMQ, 16 (1956), 459-
       484.

       Colonies recognized the Royal Navy's jurisdiction in prizes,
       wrecks, and salvage, but the means to enforce imperial legis-
       lation were as novel as the new taxes themselves.

2411. May, W.E. "The Gaspee Affair." MM, 63 (1977), 129-135.

       This is a poorly documented article about the Marblehead
       schooner, written, apparently, for a popular audience.

2412. Monahan, Clifford P. and Clarkson A. Collins, III, eds. "A
       Letter from William Ellery to Henry Marchant." RI HIST, 24
       (1965), 49-54.

       The document summarizes the events of a Tory dominated
       Newport town meeting in 1775.

2413. Polishook, Irwin W. 1774-1795: RHODE ISLAND AND THE UNION.
       Evanston, Illinois: Northwestern University Press, 1969.

       Here is a readable account of Rhode Island's erratic re-
       sponse to the organization of a national government because
       of its vulnerability to British naval attacks. The work is
       weak on local affairs, and on clarifying the issue of poli-
       tical parties during the war. But the post-1783 coverage is
       good.

2414. Revolutionary Correspondence. "Revolutionary Correspondence
       from 1775-1782." RI HIST SOC COLL, 6 (1907), 105-300.

       This is a very useful collection of letters about the state
       mobilizing for war, organizing for privateering, and seeking
       provisions for its troops.

2415. Roelker, William G., and Clarkson, A. Collins, III. "The
       Patrol of Narrangansett Bay (1774-1776) by H.M.S. Rose,
       Captain James Williams." RI HIST, 7 (1984), 12-19, 90-95;
       8 (1949), 45-53, 77-83; 9 (1950), 11-23, 52-58.

       Based at Newport to check smuggling and to collect intelli-
       gence, the frigate covered the Bay, fought privateers, cut off
       supplies to the Americans, and it threatened to bombard the
       coast.

2416. Simister, Florence Parker. THE FIRE'S CENTER. RHODE ISLAND
       IN THE REVOLUTIONARY ERA, 1763-1790. Providence, Rhode
       Island: Rhode Island Bicentennial Foundation, 1978.

       This is a well-illustrated volume. Unfortunately, it is
       poorly written, and it has no footnotes or bibliography.
       The author offers not a single fresh fact nor a novel inter-
       pretation. Perhaps high-schoolers could use this book.

2417. Thompson, Mack E. "The Ward-Hopkins Controversy and the
      American Revolution in Rhode Island: An Interpretation."
      WMQ, 16 (1957), 363-373.

      Two factions contended from 1755-1770 in Newport and
      Providence in a home rule fight to preserve the political
      structure and not to modify it.

2418. Wells, Thomas L. "An Inquiry Into the Resignation of
      Quartermaster General Nathanael Greene in 1780." RI HIST,
      24 (1965), 41-48.

      Here is a good discussion of Greene's reasons and Congres-
      sional reactions to the event.

2419. Wulsin, Eugene. "The Political Consequences of the Burning
      of the Gaspee." RI HIST, 3 (1944), 1-11, 55-64.

      The resulting court martial led to the creation of inter-
      colonial committees of correspondence, and the end of Crown
      efforts to establish extra-legal courts.

                            4. Connecticut

2420. Baldwin, Simeon E. "New Haven Convention of 1778." N HAVEN
      COL HIST SOC PAP, 3 (1862), 33-62.

      Although this meeting is sometimes overlooked by historians,
      seven states sent delegates to deal with price controls and
      credit matters.

2421. Barrow, Thomas C. CONNECTICUT JOINS THE REVOLUTION. Chester,
      Connecticut: Pequot Press, 1973.

      Intended for the general reader, this work concentrates on
      Jonathan Trumbull and Jared Ingersoll. It is repetitious,
      skims over the privotal events, and over religious contro-
      versies.

2422. Bickford, Christopher P. "In the King's Pay: Two Customs
      Officials in New Haven, 1774-1776." CONN HIST SOC BULL,
      42 (1977),

      This is a good sketch of two agents of the Crown caught up
      in the revolutionary turmoil.

2423. Boyd, Julian P. "Roger Sherman: Portrait of a Cordwainer
      Statesman." NEQ, 5 (1932), 221-236.

      A self-taught New Haven man, Sherman rose from local politics
      and was a "signer" of major constitutional documents.

2424. Buel, Richard, Jr. DEAR LIBERTY: CONNECTICUT'S MOBILIZATION
      FOR THE REVOLUTIONARY WAR. Middletown, Connecticut:
      Wesleyan University Press, 1980.

This is an original and path-breaking view about a state's
role because it challenges the standard thesis that a war of
attrition favored the American cause. Despite Saratoga and
the French alliance, Connecticut struggled to recruit, supply
and finance the war effort. By 1781 her efforts had failed,
and the state neared bankruptcy. Here is a well-written
account that weaves social, political, and military history
together in a thoughful synthesis that is amply documented.

2425. Callahan, North. CONNECTICUT REVOLUTIONARY WAR LEADERS.
       Chester, Connecticut: Pequot Press, 1973.

       There are sketches here of eleven military leaders, but the
       writing is dull.

2426. Cohen, Sheldon S. CONNECTICUT IN THE CONTINENTAL CONGRESS.
       Chester, Connecticut: Pequot Press, 1973.

       Designed for the general reader, this work contains little
       fresh information, but it provides sufficient background about
       the state Delegates, the Lee-Deanne feud, the Susquehanna
       Company, and the question of Vermont.

2427. Daniels, Bruce Collins. "Economic Development in Colonial
       and Revolutionary Connecticut - An Overview." WMQ, 37
       (1980), 429-450.

       The war stimulated manufacturing, a quest for distant markets
       and caused economic hardship.

2428. Davis, Andrew M. "The Trials of a Governor in the Revolution."
       MASS HIST SOC PROC, 47 (1914), 131-141.

       This is a good but undocumented sketch of Trumbull during
       the war.

2429. Deane, Silas. THE DEANE PAPERS. CORRESPONDENCE BETWEEN SILAS
       DEANE, HIS BROTHERS AND THEIR BUSINESS AND POLITICAL ASSOCI-
       ATES, 1771-1795. Vol. 23. Collections of the Connecticut
       Historical Society. Hartford, Connecticut: The Connecticut
       Historical Society, 1930.

       Here are 120 letters among Silas, Barnabas, Simeon, and
       Barzillai Deane about their firm in which Nathanael Greene
       and Jeremiah Wadsworth were silent partners.

2430. Destler, Chester McArthur. "Barnabas Deane and Barnabas Deane
       and Company." CONN HIST SOC BULL, 35 (1970), 7-19.

       This is a good account of a business that was engaged in
       coastal shipping, privateering, the West Indian trade as well
       as provisioning the Continental and French armies.

2431. ———. "Colonel Henry Champion, Revolutionary Commissary."
       CONN HIST SOC BULL, 36 (1971), 52-64.

Criticized for speculation in army supplies, Champion was cleared of the charges and served well in his post.

2432. ————. CONNECTICUT: THE PROVISIONS STATE. Chester, Connecticut: Pequot Press, 1973.

This is a good but un-footnoted summary of the state's role in feeding the army. It is well-researched and based mainly on the correspondence of Commissary General Jeremiah Wadsworth.

2433. ————. "Newton and the American Revolution." CONN HIST, 20 (1977), 6-26.

The town supplied Continental troops and Rochambeau's army with provisions.

2434. Dexter, Franklin D. "Notes on Some of the New Haven Loyalists Including Those Graduated at Yale." NEW HAVEN COLONY HIST SOC PAP, 9 (1918), 29-45.

This un-documented essay is useful for the data about five graduates of Yale.

2435. Gerlach, Larry R. "Connecticut and Commutation, 1778-1784." CONN HIST SOC BULL, 33 (1968), 51-58.

In the uproar in Congress about suitable pensions for Continental officers, Connecticut opposed the proposed half-pay for life.

2436. ————. "Connecticut, The Continental Congress and the Independence of Vermont, 1777-1782." VT HIST, 34 (1966), 188-193.

Lack of arable land forced many Connecticut Yankees to settle in the Hampshire Grants, and, consequently the state was concerned about the future political status of the area.

2437. ————. "Firmness and Prudence: Connecticut, the Continental Congress and the National Domain, 1776-1786." CONN HIST SOC BULL, 31 (1966), 65-75.

Because of its land shortage, Connecticut was deeply involved in politics involving western boundaries, refusing to modify its claims until it received the "Western Reserve" in Ohio for its veterans.

2438. ————. "Toward ' a more perfect Union:' Connecticut The Continental Congress, and the Constitutional Convention." CONN HIST SOC BULL, 34 (1969), 63-78.

The government of colonial Connecticut closely resembled "the new national policy" and the experienced state delegates were instrumental in preparing for the Confederation period.

2439. Kuslaw, Louis I. CONNECTICUT SCIENCE, TECHNOLOGY, AND MEDI-
       CINE IN THE ERA OF THE AMERICAN REVOLUTION. Hartford,
       Connecticut: American Revolution Bicentennial Commission,
       1978.

       This is a very superficial account of scientific and
       technological developments in the state. The section on
       medicine is very weak. But, for the general reader, it may
       be helpful.

2440. McGrath, Stephen P. "Connecticut's Tory Towns: The Loyalty
       Struggle in Newtown, Redding, and Ridgefield, 1774-1783."
       CONN HIST SOC BULL, 44 (1979), 88-96.

       Due to issues related to Anglicanism, the Stamp Act, and
       land claims, these villages had to be coerced into submission
       by the state.

2441. Mark, Edward M. "The Reverend Samuel Peters and the Patriot
       Mobs of Connecticut." CONN HIST SOC BULL, 40 (1975), 89-94.

       Peters, a prominent Tory of Hebron, wrote a history in which
       he exaggerated mob activities; he was one of the first Loyal-
       ists to be persecuted.

2442. Roth, David M. CONNECTICUT. A BICENTENNIAL HISTORY. New
       York: W.W. Norton, 1979.

       Roth wrote a fine popular history of the state. Pages 66-
       104 on the Revolution provide an adequate background for the
       era.

2443. ————. "Connecticut and the Coming of the Revolution."
       CONN REV, 7 (1973), 47-65.

       This is a readable summary of events including data about
       the Sons of Liberty, and Governor Trumbull.

2444. ————. "Connecticut in the American Revolution." CONN REV,
       9 (1975), 10-20.

       Here is a good crisp summary of developments stressing that
       Tories were neutralized, agrarian productivity was stable,
       little war damage occurred, and the state made significant
       contributions in men, ships and cannon.

2445. Stark, Bruce. "Stephen Johnson. Patriot Minister." CONN
       HIST SOC BULL, 44 (1979), 17-32.

       Johnson, the famous patriot minister whose sermons on the
       Stamp Act were widely read, became a chaplain in the Con-
       necticut line.

2446. Storch, Neil T. "The Recall of Silas Deane." CONN HIST SOC
       BULL, 38 (1973), 30-32.

       Congress was embarrassed over Deane's actions in granting
       army commissions to many European mercenaries.

2447. Taylor, Robert J. COLONIAL CONNECTICUT, A HISTORY. Millwood,
       New York: KTO Press, 1979.

       This is the best synthesis of the state prior to independ-
       ence. Gracefully written with a penetrating insight, this
       deftly researched study is a model for state histories. The
       bibliography is full and covers recent scholarship.

2448. Tyner, Wayne C. "Timothy Dwight in the American Revolution."
       CONN HIST SOC BULL, 41 (1976), 107-118.

       Grandson of Jonathan Edwards and President of Yale, Dwight
       was a typical Calvinist representative of the Revolution.

2449. Van Dusen, Albert L. "Samuel Huntington, A Leader of Revolu-
       tionary Connecticut." CONN HIST SOC BULL, 19 (1954), 38-
       62.

       Long neglected as a historical figure, Huntington merits to
       be rated in the top echelon of patriot politicians.

2450. Weaver, Glenn. JONATHAN TRUMBULL, CONNECTICUT'S MERCHANT
       MAGISTRATE (1710-1785). Hartford, Connecticut: Connecticut
       Historical Society, 1956.

       Trumbull was cursed by bad luck and poor management in his
       business career. This very readable account illustrates the
       techniques of a Yankee merchant. Weaver's handling of detail
       is clear and concise.

2451. Zeichner, Oscar. CONNECTICUT'S YEARS OF CONTROVERSY, 1750-
       1776. Chapel Hill, North Carolina: University of North
       Carolina Press, 1949.

       This is a lively and detailed account of the colony's
       problems over freedom of the press, publication of pamphlets,
       religious disputes, and quarrels over land claims.

                             5. New York

2452. Alexander, Arthur J. "Exemptions From Military Service in
       New York State During the Revolutionary War." NY HIST, 27
       (1946), 204-212.

       Exemptions were granted to clergymen, civil servants, state
       officials and to some artisans; substitutions were permitted.

2453. Alexander, De Alva S. A POLITICAL HISTORY OF THE STATE OF
      NEW YORK. 4 vols. New York, 1906-1923. Reprint. Port
      Washington, New York: Kennikat Press, 1959.

      Volume one provides a general political survey of the
      Revolution in New York. Though social and economic factors
      are overlooked, this is a reliable treatment of major events
      but with little analysis.

2454. Alexander, Edward P. "James Duane, Moderate Rebel." NY HIST,
      17 (1938), 123-134.

      Duane was a hesitant revolutionary, but he became a major
      state political figure.

2455. Bailyn, Bernard. "The Beekmans of New York: Trade, Politics,
      and Families." WMQ, 14 (1957), 598-608.

      This is a good summary of a prominent mercantile family and
      its part in the war.

2456. Barck, Oscar T., Jr. NEW YORK CITY DURING THE WAR FOR INDE-
      PENDENCE. 1931. Reprint. Port Washington: New York:
      Kennikat Press, 1966.

      Barck wrote a thorough study about Loyalism in the city
      and why New York remained committed to the British cause.
      Gracefully written, it is a solid account of civilian life in
      Manhattan. The inhabitants were generally tolerant of
      the British occupation.

2457. Becker, Carl L. "The Growth of Revolutionary Parties and
      Methods in New York Province, 1765-1774." AHR, 7 (1901),
      56-76.

      The author claims that political parties were formed due to
      concerns about equality, and that the Revolution symbolized
      the challenge to oligarchies.

2458. ———. "Election of Delegates from New York to the Second
      Continental Congress." AHR, 9 (1903), 66-85.

      Becker explains the split in factions from 1765 to 1776
      and the growing arguments over imperial issues.

2459. ———. THE HISTORY OF POLITICAL PARTIES IN THE PROVINCE OF
      NEW YORK, 1766-1776. Madison, Wisconsin: University of
      Wisconsin Press, 1909.

      This key monograph is the classic work about the Revolution
      in New York that provides insights into the Progressive inter-
      pretations. To Becker, the Revolution was a dual struggle--
      the fight against Britain and the provincial struggle over
      who should rule at home. In his class struggle view, Becker
      maintains that the war unleashed emerging republican elements
      and the voteless lower classes to wrest control from the

Loyalist aristocracy. Stressing economic issues, Becker
notes how a depressed economy added to the tension with
the Crown.

2460.   Bolton, Reginald P. "The Military Hut-Camp of the War of the
        Revolution on the Dyckman Farm, Manhattan." NY HIST SOC Q
        BULL, 2 (1918-19), 89-97, 130-136; 3 (1919-20), 15-18.

        As a result of excavations conducted between 1918 and 1919,
        historians have good descriptions of the encampment and its
        buildings.

2461.   Bonomi, Patricia U. A FACTIOUS PEOPLE: POLITICS AND SOCIETY
        IN COLONIAL NEW YORK. New York: Columbia University Press,
        1971.

        In one of the best monographs on the topic, Bonomi notes
        the emergence by 1772 of a sophisticated political culture
        in which the province's many interest groups competed for
        increased participation in government. This collective ef-
        fort represented the province's education in the art of
        politics, and in the ideology of representative government.
        The author doubts the validity of class-consicousness inter-
        pretations, shows the volatile nature of New York politics,
        the heavy patrician influence, and the response of various
        groups to public opinion. The key word is factionalism in
        the increasing political rivalry that contributed to the
        cultivation of democratic institutions.

2462.   ————. "Local Government in Colonial New York: A Base for
        Republicanism." In ASPECTS OF EARLY NEW YORK SOCIETY AND
        POLITICS. Edited by Jacob Judd and Irwin H. Polishook.
        Tarrytown, New York: Sleepy Hollow Restorations, 1974,
        pp. 29-50.

        By focusing on the village of Kingston, the author demon-
        strates that experience in local government formed the foun-
        dation for emerging republican governments during the war.

2463.   ————. "Political Patterns in Colonial New York City: The
        General Assembly Election of 1768." POL SCI Q, 81 (1966),
        423-477.

        Large numbers of non-voters in elections does not suggest
        a restricted franchise but rather public indifference to
        voting.

2464.   Boyer, Lee R. "Lobster Backs, Liberty Boys, and Laborers in
        the Streets: New York's Golden Hill and Nassau Street Riots."
        NY HIST SOC Q BULL, 57 (1973), 281-308.

        This is a little known incident in January, 1770 that is
        the New York counterpoint of the Boston Massacre as laborers
        rioted over wages.

2465.   Burrows, Edwin C. "Military Experience and the Origins of
        Federalism and Antifederalism." See 2462, pp. 83-
        92.

        Here is a unique perspective which traces the origin of
        anti-Federalism to military services; the Continental troops
        acquired a national view while militia retained a parochial
        attitude.

2466.   Caldwell, Lynton K. "A Battle of Bureaucrats - 1781." NY
        HIST, 29 (1952), 154-158.

        Udney Hay of New York feuded with New England's Timothy
        Pickering about means to provision the army.

2467.   ————. "George Clinton--Democratic Administrator." NY
        HIST, 32 (1951), 134-156.

        Clinton performed well in mobilizing militia, acquiring
        supplies, repreaving Loyalists, and participating in the
        Sullivan campaign against the Indians.

2468.   Champagne, Roger J. "Family Politics Versus Constitutional
        Principles: The New York Assembly Elections of 1768 and
        1769." WMQ, 20 (1963), 57-59.

        Politics in New York was not based on class but rivalry
        between the aristocratic Livingstons and DeLanceys who
        exploited popular agitation over imperial issue.

2469.   ————. "Liberty Boys and Mechanics of New York City, 1764-
        1774." LABOR HIST, 8 (1967), 115-133.

        Like the Sons of Liberty, the Liberty Boys was a group com-
        plex in attitudes and allegiances, and by 1774 it demonstrated
        more opposition to aristocratic domination of politics.

2470.   ————. "New York Politics and Independence, 1776." NY HIST
        SOC Q REV, 46 (1962), 281-303.

        Both the Livingston and DeLancey factions were drifting
        with events and unwilling to support the revolutionary move-
        ment, but the Livingston group took a more active role in
        response to the British capture of New York City as it was
        stronger in Albany and in upstate villages.

2471.   ————. "New York's Radicals and the Coming of Independence."
        JAH, 51 (1964), 21-40.

        By 1776, Lamb, Sears, and McDougall had been ousted from
        political power by the Livingston faction which had a free
        hand in preparing the province for statehood; that is, ex-
        tremists gave way to moderate Whigs.

2472. ————. "The Military Association of the Sons of Liberty."
      NY HIST SOC Q BULL, 41 (1957), 338-350.

      This is a good account of the popular reaction to the Stamp
      Act in New York City and efforts to resist its enforcement.

2473. Clarke, T. Wood. THE BLOODY MOHAWK. New York, 1941. Re-
      print. Port Washington, New York: Ira J. Friedman, 1968.

      One-half of this lively account of New York's upstate river
      covers the history of Indian-white relations prior to the
      Revolution. The second half is a dependable and well-written
      version of major events at pioneer settlements hit by
      Iroquois-Tory raids.

2474. Clement, John. "James Duane of New York: A Review." VT HIST
      SOC PROC, 6 (1938), 352-361.

      Duane was active in the famous dispute over the Hampshire
      land grants with prominent New Englanders.

2475. Coles, Robert R. "Historical Hempstead Harbour." LONG ISLAND
      HIST FOR, 33 (1970), 160-164.

      Patriots suffered from requisitions and the quartering of
      troops during the long British occupation.

2476. Countryman, Edward. "Consolidating Power in Revolutionary
      America: The Case of New York, 1775-1783." J INTERDISP
      HIST, 6 (1976), 645-677.

      The state's governmental structure adjusted to situations
      during the war as new groups emerged and a one-party domi-
      nated system contributed to internal stability.

2477. Crary, Catherine S. "Forfeited Loyalist Lands in the Western
      District of New York--Albany and Tryon Counties." NY HIST,
      35 (1954), 239-258.

      While the immediate effect in land sales was to enrich
      speculators, the long-term result was the democratization of
      farm property.

2478. ————. "The American Dream: John Tabur Kempe's Rise from
      Poverty to Riches." WMQ, 14 (1937), 176-195.

      One of the province's wealthiest men, Kempe lost his fortune
      during the war because of his Loyalist convictions.

2479. Dawson, Henry B. THE SONS OF LIBERTY IN NEW YORK. 1859. Re-
      print. New York: Arno Press, 1967.

      Decker wrote a pioneering work that was probably the first
      to note the divisions within the membership of New York's
      revolutionaries. His comments on the differing views of the

upper-class leaders and their lower-class followers are
lucid. He suggested the dual nature of the war as partly a
class conflict, a thesis that was developed by Carl Becker.

2480. Decker, Malcolm. BRINK OF REVOLUTION: NEW YORK IN CRISIS,
1765-1776. New York: Argosy Antiquarian, 1964.

This is a lively account of events in New York on the eve
of revolution that is based on standard secondary sources.
Although virtually no new information or fresh perspectives
emerge here, it is a dependable account for the general
reader.

2481. Ellis, David M., James A. Frost, Harold C. Syrett, and Harry
J. Carmen. A HISTORY OF NEW YORK STATE. Ithaca, New York:
Cornell University Press, 1967.

This synthesis may be the best single volume on the history
of the state. It is well organized, quite readable, and the
chapters on the colonial and revolutionary eras are perceptive. The volume has a fine bibliographical essay.

2482. Flick, Alexander C., ed. HISTORY OF THE STATE OF NEW YORK.
10 vols. New York, 1932-1937. Reprint. Port Washington,
New York: Kennikat Press, 1962.

Volumes three and four cover the Revolution. Each chapter
was written by a specialist, and each has a wealth of detail.
Although the essays need to be reviewed in light of recent
scholarship, this material represents a fine synthesis of
research for the 1930's.

2483. ———. "How New York Won and Lost and Empire." NY HIST,
18 (1937), 361-377.

The state relinquished most of its frontier land claims
to Congress in 1781 and to Pennsylvania in 1792.

2484. ———, ed. THE AMERICAN REVOLUTION IN NEW YORK: ITS POLI-
TICAL, SOCIAL AND ECONOMIC SIGNIFICANCE. 1926. Reprint.
Port Washington, New York: Ira J. Friedman, 1967.

Though somewhat dated, this is a key work with a useful
compilation of revolutionary events. It provides ample background to the outbreak of war, the Declaration of Independence, the new government under the constitution of 1777,
fiscal difficulties, military campaigns, and Loyalist activities. The author's comments about the social impact of the
war are especially penetrating.

2485. Forsyth, Mary I. "The Burning of Kingston by the British on
October 16, 1777." NY STATE HIST ASS PROC, 11 (1912), 62-
70.

The article briefly describes the damages caused by General

Henry Clinton's expedition up the Hudson along with a ballad
about the event.

2486. Fowler, William W., Jr. "A Yankee Peddler, Nonimportation,
       and the New York Merchants." NY HIST SOC Q, 56 (1972), 147-
       154.

       Fowler comments on the fate of a New Englander who violated
       the Nonimportation Agreements of 1770.

2487. Fox, Dixon Ryan. YANKEES AND YORKERS. New York: New York
       University Book Store, 1940.

       Though this work needs some revisions, it remains the best
       account of the complicated quarrels between New York and New
       England over the Hampshire Grants question. Fox provides am-
       ple background to the feud, and he notes the economic stakes in-
       volved by competing investors. He is especially astute in
       portraying the cultural milieu of the period.

2488. Friedman, Bernard. "The New York Assembly Election of 1768
       and 1769: The Disruption of Family Politics." NY HIST, 46
       (1965), 3-24.

       The successive political and economic crises that preceeded
       the Revolution wrecked the political power of the DeLancey
       and Livingston factions.

2489. ———. "The Shaping of the Radical Consciousness in Pro-
       vincial New York." JAH 56 (1970), 781-801.

       Friedman claims that the New York radicals were basically
       middle class opportunists seeking monetary opportunities
       (like the Whig aristocrats in their drive for power), but
       they differed with the oligarchy on the need for new poli-
       tical standards.

2490. Gabriel, Ralph H. "Crevecoeur. An Orange County Paradox."
       NY STATE HIST ASSOC Q J, 12 (1931), 45-55.

       Michael-Guillaume de Crevecoeur, the author of the famed
       LETTERS FROM AN AMERICAN FARMER (1782) had difficulties re-
       maining neutral during the war.

2491. Gage, Leonne. "Lake Champlain and Its Importance During the
       War." VT HIST, 29 (1961), 87-91.

       The lake was a gateway to and from the river system leading
       to the St. Lawrence, and it was a major area of warfare from
       1775 through 1778.

2492. Gerlach, Larry R. THE AMERICAN REVOLUTION: NEW YORK AS A
       CASE STUDY. New York: Wadsworth, 1972.

       Here are eighty-one contemporary writings from 1764-88 with

fine introductory essays to place them into perspective.
Even though the work is weak on Hamilton's leadership, and
particularly on the British occupation of New York, this is
a very helpful collection of documents.

2493.   Hadaway, William S., ed. THE MCDONALD PAPERS. Publications
        of the Westchester County Historical Society. Vols. 4-5.
        New York: The Society, 1926-27.

        Here is a useful collection of memoirs and interviews re-
        lating to the war in Westchester County. The material on
        the battle of White Plains, the brutal partisan warfare, the
        Danbury expedition, the services of Colonel Armand, Tarleton's
        raids, and interviews with survivors are illuminating.

2494.   Hastings, Hugh, ed. PUBLIC PAPERS OF GEORGE CLINTON, FIRST
        GOVERNOR OF NEW YORK, 1777-1795, 1801-1892. 10 vols.
        New York and Albany: The State of New York, 1899-1914.

        This collection is somewhat difficult to follow because
        of poor editing. Yet volume one is indispensable for an
        understanding of politics and the war in New York. Clinton
        emerges as a dedicated patriot, a minor general, but a cap-
        able administrator and governor.

2495.   Hendrick, Olysses P. A HISTORY OF AGRICULTURE IN THE STATE
        OF NEW YORK. New York: Hill and Wang, 1966.

        Even though most of the material in this book is chrono-
        logically beyond the war years, it should be consulted. The
        study provides unique insights about farms, tenant-landlord
        relations, agricultural productivity, and the impact of the
        war in creating a democratic farming community. Frontier
        lands and confiscated estates provided new economic oppor-
        tunities.

2496.   Higgins, Ruth L. EXPANSION IN NEW YORK, WITH ESPECIAL RE-
        FERENCE TO THE EIGHTEENTH CENTURY. Columbus, Ohio: Ohio
        State University Press, 1931.

        About one-third of this fine work treats the effects of
        the war on northern and western settlements in the state.
        The material on generally little-known communities is excel-
        lent, and the comments about land tenure and speculation are
        quite useful.

2497.   Hull, N.E.H., Peter C. Hoffer, and Steven L. Allen. "Choos-
        ing Sides: A Quantification Study of the Personality Deter-
        minants of Loyalists and Revolutionary Political Affilia-
        tion in New York." JAH, 65 (1978), 344-366.

        The authors attempt to assess the political attitudes of
        eighty prominent New York politicians.

2498.   Jones, Thomas. HISTORY OF NEW YORK DURING THE REVOLUTIONARY
        WAR. 2 vols. Edited by E.F. Delaney. New York, 1879.
        Reprint. New York: Arno Press, 1968.

        Jones, a member of a prominent New York Tory family, wrote
        a lively commentary about the causes of the Revolution. His
        language is particularly interesting as it reveals a highly
        partisan view. Yet he was also very caustic about the
        British indifference to Loyalist exiles. This is a fine
        source for a glimpse of the Loyalist mentality.

2499.   Kenny, Alice P. THE GANSEVOORTS OF ALBANY: DUTCH PATRICIANS
        IN THE UPPER HUDSON VALLEY. Syracuse: Syracuse University
        Press, 1967.

        Kenny portrays Albany as a major trading center on the
        frontier where Dutch was the main language in an English
        colony. A dozen families with wide commercial and agricul-
        tural interests - the Gansevoorts, the Schuylers, the
        Rosebooms, Lansings, Wendels, etc. - dominated the life of
        the area that was an important war center.

2500.   Klein, Milton M. "Democracy and Politics in Colonial New
        York." NY HIST, 40 (1959), 221-246.

        Examining the Becker thesis, Klein holds that political
        parties were not personal factions, that the gentry did not
        monopolize power, nor was the franchise severely restricted.

2501.   ———. "Politics and Personalities in Colonial New York."
        NY HIST, 47 (1969), 3-16.

        The pre-revolutionary political groups encompassed diver-
        gent interest groups and displayed the rudiments of party
        machines.

2502.   ———. "Prelude to Revolution in New York: Tory Trial and
        Judicial Tenure." WMQ, 17 (1960), 439-462.

        This is a good discussion of the judicial issues that placed
        many New York lawyers and the "popular" party in a lengthy
        argument with Lieutenant Governor Colden.

2503.   ———. "The Rise of the New York Bar: The Legal Career of
        William Livingston." WMQ, 15 (1958), 334-358.

        Livingston was influential in espousing legal and con-
        stitutional principles which were used against British in
        the pre-war debates on imperial petitions.

2504.   Launitz-Schurer, Leopold S., Jr. LOYAL WHIGS AND REVOLU-
        TIONARIES: THE MAKING OF A REVOLUTION IN NEW YORK, 1765-
        1776. New York: New York University Press, 1980.

        As demonstrated by the DeLancey's spirited defense of

American rights in the Stamp Act debate, the Tory leadership
was as "Whiggish" as its American opponents. Where the Tories
and Whigs in New York split was over the question of parliamentary sovereignty which the DeLanceys did not contest. This
is a well-written account of the great families in politics,
the Liberty Boys, and the impact of Townshend Acts on the
province.

2505.   ————. "Whig-Loyalists: The DeLanceys of New York." NEW
        YORK HIST SOC Q BULL, 56 (1972), 179-198.

        The DeLanceys were more Whiggish than Tory in their poli-
        tics, and that until 1775 they were active champions of the
        American cause.

2506.   Leder, Lawrence H. "The New York Election of 1769: An As-
        sault on Privilege." MVHR, 49 (1963), 675-682.

        The origins of the Constitutional requirement of residency
        for legislators was clarified by the Livingston-DeLancey feud.

2507.   Lemisch, L. Jesse. "New York's Petitions and Resolves of
        December, 1765: Liberals vs. Radicals." NY HIST SOC Q BULL,
        49 (1965), 313-326.

        These actions by the Assembly of New York were typical of
        other contemporary colonial compromises and blunted a more
        radical approach.

2508.   Levermore, Charles H. "The Whigs of Colonial New York." AHR,
        1 (1896), 238-250.

        Three Yale lawyers (William Livingston, John Morin Scott,
        William Smith, Jr.), who were Presbyterians and moderate
        Whigs, contested the power of the Episcopal-Tory party until
        violence over the Stamp Act forced moderates into the back-
        ground.

2509.   Lobell, Jared C. "Some Evidence of Price Inflation on Long
        Island, 1770-1782, From the Papers of Richard Jackson,
        Junior." J LONG ISLAND HIST, 8 (1968), 39-43.

        A merchant's accounts show the price trends for rum, tea,
        sugar, and molasses.

2510.   Lynd, Staughton. ANTI-FEDERALISTS IN DUTCHESS COUNTY, NEW
        YORK: A STUDY OF DEMOCRACY AND CLASS CONFLICT IN THE REVO-
        LUTIONARY ERA. Chicago: Loyola University Press, 1962.

        Lynd probes the question of tenant unrest during the war
        in rural New York. He claims that for the tenants and small
        farmers aligned against the great landlords, the Revolution
        was basically a question of "who should rule at home." Hence
        the issue of internal revolution and class consciousness
        is again propounded.

2511.   ———. "The Mechanics in New York Politics, 1774-1788."
        LABOR HIST, 5 (1964), 225-246.

        Lynd questions Becker's all-inclusive use of the term
        "mechanics," but he supports Becker's thesis of an urban and
        rural class conflict.

2512.   McAnear, Beverly. "The Place of the Freeman in Old New York."
        NY HIST, 21 (1940), 418-430.

        The author notes that this legal status served as a media
        of political democracy by allowing many to avoid the freehold
        requirements for the franchise.

2513.   Marting, Elizabeth. "Footnote to the Revolution: The Tribu-
        lation of William Gilliland." NY HIST SOC Q, 30 (1946),
        234-253.

        Gilliland was a frontier land speculator who complained
        about the destruction of his property by American troops and
        who was arrested as a suspected Tory.

2514.   Mason, Bernard. "Entrepreneurial Activity in New York During
        the American Revolution." BUS HIST REV, 40 (1966), 190-
        212.

        Merchants benefitted by war expenditures for the Continental
        army; the state government provided much new business; illegal
        trade with the British and privateering were additional areas
        of enterprise.

2515.   ———. "Robert R. Livingston and the Non-Exportation Policy:
        Notes for a Speech in the Continental Congress, October 27,
        1778." NY HIST SOC Q, 44 (1960), 296-306.

        Livingston opposed the proposal because it would harm the
        province's economy.

2516.   ———. "The Heritage of Carl Becker: The Historiography of
        the Revolution in New York." NY HIST SOC Q, 53 (1969),
        127-147.

        This is the best summary of Becker's thesis, stressing the
        areas of his research that still stand and other areas of
        study that need to be explored.

2517.   ———. THE ROAD TO INDEPENDENCE: THE REVOLUTIONARY MOVE-
        MENT IN NEW YORK, 1773-1777. Lexington, Kentucky: Univer-
        sity of Kentucky Press, 1966.

        Mason disputes Becker's claim that the movement to demo-
        cratize local government was a more important factor in
        New York politics than opposition to British imperial control.
        He argues that New York moved toward independence with more
        unanimity than has been generally acknowledged.

2518. O'Callaghan, E.B. and Berthold Fernow, eds. DOCUMENTS
      RELATIVE TO THE COLONIAL HISTORY OF THE STATE OF NEW YORK.
      15 vols. Albany: The University of the State of New York,
      1856-1857.

      This collection is the most important source of published
      documents and manuscripts related to the state. Volume
      fifteen has the proceedings of the New York Provincial Con-
      gress and the reports of the Committee of Safety. It also
      contains data such as casualty lists, and rosters of officers
      and men in the militia and in the Continental line.

2519. Olm, Lee F. "The Mutiny Act for America: New York's Non-
      compliance." NY HIST SOC Q, 58 (1974), 188-214.

      The renewal of the Mutiny Act for the colonies in 1765
      aroused opposition, for the province was required to provide
      provisions and transport; New York was the first colony to
      refuse compliance.

2520. Olson, James S. "The New York Assembly, the Politics of
      Religion, and the Origins of the Revolution, 1768-1771."
      HIST MAG PROT EPIS CHURCH, 43 (1974), 21-28.

      The religious issues were dormant from 1770-76 with the
      DeLanceys and Livingstons supporting religious equality,
      but the matter was revived in political controversies.

2521. Paltsits, Victor H., ed. MINUTES OF THE COMMISSIONS FOR
      DETECTING AND DEFEATING CONSPIRACIES IN THE STATE OF NEW
      YORK: ALBANY COUNTY SESSIONS, 1778-1781. 3 vols. 1909-
      1910. Reprint. New York: DeCapo Press, 1972.

      Volume one contains the origins and history of this com-
      mission. Volume two and three provide valuable insights
      about political partisanship in a state with a large number
      of Loyalists.

2522. Pell, John H.C. "Philip Skene of Skenesborough." NY STATE
      HIST ASSOC Q J, 9 (1928), 24-44.

      Skene was a Loyalist proprietor on the lower Lake George
      area who advised Burgoyne on topography of the area, who lost
      his landholdings, and who emigrated to England to request a
      pension from the Crown.

2523. Reubens, Beatrice G. "Pre-Emptive Rights in the Disposition
      of a Confiscated Estate, Phillipsburgh Manor, New York."
      WMQ, 22 (1965), 435-456.

      A social revolution occurred here through the right of pre-
      emption when former tenant farmers purchased the Tory estate
      at market value in 1779.

2524. Roberts, James A., comp. NEW YORK IN THE REVOLUTION AS
       COLONY AND STATE. 2 vols. Albany, 1901-1904.

       Volume one has a roster of New Yorkers who served in the
       regular army or the militia. The total lists nearly 52,000
       officers and men but this figure has been challenged as
       incomplete for pre-1778 service. Volume two offers a con-
       densed version of the war as traced through the documents
       cited.

2525. Roberts, Robert R. NEW YORK'S FORTS IN THE REVOLUTION. East
       Brunswick, New Jersey: Fairleigh Dickinson Press, 1980.

       The author mentions over 300 forts, redoubts, blockhouses,
       posts, and cantonments in the state. This is an admirable
       and highly specialized study about the location, building,
       staffing, and history of innumerable Continental defenses in
       the war.

2526. Schaukirk, Ewald G., ed. "Occupation of New York City by
       the British 1776; Extracts from the Diary of the Moravian
       Congregation." PA MHB, 1 (1877), 133-148, 250-262, 467-
       468; 10 (1886), 418-445.

       This religious minority kept detailed account of events,
       and as a result, this article has worthwhile clues about
       Manhattan during the war.

2527. Scott, Kenneth. "Counterfeiting in New York during the Revo-
       lution." NY HIST SOC Q, 42 (1985), 221-259.

       The Loyalists set up a press in New York City to print
       Continental currency in order to disrupt the patriot economy.

2528. Shammas, Carole. "Cadwallader Colden and the Role of the
       King's Prerogative." NY HIST SOC Q, 53 (1969), 102-126.

       The Acting Governor (1760-65) antagonized colonists who
       heretofore had little interference from the Crown, and, con-
       sequently, Colden symbolized the ruthlessness of British
       officialdom.

2529. Sherwood, Jeanette B. "The Military Tract." NY STATE HIST
       ASSOC Q J, 7 (1926), 169-179.

       New York rewarded its Continental army officers and soldiers
       with bounty lands in the state's Finger Lakes area.

2530. Smith, William Jr. THE HISTORY OF THE PROVINCE OF NEW YORK
       FROM THE FIRST DISCOVERY TO THE YEAR 1732 [AND] A CON-
       TINUATION, 1732-1762. 1st ed. in part, London, 1759. Rev.
       ed. 2 vols. Michael Kammen, ed. Cambridge, Massachusetts:
       Harvard University Press, 1972.

A member of a famous Whig trio that challenged British
officialdom in the 1760's, Smith became a Loyalist and served
as a judge in British occupied Manhattan. There have been
six editions of this work, but the latest version has the
original manuscript text and corrects mistakes made by previous editors. With a good introduction, biographical data,
and numerous headnotes, Kammen has produced a key work which
is essential to comprehending how a Whig became a Tory.

2531.   Smits, Edward J. "Long Island's Revolutionary Counterfeiting
        Plot." J LONG ISLAND HIST, 2 (1962), 16-25.

        This incident concerns a Huntington counterfeiter who
        later became engraver of United States currency.

2532.   Spiro, Robert H., Jr. "John Loudon McAdam in Revolutionary
        New York." NY HIST SOC Q, 40 (1956), 28-54.

        McAdam, the famous turnpike engineer, was a Loyalist and
        resident of New York for thirteen years.

2533.   Stokes, Isaac N.P. THE ICONOGRAPHY OF MANHATTAN ISLAND,
        1498-1909. 6 vols. New York, 1915-1928. Reprint. New
        York: Arno Press, 1967.

        Though poorly indexed, this collection is a melange of
        data about New York City from its original settlement through
        the nineteenth-century. It is useful for the Revolutionary
        era because it contains innumerable maps, pictures, anecdotes,
        and ample factual material about Manhattan taken from private
        correspondence, official records, and newspapers, many of
        which are unavailable elsewhere.

2534.   Sullivan, James, and A.C. Flick, eds. MINUTES OF THE ALBANY
        COMMITTEE OF CORRESPONDENCE, 1775-1778, AND MINUTES OF THE
        SCHENECTADY COMMITTEE, 1775-1778. 2 vols. Albany: The
        University of the State of New York, 1923-1925.

        These are the valuable minutes of the famous committees
        reproduced. It is clear that the committeemen had a multi-
        tude of responsibilities to perform while serving as interim
        officials, and that they appear to have been dedicated and
        conscious men.

2535.   Thomas, Howard. MARINUS WILLETT: SOLDIER-PATRIOT, 1740-1830.
        Prospect, New York: Prospect Books, 1954.

        This is a popular account of a Sons of Liberty leader and
        a Continental army officer who served mainly on the Mohawk
        and at Albany. The descriptions of Indian fights, Willett's
        defense of Fort Stanwix, and numerous skirmishes in the Mohawk
        Valley are well written.

2536. Tryon, Winthrop P. "Whig Strategy on the Delaware County
       Border: The Work of the Fredericksberg Precinct Committee
       and the New York Provincial Committee in Checking Tory
       Activities, (1776-1777)." NY HIST SOC BULL, 6 (1923), 111-
       127.

       These committees suppressed Loyalists, organized local
       militiamen, and they kept excellent land records for four
       towns in Duchess County.

2537. Tyler, J.E. "A British Whig's Report from New York on the
       American Situation, 1775." NY HIST SOC Q, 37 (1953), 158-
       169.

       James Murray indicated a possible peace sentiment if the
       British proposed some compromise settlement.

2538. Van Cortlandt, Philip. THE REVOLUTIONARY WAR MEMOIRS AND
       SELECTED CORRESPONDENCE OF PHILIP VAN CORTLANDT. Compiled
       and edited by Jacob Judd. New York: Sleepy Hollow Restora-
       tions, 1976.

       Cortlandt wrote his account of service in Westchester County,
       New York, at Saratoga, Valley Forge, the Sullivan Campaign,
       and Yorktown when in his seventies. The narrative is sup-
       ported by careful annotations and ample documentation. The
       material on Westchester County is quite useful.

2539. Van Wyck, Pierce C., ed. "Autobiography of Philip Van
       Cortlandt, Brigadier-General in the Continental Army." MAG
       AMER HIST, 2 (1878), 278-298.

       Van Cortlandt, a minor figure, served almost entirely in
       New York.

2540. Venables, Robert W. and Myron H. Luke. LONG ISLAND IN THE
       AMERICAN REVOLUTION. Albany: New York State American
       Revolution Bicentennial Commission, 1976.

       This crisply written booklet contains good accounts about
       the Tory cause, the battle of Long Island, and the impact of
       the British occupation on the area. The maps are particu-
       larly good.

2541. Wall, Alexander J. "New York and the Declaration of Inde-
       pendence." NY HIST SOC BULL, 10 (1926), 43-51.

       This essay explains why New York delayed in concurring with
       other colonies in approving the Declaration by July 2, 1776.

2542. ———. "The Statues of King George III and the Honorable
       William Pitt Erected in New York City 1770." NY HIST SOC
       Q BULL, (1920-21), 37-57.

       Here is a good account of the erection and the eventual de-
       struction of these statues during the revolutionary turmoil.

2543. Wertenbaker, Thomas Jefferson. FATHER KNICKENBOCKER'S REBELS:
       NEW YORK CITY DURING THE REVOLUTION. New York and London:
       Charles Scribner's Sons, 1948.

       This is one of the best treatments of events in the Revolu-
       tionary era in New York from 1765 to 1783. Written with wit
       and perception, Wertenbaker is especially capable at pro-
       viding colorful vignettes of the era. His summation of major
       figures on both sides of the conflict is nicely handled.
       For a very readable introduction to the topic, this work is
       highly recommended.

2544. Yoshe, Harry B. THE DISPOSITION OF LOYALIST ESTATES IN THE
       SOUTHERN DISTRICT OF THE STATE OF NEW YORK. New York: AMS
       Press, 1967.

       After investigating land tenure conditions in six New York
       counties, the author concludes that wealthy patriots bene-
       fitted more than the poorer classes from the sale of con-
       fiscated Loyalist property. The spoils went to merchants,
       speculators, and to the landed oligarchy. New York did not
       experience a democratizing effect in land distribution until
       the 1830's.

2545. Young, Alfred F. THE DEMOCRATIC-REPUBLICANS OF NEW YORK:
       THE ORIGINS, 1763-1797. Chapel Hill: The University of
       North Carolina Press, 1957.

       This is a fine summary, based on full documentation of
       politics in the Revolutionary era. The author concludes that
       the riots of the major political parties of the early Federal
       era had their origins in the split between 'popular' and 'con-
       servative' Whigs by 1775. Parties that developed in the state
       were based on local and not on national issues.

                        6. New Jersey

2546. Bill, Alfred H. NEW JERSEY AND THE REVOLUTIONARY WAR.
       Princeton: D. Van Nostrand Co., Inc., 1964.

       This is a colorful and lively description of major events
       that transpired in the state during the war. Undergraduates
       would enjoy the descriptions of fights and raids as narrated
       by a top historian.

2547. Coad, Okal S. "Pine Barons and Robber Barons." NJ HIST SOC
       PROC, 82 (1964), 185-199.

       Bandits who pretended to be Tories raided isolated Jersey
       villages.

2548. Cody, Edward J. THE RELIGIOUS ISSUE IN REVOLUTIONARY NEW
       JERSEY. Trenton: New Jersey Historical Commission, 1975.

       Here is a good summary of the major churches (Anglican,

Dutch Reformed, Methodist, Baptist, Quaker, Presbyterian),
the decline of religious sentiment, and the rise of deism.

2549. Cohen, Sheldon S., and Larry R. Gerlach. "Princeton and the
       Coming of the Revolution." NJ HIST, 92 (1974), 89-92.

       The fourth oldest of the nine colonial colleges, Princeton
       had campus unrest and was considered a center of sedition by
       Loyalists in 1775.

2550. Conners, Richard J. THE CONSTITUTION OF 1776. Trenton:
       New Jersey Historical Commission, 1976.

       This is a good brief summary of how the state's thirteen
       counties met to draft a state constitution in May, 1776.

2551. Cowen, David L. "Revolutionary New Jersey, 1763-1787." NJ
       HIST SOC PROC, 81 (1953), 1-23.

       With little analysis, the author relates key events during
       the war.

2552. Cunningham, John T. NEW JERSEY'S FIVE WHO SIGNED. Trenton:
       New Jersey Historical Commission, 1977.

       This pamphlet about Richard Stockton, John Witherspoon,
       Frances Hopkinson, Abraham Clark and John Hart would be inter-
       esting for high-schoolers.

2553. Docklinger, Thomas M. "Hibernia Furnace During the Revolu-
       tion." NJ HIST, 90 (1972), 97-114.

       Operating to 1779, Lord Stirling's iron foundry was plagued
       with problems - shortages of labor and raw materials, pro-
       duction difficulties, and British raids.

2554. Fennelly, Catherine. "William Franklin of New Jersey." WMQ,
       6 (1949), 301-382.

       Benjamin Franklin's son, the last royal Governor of the
       colony, remained loyal to the Crown, broke with his father
       and experienced endless difficulties during the war.

2555. Folsom, Joseph E. "New Jersey's Part in the Revolution."
       NJ HIST SOC PROC, 7 (1982), 65-74.

       Here is a useful sketch of the state's contributions in man-
       power, foodstuffs, and war material.

2556. Fuhlgruegge, Edward A. "New Jersey Finance During the Ameri-
       can Revolution." NJ HIST SOC PROC, 55 (1937), 167-190.

       The essay outlines the problems involved in credit, cur-
       rency, taxes and price regulations.

2557. Gerlach, Larry R., ed. NEW JERSEY IN THE AMERICAN REVOLU-
      TION, 1763-1783. A DOCUMENTARY HISTORY. Trenton: New
      Jersey Historical Commission, 1975.

      This work is one of the best compilation of edited docu-
      ments to appear in the Bicentennial period. There are nearly
      200 excerpts extracted from a wide variety of primary source
      material with neat introductory essays and with helpful foot-
      notes. The organization of the material into thirteen sec-
      tions (Citizen Soldiers, Government at War, etc.) makes this
      a very convenient work that deserves a wide audience.

2558. ————. PROLOGUE TO INDEPENDENCE: NEW JERSEY IN THE COMING
      OF THE AMERICAN REVOLUTION. New Brunswick, New Jersey:
      Rutgers University Press, 1976.

      Based on fresh manuscript sources, the volume is the best
      treatment of the era. A poor province, Jersey lacked the
      resources, grievances and tradition to assume a major role
      in the crisis and thus, moderate Whigs led the cause. Al-
      though few new interpretations surface here, the author's
      work on local history, social stratification, and his thorough
      documentation (one hundred pages of footnotes) provide a fine
      synthesis of recent historical investigations.

2559. ————. "Soldier and Citizen: The British Army in New Jersey
      on the Eve of the Revolution." NJ HIST, 93 (1975), 5-36.

      Quartered in Jersey since 1758, British troops respected
      property rights, and the army was not considered by civilians
      as an instrument of oppression.

2560. Haskett, Richard C. "Prosecuting the Revolution." AHR, 59
      (1954), 578-587.

      Patterson, as Attorney General was a champion of the
      patriotic cause and vigorously punished Tories.

2561. ————. "William Patterson, Attorney General of New Jersey:
      Public Office and Private Profit in the American Revolu-
      tion." WMQ, 7 (1950), 26-38.

      Patterson used his office to prosecute Loyalists and to
      purchase their property.

2562. Hixson, Richard F. THE PRESS IN REVOLUTIONARY NEW JERSEY.
      Trenton, New Jersey Historical Commission, 1976.

      This pamphlet summarizes the activities of major printers
      like Issac Collins and Sheppard Kollock as well as the impor-
      tance of five Jersey newspapers.

2563. Honeyman, A. Van Doren. "An Unwritten Account of a Spy of
      Washington." NJ HIST, 85 (1967), 219-224.

A spy who operated along the Delaware provided Washington
with information for his Trenton-Princeton campaign.

2564.   ————. "The Pension Laws Concerning Revolutionary Soldiers."
         NJ HIST SOC PROC, 6 (1921), 116-118.

         This is a pioneering essay on the subject that needs to be
         revised.

2565.   Keesey, Ruth M. "Loyalism in Bergan County, New Jersey,"
         WMQ, 18 (1961), 558-576.

         Toryism was dominant here because of the lack of class
         agitation, the absence of land squabbles, and the nearness of
         British markets in New York for the county's produce.

2566.   Kemmerer, Donald L. "Judges Good Behavior Tenure in Colonial
         New Jersey." NJ HIST SOC PROC, 18 (1938), 18-30.

         Here is a good examination of the court system, and its
         adaptation to changes on the eve of war.

2567.   Leiby, Adrian C. THE REVOLUTIONARY WAR IN THE HACKENSACK
         VALLEY, THE JERSEY DUTCH AND THE NEUTRAL GROUND, 1775-1783.
         New Brunswick, New Jersey: Rutgers University Press, 1962.

         This is a fine account of how five nationality groups ab-
         sorbed in their own cultural-religious milieu became involved
         in political and military events in the state with the ebb
         and flow of war. The book is very valuable because the
         author examines the bitter church, land, and ethnic divisions,
         and mentions the bloody partisan war in the Hackensack area.
         This is a solid, well-written study that merits a wide
         audience.

2568.   Lender, Mark Edward. THE NEW JERSEY SOLDIER. Trenton: New
         Jersey Historical Society Commission, 1975.

         The pamphlet, written for a popular audience, is a good
         summary of Jersey's contributions in manpower and material
         to the war.

2569.   ————. THE RIVER WAR. Trenton: New Jersey Historical Com-
         mission, 1979.

         Lender summarizes the British invasion of the Delaware in
         1777 by concentrating on New Jersey's role in the struggle.
         The information about the river fortresses is pertinent.

2570.   Levitt, James H. NEW JERSEY'S REVOLUTIONARY ECONOMY. Trenton:
         New Jersey Historical Commission, 1975.

         For a solid, brief treatment about the impact, of the war on
         commerce, farmers, and merchants, this pamphlet is worth con-
         sulting.

2571. McCormick, Richard P. EXPERIMENT IN INDEPENDENCE, NEW JERSEY
      IN THE CRITICAL PERIOD, 1781-1789. New Brunswick, New
      Jersey: Rutgers University Press, 1950.

      McCormick wrote a sound, thoughtful monograph. The excel-
      lent narration, good chapter organization, and careful docu-
      mentation help to delineate the discord between East and West
      Jersey. The author also covers the problem of adjustment from
      a wartime to a peace economy, the difficulties in resolving
      war debts, and the problems of currency measures.

2572. Morrin, John M. "Princeton and the American Revolution."
      PRINCETON UNIV LIB CHRON, 38 (1978), 1-10.

      Here is a sample of the college's views on the rebellion
      and its role in the war.

2573. O'Connor, John E. "William Patterson and the Ideological
      Origins of the Revolution in New Jersey." NJ HIST, 94
      (1976), 5-22.

      Patterson symbolized the intense ideological commitment of
      patriots in a province characterized by economic backwardness
      and diverse ethnic-religious groups.

2574. Owen, Lewis F. "The Town That Was Robbed." NJ HIST SOC PROC,
      81 (1963), 164-180.

      Dobbs Ferry on the Palisades was battered continually by
      raiding parties until 1782.

2575. Pierce, Arthur D. SMUGGLER'S WOODS. New Brunswick: Rutgers
      University Press, 1980.

      Originally a coastal salt works, the area became important
      for privateering during the Revolution. The author has com-
      piled some fascinating data about locations, privateer
      harbors, personnel, and their method of raiding local British
      commerce. This is a lively book.

2576. Pole, J.R. "Suffrage Reform and the American Revolution in
      New Jersey." NJ HIST SOC PROC, 74 (1956), 175-194.

      The war helped to complete political reforms underway for
      decades.

2577. Pomfrey, John E. COLONIAL NEW JERSEY: A HISTORY. New York:
      Charles Scribner's Sons, 1973.

      This is the best volume written on the pre-Revolutionary
      era. It contains full bibliographies on the eras of propri-
      etary and royal governments. Chapters eight and nine provide
      a fine coverage of social-economic patterns on the eve of war.

2578. ———. "West New Jersey: A Quaker Society, 1675-1775."
       WMQ, 8 (1950), 493-519.

       The West Jersey friends maintained their unique social
       and geographic unity until after the Revolution.

2579. Ransom, Jerome M. VANISHING IRONWORKS OF THE RAMAPOOS. New
       Brunswick, New Jersey: Rutgers University Press, 1966.

       This is a worthwhile book with unique topics. There are
       detailed chapters about Robert Erskine, the cartographer and
       entrepreneur, ironworks at Ringwood, and the foundry of Lord
       Sterling. These sites produced cannon balls and chains to
       stretch across the Hudson in order to block British ships
       sailing upstream.

2580. Riccards, Michael P. "Patriots and Plunderers: Confiscation
       of Loyalist Lands in New Jersey, 1776-1786." NJ HIST, 86
       (1968), 14-38.

       The state's efforts to acquire revenue for sales of Tory
       lands were blunted by inflation, corruption and currency
       manipulation.

2581. Robinson, Thomas P., and Lawrence Leder. "Governor Livingston
       and the 'Sun Shine Patriots'." WMQ, 13 (1950), 394-397.

       Livingston tried to check the movement of Loyalists through
       American lines during the British occupation of New York City.

2582. Rosenberg, Leonard B. "William Patterson: New Jersey's Na-
       tion Maker." NJ HIST, 85 (1967), 7-40.

       Jersey's war governor was not an original thinker; he fully
       supported the war effort and feared the lower classes.

2583. Ryan, Dennis P. "Landholding, Opportunity and Mobility in
       Revolutionary New Jersey." WMQ, 36 (1976), 571-582.

       Examining the property of 2,500 adult males (by tax rolls)
       from six towns in 1789, the author concludes that the Revolu-
       tion caused no major re-distribution of wealth.

2584. ———. NEW JERSEY IN THE AMERICAN REVOLUTION, 1763-1783. A
       CHRONOLOGY. Trenton: The New Jersey Historical Commission,
       1974.

       This is a useful guide to significant events that helped
       to shape the state's destiny for two decades.

2585. ———. NEW JERSEY'S WHIGS. Trenton: New Jersey Historical
       Commission, 1975.

       Here are brief profiles of William Patterson, William
       Alexander, John Stevens, Jr., and Nathanael Baldwin.

2586.   Salay, David L. "The Production of War Material in New Jersey
        During the Revolution." In William C. Wright, ed. NEW
        JERSEY IN THE AMERICAN REVOLUTION III. Trenton: New Jersey
        Historical Commission, 1976, pp. 7-20.

        Salay demonstrates that in the production of arms, gun-
        powder, iron products, shot and shell, and cannon that
        the basic problem was not lack of technological "know-how"
        but shortages of funds, materials, and British raids.

2587.   Shelley, Fred. "Ebenezer Hazard's Diary: New Jersey During
        the Revolution." NJ HIST SOC, 90 (1972), 40-54.

        As Postmaster of New York, Hazard made a trip through the
        state in August, 1777, noting the destruction of communities
        due to the war.

2588.   Shy, John W. "Quartering His Majesty's Forces in New Jersey."
        NJ HIST SOC PROC, 78 (1968), 82-94.

        The presence of British regulars was not a basic grievance
        until 1775.

2589.   Stewart, Bruce W. MORRISTOWN: A CRUCIBLE OF THE AMERICAN
        REVOLUTION. Trenton: New Jersey Historical Commission,
        1977.

        This summary of the encampment's importance to the state
        is suitable for high school and college undergraduates.

2590.   White, Donald W. "A Local History Apporach to the American
        Revolution: Chatham, N.J." NJ HIST, 96 (1978), 46-64.

        The social-economic changes on one village were relatively
        minor compared to the impact of the war on nearby regions.

2591.   ————. A VILLAGE AT WAR, CHATHAM, NEW JERSEY, AND THE
        AMERICAN REVOLUTION. Cranbury, New Jersey: Fairleigh
        Dickinson University Press, 1978.

        This is an excellent account of how war affected a small
        settlement. The author skillfully enlivens his narrative
        from masses of local records to show the impact of inflation,
        food shortage, small pox, and military duty on Chatham. By
        1783, little had changed in property-holdings or in political
        power.

2592.   Wright, William C., ed. NEW JERSEY IN THE AMERICAN REVOLU-
        TION, II. PAPERS PRESENTED AT THE FOURTH ANNUAL NEW JERSEY
        SYMPOSIUM, DECEMBER 2, 1772. Trenton: New Jersey Histori-
        cal Commission, 1973.

        David A. Bernstein narrated how a strong executive branch
        developed under William Livingston. Dennis P. Ryan provided
        a quantitative analysis of Whig activists in six counties.

Peter J. Guthorn summarized the work of map-makers Robert
Erskine and John Hills. Howard C. Rice, Jr. discussed the
march of Rochambeau's army through New Jersey.

7. Pennsylvania

2593. Aldrich, James M. "A Quantitative Reassessment of the Effects
of Sectionalism in Pennsylvania during the War for Independence." PA HIST, 39 (1972), 334-361.

This is a valuable article, based on a detailed statistical
analysis of voting patterns in the legislature, which shows
that both radicals and conservatives represented a broad
geographic spectrum.

2594. Anderson, James La Verne. "The Impact of the American Revolution on the Governor's Councillors." PA HIST, 34 (1967),
131-146.

Although Tories on the Council had their lands confiscated,
after the war some of them achieved high political or judicial
posts in the state.

2595. Bezanson, Anne. "Inflation and Controls, Pennsylvania, 1774-
1777." J ECON HIST, 8 Supplement (1948), 1-20.

Here is a neat summary of how the patriots tried to stem
inflation and to determine the distribution of key commodities.

2596. Bowling, Kenneth R. "New Light on the Philadelphia Mutiny
of 1783: Federal-State Confrontation at the Close of the
War for Independence." PA MHB, 101 (1977), 419-450.

The last wartime disturbance by army units over back-pay
raised questions about the police powers of the young Republic and resulted in the departure of Congressional Delegates
from Philadelphia.

2597. Brobeck, Stephen. "Revolutionary Class in Colonial Pennsylvania: The Brief Life of the Proprietary Gentry." WMQ, 33
(1976), 410-434.

This is a valuable account about 22 non-Quaker members of
an elite who dominated the government until the war disrupted
their control.

2598. Brunhouse, Robert L. THE COUNTER-REVOLUTION IN PENNSYLVANIA,
1776-1780. New York: Octagon Books, 1971.

This is a comprehensive study of the Confederation era.
The author tends to view Pennsylvania politics as a struggle
between eastern mercantile interests and western agrarian
democrats. Consequently, he neglects the essence of the
crucial ethnic and religious conflicts of the period.

2599. Crowley, James E. "The Paxton Disturbances and Ideas of
       Order in Pennsylvania Politics." PA HIST, 37 (1970), 317-
       339.

       The affair demonstrated that illegal actions against Indians
       were not tolerated by the provincial authorities.

2600. Fisher, Darlene Emmert. "Social Life in Philadelphia During
       the British Occupation." PA HIST, 37 (1970), 237-260.

       This is a well-documented article about elaborate balls and
       festivities, the quartering of troops, plundering by the army,
       and theatre presentations.

2601. Gibson, James E. "The Pennsylvania Provincial Congress of
       1776." PA MHB, 58 (1934), 312-341.

       Held June 18 to June 25, the Congress made possible the
       Declaration of Independence.

2602. Gilbert, Daniel R. "Bethlehem and the American Revolution."
       TRANS MORAVIAN SOC, 23 (1977), 17-40.

       Bethlehem was a hospital center for the Continental Army,
       and, consequently, the impact of the experience on the vil-
       lage was significant.

2603. Gough, Robert. "Notes on the Pennsylvania Revolutionaries
       of 1776." PA MHB, 76 (1972), 89-103.

       This is a detailed analysis of ninety-two patriots from
       eastern Pennsylvania who displayed a diverse but mainly a
       middle-class background.

2604. Hawke, David. IN THE MIDST OF REVOLUTION. Philadelphia:
       University of Pennsylvania Press, 1961.

       This is a lively and thoughtful account that covers May
       through July, 1776. Though the events related here are
       familiar, Hawke's exciting writing style and his familiarity
       with the sources provide a fine perspective of these dramatic
       months. Although vague on sectionalism and class strife, the
       author compiled one of the best accounts of the Founding
       Fathers at a key moment in history. The work is amply docu-
       mented, and it is a model of its kind.

2605. Jable, J. Thomas. "The Pennsylvania Sunday Blue Laws of
       1779: A View of Pennsylvania Society and Politics During
       the American Revolution." PA HIST, 40 (1973), 413-26.

       Social pressures, religious attitudes, and economic condi-
       tions were factors in requiring church attendance and prohib-
       iting amusements on Sunday.

2606.   Jordan, John W. "Bethlehem During the Revolution." PA MAG
         HIST BIOG, 12 (1888), 385-406.

         Extracts from the Moravian Archives provide a good view of
         hospital conditions here for the army.

2607.   Lucas, Stanley E. PORTENTS OF REBELLION: RHETORIC AND REVO-
         LUTION IN PHILADELPHIA, 1765-76. Philadelphia: Temple
         University Press, 1976.

         In jargon that is difficult to comprehend, the author at-
         tempts to relate the rhetoric of revolution to the clamor for
         independence. Yet this volume summarizes the views of dozens
         of groups and individuals and thereby it provides a microcosm
         of urban viewpoints on the eve of Revolution. The ideologi-
         cal factors are stressed here to almost the total exclusion
         of other causes.

2608.   Marshall, Christopher. EXTRACTS FROM THE DIARY OF CHRISTOPHER
         MARSHALL, KEPT IN PHILADELPHIA AND LANCASTER DURING THE
         AMERICAN REVOLUTION, 1774-1781. Edited by William Duane.
         Albany, New York: J. Munsell, 1877.

         An apothecary and city father, Marshall was active in
         politics. His notes about meetings that he attended, views
         on the early war years, preparations for Washington's army,
         and related matters provide useful insights.

2609.   Martin, James Kirby. "The Return of the Paxton Boys and the
         Historical State of the Pennsylvania Frontier, 1764-1775."
         PA MHB, 38 (1971), 117-133.

         The Paxton Boys were dissatisfied with rent collections,
         land sales and Indian relations; many of them moved into
         the Wyoming Valley to support a Connecticut land company.

2610.   Mishcoff, Willard O. "Business in Philadelphia During the
         British Occupation, 1777-78." PA MHB, 61 (1937), 165-181.

         The occupation stimulated the wholesale and retail trade
         to supply the British army; the data here is useful about
         price levels, food scarcities, and Whig profiteers.

2611.   Molovinsky, Lemuel. "Taxation and Continuity in Pennsylvania
         During the American Revolution." PA MHB, 104 (1980), 365-
         378.

         Provincial Pennsylvania demonstrated a remarkable continuity
         with English traditions in customs, duties, and excise taxes.

2612.   ————. "Tax Collection Problems in Revolutionary Pennsyl-
         vania." PA HIST, 47 (1980), 253-259.

         Collecting state revenues was difficult due to the British,
         Loyalists, Indians and a tradition of opposing taxes.

2613. Nash, Gary B. "Up From the Bottom in Franklin's Philadelphia."
       PAST AND PRESENT, 77 (1977), 58-83.

       For ordinary urban dwellers in the pre-industrial commercial
       seaport, chances of success were limited due to many economic
       factors.

2614. Nesbitt, John R. "Old Westmoreland's Delegates to Pennsyl-
       vania's 1776 Constitutional Convention." W PA HIST MAG,
       55 (1972), 255-267.

       The newest county formed in 1773 was virtually isolated
       by geography; it was composed of many ethnic groups, and it
       elected a diverse assortment of men.

2615. Oaks, Peter F. "Philadelphia Merchants and the Origins of
       American Independence." AMER PHIL SOC PROC, 121 (1977),
       407-437.

       This is a neat summary of the role of the merchant class
       from 1765-1776 as it shifted its rhetoric and attitudes with
       each crisis.

2616. Olton, Charles S. ARTISANS FOR INDEPENDENCE: PHILADELPHIA
       MECHANICS AND THE AMERICAN REVOLUTION. Syracuse, New York:
       Syracuse University Press, 1975.

       This is a gracefully written and solidly documented account
       about the ideology and the politics of a semi-specialized
       laboring group. Unlike an unskilled urban proletariat, the
       mechanics tended to represent a rising middle class with view-
       points similar to businessmen. The author deftly traces their
       growing political consciousness with respect to each major
       crisis with ample detail.

2617. ————. "Philadelphia's Mechanics in the First Decade of
       Revolution, 1765-1775." J AH, 59 (1972-73), 311-
       326.

       The artisans were not radical, nor keenly class-conscious,
       but they opposed the merchants over the nonimportation agree-
       ments and strove for political power.

2618. Outerhurst, Anne M. "Pennsylvania Land Confiscation during
       the Revolution." PA MHB, 102 (1978), 328-343.

       Confiscation laws on Loyalists were enacted after much de-
       bate and were generally reluctantly enforced.

2619. Smith, Charles Page. "The Attack on Fort Wilson." PA MHB,
       78 (1954), 177-194.

       This essay concerns a Philadelphia mob which attacked the
       home of conservative James Wilson because of discontent, in-
       cluding price controls.

398   THE IMPACT OF WAR ON SOCIETY

2620. Thayer, Theodore. PENNSYLVANIA POLITICS AND THE GROWTH OF
       DEMOCRACY, 1746-1776. Harrisburg, Pennsylvania: Pennsyl-
       vania Historical and Museum Commission, 1953.

       The old split between the proprietary party and the Quaker-
       led anti-proprietary faction conditioned Pennsylvania for the
       imperial conflict. The Quakers tried to persuade the Crown
       to make Pennsylvania a royal colony but they failed to satisfy
       the radicals. But rivalry about class distinctions ended in
       1776. The author stresses the absence of social or class
       conflict in this thoughtful but now outdated monograph.

2621. Ward, A. Gertrude. "John Ettwein and the Moravians in the
       Revolution." PA HIST, 1 (1934), 191-201.

       The Moravians had their property seized by the army for
       lodging and hospitals and were persecuted for their neutrality.

2622. Young, Henry J. "Treason and Its Punishment in Revolutionary
       Pennsylvania." PA MHB, 90 (1966), 287-313.

       The state punished subversives severely, and it imposed
       harsh penalities on Loyalists.

                           8. Delaware

2623. Bellas, Henry Hobart, comp., "Personal Recollections of
       Captain Enoch Anderson, an Officer of the Delaware Regi-
       ments in the Revolution." HIST SOC DEL PAPERS, 16 (1896),
       1-69.

       Anderson wrote a lively memoir about his army experiences
       in major northern campaigns.

2624. Farris, Sara Guertler. "Wilmington Maritime Commerce, 1775-
       1807." DEL HIST, 14 (1970), 22-51.

       The port's marketing facilities, tariff structure and its
       favorable location provided shipping advantages for trade
       with the West Indies and with Europe.

2625. Ferrand, Max. "The Delaware Bill of Rights of 1776." AHR,
       3 (1898), 641-649.

       Maryland is indebted to Delaware for a model of the bill
       of rights in the first Delaware constitution.

2626. Flower, Milton E. "John Dickinson, Delawarean." DEL HIST,
       17 (1976), 12-20.

       This prominent politician served his state in many capaci-
       ties, particularly in Congress.

2627. Frank, William R., and Hancock, Harold B. "Caesar Rodney's
       Two Hundred and Fiftieth Anniversary: An Evaluation."
       DEL HIST, 10 (1978), 63-74.

       Here is a good sketch of Delaware's most important patriot,
       devoid of the legends.

2628. Guertler, John Thomas. "Hezekiah Niles: Wilmington Printer
       and Editor." DEL HIST, 17 (1976), 44-62.

       Although this article covers Niles' early nineteenth-cen-
       tury career, it contains useful information about his early
       apprenticeship in printing.

2629. Hancock, Harold B. "Country Committees and the Growth of
       Independence in the Three Lower Counties on the Delaware,
       1765-1776." DEL HIST, 15 (1973), 265-294.

       These committees suppressed Tory agitators, organized
       militia, elected Delegates to Congress, and they corresponded
       with Boston and Philadelphia.

2630. ————. "Letters To and From Caesar Rodney." DEL HIST, 12
       (1966), 54-76, 147-180.

       This correspondence concerns Tories, White Plains, and
       Delaware politics.

2631. Jackson, J.B. "Our Forgotten Regiment: The Second Delaware
       Militia, 1780." DEL HIST, 9 (1960), 3-50.

       Here is a fine summary about Lieutenant-Colonel Henry
       Neill's dependable unit.

2632. Kirkwood, Robert. "The Journal and Orderly Book of Captain
       Robert Kirkwood of the Delaware Regiment of the Continental
       Line." HIST SOC DEL PAPERS, 56 (1910), 1-277.

       Kirkwood served at Princeton, Germantown, and Wilmington; he
       spent 1780-82 fighting the British in the south.

2633. Moyne, Ernest J. "Who was Colonel John Hastel of Delaware?"
       DEL HIST, 13 (1969), 283-300.

       A Scot physician and patriot who died at Princeton, Hastel
       merits a biography.

2634. Munroe, John A. "Reflections on Delaware and the American
       Revolution." DEL HIST, 17 (1976), 1-11.

       The Revolution in Delaware was moderate and its delegates
       ratified the Constitution.

2635. Powell, John H. "John Dickinson, President of the Delaware
       State, 1781-1782." DEL HIST, (1949), 1-55, 111-134.

Dickinson was one of Delaware's most active champions of the Revolution and provided leadership to the new state.

2636. Reed, H. Clay, and Palermo, Joseph A. "Justice of the Peace in Early Delaware." DEL HIST, 14 (1971), 223-237.

Justices played a vital role in local government until the Delaware constitutions stripped them of administrative and judicial functions.

2637. Rowe, G.S. "A Valuable Acquisition in Congress: Thomas McKean, Delegate to the Continental Congress, 1774-1783." PA HIST, 38 (1971), 225-264.

Due to a tradition of plural office-holding, McKean, a resident of Pennsylvania and its Chief Justice in 1777, also represented Delaware in Congress.

2638. ————. "The Travail of John McKinley, First President of Delaware." DEL HIST, 17 (1876), 21-36.

Captured by the British, McKinley was unable to be exchanged due to bitter Whig rivalries in the state.

2639. Welsh, Peter C. "Merchants, Millers and Ocean Ships: The Components of an Early American Industrial Town." DEL HIST, 7 (1957), 319-330.

Here is an excellent essay describing how various economic components aided in the rise of Wilmington as a prosperous port.

2640. ————. "The Brandywine Mills: A Chronicle of an Industry, 1762-1816." DEL HIST, 7 (1956), 17-36.

Farmers and business profited by the location near Wilmington, and the port was virtually unaffected by the enemy.

9. Maryland

2641. Alexander, Arthur J. "How Maryland Tried to Raise Her Continental Quota." MD HIST MAG, 18 (1947), 184-196.

Efforts to recruit with bounties and land, or to use black troops all failed, so compulsory military service was instituted in 1778.

2642. Ammerman, David. "Annapolis and the First Continental Congress: A Note on the Committee System in Revolutionary America." MD HIST MAG, 66 (1971), 169-180.

Marylanders voted for trade suspensions with Britain as a result of the Boston Port Act, and their committee was a precedent for calling a congress.

2643. Anderthorn, Thornton. "Maryland's Property Qualifications
       for Office: A Reinterpretation of the Constitutional Con-
       vention of 1776." MD HIST MAG, 78 (1973), 327-339.

       Even with tax reform and extension of the franchise, eighty-
       three per cent of white males were without voting rights; the
       oligarchy held control of offices for another forty years.

2644. Barker, Charles A. "Maryland Before the Revolution: Society
       and Thought." AHR, 46 (1940), 1-20.

       Enlightened thought in Maryland resembled that of New
       England and Virginia, but life was more dominated by a
       tobacco-staple economy, the lack of major cities, a de-
       centralized economy, and neither Annapolis nor Baltimore
       provided leadership.

2645. ————. "The Revolutionary Impulse in Maryland." MD HIST
       MAG, 36 (1941), 125-138.

       This is a weak summary which concentrates on legislation for
       tobacco exports.

2646. Bast, Homer. "Tench Tilghman - Maryland Patriot." MD HIST
       MAG, 41 (1947), 71-94.

       Tilghman was Washington's aide in '76, served in numerous
       military engagements, and he carried the news of Yorktown to
       Congress.

2647. Beirne, Rosamind R. "Portrait of a Colonial Governor:
       Robert Eden." MD HIST MAG, 45 (1950), 153-175, 294-311.

       Maryland's last royal governor became embroiled in en-
       forcing the Townsend Act; he served the Crown well and had
       to flee the colony in 1776.

2648. Browne, William Hand and others, eds. ARCHIVES OF MARYLAND.
       71 vols. Baltimore: The Maryland Historical Society, 1892-
       1970.

       This is one of the best printed collections of a state's
       documents during the Revolution. About ten volumes in the
       series have material on many aspects of the war. There are
       innumerable letters from Committees of Safety and to Maryland
       officers in the field as well as ample data about political
       and economic developments.

2649. Cometti, Elizabeth. "Inflation in Revolutionary Maryland."
       WMQ, 8 (1951), 228-234.

       John Galloway's account book shows changes in prices, wages,
       and rents during the war.

2650. Crowl, Philip A. MARYLAND DURING AND AFTER THE REVOLUTION.
       Baltimore: Johns Hopkins University Press, 1943.

       This work summarizes major political events in the state
       to the virtual omission of social factors. However, it is
       well-documented, stresses the concensus in government by
       Maryland's leading families, and the book's coverage of debts,
       financing, and property confiscation is ably related.

2651. Dorsey, Rhoda M. "The Pattern of Baltimore Commerce During
       the Confederation Period." MD HIST MAG, 62 (1967), 119-
       134.

       Even with increased exports from 1780-87 of flour and
       wheat, Baltimore remained a small trading center.

2652. Dowd, Mary Jane. "The State in the Maryland Economy, 1776-
       1807." MD HIST MAG, 57 (1962), 90-132, 229-258.

       The government was deeply involved in subsidies to manu-
       facturing, transportation, shipping, and agriculture.

2653. Giddens, Paul H. "Governor Horatio Sharpe and His Maryland
       Government." MD HIST MAG, 32 (1937), 156-174.

       Sharpe's long reign was characterized by endless feuds
       with the Lower House, with courts, local government, and with
       officialdom.

2654. ————. "Land Policies and Administration in Colonial
       Maryland, 1753-1769." MD HIST MAG, 28 (1933), 142-171.

       This is a valuable discussion of Governor Sharpe's policies
       concerning leases, quitrents, land speculation, and disposal
       of new lands prior to the revolution.

2655. Hanley, Thomas O'Brien. "The State and Dissenters in the
       Revolution." MD HIST MAG, 58 (1963), 325-332.

       In a weak essay, Hanley cites the negotiations by Quakers
       and Methodists with the Assembly over freedom of conscience
       issues.

2656. Hoffman, Ronald. A SPIRIT OF DISSENSION: ECONOMICS, POLITICS
       AND THE REVOLUTION IN MARYLAND. Baltimore: Johns Hopkins
       University Press, 1973.

       This significant work provides a penetrating account of the
       colony on the eve of the Revolution. It has excellent com-
       mentaries about regionalism in politics, the response of
       the merchant community to British provocations, and about the
       roles of Paca, the Dulaneys, and the Carrolls. Hoffman pro-
       vides insights about why Maryland was cautious with independ-
       ence movements, how the state approached near anarchy in
       mid-'76, why men who drafted a conservative constitution also

enacted a liberal tax code, and how the patriot leaders
handled Loyalism on the Eastern Shore. Well-documented and
gracefully written, this is one of the best state histories
during the era.

2657.   ———. "Popularizing the Revolution: Internal Conflict and
        Economic Sacrifice in Maryland, 1774-1780." MD HIST MAG,
        68 (1973), 125-139.

        This key article demonstrates the degree of lower class
        resentment, Eastern Shore agitation, and how Maryland's
        leaders restored order during the war by leniency in court
        cases and in tax legislation.

2658.   Howard, Cary. "John Eager Howard." MD HIST MAG, 82 (1967),
        300-317.

        Howard was a daring Continental colonel who fought the
        British in the south and became a Governor and Senator.

2659.   Howard, John Eager. "Col. John Eager Howard's Account of
        the Battle of Germantown." MD HIST MAG, 4 (1909), 314-
        320.

        Written in 1827, this is a vivid account of the famous fight.

2660.   Klingelhofer, Herbert E. "The Cautious Revolution: Maryland
        and the Movement Toward Independence, 1774-1776." MD HIST
        MAG, 60 (1965), 261-313.

        Here is a major article which analyzes the June, 1774 con-
        vention, the sending of delegates to Congress, the quest
        for independence, and the formation of a new state government.

2661.   Kulikoff, Allan. "The Economic Growth of the Eighteenth
        Century Chesapeake Colonies." J ECON HIST, 39 (1979), 275-
        288.

        Increased grain production, more efficient tobacco culti-
        vation, a greater extension of credit from Scot factors, and
        a larger supply of black labor enabled Maryland to prosper.

2662.   Land, Aubrey C. COLONIAL MARYLAND - A HISTORY. Millwood,
        New York: KTO Press, 1978.

        Here is the best synthesis available on Maryland's history
        to 1775. The author provides an admirable fusion of major
        social, economic, and political developments that incorporates
        interpretations from recent research by specialists. The
        bibliography is very comprehensive.

2663.   Main, Jackson Turner. "Political Parties in Revolutionary
        Maryland, 1780-1787." MD HIST MAG, 62 (1967), 1-27.

This is a detailed examination of the House of Delegates
showing constituencies, political characteristics of members,
and the nature of major issues related to sections and to oc-
cupations, demonstrating that only informal coalitions existed.

2664.   Molovinsky, Lemuel. "Maryland and the American West at
        Independence." MD HIST MAG, 72 (1977), 353-360.

        Fearful of Virginia's vast claims, Maryland, handicapped
        by the scarcity of public land, offered a reasoned response
        to the implications of gross inequities in the state domain.

2665.   Overfield, Richard A. "A Patriot Dilemma. The Treatment of
        Passive Loyalists and Neutrals in Revolutionary Maryland."
        MD HIST MAG, 68 (1913), 140-159.

        The article examines the state's dilemma in providing for
        security, quelling Loyalist agitation, and yet attempting
        to be equitable to neutral citizens.

2666.   Owen, Hamilton. BALTIMORE ON THE CHESAPEAKE. New York:
        Doubleday and Co., 1941.

        This is a readable summary of Maryland's maritime efforts
        during the war that was written for a general readership.
        The author covers privateering, and elaborates on the Maryland
        state DEFENSE, and the Continental frigate VIRGINIA.

2667.   Papenfuse, Edward C., Alan F. Day, David W. Jordan, and
        Gregory A Stiverson. A BIOGRAPHICAL DICTIONARY OF THE
        MARYLAND LEGISLATURE, 1635-1789. Vol. 1. A-H.
        Baltimore and London: The Johns Hopkins University Press,
        1979.

        This first volume of a collective biography of Maryland's
        politicians during the Revolutionary era has excellent maps.
        It provides concise, and well-written summaries about legis-
        lators during the Revolution.

2668.   ————. "Economic Analysis and Loyalist Strategy During the
        American Revolution: Robert Alexander's Remarks on the
        Economy of the Peninsula or Eastern Shore of Maryland."
        MD HIST MAG, 68 (1973), 173-195.

        This document represents one of the few comprehensive re-
        ports on regional agriculture in colonial America, and it
        shows an aspect of a Loyalist intelligence network planning
        for a British invasion of the area.

2669.   ————. IN PURSUIT OF PROFIT: THE ANNAPOLIS MERCHANTS IN THE
        ERA OF THE AMERICAN REVOLUTION, 1763-1805. Baltimore:
        Johns Hopkins University Press, 1975.

        Though this is primarily an urban history with relatively
        little on the war itself, it is a very valuable work. The

merchant community had close ties to London, the town was
prosperous, and it was a military depot before and during
the Revolution. Papenpuse deftly shows Annapolis merchants
adjusting to changing economic and demographic patterns as
trade shifted to Philadelphia and Baltimore.

2670. Pinkett, Harold T. "Maryland As a Source of Food Supply
       During the American Revolution." MD HIST MAG, 48 (1951),
       157-172.

       Relatively free from raids and civil war, Maryland's
       production of wheat and corn (usually shipped to the Elk
       River for Continentals, or to Baltimore for the French) was
       considerable.

2671. Pole, J.R. "Sufferage and Representation in Maryland from
       1776 to 1810: A Statistical Note and Some Reflections."
       JSH, 24 (1958), 218-225.

       Maryland experienced a remarkable political transformation
       as religious discrimination ended, the franchise was extend-
       ed, and the property qualifications for office were terminated.

2672. Price, Jacob M. "The Rise of Glasgow in the Chesapeake
       Tobacco Trade, 1701-1775." WMQ, 11 (1954), 179-199.

       Tobacco was king in Maryland and Virginia, and it retarded
       crop diversification; the Scot store system was efficient
       and drained the Tidewater area of American commercial talent.

2673. Rainbolt, J. Ralph. "A Note on the Maryland Delegation of
       Rights and Constitution of 1776." MD HIST MAG, 66 (1971),
       420-435.

       These documents were typical yardsticks in the democrati-
       zation process, but the executive retained much authority,
       and the Assembly's power was diffused by the electoral system.

2674. Reges, Stephen G. "A Spanish Governor's Invitation to Mary-
       land Catholics." MD HIST MAG, 60 (1965), 93-98.

       Antonio de Ulloa from 1766-1783 attempted to settle
       Louisiana with Maryland Catholics but the Marylanders were
       reluctant to move.

2675. Silverman, Albert. "William Paca, Signer, Governor, Jurist."
       MD HIST MAG, 37 (1942), 1-23.

       Paca, an outstanding patriot and politician, merits more
       attention from historians.

2676. Skaggs, David C. "Maryland's Impulse Toward Social Revolu-
       tion, 1750-1776." JAH, 54 (1964), 777-786.

       The voters wanted a drastic reform of society which was then
       dominated by the provincial elite.

2677. ————. ROOTS OF MARYLAND DEMOCRACY, 1753-1776. Westport,
       Connecticut: Greenwood Press, Inc., 1973.

       The inequities in the political system whereby forty per
       cent of white adult males were disfranchised was partially
       rectified in the Constitution of 1776. This volume pro-
       vides fine coverage about the landed gentry, political
       battles, the mobs of landless, demands for legislative re-
       form, and shifts in the tax structure.

2678. Steiner, Edward E. "Nicholas Ruxton Moore: Soldier, Farmer
       and Politician." MD HIST MAG, 73 (1978), 375-388.

       Moore served as an artillery officer at Annapolis, Balti-
       more, Brandywine, and he later organized the Baltimore
       Light Dragoons.

2679. Stewart, Arthur. "The Burning of the Peggy Stewart." MD
       HIST MAG, 5 (1910), 235-245.

       The ship-owners wrote a memorial to the British Treasury
       regarding the destruction of the vessel by patriots off
       Annapolis in 1774.

2680. Strawser, Neil. "Samuel Chase and the Annapolis Paper War."
       MD HIST MAG, 73 (1978), 375-388.

       Chase led the criticism of entrenched officialdom in Annap-
       olis with mob activities and propagandist methods to defeat
       the corrupt town government.

2681. Thompson, Tommy R. "Personal Indebtedness and the American
       Revolution in Maryland." MD HIST MAG, 73 (1978), 13-29.

       The impact of the tobacco trade and the control by credi-
       tors of the province's economy were contributing factors for
       revolution.

2682. Vivian, Jean H. "Thomas Stone and the Reorganization of the
       Maryland Council of Safety, 1776." MD HIST MAG, 69 (1974),
       271-278.

       The Council had great power to supervise defense, recruit
       militia, and punish Tories until the committee's authority
       was modified.

2683. Walker, Paul K. "Business and Commerce in Baltimore on the
       Eve of Independence." MD HIST MAG, 71 (1976), 296-309.

       Formerly dependent on Philadelphia, by a combination of
       geography, enterprise, and chance, Baltimore developed into
       a bustling port.

2684. ———. "The Baltimore Community and the American Revolution 1763-1783: A Study in Urban Development." Ph.D.
dissertation, University of North Carolina, 1973.

Based on a wide range of archival material, this monograph
deftly examines how Baltimore became a principal marketing
center, and how it developed commercial ties with Pennsylvania's Susquehanna Valley. Escaping British attacks,
Baltimore grew during the war because of shipping, privateering, and its control of the tobacco trade.

2685. Williams, George H. "William Eddis: What the Sources Say."
MD HIST MAG, 60 (1965), 121-131.

A Loyalist official in Annapolis who returned to England,
Eddis wrote a good contemporary account of events, 1767-77.

2686. Yackel, Peter G. "Criminal Justice and Loyalists in Maryland:
Maryland vs. Casper Frietschie." MD HIST MAG, 73 (1978),
46-63.

A key trial in Frederick (1781) demonstrated a traditional
respect for legal procedure and respect for common law in the
case of a Loyalist.

10. Virginia

2687. Anderson, James LaVerne. "The Virginia Councillors and the
American Revolution: The Demise of an Aristocratic Office."
VA MHB, 82 (1974), 56-74.

The Revolution completed the political erosion of this once
powerful group who lost influence during the war.

2688. Ardery, William B. "The Other Ride of the Revolution." AMER
HIST ILLUS, 6 (5) (1971), 41-42.

On June 3-4, 1781, Captain Jack Jouett rode forty miles to
warn the Virginia General Assembly about an expedition of
British troops marching into the interior.

2689. Bowman, Larry. "The Scarcity of Salt in Virginia During the
American Revolution." VA MHB, 77 (1969), 464-472.

Virginia experienced a serious crisis concerning salt; the
state tried various expedients to increase imports and production but with little success.

2690. ———. "The Virginia County Committees of Safety, 1774-1776."
VA MHB, 79 (1971), 332-337.

Forty-nine committees formed to enforce the boycott urged
by the First Continental Congress did a respectable job and
were dissolved in late 1776.

408 THE IMPACT OF WAR ON SOCIETY

2691. Brown, Douglas Summer. "Charles Cummings: The Fighting
Parson of Southwest Virginia." VA CAV, 28 (1979), 138-143.

Parsons was a Presbyterian minister, pioneer, and a folk-
hero who fought the British.

2692. Buckley, Thomas E. CHURCH AND STATE IN REVOLUTIONARY VIRGIN-
IA, 1776-1787. Charlottesville, Virginia: University of
Virginia Press, 1977.

This is a fine account of the religious debate that cul-
minated in an amendment to the Constitution. The author
deftly covers the influence of the Great Awakening, the difficulties of the Anglican Church, the roles of George Mason
and Thomas Jefferson, and the attitudes of dissenting sects
in the controversy.

2693. Cometti, Elizabeth. "Depredations in Virginia During the
Revolution." In THE OLD DOMINION: ESSAYS FOR THOMAS
PERKINS ABERNATHY. Edited by Darrett B. Rutman.
Charlottesville: The University of Virginia, 1964, pp. 135-151.

Because Virginia lacked a navy and sufficient militia, the
state was repeatedly devastated by British coastal raids and
expeditions to the interior.

2694. Curtis, George M., III. "The Goodrich Family and the Revolution in Virginia." VA MHB, 84 (1976), 49-74.

John Goodrich, a Portsmouth merchant, suffered for his
Loyalist sympathies.

2695. Dabney, Virginius. "Jack Jouett's Ride." AMER HERITAGE,
13 (1) (1961), 56-59.

Jouett raced to Monticello and Charlottesville to save
Jefferson and the legislature from a British raid.

2696. Eckenrode, H.J. THE REVOLUTION IN VIRGINIA. Boston and
New York: Houghton Mifflin, 1916.

This is a quaint, poorly written book that stresses the
virtues of Virginians. However, there is some useful information here about Portsmouth, Loyalism, ideological debates,
and the difficulties of the war governors.

2697. Ernst, Joseph. "The Robinson Scandal Redivivus: Money, Debts
and Politics in Revolutionary Virginia." VA MHB, 77 (1969),
146-173.

The embezzlement of state funds demonstrated the delicate
balance of debts, politics, and currency issues in an ex-
panding economy.

THE IMPACT OF WAR ON SOCIETY 409

2698. Evans, Emory G. "Planter Indebtedness and the Coming of the
       Revolution in Virginia." WMQ, 19 (1962), 511-533.

       This article demonstrates that debts owed British firms
       were not involved in the Revolutionary debate, that some
       prominent Virginia debtors were hesitant about independence,
       and that constitutional issues were the source of contention.

2699. ———. "Planter Indebtedness and the Revolution in
       Virginia, 1776 to 1796." WMQ, 28 (1971), 349-374.

       The debt issue was complicated by the scarcity of money,
       economic dislocation, war damages, and the British con-
       fiscation of slaves.

2700. ———. "The Rise and Decline of the Virginia Aristocracy
       in the Eighteenth Century: The Nelsons." See 2693,
       pp. 62-78.

       One of the most influential families in late colonial
       Virginia, the patriotic Nelson family lost wealth and power
       during the war, even when Thomas Nelson was Governor.

2701. Greene, Jack P. "Character, Persona, and Authority: A Study
       of Alternative Styles of Political Leadership in Revolu-
       tionary Virginia." See 855, pp. 3-42.

       This is a very perceptive essay about the political roles
       of Richard Henry Lee, George Mason and Edward Pendleton.

2702. ———. "Foundations of Political Power in the Virginia
       House of Burgesses, 1720-1776." WMQ, 16 (1959), 485-506.

       Of 630 politicians, only 110 had major influence, and no
       particular section monopolized power.

2703. ———. "'Virtus et Libertas': Political Culture, Social
       Change and the Origins of the American Revolution in
       Virginia, 1763-1766." See 1913, pp. 55-108.

       A series of political scandals mared the image of the
       oligarchy, but this group retained power for another decade
       without a serious challenge.

2704. Harrell, Isaac S. "Some Neglected Phases of the Revolution."
       WMQ, 5 (1925), 159-170.

       This article summarizes the importance of land policies,
       public finance, and private debts as related to the economic
       development of the state.

2705. Hecht, Arthur. "Lead Production in Virginia During the
       Seventeenth and Eighteenth Centuries." WEST VA HIST, 25
       (1964), 173-183.

Little production occurred until the war caused the state
to increase output of the mineral.

2706. Herndon, G. Melvin. "A War-Inspired Industry: The Manufac-
       ture of Hemp in Virginia During the Revolution." VA MHB,
       74 (1966), 301-311.

       The war stimulated the production of linen weaving.

2707. ———. "George Matthews, Frontier Patriot." VA MHB, 77
       (1967), 301-338.

       Matthews was a wealthy land speculator and prominent poli-
       tician who fought the Indians and the British.

2708. ———. "Hemp in Colonial Virginia." AGRIC HIST, 37 (1963),
       86-93.

       Hemp manufacture was an important pre-war enterprise that
       earned one-fourth the amount of the tobacco trade.

2709. Keim, C. Ray. "Primogeniture and Entail in Colonial Virginia."
       WMQ, 25 (1968), 545-586.

       The war obliterated the last vestiges of feudal tenure
       systems; by 1785 all sons could inherit equally in intestate
       cases.

2710. Klingaman, David C. "The Development of the Coastwise Trade
       of Virginia in the Late Colonial Period." VA MHB, 77 (1969),
       26-45.

       Coastal trade boomed 1768-72 with exports of corn and
       wheat in exchange for sugar and rum.

2711. Laub, C. Herbert. "Revolutionary Virginia and the Crown
       Lands (1775-1783)." WMQ, 11 (1931), 304-314.

       The disposition of lands by bounty and by speculators
       inflated their values and quickened frontier settlement.

2712. Main, Jackson Turner. "Sections and Politics in Virginia,
       1781-1787." WMQ, 12 (1935), 96-112.

       Clues to sectionalism are the Fall Line, the James River
       area, and regions without access to navigable rivers.

2713. ———. "The Distribution of Property in Post-Revolutionary
       Virginia." MVHR, 41 (1954), 241-258.

       The large planters gradually shifted their land interests
       westward leaving behind regions of economic inequality and
       diminishing wealth.

2714. ————. "The One Hundred." WMQ, 11 (1954), 355-384.

The one hundred wealthiest Virginians held six per cent of
the land, over six per cent of the slaves, and plots
averaging 3,000 acres.

2715. Miller, Elmer J. "The Virginia Committee of Correspondence."
WMQ, 24 (1913), 1-20.

The Committee symbolized the colony's first significant
protest over imperial affairs.

2716. Morris, Robert L. "Military Contributions of Western
Virginia in the American Revolution." WEST VA HIST, 23
(1962), 86-99.

One of the largest contributors of manpower to the war,
Virginian troops fought the British and the Cherokee in
many campaigns.

2717. Reardon, John J. "'The Heart is Gnawed': Edmund Randolph
and American Independence." VA CAV, 26 (1976), 20-29.

Unlike his Loyalist father, Randolph joined the Continental
army to quell doubts about his patriotism.

2718. Rhys, Isaac. "Dramatizing the Ideology of Revolution: Popular Mobilization in Virginia, 1774 to 1776." WMQ, 33
(1976), 357-385.

The author probes the processes by which the inarticulate
masses translated their attitudes into social action and
finds the local court house was the typical ritual center.

2719. Rich, Myra L. "Speculation on the Significance of Debts:
Virginia, 1781-1789." VA MHB, 76 (1968), 301-317.

Chronic debt to Britain before the war, and the scarcity
of specie, the commitment to agrarianism, the failure to
accumulate capital, and the lack of an influential merchant
class were detrimental to Virginia's economy.

2720. Riggs, A.R. "Arthur Lee: A Radical Virginian in London,
1768-1776." VA MHB, 78 (1970), 268-280.

Lee wrote 250 articles of complaint about imperial policy,
most of which were published in English newspapers.

2721. Selby, John E. A CHRONOLOGY OF VIRGINIA AND THE WAR OF
INDEPENDENCE, 1763-1783. Charlottesville: University
Press of Virginia, 1973.

This is a summary of events in the state. It is adequate
for undergraduates.

2722. Smith, Hampden, III. "The Virginia Resolutions for Independ-
       ence." VA CAV, 25 (1976), 149-157.

       Here is a well-written sketch concerning the views of
       leading Virginian politicians in 1776.

2723. Tarter, Brent. "'An Infant Borough Entirely Supported by
       Commerce': The Great Fire of 1776 and the Rebuilding of
       Norfolk." VA CAV, 28 (1978), 52-61.

       Here is a lively description of how Tidewater Virginia
       sustained and overcame a disaster.

2724. ————. "'The Very Standard of Liberty': Lord Dunmore's
       Seizure of the Virginia Gazette." VA CAV, 25 (1975), 58-
       71.

       The consequences for the freedom of the American press
       were awesome; the incident helped to rally anti-British senti-
       ment.

2725. Tate, Thad W. "The Coming of the Revolution in Virginia:
       Britain's Challenge to Virginia's Ruling Class, 1773-1776."
       WMQ, 19 (1962), 325-343.

       Constitutional issues dominated the themes of aristocratic
       protests, not complaints about debts or imperial land poli-
       cies.

2726. Thomas, Emory M. "Edmund Randolph." VA CAV, 18 (1967), 5-
       12.

       This is an excellent sketch of one of Virginia's leading
       political thinkers.

2727. Thomson, Robert P. "The Tobacco Export of the Upper James
       Naval District, 1773-1775." WMQ, 18 (1961), 393-407.

       Virginia's politics pivoted around tobacco, the colony's
       major export.

2728. Tyler, Lyon G. "The Leadership of Virginia in the War of the
       Revolution." WMQ, 18 (1910), 145-164; 19 (1910), 10-27; 19
       (1911), 219-262.

       This is a summary about how Virginia responded to successive
       crises with Britain from 1765 to 1776.

2729. Van Schreeven, William T., Robert L. Scribner, and Brent
       Tarter. REVOLUTIONARY VIRGINIA: THE ROAD TO INDEPENDENCE.
       6 vols. Charlottesville: University Press of Virginia,
       1973-

       This superbly edited collection of documents begins in
       1763 and carries the story of successive Virginia political

conventions to May, 1776. The volumes are replete with
proceedings of conventions, minutes by Committees of Safety,
proclamations, correspondence from numerous officials, and
discussions about elections. The material is well-annotated,
the index is excellent, and the footnotes are copious. In one
volume alone there are over 370 documents from a wide variety
of sources.

2730. Ward, Harry M. and Harold E. Greer, Jr. RICHMOND DURING THE
       REVOLUTION, 1775-83. Charlottesville: University Press of
       Virginia, 1978.

       This is a fine study of the impact of the war on an impor-
       tant town which was the site of conventions, the state
       capital, a supply depot, and which was wrecked by the British.
       One of the few such works on an urban society in the south
       during the Revolution, this is a very perceptive and analyti-
       cal work.

2731. Zornow, William F. "The Tariff Policies of Virginia, 1775-
       1789." VA MHB, 62 (1954), 306-319.

       Virginia developed an equitable tariff system and cooper-
       ated with Congress.

                        11. North Carolina

2732. Adams, George R. "The Carolina Regulators: A Note on Chang-
       ing Interpretations." NC HIST REV, 49 (1972), 345-352.

       Here is an excellent review of the Regulators which
       demonstrates that they were linked to class conflict and
       had revolutionary aspirations.

2733. Alexander, C.B. "Richard Caswell: Versatile Leader of the
       Revolution." NC HIST REV, 23 (1946), 119-

       Caswell was a Delegate in the Continental Congress, a
       member of three provincial congresses, and one of the best
       governors.

2734. Butler, Lindley S. NORTH CAROLINA AND THE COMING OF THE
       REVOLUTION, 1763-66. Raleigh: North Carolina Department
       of Cultural Resources, 1976.

       This booklet is a good summary of how the province - wracked
       by civil war, sectionalism, and social conflict - moved to-
       ward independence. The bibliography is excellent.

2735. Connor, R.D.W. REVOLUTIONARY LEADERS OF NORTH CAROLINA.
       1916. Reprint. Spartanburg, South Carolina: The Reprint
       Company, 1971.

       This is an excellent source for concise sketches of numerous
       North Carolinians who were active in the independence movement.

2736. Crittenden, Charles C. "Overland Travel and Transportation
       in North Carolina, 1763-1789." NC HIST REV, 8 (1931), 239-
       252.

       The lack of roads, frequency of river barriers, and sparsely
       populated areas were factors in the local military campaigns.

2737. ———. "Ships and Shipping in North Carolina, 1783-89." NC
       HIST REV, 8 (1931), 1-13.

       Regardless of the natural obstacles, the state developed a
       shipbuilding industry which expanded after the Revolution.

2738. ———. "The Sea Coast in North Carolina History, 1763-1789."
       NC HIST REV, 7 (1930), 433-442.

       Here is a fine description of why the lack of suitable
       harbors and a treacherous coastline impeded the development of
       commerce in the state.

2739. Crowe, Jeffery J. A CHRONOLOGY OF NORTH CAROLINA DURING THE
       AMERICAN REVOLUTION, 1763-1789. Raleigh: Department of
       Cultural Resources, Division of Archives and History, 1975.

       This pamphlet is a useful compilation of political and
       military events related to the Revolution.

2740. ———, and comp. by Patricia B. Moss. A GUIDEBOOK TO REVOLU-
       TIONARY SITES IN NORTH CAROLINA. Raleigh: Division of
       Cultural Resources, Division of Archives and History, 1975.

       This is a handsome booklet that covers, county by county,
       famous homes, churches, public buildings and battle sites
       associated with the Revolution.

2741. Davis, Sallie J. "North Carolina's Part in the Rebellion."
       S ATL Q, 2 (1903), 314-324; 3 (1904), 27-38, 154-165.

       This is a useful narrative about Carolina's politics and
       military contributions to the war.

2742. Delancy, Norman C. "The Outer Banks of North Carolina During
       the Revolutionary War." NC HIST REV, 36 (1959), 1-16.

       Because of the storms off Cape Hatteras, the Royal Navy
       was unable to blockade the Carolina coast.

2743. Douglass, Elisha P. "Thomas Burke: Disillusioned Democrat."
       NC HIST REV, 26 (1949), 150-186.

       Dismayed by popular government, financially hurt by the
       state's civil war, and captured by Tories, Burke became an
       embittered man.

2744. Ekirch, A. Roger. "POOR CAROLINA:" POLITICS AND SOCIETY IN
       COLONIAL NORTH CAROLINA, 1729-1779. Chapel Hill: University
       of North Carolina Press, 1980.

       This is a masterly synthesis of recent interpretations
       of late colonial North Carolina supplemented by the author's
       vast research and thorough documentation. The demographic
       and environmental material is essential to comprehend why the
       province was so sharply divided politically, why it had such
       factional politics, and why a civil war erupted on the eve of
       the Revolution. The author's emphasis on the uniqueness of
       the impoverished province compared to its southern neighbors
       is based on a detailed scrutiny of statistical data.

2745. Frech, Laura Page. "The Wilmington Committee of Public
       Safety and the Loyalist Rising of February, 1776." NC HIST
       REV, 41 (1964), 21-33.

       The Committee was unable to prevent Loyalist Governor Josiah
       Martin from inciting the Regulators and Highlanders from a
       Tory uprising.

2746. Fries, Adelaide L. "North Carolina Certificates of the
       Revolutionary Period." NC HIST REV, 9 (1932), 225-241.

       This article examines the complexities of Carolina's finan-
       cial problems with taxes, bounties, credit, and currency
       issues to pay for troops and supplies.

2747. Ganyard, Robert L. "Radicals and Conservatives in Revolu-
       tionary North Carolina: A Point at Issue, the October
       Election, 1776." WMQ, 24 (1967), 568-587.

       The State's fifth revolutionary Congress was significant
       as a constitutional contest that ended in a moderate-conserva-
       tive electoral victory.

2748. ————. THE EMERGENCE OF NORTH CAROLINA'S REVOLUTIONARY STATE
       GOVERNMENT. Raleigh: North Carolina Department of Cultural
       Resources, Division of Archives and History, 1978.

       Ganyard wrote a useful synthesis about the end of royal
       government, the ill-fated Regulator movement, and the develop-
       ment of the network of committees, congresses, and councils
       in the patriotic cause. His comments about the state's con-
       stitution in 1776 are incisive.

2749. Henderson, Archibald. "The Origins of the Regulators in
       North Carolina." AHR, 21 (1916), 320-332.

       A petition by some back countrymen of Grenville County pro-
       vides a valuable insight into their grievances in the 1760s
       against the government.

2750. Higginbotham, R. Don. "James Iredell's Efforts to Preserve
       the First British Empire." NC HIST REV, 49 (1972), 127-145.

       Iredell's seven essays display his efforts to find a com-
       promise between the British empire and the American republic.

2751. Hildrun, Robert L. "The Salt Supply of North Carolina During
       the Revolution." NC HIST REV, 22 (1945), 393-417.

       Salt was important as gasoline to a modern army because it
       was a preservative for meat and fish; hence the state was in-
       volved in rationing, price control, and promoting salt farms.

2752. Kay, Marvin L., and Lorin Lea Cary. "Class, Mobility, and
       Conflict in North Carolina on the Eve of Revolution." See
       1913, pp. 109-157.

       Here is a fine discussion, based on quantifiable data, of
       the most bitter and prolonged attack by poor farmers upon a
       provincial elite in North America.

2753. ————. "Provincial Taxes in North Carolina During the
       Administration of Dobbs and Tryon." NC HIST REV, 42 (1965),
       440-453.

       An inequitous tax structure based on polls, liquor, imports,
       and fees led to numerous quarrels between county sheriffs and
       revenue collectors.

2754. ————. "The North Carolina Regulation: A Class Conflict."
       See 3335, pp. 74-123.

       This is a detailed explanation of why Alamance was not a
       sectional struggle but an attempt to democratize local govern-
       ment.

2755. ————. "The Payment of Provincial and Local Taxes in North
       Carolina, 1748-1771." WMQ, 26 (1969), 218-240.

       Kay explains why a shortage of currency, an unfair tax
       system, and official corruption were vital forces in arousing
       provincial discontent.

2756. Ketcham, Earle H. "The Sources of the North Carolina Con-
       stitution of 1776." NC HIST REV, 6 (1929), 215-230.

       The origins of the constitution were from the province's
       own political development, the examples of nearby states,
       and the English legal heritage.

2757. Lefler, Hugh T., and William S. Powell. COLONIAL NORTH
       CAROLINA. New York: Charles Scribner's Sons, 1973.

       This is the best synthesis of early Carolina to the eve of
       the Revolution. It is quite readable, lively in style, well-
       organized, and it has a fine bibliography.

2758. Lutz, Paul V. "A State's Concern for the Soldier's Welfare:
       How North Carolina Provided for Her Troops during the
       Revolution." NC HIST REV, 42 (1965), 315-318.

       North Carolina rewarded veterans with land grants, cash
       bounties, and attempted to compensate them for inflation.

2759. Mathews, Alice Elaine. SOCIETY IN REVOLUTIONARY NORTH
       CAROLINA. Raleigh: North Carolina Department of Cultural
       Resources, 1976.

       This is an outstanding summary about social structure, land
       tenure, slavery, class, and manners in the state.

2760. Morgan, Daniel T. "Cornelius Harnett: Revolutionary Leader
       and Delegate to the Continental Congress." NC HIST REV, 49
       (1972), 229-241.

       This article covers Harnett's anti-British activities and
       his role as a minor statesman.

2761. ————, and Schmidt, William J. "From Economic Sanctions to
       Political Separation: The North Carolina Delegates to the
       Continental Congress, 1774-1776." NC HIST REV, 52 (1975),
       215-234.

       The Delegates examined here - William Hooper, Joseph Hewes,
       Richard Caswell, John Penn - made no significant contributions
       in Congress, but they voted for independence.

2762. ————. NORTH CAROLINA IN THE CONTINENTAL CONGRESS. Winston-
       Salem: Blair, 1976.

       The authors study seventeen Delegates to show their atti-
       tudes on independence, their political service, and their
       viewpoints on North Carolina's role in the war. Only a few
       Delegates merit praise, state the authors. Most considered
       Carolina first, and they tried to prevent Massachusetts and
       Virginia from dominating Congress.

2763. Morris, Francis G., and Phyllis Mary Morris. "Economic Condi-
       tions in North Carolina About 1780." NC HIST REV, 16 (1939),
       107-133, 296-327.

       This is an excellent discussion about the distribution of
       wealth showing land and slave ownership, tax lists, and size
       of properties.

2764. North Carolina. THE COLONIAL RECORDS OF NORTH CAROLINA.
       Edited by William L. Sanders. 10 vols. Raleigh and
       Goldsboro: P.M. Hale and others, 1886-1890.

       This is a wealth of information in this excellent compilation
       of official documents about the colonial and revolutionary era.
       These volumes are an indispensable source of information for
       innumerable topics about the colony.

2765. ———. THE STATE RECORDS OF NORTH CAROLINA. Edited by
       Walter Clark. 11 vols. Winston-Salem and Goldsboro: M.I.
       and J.C. Stewart and others, 1895-1914.

       This collection is well-edited, reliable, and it contains
       a vast amount of data and clues about the state during the
       war. The index is particularly good. Many letters repro-
       duced in their entirety.

2766. Olds, Fred A. "The Celebrated Edenton, North Carolina Tea
       Party." DAR MAG, 16 (1922), 327-333.

       The refusal by ladies to drink tea was the state's first
       patriotic gesture of rebellion by women.

2767. Powell, William S. and others, comps. THE REGULATORS IN NORTH
       CAROLINA: A DOCUMENTARY HISTORY, 1759-1776. Raleigh: State
       Department of Archives and History, 1971.

       Here is a full collection of documents about the Regulators;
       much of this correspondence has not heretofore been published.
       The compilers provide ample information about this demon-
       stration of armed resistance to royal authority.

2768. Price, William S., Jr. NOT A CONQUERED PEOPLE: TWO CAROLI-
       NIANS VIEW PARLIAMENTARY TAXATION. Raleigh: Department of
       Cultural Resources, Division of Archives and History, 1975.

       Price extracts the political views of a Tory and a Whig
       from their contemporary phamphlets.

2769. Robinson, Blackwell Pierce. "Willie Jones of Halifax County."
       NC HIST REV, 18 (1941), 1-26, 133-170.

       Jones, the state's foremost radical, was an aristocrat like
       Jefferson with a deep concern for society's welfare.

2770. Salley, Alexander S. "The Mecklenberg Declaration, The Pre-
       sent Status of the Question." AHR, 13 (1907), 16-43.

       This is a sound examination of the famous convention at New
       Bern in August, 1774 in response to the Boston Port Bill.

2771. Sanders, Jennings B. "Thomas Burke in the Continental Con-
       gress." NC HIST REV, 9 (1932), 22-37.

       Burke served in Congress, fought at Brandywine, defended
       state land policies, and became Governor in 1781.

2772. Sellers, Charles C., Jr. "Making a Revolution: The North
       Carolina Whigs, 1765-1775." In Joseph C. Sitterson, ed.,
       STUDIES IN SOUTHERN HISTORY. Chapel Hill: University of
       North Carolina Press, 1957, pp. 23-46.

       Sellers provides a comprehensive coverage of politics in a
       crucial decade for the state.

2773. Spindel, Donna J. "Law and Disorder: The North Carolina
       Stamp Act Crisis." NC HIST REV, 57 (1980), 1-16.

       A precedent for future rebellious activity was established
       in 1768 when Crown officials were unable to enforce the law
       in the Wilmington area.

2774. Stumpf, Vernon O. "Josiah Martin and the Search for Success:
       The Road to North Carolina." NC HIST REV, 53 (1976), 55-
       79.

       The first royal governor of the colony became a convenient
       symbol of royal oppression for the patriots.

2775. Tilley, Nannie M. "Political Disturbances in Colonial Gran-
       ville County." NC HIST REV, 14 (1941), 339-359.

       Here is a good account of the difficulties encountered by
       justices of the peace who were hampered by the court system
       and militia mismanagement.

2776. Walterson, John S. "The Ordeal of Governor Burke." NC HIST
       REV, 48 (1971), 95-117.

       Dr. Thomas Burke served four trying years in Congress and
       ten months as governor.

2777. ————. "Thomas Burke, Paradoxical Patriot." HISTORIAN, 41
       (1979), 664-681.

       Burke's ideological transformation from a champion of the
       masses in 1776 to a distrust of popular government by 1783
       remains a puzzle.

2778. Zornow, W.F. "North Carolina Tariff Policies, 1775-1789."
       NC HIST REV, 32 (1955), 151-164.

       By 1781 the state demonstrated willingness to cooperate
       with Congress and other states on tariff and revenue schedules.

12. South Carolina

2779. Cote, Richard. SOUTH CAROLINA FAMILY AND LOCAL HISTORY. A
       BIBLIOGRAPHY. Easley, South Carolina: Southern Historical
       Press, 1981.

       Although this work is for genealogists, it has abundant
       clues about materials for historians. It lists headings of
       manuscript collectors, census schedules, local and state
       histories, indices to the state's published documents, and to
       its historical journals.

2780. Crouse, Maurice A. "A Cautious Resistance. South Carolina's
      Opposition to the Stamp Act." SC HIST MAG, 75 (1972), 59-
      71.

      Lieutenant Governor William Bull refused to appoint agents
      to distribute the stamps.

2781. ————. "Gabriel Manigault: Charleston Merchant." SC HIST
      MAG, 68 (1967), 220-231.

      Manigault was a prominent exporter and importer.

2782. ————, ed. "Papers of Gabriel Manigault, 1771-1784." SC
      HIST MAG, 64 (1963), 1-13.

      The son of a prominent Carolina politician, Manigault's
      letters and diary mention a number of contemporary provincial
      developments during the war.

2783. Dabney, William M., and Marion Dargar. WILLIAM HENRY DRAYTON
      AND THE AMERICAN REVOLUTION. Albuquerque: University of
      New Mexico Press, 1962.

      Dabney was an active Whig, commander of a frigate, Chief
      Justice of the state, and President of the Provincial Congress.
      As a Carolina Delegate to Congress, he feuded with the Lee-
      Adams Junto and with Henry Laurens. Dabney merits a better
      study than this for the authors are vague about the terms
      "conservative" or "radical," and they perceived politics as
      mired in economic conflicts.

2784. Davidson, Philip. "Southern Back Country on the Eve of the
      Revolution." See 2772, p. 1-14.

      This is a pioneering essay about sectional differences with
      the coastal area over taxes, representation, transportation,
      land claims, religious differences, and Indian problems.

2785. Ford, Paul Leicester. REPORT OF THE MANAGEMENT OF THE ES-
      TATES SEQUESTERED IN SOUTH CAROLINA, BY ORDER OF LORD
      CORNWALLIS, 1780-1782, BY JOHN CRUDEN, COMMISSIONER.
      Brooklyn, New York: History Printing Club, 1890.

      In a useful compilation of material, Ford documents how the
      property of patriot leaders in Carolina was administered by
      British officials.

2786. Fraser, Walter J., Jr. "Reflections of Democracy in South
      Carolina? The Composition of Militia Organizations and
      the Attitudes and the Relationship of the Officers and Men,
      1775-1780." SC HIST MAG, 78 (1977), 202-212.

      Poor whites in the ranks displayed intense dislike for their
      aristocratic officers, and consequently, they deserted and
      performed poorly in combat.

2787. Higgins, W. Robert. "The South Carolina Revolutionary Debt
       and Its Holders, 1776-1780." SC HIST MAG, 72 (1971), 15-
       29.

       This is a valuable summary of the state's largest creditors
       during the war; the fact that 700 citizens loaned money to the
       state indicated wide support for the cause.

2788. Kirkland, Thomas J., and Robert M. Kennedy. HISTORIC CAMDEN.
       Columbia, South Carolina: State Co., 1905, 1926.

       Chapters five through fourteen provide some colorful
       vignettes about the fighting in the back country during the
       partisan warfare with the Loyalists and British.

2789. Landrum, J.B.O. COLONIAL AND REVOLUTIONARY HISTORY OF UPPER
       SOUTH CAROLINA. 1879. Reprint. Spartanburg, South
       Carolina: Reprint Co., 1959.

       Chapters seven through eleven are uneven in scope but are
       still useful in covering events during the war.

2790. McCowen, George S. Jr. THE BRITISH OCCUPATION OF CHARLESTON,
       1780-1782. Columbia, South Carolina: University of South
       Carolina Press, 1972.

       This is a brief but perceptive treatment about how the
       British attempted to rule the port under martial law, pacify
       the interior, and how they tried to establish the framework
       for civil government in the province. The work is readable
       and scholarly.

2791. ————. "The Charles Town Board of Police, 1780-1782: A
       Study of Civil Administration Under Military Occupation."
       SC HIST ASSOC PROC, 3 (1964), 25-42.

       After the British captured Charleston in May, 1780, they
       established quasi-military rule as a temporary government
       until they evacuated the city in December, 1782.

2792. McCrady, Edward. THE HISTORY OF SOUTH CAROLINA IN THE
       REVOLUTION, 1775-1783. New York and London: Macmillan, 1901.

       This is a lengthy account of the turmoil in the province
       during the war with adequate descriptions of major battles and
       sieges. McCrady provided a commendable, but a now outdated,
       synthesis of the war in Carolina.

2793. ————. THE HISTORY OF SOUTH CAROLINA UNDER THE ROYAL GOVERN-
       MENT, 1719-1776. London and New York: Macmillan, 1899.

       Chapters twenty-seven through forty-one provide a standard
       but a still helpful account of political developments in the
       province in the late colonial era.

2794. Meroney, Geraldine M. "William Bull's First Exile From
      South Carolina, 1777-1781." SC HIST MAG, 80 (1979), 150-
      156.

      The Lieutenant Governor was expelled by the Assembly to
      England; in 1780 he returned with the British army to flee
      again in 1782.

2795. Merrens, H. Roy. "A View of Coastal South Carolina in 1778:
      The Journal of Ebenezer Hazard." SC HIST MAG, 73 (1972),
      177-183.

      Hazard wrote a lucid commentary on the social, geographic,
      and political factors of the area.

2796. Milling, Chapman J. RED CAROLINIANS. Chapel Hill: The Uni-
      versity of North Carolina Press, 1940.

      Chapter sixteen deals with the threat from the Cherokees
      on the Carolina frontier in an incisive manner.

2797. Nadelhoft, Jerome. "Ending South Carolina's War: Two 1782
      Agreements Favor the Planters." SC HIST MAG, 80 (1979),
      50-64.

      Patriot merchants and landowners attempted to apply vindic-
      tive legislation on Loyalist enemies, but the laws were soon
      repealed.

2798. ————. "The 'Havoc of War' and Its Aftermath in Revolu-
      tionary South Carolina." SOC HIST, 12 (1979), 97-121.

      The inhabitants of the backcountry, harmed by civil war and
      Indian raids, emerged from the war as an embittered group.

2799. O'Donnell, James H., ed. "A Loyalist View of the Drayton-
      Tennent-Hart Mission to the Upcountry." SC HIST MAG, 67
      (1966), 15-26.

      Thomas Brown, a prominent Tory leader, stated his hatred
      of the group sent by the Council of Safety for support in the
      interior.

2800. Ramsey, David. THE HISTORY OF THE REVOLUTION OF SOUTH-
      CAROLINA, FROM A BRITISH PROVINCE TO AN INDEPENDENT STATE.
      2 vols. Trenton, New Jersey: Issac Collins, 1785.

      The most prominent physician of Charleston and a gifted
      man of letters, Ramsay wrote in volume two of the most per-
      ceptive and comprehensive descriptions of the war. Considering
      the publication date, this is a remarkably visionary book with
      valuable insight into war-time society.

2801. Rogers George C. "Aedanus Burke, Nathanael Greene, Anthony
       Wayne and the British Merchants of Charleston." SC HIST
       MAG, 67 (1968), 75-83.

       The evidence indicates that British and Loyalist merchants
       in Charlestown successfully survived the social upheaval of
       the Revolution.

2802. Salley, A.S. DOCUMENTS RELATING TO THE HISTORY OF SOUTH
       CAROLINA DURING THE REVOLUTIONARY WAR. Columbia, South
       Carolina: South Carolina Historical Commission, 1908.

       This is a prime source of information about the war in
       Carolina. There is correspondence here on virtually every
       aspect of the war. The material is generally unavailable
       elsewhere.

2803. Tobias, Thomas J. "Charlestown in 1764." SC HIST MAG, 67
       (1976), 63-74.

       Rhode Island entrepreneur Moses Lopez wrote keen observa-
       tions about the port and its commercial activities.

2804. Walsh, Richard. CHARLESTON'S SONS OF LIBERTY: A STUDY OF THE
       ARTISANS, 1764-1789. Columbia, South Carolina: University
       of South Carolina Press, 1959.

       These artisans were prime movers in the thrust to Revolu-
       tion. This is a fine account about their work functions,
       technological changes, industrial activities, and about some
       who became businessmen. This group was more politically
       articulate by 1775.

2805. ————. "Christopher Gadsden: Radical or Conservative Revo-
       lutionary." SC HIST MAG, 63 (1962), 195-203.

       Called the "Sam Adams of the South", Gadsden was actually a
       conservative like John Jay or Alexander Hamilton.

2806. Weir, Robert M. "Rebelliousness, Personality Development and
       the American Revolution in the Southern Colonies." See
       1913, pp. 25-54.

       Weir claims that families were experiencing severe personal
       tensions between children and parents, an attitude which was
       extended against the mother country.

2807. ————. "The Harmony That We Were Famous For: An Interpreta-
       tion of Pre-Revolutionary South Carolina Politics." WMQ,
       26 (1969), 473-491.

       Carolina politics displayed a "country ideology," community
       solidarity, little factionalism, and "Negrophobia."

2808. Zornow, William F. "Tariff Policies in South Carolina, 1775–
       1789." SC HIST MAG, 56 (1955), 31–44.

       South Carolina politician regarded tariffs as essential for
       revenues and retaliation but the state was cooperating with
       Congress and other states on this matter by 1781.

13. Georgia

2809. Abbot, William W. "A Cursory View of Eighteenth Century
       Georgia." S ATL Q, 61 (1962), 339–344.

       Due to a unique pattern of colonial development, Georgia
       joined the Revolution not because of Parliamentary oppression,
       but to "the pull of American nationalism."

2810. ————. THE ROYAL GOVERNORS OF GEORGIA, 1754–1775. Chapel
       Hill: The University of South Carolina Press, 1959.

       Georgia, the youngest of the thirteen colonies, generally
       lacked economic and social conflicts. As a result of politi-
       cal immaturity, Georgia was drawn into the Revolution by out-
       side forces. This is a nicely written, well-documented ac-
       count that provides an excellent portrait of the colony on
       the eve of the Revolution.

2811. ————. "The Structure of Politics in Georgia, 1782–1789."
       WMQ, 14 (1957), 47–65.

       The House of Assembly brought order and stability out of
       confusion and prepared Georgia for statehood in the Union
       after a perilous period of invasion and partisan war.

2812. Cashin, Edward J. "The Famous Colonel Wells: Factionalism
       in Revolutionary Georgia." GA HIST Q, 58 (1974), 151–156.

       Wells was a militia officer, Indian fighter, and political
       radical whose career signalled party factions in Georgia.

2813. Chamblis, Amy. "Three Georgians Among Signers of the Declara-
       tion of Independence." GA MAG, 15 (2) (1971), 10–11.

       Here are brief sketches of George Walton, Button Gwinnett,
       and Lyman Hall.

2814. Charlton, Walter G. "Button Gwinnett." GA HIST Q, 8 (1924),
       146–158.

       This is a brief sketch of the state's most prominent poli-
       tician who was killed in a duel.

2815. Coleman, Kenneth. COLONIAL GEORGIA. A HISTORY. New York:
       Scribners, 1976.

Here is a well-organized and detailed account about the
colony's development to 1776. The emphasis, however, is
heavily political. The bibliography is helpful.

2816. ————. "Restored Colonial Georgia (1779-1782)." GA HIST Q,
40 (1956), 1-20.

All branches of the civil government were soon restored
after the British evacuation but hostility remained in the
Whig back country.

2817. ————. THE AMERICAN REVOLUTION IN GEORGIA, 1763-1789.
Athens, Georgia: University of Georgia Press, 1958.

This is the standard source for a traditional narrative that
concentrates almost entirely on political life. The book is
extremely weak on other aspects of the war, and it is very
dull to read.

2818. Crout, Robert Rhodes. "Pierre-Emmanuel de la Plaigne and
Georgia's Quest for French Aid During the War of Independence." GA HIST Q, 60 (1976),

Georgia had her own agent in Paris negotiating for weapons
and clothing from 1776 to 1780.

2819. Davis, Harold E. THE FLEDGING PROVINCE: SOCIAL AND CULTURAL
LIFE IN COLONIAL GEORGIA, 1773-1776. Chapel Hill: University of North Carolina Press, 1976.

Although there are few fresh interpretations here, this work
is a satisfactory account of class, society, slavery, and
numerous other topics. Georgia was generally similar to
other southern colonies and grew rapidly after 1750 due to free
land, productive agriculture, and the availability of slave
labor.

2820. ————. "The Scissors Thesis, or Frustrated Expectations as
a Cause of Revolution of the Revolution of Georgia." GA
HIST Q, 61 (1977), 246-257.

The colony had high expectations of self-rule in the 1760s,
but its leadership became frustrated over British imperial
legislation by 1774.

2821. Davis, Robert Scott, Jr. "Georgia History and the American
Revolution." GA SOC SCI J, 10 (1979), 12-13, 21.

Here is a thoughtful essay about methods of interpretating
the Revolution in the south.

2822. Ellefson, C. Ashley. "Loyalists and Patriots in Georgia During the American Revolution." HISTORIAN, 24 (1961-62),
347-356.

426

Here is a superficial examination of wealth as a factor in determining political attitudes toward the war.

2823. Flippen, Percy Scott. "The Royal Government in Georgia, 1752–1776." GA HIST Q, 8 (1924), 1–37, 81–120, 243–291; 9 (1925), 187–245; 10 (1926), 1–25, 251–276; 12 (1928), 326–352; 13 (1929), 128–153.

Here is a convenient summary about the colony's administration – land, taxes, slaves, courts, local governments, land surveys, and the militia system.

2824. Foster, William O. "James Jackson in the American Revolution." GA HIST Q, 21 (1947), 249–281.

Jackson led the Georgia Legion to Savannah when the British invaded in 1782.

2825. Graham, John M. "The Exclusion of the Scotch from Georgia." GA HIST Q, 17 (1933), 37–39.

In 1782 a Georgia law punished Tory Scots who constituted a large percentage of the state's population.

2826. Hardern William. "Sir James Wright: Governor or Georgia by Royal Commission, 1780–1782." GA HIST Q, 2 (1918), 22–36.

This is a fine sketch of the troubles Wright had in governing a conquered province.

2827. Hawes, Lilla Mills, ed. "Some Papers of the Governor and Council of Georgia, 1780–1781." GA HIST Q, 46 (1962), 280–296, 395–417.

This set of documents provide a glimpse of the restored royal government.

2828. Hefferman, John B. "The Influence of Naval and Maritime Developments on the History of Georgia." GA HIST Q, 39 (1955), 240–252.

The article is a brief summation of maritime events related to Georgia in the eighteenth century.

2829. Hitz, Alex M. "Georgia Land Bounty Grants." GA HIST Q, 38 (1954), 337–348.

Here is a useful commentary about the manner in which the state awarded land bounties to deserving men.

2830. Huhner, Leon. "Captain Abraham Simon of the Georgia Line in the Revolution." AMER JEW HIST SOC PUB, 33 (1954), 231–236.

An officer in the army, Simon was one of the first Jews to be elected to a state legislature in the United States.

2831. Jackson, Harvey H. "Consensus and Conflict: Factional Conflict
       in Revolutionary Georgia, 1774-1777." GA HIST Q, 59 (1975),
       388-401.

       Only in fighting the British was there consensus in Georgia
       politics as demonstrated by feuds in the House of Assembly.

2832. ————. LACKLAN MCINTOSH AND THE POLITICS OF REVOLUTIONARY
       GEORGIA. Athens, Georgia: University of Georgia Press,
       1979.

       This is a good biography about an ambitious figure who
       sought to break the traditional political power structure.
       Although the author is unconvincing in explaining the fac-
       tional strife of the Whig partisans, and his treatment of
       McIntosh's military career is too brief, this is a well-
       researched monograph.

2833. King, Spencer Bidwell, Jr. "Georgia and the Revolution: Three
       Shades of Opinion." GA REV, 23 (1969), 44-50.

       This essay would be suitable for high-school use.

2834. Lambert, Robert S. "The Confiscation of Loyalist Property
       in Georgia, 1781-1786." WMQ, 20 (1963), 80-94.

       Triumphant Whigs punished only some wealthy Tories as a
       means to finance the state government; the Loyalists lost
       relatively few estates as bounty lands on the frontier were
       available.

2835. ————. "The Repossession of Georgia, 1782-1784." SC HIST
       ASSOC PROC, 2 (1957), 14-25.

       Here is a very clear picture of the restoration of the
       colony in late 1778 by Sir James Wright.

2836. Lamplugh, George R. "Farewell to the Revolution: Georgia in
       1785." GA HIST Q, 56 (1975), 387-403.

       The politicans were intent on a quick recovery of the
       state after the war, were concerned with land policies, and
       they worried about relations with the Creeks and Cherokees.

2837. Lawrence, Alexander A. "James Jackson: Passionate Patriot."
       GA HIST Q, 34 (1950), 75-86.

       Jackson, a fine soldier, fought at Savannah against the
       British.

2838. ————, and Gordon T. Banks. "Lachlan McIntosh vs. George
       Walton." MANUSCRIPTS, 7 (1955), 224-228.

       The article covers a famous duel, a forged petition, and
       the dismissal of McIntosh from the army.

2839. Lutz, Paul V. "The Oath of Absolutism." GA HIST Q, 53
       (1969), 330-334.

       The problem of double allegiances (American or British) is
       discussed in this petition by Loyalists to General Anthony
       Wayne.

2840. Martin, Harry W. "Official Letters of Governor John Martin,
       1782-1783." GA HIST Q, 1 (1917), 281-335.

       This correspondence delineates the problems of a war-
       ravaged state.

2841. Mebane, John. "Joseph Habersham in the Revolutionary War."
       GA HIST Q, 47 (1963), 76-83.

       Habersham was a leader of the Liberty Boys in 1775, served
       on the Council of Safety, helped to capture a British supply
       ship, and arrested the royal governor.

2842. Miller, Randall M. "The Stamp Act in Colonial Georgia." GA
       HIST Q, 56 (1972), 318-331.

       Governor Sir James Wright managed to control the Assembly,
       pacify frontiersmen, and to keep the peace.

2843. Mitchell, Robert Grey, ed. "Sir James Wright Looks at the
       American Revolution." GA HIST Q, 53 (1969), 509-518.

       Wright's letter of February, 1777 offers a fine explanation
       of the turmoil in Georgia.

2844. Perkins, Eunice Ross. "The Progress of the Revolution in
       Georgia." GA HIST Q, 17 (1933), 259-275.

       This is a simplified summary of events without any analysis
       or fresh materials.

2845. Reese, Trevor R. COLONIAL GEORGIA: A STUDY IN BRITISH IM-
       PERIAL POLICY IN THE EIGHTEENTH CENTURY. Athens, Georgia:
       University of Georgia Press, 1963.

       This work is a judicious assessment of standard interpreta-
       tions. There is little novel here in fact or in analysis.
       But as a case study of how a young Crown colony was organized
       by experienced administrations, it does provide a good summary
       written in lucid prose.

2846. Roberts, William L. "The Losses of a Loyalist Merchant in
       Georgia During the Revolution." GA HIST Q, 52 (1968), 270-
       276.

       William Mass's business in Savannah was destroyed by the
       severence of trade with Britain.

2847. Robertson, Heard, ed. "Georgia's Banishment and Expulsion
       Act of September 16, 1777." GA HIST Q, 55 (1971), 274-281.

       Here is the complete text of a repressive law on Loyalists
       enacted by Georgia, the last colony to do so in the early war
       years.

2848. Robertson, William F. "Rare Button Gwinnett." GA HIST Q, 30
       (1946), 297-307.

       This is a brief sketch of a famous Delegate to Congress.

2849. Scruggs, Carroll Proctor. GEORGIA DURING THE REVOLUTION.
       Norcross, Georgia: Bay Tree Grove, 1975.

       Here is a very useful and colorful guide to Revolutionary
       war sites in Georgia.

2850. Wilkins, Barratts. "A View of Savannah on the Eve of Revolu-
       tion." GA HIST Q, 54 (1970), 577-584.

       Savannah by 1774 was a prosperous city experiencing rapid
       commercial expansion and competing with Charleston.

2851. Zornow, William Frank. "Georgia Tariff Policies, 1775 to
       1789." GA HIST Q, 38 (1954), 1-10.

       Georgia's politicians needed revenues for the state but
       they were generally cooperative in tariff legislation with
       Congress and other states.

                        C. THE LOYAL AMERICAN COLONIES

                              1. Canada

2852. Burt, Alfred L. "The Quarrel Between Germain and Carleton:
       An Invented Story." CAN HIST REV, 11 (1930), 202-220.

       Burt examines the causes of an old grudge and gives Germain
       some credit for selecting able officials for the civil ad-
       ministration.

2853. Cecil, Robert. "When Canada Did Not Choose Freedom." HIST
       TODAY, 13 (1963), 511-519.

       This is a fine summary of why Quebec and the Maritimes -
       exposed to British seapower, possessing economic advantages,
       and having fewer grievances - remained loyal to the empire.

2854. Lanctot, Gustave. CANADA AND THE AMERICAN REVOLUTION, 1774-
       1781. Translated by Margaret W. Cameron. London and
       Toronto: George G. Harrapp Co., Ltd., 1967.

       This is a fine narrative that is filled with fresh docu-
       mentary material. After a long discussion about the

ramifications of the Quebec Act, the author devotes six
chapters to the American invasion of 1775-76, its aftermath,
and the unsuccessful efforts to re-invade after 1778. The
Catholic clergy was the key in determining the degree of
French Canadian support to the American cause. The war almost made Quebec into an American state. Here is a definitive
work for specialists that contains twenty-six pages of footnotes and fifty pages of appendices.

2855.   Neatby, Hilda. "French Canadian Nationalism and the American
        Revolution." CENTENNIAL REV, 10 (1966), 505-522.

        French nationalism was unintentionally assisted by Sir Guy
        Carleton who supported the Catholic Church and the social
        distinctions; other factors were the American Revolution and
        the Loyalist influx.

2856.   ————. "The Impact of the American Revolution On Canada:
        Some Neglected Aspects." In John Browning and Robert Norton.
        1776. Toronto and Sarasota: Samuel Stevens Hakkert and
        Co., 1976, pp. 93-108.

        The Revolution and the American invasion shook Canada out
        of its provincialism.

2857.   Scott, S. Morley. "Civil and Military Authority in Canada,
        1764-1766." CAN HIST REV, 9 (1928), 117-136.

        General James Murray, heading the civil government, has
        innumerable problems with billeting troops, impressment, and
        with Generals Gage and Haldimand.

2858.   Whitbridge, Arnold. "Canada: The Struggle For the 14th State."
        HISTORY TODAY, 17 (1967), 13-21.

        Five prominent American politicians voiced their attitudes
        about acquiring Canada, as summarized in this article.

2859.   Willson, William S. "The Beginning of British Rule in
        Canada." CAN HIST REV, 6 (1925), 208-221.

        Problems with land claims, the Catholic population, and the
        uncertainty of civil laws made Quebec a discontented province
        until 1774.

2860.   Wilson, Samuel Knox. "Bishop Briand and the American Revolu-
        tion." CATH HIST REV, 19 (1948), 133-147.

        Quebec's Catholic bishop was very influential in keeping
        French Canadians neutral in the war.

2861.   Wrong, George M. CANADA AND THE AMERICAN REVOLUTION, THE
        DISRUPTION OF THE FIRST BRITISH EMPIRE. New York: Macmillan
        Co., 1935.

This is a very readable summary of the war in Canada including American plans to re-invade in 1777 and 1778. Wrong
demonstrates how the Revolution helped to found a nation
above the St. Lawrence. The volume is particularly useful
for material about the French-Candians, military operations,
and the American peace commissions. Though there is little
here for specialists, the work is a graphic and dependable
account for a general audience.

2. The Maritime Provinces

2862. Armstrong, Maurice W. "Neutrality and Religion in Revolu-
        tionary Nova Scotia." NEQ, 19 (1946), 50-62.

        The colonists were influenced by profits of imperial trade,
        the proximity of Halifax, by the Great Awakening, and by their
        general isolation.

2863. Barnes, Viola F. "Frances Legge, Governor of Loyalist Nova
        Scotia, 1773-1776." NEQ, 4 (1931), 420-447.

        An unpopular governor, Legge managed to keep the colony
        Loyalist.

2864. Blakely, Phyllis R. "An Adventure with a Privateer." NOVA
        SCOTIA HIST Q, 2 (1972), 163-171.

        The uproar over an American seizure of a Nova Scotia
        schooner was influential in the colony's Toryism.

2865. ————. "Boston King: A Negro Loyalist Who Sought Refuge in
        Nova Scotia." DALHOUSIE REV, 48 (1968-79), 347-356.

        This is a fine account of a New England black who sup-
        ported the Crown and found a haven in the Maritimes.

2866. Brebner, John B. "Nova Scotia's Remedy for the American
        Revolution." CAN HIST REV, 15 (1934), 171-181.

        On June 24, 1775 a committee of the Assembly acknowledged
        Parliamentary supremacy in return for a redress of grievances.

2867. ————. THE NEUTRAL YANKEES OF NOVA SCOTIA: A MARGINAL COLONY
        DURING THE REVOLUTIONARY WAR. New York: Columbia University
        Press, 1937.

        This is a useful work for specialists. Unfortunately, the
        work lacks a central theme although it does stress the poverty
        of the area, the lack of unity among the scattered ethnic
        groups, and the differences of the population compared to
        New England. The author demonstrates a mastery of the
        material for this local history. The wealth of often unimpor-
        tant detail, and the absence of a synthesis suggest the need
        for further research on this topic.

2868.   Kerr, Wilfred B. "Newfoundland in the Period Before the
        American Revolution." PA MHB, 65 (1941), 56-78.

        The 16,000 inhabitants were uninvolved in the disputes over
        imperial policies.

2869.   ————. "The Merchants of Nova Scotia and the American Revo-
        lution." CAN HIST REV, 13 (1932), 20-36.

        Not the merchants, but the artisans, farmers, and fisher-
        men were the key groups in maintaining loyalty to the crown.

2870.   Raddall, Thomas H. "Tarleton's Legion." NOVA SCOTIA HIST
        SOC COLL, 28 (1949), 1-50.

        Many Loyalists in the famous legion settled in Nova Scotia,
        1778-83.

2871.   Rawlyk, George A. "The American Revolution and Nova Scotia
        Reconsidered." DALHOUSIE REV, 43 (1963), 379-384.

        Even with strong cultural and economic ties to New England,
        Nova Scotia remained loyal.

2872.   Spindel, Donna J. "Anchors of Empire: Savannah, Halifax, and
        the Atlantic Frontier." AMER REV CAN STUD, 6 (1976), 88-
        103.

        This is a unique comparison of the reasons why these major
        ports took divergent political routes.

2873.   Stewart, Gordon, and George Rawlyk. A PEOPLE HIGHLY FAVORED
        OF GOD: THE NOVA SCOTIA YANKEES AND THE AMERICAN REVOLUTION.
        Hamden, Connecticut: Archon Books, 1972.

        The authors explain why a province with two-thirds of New
        England stock remained neutral. Citing the standard reasons -
        economic benefits, the naval base at Halifax, the general
        lack of complaints about civil government, the Great Awaken-
        ing - they have compiled a serviceable account of the topic
        that is useful for a general audience.

2874.   Varney, George J. "Acadia in the Revolution." MAG AMER HIST,
        8 (1882), 486-495.

        New Brunswick's role is probed here indicating some early
        sympathy for the patriots but a change after the Machias
        expedition.

2875.   Weaver, Emily P. "Nova Scotia and New England during the
        Revolution." AHR, 10 (1904), 52-71.

        This is a fine analysis of why the two areas were different
        in political viewpoints by 1775.

2876. Whiteley, William H. "Governor Hugh Palliser and the New-
       foundland Fisheries, 1764-1768." CAN HIST REV, 50 (1964),
       141-163.

       Palliser revived the fishing trade, policed the Labrador
       coast, had the area mapped, and he curtailed French fishing
       off Newfoundland.

                         3. The Floridas

2877. Abbey, Kathryn T. "Peter Chester's Defense of the Missis-
       sippi; After the Willing Raid." MVHR, 22 (1935),
       17-32.

       The inept American raid caused the British to re-organize
       West Florida in order to check American and Spanish invasions
       of the lower Mississippi area.

2878. Barrs, Barton. EAST FLORIDA IN THE AMERICAN REVOLUTION.
       Jacksonville, Florida: Guild Press, 1932.

       Now outdated, this is a readable summary about the last
       years of British rule in Florida. The coverage of military
       activities on the Florida-Georgia border needs to be revised.

2879. Boyd, Mark F., ed. "From a Remote Frontier ... " FLA HIST Q,
       19 (1941), 179-245, 402-412; 20 (1942), 382-397; 12 (1943),
       44-52, 135-140.

       These articles cover the correspondence between British
       commanders at St. Marks, St. Augustine, and Pensacola with
       General Gage in New York.

2880. Boyd, Mark F. and Jose Navarro Latorre. "Spanish Interest in
       Florida and the Progress of the American Revolution." FLA
       HIST Q, 32 (1953), 92-130.

       Because of the Creek and Seminole Indians, as well as the
       need for naval stores, the Spanish became increasingly in-
       terested in Florida.

2881. Bragg, Marion B. "British Land Grants in Warren County,
       Mississippi." J MISS HIST, 26 (1964), 229-234.

       Governor Peter Chester of West Florida issued seventeen
       land grants to retired naval officers in 1776-79 but few
       tracts were developed.

2882. Buker, George E. "Governor Tonyn." FLA HIST Q, 58 (1978),
       58-71.

       The British Governor's naval policy protected East Florida
       from attacks by Americans in Georgia.

2883. Clinton, L. Howard. "Colonial Pensacola in the British
       Period: Part III." FLA HIST Q, 19 (1941), 368-401.

       This is a good summary of the administration of Governor
       Peter Chester, 1770-1781.

2884. Conover, Bettie Jones. "British West Florida's Mississippi
       Frontier Posts, 1763-1779." ALA REV, 29 (1976), 177-207.

       For information about Britain's three main fortresses here
       and American raids in the area, this article is worth con-
       sulting.

2885. Corse, Carita Doggett. "De Braham's Report on East Florida."
       FLA HIST Q, 17 (1939), 219-226.

       This was the most detailed report on the topography of the
       area by a Surveyor-General in the Southern District.

2886. Drude, Kenneth. "Fort Baton Rouge." LA STUD, 7 (1968), 258-
       269.

       The fortress was established by the British in 1779.

2887. Griffith, Lucille. "Peter Chester and the End of the British
       Empire in West Florida." ALA REV, 30 (1977), 14-33.

       Britain's last Governor had problems with settlers, Indians,
       the Spanish, and the Americans.

2888. Howard, Clinton N. "Some Economic Aspects of British West
       Florida, 1762-1768." JSH, 6 (1940), 201-221.

       The first British colony west of the Appalachians, the area
       developed quickly.

2889. ————. "The Interval of Military Government in West Florida."
       LA HIST Q, 22 (1938), 181-553.

       As a result of the French and Indian War, the British
       established a government by late 1765 in the area.

2890. Johnson, Cecil. "Expansion in West Florida, 1770-1779."
       MVHR, 20 (1934), 481-490.

       Rapid British penetration by settlers and then Loyalist
       refugees helped develop the area.

2891. ————. "West Florida Reunited." J MISS HIST, 28 (1966),
       121-132.

       This area was important to the British and Spanish but the
       British were willing to cede it to retain Gibraltar.

2892. Kennett, Lee. "A French Report on St. Augustine in the
       1770's." FLA HIST Q, 44 (1963), 133-135.

       This concerns a secret report to Paris in 1777 about
       methods to capture the British fortress.

2893. Kleber, Louis C. "Spain and England in the Floridas." HIST
       TODAY, 19 (1969), 49-52.

       Although Spain eventually wrested Florida from Britain,
       she was unable to develop it economically and militarily to
       ward off the Americans.

2894. Manuey, Albert, and Alberta Johnson. "Castle St. Mark and
       the Patriots of the Revolution." FLA HIST Q, 21 (1942), 3-
       24.

       The fortress was the major defense of St. Augustine.

2895. Mowat, Charles Loch. "St. Augustine Under the British Flag,
       1763-1775." FLA HIST Q, 20 (1941), 131-150.

       This is a good summary about trade, artisans, and immigra-
       tion.

2896. ————. "St. Francis Barracks, St. Augustine; a Link with
       the British Regime." FLA HIST Q, 23 (1943), 266-280.

       It required considerable engineering skill to make the
       fortress defensible.

2897. ————. "The Enigma of William Drayton." FLA HIST Q, 22
       (1943), 3-33.

       The quarrelsome Chief Justice of East Florida was suspended
       from office, but he was reinstated in 1778.

2898. Pennington, Edgar L. "East Florida in the American Revolu-
       tion, 1775-1778." FLA HIST Q, 9 (1930), 24-46.

       This is an edited letter from Florida to Lord Germain about
       potential American and Spanish invasions.

2899. Pittman, Lieutenant. "Apalachee During the British Occupa-
       tion; A Description Contained In a Series of Four Reports
       by Lieut. Pittman, R.E." FLA HIST Q, 12 (1934), 114-132.

       A British engineer reported about his outpost, a hundred
       miles west of St. Augustine.

2900. Proctor, Samuel, ed. EIGHTEENTH-CENTURY FLORIDA: LIFE ON THE
       FRONTIER. Gainesville, Florida: University Press of Florida,
       1976.

In a series of essays, specialists examine West Florida
as a political entity that failed to become a cohesive colony.
Roland McConnell surveys slaves; James O'Donnell comments on
how Indian trade was dependent on the exchange of rum and deer-
skins; Bertram Korman discusses the problems of Jewish merchants and peddlers; Mary Beth Norton and Robert Calhoon com-
ment on British troops and the influx of Tories. This is a
useful and well-footnoted volume.

2901. Rea, Robert R. "A Naval Visitor in British West Florida."
      FLA HIST Q, 40 (1961), 142-153.

      The essay covers the frustrated effort to build a fort on
      the Mississippi, and to open a canal along the Iberville
      River in order to by-pass New Orleans for access to the
      Indian trade.

2902. ————. "Brigadier Frederick Haldimand - The Florida Years."
      FLA HIST Q, 54 (1976), 512-531.

      Haldimand was a capable military administrator (1767-1773),
      whose troops provided some stability to the Florida frontier.

2903. ————. "Graveyard for Britons', West Florida, 1763-1781."
      FLA HIST Q, 69 (1947), 345-364.

      Climate, disease, and lack of medical supplies decimated
      British troops at Mobile and Pensacola.

2904. ————. "The King's Agent for British West Florida." ALA
      REV, 18 (1963), 141-153.

      Rea describes the activities of John Elles who assisted
      the new colony from 1763-76 in improving its commercial ties
      with older British colonies in the Americas.

2905. Rowland, Mrs. Dunbar. "Peter Chester: Third Governor of the
      Province of British West Florida Under British Dominion,
      1776-1781." MISS HIST SOC PUB, 5 (1925), 1-183.

      This is an excellent source for Florida history; it is
      replete with documents concerning land policies, Indian prob-
      lems, and it provides a good view of the colony.

2906. Rush, N. Orwin. SPAIN'S FINAL TRIUMPH OVER GREAT BRITAIN IN
      THE GULF OF MEXICO: THE BATTLE OF PENSACOLA, MARCH 9 TO
      MAY 8, 1781. Tallahassee: Florida State University Press,
      1968.

      The cockpit of the Anglo-Spanish rivalry was the Gulf of
      Mexico where Galvez was the key figure in the conquest of
      Florida. His diary of the campaign is well reproduced here
      along with excellent maps and illustrations. But Rush did
      not critically evaluate the problems of General John Campbell
      in defending the fortress.

2907. Starr, Joseph Barton. TORIES, DONS AND REBELS. THE AMERICAN
       REVOLUTION IN BRITISH WEST FLORIDA. Gainesville, Florida:
       The University Presses of Florida, 1976.

       This is a very detailed and meticulously researched mono-
       graph which corrects assumptions made about Florida's Tories
       by specialists. The book is full of information about here-
       tofore obscure figures and relatively unknown posts from
       Florida to the upper Mississippi. Starr provides the best
       and most comprehensive treatment of the struggle in relation
       to the European war, the achievements of Bernardo de Galvez,
       Spanish aid to the patriots, Indian problems, and the influx
       of Loyalists to the area. Here is a fine synthesis about
       Florida in the Revolution.

2908. Tingley, Helen Eliose Boor. "Florida Under the British Flag,
       1763-1783." JAH, 11 (1917), 86-102.

       This is an adequate summation of British rule during the
       war.

2909. Wright, J. Leitch, Jr. FLORIDA IN THE AMERICAN REVOLUTION.
       Gainesville, Florida: The University Presses of Florida,
       1976.

       In the best book on the subject, Wright presents a concise,
       readable and copiously documented account which brings a new
       perspective to the barely charted territory. The volume is
       packed with information about English and Spanish garrisons
       and settlements, negotiations with Indians, the invasion from
       other southern colonies during the war, the flight of Loyalists
       to the area, the Spanish conquest of the area, and the re-
       lationship of the Floridas to diplomatic negotiations. Well
       organized, with excellent maps, and a thoughtful bibliographical
       essay, this account merits a wide audience.

                        4. The British West Indies

2910. Bell, Herbert C. "The West Indies Trade Before the Revolu-
       tion." AHR, 22 (1917), 272-287.

       The commerce between the Caribbean and the northern colonies
       was extensive, and the severance of trade with the British
       West Indies hurt the American economy from the Kennebec to
       Savannah.

2911. Kerr, Wilfred B. BERMUDA AND THE AMERICAN REVOLUTION: 1763-
       1783. Hamden, Connecticut: Archon Books, 1969.

       This is a thoroughly researched, well-written account of the
       imperial ties between Bermuda and the colonies to the north.
       Although economically dependent on the rebelling colonies for
       foodstuffs, Kerr notes that the small number of whites in a
       plantation economy needed Crown protection from slave revolts.

2912. Toth, Charles, ed. THE AMERICAN REVOLUTION AND THE WEST
       INDIES. New York: Kennikat Press, 1975.

       This collection of nineteen essays covers the eight major
       British Caribbean islands, commerce, Loyalists, smuggling,
       and shipbuilding. Most of the material has been printed else-
       where (some in text books), some of the articles are quite
       out-dated, and they are too diffused in content for a
       synthesis. The editor seems unfamiliar with recent inter-
       pretations of the area during the Revolution.

2913. Tucker, Terry. "Reverberations in Bermuda of the American
       Revolutionary War." CONTEMP REV, 30 (1977), 32-42.

       The profitable Bermuda trade was a source of growing ten-
       sion between Britain and the American colonies, 1773-1776.

2914. Whitson, Agnes M. "The Outlook of the Continental American
       Colonies in the British West Indies, 1760-1775." POL SCI
       Q, 45 (1930), 56-86.

       While alike in cultural backgrounds, the British settlers
       in the Caribbean and the northern colonies viewed trade
       restrictions quite differently.

2915. Wright, Esmond. "Bermuda in 1776: Loyalist or Neutral."
       HIST TODAY, 26 (1976), 118-126.

       This is a fine summary of the economic and strategic factors
       that kept Bermuda loyal to the Crown.

D. THE LOYALISTS

2916. Adair, Douglass, and John A Schutz, eds. PETER OLIVER'S
       ORIGIN AND PROGRESS OF THE AMERICAN REVOLUTION: A TORY
       VIEW. San Marino, California: Huntington Library, 1961.

       The editors have produced an excellent version of Oliver's
       famous history. Written in exile by the former Chief Justice
       of Massachusetts, the memoir concentrates on the 1760-1775 era,
       and it offers a unique insight into a Tory mentality. Oliver
       was caustic about the patriots and some fellow Loyalists. The
       work is carefully annotated, items are clearly identified, and
       the index is a model. This volume is a fine contribution to
       the field.

2917. Andreano, Ralph L. and Herbert D. Wierner. "Charleston
       Loyalists: A Statistical Note." SC HIST MAG, 60 (1959),
       164-168.

       The Loyalists here represented the professional and govern-
       ing elite.

2918. Baker, Donald S. "Charles Wesley and the American Loyalists."
       WESLEYAN HIST SOC PROC, 35 (1965), 5-9.

       Wesley was aghast at the callous treatment of Loyalist
       refugees by the British Crown.

2919. Bargar, B.D., ed. "Charles Town Loyalists in 1775; The
       Secret Reports of Alexander Innes." SC HIST MAG, 63 (1960),
       125-136.

       Here is a good summary of a Tory's correspondence with the
       Lord North Cabinet.

2920. Barnwell, Robert W. "The Migration of Loyalists from South
       Carolina." SC HIST ASSOC PROC, 3 (1937), 34-38.

       The exodus occurred mainly after the British evacuated
       Charleston in 1782, and it may have amounted to 5,000 exiles.

2921. Basil, Hamilton Vaughn. "Zadock Wright: That Devilish Tory
       of Hartland." VT HIST, 36 (1968), 186-203.

       Captured in a Loyalist regiment at Saratoga, Wright lost
       his property but became a Shaker leader at Enfield and
       Canterbury.

2922. Behrens, John F. "'A God of Order and Not of Confusion':
       The American Loyalists and Divine Providence, 1774-1783."
       HIST MAG PROT EPIS CHURCH, 47 (1978), 211-219.

       This is a fine summary about the views of Boston Tories who
       viewed the Revolution within a conceptualized religious frame-
       work and whose rhetoric about Divine Providence diverted from
       patriot views.

2923. Benton, William A. WHIG-LOYALISM: AN ASPECT OF POLITICAL
       IDEOLOGY IN THE AMERICAN REVOLUTIONARY ERA. Rutherford,
       New Jersey: Fairleigh Dickinson University Press, 1969.

       The author probes a relatively untouched area of scholar-
       ship - the response to the Revolution of many Loyalists with
       Whig principles. The summaries about William Smith, Jr., and
       Peter Van Schaack are incisive. Benton claims such Whigs were
       Loyalists because they were unwilling to resign their posi-
       tions of local leadership to lesser men.

2924. Berkin, Carol R. JONATHAN SEWELL: ODYSSEY OF AN AMERICAN
       LOYALIST. New York: Columbia University Press, 1974.

       Berkin wrote a thoughtful and carefully researched monograph
       that is quite readable. A former Attorney General in Massa-
       chusetts, Sewell spent a bitter exile in England and Canada.
       Uprooted, ignored by Cabinets, his life became somewhat
       meaningless as he meditated on the forces leading to rebel-
       lion. Written in crisp, concise sentences, this work is a

deft analysis of the motives and attitudes of a prominent
pamphleteer and defender of the Empire.

2925.   Bradley, A.G. THE UNITED EMPIRE LOYALISTS, FOUNDERS OF
        BRITISH CANADA. 1932. Reprint. New York: AMS Press, 1980.

        About one-half of this work covers the Revolution. The
        work is a good summary about the expulsion of Loyalists and
        about their settlement in Upper Canada bringing to the St.
        Lawrence area a large English contingent. It contains de-
        tails about their adaptations to living in Nova Scotia and
        New Brunswick and covers the story of this Tory migration
        through the War of 1812.

2926.   Braydon, Joseph. "Cadwallader Colder, II: An Ulster County
        Tory." NY HIST, 14 (1933), 411-421.

        The third son of New York's royal governor was a pivotal
        figure in Loyalist activities.

2927.   Brown, Alan S., ed. "James Simpson's Report on the Carolina
        Loyalists, 1779-1780." JSH, 21 (1955), 513-519.

        The former royal attorney-general of the colony provided
        Lord Germain and General Clinton with estimates of Tory
        strength as a basis for a southern campaign.

2928.   Brown, Richard D. "The Confiscation and Disposition of Loy-
        alist Estates in Suffolk County, Massachusetts." WMQ, 21
        (1964), 534-550.

        The confiscation of Tory property in a wealthy, populated
        area was slow until 1779 when legislation was enacted to
        punish political dissent and not to alter the social structure
        or to acquire assets for the state.

2929.   Brown, Wallace. "American Loyalists in Britain." HIST TODAY,
        19 (1968), 672-678.

        Here is a brief summary about the thousands of Tories who
        migrated to London where they formed immigrant communities.

2930.   ————. "Escape From the Republic: The Dispersal of American
        Loyalists." HIST TODAY, 22 (1972), 94-102.

        Here is a resume of why 100,000 Tories migrated overseas,
        and why one-fifth of the white American population in the
        thirteen colonies actively opposed the Revolution.

2931.   ————. THE GOOD AMERICANS; THE LOYALISTS IN THE AMERICAN
        REVOLUTION. New York: William Morrow, 1969.

        This is a good account of the development and motivation of
        the Loyalist bloc, their involvement in the war, how they were
        treated by the patriots and by the British, and how complex

were their difficulties. New York was the source of greatest
Loyalist strength and provided the largest number of Tory
regiments. This is a good general summary for a wide audience.

2932. ————. THE KING'S FRIENDS: THE COMPOSITION AND MOTIVES OF
THE AMERICAN LOYALIST CLAIMANTS. Providence, Rhode Island:
Brown University Press, 1965.

Brown made a systematic analysis of the diverse background
of 2,900 Loyalists who submitted claims for compensation to
the Crown. The study demonstrates that Tory strongholds were
relatively few, mainly in New York and Georgia. The author
also studies the pattern and character of Loyalism in the
other colonies. Unfortunately, this study covers a selected group who migrated overseas, and hence the samples
may not be adequate for generalizations about an area. Yet
this is a major work that merits attention.

2933. ————. "The Loyalists and the American Revolution." HIST
TODAY, 12 (1962), 147-157.

The author surveys the plight of Loyalists who sought haven
in England, Canada, and the West Indies, including some who
returned to the United States.

2934. ————. "The View at 200 Years: The Loyalists of the American
Revolution." AMER ANTIQ SOC PROC, 80 (1970), 25-47.

Brown calls for a Namier-style collective biography to
identify Loyalist motives and organizations and to determine
why many became successful after the war in the United States.

2935. ————. "Tories in the Revolution." AMER HIST ILLUS, 7 (5)
(1972), 36-43.

Here is a good popular summary of the topic which mentions
that 3,600 black Loyalists fled the country.

2936. Bryce, Peter H. "Sir John Johnson; Baronet: Superintendent-
General of Indian Affairs, 1743-1830." NY HIST ASSOC Q J,
9 (1928), 233-271.

This is a good summary of Johnson's career and the assistance
he rendered to the United Empire Loyalists.

2937. Burton, Clarence M. "Charles Wesley and the American War of
Independence." METH HIST, 5 (1965), 5-37.

A dedicated follower of George III, Wesley assumed that
peace with the United States would symbolize the end of the
British empire.

2938. ————. "John Connolly, a Tory in the Revolution." AMER
ANTIQ SOC PROC, 14 (1909), 70-105.

Connelly of Pennsylvania was a key figure in efforts to keep Indian tribes on the British side.

2939.   ———. "Patriots - And Howe!" CONTEMP REV, 230 (1977), 15-23.

Charles Wesley wrote a famous poem which ridiculed the American cause and also General William Howe's strategy.

2940.   Caley, Percy B. "The Life and Adventures of Lieutenant-Colonel John Connelly: The Story of a Tory." W PA HIST MAG, 17 (1928), 16-49, 76-111.

Connelly was Lord Dunmore's agent at Fort Pitt, was involved in intrigue with the Indians, and he was finally imprisoned by patriots.

2941.   Calhoon, Robert M. THE LOYALISTS IN REVOLUTIONARY AMERICA, 1760-1781. New York: Harcourt, Brace and Jovanovich, 1973.

This is a scholarly, insightful work. Half the book is devoted to examining the ideas of some twenty dedicated Loyalists in order to provide a synthesis of the Tory mentality; the remaining portion covers the activities of prominent Loyalists by areas. This is a readable summary but it is almost an encyclopedia of Tories. The author does not quantify his data nor does he organize it into a conceptual framework. The work is weak on the impact of the Great Awakening, on the psychological probing of the minds of Peter Oliver and Jonathan Boucher, the importance of many Tory organizations, and on the post-war impact of the Loyalists. Yet even with these flaws and omissions, the book is worthwhile.

2942.   ———. "William Smith Jr.'s Alternative to the American Revolution." WMQ, 22 (1965), 105-118.

A New York Loyalist, Smith saw flaws in imperial legislation and urged an arbitration court to settle disputes with the colonies.

2943.   Callahan, North. FLIGHT FROM THE REPUBLIC: THE TORIES OF THE AMERICAN REVOLUTION. Indianapolis: Bobbs-Merrill, 1963.

For a useful account about the exodus of Loyalists overseas, this is adequate. The sections on the Philipses, DeLanceys and other prominent Tory families are colorful.

2944.   Carr, Patrick. "Letters of Patrick Carr, Terror to British Loyalists, to Governor John Martin and Lyman Hall, 1782 and 1783." GA HIST Q, 1 (1917), 337-343.

This correspondence provides clues about Tory activities in Georgia and South Carolina during the war.

2945.   Cary, John H.   "'The Judicious are Entirely Neglected': The
        Fate of a Tory."   NE HIST GEN REG, 134 (1980), 99-114.

        Tory Jonathan Sayward of York (Maine) remained in America
        and prospered.

2946.   Chase, Virginia.   "A Loyalist of the Kennebec."   DOWN EAST,
        9 (1963), 26-28, 49, 53, 55-56.

        Reverend Jacob Bailey was a prominent Loyalist on the Maine
        frontier.

2947.   Clark, Michael D.   "Jonathan Boucher: The Mirror of Reaction."
        HUNTINGTON LIB Q, 33 (1969), 19-32.

        An Anglican clergyman of Maryland, Loyalist Boucher stressed
        a stable hierarchical structure, disdained Lockian theories of
        contractual relations in government and had pseudo-Burkian
        views about the need for a tested establishment.

2948.   Cohen, Joel A.   "Rhode Island Loyalism and the American Revo-
        lution."   RI HIST, 27 (1966), 97-112.

        This is a neat summary of the penalties, loyalty oaths, and
        property confiscations imposed on Tories.

2949.   Coleman, John M.   "Joseph Galloway and the British Occupation
        of Philadelphia."   PA HIST, 30 (1963), 272-300.

        A superintendent general under General Howe, Galloway at-
        tempted to regulate commerce and to curtail aid to the
        patriot forces.

2950.   Coles, Robert R.   "Historical Hempstead Harbor."   LONG ISLAND
        FORUM, 32 (1970), 160-164.

        The famous port became a Loyalist haven during the war.

2951.   Connolly, John.   "A Narrative of the Transactions, Imprison-
        ment, and Sufferings of John Connolly, an American Loyalist
        and Lieutenant-Colonel in His Majesty's Service."   PA MHB,
        12 (1888), 310-324, 407-437.

        Connolly wrote a fine account of his experiences during the
        war.

2952.   Coughlin, Robert C.   "Jonathan Ashley: Tory Minister."   WEST
        MASS HIST J, 7 (1979), 35-40.

        Because of Ashley's Toryism, his Deerfield, Massachusetts,
        parishioners cut off his supply of firewood.

2953.   Crary, Catherine S.   "Cadwallader Colden II: True Lover of
        His Country or Enemy of the State."   J LONG ISLAND HIST, 10
        (1973), 7-13.

444   THE IMPACT OF WAR ON SOCIETY

Here is a sympathetic portrayal of a Tory Governor of New
York who had to choose sides by the impact of circumstances.

2954.   ————. "Forfeited Lands in the Western District of New York-
Albany and Tryon Counties." NY HIST, 35 (1954), 239-258.

In a solid statistical study of forfeited sales, the author
contends that while speculators benefitted, the long-range
effect was to democratize land holding.

2955.   ————. THE PRICE OF LOYALTY: TORY WRITINGS FROM THE REVOLU-
TIONARY ERA. New York: McGraw-Hill, 1973.

De-emphasizing the more prominent Loyalists in order to
concentrate on relatively minor figures, Crary presents a
nicely balanced anthology of the Tory mind and the Loyalist
degree of unity on certain issues to demonstrate that they
were a heterogeneous group with firm convictions. This is a
well-edited work with a valuable bibliography of current
scholarship on the tragic treatment of the Tories.

2956.   Crowe, Jeffrey J. "Tory Plots and Anglican Loyalty: The
Llewelyan Conspiracy of 1777." NC HIST REV, 55 (1978), 1-
17.

Offended by punitive measures in North Carolina and by the
disestablishment of Anglicanism, the Loyalists of the eastern
area rebelled, were defeated, were convicted, but they were
released.

2957.   Curry, Richard O. "Loyalism in Western Virginia During the
American Revolution." WEST VA HIST MAG, 14 (1953), 269-
274.

Loyalism here was related to Governor Dunmore, John Connolly,
land quarrels, and Indian affairs.

2958.   Curwen, Samuel. JOURNAL OF SAMUEL CURWEN, LOYALIST. 2 vols.
Edited by Andrew Oliver. Cambridge, Massachusetts: Harvard
University Press, 1972.

This is a meticulously edited, handsomely reproduced account
of a Tory's flight from Boston to Philadelphia, then to
England, and his return to the United States in 1784. Curwen
wrote a fine commentary about social life in New England and
his travels in southern England in which he indicated his
dislike of armed rebellion.

2959.   Daniel, Majorie. "John Joachin Zubly - Georgia Phamphleteer
of the Revolution." GA HIST Q, 19 (1935), 1-10.

Zubly, a prominent clergyman, was not an original political
thinker but his writings represented the typical Tory mind in
Georgia.

2960. Davis, Andrew M. "The Confiscation Laws of Massachusetts."
       COL SOC MASS PUB, 8 (1906), 50-72.

       This narrative concisely summarizes the issue.

2961. Dean, David M., ed. "The End of a Siege. A Silent Loyalist
       Becomes a Reluctant Patriot: A Letter from John Andrews to
       William White, December 14, 1779." PA HIST, 37 (1970),
       381-386.

       Andrews, an Anglican minister from Maryland, was evicted
       to York, Pennsylvania, penalized under the state's Test Act,
       but he eventually supported Congress.

2962. De Mond, Robert O. THE LOYALISTS IN NORTH CAROLINA DURING
       THE REVOLUTION. Durham, North Carolina: Duke University
       Press, 1940.

       Although this work suggests why tax, land, and religious
       issues as well as the aftermath of the Regulators were
       influential in molding a Tory mind, it needs to be revised
       in the light of current research. The lists of hundreds of
       Loyalists are useful.

2963. Eddis, William. LETTERS FROM AMERICA. Edited by Aubrey C.
       Land. Cambridge, Massachusetts: The Belknap Press, 1969.

       This is a handsome, well-edited volume with ample footnotes
       about the career of a British official in Annapolis who re-
       mained a Loyalist. His descriptions of events that he wit-
       nessed provide one of the best eye-witness accounts of cer-
       tain incidents.

2964. Egerton, Hugh Edward, ed. THE ROYAL COMMISSION ON THE LOSSES
       AND SERVICE OF AMERICAN LOYALISTS, 1783-1785. 1815. Re-
       print. New York: Arno Press, 1965.

       This is an excellent contemporary summary of how the British
       government handled the claims for compensation by exiled
       Loyalists. There is worthwhile statistical data here which
       helps to provide an understanding of the administrative
       machinery involved in processing appeals.

2965. Einstein, Lewis D. DIVIDED LOYALTIES: AMERICANS IN ENGLAND
       DURING THE WAR OF INDEPENDENCE. London: Cobden-Sanderson,
       1933.

       This is a pioneering work which described the problems of
       Tory exciles in London, the general insensitivity by official-
       dom to their plight, and their difficulties in acquiring com-
       pensation from the Crown for their sufferings and property
       losses. It is an interesting book and suitable for a general
       audience.

2966. Ellefson, C. Ashley. "James Habersham and Georgia Loyalism,
       1764-1775." GA HIST Q, 44 (1980), 395-380.

       Acting Governor in 1771, Tory Habersham questioned Parlia-
       ment's right to tax the colonies, but he had difficulties
       with Whig opponents over veto powers and the choice of a
       Speaker of the Assembly.

2967. Ernst, Robert. "Andrew Elliot, Forgotten Loyalist of Oc-
       cupied New York." NY HIST, 57 (1976), 285-320.

       The most important Loyalist in the colony, Elliot was a
       customs collector, Lieutenant Governor, and Governor and held
       power during the eight-year British occupation of the city.

2968. Evanson, Philip. "Jonathan Boucher: The Mind of an American
       Loyalist." MD HIST MAG, 58 (1953), 123-136.

       This outspoken Anglican clergyman of Virginia and Maryland
       rejected the social contract theory and returned to England
       in late 1775.

2969. Everest, Allan Seymour. MOSES HAZEN AND THE CANADIAN REFUGEES
       IN THE AMERICAN REVOLUTION. Syracuse, New York: Syracuse
       University Press, 1976.

       Here is a fine scholarly work, compiled from a mass of docu-
       ments, that explains the role of Hazen in recruiting Loyalist
       refugees in Quebec and Nova Scotia. The author's sketches of
       the Tory sufferings and the mismanagement of their efforts
       by British officials is illuminating. The work fills in a
       gap in understanding the complexity of the Loyalist exodus.

2970. Fall, Ralph Emmett. "The Rev. Jonathan Boucher, Turbulent
       Tory (1738-1804)." HIST MAG PROT EPIS CHURCH, 36 (1967),
       323-356.

       Boucher opposed resistance to the Crown, and he was com-
       pelled to preach with loaded pistols in his pulpit.

2971. Ferling, John E. "Joseph Galloway's Military Advice: A
       Loyalist's View of the Revolution." PA MHB, 98 (1974),
       171-188.

       He provided intelligence reports and recommendations to
       London which were usually ignored in strategic planning.

2972. Fingerhurst, Eugene R. "Use and Abuses of the American
       Loyalist's Claims: A Critique of Quantitative Analyses."
       WMQ, 24 (1968), 245-258.

       The author emphasizes that the documents traditionally used
       by historians to study Loyalist petitions for compensation are
       too limited for an actual profile of the Tories for many types
       of property and numerous petitions were excluded for consider-
       ation by the Crown.

2973. Flanagan, Vincent. "Stephen Kemble: New Jersey Loyalist."
       NJ HIST, 90 (1972).

       Kemble fought the rebels and quarreled with General Clinton.

2974. Flick, Alexander C. LOYALISM IN NEW YORK DURING THE AMERICAN
       REVOLUTION. London and New York, 1901. Reprint: Arno
       Press, 1969.

       This was a major attempt to view the attitudes of the
       Loyalists. Flick demonstrated that Toryism was not entirely
       related to wealthy landowners, prominent merchants, or Crown
       officials, but that the political attitudes representative
       of Loyalism reflected views from a wide spectrum of society.
       He showed their property losses, and the wretched treatment
       Tories received from the British. The confiscation and re-
       distribution of Loyalist lands had a beneficial effect in
       democratizing the landholding system in New York.

2975. ————. "The United Empire Loyalists." NY STATE HIST ASSOC
       Q J, 6 (1925), 197-222.

       This Tory group was mistreated by the British and its con-
       tributions to the British empire have been overlooked by
       historians.

2976. Gandy, William E. "The Colonists Who Wouldn't Rebel." SOC
       EDUC, 27 (1963), 385-389.

       This essay about Loyalists is suitable for high-schoolers.

2977. Gilbert, G.A. "The Connecticut Loyalist." AHR, 4 (1899),
       273-291.

       Connecticut was not vindicative to its Tories, no civil war
       erupted here, and terms of pardon and repentence were lenient.

2978. Hammond, Otis G., ed. TORIES OF NEW HAMPSHIRE IN THE WAR OF
       INDEPENDENCE. 1917. Reprint. New York: Gregg Press, 1972.

       Though statistically unreliable due to recent studies, this
       account is useful for an examination about the prevalence of
       Loyalism in a state. The author identified Tories by resi-
       dence, occupation, religion, and political ties.

2979. Hancock, Harold B. "A Loyalist in Sussex County: The Ad-
       ventures of J.F.D. Smyth in 1777." DEL HIST, 16 (1975),
       325-336.

       Smyth performed minor service for the British cause and
       pursued his claims for rewards for twenty-five years.

2980. ————. THE LOYALISTS OF REVOLUTIONARY DELAWARE. Newark,
       Delaware: The University of Delaware Press, 1977.

Here is a solid and thoughtful monograph based on the
author's numerous articles on the subject. Hancock presents
fine descriptions about Loyalism in Kent and New Castle
Counties. He also describes the contributions made to the
Tory cause by numerous Delawareans such as Thomas Robinson
and John F.D. Smyth.

2981. ———, ed. "The Revolutionary War Diary of William Adair."
        DEL HIST, 13 (1968), 154-168.

The diary provides interesting data about sighting British
vessels on the Delaware coast, and it provides a good view
of Sussex County in the war.

2982. Harrell, Issac S. "North Carolina Loyalists." NC HIST REV,
        3 (1926), 575-590.

Small in number, these Loyalists provided little aid to the
British after 1776; data on their confiscated estates is
edited here.

2983. Hast, Adele. "Loyalism in Virginia During the American Revo-
        lution." Ph.D. dissertation, University of Iowa, 1979.

Hast concentrates on the thought and activities of 550
Tories in two areas bordering Chesapeake Bay to demonstrate
that Loyalism here was based on local issues and not on broad
ideological ones. The state punished relatively few Loyalists
who readily accommodated themselves into post-war society.

2984. Hoberg, Walter. "A Tory in the Northwest." PA MHB, 59 (1935),
        32-41.

Alexander Mckee was a Loyalist Colonel active in partisan
warfare on the northern frontier.

2985. Hogan, Neil. "A Loyalist Execution." NE GALAXY, 20 (1948),
        52-60.

Moses Dunbar of Waterbury, Connecticut, was executed for
enlisting in the British army.

2986. Honeyman, A. Van Doren. "Concerning the New Jersey Loyalists
        in the Revolution." NJ HIST SOC PROC, 51 (1933), 117-133.

This is a good summary about the exodus of Loyalists from
such areas as Bergen County.

2987. Humphreys, R.A. "Richard Oswald: Plan for a English and
        Russian Attack on Spanish America, 1781-1782." HISP AMER
        HIST REV, 18 (1935), 95-101.

Oswald, a peace commissioner from England had an imaginative plan to invade the Spanish borderlands with 6,000
Russian troops.

2988.   Johnson, William T. "Alan Camerson, a Scotch Loyalist in
        the American Revolution." PA HIST, 8 (1941), 29-46.

        Camerson was a Scot immigrant who campaigned in Maryland,
        Virginia, and South Carolina before he was captured in 1778.

2989.   Jones, Alfred E. "The Loyalists of New Jersey in the Revolu-
        tion." NJ HIST SOC PROC, 11 (1926), 77-87, 213-282, 289-
        353, 433-475; 12 (1927), 1-55, 144-213.

        Here are detailed statistics, by area and occupation about
        the centers of Loyalism in the state.

2990.   Kenny, Alice P. "Loyalism in Bergen County, New Jersey."
        WMQ, 18 (1961), 558-576.

        Traditionally inclined toward conservatism, Tories here
        were rarely officials or landlords and their nearness to
        profitable British markets in New York City colored their
        viewpoints.

2991.   ————. "The Albany Dutch: Loyalists and Patriots." NY HIST,
        42 (1961), 331-350.

        This is a fine statistical analysis of twenty Dutch Re-
        formed congregations in Albany County and the leading patroons
        of the area showing that this ethnic group was neither
        solidly Tory or Whig, but that the war shattered their unity.

2992.   Kornhizer, Robert. "Tory and Patriot: Love in the Revolution."
        L I HIST J, 12 (1976), 36-45.

        This essay concerns the love affair of an imprisoned Yankee
        officer and a Loyalist woman in New York City.

2993.   Kurland, Gerald, and Flanagan Vincent. "Stephen Kemble: New
        Jersey Loyalist." NJ HIST, 90 (1972), 6-26.

        Kemble, an officer in the New Jersey Volunteers, fought the
        rebels in several campaigns, quarreled with General Clinton,
        and he sailed on a British expedition to Nicaragua.

2994.   Kyte, George W. "Some Plans for Loyalist Strongholds in the
        Middle Colonies." PA HIST, 16 (1949), 177-190.

        Lord Germain pondered the possibility of conquering and
        holding the Delaware River area as a Tory base of operation.

2995.   Labaree, Leonard W. "The Nature of American Loyalism." AMER
        ANTIQ SOC PROC, 54 (1945), 15-58.

        The Tories were dubious about the future of mankind and
        feared that violence and disorder would errupt if a new
        political state were created.

2996. Lambert, Robert S. "The Confiscation of Property in Georgia,
       1782-1786." WMQ, 20 (1963), 80-94.

       Georgia's punitive laws of 1778 were inoperative until
       1782 when neither the state nor landless Whigs benefitted
       from the disposal of sequestered estates; land grants on
       the frontier to veterans were more important in creating
       more property owners.

2997. ————. "The Flight of Georgia Loyalists." GA REV, 17 (1963),
       435-448.

       This is a good account of the retaliatory measures that the
       state imposed on the Tories.

2998. Lamplugh, George R. "'To Check and Discourage the Wicked and
       Designing': John Wereat and the Revolution in Georgia."
       GA HIST Q, 61 (1967), 295-307.

       A conservative Whig, Wereat fluctuated between radicalism
       and conservatism depending on the nearness of the British
       army.

2999. Launitz-Schurer, Leopold S., Jr. "A Loyalist Clergyman's
       Response to the Imperial Crisis in the American Colonies:
       A Note on Samuel Seabury's Letters of a Westchester Farmer."
       HIST MAG PROT EPIS CHURCH, 44 (1975), 107-119.

       A good clue to the ideology of Toryism can be found in four
       pamphlets printed in 1774-75 by Seabury who later became the
       first Episcopal bishop in the United States.

3000. ————. "Whig-Loyalists: The DeLanceys of New York." NY HIST
       Q, 56 (1972), 178-198.

       The prominent DeLancey family lost its political influence
       in the early war years because of its pronounced Loyalism.

3001. Levett, Ella P. "Loyalism in Charleston, 1761-1784." SC HIST
       ASSOC PROC, 6 (1935), 3-17.

       There are hundreds of Tory names edited in this useful
       article.

3002. Lockwood, Allison. "The Times of Samuel Curwen." AMER HIST
       ILLUS, 12 (1) (1978), 22-32.

       Judge Curwen of Salem, Massachusetts, was tarred and
       feathered for his Tory views.

3003. Lorenz, Alfred L. HUGH GAINE: A COLONIAL PRINTER-EDITOR'S
       ODYSSEY TO LOYALISM. Carbondale, Illinois: Southern
       Illinois University Press, 1972.

       Gaine was the publisher of the NEW YORK MERCURY (1752-83).

With subsidies, he molded his newspaper into a Tory tract
during the British occupation of New York City. Well researched
and written with verve, this work provides a valuable insight
into the Tory mentality and into the journalistic world.

3004. Lutz, Paul V. "The Damnation of the Disaffected." MANUSCRIPTS,
      31 (1979), 25-45, 108-126.

      The Albany Committee of Safety in 1776 convicted seven Tories
      such as Henry Cuyler, Cornelius Glen, and Stephen DeLancey.

3005. McKeel, Arthur J. "The Quaker-Loyalist Migration to New
      Brunswick and Nova Scotia in 1783." FRIENDS' HIST ASSOC
      BULL, 32 (1943), 63-75.

      The lure of land, and the persecution at home were the
      motives for 200 New Yorkers to migrate northward.

3006. Maguire, James H. "Elisium and the Wilds: A Loyalist's
      Account of Experiences in America at the Beginning of the
      American Revolution." HIST NH, 26 (1971), 31-44.

      Tory Edward Parry, a mast agent in Portsmouth, New Hamp-
      shire, was arrested in 1775, paroled, shipped to Halifax in
      1777 in an exchange; he finally reached England.

3007. Merritt, Bruce G. "Loyalism and Social Conflict in Revolu-
      tionary Deerfield, Massachusetts." JAH, 57 (1970), 277-289.

      Class differences here were not based on rich versus poor,
      but were caused by Whig farmers versus Tory artisans, mer-
      chants and professionals; the war hurt both former Whig and
      Tory leaders and a new breed of citizens assumed leadership.

3008. Moody, Robert Earle, and Charles Christopher Crittenden. "The
      Letterbook of Mills and Hicks...." NC HIST REV, 14 (1937),
      39-83.

      Nathaniel Mills and John Hicks, Loyalist printers and mer-
      chants, went from Charleston to exile in Florida, New York,
      Nova Scotia, and England.

3009. Morgan, Daniel T. "'The Dupes of Designing Men': John Wesley
      and the American Revolution." HIST MAG PROT EPIS CHURCH,
      44 (1975), 121-131.

      Wesley considered the rebels as pawns of British radical
      Whigs and as "evil men" in a society that should have been
      loyal to the Crown.

3010. Morrison, Samuel E. "The Property of Harrison Gray, Loyalist."
      COL SOC MASS PUB, 14 (1913), 320-350.

      Gray, one of twenty-nine "Notorious Conspirators" proscribed
      under Massachusetts' Banishment Act of 1778, had his valuable
      tract sold by the state as a punitive measure.

452   THE IMPACT OF WAR ON SOCIETY

3011. Morse, Jarvis M. "The Wanton Family and Rhode Island
       Loyalism." RI HIST SOC COLL, 31 (1938), 33-44.

       This article describes the confiscation of a former royal
       governor's property in a state where such seizures were re-
       latively few.

3012. Mullett, Charles F. "Tory Imperialism on the Eve of the
       Declaration of Independence." CAN HIST REV, 12 (1931),
       262-282.

       This is a fine summary of Tory legal and constitutional
       theories which centered on the experiences of Parliament
       versus the Whig view of supremacy of the law.

3013. Nelson, William H. THE AMERICAN TORY. London: Oxford Uni-
       versity Press, 1980.

       Though Nelson claims to fuse the viewpoints of Loyalists
       from all thirteen colonies in this synthesis, he relies al-
       most entirely on New York, only touches the Middle States,
       and virtually ignores the south, especially Georgia. New
       York was the most conservative of the provinces, and its Tory
       strength was derived from many groups, classes, religion,
       and regions. This is well-written, stimulating but not a
       definitive work.

3014. ————. "The Last Hopes of the American Loyalists." CAN HIST
       REV, 32 (1951), 22-42.

       Tory hopes dissolved during the war as a plan for a colonial
       federation was considered unworkable.

3015. Norton, Mary Beth. "Eighteenth Century American Women in
       Peace and War: The Case of the Loyalists." WMQ, 33 (1976),
       386-409.

       A study of the petitions to the Crown of some 460 American
       refugee females shows them not completely passive but still
       viewing themselves in traditional domestic roles.

3016. ————, ed. "John Randolph's Plan of Accommodations." WMQ,
       28 (1971), 103-120.

       Randolph, Virginia's most important Loyalist, indicated in
       his letter to Lord Germain, that the colonies were in discord
       and could be easily conquered.

3017. ————. THE BRITISH AMERICANS: THE LOYALISTS EXILES IN
       ENGLAND, 1774-1789. Boston: Little, Brown, and Co., 1972.

       This is a definitive account about Tory refugees in London,
       many of them from New York. These exiles yearned for a
       Utopian British Empire and were never at home in the nation
       for which they sacrificed. Norton is especially capable in

examining the Loyalists' communities, their plight in a new
land, and their frustrations over petitions to the Crown for
relief. Gracefully written and thoroughly documented, this
is the best volume on this subject.

3018. ————. "The Fate of Some Black Loyalists of the American
        Revolution." J NEGRO HIST, 58 (1973), 402-426.

        This is a grim tale of the British government's attempt to
        resettle some 700 American blacks living in London in Sierra
        Leone after the war.

3019. Nye, May G. "Loyalists and Their Property." VT HIST SOC, 10
        (1942), 36-44.

        This is a summary of Vermont's law regarding the con-
        fiscation of Tory holdings.

3020. Nye, Wilbur S. "Aftermath of Moore's Creek: Plight of the
        Tories." AMER HIST ILLUS, 4 (2) (1970), 15-17.

        Centering around the claims of Alexander Morrison in 1783
        for the loss of his plantation, this article stresses the
        harsh treatment of Loyalists in the Carolinas.

3021. Oaks, Robert F. "Philadelphians in Exile: The Problem of
        Loyalty During the American Revolution." PA MHB, 96 (1973),
        298-325.

        Here is a well-documented essay concerning the persecution
        of Philadelphia Quakers and their confinement in Virginia for
        espousing non-resistance.

3022. Overfield, Richard A. "A Patriot Dilemma: The Treatment of
        Passive Loyalists and Neutralists in Revolutionary Maryland."
        MD HIST MAG, 68 (1973), 140-159.

        Only lightly penalized until 1777, Maryland's Tories and
        neutrals - such as Quakers and Methodists - were subject to
        increasingly harsh legislation under the Security Act.

3023. Pauley, William E., Jr. "Tragic Hero: Loyalist John J. Zubly."
        J PRESBY HIST, 54 (1970), 61-81.

        An original thinker on several subjects, this Savannah pastor
        was a Delegate to Congress in 1775, but he refused to champion
        independence and died a broken man.

3024. Perkins, Eunice Ross. "John Joachim Zubly, Georgia's Con-
        scientious Objector." GA HIST Q, 15 (1931), 313-323.

        Zubly, pastor of the largest Presbyterian church in Georgia,
        was a Tory who was arrested, persecuted and barred from poli-
        tics.

3025.   Perry, William Stevens. "The Alleged 'Toryism' of the Clergy
        of the United States at the Breaking Out of the War of the
        Revolution: An Historical Examination." HIST MAG PROT
        EPIS CHURCH, 45 (1976), 133-144.

        Perry maintains that most of the Protestant clergy were
        supporters of the Revolution.

3026.   Peters, Thelma. "The American Loyalists in the Bahama Is-
        lands: Who They Were." FLA HIST Q, 40 (1962), 226-240.

        This study concentrates on eighty Loyalist families, former
        British soldiers, and freedmen who, in general, failed to
        establish themselves in exile.

3027.   ————. "The Loyalist Migration from East Florida to the
        Bahama Islands." FLA HIST Q, 40 (1961), 123-141.

        About 12,000 Loyalists entered East Florida during the
        war; after Spain received the Floridas in 1783, some 4,000
        to 7,000 of them migrated to the Bahamas.

3028.   Preston, Howard. "Rhode Island and the Loyalists." RI HIST
        SOC COLL, 21 (1928), 109-114; 22 (1929), 5-10.

        Preston summarizes the mob violence directed at Tories and
        the confiscation of the Wanton estates.

3029.   Raymond, Allen. "'I Fear God and Honour the King': John
        Wesley and the American Revolution." CHURCH HIST, 45
        (1976), 316-326.

        Opposing revolution and believing that the Ministry had
        bungled negotiations with the colonies, the Methodist leader
        claims there were links between English and American radicals
        and when France entered the war, he pursued an anti-Catholic
        tone.

3030.   Raymond, William O. "Loyalism in Arms." NEW BRUNS HIST SOC
        COLL, 5 (1904), 189-223.

        This article lists the officers, regiments, and corps re-
        cruited in the Maritimes.

3031.   Reubens, Beatrice G. "Pre-Emptive Rights in the Disposition
        of a Confiscated Estate: Philipsburgh Manor, New York."
        WMQ, 22 (1965), 435-456.

        Patriot tenants of confiscated estates had the final claims
        to purchase land by law; eighty per cent of the new owners
        were small farmers, many of who were former tenants.

3032.   Robbins, Peggy. "Benjamin Franklin and His Son, A Tory."
        AMER HIST ILLUS, 15 (5) (1980), 38-46.

Franklin bemoaned the fact that son William Franklin,
Governor of New Jersey, remained a Loyalist and broke with
him.

3033.   Roberts, William L., III. "The Losses of a Loyalist Merchant
        in Georgia During the Revolution." GA HIST Q, 52 (1968),
        270-276.

        William Moss's thriving business in Savannah with Liverpool
        was destroyed by his inability to collect debts and the
        severance of trade with Britain.

3034.   Robertson, Heard. "A Revised or Loyalist Perspective of
        Augusta During the American Revolution." RICHMOND CTY
        HIST, 1 (1969), 5-24.

        Here is a well-balanced view of the myths and folk-lore,
        particularly those surrounding Elijah Clark of the Georgia
        back country during the era of partisan warfare.

3035.   ————. "Georgia's Banishment and Expulsion Act, September
        16, 1777." GA HIST Q, 55 (1971), 274-282.

        Not until late 1777 did the state enact repressive anti-
        Tory legislation - expulsion, banishment, and confiscation
        of one-half of their property.

3036.   Ryan, Dennis P. NEW JERSEY'S LOYALISTS. Trenton, New Jersey:
        New Jersey Historical Commission, 1975.

        This is a convenient booklet with a neat summary of the
        topic. The material about Stephen Skinner, Cortlandt Skinner,
        William Franklin, and the hounding of other prominent Tories
        is useful.

3037.   Sabine, Lorenzo. BIOGRAPHICAL SKETCHES OF LOYALISTS OF THE
        AMERICAN REVOLUTION WITH AN HISTORICAL ESSAY. 2 vols. 1864.
        Reprint. Port Washington, New York: Kennikat Press, 1966.

        This is a classic work. It provides detailed information
        on Loyalists, particularly those from New York and New England.
        For the South, it is not too reliable. However, it is a
        standard reference, and it represents one of the first Ameri-
        can literary efforts to rehabilitate the Loyalists.

3038.   Sabine, William H.W., ed. HISTORICAL MEMOIRS FROM 16 MARCH
        1763 TO 12 NOVEMBER 1783. 3 vols. 1956-1958. Reprint.
        New York: Arno Press, 1969-71.

        This work is the edited version of the diary of William
        Smith, Jr. It is essential to appreciate the course of the
        Revolution in New York because Smith was prominent in politics
        for twenty-five years. He knew many patriots and British
        officers; and he ranked high in Tory circles. His observa-
        tions about life in New York during the war are penetrating.

3039. Schutz, John A. "Those Who Became Tories: Town Loyalty and
       Revolution in New England." NE HIST GEN REG, 129
       (1975), 94-105.

       In rural New England, Tories were treated as a local pro-
       blem by individual villages and were watched; but they were
       not unduly terrorized.

3040. Scott, Kenneth. "Colonel Stephen Holland of Londonderry."
       HIST NH, 3 (1947), 15-27.

       The most important Loyalist in New Hampshire, Holland was
       wounded in 1778 and fled to join the British.

3041. ———. "New Hampshire Tory Counterfeiters: Operating from
       New York City." NY HIST SOC Q, 34 (1950), 31-57.

       The printing and distribution of spurious Continental cur-
       rency was intended to inflict economic damage to the American
       cause.

3042. ———. "Tory Associators of Portsmouth (N.H)." WMQ, 17
       (1960), 509-512.

       Here is a list of names of the fifty-nine Loyalists who
       formed a bodyguard for Governor John Wentworth in 1775.

3043. Shelton, W.G. "The United Empire Loyalists: A Reconsidera-
       tion." DALHOUSIE REV, 45 (1965), 5-16.

       The writer calls attention to this Tory group, a large
       portion of which fought with the British army.

3044. Siebert, Wilbur H. "East Florida As A Refuge of Southern
       Loyalists." AMER ANTIQ SOC PROC, 37 (1927), 226-246.

       Here is a good analysis of why the area remained Tory and
       how it was a base for raids into Georgia and the Carolinas.

3045. ———. "General Washington and the Loyalists." AMER ANTIQ
       SOC PROC, 43 (1933), 34-48.

       Washington watched the Tories, suppressed them, and warded
       off plots on his life; yet he treated the Tories decently and
       forgave them.

3046. ———. "The Dispersion of the American Tories." MVHR, 1
       (1913), 185-197.

       This is a good review of the distress of the Loyalists and
       why they migrated to ten major centers.

3047. ———. "The Loyalists in West Florida and the Natchez Dis-
       trict." MVHR, 2 (1916), 465-483.

Florida became a haven for Tories fleeing Georgia and the
Carolinas; but the colony was poorly garrisoned and subject
to raids by Indians, Americans, and, eventually, it was conquered by the Spanish.

3048.   Slaski, Eugene R. "Thomas Willing: A Study in Moderation,
        1774-1778." PA MHB, 100 (1976), 491-506.

A delegate to Congress who voted against independence,
Willing was an intermediary between Congress and General
William Howe; he later converted to the patriotic cause.

3049.   Smith, Jonathan. "Toryism in Worcester County During the War
        for Independence." MASS HIST SOC PROC, 48 (1915), 15-25.

This is a general view of Whig and Tory differences which
overlooks shades of opinion; however it cites numerous court
cases against the Loyalists and the state's legislation on
the matter.

3050.   Smith, Paul H. "The American Loyalists: Notes on Their
        Organization and Numerical Strength." WMQ, 25 (1968), 259-
        277.

Smith provides an excellent analysis of Loyalist strength
in regions by determining the numbers of volunteers for
provincial military units, concluding that 19,000 out of
21,000 troops in provincial corps were Tories.

3051.   Spiro, Robert H., Jr. "John L. McAdam in Revolutionary New
        York." NY HIST SOC Q, 40 (1956), 28-54.

McAdam was the famous turnpike engineer who prospered in
New York as a Loyalist merchant during the British occupation.

3052.   Starr, J. Barton. "The Case and Petition of His Majesty's
        Loyal Subjects, Late of West Florida." FLA HIST Q, 59
        (1980), 199-212.

The memorial of thirty-eight Florida Tories to Lord North
in 1787 provides much useful information about their problems.

3053.   Steele, David Hamilton. "William Mason: British Loyalist
        in the Georgia Back Country." RICHMOND CTY HIST, 11 (1979),
        30-40.

Mason was persecuted for his views and fled to England
while his land was being confiscated.

3054.   Talman, James J. LOYALIST NARRATIVES FROM UPPER CANADA. 1946.
        Reprint. New York: Greenwood Press, 1969.

This is a fine collection about the sufferings endured by
Tories who emigrated from the colonies (especially New York)

to Canada. The letters of John Stewart, a former Anglican
missionary to the Iroquois, are revealing.

3055.   Troxler, Carole W. THE LOYALIST EXPERIENCE IN NORTH CAROLINA.
        Raleigh: Division of Cultural Resources, Department of
        Archives and History, 1976.

        Here is a fine summary of the Tories in the state. The
        writer provides excellent summaries about the Loyalist re-
        sponse to the Revolution, the partisan warfare, and the
        banishment or self-imposed exile for many. About 226 North
        Carolinians applied to the Crown for compensation.

3056.   ————. "'To Sit Out of a Troublesome Neighborhood': David
        Fanning in New Brunswick." NC HIST REV, 56 (1976), 343-364.

        This is an excellent commentary on the civil war in North
        Carolina by a Tory raider who migrated to the Maritimes.

3057.   Tyler, Moses Coit. "The Party of the Loyalists in the Ameri-
        can Revolution." AHR, 1 (1895), 24-45.

        This is a useful article which demonstrates the variety of
        Tory views, that Loyalists were not mere obstructionists nor
        opposed to reform, and that the majority loved America.

3058.   Upton, L.F.S. THE LOYAL WHIG: WILLIAM SMITH OF NEW YORK AND
        QUEBEC. Toronto: University of Toronto Press, 1969.

        Smith was a major political figure in New York who became
        a Loyalist by 1778 after much soul-searching. Though the
        author writes coherently about Smith's dilemma between Crown
        and country, the development of his public career, and his
        hope for the success of the British empire, the explanations
        for his decisions are not entirely convincing.

3059.   Vail, R.W.G. "The Loyalist Declaration of Independence of
        November 22, 1776." NY HIST SOC Q, 32 (1947), 68-71.

        Here is a replica of the Tory equivalent of the Declaration
        of Independence, signed by 950 Loyalists and published in New
        York.

3060.   Vermuele, Cornelius C. "The Active New Jersey Loyalists."
        NJ HIST SOC PROC, 52 (1934), 87-95.

        The writer contends that only 1,100 Tories were active
        in the state.

3061.   Vernon-Jackson, H.O.H. "A Loyalist's Wife: Letters of Mrs.
        Philip Van Cortlandt, 1776-77." HIST TODAY, 14 (1964),
        574-580.

        Married to a prominent New Jersey Tory, the lady describes
        how her home near Morristown was sequestered in February, 1777
        as a Continental army hospital.

3062. Wade, Mason. "Odyssey of a Loyalist Rector." VT HIST, 48
(1980), 96-113.

Reverend Ranna Cossit of New Hampshire tried to lead a
Loyalist migration of Anglicans to Quebec and ended up in
Nova Scotia.

3063. Walker, Mabel G. "Sir John Johnson, Loyalist." MVHR, 3
(1916), 318-346.

Johnson who assumed his father's role in 1774 as the chief
British official for Iroquois relations was expelled from
the Mohawk Valley by General Schuyler; but he returned to
invade New York with General Burgoyne.

3064. Walker, Robert G. "Jonathan Boucher: Champion of the Minority." WMQ, 2 (1945), 3-14.

A Tory divine, Boucher preached "quaint, confused, naive
political doctrine" that actually contained more in common
with the patriotic cause than he realized.

3065. Wallace, William S. "The Loyalist Migration Overland." NY
HIST ASSOC PROC, 13 (1914), 159-167.

This is a sympathetic treatment of the Tory exodus from
New York which stresses the "humble" origins of the majority.

3066. Waugh, John T. "The United Empire Loyalists: With Particular
Reference to the Niagara Frontier." UNIV BUFF STUD, 4
(1956), 72-123.

Most New York Catholics were Tory; one-third the colony's
population was Tory; and social class was not a dominant dis-
tinction between Tory and Whig.

3067. Wemmensten, John R. "The Travail of a Tory Parson: Reverend
Philip Hughes and Maryland Colonial Politics, 1767-1777."
HIST MAG PROT EPIS CHURCH, 44 (1975), 409-416.

The controversial clergymen of the Eastern Shore was persecuted for his beliefs in a state where eighteen out of
forty-five parishes were vacant by 1776.

3068. Werner, Raymond C., ed. "Diary of Grace Crowden Galloway."
PA MHB, 58 (1931), 32-94; 58 (1934), 152-189.

Mrs. Galloway, the wife of Philadelphia's famous Loyalist,
left colorful impressions of her experiences.

3069. Wierner, Frederick B. "The Signer Who Recanted." AMER
HERITAGE, 26 (5) (1975), 22-25.

Richard Stockton of New Jersey, a signer of the Declaration
of Independence, was imprisoned by the British and harshly
treated; for a pardon from the Crown, he recanted.

3070.   Williams, Edward G. "The Prevosts of the Royal Americans."
        WEST PA HIST MAG, 56 (1973), 1-38.

        This is an adequate summary about the military careers of
        the three Prevost brothers and a nephew who fought for the
        British.

3071.   Williams, Linda K. "East Florida as a Loyalist Haven." FLA
        HIST Q, 54 (1976), 465-478.

        St. Augustine was a refugee base and a center of military
        operations against Georgia and South Carolina.

3072.   Wright, J. Leitch, Jr. "Lord Dunmore's Loyalist Asylum in
        the Floridas." FLA HIST Q, 49 (1971), 370-379.

        The post-war Governor of the Bahamas attempted to recover
        former British grants in the Ohio Valley by trying to estab-
        lish a Loyalist-Indian colony in the Spanish Southwest.

3073.   Zeichner, Oscar. "The Loyalist Problem in New York After the
        Revolution." NY HIST, 21 (1940), 284-302.

        This is a good summary of "Tory-baiting" for the two-thirds
        of the Loyalists who remained in the state after the war.

3074.   ———. "The Rehabilitation of Loyalists in Connecticut."
        NEQ, 11 (1938), 308-330.

        Out of 2,000 Tory males, 1,000 remained after the war to
        receive fairly lenient treatment by the state except for
        confiscation laws which remained until 1787.

3075.   ———, ed. "William Smith's Observations on America." NY
        HIST, 23 (1942), 328-340.

        Writing in 1785, Smith gave his retrospective views on how
        the war could have been averted, and how the British Empire
        could learn from the experience.

3076.   Zimmer, Anne Young and Alfred H. Kelly. "Jonathan Boucher:
        Constitutionalist Conservative." JAR, 58 (1972),
        897-922.

        Boucher rejected the Lockian social contract theory and had
        a Burkian concept of stable, conservative society with respect
        for authority.

3077.   Zubly, J.J. "Rev. J.J. Zubly's Appeal to the Grand Jury,
        October 8, 1777." GA HIST Q, (1917), 161-165.

        The Savannah Loyalist minister was banished from the state
        and half his estate was confiscated.

E. WOMEN IN THE REVOLUTION

3078.   Adams, Abigail and John Adams. THE BOOK OF ABIGAIL AND JOHN:
        SELECTED LETTERS OF THE ADAMS FAMILY 1762-1784. Edited
        and with an introduction by L.H. Butterfield, Marc
        Friedlaeander, and Mary-Jo Kline. Cambridge, Massachusetts:
        Harvard University Press, 1975.

        The 226 letters, many of which are printed for the first
        time, reflect the intelligence of the husband and wife, and,
        particularly, the captivating personal style of Abigail who
        wrote with clarity and perception. This is one of the most
        significant documentary collections about the reflections of
        an influential lady during the war.

3079.   Akers, Charles W. ABIGAIL ADAMS: AN AMERICAN WOMEN. Boston,
        Massachusetts: Little, Brown and Co., 1980.

        In a lively writing style, the writer demonstrates that
        Abigail refused to accept a position of female inferiority
        in society or legal subjugation to her husband. She ex-
        pected that the emancipation of her sex was soon dawning.
        Samples from 2,000 letters show her wide interests and her
        witty comments.

3080.   Beard, Mary Ritter. WOMEN AS A FORCE IN HISTORY. New York:
        Macmillan Co., 1946.

        While weak on the American Revolution, the book emphasizes
        the role of women in history and thereby provides a useful
        perspective. The author mentions some historical works which
        treat feminism in the war era.

3081.   Benson, Mary Summer. WOMEN IN EIGHTEENTH CENTURY AMERICA.
        New York: Columbia University Press, 1935.

        A well-documented study which investigates the status of
        women in the century, this work has excellent descriptions
        of their abilities and obligations. The bibliography is very
        helpful, and chapter nine is a humorous commentary on customs
        and manners.

3082.   Berkin, Carol Ruth. "Remembering the Ladies: Historians and
        the Women of the American Revolution." See 1799,
        pp. 47-67.

        This is a historiographical essay about how women have been
        considered in the Revolution by writers. In this article,
        which is weak on facts, Berkin claims that women realized a
        new self-identity in the era.

3083.   Blake, John B. "The Compleat Housewife." BULL HIST MED, 49
        (1975), 30-42.

        The first cookbook printed in North America (1742) had
        numerous medical remedies and drug recipes for household use.

3084. Blumenthal, Walter H. WOMEN CAMP FOLLOWERS OF THE AMERICAN
       REVOLUTION. Philadelphia: George S. MacManus Co., 1952.

       Although outdated and with a title that is insulting to women,
       this is one of the few comprehensive studies which shows that
       women on both the American and British sides performed in-
       numerable useful tasks for their husbands and lovers. The
       author cites the exploits of several American female com-
       batants. The bibliography is useful.

3085. Bolar, Mary. "Jane Wilson McKissack: Patriot of the American
       Revolution." DAR MAG, 114 (1980), 152-155.

       This article concerns a heroine of Lincoln County, North
       Carolina, who cared for wounded troops after the fight at
       Ramsour's Mill in 1780.

3086. Booth, Sally Smith. THE WOMEN OF '76. New York: Hastings
       House, Philadelphia, 1973.

       This is a helpful introduction to the subject because of
       its simplistic style and organization. It may appeal to
       high-schoolers.

3087. Botti, Priscilla Smith. "Elizabeth Whitmore: Midwife of
       Mayboro." VT HIST, 39 (1971), 98-100.

       A tinker's wife, Whitmore supported her family with delivery
       fees while her patriotic husband fought in the war.

3088. Brown, Marvin L., Jr. BARONESS VON RIEDESEL AND THE AMERICAN
       REVOLUTION: JOURNAL AND CORRESPONDENCE OF A TOUR OF DUTY
       1776-1783. Chapel Hill: The University of North Carolina
       Press, 1965.

       The wife of a Hessian general on Burgoyne's ill-fated cam-
       paign in New York, the Baroness provided some fascinating
       anecdotes about the life of a mercenary's wife with three
       children in an alien land. Her descriptions of Saratoga,
       life under confinement, and her comments about the Americans
       are perceptive. This is an interesting book for a wide
       audience.

3089. Bruce, Henry Addington. WOMEN IN THE MAKING OF AMERICA.
       Boston: Little, Brown and Co., 1933.

       This is an antiquarian work that has one chapter about the
       various roles performed by women in the war. The glimpses
       of Molly Pitcher, Deborah Sampson, Lydia Darragh, and Martha
       Washington, among others, are helpful.

3090. Brush, Ted. "Sussex County's Loyalist Heroine." NORTH JERSEY
       HIGHLANDER, 9 (1973), 23-25.

       Loyalist Nancy Nevil aided captured British soldiers en route
       to confinement in Virginia to escape to New York City.

3091. Bushnell, Charles I., ed. "Women of the Revolution." HIST
      MAG, 5 (1869), 105-112.

      This essay contains numerous brief letters about the war
      written by distinquished women from New York.

3092. Campbell, Amelia D. "Women of New York State in the Revolu-
      tion." NY STATE HIST ASSOC Q J, 3 (1922), 155-168.

      Campbell helps to rescue from obscurity a dozen women whom
      history has overlooked and who merit further research.

3093. Cheny, Cora. THE INCREDIBLE DEBORAH, A STORY BASED ON THE
      LIFE OF DEBORAH SAMPSON. New York: Charles Scribner's Sons,
      1967.

      Although supposedly based on facts, this is a fictionalized
      biography about this remarkable woman. Youngsters may enjoy
      it.

3094. Coghlan, Margaret. MEMOIRS OF MRS. COGHLAN, DAUGHTER OF THE
      LATE MAJOR MONCRIEFFE. 1865. Reprint. New York: New York
      Times, 1971.

      Here is a good contemporary version by the wife of a British
      officer stationed in New York City. It shows glimpses of
      the manners and etiquette of army life.

3095. Coit, Margaret L. "Dearest Friends." AMER HERITAGE, 19 (4)
      (1968), 9-13.

      This is a thoughtful and well-illustrated article about the
      marriage of Abigail and John Adams with some useful quotations
      from their letters.

3096. Cole, Adelaide M. "Anne Bailey: Woman of Courage." DAR MAG,
      114 (1980), 322-325.

      Bailey of the Shenandoah Valley was famous as a scout and
      messenger for the Continental army.

3097. ———. "Did Betty Zane Save Fort Henry?" DAR MAG, 114
      (1980), 672-675.

      Here is the exciting legend of a woman's flight from a
      besieged fortress in (West) Virginia in order to procure gun-
      powder.

3098. Cometti, Elizabeth. "Women in the Revolution." NEQ, 20
      (1947), 329-346.

      In a fine summary about females in the war, the author ex-
      plains their work, hardships, and life styles by covering a
      wide social and geographical spectrum with ample documentation.

464

THE IMPACT OF WAR ON SOCIETY

3099. Cook, Fred J. WHAT MANNER OF MEN, FORGOTTEN HEROES OF THE
REVOLUTION. New York: William Morrow and Co., 1959.

In one chapter about women, the author covers popular and,
sometimes, legendary versions of Ann Bailey, Margaret Corbin,
Nancy Hart, Mary Hayes, Deborah Sampson, and Betty Zane.

3100. Copeland, Edna Arnold. "Nancy Hart - A Revolutionary Heroine."
GA MAG, 8 (1965), 30-31.

Nancy carried dispatches, spied on Tories and captured some
of them.

3101. Cott, Nancy F. "Divorce and the Changing Status of Women in
Eighteenth Century Massachusetts." WMQ, 33 (1976), 586-
614.

A detailed study of 229 divorce petitions discloses the
legal grounds for divorce; the number of such cases increased;
more women than men sought divorce but men were more successful in obtaining it. The Revolution brought stricter stand-
ards for marital fidelity.

3102. Coulter, E. Merton. "Nancy Hart, Georgia Heroine of the
Revolution; The Story of a Growth of a Tradition." GA HIST
Q, 39 (1955), 118-151.

This article traces the growth of the legend, and the development of folklore about Hart.

3103. Criss, Mildred. ABIGAIL ADAMS. New York: Dodd, Mead and Co.,
1952.

Although generally historically correct, the author in-
vents scenes and dialogue about the ordeal and triumphs of
Abigail. Youngsters might enjoy the book.

3104. Danielson, Helga. "When Lydia Darragh Saved the Day for George
Washington." AMER MERCURY, 88 (1959), 79-81.

Here is a good example of how an excessively imaginative
writer unfamiliar with the documents concluded that Lydia
practically rescued the American army at a crisis in
Pennsylvania.

3105. Darragh, Henry. "Lydia Darragh, One of the Heroines of the
Revolution." PHIL CITY HIST SOC PUB, 13 (1916), 277-303.

Darragh was active in Philadelphia as a business woman, a
nurse, and an undertaker; she provided Washington with some
useful intelligence.

3106. DePauw, Linda Grant. FOUR TRADITIONS: WOMEN OF NEW YORK DUR-
ING THE AMERICAN REVOLUTION. Albany: New York State Revolution Bicentennial Commission, 1974.

This is a brief convenient summary of some famous New York women during the war. It is useful as an introduction to the subject and stresses the need to incorporate material about women in the war into standard accounts.

3107.   ———. "Land of the Unfree: Legal Limitations on Liberty in Pre-Revolutionary America." MD HIST MAG, 68 (1973), 355-368.

DePauw claims that only fifteen per cent of the revolutionary population was actually free to enjoy the promises of the Declaration of Independence; women, blacks, indentured servants, and Indians were excluded from free, white male legal privileges.

3108.   ———. "Stories for Free Children: The Forgotten Spirit of '76: Women in the Revolutionary Era." MS. (1974), 51-56, 100-102.

This is a good article which examines the plight of late colonial women (white, black, red) from numerous angles. It contains a good bibliography.

3109.   Desmond, Alice C. "Mary Philipes-Heiress." NY HIST, 28 (1947), 22-32.

The lady was the sister of a prominent New York patroon and the wife of Beverly Robinson.

3110.   Dexter, Elizabeth and Anthony Williams. COLONIAL WOMEN OF AFFAIRS: A STUDY OF WOMEN IN BUSINESS AND THE PROFESSIONS BEFORE 1776. Boston: Houghton Mifflin, Co., 1924.

While this work needs serious revision, it is useful introduction to the multitude of roles women played outside the home on the eve of the Revolution.

3111.   Donnelly, Lucy M. "The Celebrated Mrs. Macauley." WMQ, 6 (1949), 173-207.

Mrs. Macauley's accomplishments as a historian of the era are nicely summarized here.

3112.   Downey, Fairfax. "Girls Behind the Guns." AMER HERITAGE, 8 (1) (1956), 46-48.

This is a good popular account of how Molly Corbin at Fort Washington, and Molly Pitcher at Monmouth became legends.

3113.   Edgerton, Samuel Y., Jr. "The Murder of Jane McCrae." EARLY AMER LIT, 8 (1973), 28-30.

This is an adequate summary about the famous Indian scalping of a Tory woman whose death was used as propaganda material by Gates to arouse American frontiersmen in New York and western New England against Burgoyne.

3114. Ellet, Elizabeth F. THE WOMEN OF THE AMERICAN REVOLUTION. 3
       vols. 1848-50. Reprint. New York: Haskell House, 1969.

       This is one of the earliest, and the most famous books about
       female contributions to the war. Although not dependable as
       a historical source, it is an interesting period piece with
       adequate sketches of Peggy Arnold, Catherine Schuyler, Jane
       McCrae, and other famous American women of the era.

3115. Engle, Paul. WOMEN IN THE AMERICAN REVOLUTION. New York:
       Follett Publishing Co., 1976.

       This highly simplistic account consists of an old-fashioned
       reworking of standard sources about eighteen patriotic women.
       It may be helpful in high schools.

3116. Evans, Elizabeth. WEATHERING THE STORM; WOMEN OF THE AMERICAN
       REVOLUTION. New York: Charles Scribner's Sons, 1975.

       This book contains material about eleven women familiar to
       students of the era. It is not footnoted, it has a very
       poor bibliography, and it does not examine the role of women
       in revolutionary society. Apparently timed for the Bicenten-
       nial era, it may be helpful for high-schoolers.

3117. Farley, M. Foster. "South Carolina Women in the American
       Revolution." DAR MAG, 113 (1979), 356-361.

       Four prominent Carolina women, including Eliza Wilkinson,
       are cited here.

3118. Forbes-Robinson, Diana. "Lady Knox." AMER HERITAGE, 17 (4)
       (1966), 46-47, 74-79.

       Here is a neat summary of a Tory heiress who married Henry
       Knox, Washington's artilleryman, and her tribulations as an
       army wife during the war.

3119. Fritz, Jean. CAST FOR A REVOLUTION: SOME AMERICAN FRIENDS AND
       ENEMIES, 1728-1814. Boston: Houghton Mifflin, 1972.

       Mercy Warren dominates this collective biography which fuses
       the lives of numerous important individuals of the era in this
       interesting volume written for the general reader. The notes,
       index, bibliography and illustrations are commendable.

3120. Galloway, Grace Crowden. DIARY OF GRACE CROWDEN GALLOWAY:
       JOURNAL KEPT JUNE 17, 1778 THROUGH SEPTEMBER 30, 1779. New
       York: New York Times, 1971.

       The devoted wife of famed Loyalist Joseph Galloway of
       Philadelphia penned a provocative and embittered account of
       the difficulties she encountered as a Tory woman. Her com-
       ments are valuable reflections of contemporary social life
       during the war.

3121. Gelles, Edith B. "Abigail Adams: Domesticity and the Ameri-
       can Revolution." NEQ, 52 (1979), 500-521.

       Abigail clearly did "a man's job" during the war by managing
       a farm, handling family finances, and retailing merchandise
       shipped to her from Europe by John Adams.

3122. Gilman, Caroline, ed. LETTERS OF ELIZA WILKINSON DURING THE
       POSSESSION OF CHARLESTOWN, S.C. BY THE BRITISH IN THE REVO-
       LUTIONARY WAR. New York: New York Times, 1969.

       Although this is not a perceptive commentary about the im-
       pact of the British invasion of South Carolina, it is one of
       the few extant memoirs about the event by a southern lady.
       Some passages about the effects of the siege are quite vivid.

3123. Gray, Elizabeth Janet (Vining). MEGGY MACINTOSH. New York:
       Doubleday, Doran and Co., Inc., 1930.

       This is a lively account of Flora MacDonald of North
       Carolina, the intensive rivalry that Scot clannish settlers
       maintained after their migration to America, and the events
       leading to the fierce battle of Moore's Creek Bridge in 1776
       which destroyed Loyalist hopes of holding the province for
       the crown.

3124. Henry, Susan. "Colonial Women Printers as Prototype: Toward
       A Model for the Study of Minorities." JOURN HIST, 3 (1976),
       20-24.

       The author concentrates on the careers of thirteen female
       printers in 1776 who published newspapers and almanacs; she
       demonstrates how this sample could be extended to other
       women in business activities.

3125. ————. "Margaret Draper: Colonial Printer Who Challenged the
       Patriots." JOURN HIST, 1 (1974-75), 141-144.

       This is a good account of the courageous Loyalist editor of
       the MASSACHUSETTS GAZETTE AND BOSTON NEWS-LETTER who was
       evicted from her business by patriots.

3126. Holbrook, Stewart Hall. LOST MEN IN AMERICA. New York:
       Macmillan Co., 1964.

       In a volume that has relatively little value for the Revolu-
       tion, the author includes a colorful sketch of soldier Deborah
       Sampson who fought in combat.

3127. Holden, James A. "The Influence of the Death of Jane McCrae
       on the Burgoyne Campaign." PROC NY STATE HIST ASSOC, 12
       (1913), 249-310.

       Holden has compiled a detailed account about the famous
       Indian scalping of the young Tory woman who waited for her

lover (on Burgoyne's staff), and how the atrocity helped to
mold American opinion for the pending Saratoga campaign.
Unfortunately, the author accepts all the legends without
question.

3128. Holliday, Carl. WOMEN'S LIFE IN COLONIAL DAYS. Boston:
       Cornhill Publishing, 1922.

       The writer includes one chapter about women in the Revolu-
       tion from the north and south to demonstrate how important
       females were for morale and for acquiring supplies. There
       are brief sketches of Abigail Adams, Eliza Pinckney, Nancy
       Warren, and Catherine Schuyler.

3129. Hutcheson, Maud MacDonald. "Mercy Warren, 1728-1814." WMQ,
       10 (1953), 378-402.

       A prominent pamphleteer, poetress, playwright, and historian
       in the patriotic cause, Mrs. Warren had a remarkable literary
       career.

3130. Hutson, James H. "Women in the era of the American Revolu-
       tion: The Historian as Suffragist." Q J LIB CONG, 35
       (1975), 290-303.

       In a key article, Hutson shows the impact of the women's
       suffrage movement on interpretations of the Revolution. He
       notes the importance of Elizabeth F. Ellet's THE WOMEN OF THE
       AMERICAN REVOLUTION (1848-50) which is the second most im-
       portant classic in the field of women's rights in America.

3131. Hutton, Ann. LETTERS OF A LOYALIST LADY: BEING THE LETTERS
       OF ANN HUTTON, SISTER OF HENRY HUTTON, COMMISSIONER OF
       CUSTOMS AT BOSTON, 1767-1776. 1927. Reprint. New York:
       New York Times, 1971.

       Hutton's letters to London friends depict the turbulence in
       Boston through the eyes of a Loyalist woman. Her comments
       about the Boston Massacre, Bunker Hill, and contemporary
       political developments provide valuable insights.

3132. Ireland, Norman Olin. INDEX TO WOMEN OF THE WORLD FROM AN-
       CIENT TIMES TO MODERN TIMES. Westwood, Massachusetts: F.W.
       Faxon Co., 1970.

       Although some key American females of the era are overlooked,
       this is a generally reliable and extensive reference tool to
       prominent women of the Revolution. The sketches provide ample
       bibliographic references about their careers.

3133. Jacob, Kathryn, Allamony. "The Woman's Lot in Baltimore Town:
       1729-97." MD HIST MAG, 71 (1976), 283-295.

       Jacob neatly demonstrates how women's lives were effected by
       their economic status, their menfolk, and consequently, most
       were homemakers. The comments about "runaway wives" are fasci-
       nating.

3134.   James, Edward T., Janet Wilson James, and Paul S. Boyer.
         NOTABLE AMERICAN WOMEN 1607-1950: A BIOGRAPHICAL DICTIONARY.
         3 vols. Cambridge, Massachusetts: Harvard University Press, 1971.

         Similar in style to the DICTIONARY OF AMERICAN BIOGRAPHY,
         these books are very useful for background material on many
         prominent women of the era. There are numerous cogent sum-
         maries with quotations from documentary sources in these
         brief biographies. This is the best general reference for
         research on the topic, but with the emphasis on the 1825-1920
         years.

3135.   Johnston, Jean. "Molly Brant: Mohawk Matron." ONTARIO HIS-
         TORY, 56 (1965), 105-124.

         Mistress to Sir William Johnson, the British Indian agent
         for the Iroquois, Molly was influential in keeping the Six
         Nations Confederacy on the British side.

3136.   Jordan, Jean P. "Women Merchants in Colonial New York." NY
         HIST, 58 (1977), 412-39.

         From a wealth of documentary sources, the essayist demon-
         strates that "she Merchants" had influential positions in
         New York's mercantile activities.

3137.   Keller, Allan. "'Private' Deborah Sampson." AMER HIST ILLUS,
         11 (4) (1976), 30-33.

         This is a readable and dependable summary about a woman who
         participted in combat against British troops.

3138.   Kerber, Linda. "The Republican Mother: Women and the En-
         lightenment - An American Perspective." AMER Q, 28 (1976),
         187-205.

         In a key article, Kerber summarizes the ideas of prominent
         historians of the eighteenth-century about the role of women
         in politics.

3139.   ————. WOMEN OF THE REPUBLIC: INTELLECTUAL IDEOLOGIES IN
         REVOLUTIONARY AMERICA. Chapel Hill: The University of North
         Carolina Press, 1980.

         This prize-winning book is the best survey of the topic.
         Thoroughly researched from voluminous manuscript sources,
         Kerber shows in an eloquently constructed and provocative
         study that colonial women - who were usually barely literate
         and politically apathetic - modified their views and their
         status to some degree during the Revolution because of the
         war, changing technology, the shouldering of men's burdens at
         home and on the front, and, particularly, a gradual political
         consciousness. Yet, as the author shows, the only major
         change for women after the war was not in political and legal
         reforms, but in educational opportunities. Divorce was still
         very difficult to obtain, but the ideal of a "republican mother"
         had dawned.

3140. Lacey, Barbara E. "Women in the Era of the American Revolu-
       tion: The Case of Norwich, Connecticut." NEQ, 53 (1980),
       527-543.

       In Connecticut's second largest town, the author contends
       that the status of women definitely improved during the
       Revolution as demonstrated in wills, distribution of property,
       divorce petitions, new types of work, and more interests out-
       side of the home.

3141. Landis, John A. "Investigation Into The Tradition of
       Women Known as Molly Pitcher." JAR, 5 (1911), 83-
       96.

       Landis attempted to separate the facts from the fiction
       about the legendary woman who fought at Monmouth Court House.

3142. Leonard, Eugenie Andruss, Drinker Hutchinson, and Miriam
       Young Holden. THE AMERICAN WOMAN IN COLONIAL REVOLUTIONARY
       TIMES, 1565-1800; A SYLLABUS WITH BIBLIOGRAPHY.
       Philadelphia: University of Pennsylvania Press, 1962.

       Although this is a poorly-organized work, it contains much
       valuable data and is an essential reference tool. It lists
       over one hundred prominent women of the eighteenth century,
       provides essential bibliographic entries, and suggests a re-
       search technique to extract information about these heroines
       and prominent females.

3143. Leonard Eugenie. THE DEAR-BOUGHT HERITAGE. Philadelphia:
       University of Pennsylvania Press, 1965.

       Though inadequately documented and based on standard sources,
       this readable work is a convenient summary of the position of
       women - their hardships, their social activities, their par-
       ticipation in political issues, and their contribution to
       the cause. This book is especially worthwhile for the general
       reader. The bibliography is extensive.

3144. Lupton, Mary Hosner. "Journal of Lucy Barnes Homes: Tuesday
       18 April - Wednesday 19 April, 1775, Concord, Massachusetts."
       DAR MAG, 114 (1980), 14-17.

       Here is an excellent extract about preparations in Concord
       for the famous incident.

3145. Logan, Mary S. THE PART TAKEN BY WOMEN IN AMERICAN HISTORY.
       1912. Reprint. New York: Arno Press, 1972.

       Written in a late Victorian style, this collection is worth
       perusing because it provides a long list of Revolutionary
       women and their contributions in one helpful chapter.

3146. Long, J.C. "Patience Wright of Bordentown." PROC NJ HIST
       SOC, 79 (1961),

       An eccentric artist who specialized in making wax figures,
       Wright won fame in New York and London; she knew Franklin and
       Josiah Wedgwood.

3147. Lutz, Paul V. "An Army Wife in the Revolution." MANUSCRIPTS,
       23 (1971), 124-130.

       Lutz contrasts the life of a Hessian soldier's wife with
       that of Baroness von Riedesel.

3148. Lyman, Susan E. "Three New Women of the Revolution." NY HIST
       SOC Q, 29 (1945), 77-82.

       The essay concerns Sarah Todd, Margaret Whetter and Sarah
       Whaley who made uniforms, gathered intelligence and visited
       American prisoners.

3149. Mann, Herman. THE FEMALE SOLDIER: LIFE OF DEBORAH SAMPSON,
       THE FEMALE SOLDIER IN THE WAR OF REVOLUTION. 1866. Reprint.
       New York: Arno Press, 1972.

       Here is a summary of the legends about the famous woman
       soldier. The footnotes by John Adams Vinton provide a neces-
       sary and correct perspective to this romantic tale.

3150. Martin, Wendy. "Women and the American Revolution." EARLY
       AM LIT, 11 (1976-77), 322-335.

       From numerous letters and diaries, the author has compiled
       a serviceable review about influential patriotic women in the
       war.

3151. Mayer, Jane Rothchild. BETSY ROSS AND THE FLAG. New York:
       Random House, 1952.

       With some documentary evidence, the author wrote a fiction-
       alized account of the famous legend. Youngsters may find it
       helpful, but the writing style is dull.

3152. Meehan, Thomas. "'Not Made Out of Levity': Evolution of Di-
       vorce in Early Pennsylvania." PA MHB, 92 (1968), 441-464.

       This is an excellent account of the development of divorce
       cases; over 100 were in the state courts from 1785 to 1801.

3153. Miller, William C. "The Betsy Ross Legend." SOCIAL STUDIES,
       37 (1946), 317-323.

       Apparently there is little supporting evidence to indicate
       that Betsy Ross sewed the first American flag.

3154. Morgan, Medel Jacobs. "Sarah Truly, A Mississippi Tory."
       J MISS HIST, 37 (1975), 87-95.

       Useful as a sketch of the Old Natchez District, the article
       shows a Loyalist heroine who was a successful farmer and grist-
       mill owner.

3155. Morison, Samuel Eliot. "Three Great Ladies Helped Establish
       the United States." SMITHSONIAN, 6 (1975), 96-103.

       A famed historian comments about Abigail Adams, Mercy Otis
       Warren, and Martha Washington.

3156. Morris, Margaret. PRIVATE JOURNAL KEPT DURING A PORTION OF
       THE REVOLUTIONARY WAR, FOR THE AMUSEMENT OF A SISTER. 1855.
       Reprint. New York: New York Times, 1969.

       This is a lively view about the ravaging of New Jersey by
       opposing forces as described by a Burlington, New Jersey woman.

3157. Myers, Albert Cook, ed. SALLEY WISTER'S JOURNAL: A TRUE NAR-
       RATIVE BEING A QUAKER MAIDEN'S ACCOUNT OF HER EXPERIENCE
       WITH OFFICERS OF THE CONTINENTAL ARMY 1777-1778.
       Philadelphia: Ferris and Leach, 1902.

       Miss Wister wrote her impressions about the officers on
       Washington's staff that are perceptive and humorous.

3158. Newman, Debra L. "Black Women in the Era of the American Rev-
       olution of Pennsylvania." J NEGRO HIST, 61 (1978), 275-289.

       In an article replete with insight, Newman studies the im-
       pact of the war on some black women and the influence of the
       Abolition Law (1780) in Pennsylvania.

3159. Norton, Mary Beth. "A Cherished Spirit of Independence: The
       Life of an Eighteenth-Century Boston Businesswoman." In
       Carol Ruth Berkin and Mary Beth Norton, eds. WOMEN OF
       AMERICA: A HISTORY. Boston: Houghton Mifflin Co., 1979,
       pp. 48-67.

       This article concerns a female manager who managed a dry
       goods store, handled her own property, and became a Loyalist.

3160. ————. LIBERTY'S DAUGHTERS: THE REVOLUTIONARY EXPERIENCE OF
       AMERICAN WOMEN. New York: Little, Brown, and Co., 1980.

       Although the author barely mentions women who participated
       in the war effort, she does stress that "the legacy of the
       American Revolution was ambiguous." Republican womanhood
       ideals eventually became concepts for Victorian women. But
       the egalitarian rhetoric of the Revolution provided the women's
       right movement with its earliest vocabulary. This is a very
       thoughtful, provocative, and well-researched study which shows
       how attitudes about femininity were undergoing subtle trans-
       formations. Norton studied materials on 450 eighteenth-
       century families.

3161. ————. "'What an Alarming Crisis Is This': Southern Women
       and the American Revolution. See 1919, pp. 203-224.

       Whether rich or poor, black or white, rebel or Loyalist, the
       Southeners were badly shattered by the war. The result was a
       society rebuilt upon slavery in which southern white women had
       a restricted role compared to northern females.

3162. Parry, Edward Owen. "Mary Frazer: Heroine of the American
       Revolution." DAR MAG, 113 (1979), 766-775.

       A wife of a captured American general managed to aid her
       imprisoned husband and to help supply the army at Valley Forge.

3163. Pinckney. Eliza, ed. "Letters of Eliza Lucas Pinckney, 1768-
       1782." SC HIST MAG, 76 (1975), 143-170.

       This essay concerns the pattern of births, illnesses, and
       hardships of Carolina women during the war.

3164. Potter, Gail M. "Maid of Marblehead." NE GALAXY, 16 (1975),
       34-40.

       The essayist wrote a good tale about Agnes Surriage, a
       "rags to riches" female who married into a prominent Boston
       family and who remained a Loyalist.

3165. Pumpelly, Joseph. "Some of the Women who Skillfully Planned
       and Heroically Suffered in the Revolution for the Cause of
       American Independence." AMERICANA, 10 (1915), 647-659, 791-
       792, 818-827, 894, 900, 945-950, 1045-1049; 11 (1916), 116-
       120, 227-235, 281-284.

       Although this is an excessively patriotic essay with a
       patronizing tone, it is a useful sample of how American
       heroines of the war were described until fairly recently.

3166. Radbill, Kenneth A. "The Ordeal of Elizabeth Drinker." PA
       HIST, 47 (1980), 147-172.

       In a touching essay, Radbill depicts the sufferings of
       pacifist Quakers in Philadelphia including their arrest, de-
       struction of property, assault by mobs, and their confinement
       in Winchester, Virginia.

3167. Rawley, James A. "The World of Phillis Wheatley." NEQ, 50
       (1977), 666-677.

       Although not a revolutionary heroine, this young slave dis-
       played remarkable literary talents and her poems were pub-
       lished in London (1773).

3168. Reed, Esther De Berdt. THE LIFE OF ESTER DE BERDT, AFTERWARDS
       ESTER REED OF PENNSYLVANIA. 1853. Reprint. New York: New
       York Times, 1971.

The wife of the influential Joseph Reed, Esther narrated in simple but moving prose a graphic account of life in the Middle States in the Revolutionary era.

3169. Rodman, Linda T. "Patriotic Women of North Carolina in the Revolution." DAR MAG, 45 (1914), 145-152.

Over fifty Carolina women are mentioned here, including Elizabeth Ashe and Mrs. Willie Jones.

3170. Rogers, George V. "Woman's Liberation, c. 1781." NE GALAXY, 16 (1975), 3-12.

This is a popular account of Deborah Sampson who masqueraded as Private Robert Shurtleff of the 4th Massachusetts Regiment, and who served in combat and on garrison duty.

3171. Ross, Emily. "Captain Molly: Forgotten Heroine of the Revolution." DAR MAG, 106 (1972), 108-111.

The writer provides a standard rendition about Margaret Corbin, the first patriotic women to sustain injuries in battle with British soldiers.

3172. Singer, Jurt and Jane Sherrod. SPIES FOR DEMOCRACY. Minneapolis: T.S. Denison, 1960.

There are numerous romantic accounts here of espionage and intelligence - gathering by several patriotic women (notably Lydia Barrington Darragh) that might appeal to young readers.

3173. Sinnickson, Lina. "Frederika Baroness Riedesel." PA MHB, 30 (1900), 385-408.

Although the writer quotes from documents, she does not authenticate them for this out-dated but still interesting tale about the tribulations of a Hessian general's wife with Burgoyne.

3174. Slaymaker, Samuel R., II. "Mrs. Frazer's Philadelphia Campaign." J LANCASTER CTY HIST SOC, 73 (1969), 165-209.

A local historian provides a rousing tale about a general's wife who visited her imprisoned husband, had her home plundered by enemy troops, and who did reconnaissance work at Brandywine.

3175. Smith, Eleanor. "Phillis Wheatley: A Black Perspective." J NEGRO EDUC, 43 (1974), 400-407.

A highly intelligent slave girl who wrote remarkable poetry, Phillis did little to help the black cause.

3176. Smith, Samuel Stelle. "The Search for Molly Pitcher." DAR MAG, 109 (1976), 292-295.

A noted military historian probed the legends about Molly's
performance in action at Monmouth, New Jersey to discover
that her maiden name is unknown, but that her married name
was Mary Hayes McCauley.

3177. Somerville, Mollie, comp. WOMEN AND THE AMERICAN REVOLUTION.
        Washington, DC: Daughters of the American Revolution, 1974.

        Assembled from articles in the DAR MAG, this is a useful
        anthology of lesser-known heroines of the Revolution. It is
        particularly good for material about women in the south.

3178. Spalatta, Matteo. "Divorce in Colonial New York." NY HIST
        SOC Q, 39 (1955), 422-440.

        Although the essay is weak after the Dutch era, it does
        attempt a systematic analysis about divorce procedures from
        1655 to 1787.

3179. Spruill, Julia Cherry. WOMEN'S LIFE AND WORK IN THE SOUTHERN
        COLONIES. Chapel Hill: The University of North Carolina
        Press, 1938.

        In a now classic work in women's history, Spruill comments
        about women at home, in society, and their rights under state
        laws. Although it does not include material on the Revolution,
        there is ample data here for a penetrating view of the white
        female in the late colonial south.

3180. Stevenson, Augusta. MOLLY PITCHER, GIRL PATRIOT. Indianap-
        olis: Bobbs-Merrill, 1952.

        A work for young readers, this story begins in Trenton, New
        Jersey with the imagined dialogue of young Mary Ludwig Hayes.
        A decade's jump in the narrative suddenly ends on the battle-
        field at Monmouth.

3181. Stickley, Julia Ward. "The Records of Deborah Sampson Gannett,
        Woman Soldier of the Revolution." PROLOGUE, 4 (1972), 233-
        241.

        This is a valuable documented account of Robert Shurtleff,
        a woman disguised in uniform, who campaigned three years,
        married in 1784 and had three children. Her husband was the
        first American to receive a pension as a soldier's widower.

3182. Straub, Jean S. "Benjamin Rush's Views on Women's Education."
        PA HIST, 34 (1967), 147-159.

        His suggested curriculum for educated females was a curious
        blend of basic fundamentals with elements of a liberal educa-
        tion, particularly civics.

3183.   Stryker-Roda, Harriet. "Militia Women of 1780." DAR MAG,
        113 (1979), 308-312.

            This survey concerns nineteen women from Monmouth County,
        New Jersey, who performed military service.

3184.   Tharp, Louisa Hall. THE BARONESS AND THE GENERAL. Boston:
        Little, Brown and Co., 1962.

            This is a joint biography about Baron von Riedesel and his
        wife on Burgoyne's campaign that might appeal to high school
        readers.

3185.   Tonkinson, Grace. "Jane McCrae: A Martyr of the Revolutionary
        War." DALHOUSIE REV, 49 (1969), 399-403.

            Here is a standard account of how a famous atrocity com-
        mitted on a Tory girl by Indians was cleverly dramatized
        into effective propaganda to rally Americans at Saratoga.

3186.   Uttey, Beverly. "Brave Women: Distaff Side of Revolution."
        AMER HIST ILLUS, 3 (5) (1968), 10-18.

            Here is an example of all the legends - many long disproved -
        summarized in a vague essay.

3187.   Warren, Mercy Otis. HISTORY OF THE RISE, PROGRESS AND TER-
        MINATION OF THE AMERICAN REVOLUTION, INTERSPERSED WITH
        BIOGRAPHICAL, POLITICAL AND MORAL OBSERVATIONS. 3 vols.
        1878. Reprint. New York: Arno Press Co., 1972.

            While difficult to read and to comprehend, this collection
        is pertinent as a prominent observer's account of the Revolu-
        tion. Clearly, Mrs. Warren had a fine mind and was a gifted
        commentator.

3188.   Weil, Ann. BETSY ROSS; GIRL OF OLD PHILADELPHIA. Indianap-
        olis: Bobbs-Merrill Co., 1954.

            Weil stresses young Betsy's life to the age of fourteen,
        and only a final chapter places the woman in perspective as
        the famous seamstress. Where the author obtained her factual
        material is not explained. Perhaps youngsters might enjoy
        this tale.

3189.   Wells, Louisa Susannah. THE JOURNAL OF A VOYAGE FROM
        CHARLESTON, S.C. TO LONDON UNDERTAKEN DURING THE AMERICAN
        REVOLUTION BY A DAUGHTER OF AN EMINENT AMERICAN LOYALIST IN
        THE YEAR 1778 ... n.p., 1903.

            This is an excellent travel account of an ocean voyage to
        the south's major city. The writer had a sharp eye for de-
        tail and duly recorded her impressions of the revolutionary
        turmoil in the Carolinas.

3190.   White, John Todd. "The Truth About Molly Pitcher." In James
        Kirby Martin, ed. THE AMERICAN REVOLUTION: WHOSE REVOLU-
        TION. Huntington, New York: Robert E. Krieger Pub. Co.,
        1977, pp. 40-48.

        White doubts that Molly actually existed, and he notes that
        it was common practice for women in battle to carry water, not
        for drinking, but for swabbing the muzzles of overheated can-
        non.

3191.   Whitton, Mary Ormsbee. THESE WERE THE WOMEN, U.S.A. 1776-
        1860. New York: Hastings House Publishers, 1954.

        This is a full scale treatment about women in the United
        States to the Civil War. It includes thirty pages of sketches
        about such females as Peggy Shippen Arnold, Catherine Schuyler,
        Dorothy Hancock, Martha Washington, and many others.

3192.   Wilson, Joan Hoff. "Dancing Dogs of the Colonial Period:
        Women Scientists." EARLY AMER LIT, 7 (1973), 225-235.

        Wilson notes some females were medical practitioners, but
        with the exception of four prominent women scientists, few
        were active in the botany, astronomy, or agronomy.

3193.   ————. "The Illusion of Change: Women and the American
        Revolution." See 3335, pp. 385-445.

        The author contends the Revolution brought no tangible
        benefits to females, that the war retarded some societal
        functions, and that by 1800 their economic and legal privi-
        leges were curtailed. Though the writing here is murky and
        the conceptual framework is puzzling, it is a provocative
        article.

                            F. THE INDIANS

3194.   Almeida, Deirdre. "The Stockbridge Indians in the American
        Revolution." HIST J WEST MASS, 4 (1975), 34-39.

        A branch of the Algonquins served the patriots well in the
        war.

3195.   Bast, Homer. "Creek Indian Affairs, 1775-1778." GA HIST Q,
        33 (1949), 1-25.

        This is a valuable essay which surveys the importance of
        British gunpowder to the Creeks and Choctaws in their stand
        against American encroachments on tribal lands.

3196.   Beauchamp, William M. "Indian Raids in the Mohawk Valley."
        NY STATE HIST ASSOC PROC, 14 (1915), 195-206.

        Here is a brief and adequate summary of Loyalist-led war-
        fare in upper New York.

3197. Beers, Paul. "Simon Girty - 'Beast in Human Form'." AMER
       HIST ILLUS, 3 (8) (1968-69, 20-24.

       Girty was the famous renegade who led the Senecas on the
       warpath on the Ohio and Kentucky frontiers.

3198. Bishop, Morris. "The End of the Iroquois." AMER HERITAGE,
       20 (6) (1969), 28-33, 77-81.

       This is a colorful summary of how Sullivan's expedition
       crippled the Indian allies of George III in western New York.

3199. Bogert, Frederick W. "Marauders in the Minisink."   NJ HIST,
       82 (1964), 271-282.

       Minisink, covering a three state area, was frequently
       devestated by Indian raids.

3200. Clark, Donald F. "Joseph Brant and the Battle of the Minisink."
       DAR MAG, 113 (1979), 785-795.

       The essay summarizes a bloody Indian raid on an isolated
       village in New York (July, 1777).

3201. Covington, James W. "Migration of the Seminoles into the
       Floridas, 1700-1820." FLA HIST Q, 46 (1768), 340-357.

       The Lower Creeks migrated in three phases over a century.

3202. Culturill, Robert S. "The Virginia-Chickasaw Treaty of 1763."
       JSH, 8 (1942), 482-496.

       No Delaware, Choctaw or Creek signed the curious document
       for a peace made by whites with the Chickasaws; it was a
       treaty that did not specify land cessions.

3203. Davis, Andrew M. "The Employment of Indian Auxiliaries in
       the American War." ENG HIST REV, 1 (1887), 709-729.

       The author places more blame on the British for Indian
       atrocities than on the Yankees.

3204. De Vorsey, Louis, Jr. "Indian Boundaries in Colonial Georgia."
       GA HIST Q, 54 (1970), 63-78.

       Discussing the shifting boundary settlements here with the
       Creeks and Cherokees, the author notes that by 1775 most of
       Georgia was still Indian country.

3205. ————. THE INDIAN BOUNDARY IN THE SOUTHERN COLONIES, 1763-
       1775. Chapel Hill: The University of North Carolina Press,
       1968.

       The British merit praise for careful negotiations with the
       Indians in their jurisdiction. Concentrating on the Creeks,

Choctaws, Seminoles, and Cherokees in four future states and
the Floridas, the author compiled a thoughtful and comprehensive treatment of this topic. The thirty maps are excellent.

3206. Downes, Randolph C. "Creek American Relations, 1782-1790."
       GA HIST Q, 29 (1937), 142-181.

       The Creeks emerged from the war with their territories
       relatively intact due to Spanish protection, but they lost
       huge holdings to Georgia in 1783 through a fraudulent treaty.

3207. Dunn, Walter S. "The Frontier on the Eve of the Revolution."
       NIAG FRONT, 20 (1973), 98-111.

       Even though only a few whites resided in the area between
       the Great Lakes and the Ohio River, British officers were
       active here in establishing ports, aiding commerce, and
       negotiating trade treaties.

3208. Edward, C. "The Wyoming Valley Massacre." AMER HIST ILLUS,
       13 (6) (1978), 32-40.

       The brutal raid by John Butler's 1,000 Tories and Indians
       here in 1778 was a prime factor for the Sullivan expedition in
       1779 against the Iroquois.

3209. Farrand, Max. "The Indian Boundary Line." AHR, 10
       (1905), 782-791.

       This is a fine summary of the effort to separate Indian
       lands from white settlements, 1763-83.

3210. Ganyard, Robert L. "Threat From the West: North Carolina and
       the Cherokee, 1776-1778." NC HIST REV, 45 (1968), 47-66.

       Aroused by encroachments on their lands, the Cherokees at-
       tacked white settlements; but they were smashed by southern
       militia in 1776 and remained passive until 1780.

3211. Gold, Robert L. "The East Florida Indians Under Spanish and
       English Control: 1763-1765." FLA HIST Q, 44 (1965), 105-
       120.

       This is a good summary of how the quest for trade and Indian
       alliances led two European nations into conflict on the
       southern frontier.

3212. Graymont, Barbara. THE IROQUOIS IN THE AMERICAN REVOLUTION.
       Syracuse, New York: Syracuse University Press, 1972.

       This is a scholarly work which explains why the Iroquois
       were valuable allies to the British, why they were formidable
       enemies, and how they restrained American expansion. By ex-
       amining the diplomacy of the Six Nations with the British

and Americans, Graymont demonstrates in this ethno-history
the pressures exerted on the tribes, why it was difficult for
them to remain neutral, and how the struggle degenerated into
an Indian civil war in which the Oneidas were generally pro-
Yankee. The study is especially good on Indian raids, the
Sullivan expedition to the Finger Lakes, and how the Indians
viewed the white man's struggle. Regardless of the outcome
of the Revolution, due to land pressure by settlers, the
Iroquois were doomed as a Confederacy.

3213. Guzzardo, John C. "The Superintendent   and the Ministers:
        The Battle for Oneida Allegiances, 1761-65." NY HIST, 57
        (1976), 255-283.

        The friction between Sir William Johnson and two Presby-
        terian ministers over handling of this tribe pressaged the
        disruption of the Iroquois nation.

3214. Hamer, Philip M. "John Stuart's Indian Policy During the Early
        Months of the Revolution." MVHR, 17 (1930), 351-
        366.

        For fifteen months of the war, Britain's Indian agent in
        the south tried to restrain the Cherokee from raiding American
        settlements, and, thereby, he ignored the orders of his supe-
        riors in Boston and Savannah.

3215. Hamilton, Milton W. "Joseph Brant - The Most Painted Indian."
        NY HIST, 39 (1938), 119-132.

        Less cruel than described by American historians, Brant had
        portraits painted of him by five artists, including Gilbert
        Stuart, Benjamin West, and Charles Wilson Peale.

3216. Henderson, Archibald. "The Treaty of Long Island Holston,
        July, 1777." NC HIST REV, 8 (1931), 53-116.

        This is a key article which documents the Cherokee cession
        of all lands east of the Blue Ridge Mountains after their
        defeat in 1776.

3217. Jennings, Francis. "The Indians' Revolution." See
        3325, pp. 321-348.

        Though the article concentrates on the pre-1774 era, it
        notes that the tribes had to fight for independence from the
        states and stresses the significance of the tribe-nation
        governments confronted by European legal-political traditions.

3218. Kelsay, Isabelle T. "Joseph Brant: The Legend and the Man."
        NY HIST, 40 (1959), 368-379.

        Here is a solid bibliography essay about the life and times
        of the famous warrior.

3219. Knapp, David, Jr. "The Chickamaugas." GA HIST Q, 51 (1967),
       194-196.

       This tribe seceded from the Cherokee nation, fought with
       the British, and it was finally reintegrated with the Cherokees
       in 1792.

3220. Little, Mrs. William S. "The Massacre of Cherry Valley."
       ROCH HIST SOC PUB, 6 (1927), 99-128.

       Little wrote a highly dramatic description of one of the
       most famous Indian raids of the Revolution.

3221. Mahon, John K. "Anglo-American Methods of Indian Warfare,
       1676-1794." MVHR, 45 (1958), 254-275.

       Here is a thoughtful essay about how weapons and tactics
       adopted from European traditions were used by the American
       and British to combat Indians whose techniques in warfare and
       in combat were usually inferior to that of the whites.

3222. Moore, John H. "A Captive of the Shawnee, 1779-1784." W VA
       HIST, 23 (1962), 287-296.

       Margaret Handley Erskine related her tale in the 1840s.

3223. O'Donnell, James H. Jr. "Alexander McGillivray: Training for
       Leadership, 1777-1778." GA HIST Q, 49 (1965), 172-186.

       The article summarizes the career of the Creek "Head War-
       rior" and his influence with the British Indian Departments
       while he negotiated with the Americans and Spanish.

3224. ————. "More Apologies: The Indian in New York Fiction."
       NY FOLKLORE Q, 23 (1967), 243-252.

       This is an imaginative sketch of how the Iroquois were
       stereotyped by James Fennimore Cooper as noble savages or
       as fierce warriors.

3225. ————. SOUTHERN INDIANS IN THE AMERICAS IN THE REVOLUTION.
       Knoxville, Tennessee: University of Tennessee Press, 1973.

       This is a solidly researched book about the fate of four
       major tribes--the Creeks, Cherokee, Choctaw and Chickasaw.
       Victimized by the white's greed for land and by military
       alliances (usually with the British) these Indians were
       invariable pawns who were destined to be losers. The British
       were generally better able to supply these tribes but were
       unable to protect them from devastating American raids. Al-
       though criticized for being too brief considering the scope of
       the subject and for overlooking the ethnohistorical ramifi-
       cations of Indian attitudes, nevertheless this is a fine
       work that merits attention.

3226. ————. THE CHEROKEES OF NORTH CAROLINA IN THE AMERICAN
       REVOLUTION. Raleigh, North Carolina: Department of Cul-
       tural Resources, Division of Archives and History, 1976.

       Hurt by successive invasions of Cherokee land, tribal unity
       deteriorated. The notes and bibliography in this booklet are
       excellent.

3227. ————. "The Native American Crisis in the Ohio Country,
       1774-1783." See 1063, pp. 151-160.

       The Anglo-Americans displayed murderous attitudes toward
       the splintered tribal groups of the Ohio area.

3228. ————. "The Native Americans." See 855, pp. 64-78.

       Conflicting allegiances, trade problems, the influx of white
       settlers, and the erosion of tribal lands in the south were
       all factors in the pending factionalism of southern tribes
       during the war.

3229. ————. "The Virginia Expedition Against the Overhill
       Cherokees, 1776." E TENN HIST SOC, 39 (1967), 13-25.

       The invasion by Virginians and Carolinians virtually smashed
       Cherokee resistance for years and awed other tribes.

3230. Osborn, George C. "Relations with the Indians in West Florida
       During the Administration of Governor Peter Chester." FLA
       HIST Q, 31 (1953), 239-272.

       At Pensacola, Chester dealt skillfully with Indians, com-
       merce, land policies, the American invasion at Natchez, and
       the Spanish conquest of East Florida.

3231. Parker, Arthur C. RED JACKET: LAST OF THE SENECAS. New York:
       McGraw Hill, 1952.

       This is a scholarly and readable account of the famous
       Seneca chief by a noted authority of Indian lore. It is a
       lively and perceptive treatment that carries the story to the
       1830s.

3232. Pastore, Ralph T. "Congress and the Northern Department."
       NIAG FRONT, 20 (1973), 80-95.

       Here is a worthwhile summary of how the Board of Commissions
       for Indian Affairs of the Continental Congress handled the
       Iroquois Confederacy.

3233. Rea, Robert R. "Redcoats and Redskins on the Lower Missis-
       sippi, 1763-1776, The Career of Lt. John Thomas." LA HIST,
       11 (1970), 5-36.

       Thomas served at Fort Bute and Fort Pammure at the Iberville-
       Mississippi River junction where relations with the Spanish and
       Indians were tense.

3234. Rogers, T.L. "Simon Girty and Some of His Contemporaries."
       W PA HIST MAG, 8 (1925), 140-158.

       This biographical sketch is adequate for high school use.

3235. Rossie, Jonathan G. "The Northern Indian Department and the
       American Revolution." NIAG FRONT, 20 (1973), 52-65.

       The stress here is on the British links to their Indian
       allies in New York, particularly the Johnson family, Sir Guy
       Carleton, and the massacres at Wyoming Valley and Cherry
       Valley.

3236. Russell, Nelson Vance. "The Indian Policy of Henry Hamilton:
       A Reevaluation." CAN HIST REV, 11 (1930), 20-37.

       The Lieutenant-Governor of Detroit should not be censured
       for being a "hair-buyer" for there is no evidence that he
       paid for scalps or instigated Indian raids.

3237. Sahli, John R. "The Growth of British Influence Among the
       Senecas to 1768." W PA HIST MAG, 49 (1965), 127-139.

       Due to possession of Fort Niagara, Sir William Johnson and
       other British Indian agents rapidly supplanted the former
       French influence.

3238. Scott, John A. "Joseph Brant at Fort Stanwix and Oriskany."
       NY HIST, 19 (1938), 399-406.

       Scott explains the Indian leader's alleged failure to cap-
       ture Fort Stanwix for the British.

3239. Sheehan, Bernard W. "Ignoble Savagism and the American Revo-
       lution." In Larry R. Gerlach, ed. LEGACIES OF THE AMERI-
       CAN REVOLUTION, n.p.: Utah State University, 1978, pp. 151-
       181.

       The Revolution caused a major defeat of Indian tribes and
       led to their disintegration as they became more dependent on
       whites.

3240. Sosin, Jack M. "The British Indian Department and Dunmore's
       War." VA MHB, 74 (1966), 34-50.

       Due to quarrels over land, the Indians and Virginians raided
       each other's settlements; the result was the ejection of the
       Shawnee and Delaware to the Ohio River while the British kept
       other tribes neutral.

3241. ————. "The Use of Indians in the War of the American Revo-
       lution." CAN HIST REV, 46 (1965), 101-121.

       Massachusetts Whigs and Carolina Loyalists were inclined to
       use Indian allies, as did British General Gage; but Carleton
       and Stuart were cautious and gave the Yankees two years of
       border peace.

3242. Stanley, George G. "The Six Nations and the American Revolu-
       tion." ONT HIST, 56 (1956), 217-232.

       Holding a buffer zone between competing colonial powers, the
       Iroquois were forced to fight the Yankees; later they re-
       ceived new land grants from the British in Canada.

3243. Stone, William L. LIFE OF JOSEPH BRANT. 2 vols. 1878. Re-
       print. New York: Kraus Reprint Co., 1969.

       This is an awkward, rambly narrative that is somewhat better
       concerning battles in which British troops were not involved.
       While not a detailed study of Brant and his family's influence
       with the Iroquois, the volume contains now-lost documents and
       interviews with survivors from the Indian wars in New York.
       The material on frontier warfare and the Sullivan expedition
       is useful.

3244. Wallace, Arthur F.C. THE DEATH AND REBIRTH OF THE SENECA.
       New York: Alfred A. Knopf, 1970.

       This is a rare and successful blend of history and anthro-
       pology that makes fascinating reading. It shows how Seneca
       leaders like Handsome Lake managed to revive the dignity of
       their tribe which had been battered by the Revolution.

3245. Weeks, Philip. "Genocide in Ohio. Gnadenhutten, 1782."
       WASSAJA THE IND HIST, 13 (1980), 32-33.

       The Pennsylvania militia butchered 100 peaceful Delaware
       Indians.

3246. Whitaker, Arthur Preston. "Alexander McGillivray." NC HIST
       REV, 5 (1928), 181-203, 289-309.

       Here is a fine sketch of the Tory half-breed leader of the
       Creeks who terrorized the Georgia-Carolina borderlands, and
       who negotiated successfully with the Spanish after 1783.

3247. Young, Henry J. "A Note on Scalp Bounties in Pennsylvania."
       PA HIST, 24 (1957), 207-218.

       The Pennsylvania government offered bounties for Indian
       scalps in 1756, 1760 and 1780 which were paid from the public
       treasury.

                          G. THE BLACKS

3248. Akers, Charles W. "Our Modern Egyptians: Phillis Wheatley
       and the Whig Campaign Against Slavery in Revolutionary
       Boston." J NEGRO HIST, 60 (1975), 397-410.

       Wheatley, a talented black poet and author, represents a
       landmark in the emergence of a black American literature and
       a symbol of the anti-slavery movement in Massachusetts.

3249. Babuscio, Jack. "Crevecoeur in Charlestown: The Negro in
       the Cage." J HIST STUD, 2 (1967), 283-286.

       Crevecoeur was stunned at the sight of a condemned black
       who was pecked to death by birds.

3250. Berlin, Ira. "The Revolution in Black Life." See
       3335, pp. 351-382.

       The revolutionary era was characterized by an abolition
       movement, many manumissions in the south, naturalization of
       native-born Afro-Americans, and a short-lived flexibility in
       white racial attitudes. This article has an excellent
       bibliography.

3251. Bruns, Roger. "Anthony Benezet's Assertion of Negro Equality."
       J NEGRO HIST, 56 (1971), 230-238.

       A Quaker schoolmaster, a leading anti-slavery figure, claimed
       that blacks were biologically, morally, and intellectually
       equal to whites.

3252. Cantor, Milton. "The Image of the Negro in Colonial Litera-
       ture." NEQ, 36 (1963), 452-477.

       Pro-slavery and anti-slavery arguments were well established
       in poetry, prose, and pamphlets by 1775.

3253. Carpenter, Joseph. "The Bicentennial and the Black Revolu-
       tion: Is It a Myth or a Reality?" NEGRO HIST BULL, 39
       (1976), 496-499.

       The author claims that George Washington and Thomas
       Jefferson "were racist slaveowners who fathered black slave
       children."

3254. Cohen, William. "Thomas Jefferson and the Problem of Slavery."
       JAH, 56 (1969), 503-526.

       Jefferson owned 180 slaves, 10,000 acres and considered
       blacks as "innately inferior."

3255. Conforti, Joseph. "Samuel Hopkins and the Revolutionary
       Antislavery Movement." RI HIST, 58 (1979), 39-49.

       The pastor of the First Congregationalist Church in Newport
       was a leading advocate of anti-slavery reform.

3256. Crowe, Jeffrey J. "Slave Rebelliousness and Social Conflict
       in North Carolina, 1775-1802." WMQ, 37 (1980), 79-102.

       This is an excellent summary about the blacks' quest for
       freedom and their efforts to oppose slaveholders in a state
       ravaged by war.

486   THE IMPACT OF WAR ON SOCIETY

3257. Davis, David Brian. THE PROBLEM OF SLAVERY IN THE AGE OF
       REVOLUTION: 1770-1783. Ithaca, New York: Cornell University
       Press, 1975.

       The long and detailed account here and the cumbersome prose
       are relatively minor flaws in one of the most scholarly and
       absorbing accounts of the topic. Davis has clearly mastered
       an enormous amount of source material, and he navigates deftly
       through the complex factors that determined public opinion
       about slavery. The best part of the book is how slavery was
       viewed in the Anglo-American judicial systems and how influ-
       ential were the early abolitionists. The analysis of atti-
       tudes, local cases, social conditions and a variety of other
       related topics is skillfully handled. This is a remarkable
       and provocative work that deserves the acclaim that it has
       received.

3258. Diggins, John P. "Slavery, Race, and Equality: Jefferson and
       the Pathos of the Enlightenment." AMER Q, 26 (1976), 206-
       228.

       This is a good review essay of how four prominent historians
       have probed Jefferson's writing on the question of slavery.

3259. Dobbs, John Wesley. "Crispus Attucks: One of America's First
       and Noblest Heroes." NEGRO HIST BULL, 34 (1971), 55-56.

       Attucks, a Bostonian freedman, was killed in the "Boston
       Massacre."

3260. Donnan, Elizabeth. "The New England Slave Trade After the
       Revolution." NEQ, 3 (1930), 251-278.

       Massachusetts and Rhode Island vessels were active to 1808
       in shipping blacks, mainly to Charleston.

3261. ———. "The Slave Trade in South Carolina Before the Revolu-
       tion." AHR, 33 (1938), 804-833.

       This is a fine article about the importance to Charlestonian
       merchants and shippers of the slave trade with the Gold Coast.

3262. Foster, Joseph. "Prince Whipple of Portsmouth, a Colored
       Veteran of the American Revolution." GRANITE MONTHLY, 40
       (1908), 287-288.

       A slave of General William Whipple, Prince fought the British
       at Saratoga, Newport, and was freed by his master at Yorktown.

3263. Franklin, John Hope. "The North, the South and the American
       Revolution." JAH, 62 (1975), 5-23.

       Here is a fine account of how early nineteenth-century south-
       ern historians, preparing to defend the institution of slavery,
       interpreted the Revolution.

3264. Freehling, William W. "The Founding Fathers and Slavery."
       AHR, 77 (1972), 81-93.

       The author explores the ideological opposition to slavery,
       and the ambiguities of anti-slavery thought.

3265. Frey, Sylvia R. "The British and the Black: A New Perspective."
       HISTORIAN, 38 (1976), 225-238.

       This is a key article about the problems of using black
       labor, arming slaves, and about racial prejudice in the British
       military.

3266. Greene, Jack P. "Slavery or Independence: Some Reflections
       on the Relationship Among Liberty, Black Bondage, and
       Equality in Revolutionary South Carolina." SC HIST MAG,
       80 (1979), 193-214.

       A leading colonial historian explores the paradox of slavery
       within the context of liberty and independence.

3267. Hammond, Isaac W. "Slavery in New Hampshire." MAG AMER HIST,
       21 (1889), 62-65.

       Here is a replica of a petition for freedom drafted by
       nine black slaves in 1777.

3268. Haywood, C. Robert. "Mercantilism and Colonial Slave Labor,
       1700-1763." JSH, 23 (1937), 454-469.

       The necessity to maintain the close link between slavery
       and the production of staple commodities ended abolition
       arguments in the south.

3269. Higginbotham, Don and William S. Price, Jr. "Was It Murder
       for a White Man to Kill a Slave? Chief Justin Martin Howard
       Condemns the Peculiar Institution in North Carolina." WMQ,
       36 (1976), 593-601.

       A key case in 1771 led to laws making it a crime for a white
       to kill a Negro.

3270. Ireland, Owen. "Germans Against Abolition: A Minority View
       of Slavery in Pennsylvania." J INTERDIS HIST, 3 (1973),
       685-706.

       Luthern and Reformed Germans opposed abolition due to reli-
       gious reasons and fears of social change.

3271. Jordan, Winthrop. WHITE OVER BLACK: AMERICAN ATTITUDES TOWARD
       THE NEGRO, 1550-1812. Chapel Hill: University of North
       Carolina Press, 1968.

       This significant study is indispensable for an understanding
       of race relations in America. The author provides a detailed

coverage about the status of slavery in the colonies through
virtually all-encompassing chapters. Though critics have
faulted the author for conceptual or methodological flaws,
this is a sensitive, thoughtful work about the origins of an
acute color consciousness in the new republic. Jordan explains
that slavery was much more than economic exploitation - it
was a systematic psychological debasement of Negroes. The
material on Jefferson's views, the slave codes, restraints on
freed blacks, and attitudes about racial mixtures is fascinating. This may be one of the best books on early race
relations in the United States.

3272. Kaplan, Sidney. "The 'Domestic Insurrection' of the Declara-
       tion of Independence." J NEGRO HIST, 61 (1976), 243-255.

       Questioning why the document omitted references to slavery,
       the author claims that 'domestic insurrections' were not linked
       to slave revolts.

3273. Kobrin, David. THE BLACK MINORITY IN EARLY NEW YORK. Albany,
       New York: Office of State History, New York State Education
       Department, 1971.

       This is a brief assessment about white attitudes to blacks
       in the state, and about the legislation regarding slavery
       and manumission. New York had the largest black population
       of the northern states.

3274. Logan, Gwendolyn Evans. "The Slave in Connecticut During the
       American Revolution." CONN HIST SOC BULL, 30 (1965), 73-
       80.

       In a weak essay, the author notes that in 1775 the state
       had over 6,400 blacks out of New England's total of 16,000,
       but it is unclear how many served in the armed forces or how
       many received freedom.

3275. Lovejoy, David S. "Samuel Hopkins: Religion, Slavery and the
       Revolution." NEQ, 40 (1947), 227-243.

       A minister of Massachusetts and Rhode Island vigorously
       opposed slavery due to religious convictions and to the Decla-
       ration of Independence.

3276. McManus, Edgar J. "Anti-Slavery Legislation in New York."
       J NEGRO HIST, 46 (1961), 207-216.

       A convention in 1777 urged abolition, and by 1785 most
       legislators favored some form of emancipation.

3277. MacLeod, Duncan J. SLAVERY, RACE, AND THE AMERICAN REVOLU-
       TION. London: Cambridge University Press, 1974.

       This is a compact, well-written synthesis of the problem.
       It shows the divergence of revolutionary political theory

about the treatment of blacks along with a glimpse of the
slave system. The author examines the heated discussions on
the subject, the conflict of values, and the ambivalence about
slavery in the Revolution that was transformed into a positive
commitment. In the post-war era, all slave states soon
adapted stringent laws against freed Negroes and caused
Americans to view revolutionary ideology exclusive of a
serious consideration of slaves or freedmen, and to reinforce
that concept with racism.

3278. MacMaster, Richard K. "Anti-Slavery and the American Revolu-
        tion." HIST TODAY, 21 (1971), 715-723.

        Quakers and clergymen led the struggle for abolition during
        the Revolution.

3279. ———. "Arthur Lee's Address on Slavery: An Aspect of
        Virginia's Struggle to End the Slave Trade, 1765-1774."
        VA MHB, 80 (1972), 141-157.

        Lee claimed that slavery was indefensible and hurt white
        society.

3280. Miller, William. "The Effect of the American Revolution on
        Indentured Servitude." PA HIST, 7 (1940), 131-141.

        The war did not relax the (white) indenture system except
        to halt immigration and to require servants for military duty.

3281. Morgan, Edmund S. "Slavery and Freedom: The American Paradox."
        JAH, 59 (1972), 5-29.

        The Revolution made slavery a paradox in a supposedly free
        society, especially in Virginia where slavery actually
        nourished a white representative government.

3282. Mullin, Michael. "British Caribbean and North American Slaves
        in an Era of War and Revolution, 1775-1807." See
        1913, pp. 232-267.

        In a comparative hemispheric perspective, the author probes
        two types of slave rebellions and attributes differences to
        acculturation rates, African ethnicity, urbanization, and the
        type of plantation management.

3283. Nash, Gary B. "Slaves and Slaveowners in Colonial Philadel-
        phia." WMQ, 30 (1973), 223-226.

        Philadelphians, including Quakers, avidly sought slave
        labor for manpower until more white indentured servants came
        to the colony.

3284. O'Brien, William. "Did the Jennison Case Outlaw Slavery in
        Massachusetts." WMQ, 17 (1960), 219-241.

The state's supreme Judicial Court, sometime in 1780 or
1781, held slavery to be unconstitutional.

3285. Okoye, F. Nwabueze. "Chattel Slavery as the Nightmare of the
       American Revolution." WMQ, 37 (1980), 5-28.

       This is a study of contemporary literature that shows the
       ambivalent views about racial prejudice and the typical
       fear of whites concerning equality with blacks.

3286. Pingeon, Frances D. "Slavery in New Jersey On the Eve of
       Revolution." NEW JERSEY IN THE AMERICAN REVOLUTION. Trenton:
       New Jersey Historical Commission, 1970, pp. 48-65.

       The author inquires why the state maintained slavery after
       New York and Pennsylvania had abolished it and why blacks
       were prohibited from serving in the army or militia.

3287. Porter, Dorothy Burnett. "Early Negro Writings: A Bibliog-
       raphical Study." BIB SOC AMER PAP, 39 (1945), 192-268.

       Here is a useful list of black literature that appeared
       from 1760 with data about leading black authors.

3288. Quarles, Benjamin. "Lord Dunmore as Liberator." WMQ, 15
       (1958), 494-507.

       Over 800 slaves in the Virginia area joined the Loyalist
       forces under Dunmore in 1775-76.

3289. Robert Wesley A. "The Black Experience and the American
       Revolution." FIDES ET HISTORY, 8 (1976), 50-62.

       Based on secondary sources, this article shows how both
       the American and British capitalized on the desires of Ameri-
       can blacks for freedom.

3290. Rose, Willie Lee. "The Impact of the American Revolution on
       the Black Population." See 3239, pp. 183-187.

       This is a rambling essay, with little documentation, that
       states how the war effected slavery in the early Republic.

3291. Schwarz, Philip J. "Clark T. Moorman, Quaker Emancipator."
       QUAKER HIST, 69 (1980), 27-33.

       In 1782, a Virginia farmer freed two slaves that he had
       inherited.

3292. Sheeler, J. Reuben. "The Negro on the Virginia Frontier."
       J NEGRO HIST, 43 (1958), 279-297.

       This is a confusing essay which suggests that blacks were
       rarely found in frontier areas.

3293. Sheridan, Richard B. "The Crisis of Slave Subsistence in the
       British West Indies During and After the American Revolu-
       tion." WMQ, 33 (1976), 615-641.

       Due to the curtailment of foodstuffs from the north, high
       prices for basic commodities, diseases, and hurricanes, the
       slaves suffered severely.

3294. ————. "The Jamaican Slave Insurrection Scare of 1776 and
       the American Revolution." J NEGRO HIST, 61 (1976), 290-308.

       Like similar slave revolts of the era, this uprising was
       partially inspired by revolutionary ideology.

3295. Spector, Robert M. "The Quock Walker Case (1781-83) –
       Slavery, Its Abolition, and Negro Citizenship in Early
       Massachusetts." J NEGRO HIST, 53 (1968), 12-32.

       In the most famous case of its kind before the Dred Scott
       decision, the author argues that it was a series of court
       decisions which created a "common law" of abolition rather
       than a departure from legal tradition.

3296. Thompson, J. Earl, Jr. "Slavery and Presbyterianism in the
       Revolutionary Era." J PRESBY HIST, 54 (1976), 121-141.

       The views of seven Presbyterian leaders are reviewed here
       to demonstrate the dichotomy of attitudes towards blacks and
       the stress on gradualism concerning manumission.

3297. Watson, Alan D. "Impulse Toward Independence: Resistance
       and Rebellion among North Carolina Slaves, 1770-1775."
       J NEGRO HIST, 63 (1978), 317-328.

       This is a good summary of black hopes for emancipation on
       the eve of the Revolution.

3298. Wax, Darold D. "Georgia and the Negro Before the American
       Revolution." GA HIST Q, 51 (1967), 63-77.

       For economic reasons in a basically plantation economy,
       the earlier ban on slavery was repealed in 1750, and slavery
       became institutionalized.

3299. ————. "Reform and Revolution: The Movement Against Slavery
       and the Slave Trade in Revolutionary Pennsylvania." WEST
       PA HIST MAG, 57 (1974), 403-429.

       Pennsylvania, under the influence of the Society of Friends,
       led the states in the anti-slavery movement.

3300. ————. "The Demand for Slave Labor in Colonial Pennsylvania."
       PA HIST, 34 (1967), 331-345.

In a highly diversified economy with much European immigration, whites tended to prefer white labor, although blacks
were used on farms, foundries, and shipyards.

3301. Wood, Peter H. "'Taking Care of Business' in Revolutionary
      South Carolina: Republicans and the Slave Society." See
      1913, pp. 268-293.

      The paradox about how the whites fought the war while the
      slaves toiled is traced in this thoughtful essay.

3302. Wright, J. Leitch, Jr. "Blacks in British East Florida."
      FLA HIST Q, 54 (1976), 425-442.

      Blacks outnumbered whites here in the 1763-84 era by two
      to one, or in greater numbers than the other southern colonies.

3303. Zilversmit, Arthur. "Quock Walker, Mumbet, and the Abolition
      of Slavery in Massachusetts." WMQ, 25 (1968), 614-24.

      This is a key article about the famous case (1780) in which
      the author clarifies the ambiguity of the matter by stressing
      that the jury did not decide that a slave was a free man or
      that slavery was in conflict with the Massachusetts con-
      stitution.

                          H. CLASS TENSIONS

3304. Alexander, John K. "Urban America in the Revolutionary Era:
      Studies in the Neglected Period of American Urban History."
      J URBAN HIST, 5 (1979), 241-254.

      This is a solid review article that covers recent works
      about the importance of the city by Stephen E. Lucas, Edward
      C. Papenfuse, Charles S. Olton, and Philip S. Foner.

3305. Ashton, Richard J. "Fathers, Sons, and Displaced Persons in
      the American Revolution." REV AMER HIST, 6 (1978), 203-208.

      Here is a perceptive comparison of books by Allen S. Everest
      and Kenneth S. Lynn.

3306. Cary, John. "Statistical Method and the Brown Thesis on
      Colonial Democracy, With a Rebuttal by Robert E. Brown."
      WMQ, 20 (1963), 251-276.

      Cary challenges the thesis that pre-war Massachusetts had
      a high degree of democracy, because of limited samples from
      tax and voting records; Brown claims that his statistical
      evidence is adequate.

3307. Crary, Catherine S. "The American Dream: John Tabor Kempe's
      Rise from Poverty to Riches." WMQ, 14 (1957), 176-195.

A prominent New York Tory jurist had acquired over 160,000 acres of land in ten years but only recovered ten per cent of the value in compensation from the Crown after the war.

3308. ————. "The Humble Immigrant and the American Dream: Some Case Histories, 1746-1775." MVHR, 46 (1959), 46-68.

After studying thirty case histories of Tories who appealed to the Crown for compensation, the author concludes that opportunities for pre-war self-advancement were abundant.

3309. Cullen, Joseph P. "Indentured Servants." AMER HIST ILLUS, 2 (1) (1967), 32-38.

This is a good summary of the service, duties, and terms of indentured laborers.

3310. DePauw, Linda Grant. "Politicizing the Politically Intent. The Problem of Leadership in the American Revolution." See 1799, pp. 3-26.

In an essay heavy on theory and weak with examples, the author denegrates the impact of ideas and rhetoric on the Revolution and claims colonists joined the war due to hardships and for opportunities in local politics.

3311. Foner, Philip Sheldon. LABOR AND THE AMERICAN REVOLUTION. Westport, Connecticut: Greenwood Press, 1977.

In a thoroughly researched monograph, Foner claims that mechanics, artisans, laborers, and seamen played a vital revolutionary role in this pre-industrial era. Stressing a class conflict view in shaping historical developments, Foner comments at length on the traditional restrictions on the white labor force and on the disparity of incomes. Many of the working class were represented in the Sons and Daughters of Liberty. This is a provocative study with a full bibliography and citations.

3312. Harrower, John. "Diary of John Harrower, 1773-76." AHR, 6 (1900), 65-107.

A Scot indentured servant left a unique account of life and toil in Virginia.

3313. Hoffman, Ronald. "The Disaffected in the Revolutionary South." See 3335, pp. 275-316.

A ferocious internal political struggle occurred in the wartime south against the Whigs who hung on tenuously through a civil war.

3314. Jensen, Merrill. "Democracy and the American Revolution."
        HUNT LIB Q, 20 (1956-57), 321-341.

        Though not democratic in origin, the Revolution was demo-
        cratic in results.

3315. ————. "The American People and the American Revolution."
        JAH, 57 (1970), 5-35.

        Jensen offers an evaluation of the "new left" history by
        noting that the lower classes were generally involved in
        every aspect of the war, and that the Revolution was "a
        people's revolution."

3316. Kim, Sung Bok. "A New Look at the Great Landlords of Eight-
        eenth-Century New York." WMQ, 37 (1940), 581-614.

        The pre-war landlords (Beekmans, Van Cortlands) were not
        manorial types and possessed few feudal powers.

3317. Kulikoff, Allan. "The Progress of Inequality in Revolutionary
        Boston." WMQ, 28 (1971), 375-412.

        This is a key article that demonstrates how the deference
        of the lower class to the elite continued after the war even
        with increased degrees of economic inequality.

3318. Lemisch, Jesse. "Jack Tar in the Streets: Merchant Seamen
        in the Politics of Revolutionary America." WMQ, 25 (1968),
        371-407.

        Here is an excellent view of the harsh labor conditions for
        seamen which frequently led to riots.

3319. ————, and Alexander, John K. "The White Oaks, Jack Tar,
        and the Concept of the 'Inarticulate'." WMQ, 29 (1972),
        108-142.

        The authors respond to critics about the degree of violence
        used by seamen and ships' carpenters as well as the word
        'inarticulate.'

3320. Lemon, James T., and Nash, Gary B. "The Distribution of
        Wealth in Eighteenth Century America: A Century of Change
        in Chester County, Pennsylvania, 1693-1802." J SOC HIST,
        2 (1968), 1-24.

        Studying poll tax records to examine a microcosm of America,
        the authors suggest an increasing degree of stratification in
        a comparatively open society; they also are dubious of exces-
        sive reliance on quantitative data acquired from tax and
        property rolls.

3321. Main, Jackson Turner. "Social Origins of the Political Elite:
       the Upper House of the Revolutionary Era." HUNT LIB Q, 27
       (1964), 147-158.

       In contrast to the membership of the colonial councils, the
       new wartime state senates were composed of newcomers, often
       self-made men.

3322. ————. THE SOCIAL STRUCTURE OF REVOLUTIONARY AMERICA.
       Princeton: Princeton University Press, 1965.

       This is a seminal work about wealth, power, prestige, oc-
       cupations, income levels, and land holding in the era. It
       is a valuable introduction to an understanding of eighteenth-
       century class structure. The commentaries about the charac-
       teristics of certain groups and the information compiled from
       court records, tax lists, and newspapers are impressive.
       Generally, Main concludes that the legislatures were dominated
       by wealthy classes.

3323. Marshall, Peter. "Radicals, Conservatives, and the American
       Revolution." PAST AND PRESENT, 23 (1962), 44-56.

       In a very fine summary of recent interpretations, the author
       claims that historians still lack adequate data about the
       extent of change in America's social structure, 1760-90.

3324. Martin, James Kirby. "Men of Family Wealth and Personal
       Merit: The Changing Social Bases of Executive Leadership
       Selection in the American Revolution." SOCIETAS: REV SOC
       HIST, 2 (1972), 43-70.

       Men of ambition, who were not wealthy by inheritance,
       entered wartime politics with the exception of Maryland where
       politics remained dominated by the well-to-do.

3325. Morris, Richard B. "Class Struggle and the American Revolu-
       tion." WMQ, 19 (1962), 3-29.

       In a key essay, Morris reviews the opinions of leading
       historians and doubts that the Revolution - even with its
       egalitarian and democratic impulses - was a class war.
       This is a useful summary of the dual nature of the Revolution.

3326. Nash, Gary B. "Social Change and the Growth of Pre-Revolu-
       tionary Urban Radicalism." See 3335, pp. 5-36.

       Deploring an ideological emphasis, Nash sees growing class
       antagonisms in the cities before 1775 as statistically demon-
       strated in this fine analysis.

3327. ————. "The Transformation of Urban Politics, 1700-1765."
       JAH, 60 (1973), 605-32.

Nash concentrates on the north to demonstrate that a
transformation of the political milieu was underway by 1765
which had Revolutionary overtones.

3328.   ———. THE URBAN CRUCIBLE: SOCIAL CHANGE, POLITICAL CON-
SCIOUSNESS AND THE ORIGINS OF THE AMERICAN REVOLUTION.
Cambridge, Massachusetts: Harvard University Press, 1979.

This is a ground-breaking study of laboring classes in
northern port cities. Here is a fresh portrait of a developing
class consciousness in a weakened economy which created increasing degrees of social divisions based on the growing
impoverishment of the poor. Impressively researched, finely
crafted, gracefully written, and bulging with examples of
provocative thoughts about pre-war society, this book demonstrates that cities were the cutting edge of change.

3329.   ———. "Urban Wealth and Poverty in Pre-Revolutionary
America." J INTERDISP HIST, 6 (1976), 545-584.

Examining this problem in three northern cities, Nash concludes that the changing economic-social structure eroded
traditional allegiances by urban dwellers.

3330.   Rhys, Isaac. "Preachers and Patriots: Popular Culture and
the Revolution in Virginia." See 3335, pp. 127-156.

Here is a unique study about the clash of the evangelical
movement clashing with gentry life styles, stressing importance
of the church, courthouse, the militia and the folk culture
of the lower and elite classes.

3331.   Schlesinger, Arthur M. "The Aristocracy in Colonial America."
MASS HIST SOC PROC, 74 (1962), 3-21.

Unlike Europe, the American aristocracy was more open,
flexible, welcomed new blood, and it was not resented by common folk.

3332.   Schutz, Stanley K. "The Growth of Urban America in War and
Peace, 1740-1810" See 1799, pp. 123-148.

Cities in America provided the leadership for the Revolution, and the war caused innumerable changes in population,
social inequality, and the end of closed corporative urban
politics.

3333.   Simmons, R.C. "Class Ideology and the Revolutionary War."
HISTORY, 62 (1977), 62-70.

The author is very critical of ten recent books about the
impact of the war on class consciousness, noting the lack of
synthesis.

3334. Weir, Robert M. "Who Shall Rule at Home: The American Revo-
       lution as a Crisis of Legitimacy for the Colonial Elite."
       J INTERDISC HIST, 6 (1976), 679-700.

       Stressing the essential validity of the Becker thesis, Weir
       concentrates on South Carolina where the question of who
       should rule at home was related to emotional issues, and the
       rise of indigenous political leaders.

3335. Young, Alfred F., ed. THE AMERICAN REVOLUTION: EXPLORATIONS
       IN THE HISTORY OF AMERICAN RADICALISM. Dekalb, Illinois:
       Northern Illinois University Press, 1976.

       This is a major collection of essays stressing social class,
       and the role of commoners in shaping events. It explores radi-
       cal movements, groups "at the bottom" of society, and the
       responses of elites to these challenges. The best articles
       are cited elsewhere in this bibliography.

                              I. CROWD BEHAVIOR

3336. Alexander, John K. "The Fort Wilson Incident of 1779; A Case
       Study of the Revolutionary Crowd." WMQ, 31 (1974), 589-612.

       Alexander questions if "mob" is the correct term for the
       frustrated militia and townsmen who rioted at the home of
       conservative lawyer James Wilson of Philadelphia over Toryism
       and price controls.

3337. Brown, Richard Maxwell. "Violence and the American Revolu-
       tion." See 19, pp. 81-120.

       This is a fine summary of the numerous urban riots in the
       pre-war colonies with a good synthesis of recent literature
       on the "mob."

3338. Cecil, Robert. "Oligarchy and Mob-Rule in the American Revo-
       lution." HIST TODAY, 13 (1963), 197-204.

       Mobs were the "sinews" and committees led by Samuel Adams
       were the "nerves" in creating anti-British sentiments.

3339. Crackel, Theodore, and Martin Andresen. "Fort William and
       Mary: A Case Study in Crowd Behavior." HIST NH, 29 (1974),
       203-228.

       Community leaders from Durham and elsewhere were active in
       the attack to secure gunpowder (December 14-15, 1774).

3340. Countryman, Edward. "The Problem of the Early American Crowd."
       J AMER STUD, & (1973), 77-90.

       The writer notes the significant differences about rioting
       by area, circumstances, causes, and class composition in an
       essay that suggests that more sophisticated essays on this
       topic are needed.

3341. Dorman, James H. "Collective Behavior in the American Popular
       Resistance, 1766-1775: A Theoretical Prospectus." HISTORIAN,
       42 (1979), 1-17.

       Dorman urges better analytical precision in dealing with
       episodes of collective behavior.

3342. Hoerder, Dirk. "Boston Leaders and Boston Crowds, 1765-1775."
       See 3335, pp. 235-271.

       Showing a long tradition of crowd action, Hoerder notes that
       the nature of the crowd changed due to the Stamp Act, to
       symbolic rituals, and the wealthy as a target.

3343. ————. CROWD ACTION IN REVOLUTIONARY MASSACHUSETTS, 1765-
       1780. New York: Academic Press, 1977.

       Though there is little data here on mob activity outside of
       Boston, and the 1775-80 period is imperfectly covered, never-
       theless this is a key book on the subject. The author demon-
       strates how important fundamental social, economic, and poli-
       tical issues were to commoners, how the fragmented mobs be-
       came institutionalized as a propaganda vehicle by fiery Whigs
       who lost control of the process of urban upheaval. Local
       issues tended to become imperial issues, and new leaders
       emerged with fresh ideological themes. This is an exhaustive
       piece of research that merits careful reading.

3344. Hutson, James H. "An Investigation of the Inarticulate:
       Philadelphia's White Oaks." WMQ, 28 (1971), 3-25.

       Here the ship carpenters supported Franklin, law and order,
       and like other artisans, had few ideological links with farmers.

3345. Longley, R.S. "Mob Activities in Revolutionary Massachusetts."
       NEQ, 6 (1933), 98-130.

       In this narrative, the author notes mobs were traditional
       in Britain and were used by James Otis and Sam Adams to their
       advantage in Boston.

3346. Lynd, Staughton. "The Tenant Rising at Livingston Manor,
       May 1777." NY HIST SOC Q, 48 (1964), 163-177.

       Hoping for British aid, 500 tenants rebelled in a riot that
       was crushed but one that symbolized the erosion of the
       Livingston's power.

3347. ————. "Who Should Rule at Home: Duchess County, NY in the
       American Revolution." WMQ, 18 (1961), 330-359.

       In a hierarchial social order, the sale and title confirma-
       tion of Tory lands marked a major break-through for the lower
       classes and the end of "feudal society" here.

3348. Maier, Pauline. "Popular Uprisings and Civil Authority in
      Eighteenty-Century America." WMQ, 27 (1970), 3-35.

      Mobs contributed to the concept that civil authority should
      be controlled by popular participation, mobs varied consider-
      ably in composition, and they were quite different from the mob
      violence of today.

3349. ————. "The Charleston Mob and the Evolution of Popular
      Politics in Revolutionary South Carolina, 1765-1784."
      PERSP AMER HIST, 4 (1970), 173-196.

      Not until the war did mobs act violently and then on Tories;
      soon, popular, organized politics returned to patrician control.

3350. Rudolph. Lloyd I. "The Eighteenth Century Mob in America
      and Europe." AMER Q, 11 (1959), 447-469.

      Mobs in America were less violent and pursued middle-class
      objectives compared to those in Britain and France.

3351. Schlesinger, Arthur M. "Political Mobs and the American
      Revolution, 1765-1776." AMER PHIL SOC PROC, 99 (1955), 244-
      250.

      Mob violence was highly instrumental in forming public
      opinion; some crowd actions were planned and some were
      spontaneous.

3352. Wood, Gordon S. "A Note on Mobs in the American Revolution."
      WMQ, 23 (1966), 635-642.

      Comparing mobs in France and North America, Wood claims
      that legal, political and social differences compared to
      Europe caused less social eruptions.

                    J.   RELIGIOUS FACTORS

3353. Akers, Charles W. "Religion and the American Revolution:
      Samuel Cooper and the Brattle Street Church." WMQ, 35
      (1978), 477-498.

      Cooper's sermons in his influential parish had many covenant
      theological references to revolutionary ideology.

3354. Bailyn, Bernard. "Religion and Revolution: Stephen Johnson."
      PERS AMER HIST, 4 (1970), 125-139, 144-169.

      Bailyn shows here how religious attitudes provided back-
      ground to political rhetoric. In the same issue are lengthy
      commentaries on Jonathan Mayhew (pp. 111-124, 140-143), and
      Andrew Eliot (pp. 87-110) which suggest how religion was both
      a stimulus and a deterrant to the Revolution.

3355. Baker, Robert A. "Baptists and the American Revolution."
       BAPT HIST HERITAGE, 11 (1976), 149-159.

       "God used the Baptists as a signal instrument in working at
       what may have been man's greatest step forward in all political
       history."

3356. Baldwin, Alice M. NEW ENGLAND CLERGY AND THE AMERICAN REVOLU-
       TION. Durham: Duke University Press, 1928.

       Baldwin carefully examines the studies of several major
       historians on this topic. The author perceives a direct line
       of descent from Puritan concepts to revolutionary rhetoric, all
       of which was discussed among the clergy by 1763. The dis-
       senting clergy, especially Congregationalists, were among
       the chief agitators of the Revolution. This is a solid study,
       well-written, and impressively documented with useful append-
       ices.

3357. ————. "Sowers of Sedition: The Political Theories of Some
       of the New Light Presbyterian Clergy of Virginia and North
       Carolina." WMQ, 5 (1948), 52-76.

       This clergy regarded their political rights as inalienable,
       God-given, and natural.

3358. Beardslee, John W., III. "The Dutch Reformed Church and the
       American Revolution." J PRESBY HIST, 76 (1954), 165-181.

       This church was wracked by controversy over Whig and Tory
       attitudes; amity emerged after the war when the church be-
       came involved in foreign missions.

3359. Blackwelder, Ruth. "The Attitude of the North Carolina
       Moravians Toward the American Revolution." NC HIST REV, 9
       (1932), 1-21.

       Some took the state oath, many petitioned for relief from
       war service or to pay for substitutes; generally the
       Moravians were friendly neutrals helping at Guilford Court
       House.

3360. Bockelman, Wayne L., and Ireland, Owen S. "The Internal
       Revolution in Pennsylvania: An Ethnic-Religious Interpre-
       tation." PA HIST, 41 (1974), 125-157.

       The authors note that the Quakers lost their dominance over
       the legislature by 1776, and that religious and ethnic con-
       flicts were more crucial issues than sectional and class dif-
       ferences.

3361. Boller, Paul F., Jr. "George Washington and Religious Liberty."
       WMQ, 17 (1960), 486-506.

Along with other Founding Fathers, Washington merits credit
for helping to establish liberty and freedom of conscience.

3362. Brock, Peter. "The Spiritual Pilgrimage of Thomas Watson:
       From British Soldier to American Friend." QUAKER HIST, 53
       (1965), 81-86.

       A British soldier deserted in 1778; he married and became
       a Quaker.

3363. Burnbaugh, Donald F. "Religion and Revolution: Options in
       1776." PA MENNON HERITAGE, 1 (1978), 2-9.

       This group attempted to remain neutral and claimed non-
       resistance as their creed; but some members were pro-British.

3364. Byrdon, G. MacLaren, ed. "'Passive Obedience Considered,' A
       Sermon by the Rev. David Griffiths before the Virginia Con-
       vention, December, 1775." HIST MAG PROT EPIS CHURCH, 44
       (1975), 78-93.

       The entire sermon of a future chaplain in the Continental
       army is reproduced here.

3365. Calhoon, Robert M. RELIGION AND THE AMERICAN REVOLUTION IN
       NORTH CAROLINA. Raleigh, North Carolina: Department of
       Cultural Resources. Division of Archives of History, 1976.

       This booklet contains a brisk and cogent summary of some
       ten major religious groups in the state. The material about
       religion and civil liberties and the sects' views on slavery
       is good.

3366. Cecil, Robert. "'Pulpit Incendiaries' in the American Colo-
       nies." HIST TODAY, 16 (1966), 773-780.

       The preachers' influence by 1775 was comparable to the press,
       especially in New England.

3367. Colburn, Dorothy. "No More Passive Obedience and Non-Resist-
       ance." HIST MAG PROT EPIS CHURCH, 46 (1977), 455-461.

       An Anglican clergyman of Delaware regarded his church more
       crucial than the patriotic cause.

3368. Conkin, Paul. "The Church Establishment in North Carolina,
       1765-1776." NC HIST REV, 32 (1955), 1-30.

       As seen in the religious provisions of the State Constitu-
       tion of 1776, liberalizing tendencies changed the powers of
       the established church.

3369. Currey, Cecil B. "Eighteenth-Century Evangelical Opposition
       to the American Revolution: The Case of the Quakers."
       FIDES ET HIST, 4 (1971), 17-35.

       This is a penetrating analysis of how the Society of Friends,
       due to their pacifism, were punished by both sides in the war.

3370. Daniel, Marjorie. "Anglicans and Dissenters in Georgia, 1758-
       1777." CHURCH HIST, 7 (1938), 247-262.

       Here is a convenient summary about ecclesiastical issues and
       grievances which typified part of the revolutionary argument.

3371. Elliott, Emory. "The Dove and the Serpent: The Clergy in the
       American Revolution." AMER Q, 31 (1979), 186-203.

       The old Puritan language stirred emotions and the clergy
       used a flexible, religious rhetoric against a new enemy.

3372. Erwin, S. "The Anglican Church in North Carolina." HIST
       MAG PROT EPIS CHURCH, 25 (1955), 102-161.

       This church declined due to a shortage of clergy, lack of
       bishops, indifference of royal officials, and the opposition
       of Nonconformists.

3373. ————. "The Established Church in Maryland." HIST MAG PROT
       EPIS CHURCH, 24 (1955), 232-292.

       Because of the dependence on Crown officialdom, the Anglican
       Church was badly shaken by the war.

3374. Fingard, Judith. "The Establishment of the First Colonial
       Episcopate." DALHOUSIE REV, 47 (1967), 475-491.

       The first Anglican episcopate in North America was estab-
       lished in 1787 to stem political unrest, to restore Angli-
       canism, and to end the split between American and English
       Anglican bishops.

3375. Fox, Dixon Ryan, ed. "Minutes of the Presbytery of New York,
       1775-1776." NY HIST, 50 (1969), Supplement, 22-34.

       The Presbyterian Church, strong in the Middle Colonies, drew
       middle class support and championed independence.

3376. Freeman, Stephen A. "Puritans in Rutland, Vermont, 1770-
       1818." VT HIST, 33 (1965), 342-347.

       A congregation, which split with the Congregational church
       in Connecticut, symbolized a break with traditional orthodoxy.

3377.   Gifford, Frank D.   "The Influence of the Clergy on American
        Politics from 1773 to 1776."   HIST MAG PROT EPIS CHURCH, 10
        (1941), 104-123.

        The pulpit was the major agency for disseminating Lockian
        ideas and concepts of natural law, especially in New England.

3378.   Gross, Leonard, ed.   "Mennonites and the Revolutionary Era."
        MENNON HIST BULL, 35 (1974), 3-11.

        Christian Funk of Pennsylvania was excommunicated by his
        church and formed a controversial sect called the "Funkites"
        which flourished as a pro-patriot group during the war.

3379.   ————, and Olle, Robert F., eds.   "Mennonites Before the
        Revolution."   MENN HIST BULL, 53 (1974), 1-7.

        Prior to the war, the Mennonites petitioned the Pennsylvania
        House of Assembly about their own refusal to serve in the
        militia.

3380.   Hanley, Thomas O.   "The Catholic and Anglican Gentry in
        Maryland Politics."   HIST MAG PROT EPIS CHURCH, 38 (1969),
        143-151.

        This is a weak article about the views of politicians like
        Daniel Dulaney and William Paca concerning the appointment of
        a bishop.

3381.   Hanley, Thomas O'Brien.   THE AMERICAN REVOLUTION AND RELIGION:
        MARYLAND, 1770-1800.   Washington, DC: The Catholic Univer-
        sity of America Press, 1971.

        The author claims that the Revolution brought an era of
        religious growth and a movement from "a confessional state"
        to the establishment of "a Christian state."   Though useful
        in examining the religious controversies in Maryland, this
        study has major weaknesses.   The author is unable to support
        his generalizations regarding the changing views of clerical
        groups; he is vague about the meaning of a "Christian-state;"
        and he neglects to provide adequate details about Catholic and
        Presbyterian attitudes toward slavery.

3382.   Harrison, Daniel W.   "The Significance of the American Revolu-
        tion in American History."   BAPTIST HIST HERITAGE, 11 (1976),
        130-148, 159.

        This is a very sweeping, but a convenient summary, of how
        the war affected the major denominations, suggesting why some
        churches declined while others grew.

3383.   Heimert, Alan.   RELIGION AND THE AMERICAN MIND FROM THE GREAT
        AWAKENING TO THE REVOLUTION.   Cambridge: Harvard University
        Press, 1966.

In a seminal work, the author calls for a drastic revision
of an important segment in American culture. He contends that
the democratic spirit originated not from Lockian concepts but
from the Great Awakening with Jonathan Edwards as the major
influence. Religious ideology paved the road to political
rhetoric about independence. Heimert apparently read all the
published sermons,and his erudition is obvious. Some 2,000
citations, a 100 page appendix make this a necessary study for
specialists.

3384. Heisky, John W., ed. and trans. "Extracts form the Diary of
       the Moravian Pastors of the Hebrown Church, Lebanon, 1755-
       1815." PA HIST, 34 (1967), 44-63.

       The diary mentions a Hessian occupation, rumors of French
       troops, Yorktown, and Lutherans.

3385. Hogue, William M. "The Religious Conspiracy Theory of the
       American Revolution: Anglican Motives." CHURCH HIST, 45
       (1976), 277-292.

       Non-Anglicans feared that the Church of England was part of
       a conspiracy to thwart their liberties, but such views were
       not strong enough to motivate revolutionary political attitudes.

3386. Holland, Lynwood M. "John Wesley and the American Revolution."
       J CHURCH STATE, 5 (1963), 197-213.

       The author examines Wesley's tracts to stress his political
       creed of loyalty to the Crown.

3387. Holmes, David L. "The Episcopal Church and the American Revo-
       lution." HIST MAG PROT EPIS CHURCH, 47 (1978), 261-291.

       Anglican clergy were "loyalists in direct proportion to the
       weakness of Anglicanism in their colony ...," especially in
       the south; the Church was the second largest in the colonies.

3388. Hood, Fred J. "Revolution and Religious Liberty: The Con-
       servation of the Theocratic Concept in Virginia." CHURCH
       HIST, 40 (1971), 170-181.

       Virginia Presbyterians viewed religious liberty as a reli-
       gious dogma, and the legal separation of church and state did
       not alter that belief.

3389. Ireland, Owen S. "The Ethnic-Religious Dimensions of Penn-
       sylvania Politics, 1778-1779." WMQ, 30 (1973), 425-448.

       This is a detailed analysis of legislative voting patterns
       by various religious denominations.

3390. James, Sydney V. "The Impact of the American Revolution On
       Quakers' Ideas About Their Sect." WMQ, 19 (1962), 360-382.

The war caused a probing of conscience about oaths and conscription, and it resulted in greater uniformity in the sect.

3391. Kramer, Leonard J. "Muskets in the Pulpit: 1776-1783." PRESBY HIST SOC J, 31 (1953), 229-244; 32 (1954), 37-51.

This is a vague article about the role of Presbyterians in Pennsylvania and the views of John Witherspoon in Congress.

3392. ―――. "Presbyterians Approach the American Revolution." PRESBY HIST SOC J, 31 (1953), 71-80, 167-180.

The strongest denomination in the Middle Colonies, the Presbyterians were heavily committed to the patriotic cause.

3393. Lehman, James O. "The Mennonites of Maryland During the Revolutionary War." MENNON Q REV, 50 (1976), 200-229.

The Mennonites wished to be neutral but contributed supplies for the army; nevertheless they were fined for their pacifist views.

3394. Lewis, Andrew W., ed. "Henry Muhlenberg's Georgia Correspondence." GA HIST Q, 49 (1965), 424-454.

The letters (1777-84) show constant strife in the Lutheran ranks due to theological arguments and the war.

3395. Leyburn, James G. "Presbyterian Immigrants and the American Revolution." J PRESBY HIST, 54 (1976), 9-32.

Presbyterians from Maine to Georgia remained in close contact during the war to create a unified church in 1789.

3396. MacMaster, Richard R. "Liberty or Property? The Methodist Petition for Emancipation in Virginia, 1785." METH HIST, 10 (1971), 44-55.

Methodist ministers carried petitions in their saddlebags (beginning in 1775) to free the slaves, but the Assembly took no legislative action.

3397. ―――. "Neither Whig nor Tory: The Peace Churches in the American Revolution." FIDES ET HIST, 9 (1977), 8-24.

Quakers, Mennonites, Brethern, Schwenkfelders, and Moravians tried to remain neutral but were penalized for their conscientious objections.

3398. McKeel, Arthur J. THE RELATION OF THE QUAKERS TO THE AMERICAN REVOLUTION. Washington, DC: The University Press of America, 1979.

This is a competent and well-researched study. Part of the book covers Quaker efforts to find a solution to tensions in politics and the trans-Atlantic links among the Society of Friends. The best portion of this work concerns the activities

and the persecution of Quakers. Some were neutral, some
Loyalist, and some fought on the American side. Though there
is little fresh information here, the study is a valuable
synthesis.

3399. McLemore, Richard A. "Tumult, Violence, Revolution, and
        Migration." BAPT HIST HERITAGE, 9 (1974), 230-236.

        Scattered in every colony, and a religious minority virtually
        everywhere, the Baptists generally came from the lower classes
        and had few dynamic leaders.

3400. McLoughlin, William C. "'Enthusiasm for Liberty': The Great
        Awakening as the Key to Revolution." AMER ANTIQ SOC PROC,
        87 (1977), 69-95.

        Pietistic religious fervour, with its emphasis on God's power
        and on individualism, provided the ideological impetus for re-
        bellion.

3401. ————. "Liberty of Conscience and Cultural Cohesion in the
        New Nation." See 19, pp. 197-255.

        This is a thoughtful review about the role of religion in
        the war, with imaginative commentaries on how the Revolution
        influenced religious liberty and equality.

3402. ————. "Mob Violence Against Dissent in Revolutionary
        Massachusetts." FOUNDATIONS, 14 (1971), 294-317.

        This well-documented essay demonstrates an example of
        bigotry by Congregationalists against Baptists in Pepperell,
        June 26, 1778.

3403. ————. "Patriotism and Pietism, the Dissenting Dilemma:
        Massachusetts Rural Baptists and the American Revolution."
        FOUNDATIONS, 19 (1976), 121-141.

        The author demonstrates that the Baptist quest for religious
        liberty was linked to the Congregationalist search for poli-
        tical liberty, and that the Baptists viewed imperial legisla-
        ture with alarm.

3404. Marietta, Jack D. "Wealth, War and Religion: The Perfecting of
        Quaker Ascetism, 1740-1783." CHURCH HIST, 43 (1974), 230-241.

        This is a fine essay about the treatment of Quakers during
        the war, and the thoughts of John Woolman and Anthony Benezet.

3405. Mead, Sidney E. "American Protestantism during the Revolu-
        tionary Epoch." CHURCH HIST, 22 (1953), 279-297.

        Here is a solid discussion of the difference between the
        rationalists and the sectarians in the era.

3406. Miller, Glenn. "Fear God and Honor the King: The Failure of
       Loyalist Civil Theology in the Revolutionary Crisis." HIST
       MAG PROT EPIS CHURCH, 47 (1978), 221-242.

       The failure of the Tory divines to provide a theological
       base to satisfy religious minorities may have been a factor
       in the British military defeat.

3407. ————. "The American Revolution as a Religious Event - An
       Essay in Political Theology." FOUNDATIONS, 19 (1976), 111-
       120.

       The primary role of the churches was to help win the war,
       and to participate in the maturation of American culture.

3408. Miller, Howard. "The Grammar of Liberty: Presbyterians and
       the First American Constitution." J PRESBY HIST, 54 (1976),
       142-164.

       Most Presbyterians shared fundamental constitutional beliefs.

3409. Miller, Rodney K. "The Influence of the Socio-Economic Status
       of the Anglican Clergy of Revolutionary Maryland on their
       Political Organization." HIST MAG PROT EPIS CHURCH, 47
       (1978), 197-210.

       This thoroughly documented essay about forty-four Anglican
       ministers concentrates on social and political pressures on
       their consciences and convictions.

3410. Mills, Frederick V. "Anglican Expansion in Colonial America,
       1761-1775." HIST MAG PROT EPIS CHURCH, 39 (1970), 315-324.

       The Anglican Church experienced a remarkable boom in church
       construction, clerical education, and ministerial enlistments.

3411. ————. "The Internal Anglican Controversy Over an American
       Episcopate, 1763-1775." HIST MAG PROT EPIS CHURCH, 44
       (1975), 257-276.

       Here is the paradox (after the Stamp Act) of Anglican op-
       position to bishops, a factor which varied considerably by
       area.

3412. Monk, Robert C. "Unity and Diversity Among Eighteenth Century
       Colonial Anglicans and Methodists." HIST MAG PROT EPIS
       CHURCH, 38 (1969), 51-67.

       The author classifies the nature of this disharmony which
       increased with the tension of revolutionary dialogues.

3413. Morgan, Daniel T., Jr. "The Great Awakening in North Carolina,
       1740-1775: The Baptist Phase." NC HIST REV, 45 (1968), 264-
       283.

Morgan comments on the impact of George Whitefield's
journeys in the south and the consequent splintering of Baptist
ranks.

3414. Morgan, Edmund S. "The Puritan Ethic and the American Revolution." WMQ, 24 (1967), 3-43.

This is a key article which traces the evolution of revolutionary ideology from the Puritan inheritance as shown in the
speeches of patriots and in the formation of capitalism.

3415. Morgan, George T. "Judaism in Eighteenth-Century Georgia."
GA HIST Q, 58 (1974), 41-54.

Due to the remarkable efforts of Mordecai and Levi Sheftall,
the state gave equality to Jews by 1790.

3416. Mulder, John M. "William Livingston: Propagandist Against
Episcopacy." J PRESBY HIST, 54 (1976), 83-104.

Thoroughly anti-clerical and yet a staunch Presbyterian,
Livingston of New Jersey waged a fierce fight against
Anglicanism.

3417. Nichols, John Hastings. "John Witherspoon on Church and State."
J PRESBY HIST, 42 (1964), 166-174.

Witherspoon, a member of the New Jersey legislature, Continental Congress, signer of the Declaration of Independence,
and President of the College of New Jersey, was the most
influential clergyman of the war era.

3418. Noll, Mark A. "Ebenezer Devotion: Religion and Society in
Revolutionary Connecticut." CONN HIST, 45 (1976), 293-307.

This New England minister's political attitudes reflected
his religious convictions and ecclesiastical viewpoints.

3419. Parramore, Thomas C. "John Alexander, Anglican Missionary."
NC HIST REV, 43 (1966), 305-15.

Alexander managed to overcome incredible obstacles as a
minister and survived the Revolution.

3420. Payne, Ernest A. "British Baptists and the American Revolution." BAPTIST HIST HERITAGE, 11 (1976), 3-15.

Resented by Congregationalists in New England and by Anglicans in the south, Baptist exiles considered themselves
unfairly treated in Britain.

3421. Pennington, Edgar L. "The Anglican Clergy of Pennsylvania
in the American Revolution." PA MHB, 63 (1939), 401-431.

This is a reliable roster of over twenty clergyman in the
state for whom a decisive factor was the issue of prayers for
the King.

3422. Radbill, Kenneth A. "Quaker Patriots: The Leadership of Owen
       Biddle and John Lacey, Jr." PA HIST, 45 (1978), 47-60.

       Two former pacifists served their country well in admin-
       istrative duties, and in military commands.

3423. Rainbolt, John Corbin. "The Struggle to Define 'Religious
       Liberty' in Maryland, 1776-85." J CHURCH STATE, 17 (1975),
       44-458.

       The war brought a more radical conception of religious
       liberty to the state, a variety of denominations flourished;
       alleged corruption and Toryism eroded the power of Anglicanism.

3424. Rezneck, Samuel. UNRECOGNIZED PATRIOTS, THE JEWS IN THE
       AMERICAN REVOLUTION. Westport, Connecticut: Greenwood
       Press, 1975.

       This is a serviceable synthesis of generally familiar mate-
       rial. Though the author has overlooked many significant
       archival collections on the subject, and although he writes
       dull prose, the book is quite useful in noting the achieve-
       ments of a small Jewish minority in the war effort. The
       Jewish role as financiers and suppliers to the army is covered
       as well as Jews who served as officers in the army. The work
       is useful on the plight of Jewish Loyalists; it is weak on the
       slave trade.

3425. Rightmyer, Nelson W. "The Anglican Church in Maryland: Factors
       Contributing to the American Revolution." CHURCH HIST, 19
       (1950), 187-198.

       Marylanders who were taxed to support the Church demanded
       a role in appointing clergy and dismissing inept ministers.

3426. Roberts, Lucien E. "Quakers in Georgia: The Rise and Fall of
       the Wrightsborough Community (1768-1803)." GA REV, 4 (1950),
       297-303.

       Settling in the Georgia backcountry in 1750 and 1768, the
       Quakers were hurt by the war and their villages were virtually
       gone by 1793.

3427. Sappington, Roger E. "North Carolina and the Non-Resistance
       Sects During the American War of Independence." QUAKER HIST,
       60 (1971), 29-47.

       Although the neutral and pacifist churches were penalized
       heavily in lieu of military service, the state legislature
       demonstrated some restraint and flexibility in applying puni-
       tive measures.

510   THE IMPACT OF WAR ON SOCIETY

3428. ———. "Two Eighteenth Century Dunker Congregations in North
       Carolina." NC HIST REV, 47 (1970), 176-204.

       Fined for their neutralism, the communities at Winston-Salem
       and New River survived the war.

3429. Scheidt, David L. "The Lutherans in Revolutionary Philadel-
       phia." CONCORDIA HIST INSTIT Q, 49 (1976), 62-78.

       This is a good summary about the burdens on, and the con-
       tributions of, the Lutherans in the war effort.

3430. Simpson, Robert Drew. "The Lord's Rebel: Freeborn Garrettson -
       A Methodist Preacher During the American Revolution."
       WESLEYAN Q REV, 2 (1965), 194-211.

       Garrettson, unlike his clerical colleagues who were pacifists,
       suffered for his political views.

3431. Stokes, Durward T. "The Baptist and Methodist Clergy in South
       Carolina and the American Revolution." SC HIST MAG, 71
       (1970), 270-282.

       This is a good comparison of why Baptist ministers sup-
       ported and why Methodist ministers generally opposed the
       Revolution.

3432. Sweet, William W. "The Role of Anglicans in the American
       Revolution." HUNT LIB Q, 11 (1947), 51-70.

       The Church of England had the largest numbers of Loyalists
       compared to other denominations; yet the contradiction is that
       the greatest percentage of the "Signers" were Anglicans.

3433. Sydnor, William. "David Griffith - Chaplain, Surgeon, Patriot."
       HIST MAG PROT EPIS CHURCH, 44 (1975), 247-265.

       Griffith, the first Bishop-elect of the Episcopal Church in
       Virginia, served in the Continental army as a surgeon and
       chaplain.

3434. Tanis, James. "The Dutch Reformed Church and the American
       Revolution." HALVE MAEN, 52 (2), 1-2, 15; 52 (3) 1-2, 12
       (1977).

       The pre-war factionalism within this church became especially
       acrimonious during the war in New York City and in Hackensack,
       New Jersey.

3435. Taussig, Harold E. "Deism in Philadelphia During the Age of
       Franklin." PA HIST, 37 (1970), 217-236.

       The prevailing deism of forty-eight members of the elite American
       Philosophical Society before the war shows the influence of
       the Enlightenment.

3436.   Thorne, Dorothy G. "North Carolina Friends and the Revolu-
        tion." NC HIST REV, 38 (1961), 323-340.

        After the battle of Guilford Court House, Quakers at New
        Garden treated hundreds of casualties, including wounded left
        by Cornwallis.

3437.   Van Tyne, C.F. "Influence of the Clergy, and of Religious
        and Sectarian Forces on the American Revolution." AHR, 19
        (1913), 44-64.

        The author discounts economic causation in formenting the
        Revolution and stresses religious issues voiced by Calvinistic
        clergy.

3438.   Vassar, Rena. "The Aftermath of Revolution: Letters of
        Anglican Clergymen in Connecticut, 1781-1785." HIST MAG
        PROT EPIS CHURCH, 41 (1972), 429-61.

        Five Loyalist ministers, all Yale graduates, reported to
        their superiors about local problems.

3439.   Walker, Robert G. "Jonathan Boucher: Champion of the Minority."
        WMQ, 2 (1945), 3-14.

        This Tory divine, with a quaint political doctrine and blind
        faith in the Crown, displayed some progressive ideas in his
        famous writings.

3440.   Weaver, Glenn. "Anglican-Congregationalist Tension in Pre-
        Revolutionary Connecticut." HIST MAG PROT EPIS CHURCH, 26

        These groups debated about an episcopate and about the
        ramifications of religious liberty.

3441.   Weinlich, John R. "The Moravians and the American Revolution:
        An Overview." TRANS MORAVIAN HIST SOC, 23 (1977), 1-16.

        The neutral Moravians contributed supplies to the American
        army and had six of their villages in Pennsylvania commandeered
        for sick and wounded troops.

K. JOURNALISM AND PRINTING

3442.   Adams, Thomas R. "The British Pamphlet Press and the American
        Controversy, 1704-1783." AMER ANTIQ SOC PROC, 89 (1979),
        33-88.

        Adams demonstrates in a fine study of English pamphleteers
        (citing their numbers, items printed, and publication dates)
        how London printers and booksellers reflected the British
        response to the Revolution.

3443.   Adams, William Paul. "The Colonial German-Language Press and
        the American Revolution." See 3447, pp. 151-228.

In a fine essay, the author demonstrates how influential
were editors Henry Miller and Christopher Sower in translating
Whig rhetoric to enlighten their German compatriots.

3444. Aldridge, A. Owen. "The Influence of New York Newspapers
       on Paine's COMMON SENSE." NY HIST SOC Q, 60 (1976), 53-80.

The article concerns Tom Paine's verbal attack on the NEW
YORK GAZETEER and other Tory journals, an experience which
influenced the writing of his classic book.

3445. Ascoli, Peter M. "The French Press and the American Revolu-
       tion: The Battle of Saratoga." WEST SOC FRENCH HIST, 5
       (1977), 46-55.

Here is a good summary of the Parisian press coverage of the
American victory.

3446. Bailyn, Bernard. "The Index and Commentaries of Harbottle
       Dorr." MASS HIST SOC PROC, 85 (1975), 21-35.

A Boston shop-keeper collected 3,280 pages of information
extracted from Massachusetts newspapers that show an ordinary
citizen's concern with current events.

3447. ————, and John B. Hench, eds. THE PRESS AND THE AMERICAN
       REVOLUTION. Charlottesville: Published for the Antiquarian
       Society, University Press of Virginia, 1980.

This is an indispensable source for understanding the role
of newspapers during the Revolution. It supplants virtually
all previous works on the subject. The eight essays, which
are cited in this bibliographic section, are preceded by an
excellent introductory essay.

3448. Barnes, Timothy M. "Loyalist Newspapers of the American
       Revolution, 1763-1783: A Bibliography." AMER ANTIQ SOC PROC,
       83 (1973), 214-240.

This is an excellent summary of the subject with citations
about printers, publication dates, biographical sketches of
editors, and the availability on microfilm of Tory newspapers
in eight American states.

3449. Barthold, Allen J. "'Gazette Francoise,' Newport, R.I., 1780-
       81." PAP BIB SOC AMER, 28 (1938), 64-79.

The GAZETTE was printed for French soldiers and seamen
stationed with de Ternay's fleet at Newport.

3450. Bates, Albert Carlos. "Fighting the Revolution with Printers
       Ink in Connecticut; The Official Printing of that Colony from
       Lexington to the Declaration." NEW HAVEN COL HIST SOC PAP,
       9 (1918), 129-160.

Here is a concise essay about the importance of printing
contracts authorized by the General Assembly to patriotic
editors in the state.

3451. Buel, Richard, Jr. "Freedom of the Press in Revolutionary
        America: The Evolution of Libertarianism, 1750-1820." See
        3447, pp. 59-98.

        Biel stresses the value of press freedom to patriotic leaders,
        why printing was essential to the spread of revolutionary
        concepts, and how these attitudes were reflected in the state
        and federal constitutions.

3452. Bond, Donavan H., and W. Reynolds McLead. NEWSLETTERS TO
        NEWSPAPERS: EIGHTEENTH CENTURY JOURNALISM. Morgantown,
        West Virginia: The School of Journalism, West Virginia
        University, 1977.

        This collection of essays concerns the state of journalism
        in eighteenth-century Britain and North America.

3453. Botein, Stephen. "Printers and the American Revolution."
        See 3447, pp. 11-57.

        Botein stresses the shift in entrepreneurial activities of
        newspapermen from craft skills to a more sophisticated
        technology, and the importance of journalism in the revolu-
        tionary turmoil.

3454. Brigham, Clarence S., ed. HISTORY AND BIOGRAPHY OF AMERICAN
        NEWSPAPERS, 1690-1820. 2 vols. Worcester, Massachusetts:
        The American Antiquarian Society, 1947.

        Here is the most useful tool and source of information about
        colonial American newspapers. This work is replete with de-
        tails about titles, locations, ownerships, editors, duration
        of publication, changes of titles, and locations of sur-
        viving newspaper files.

3455. Brown, Ralph A. "New Hampshire Editors Win the War: A Study
        in Revolutionary Press Propaganda." NEQ, 12 (1939), 35-51.

        Brown notes the importance of four Whig editors, and the
        NEW HAMPSHIRE GAZEETE in a state without a Tory press.

3456. ———. "The Philadelphia Ledger: Tory News Sheet." PA HIST,
        9 (1942), 161-175.

        From late 1777 to early 1778, this influential Loyalist
        periodical lashed out at the patriots and appealed for enlist-
        ments in British provincial corps.

3457. Cullen, George Edward, Jr. "Talking to a Whirlwind: The
        Loyalist Printers in America, 1763-1783." Ph.D. disserta-
        tion, West Virginia University, 1979.

This is a thoroughly researched study that provides many
fresh insights about the role of Tory newspapers in the war.
The author notes that 30 newspapers in 9 colonies were
Loyalist in the 20 year period, that 15 Loyalist presses
published in 1775, and from 1781 to 1783, 80 presses continued to support the royal cause. After a good analysis
of 34 Tory publishers – their background, influence, contributions – Cullen concentrates on the Loyalist press in
Philadelphia and New York.

3458.   Cullen, Maurice R. "Middle-Class Democracy and the Press
        in Colonial America." JOURN Q, 46 (1959), 531-534.

        The author summarizes the role of colonial journalism as
        vital in the propaganda war.

3459.   Davidson, Alexander, Jr. "James Rivington and Silas Deane."
        PAP BIB SOC AMER, 52 (1958), 173-178.

        The Tory journalist published Deanne's intercepted cor-
        respondence to Congress from Paris.

3460.   Dickerson, Oliver M. "British Control of American Newspapers
        on the Eve of Revolution." NEQ, 24 (1951), 453-468.

        This is a fascinating report of British efforts to sub-
        sidize several Tory Boston and New York newspapers on the
        eve of the war.

3461.   Echeverria, Durand. "French Publication of the Declaration
        of Independence and the American Constitutions, 1776-1783."
        PAP BIB SOC AMER, 47 (1953), 313-338.

        This is a solid study which demonstrates how the Parisian
        publication of key patriotic writings, declarations, and
        state constitutions created what Tom Paine termed "the gram-
        mar of French Liberty."

3462.   Ford, Paul Leicester. THE JOURNALS OF HUGH GAINE: PRINTER.
        2 vols. 1902. Reprint. New York: Arno Press, 1970.

        Gaine was one of the most prominent Tory news editors
        whose editorials infuriated American patriots for years
        while New York was under British occupation. Volume 1 con-
        tains mainly biographical data containing interesting anec-
        dotes about his life; volume 2 has his letters and journals
        about the NEW YORK-MERCURY (1752-83).

3463.   Frank, Willard C., Jr. "Error, Distortion and Bias in the
        VIRGINIA GAZETTE, 1773-74." JOURN Q, 49 (1972), 729-737.

        Frank stresses the significance of the Williamsburg press
        (which sided with the Whigs in 1773-74) in a prevailing mood
        of political neutrality in Virginia.

3464. George, Mary D. "American English Satirical Prints." WMQ,
      10 (1953), 511-537.

      Here is a humorous article about how ridicule and scurrility
      were used as political weapons by the London press which was
      frequently sympathetic to American complaints.

3465. Graffino, J. Kevin. "'We Have Long Been Wishing for a Good
      Printer in this Vicinity': the State of Vermont." VT HIST,
      47 (1979), 121-36.

      The essayist outlines the influence of the Spooner family
      in influencing settlers in the Connecticut River Valley about
      statehood.

3466. Harlan, Robert D. "David Hall and the Stamp Act." PAP BIB
      SOC AMER, 61 (1967),

      Here is a detailed account about the PENNSYLVANIA GAZETTE'S
      protests over British policies in the colonies.

3467. Harrison, John M. "The War and Words: The Role of Our First
      Editorial Writers in Making a Revolution." See
      3452, pp. 207-217.

      The author explains how the colonial news media influenced
      American public opinion and helped to precipitate action.

3468. Hawkins, Dorothy Lawson. "James Adams, the First Printer of
      Delaware." PAP BIB SOC AMER, 28 (1934), 28-55.

      This is a good account about the lack of printing in
      Delaware until 1761, the dependence on Philadelphia for news,
      and Delaware's first editor in Wilmington.

3469. Henry, Susan. "Ann Franklin of Newport, Rhode Island's Woman
      Printer." See 3452, pp. 129-144.

      Henry provides insight into the career of a woman who pub-
      lished a newspaper, almanacs, and printed the colony's laws
      prior to the Revolution.

3470. ———. "Sarah Goddard, Gentlewoman Printer." JOURN Q, 57
      (1980), 23-30.

      Goddard was a clever and wealthy Rhode Islander who super-
      vised a printshop, served the community, and championed
      radical Whig rhetoric in her newspaper.

3471. Hixson, Richard F. "'Faithful Guardian' of Press Freedom."
      NJ HIST SOC PROC, 81 (1963), 155-163.

      Issac Collins founded Jersey's first permanent newspaper
      in late 1777 with legislative funding.

3472. ————. "Founder of New Jersey's First Permanent Newspaper."
       JOUR Q, 40 (1963), 233-235.

       Virtually the last of the thirteen colonies to have a news-
       paper, New Jersey had a press by 1776 which was subsidized by
       its governor.

3473. Hoffman, Ronald. "The Press in Mercantile Maryland: A
       Question of Utility." JOUR Q, 46 (1969), 536-544.

       This excellent summary explains the importance of five
       newspapers which reflected the development of Maryland's
       tobacco and wheat trade in the Chesapeake area.

3474. Kobre, Sidney, THE DEVELOPMENT OF THE COLONIAL NEWSPAPER.
       1974. Reprint. Glouster, Massachusetts: Peter Smith, 1980.

       Although there are numerous inconsistencies in this nar-
       rative, this is a useful volume for tracing the emergence of
       American journalism through the Revolution. Its detailed
       descriptions of economic aspects about the press, and how
       newspapers went through a gradual transformation are partici-
       larly valuable.

3475. Langford, Paul. "British Correspondence in the Colonial
       Press: A Study in Anglo-American Misunderstanding before
       the American Revolution." See 3447, pp. 273-313.

       Here is a penetrating essay which explains how news from
       London was disseminated in the American press and why the
       patriots may have misunderstood the political realities con-
       fronting the British government.

3476. Leder, Lawrence. "The Role of Newspapers in Early America,
       'In Defense of Their Own Liberty'." HUNT LIB Q, 30 (1966),
       1-16.

       Leder explains why the press in 1774-75 was the dominant
       force in providing political insight for the average American
       colonist.

3477. Leonard, Thomas C. "News for a Revolution: The Expose in
       America 1768-1773." JAH, 67 (1980), 26-42.

       The author notes how political scandals on the eve of
       Revolution shaped views about virtue and corruption related
       to imperial policies, and how such information was infused
       with revolutionary ideology for the common man.

3478. Lutnick, Solomon M. "The Defeat at Yorktown: A View from
       the British Press." VA MHB, 72 (1964), 471-478.

       In a sampling of London newspapers, the author related how
       the English press explained that the war with America was lost.

3479. McCorison, Marcus A. "The Wages of John Carter's Journeymen
       Printers, 1771-1779." AMER ANTIQ SOC PROC, 81 (1971),
       273-303.

       Here is a reproduction of an account book which shows the
       effects of the war on inflation and wage scales.

3480. McMurtrie, Douglas C. "The Correspondence of Peter Timothy,
       Printer of Charleston with Benjamin Franklin." SC HIST MAG,
       35 (1935), 123-129; 36 (1935), 105-112.

       The letters offer a good insight into the economic and
       political problems of a southern printer, 1754-77.

3481. Merrill, Elizabeth. "The Lexington Alarm, April 19, 1775:
       Messages Sent to the Soutwaid (sic) after the Battle."
       MD HIST MAG, 41 (1946), 89-114.

       This is a good description of how the news of the fighting
       was transmitted to Maryland and Virigina by the press.

3482. Merritt, Richard L. "The Colonists Discover America: Atten-
       tion Patterns in the Colonial Press, 1735-1775." WMQ,
       21 (1964), 270-287.

       This article demonstrates, by a sampling analysis, that
       the colonial press (especially in Massachusetts and South
       Carolina) increasingly referred to its readers as "Americans."

3483. Mooney, James. "Loyalist Imprints Printed in America, 1774-
       1785." AMER ANTIQ SOC PROC, 84 (1974), 105-218.

       Mooney provides a valuable reference tool by citing details
       on Tory newspapers, many of which carried requests by the
       British army for wood and blankets.

3484. Mott, Frank Luther. "The Newspaper Coverage of Lexington and
       Concord." NEQ, 17 (1944), 489-505.

       This is a fine summary of the rudimentary news-gathering
       techniques used by some thirty-seven colonial newspapers
       which reported the incident.

3485. Ours, Robert M. "James Rivington: Another Viewpoint." See
       3452, pp. 219-233.

       Ours provides a good sketch of the hated Tory editor of
       New York's ROYAL GAZETTE, who tried to be judicious in his
       reporting.

3486. Parker, Peter J. "The Philadelphia Printer: A Study of an
       Eighteenth-Century Businessman." BUS HIST REV, 40 (1966),
       24-46.

       Parker notes that colonial printers in Philadelphia were
       both businessmen and publicists.

3487.   Polter, Janice, and Robert M. Calhoon. "The Character and
        Coherence of the Loyalist Press." See 3447, pp. 229-
        271.

        Loyalist newspapers provide unique clues about the behavior
        and expectations of the Tories.

3488.   Randolph, J. Ralph. "The End of Impartiality: SOUTH-CAROLINA
        GAZETTE, 1763-75." JOURN Q, 49 (1972), 702-709, 720.

        This is an account of how a major southern newspaper dis-
        seminated radical political views by 1775.

3489.   Raymond, Allen R. "To Reach Men's Minds: Almanacs and the
        American Revolution, 1760-1777." NEQ, 51 (1978), 370-395.

        Here is a fine summary of how almanacs were influential
        in translating Whig rhetoric into terms comprehensible to the
        average readers.

3490.   Roach, S.F., Jr. "The Georgia Gazette and the Stamp Act: A
        Reconsideration." GA HIST Q, 55 (1971), 471-491.

        In a thoroughly documented article, Roach explains that the
        GAZETTE made public opinion and made Georgians part of the
        revolutionary upheaval of 1775.

3491.   Schlesinger, Arthur M. PRELUDE TO INDEPENDENCE: THE NEWSPAPER
        WAR ON BRITAIN, 1764-1776. New York: Alfred A. Knopf, 1958.

        A master historian wrote this superb synthesis about the
        importance of newspaper editorials and letters to the editor
        in the shaping of a patriotic ideology. Schlesinger made a
        persuasive case that the impassioned arguments and virtual
        unanimity of opinion represented in the American press were
        vital forces in making the rebellion. Clearly written, in-
        cisive, and based on exhaustive research, this is the classic
        book on the subject which demonstrates the power of the pen
        over the sword, and that newspapers were "engines of opinion."

3492.   ————. "Propaganda and the Boston Newspaper Press, 1767-
        1770." COL SOC MASS TRANS, 32 (1933-37), 399-416.

        The author contends that the Stamp Act caused a revolution
        in American journalism as the Boston press became a maker
        and shaper of public opinion.

3493.   Silver, Rollo G. "Aprons Instead of Uniforms: The Practice
        of Printing, 1776-1789." AMER ANTIQ SOC PROC, 87 (1977),
        111-194.

        This is a fine analysis about the relationship among
        printers, state assemblies, and Congress which shows that
        publishing was a risky business, and that states needed to
        maintain the loyalty of printers during the war.

3494. ————. "Benjamin Eden, Trumpeter of Sedition." PAP BIB SOC
       AMER, 48 (1953), 248-258.

       Here are ample details of how the BOSTON GAZETTE became
       the most influential New England newspaper in the 1760's.

3495. Skaggs, David C. "Editorial Policies of the MARYLAND GAZETTE."
       MD HIST MAG, 59 (1964), 341-349.

       Maryland's only wartime newspaper was highly influential
       in sustaining patriotic zeal during the struggle.

3496. Steirer, William F., Jr. "A Study in Prudence: Philadelphia's
       Revolutionary Journalists." JOURN HIST, 3 (1978), 16-19.

       This summary notes that some Philadelphia editors were
       not brave crusaders; several hedged on the controversial
       issue of abolition for slaves.

3497. Sticke, Warren E., III. "State and Press in New Jersey During
       the American Revolution." NJ HIST, 86 (1968), 156-170,
       236-249.

       New Jersey subsidized two newspapers during the war which
       were handicapped by financial problems and shortages of
       printing supplies.

3498. Stoudt, John Joseph. "The German Press in Pennsylvania and
       the American Revolution." PA MAG HIST, 59 (1935), 174-90.

       The article explains the Tory view of Germantown's Saur
       family in contrast to the patriot editorials of John Heinrich
       Miller.

3499. Tanselle, G. Thomas. "Some Statistics on American Printing,
       1764-1783." See 3447, pp. 315-372.

       Tanselle provides impressive details about the output of
       American presses (books, broadsides, newspapers) along with
       a valuable commentary about the subjects which were covered.

3500. Teeter, Dwight, L. "Benjamin Towne: The Precarious Career
       of a Persistent Printer." PA MHB, 89 (1965), 316-330.

       Teeter relates an account about the wavering political
       loyalties of one editor who was patriotic in 1775-76, Tory
       in 1777, and then patriotic again in 1778.

3501. ————. "John Dunlap: The Political Economy of a Printer's
       Success." JOURN Q, 52 (1975), 3-8.

       Dunlap, a Philadelphia printer, became wealthy during the
       war because of Congressional printing contracts and because
       of his connections with land speculators.

3502. ————. "King Sears, the Mob and Freedom of the Press in New
       York, 1765-1776." JOURN Q, 41 (1964), 539-544.

       This is a good discussion of an early debate in New York
       about freedom of the press and its relationship to mob
       behavior when a patriot leader attempted to suppress Tory
       pamphleteers.

3503. ————. "Press Freedom and the Public Printing: Pennsylvania,
       1775-83." JOURN Q, 145 (1968), 445-451.

       Here is a good account of how Pennsylvania editors could
       freely criticize the state government if they were not
       financially dependent on government printing contracts,
       while other editors were necessarily more reticent about
       politics.

3504. ————. "The Printer and the Chief Justice: Seditious
       Libel in 1782-83." JOURN Q, 45 (1968), 235-242.

       A key case about an editor's charges about peculation by
       army officers led to a controversial discussion about the
       role of chief justices in such matters.

3505. Thomas, Charles M. "The Publication of Newspapers During
       the American Revolution." JOURN Q, 9 (1932), 358-373.

       This is a weak summary about the publishing world of John
       Holt, Hugh Gaine, and James Rivington.

3506. Thorton, Mary Lindsay. "Public Printing in North Carolina,
       1749-1815." NC HIST REV, 21 (1944), 181-202.

       James Davis, the publisher of the NORTH CAROLINA GAZETTE,
       was subsidized by the state to print and distribute its laws.

3507. Walett, Francis G. "The Impact of the Stamp Act on the
       Colonial Press." See 3447, pp. 134-170.

       Though most American editors avoided the issue in print,
       journalists generally gained more press freedom after the
       crisis, and they continued to defy British authority.

3508. Wall, Alexander J. "Samuel Loudon, 1727-1813, Merchant,
       Printer, and Patriot With Some of His Letters." NY HIST
       SOC Q BULL, 6 (1922-23), 75-92.

       This is a brief summary of a patriot printer in New York.

3509. Weir, Robert M. "The Role of the Newspaper Press in the
       Southern Colonies on the Eve of the Revolution: An Inter-
       pretation." See 3452, pp. 99-150.

       This is a thorough discussion of how southern newspapers
       tended to display similar views; but due to sectional

attitudes, the reliance on official printing contracts, and
the local degree of literacy, they varied considerably on
key issues.

3510. Weisberger, Bernard A. "Newspapers of the American Revolution." AMER BOOK COLL, 26 (1976), 20-26.

Here is a convenient summary of political attitudes demonstrated by leading Whig and Tory newspapers.

3511. Wolf, Edwin, II. "The American Printings of the Definitive
Treaty of Peace of 1783 Freed of Obfuscation." BIB SOC AMER
PROC, 65 (1971), 272-278.

The first printing of the Treaty was done by William Ross
of New York.

L.   AGRICULTURE

3512. Bowers, Douglas, comp and ed. A LIST AND REFERENCES FOR THE
HISTORY OF THE FARMER AND THE REVOLUTION, 1763-1790. Davis,
California: Agricultural History Center, 1971.

There are some 220 bibliographic items here about the impact
of the war on agricultural productivity.

3513. Bradford, S. Sydney. "Hunger Menaces the Revolution, December
1779-January 1780." MD HIST MAG, 61 (1965), 1-23.

Due to the near-starvation of troops at Morristown, the
army had to commandeer provisions from the Middle States.

3514. Brown, Wallace. "The American Farmer During the Revolution:
Rebel or Loyalist." AGRIC HIST, 42 (1968), 327-338.

Farmers, constituting ninety per cent of the population,
were either neutral, Whig, Loyalist or were politically in-
different.

3515. Burnett, Edmund C. "The Continental Congress and Agricultural
Supplies." AGRIC HIST, 2 (1928), 111-128.

By 1777, Congress was frantically searching for provisions
to feed the army.

3516. Jensen, Merrill. "The American Revolution and American
Agriculture." AGRIC HIST, 43 (1959), 107-124.

The colonial pattern of exports generally continued after
the war; the farmers' financial plight determined state
financial policies.

3517. Mark, Irving. "Agrarian Conflicts in New York and the American Revolution." RURAL SOC, 7 (1942), 275-293.

The fight by tenants for their own land and for positions of confiscated Loyalist estates was a long and bitter episode suggesting class warfare.

3518. Mitchell, Robert D. "Agricultural Change and the American Revolution: A Virginia Case Study." AGRIC HIST, 47 (1973), 110-132.

Few qualitative changes occurred in the Shenandoah Valley agriculture although there were some significant adjustments in the production of certain crops.

3519. Newcomer, Lee N. THE EMBATTLED FARMERS: A MASSACHUSETTS COUNTRYSIDE IN THE AMERICAN REVOLUTION. New York: Columbia University Press, 1953.

This is an excellent study of how the war effected one occupational group in a region. The book demonstrates, with ample documentation, the role of the farmer in the war, the effects of war on agricultural productivity, the degree of agrarian-discontent, and the problems of paper currency in relation to commodities. It contains a summary about the aftermath of war.

3520. Pinkett, Harold T. "Maryland as a Source of Food Supplies During the American Revolution." MD HIST MAG, 46 (1951), 157-172.

The state's grain, livestock, and fish were essential in provisioning troops of the Middle States.

M. COMMERCE

3521. Ames, Susie M. "A Typical Virginian Business Man of the Revolutionary Era: Nathaniel Littleton Savage and His Account Book." J ECON BUS HIST, 3 (1931), 407-423.

From Littleton's records, the author provides a neat sketch of a merchant's activities.

3522. Baldwin, Simeon E. "American Business Corporations Before 1787." AHR, 8 (1903), 449-465.

The states provided legislation to incorporate for business purposes; only six companies were incorporated by 1777 and over 200 by 1800.

3523. Bezanson, Anne. PRICES AND INFLATION DURING THE AMERICAN REVOLUTION: PENNSYLVANIA 1770-1776. Philadelphia: University of Pennsylvania Press, 1951.

Bezanson has compiled vast quantities of data about the production and distribution of many basic commodities. There are chapters here about wheat, corn, beef and pork, salt mining, naval stores, tobacco, and cotton. The book's value is considerably enhanced by tables, charts, and detailed notes.

3524. Bjork, Gordon C. "The Meaning of the American Economy:
       Independence, Market Changes and Economic Development."
       J ECON HIST, 24 (1964), 541-566.

       There is ample data here about foreign trade during the war
       and about a modest increase in exports in the 1780s.

3525. Cometti, Elizabeth. "Inflation in Revolutionary Maryland."
       WMQ, 8 (1951), 228-254.

       Cometti lists tables for prices from the account book
       (1777-1780) of John Galloway.

3526. Crittenden, Charles C. THE COMMERCE OF NORTH CAROLINA, 1763-
       1787. New Haven: Yale University Press, 1976.

       Chapter nine, entitled "War and Commerical Disorder,"
       has an excellent treatment of how warfare from 1779-82 virtu-
       ally wrecked the state's commerce.

3527. Devine, T.M. "A Glasgow Merchant During the American War of
       Independence: Alexander Spicks of Eldershire, 1775 to 1781."
       WMQ, 33 (1976), 501-513.

       Here is a fine summary of how a speculator in tobacco
       managed to weather crises in the Tidewater economy.

3528. East, Robert A. BUSINESS ENTERPRISE IN THE AMERICAN REVOLU-
       TIONARY ERA. 1928. Reprint. Gloucester, Massachusetts:
       Peter Smith, 1964.

       This is the best book on the topic, for it is a readable
       study about the activities of merchants, shippers, bankers,
       and entrepreneurs in the era. East suggests that the war
       resulted in the emancipation of American business enterprise,
       that numerous corporations were founded, new markets were
       opened, and that mercantile capitalism triumphed, particularly
       with the aid of a banking system by 1782.

3529. Ernst, Joseph A. "Economic Change and the Political Economy
       of the American Revolution." See 3239, pp. 103-125.

       There were few economic changes due to the Revolution, but
       a stimulus occurred in reforms for the business-financial com-
       munity; however the stress here is on pre-1775 conditions.

3530. Greene, Richard. "The American Revolution Comes to Hanover."
       WMQ, 20 (1963), 246-250.

       Baltic trade with the patriots continued despite British
       efforts to cut off European supplies.

3531. Jones, Robert F. "William Duck and the Business of Government
       in the Era of the American Revolution." WMQ, 32 (1975),
       393-416.

This is a lively sketch of a New Yorker who was active in
the business of contracting supplies for the American army.

3532. McMaster, Richard K., and Skaggs, David C., eds. "The Letter-
        book of Alexander Hamilton, Piscataway Factor, 1774-1776."
        MD HIST MAG, 61 (1966), 141-165, 305-328; 62 (1967), 135-169.

        Hamilton was active in the Maryland tobacco trade and in
        Virginia flour mills and iron foundries.

3533. Mason, Bernard. "Entrepreneurial Activity in New York During
        the American Revolution." BUS HIST REV, 40 (1966), 190-212.

        Here is a good summary of how leading businessmen handled
        commercial problems during the war. The war wrecked com-
        merce, but it opened up new opportunities in state and
        Congressional contracts, in exports to New England, in
        privateering, and in illicit trade.

3534. Morris, Richard B. GOVERNMENT AND LABOR IN EARLY AMERICA.
        New York: Columbia University Press, 1946.

        Chapter two has a thorough study of wage and price controls
        during the rebellion.

3535. Nettels, Curtis P. THE EMERGENCE OF A NATIONAL ECONOMY, 1775-
        1815. Economic History of the United States. Vol. 2. New
        York: Holt, Rinehart and Winston.

        Chapter 1 covers the initial disruption of the colonial
        economy due to the war. Chapter 2 concentrates on the devel-
        opment of a national economy.

3536. Platt, Virginia Bever. "Tar, Staves and New England Rum: The
        Trade of Aaron Lopez of Newport, Rhode Island with Colonial
        North Carolina." NC HIST REV, 48 (1971), 1-22.

        There is some data here about the wide-ranging commercial
        activities of the famed Lopez family of merchants.

3537. Robertson, M.L. "Scottish Commerce and the American War of
        Independence." ECON HIST REV, 9 (1958), 123-131.

        The Glasgow-dominated tobacco monopoly, which accounted for
        large percentages of Scotland's imports from America and ex-
        ports to Europe, was shaken by the war; but the Scots quickly
        shifted to weaving and spinning for foreign markets.

3538. Sellers, Leila. CHARLESTON BUSINESS ON THE EVE OF THE AMERI-
        CAN REVOLUTION. Chapel Hill: University of North Carolina
        Press, 1954.

        This useful work covers the role of Charleston factors in
        the Carolina economy, the importance of the city as the south's
        major port, and the production and export of rice, indigo, and
        deerskins.

3539. Shepherd, James F. "Commodity Exports From the British
       North American Colonies to Overseas Areas, 1768-1782; Magni-
       tude and Patterns of Trade." EXPLORATIONS IN ECON HIST, 8
       (1970), 5-76.

       Noting the size and importance of major commodities, the
       author stresses how vital was overseas trade for the develop-
       ment of the thirteen colonies.

3540. Ver Steeg, Clarence L. "Financing and Outfitting the First
       United States Ship to China (1784)." PAC HIS REV, 22
       (1953), 1-12.

       The EMPRESS OF CHINA symbolized a trade link to the Far East.

3541. ————. "Stacey Hepburn and Company: Entrepreneurs in the
       American Revolution." SC HIST MAG, 55 (1954), 1-5.

       A northern firm did a thriving business in Charleston.

3542. Williams, William A. "The Age of Mercantilism: An Interpre-
       tation of the American Political Economy, 1763-1828." WMQ,
       15 (1958), 419-437.

       Williams stresses the maturation of the American economy
       based upon the principles of Adam Smith.

XII. PERSPECTIVES ON THE AMERICAN REVOLUTION

3543. Archdeacon, Thomas J. "American Historians and the American
        Revolution: A Bicentennial Overview." WIS MAG HIST, 63
        (1980), 278-298.

        This is a convenient summary of how historians (Progres-
        sives, Neo-Whigs, etc.) have interpreted the war.

3544. Bailyn, Bernard. "Central Themes of the Revolution."
        See 191, pp. 3-31.

        Here is a provocative essay about politics, propaganda and
        Loyalism.

3545. Barrow, Thomas C. "The American Revolution as a Colonial
        War for Independence." WMQ, 25 (1968), 452-464.

        Barrow offers a sound analogy of the Revolution within the
        perspective of the twentieth century.

3546. Billias, George A. "The American Revolution: A Measure of
        America's Maturity." NE SOC STUD BULL, 22 (1964), 7-9.

        This is a helpful summary of interpretations written for
        high school teachers.

3547. —————, ed. THE AMERICAN REVOLUTION, HOW REVOLUTIONARY WAS
        IT? New York: Holt, Rinehart & Winston.

        The editor offers excerpts from the works of thirteen
        prominent writers on the Revolution along with a useful
        bibliographic essay.

3548. Boyd, Julian P. "A People Divided." NC HIST REV, 47 (1970),
        161-175.

        The American Revolution was a turning point in world
        history.

3549. Burrows, Edwin G., and Michael Wallace. "The American
        Revolution: The Ideology and Psychology of National Libera-
        tion." PERS AMER HIST, 6 (1972), 167-306.

        The colonials were children and Britain the authoritarian-
        parent until the Stamp Act disrupted the relationship.

3550. Chappin, Robert J. "Was the American Revolution Really Neces-
       sary?" MIDWEST Q, 19 (1977), 7-23.

       The war was fought to preserve and not to change traditional
       institutions.

3551. Cohen, Lester H. "Narrating the Revolution: Ideology, Langu-
       age and Form." STUDIES IN EIGHTEENTH CENTURY CULTURE, 9
       (1979), 455-476.

       As observers of the war, participants could not be objective
       historians.

3552. ————. THE REVOLUTIONARY HISTORIES: CONTEMPORARY NARRATIVES
       OF THE AMERICAN REVOLUTION. Ithaca: Cornell University
       Press, 1980.

       Cohen attempts an intellectual history by showing how nine
       historians writing from 1785 to 1822 viewed the struggle,
       along with prominent later historians. The author shows a
       shift from a concern with causes of the war to questions
       about consequences of the war. The book is marred by stylistic
       flaws, excessive quotations, and a faulty organization about
       the impact of ideas.

3553. Detweiler, Philip F. "The Changing Reputation of the Declara-
       tion of Independence: The First Fifty Years." WMQ, 19
       (1963), 557-574.

       The Virginia Declaration of Rights had more importance in
       political thought until the 1790s.

3554. Echeverria, Durard, ed. and trans. "The American Character:
       A Frenchman Views the New Republic from Philadelphia, 1777."
       WMQ, 16 (1959), 376-413.

       A French officer wrote some thoughtful views about American
       cities, society, and its women.

3555. Egnal, Marc and Joseph Ernst. "An Economic Determination of
       the American Revolution." WMQ, 29 (1972), 3-32.

       The authors stress the importance of a self-conscious
       colonial elite, British mercantilism, and a contraction of
       colonial business as causes.

3556. Eisenach, Eldon J. "Cultural Policies and Political Thought:
       The American Revolution Made and Remembered." AMER STUD,
       20 (1979), 71-97.

       Eisenach stresses law, religion, and constitutions to
       explain varying interpretations of the Revolution.

3557. Ernst, Joseph. "'Ideology' and an Economic Interpretation of
the Revolution." See 3335, pp. 161-85.

In a brilliant essay, Ernst probes the viewpoints of modern
historians, particularly the "New Left" scholars and stresses
the influence of pre-war economic conditions.

3558. Friedman, Lawrence J., and Arthur H. Shaffer. "History,
Politics and Health in Early American Thought: The Case of
David Ramsay." J AMER STUD, 13 (1970), 37-56.

Here is an excellent sketch of a leading South Carolinian
physician and early historian of the war.

3559. Fursenko, A.A., and Gilbert H. McArthur, trans. "The American and French Revolution Compared: The View From the USSR."
WMQ, 33 (1976), 481-500.

This is an extremely valuable article comparing the historiography of the two Revolutions from a Marxian viewpoint; the
two events were similar, signalling the rise of capitalism.

3560. Gephart, Ronald M. PERIODICAL LITERATURE ON THE AMERICAN
REVOLUTION. HISTORICAL RESEARCH AND CHANGING INTERPRETA-
TIONS 1895-1970. Washington, DC: Library of Congress, 1971.

This is the best selection of (un-annotated) articles that
has been compiled on the Revolution. There are some 1,100
entries cited from a wide range of journals.

3561. Greene, Jack P., comp. THE AMBIGUITY OF THE AMERICAN REVO-
LUTION. New York: Harper and Row, 1968.

This is an excellent selection of writing on the Revolution by ten historians including Louis Hartz, Benjamin F.
Wright and Gordon S. Wood.

3562. ————. REAPPRAISAL OF THE AMERICAN REVOLUTION IN RECENT
HISTORICAL LITERATURE. Washington, DC: American Historical
Association, 1967.

Greene wrote a very stimulating review about current trends
in historical thought about the Revolution. Although designed
for high school teachers, there are abundant clues here about
the literature of the era for other audiences.

3563. ————. "Values and Society in Revolutionary America." ANN
AMER ACAD POLI SOC SCI, 26 (1975), 53-69.

By 1775, a distinctly American body of tradition had emerged
stressing limited government, sovereignty of the people, and
the natural rights concepts.

3564. Gruber, Ira D. "The American Revolution as a Conspiracy:
The British View." WMQ, 26 (1969), 350-372.

After April 1775, British Cabinets saw the war as a long-planned plot and based their strategy on the assumption that most of the colonial population was Loyalist.

3565. Hartz, Louis. "American Political Thought and the American Revolution." AM POL SCI REV, 46 (1952), 321-342.

Compared to Europe, American society was unique and by 1775 had virtually the social goals that were confirmed by 1783.

3566. Hawke, David. "The American Revolution - Was it a Real One." AMER BOOK COLL, 17 (1967), 27-29, 31-32.

The war produced a different outlook on life, a republic, not a hierarchy, and the emergence of new entrepreneurs.

3567. Herbert, Jurgen. "The American Revolution and the American University." PERS AMER HIST, 10 (1975), 279-354.

State legislatures protected colleges from radicals - who saw such institutions as elitist - in order to prepare future citizens for political roles.

3568. Higginbotham, Don. "The American Revolution: Yesterday and Today." HIST NH, 31 (1975), 1-15.

Here is a convenient summary for undergraduates concerning the implications of the struggle for modern society.

3569. Hooker, Richard J., ed. THE AMERICAN REVOLUTION: THE SEARCH FOR MEANING. New York: J. Wiley and Sons, Inc. 1970.

There are sixteen thoughtful essays in the collection with samples from John Adams to Hannah Arendt. The articles by Bernard Bailyn, Gordon S. Wood, Benjamin Quarles and Jesse Lemisch are provocative.

3570. Jacobson, David L., comp. ESSAYS ON THE AMERICAN REVOLUTION. New York: Holt, Rinehart and Winston, 1970.

This is the best collection of essays available on the subject. Some twenty-two historians present their viewpoints on a wide variety of topics. The material covered here represents a good sampling of current literature on the Revolution.

3571. Jensen, Merrill. "Democracy and the American Revolution." HUNT LIB Q, 20 (1975), 321-341.

The Revolution was democratic in origins and in results, with political reforms as the major area of change.

3572. ————. "The American People and the American Revolution." JAR, 57 (1975), 5-34.

In a model essay, Jensen focuses on the contemporary view of democracy and how institutions can be adapted to a changing society.

3573.   Ketchum, Richard M. "England's Vietnam: The American Revolution." AMER HERITAGE, 22 (4) (1971), 6-11, 81-83.

Here is a good comparison of two colonial wars, two centuries apart, which were impossible for Britain or for the United States to win.

3574.   Klein, Milton M. "The American Revolution in the Twentieth Century." HISTORIAN, 34 (1972), 213-239.

Noting the exclusive nature of the Revolution, Klein claims that the dreams of 1776 have still not been played out in the present world.

3575.   Leder, Lawrence H., comp. THE MEANING OF THE AMERICAN REVOLUTION. Chicago: Quadrangle Books, 1969.

This collection contains fifteen extremely penetrating articles about the war and its results, written by authors who originally published these essays in the NEW YORK TIMES.

3576.   Lockridge, Kenneth A. "Social Change and the Meaning of the American Revolution." J SOC HIST, 6 (1973), 403-449.

This is a perceptive article, centering on the theory of modernization, which questions if much change actually occurred by 1783.

3577.   Lokken, Roy N. "The Political Theory of the American Revolution: Changing Interpretations." HIST TEACHER, 8 (1974), 81-95.

Lokken examines the views of Bernard Bailyn and Gordon Wood to demonstrate the varying expressions of revolutionary ideology.

3578.   McNeil, William H. "The American War of Independence in World Perspective." See 414, pp. 3-13.

McNeil places the Revolution within the context of the revolts in Brazil, Corsica, and Russia in the eighteenth-century.

3579.   Maier, Pauline. "Why Revolution? Why Democracy?" J INTERDISP HIST, 6 (1976), 711-732.

Analyzing recent writings, Maier concludes that the methodology of some historians is new but the questions they ask are old ones.

3580. Main, Jackson Turner. "Government By the People: The Ameri-
       can Revolution and the Democratization of the Legislature."
       WMQ, 23 (1966), 391-407.

       A wider franchise, a new elite, and increased power to the
       back country resulted.

3581. ————. "The Results of the American Revolution Reconsidered."
       HISTORIAN, 3 (1969), 539-554.

       This is a refreshing essay about the need to probe the re-
       sults and to assess social, economic and intellectual change.

3582. Martin, James Kirby. IN THE COURSE OF HUMAN EVENTS: AN
       INTERPRETATIVE EXPLORATION OF THE AMERICAN REVOLUTION.
       Chicago: AHM Publishing, 1979.

       The author has compiled an excellent synthesis of recent
       scholarship on the Revolution. The essays are concise, pro-
       vocative and reflect trends in current interpretations. This
       is a handy volume for college students.

3583. Mason, Bernard. "The Heritage of Carl Becker: The Histori-
       ography of the American Revolution." NY HIST SOC Q, 53
       (1959), 127-147.

       Becker's monograph (1909) about the dual revolution of the
       war was highly influential and is still a valuable starting
       point for a discussion about social change.

3584. Middleton, Richard. "British Historians and the American
       Revolution." J AMER STUD, 5 (1971), 43-58.

       This is a fine summary of the viewpoints of fourteen
       British writers which shows a revival of interest in the war
       since the 1950s.

3585. Miller, William. "The Effects of the American Revolution on
       Industrial Servitude." PA HIST, 7 (1940), 131-144.

       An examination of statutory law from 1775 to 1782 shows
       little change.

3586. Morgan, Edmund S., ed. THE AMERICAN REVOLUTION: TWO CENTURIES
       OF INTERPRETATION. Englewood Cliffs, New Jersey: Prentice-
       Hall, 1965.

       Morgan presents writings from the early National period
       to the present. Included here, among others, are essays by
       David Ramsay, George Bancroft, Daniel J. Boorstein, and Eric
       Robson.

3587. ————. THE CHALLENGE OF THE AMERICAN REVOLUTION. New York:
       Norton, 1976.

A foremost authority presents here a collection of his
writings. Six essays have been published before, the seventh
is new. Each chapter has an introduction which indicates how
the author's views have been modified over decades. This is
a very provocative volume replete with insight and imagination.

3588. Morris, Richard B. THE AMERICAN REVOLUTION RECONSIDERED.
        New York: Harper and Row, 1957.

        Here is a well-written, amply documented summary of the war.
        Morris demonstrates the wide-ranging effects of key events
        with admirable skill. His comparison of the historians on
        the Revolution is refreshing, and his analogy between the
        American and French Revolutions is stimulating.

3589. ————. "'We the People of the United States': The Bicenten-
        nial of a People's Revolution." AHR, 82 (1977), 1-19.

        The Revolution brought nationhood, new men to power, raised
        political aspirations, and it made state governments more
        responsive to social inequities.

3590. Nelson, Paul David. "British Conduct and the American Revolu-
        tionary War: A Review of Interpretations." JAH, 65 (1978),
        623-653.

        Current trends place the blame for British failure on the
        incompetence of key political and military figures.

3591. Nelson, William H. "The Revolutionary Character of the Ameri-
        can Revolution." AHR, 70 (1965), 998-1014.

        The Founding Fathers built a solid political foundation but
        the precise nature of revolutionary change is difficult to
        delineate.

3592. Paret, Peter. "The Relationship between the Revolutionary
        War and European Military Thought and Practice in the
        Second Half of the Eighteenth Century." See 414, pp.
        144-157.

        The Revolution was different from the contemporary European
        conflict mainly due to its ideological thrust.

3593. Pohl, James W. "The American Revolution and the Vietnamese
        War: Pertinent Military Analogies." HIST TEACHER, 7 (1974),
        255-265.

        This is a suggestive essay, touching on atrocities and
        emotional attitudes of the two struggles; but the author
        seems unfamiliar with the Revolutionary era.

3594. Reibel, John C. "America's Initial View of their Revolution;
        Significance for Other Peoples, 1776-1788." HISTORIAN, 35
        (1973), 418-433.

Americans of the era saw the Revolution as a reforming force but few expected its example to be duplicated elsewhere.

3595.   Robson, Eric. "The American Revolution Reconsidered." HIST TODAY, 2 (1952), 126-132, 314-322.

A talented British historian explains why capable politicians and soldiers were destined to fail in the struggle.

3596.   Root, Winfred Frexler. "The American Revolution Reconsidered." CAN HIST REV, 23 (1942), 16-29.

Noting the hopeless situation of the colonists in winning the war by 1778, the author stresses the importance of French military and moral assistance.

3597.   Royster, Charles. A REVOLUTIONARY PEOPLE AT WAR: THE CONTINENTAL ARMY AND AMERICAN CHARACTER, 1775-1783. Chapel Hill: University of North Carolina Press, 1979.

In an imaginative attempt to stress the contrast between national ideals for freedoms and the reality of military necessary (such as conscription and army discipline), Royster notes that not until Valley Forge did an American sense of military professionalism emerge. This work is not traditional military history but it is a social-psychological study of ideals and attitudes. Though it is thoroughly documented, it is a very difficult book to read and it is replete with numerous questionable assumptions not supported by fact or analysis.

3598.   Schlesinger, Arthur M. "The American Revolution Reconsidered." POL SCI Q, 34 (1919), 61-78.

The author stresses economic forces, rival capitalistic systems and lower class aspirations.

3599.   Seller, Maxine and Andrew Trusz. "High School Textbooks and the American Revolution." HIST TEACHER, 9 (1973), 535-594.

This is a fine article to help high school teachers to select a textbook; the authors note the weaknesses in most books on the subject and suggest how to fill in topical gaps with various materials.

3600.   Shy, John. A PEOPLE NUMEROUS AND ARMED: REFLECTIONS ON THE AMERICAN STRUGGLE FOR AMERICAN INDEPENDENCE. New York: Oxford University Press, 1966.

The focus of this collection of ten essays (of which eight were previously published) is the impact of the war on society. Shy suggests that military operations should be considered within a social and political context, that the nations found it difficult to mobilize for warfare, and that a civil war was fundamental to the conflict. This is a useful work for a

different perspective of the war, but the author's rambling
narrative inhibits his ability to stress his points with
clarity.

3601. Spector, Robert M. "The American Revolution: Something Beyond the Causes." SOC STUD, 62 (1971), 99-106.

The author claims that historians have stressed causes to
the neglect of issues in the war.

3602. Streiker, William F., Jr. "Conflict or Consensus? Recent
Trends in the Historiography of the American Revolution."
PROC SC HIST ASSOC, 6 (1967), 32-42.

The "consensus" school dominates the work of ten experts
on the Revolution cited here.

3603. Tolles, Frederick B. "The American Revolution Considered as
a Social Movement: A Re-Evaluation." AHR, 60 (1954), 1-12.

In reviewing J. Franklin Jameson's famous work (1925) about
the degree of social upheaval, Tolles asserts that despite
some oversights, the Jameson thesis is still sound and viable.

3604. Underdal, Stanley J. MILITARY HISTORY OF THE AMERICAN REVOLU-
TION: THE PROCEEDINGS OF THE 6TH MILITARY HISTORY SYMPOSIUM,
UNITED STATES AIR FORCE ACADEMY, 10-11 OCTOBER, 1974.
Washington: Government Printing Office, 1974.

There are interesting papers done by Ira Gruber, David
Palmer, John Shy, and Robert Calhoon among other authorities.
Unfortunately, the writers cover familiar ground (often from
their own works) and borrow heavily with each other's writings.
The symposium appears to have moved in circles.

3605. Ver Steeg, Clarence L. "The American Revolution Considered
as an Economic Movement." HUNT LIB Q, 20 (1956-57), 361-
372.

The author calls for investigation of mining, farming, land
tenure, trade routes, and business enterprise.

3606. Wright, Esmond, ed. CAUSES AND CONSEQUENCES OF THE AMERICAN
REVOLUTION. Chicago: Quadrangle Books, 1966.

The author assembled the views of eighteen distinguished
writers on the Revolution. This is a very convenient summary
of some five 'schools' of interpretation. It contains excellent introductory essays, and suggestive extracts from
scholarly works.

XIII. BIOGRAPHY

3607. Alberts, Robert C. THE GOLDEN VOYAGE: THE LIFE AND TIMES OF
       WILLIAM BINGHAM, 1752-1804. Boston: Houghton Mifflin, 1969.

       Bingham was a Continental Commercial Agent in the West Indies,
       1776-1780. This work is a carefully written and amply docu-
       mented account of his successful efforts to procure and to
       transport essential commodities for the Continental Army.

3608. Alden, John Richard. GENERAL CHARLES LEE: TRAITOR OR PATRIOT?
       Baton Rouge: Louisiana State University Press, 1951.

       This is a fine book for students and general readers for it
       is colorful and readable. Yet the specialist could gain from
       this insightful account of the controversial American general
       disgraced for his conduct at Monmouth. Alden provides ample
       detail and a sound perspective of this puzzling figure.

3609. Aldridge, Alfred Owen. MAN OF REASON: THE LIFE OF TOM PAINE.
       Philadelphia: J.B. Lippincott, 1957.

       Here is a good analysis of a famed propagandist who seized
       a unique opportunity to popularize the American cause.
       Though the author delineates unsavory aspects of Paine's
       personality and praises him as a champion of freedom, he did
       not write a balanced account. Aldridge used excessive quota-
       tions without placing them in perspective, and he seems
       unfamiliar with the essential literature of the era.

3610. Allan, Herbert S. JOHN HANCOCK. PATRIOT IN PURPLE. New
       York: The Macmillan Co., 1948.

       This is a useful work with some major flaws. The coverage
       is judicious, the documentation copious, the material is
       readable, and the author presents an objective view of this
       prominent merchant and flamboyant politician. However, some
       chapters detract from the story due to excessive background
       material, and the author neglected to provide enough informa-
       tion about Hancock himself.

3611. Ammon, Harry. JAMES MONROE: THE QUEST FOR A NATIONAL IDENTITY.
       New York: McGraw-Hill Publishing Co., 1971.

       Though only a portion of this excellent work covers the
       Revolution, this meticulously researched and nicely paced
       narrative merits a wide readership. There are some new in-
       sights and some novel perspectives about this prominent poli-
       tician who apparently was not a significant thinker but a
       remarkable patriot.

3612. Ayling, Stanley. GEORGE THE THIRD. New York: Alfred C. Knopf, 1972.

America's last king had a long reign and hence about one-half of this excellent work applies to the Revolution. This is a very engrossing, thoroughly researched study which shows that the monarch was devoted to his duties. There are few revisions here of traditional appraisals of this complex personality, but the study is fair, judicious and eminently interesting.

3613. Bailyn, Bernard. THE ORDEAL OF THOMAS HUTCHINSON. Cambridge: Harvard University Press, 1974.

This is one of the best biographies about a key Massachusetts figure caught in the pre-revolutionary turmoil. Devoted to America, yet loyal to the Crown, Hutchinson faced successful crises as a leading Tory. This work is meticulously documented, written with verve, and it contains insights about politics in the era that are masterly. Bailyn presents a well-balanced and thoughtful assessment of this leading figure.

3614. Bass, Robert Duncan. GAMECOCK: THE LIFE AND CAMPAIGNS OF GENERAL THOMAS SUMTER. New York: Holt, Rinehart, and Winston, 1961.

Here is a readable, interesting story of a famous southern partisan leader. The material on guerrilla warfare in the Carolinas is intriguing. However, even with careful research, due to the lack of existing documentation and excessive reliance on folktales, the author is unable to clarify much about Sumter's career that remains vague and inexplicable.

3615. ————. SWAMP FOX; THE LIFE AND CAMPAIGNS OF GENERAL FRANCIS MARION. New York: Henry Holt and Co., 1959.

Bass recaptures the wartime experience of this romantic guerrilla leader who hounded Tories and raided British outposts in the Carolinas. This is a fine biography that reads more like a novel than an account of partisan fighting. The author has done a fine job of examining his subject and placing him in the southern milieu of the war.

3616. ————. THE GREEN DRAGOON: THE LIVES OF BANASTRE TARLETON AND MARY ROBINSON. New York: Henry Holt and Co., 1957.

Here is a lively, colorful story of the famed British cavalry leader who was hated and feared by southern patriots. Though the book is entertaining about the mannerisms of the late Hanoverian era and replete with documentation, the major flaws here are the author's unexplained detachment about his subject and his inability to examine Tarleton's vicious method of waging warfare.

3617. Beach, Stewart. SAMUEL ADAMS: THE FATEFUL YEARS, 1764-1775.
       New York: Dodd, Mead, and Co., 1965.

       This is a well-researched, conscientious effort to place
       one of America's famed propagandists into perspective. The
       coverage of imperial relations on Massachusetts politics,
       and on the successive pre-war crises is excellent. Beach
       views Adams less as a radical but as one who viewed inde-
       pendence as inevitable.

3618. Boardman, Roger S. ROGER SHERMAN, SIGNER AND STATESMAN.
       Philadelphia: University of Pennsylvania Press, 1938.

       Sherman had a varied career in business, law, and as a
       politician. He was particularly astute on Congressional com-
       mittees and resolved many irksome problems confronting the
       Delegates. This is a carefully documented history that pro-
       vides much information about politics during the Revolution
       and the Confederation.

3619. Bowen, Catherine Drinker. JOHN ADAMS AND THE AMERICAN REVOLU-
       TION. Boston: Little, Brown, and Co., 1950.

       Bowen writes well, manages to re-create an era with zest
       and color, and tries to assess a complex figure. Though
       this work is adequate for general readers (who should be
       warned of innumerable imagined conversations in the narra-
       tive), specialists can overlook this work because of its
       superficiality.

3620. ————. THE MOST DANGEROUS MAN IN AMERICA: SCENES FROM THE
       LIFE OF BENJAMIN FRANKLIN. Boston: Little Brown, and Co.,
       1974.

       By using Franklin's innumerable published papers and letters
       and standard scholarly works, the author has attempted to
       present a vivid portrayal of Franklin for young adults.

3621. Boyd, George Adams. ELIAS BOUDINET, PATRIOT AND STATESMAN.
       Princeton: Princeton University Press, 1952.

       Though this is ponderous to read, it is a useful portrayal
       of a prominent figure. The author made an exhaustive re-
       search of his subject's career, and, consequently, he has
       broadened our knowledge of the era. Boudinet's work as Com-
       missary-General of Prisons is well-related in this useful
       work.

3622. Boyd, Thomas A. MAD ANTHONY WAYNE. New York: Scribner's Sons,
       1947.

       Boyd wrote a popular account of a famed war hero. Wayne was
       involved in major engagements of the war, was a fine field com-
       mander, and led the successful assault on Stony Point. The
       author mastered the source material and re-created a romantic
       figure who throve on excitement.

3623. Brant, Irving. JAMES MADISON. 6 vols. Indianapolis:
       Bobbs-Merrill Co., 1941-1961.

       Volumes one and two are pertinent to the Revolution. These
       books may be the best written about Madison. Brant compiled
       a scholarly narrative that would interest specialists, but
       one that would probably bore a general audience. The works
       cover the years through the Confederation era and provide a
       sound probing of the statesman's mind. Though somewhat
       ponderous to read, the volumes provide illuminating insights
       into the thinking of a key statesman.

3624. Brooke, John. KING GEORGE III. New York: McGraw-Hill Book
       Co., Inc., 1972.

       This is a fine biography of the monarch for it reveals much
       about the man, his family, and his public life. Brooke tends
       to defend his subject against the traditional "Whig" historians,
       but his mastery of the documents, his cautious assessments,
       and his knowledge of the politics of the era require the
       reader to re-appraise the King in a different manner. This is
       a splendid work, written for specialists.

3625. Bush, Martin H. REVOLUTIONARY ENIGMA: A REAPPRAISAL OF
       GENERAL PHILIP SCHUYLER OF NEW YORK. Port Washington, New
       York: Ira J. Friedman, Inc., 1969.

       Here is a sound, thoughtful analysis of the early career of
       a wealthy patroon who was influential in New York politics
       and in military campaigns in the North. Bush tends to over-
       look the General's character flaws and credits him as an
       astute statesman, an able negotiator with the Six Nations, as
       a logistics specialist, and one who prepared the army for the
       victory at Saratoga. This is a well-written account.

3626. Callahan, North. DANIEL MORGAN, RANGER OF THE REVOLUTION.
       New York: Holt, Rinehart, and Winston, 1951.

       This exciting tale is suitable for college students who
       desire a simple narrative and good description of battles
       such as Quebec, Saratoga, and Cowpens. Callahan tended to
       overrate Morgan's contributions and to romanticize his career.

3627. Campbell, Norine Dickson. PATRICK HENRY: PATRIOT AND STATES-
       MAN. New York: Devin-Adair Co., Publishers, 1969.

       Though adequately written, this work is too laudatory of
       the famous Virginia orator, and it is marred by the inclusion
       of many generally irrelevant letters. For the general reader,
       however, this work is suitable.

3628. Cary, John H. JOSEPH WARREN: PHYSICIAN, POLITICIAN, PATRIOT.
       Urbana: University of Illinois, 1961.

       Warren was a Bostonian doctor and a patriot leader. Cary
       researched thoroughly, he organized his material well, and he

attempted to re-capture the pre-war excitement. This is an
interesting, thoughtful book that provides one with some fresh
viewpoints about Massachusetts politics.

3629. Champagne, Roger J. ALEXANDER MCDOUGALL AND THE AMERICAN
       REVOLUTION IN NEW YORK. Schnectady, New York: Union College
       Press, 1975.

       From humble origins, McDougall rose to leadership in poli-
       tics and in the army. Here is a nicely crafted work that
       demonstrates the author's mastery of the source material and
       the nature of radicalism in New York. This is a traditional
       type of biography with sufficient attention to McDougall's
       military achievements.

3630. Chinard, Gilbert. THOMAS JEFFERSON: THE APOSTLE OF AMERICAN-
       ISM. New York: Little, Brown, and Co., 1929.

       In the 1930s, this reverential appraisal of Jefferson was
       regarded as the definitive study. It contained fresh data,
       new perspectives, and the author had probed his subject's
       complexities. Although supplanted by more recent works,
       Chinard's study remains one of the best portraits of this
       key figure.

3631. Clark, William B. CAPTAIN DAUNTLESS: THE STORY OF NICHOLAS
       BIDDLE OF THE CONTINENTAL NAVY. Baton Rouge: Louisiana
       State University Press, 1949.

       This is a thrilling saga for naval "buffs." Clark research-
       ed this topic carefully and wrote a colorful narrative about a
       remarkable seaman. The book contains an abundance of material
       about maritime lore.

3632. ————. GALLANT JOHN BARRY, 1745-1803. THE STORY OF A NAVAL
       HERO OF TWO WARS. New York: The Macmillan Co., 1938.

       Here is a readable, scholarly account about a distinguished
       seaman. Though the study is excessively detailed, contains
       unnecessary quotations, and covers some obscure events, it
       is reliable and the definite work on Barry.

3633. ————. LAMBERT WICKES: SEA RAIDER AND DIPLOMAT. New Haven:
       Yale University Press, 1932.

       Here is a well-researched study for specialists. The book
       has ample data about diplomatic relations in London and at
       Versailles; it is crammed with fascinating documentation, and
       it presents a fine portrayal of life under sail. The data
       about sea fights is exciting.

3634. Coleman, John M. THOMAS MCKEAN: FORGOTTEN LEADER OF THE
       REVOLUTION. Rockaway, New Jersey: American Faculty Press,
       1975.

For a solid account of politics in Delaware and to a lesser
degree in Pennsylvania, this well-researched book is recommended. McKean held such a number of political and judicial
posts during the Revolution, and his biographer provides much
data about the impact of the war in the Middle States.

3635.   Collier, Christopher. ROGER SHERMAN'S AMERICA: YANKEE POLITICS
        AND THE AMERICAN REVOLUTION. Middletown, Connecticut:
        Wesleyan University Press, 1971.

        Here is a convincing and detailed examination into the
        nature of Connecticut politics. Though somewhat weak in
        placing Sherman into a national perspective, and flawed by
        perplexing footnoting, this volume does provide a fresh
        viewpoint of a minor figure.

3636.   Cunliffe, Marcus. GEORGE WASHINGTON: MAN AND MONUMENT.
        Boston: Little, Brown and Co., 1958.

        Here is a thoughful, well-balanced biography that clears
        away the myths and legends surrounding the great Virginian.
        This is a penetrating commentary on Washington's major con-
        tributions with sufficient coverage on the war. The work is
        highly recommended for undergraduates.

3637.   Dangerfield, George. CHANCELLOR ROBERT R. LIVINGSTON OF NEW
        YORK, 1746-1813. New York: Harcourt, Brace, and Jovanovich,
        1980.

        Dangerfield wrote a compelling and fascinating biography of
        a New York aristocrat who attempted to adapt to concepts of
        popular sovereignty. The author contends that Livingston joined
        the Revolution in order to retain the liberties that he had
        acquired and not to obtain extensions of civil freedom for the
        populace. The writing style here is admirable.

3638.   Darrow, Jane. NATHAN HALE: A STORY OF LOYALTIES. New York:
        Century Company, 1922.

        Here is a reliable account of the famous martyr of the Ameri-
        can cause that is suitable for a general audience. Though
        the work nears fiction with its pages of faked conversations,
        it was designed to strengthen patriotism and to romanticize
        a folk hero.

3639.   Davidson, Chalmers G. PIEDMONT PARTISON: THE LIFE AND TIMES
        OF BRIGADIER GENERAL WILLIAM LEE DAVIDSON. Davidson, North
        Carolina: Davidson College, 1951.

        Davidson was one of North Carolina's most ingenious war
        leaders. This is a carefully researched, cogently written
        account of his career. Unfortunately, due to limited source
        material, important aspects of the subject's life are not
        clarified.

3640. Davis, Burke. GEORGE WASHINGTON AND THE AMERICAN REVOLUTION.
       New York: Random House, 1975.

       Here is a readable summary of some military operations con-
       ducted by Washington with ample quotations from reliable
       sources. The work would be useful for high school students.

3641. Dillon, Dorothy R. THE NEW YORK TRIUMVIRATE: A STUDY OF
       THE LEGAL AND POLITICAL CAREERS OF WILLIAM LIVINGSTON, JOHN
       MORIN SCOTT, WILLIAM SMITH, JR. New York: Columbia
       University Press, 1949.

       This is an excellent account about three politicians who
       dominated the New York scene in the early 1770's. They
       agitated successfully on innumerable matters involving civil
       liberties and invariably championed the cause of civil and
       religious freedom.

3642. Evans, Emory G. THOMAS NELSON OF YORKTOWN. Charlottesville:
       The University Press of Virginia, 1975.

       This is a satisfactory summary of Nelson's career as a
       leading Virginian and as Governor of the state in 1781. The
       book is useful for information about the impact of the war
       on Virginia. It is carefully researched, but the thesis of
       the work remains unclear. A general audience might enjoy it.

3643. Ferling, John E. THE LOYALIST MIND; JOSEPH GALLOWAY AND THE
       AMERICAN REVOLUTION. University Park, Pennsylvania:
       Pennsylvania State University Press, 1977.

       This is a helpful narrative that aids one in comprehending
       the Loyalist mind. Galloway was an articulate politician and
       a prolific writer who was unable to resolve the imperial crisis
       in 1775. The study is weak on intellectual trends of the era
       and is characterized by some major factual mistakes. However,
       college students may find the work helpful.

3644. Fleming, Thomas. THE MAN FROM MONTICELLO; AN INTIMATE LIFE
       OF THOMAS JEFFERSON. New York: William Morrow and Co.,
       1969.

       The book is well-written, it had excellent plates, and it is
       nicely organized. This is a very readable work that comes
       close to explaining some of the paradoxes in the life of a
       very complex thinker and activist. The work merits a large
       readership.

3645. Flexner, James Thomas. GEORGE WASHINGTON IN THE AMERICAN
       REVOLUTION, 1775-1783. Boston: Little Brown and Co., 1968.

       For a quick, vivid summary of Washington's career in this
       war, this work is highly recommended. The chapters are lively;
       the descriptions colorful and the portraits of generals and
       politicians are astute. This is an excellent work for under-
       graduates and for a popular readership.

3646.   ———. WASHINGTON: THE INDISPENSABLE MAN. BOSTON: Little
         Brown and Co., 1974.

         Flexner does make Washington the truly indispensable man of
         war, but the author relates his story without hero-worship
         and with candor about the General's errors and faults. While
         Washington was relatively unsuccessful in military operations,
         Flexner stresses how he persevered to continue the struggle
         for independence. This may be the best, single volume on
         Washington. It certainly deserves a wide audience.

3647.   Franklin, Benjamin. BENJAMIN FRANKLIN; A BIOGRAPHY IN HIS
         OWN WORDS. Edited by Thomas Fleming. New York: Newsweek,
         1972.

         Fleming does a remarkable job of compressing the essence of
         Franklin's incredible interests, connections, and achievements
         into one volume. The author is particularly capable in con-
         veying to the reader some of Franklin's wit and wisdom. The
         value of the book is enhanced by numerous portraits, woodcuts,
         and cartoons.

3648.   Freeman, Douglas S. GEORGE WASHINGTON: A BIOGRAPHY. 7 vols.
         New York: C. Scribner's Sons, 1948-1957.

         Volumes four and five of the superb biography are pertinent
         to the Revolution. Though the narration may move too slowly
         for general readers, it had intrigued scholars. Freeman does
         not make a literary monument of Washington, for he clearly
         delineates the man's flaws, particularly as a general. There
         are numerous excellent descriptions of battles, personality
         clashes, and of the army at Valley Forge. Freeman wrote the
         best summary of Washington's wartime career and portrayed
         his hero with clear and precise prose.

3649.   Gerlach, Don R. PHILIP SCHUYLER AND THE AMERICAN REVOLUTION
         IN NEW YORK, 1733-1777. Lincoln, Nebraska: University of
         Nebraska Press, 1964.

         Noting that Schuyler has been underrated by historians, the
         author provides a good account of the conservative politician
         and general. Though weak on Schuyler's early career and in
         probing his subject's motives, the book is especially valuable
         for its coverage of New York politics. Gerlach credits him
         as a skillful diplomat with the Iroquois but stresses that
         he was an unlucky field commander.

3650.   Goodman, Nathan G. BENJAMIN RUSH, PHYSICIAN AND CITIZEN,
         1746-1813. Philadelphia: University of Pennsylvania Press,
         1934.

         This is a good general account of America's foremost physician
         of the era and one of the nation's most original thinkers and
         reformers. The material is well-written, the chapters soundly
         organized, and the author came close to comprehending this
         remarkable man. College students would enjoy this volume.

3651. Gottschalk, Louis M. LAFAYETTE.... 5 vols. Chicago:
       University of Chicago Press, 1935-1969.

       Three volumes in this definitive collection relate to this
       Revolution. Here is meticulously researched scholarship about
       the famous French romantic which is written gracefully, and
       with a penetrating character analysis. Though not for general
       readers because of excessive detail and the lack of sustained
       dramatic appeal, nevertheless, because of the huge amount of
       fresh factual data and novel interpretations, this work re-
       mains the definitive one on Lafayette.

3652. Hawke, David Freeman. BENJAMIN RUSH: REVOLUTIONARY GADFLY.
       Indianapolis: Bobbs-Merrill Co., 1971.

       Politician, physician, and social reformer, Rush had a
       diverse and intriguing career. The book demonstrates a keen
       appreciation of the Philadelphia milieu, it shows the results
       of extensive research, and it is a delight to read. This is
       the definitive work on Rush the politician - not the physician -
       and it should appeal to a wide audience.

3653. ————. PAINE. New York: Harper and Row, Publishers, 1974.

       This is the best biography of the controversial patriot.
       Though Hawke neglects to penetrate his subject's personal life,
       he wrote a judicious, thoughtful, and provocative study of the
       man. The author rates high praise for his exhaustive research
       and for his clear, coherent descriptions of Paine's life and
       times.

3654. Higginbotham, Don. DANIEL MORGAN: REVOLUTIONARY RIFLEMAN.
       Chapel Hill: The University of North Carolina Press.

       Here is a lucid, highly readable narrative about a fine Ameri-
       can field commander. The material about Morgan at Quebec,
       Saratoga and Cowpens demonstrates a mastery of the documenta-
       tion. The book is recommended for both specialists and for
       general readers.

3655. Jellison, Charles A. ETHAN ALLEN: FRONTIER REBEL. Syracuse:
       Syracuse University Press, 1959.

       Of the many biographies of the brawling, aggressive Allen,
       this is clearly the best. As a folk-hero of Vermont, Allen
       was a soldier, a champion of local autonomy, and a profound
       theological thinker. The book is especially worthwhile in
       its coverage of military events in some northern campaigns.
       Though not well-documented, the work is nicely written.

3656. Knollenberg, Bernhard. WASHINGTON AND THE REVOLUTION. A RE-
       APPRAISAL: GATES, CONWAY, AND THE CONTINENTAL CONGRESS.
       New York: The Macmillan Co., 1940.

Knollenberg faults Washington for key errors in major battles; he gives full credit to Gates for victory at Saratoga;
and he is dubious about the Conway Cabal. This is a careful
and provocative assessment of Washington that is based on
exhaustive research. The study should attract specialists.

3657. Lewis, Paul. THE MAN WHO LOST AMERICA: A BIOGRAPHY OF GENTLE-
        MAN JOHNNY BURGOYNE. New York: The Dial Press, 1973.

Here is a good summary of the ruthless, ambitious British
warrior who almost won the war in the north. While weak on military matters, Lewis presents an adequate portrait of Burgoyne
as a politician, and as an intellectual. College students
would enjoy this work.

3658. Lunt, James. JOHN BURGOYNE OF SARATOGA. New York: Harcourt,
        Brace and Jovanovich, 1975.

Though the author cites no fresh sources nor does he offer
any novel interpretations, this volume is useful for the lucid
descriptions of battles and campaigning in upper New York.
Lunt claims that Burgoyne was unlucky and tends to blame other
generals for the disaster at Saratoga. This is a good account
for the general reader.

3659. Meade, Robert Douthart. PATRICK HENRY. 2 vols. Philadelphia:
        J.B. Lippincott, Co., 1957, 1959.

This work has excellent coverage on Henry's remarkable political career. Though the author was unable to probe the com-
plexities of his subject's character, and though he left unanswered a number of puzzles about the Virginian's personality,
this is a fine study. It shows the result of wide-ranging
research, a crisp writing style, and a keen appreciation of the
era. This may be the definitive work on Henry.

3660. Malone, Dumas. JEFFERSON AND HIS TIMES. 4 vols. Boston:
        Little, Brown and Co., 1948-1963.

This may be the best biography of Jefferson. Volumes one
and two are pertinent to the Revolution. Malone shows the
historian's work at its best - he demonstrates his mastery of
an enormous amount of records, he writes exceedingly well, and
he renders cautious judgments. The fine bibliography and detailed footnotes are highly useful; the penetrating insights
into Jefferson's complex mind are thoughtful; the smooth narrative should appeal to a broad audience.

3661. Miller, John C. SAM ADAMS; PIONEER IN PROPAGANDA. Boston:
        Little, Brown and Co., 1936.

Here is a very engaging work about the famous radical of
Boston. The book is especially valuable for interpretations
of the pre-revolutionary turmoil, and for sketches of Adams's
contemporaries. This is a highly detailed work; it is judicious
in evaluating Adams; and it shows a dramatic literary style.

3662. Morison, Samuel Eliot. JOHN PAUL JONES: A SAILOR'S BIOGRAPHY.
       Boston: Little, Brown and Co., 1959.

       Here is the definitive work on America's famous naval hero.
       More than a biography, the book is crammed with information
       about maritime lore, and data about forming a new fleet.
       Morison, who knew his ships and seamen well, wrote so smoothly
       that his passages almost conceal the degree of profound
       scholarship in this superb saga of the sea.

3663. Nelson, Paul David. GENERAL HORATIO GATES: A BIOGRAPHY.
       Baton Rouge: Louisiana State University Press, 1976.

       Nelson portrays Gates as neither a bungler nor a military
       genius but as a sensible general who could handle his troops.
       The information here on Gates's rivalries with Schuyler and
       Washington is adroitly covered. Unfortunately, the author
       tends to exaggerate his subject's role at Saratoga, and to
       excuse his blunders at Camden.

3664. Nettels, Curtis P. GEORGE WASHINGTON/AND AMERICAN INDEPENDENCE.
       Boston: Little, Brown and Co., 1951.

       Except for the first sixty-five pages, this is an exception-
       ally well-paced and stimulating account of Washington's role
       in the war. It merits a wide reading audience, especially
       those who wish to see Washington portrayed without flaws.

3665. Palmer, John M. GENERAL VON STEUBEN. 1937. Reprint. Port
       Washington, New York: Kennikat Press, 1966.

       This is a rather uninspiring but a dependable treatment of
       the famous Prussian who became Inspector General at Valley
       Forge. Palmer wrote a cautious appraisal of his hero, delved
       deeply into the source material and he placed von Steuben in
       proper perspective, particularly in the Virginia campaigns
       of 1780-81.

3666. Rankin, Hugh F. FRANCIS MARION, THE SWAMP FOX: THE GREAT
       GUERRILLA LEADER OF THE AMERICAN REVOLTUION - HIS LIFE AND
       HIS CAMPAIGN. New York: Thomas Y. Crowell Co., 1973.

       Though there is little information about the man himself,
       this is a solid account about the importance of partisan war-
       fare in the Carolinas and how it helped to blunt the British
       conquest of the south. College students would enjoy it.

3667. Sellers, Charles Coleman. BENEDICT ARNOLD: THE PROUD WARRIOR.
       New York: Minton, Balch and Co., 1930.

       Here is a good factual account of a remarkable American
       soldier and, perhaps, the nation's most infamous traitor.
       Though there is little new revealed here about Arnold, the
       story of his dramatic career is well-related, and the material
       is nicely plotted. Sellers did not attempt to exonerate Arnold,

but instead he explained that Arnold believed that the American
cause was doomed and that he was tempted by British offers
of bribes and rank.

3668.   Smith, Page. JOHN ADAMS. 2 vols. Garden City, New York:
        Doubleday and Co., Inc., 1962.

        This may be the best work on Adams. Though it includes
        excessive trivia and delves into a psychological study of the
        man, the work is a lively, imaginative commentary on the key
        statesman. There is abundant material here about the Adams
        family, contemporary political thought, and developments in
        the Continental Congress. College students and specialists
        alike can obtain a mass of information and some stimulating
        interpretations from these books.

3669.   Thayer, Theodore. NATHANAEL GREENE: STRATEGIST OF THE REVOLU-
        TION. New York: Twayne Publishers, Inc., 1960.

        A long bibliography and copious footnotes attest to the
        author's thorough research on the fascinating Quaker general.
        The writing style is adequate for general readers. However,
        Thayer's stress is on Greene's personality and not on his
        battles. Thus, the information about campaigns in the south
        is weak in depth and in analysis.

3670.   Van Doren, Carl C. BENJAMIN FRANKLIN. New York: Viking Press,
        Inc., 1938.

        This remains the best work on Franklin. It neatly demon-
        strates Franklin's incredible energy, his endless range of
        interests, his degree of influence in politics and diplomacy,
        and samples of his wisdom. However, the book is basically a
        narrative, it is weak on Franklin's scientific efforts, and
        the author seemed reticent to explore his subject's person-
        ality. Nevertheless, this highly readable book is excellent
        for college students.

3671.   Wallace, Willard M. TRAITOROUS HERO: THE LIFE AND FORTUNES OF
        BENEDICT ARNOLD. New York: Harper and Row, 1954.

        The subject is naturally a fascinating one, and this book
        is suitable for a general audience. Wallace provides adequate
        coverage on most phases of Arnold's career, but the attempted
        psychological analysis is weak. However, this is a judicious
        and well-written work.

3672.   Whitbridge, Arnold. ROCHAMBEAU. New York: The Macmillan Co.,
        1965.

        Here is a fine study of the famed French general who patiently
        assisted the collapsing American army in 1780-1781. The book
        contains vivid descriptions of French military activities in
        the war, and it stresses the highly significant role the French
        had at Yorktown. Thoroughly documented and gracefully written,
        this is a model biography.

3673. Whittemore, Charles P. A GENERAL OF THE REVOLUTION: JOHN
       SULLIVAN OF NEW HAMPSHIRE. New York: Columbia University
       Press, 1961.

       The author tends to overestimate Sullivan's limited abi-
       lities as a solider. The "Luckless Irishman" quarreled in-
       cessantly with colleagues and politicians, he bungled military
       operations, and only on his expedition to the Iroquois country
       did he really achieve success. Until a better evaluation of
       Sullivan is available, this work will have to suffice.

3674. Wickwire, Frank B., and Mary Wickwire. CORNWALLIS: THE
       AMERICAN ADVENTURE. Boston: Houghton-Mifflin, 1970.

       Cornwallis was an aggressive soldier but was hampered by
       serving under Howe. Virtually unrestrained in his southern
       campaign, however, Cornwallis nearly won the war for the
       British. Though this work is carefully researched, it has
       major flaws. The authors overrate Cornwallis's abilities and
       tend to blame Clinton and the admirals for Yorktown. Further-
       more, they added little fresh information or novel interpre-
       tations about their topic. Undergraduates, however, could
       profit from reading this book.

3675. Willcox, William B. PORTRAIT OF A GENERAL: SIR HENRY CLINTON
       IN THE WAR OF INDEPENDENCE. New York: Alfred A. Knopf,
       1964.

       Here is a heavily detailed and scholarly analysis of why
       Clinton, seemingly with all the advantages for victory, could
       not defeat Washington. There is fascinating information here
       about the British army, its difficulties in fighting an
       elusive foe, and Clinton's protracted arguments with fellow
       generals, admirals, and ministers of state. Unfortunately,
       Willcox attempted to probe Clinton's psyche through the man's
       correspondence in order to explain Clinton's peculiar person-
       ality. Willcox tried an interesting literary experiment but
       not a successful one. Clinton still remains an enigma.

XIV. BIBLIOGRAPHY

3676. Albion, Robert G. NAVAL AND MARITIME HISTORY; AN ANNOTATED
BIBLIOGRAPHY. 4th ed. Mystic, Connecticut: Munson Institute of American Maritime History, 1972.

This volume contains a wealth of data about warships, mer-
chantmen, captains, crews, and maritime lore. Unfortunately,
the coverage is limited to books, official documents, and unpublished dissertations; articles on naval history are not
cited. However, once one masters the bewildering topical and
chronological arrangement, he can find numerous valuable
and obscure items listed here.

3677. Allard, Jean C., Martha L. Crawley, and Mary W. Edmison, comps.
and eds. US NAVAL HISTORY SOURCES IN THE UNITED STATES
NAVAL HISTORY CENTER. Department of the Navy, Washington,
DC, 1975.

Although this publication concentrates on archival holdings
of manuscript collections relating to the United States Navy,
it is useful for naval history "buffs" because it lists over
250 locations which contain large collections of books on
naval history, much of which deals with the Revolution.

3678. Bassett, T.D. Seymour. "A List of New England Bibliographies."
NEQ, 44 (1971), 278-300.

The author cites 217 items related to the region.

3679. Bloxom, Marguerite D., comp. "Winter at Valley Forge: A
Selected List of References." LIB CONG INFO BULL, 37 (1978),
93-96.

Here are 100 items cited that would be useful for term papers.

3680. Boatner, Mark Mayo, III. ENCYCLOPEDIA OF THE AMERICAN REVOLU-
TION. Rev. ed. New York: David McKay Co., 1976.

This work contains over 2,000 entries. It is cross-indexed,
contains a list of abbreviations, and a good bibliography.
The material on military leaders, battles and campaigns is
terse and reliable. However, the book is weak on political and
other developments. For the non-specialist, however, this is a
very useful book.

3681. Brigham, Clarence S. "Additions and Corrections to the History
and Bibliography of American Newspapers, 1690-1820." AMER
ANTIQ SOC PROC, 71 (1961), 15-62.

This article is a valuable corrective to Brigham's magisterial work on journalism.

3682. Bruce, A.P.C. AN ANNOTATED BIBLIOGRAPHY OF THE BRITISH ARMY, 1600-1914. New York: Garland Publishing, Inc., 1975.

This excellent reference of 255 pages has a necessarily broad coverage, and, thereby, the material devoted to the Revolution is quite restricted. However, it is nicely written and the author demonstrates a firm control of his material and organization. For military "buffs," it is invaluable.

3683. Burr, Nelson R. A NARRATIVE AND DESCRIPTIVE BIBLIOGRAPHY OF NEW JERSEY. New Jersey, Toronto, and London: D. Van Nostrand Co., Inc., 1964.

This bibliography covers material on the state from 1609 to 1964. Pages 54-71 are replete with references to New Jersey in the Revolution.

3684. Churchill, Edward A., and James S. Leamon. "Maine in the Revolution: A Reader's Guide." MAINE HIST SOC Q, 15 (1975-76), 145-195.

This is a fine bibliography containing 325 items. The stress is on relatively obscure events and personages in local history of the state with only a handful of useful citations on the Revolution.

3685. Coakley, Robert W., and Stetson Conn. THE WAR OF THE REVOLUTION: NARRATION, CHRONOLOGY, AND BIBLIOGRAPHY. Washington: Center of Military History, 1975.

This work contains a highly simplistic summary of the major military campaigns. The maps are excellent, and the chronology of events is useful. The list of books on the war and especially the citations of periodical literature, however, are quite outdated and are very limited in scope.

3686. Cone, Gertrude E., comp. A SELECTIVE BIBLIOGRAPHY OF PUBLICATIONS ON THE CHAMPLAIN VALLEY. Plattsburgh, New York: North County Life, 1959.

Here are over 800 items, many of which deal with the area during the late colonial era.

3687. Coughlin, Margaret N. CREATING INDEPENDENCE, 1763-1789: BACKGROUND READING FOR YOUNG PEOPLE. Washington, DC: Library of Congress, 1972.

Here is a handsomely printed booklet which annotates a good sample of the literature available for youngsters about battles, biographies, seafights, the Founding Fathers, and related topics.

3688. Cowen, David L. A BIBLIOGRAPHY OF THE HISTORY OF COLONIAL
      AND REVOLUTIONARY MEDICINE AND PHARMACY. Madison, Wisconsin:
      American Institute of Pharmacy, 1976.

      This 16 page booklet contains nearly 200 references to medi-
      cine, much of it relating to the war.

3689. Dickinson, A.T. AMERICAN HISTORICAL FICTION. New York: The
      Scarecrow Press, 1963.

      With very brief commentaries, the author covers (pages 29-
      45) the best novels about the Revolution.

3690. Eakin, Joyce L. COLONIAL AMERICA AND THE WAR OF INDEPENDENCE.
      Carlisle Barracks, Pennsylvania: US Army Military History
      Research Collection, 1976.

      This is merely a listing of books held by the United States
      Army at Carlisle Barracks on the Revolution. The items are
      not annotated, no periodical literature is cited, much of the
      material is quite outdated, and the topical organization is
      quaint.

3691. Easterby, J.H. GUIDE TO THE STUDY AND READING OF SOUTH
      CAROLINA HISTORY. A GENERAL CLASSIFICATION BIBLIOGRAPHY
      WITH A SUPPLEMENT OF BOOKS AND REPRINTS ON SOUTH CAROLINA
      HISTORY PUBLISHED SINCE 1950 BY NOEL PALK. Spartansburg,
      South Carolina: The Reprint Co., 1975.

      Some thirty pages here are relevant to the era. The annota-
      tions are brief, and the authors have omitted many valuable
      essays from prominent journals.

3692. Estler, Chester Arthur. "Bibliography of Connecticut During
      the American Revolution." CONN HIST, 16 (1976), 7-36.

      Although the entries are not annotated, this is the best
      source of published material about the state in the war.

3693. Flagg, Charles A., and Judson T. Jennings. "A Bibliography
      of New York Colonial History." NY STATE LIB BULL, 56
      (1901), 291-558.

      This lengthy article contains an extensive listing on printed
      materials related to the Revolution in New York.

3694. Forbes, Harriet M. NEW ENGLAND DIARIES, 1602-1800: A DESCRIP-
      TIVE CATALOG OF DIARIES, ORDERLY BOOKS, AND JOURNALS.
      Topsfield, Massachusetts: priv. ptd., 1923.

      There are over 120 printed items here about the war and the
      late colonial period that are usually not cited elsewhere.
      This is a valuable reference for researchers.

3695.   Foster, Olive S., and M.C. Hempstead. "The Revolutionary War
        Period, 1763-1787." In PUBLICATIONS OF THE ILLINOIS STATE
        HISTORICAL LIBRARY AND SOCIETY. Springfield, Illinois:
        Illinois Bicentennial Commission, 1973.

        Here are eighteen pages of items related to George Rogers
        Clark and the Old Northwest.

3696.   Fox, Vicki G., and Althea L. Stoeckel. "The Role of Women in
        the American Revolution: An Annotated Bibliography." IND
        SOC STUD Q, 28 (1977), 14-27.

        This is the most thoughtful and comprehensive essay on the
        topic with a good sample of biographies, juvenile material,
        and contemporary accounts.

3697.   Friedel, Frank, and Richard K. Showman, eds. HARVARD GUIDE TO
        AMERICAN HISTORY. 2 vols. Rev. ed. Cambridge, Massachu-
        setts: Harvard University Press, 1974.

        Information about the Revolution is scattered in many topical
        categories in volume one. However, pages 665-706 in volume
        two contain a satisfactory listing of books and articles on
        the 1775-1783 era.

3698.   Gephart, Ronald Michael. "Revolutionary America, 1763-1789:
        A Bilbiography." Ph.D. dissertation, Northwestern University,
        1980.

        Here is a well-written discussion in 81 pages about how
        archives and libraries developed methods for collecting materi-
        als on the Revolution. There are abundant hints here about
        special manuscripts that would interest the specialist. The
        last 36 pages contain an outline for a forthcoming bibliography
        on the Revolution to be published by the Library of Congress.

3699.   Greene, Evarts B., and Richard B. Morris. A GUIDE TO THE
        PRINCIPAL SOURCES FOR EARLY AMERICAN HISTORY, (1600-1800)
        IN THE CITY OF NEW YORK. New York: Columbia University
        Press, 1929. 2nd ed. 1953.

        This is an essential work for specialists. Though the book
        concentrates on manuscript holdings, there are hundreds of
        references to printed materials about New York during the
        Revolution.

3700.   Greene, Jack P. THE AMERICAN COLONIES IN THE EIGHTEENTH
        CENTURY, 1689-1763. New York: Appleton-Century-Crofts, 1969.

        Although many of the books and articles cited in this fine
        listing of un-annotated material pre-date the Revolution, the
        material on developments during the French and Indian War is
        particularly useful for college students.

3701. Guerra, Francisco. AMERICAN MEDICAL BIBLIOGRAPHY, 1639-1783.
       New York: Lathrop C. Harper, 1962.

       Here is an excellent reference tool for medical historians.
       It lists, apparently, all books and pamphlets related to medi-
       cine and pharmacy during the era. The most valuable section
       of the work, however, is the citation of medical items and
       personages in the medical world through a detailed coverage of
       colonial newspapers.

3702. Harper, Lawrence A. "Recent Contributions to American Economic
       History: American History to 1789." J ECON HIST, 19 (1959),
       1-24.

       Harper wrote an extremely valuable compilation of books and
       articles related to the era.

3703. Harris, Michael H., comp. FLORIDA HISTORY: A BIBLIOGRAPHY.
       Metuchen, New Jersey: The Scarecrow Press, Inc., 1972.

       On pages fifty-four to sixty-three are un-annotated citations
       of books and essays about Florida in the war.

3704. Haskell, John D., Jr., ed. MAINE: A BIBLIOGRAPHY OF ITS HIS-
       TORY. Boston: G.K. Hall, 1977.

       While excellent for local history, there is surprisingly
       little reference material here on the American Revolution.

3705. ————. MASSACHUSETTS: A BIBLIOGRAPHY OF ITS HISTORY. Boston:
       G.K. Hall, 1978.

       Again, the author has done an excellent job in compiling
       masses of data about towns and villages. But, surprisingly
       enough, he has nearly ignored the American Revolution.

3706. ————, and F.D. Seymour Bassett. NEW HAMPSHIRE: A BIBLIOGRAPHY
       OF ITS HISTORY. Boston: G.K. Hall, 1979.

       Although very useful for historians concentrating on local
       events, this bibliography overlooks numerous items on the war
       period.

3707. Hecht, J. Jean. "The Reign of George III in Recent Histori-
       graphy: A Bibliographic Essay." BULL NY PUB LIB, 14 (1960),
       279-304.

       Though many works cited here relate to the post-1783 era,
       this essay is valuable as a guide to British politics during
       the Revolution.

3708. Higham, Robin, ed. A GUIDE TO THE SOURCES OF UNITED STATES
       MILITARY HISTORY. Hamden, Connecticut: Archon Books, 1975.

       Hugh Rankin merely lists 309 books on the Revolution without
       explanations of their usefulness.

3709.   ————, and Donald J. Mrozek, eds. A GUIDE TO THE SOURCES OF
        UNITED STATES MILITARY HISTORY: SUPPLEMENT I. Hamden,
        Connecticut: Archon Books, 1981.

        Rankin cites another eighty books without commentaries.

3710.   Holmes, Jack D.L. "The Historiography of the American Revolu-
        tion in Louisiana." LA HIST, 19 (1978), 309-326.

        This is a superb essay on the area which mentions books,
        articles, theses, dissertations, as well as the state of cur-
        rent research on the war.

3711.   Ingelsbe, Granville M. "A Bibliography of Sullivan's Indian
        Expedition." NY STATE HIST ASSOC PROC, 6 (1906), 37-70.

        Though this essay is badly in need of revision, it is ex-
        tremely helpful in locating obscure items about the campaign.

3712.   James, Sydney V. COLONIAL RHODE ISLAND: A HISTORY. New York:
        Charles Scribner's Sons, 1978.

        Pages 397-401 have ample references to the background of
        the war and the impact of the Revolution on the state.

3713.   Jessup, John E., Jr. and Robert W. Coakley. A GUIDE TO THE
        STUDY AND USE OF MILITARY HISTORY. Washington, DC: Center of
        Military History, 1975.

        Chapter seven deals with the 1609-1815 era. It barely
        touches the subject, offers little analysis and overlooks
        innumerable pertinent books and articles.

3714.   Jones, Lewis P. BOOKS AND ARTICLES ON SOUTH CAROLINA HISTORY:
        A LIST FOR LAYMEN. Columbia, South Carolina: The University
        of South Carolina Press, 1965.

        Pages forty to fifty-one have citations on the Revolution.

3715.   Keegan, John, and Andrew Wheatcroft. WHO'S WHO IN MILITARY
        HISTORY FROM 1453 TO THE PRESENT DAY. New York: William
        Morrow and Co., Inc., 1976.

        Although there are relatively few American ranking officers
        cited here, the brief descriptive entries of prominent
        European military leaders of the late eighteenth-century are
        of value. There is a brief glossary, and the plates are
        excellent.

3716.   Klein, Milton M., comp. NEW YORK IN THE REVOLUTION: A BIBLI-
        OGRAPHY. Albany: New York State American Revolution Bi-
        centennial Commission, 1974.

        This is one of the best bibliographies that has recently
        been published on the subject. It contains over 1,100 entries,

many of which are briefly annotated. The volume has headnotes
for each section, thoughtful bibliographic essays (especially
on Carl Becker's influence), and a unique chapter entitled
"The Revolution in New York Fiction."

3717. Labaree, Benjamin W. COLONIAL MASSACHUSETTS: A HISTORY.
Millwood, New York: KTO Press, 1975.

Pages 275-280 contain a concise summary of the best book
and articles on late colonial and early revolutionary Massachusetts.

3718. Lefler, Hugh T. A GUIDE TO THE STUDY AND READING OF NORTH
CAROLINA HISTORY. 3rd ed. Chapel Hill: The University
of North Carolina Press, 1969.

This work provides a good starting point for works on the
state. Due to the large scope of the numerous topics summarized and to the broad chronological span, however, the
material on the Revolution is sparce.

3719. Library of Congress. THE AMERICAN REVOLUTION: A SELECTED
READING LIST. Washington, DC: Library of Congress, 1968.

Here is a thoughtful compilation of books on the Revolution
arranged into fourteen sections. For students and a general
audience, this may be the best, quick reference to a topic.

3720. Lloyd, Christopher. THE BRITISH NAVY IN THE EIGHTEENTH CEN-
TURY. In Robin Higham, ed. A GUIDE TO THE SOURCES OF
BRITISH MILITARY HISTORY. Berkeley: University of California
Press, 1971.

There is a useful annotated bibliography on the Royal Navy
in the war on pages 152-176.

3721. Lynch, Barbara A., comp. THE WAR AT SEA: FRANCE AND THE
AMERICAN REVOLUTION: A BIBLIOGRAPHY. Washington, DC:
Naval History Division, Department of the Navy, 1976,

This is an excellent reference work which contains forty-
four citations to material about the role of the French navy
in the Revolution.

3722. Manwaring, George E. A BIBLIOGRAPHY OF BRITISH NAVAL HISTORY:
A BIOGRAPHICAL AND HISTORICAL GUIDE TO PRINTED AND MANUSCRIPT
SOURCES. Cardiff, United Kingdom: Conway Maritime, 1970.

This useful work contains a two part index of authors and
subject. Unfortunately, Manwaring did not list articles on
merchant ships.

3723. Millett, Allan R., and B. Franklin Cooling, III, comps.
DOCTORAL DISSERTATIONS IN MILITARY AFFAIRS. Manhattan,
Kansas: State University Library, 1972.

On pages 122-124 the compilers listed some forty dissertations on the Revolution about one-half of which have not
been published. Yearly "up-dates" have appeared on dissertations in MILITARY AFFAIRS.

3724. Monroe, John A. COLONIAL DELAWARE: A HISTORY. Millwood, New
York: KTO Press, 1976.

On pages 275-280 are citations for the most reliable printed
material about Delaware in the late colonial and revolutionary
era.

3725. Naval History Division. UNITED STATES NAVAL HISTORY: A
BIBLIOGRAPHY. 6th ed. Washington, DC: Department of the
Navy, 1972.

Pages five to ten contain familiar references to the birth
of the American Navy in the war.

3726. New Hampshire Bicentennial Commission. NEW HAMPSHIRE'S ROLE
IN THE AMERICAN REVOLUTION, 1763-1789. Concord: New
Hampshire: New Hampshire State Library, 1974.

This is a model compilation of printed material about a
state's role in the war. It contains citations to 138 books
and monographs and to 482 printed articles. Most of the
entries are annotated.

3727. Northrup, Everett H., comp. "Burgoyne's Invasion, 1777; A
Selected List of Published Sources Both Primary and Secondary." BULL BIB, 16 (1939), 175-176, 197-199; 7 (1940), 12-
14.

Though now outdated, this essay - which contains some an-
notation - is a good departure point for material on the
topic.

3728. Reed, H. Clay, and Morier B. Reed, comp. A BIBLIOGRAPHY OF
DELAWARE HISTORY THROUGH 1960. Newark, Delaware: University
of Delaware Press, 1966.

The 4,700 entries here cover a broad social-cultural spectrum,
but data on the Revolution is sparse.

3729. Rowland, Arthur Key, and James E. Dorsey. A BIBLIOGRAPHY ON
THE WRITINGS OF GEORGIA HISTORY, 1900-1970. Spartansburg,
South Carolina: The Reprint Co., 1972.

Here are over 5,000 references to published books and
articles about Georgia. Unfortunately, the coverage on the
Revolution is limited.

3730. Shy, John, comp. THE AMERICAN REVOLUTION. Northbrook, Illinois: AMH Publishing Corporation, 1972.

This listing of references is flawed. Over one-half of the
booklet is concerned with the coming of the Revolution, the
data on the war and on wartime society is very sparse, and
there are innumerable spelling and typographical errors.

3731. Simpson, John Eddins, comp. GEORGIA HISTORY: A BIBLIOGRAPHY.
Metuchen, New Jersey: The Scarecrow Press, 1976.

This is a well-organized bibliography that covers virtually
all phases of Georgia's social-economic background. The
references to late colonial Georgia and the Revolution are
helpful.

3732. Smith, Dwight L., ed. ERA OF THE AMERICAN REVOLUTION: A
BIBLIOGRAPHY. Santa Barbara, California: ABC-CLIO Press,
1975.

The editor lists hundreds of periodical citations that have
been abstracted in AMERICA: HISTORY AND LIFE: A GUIDE TO
PERIODICAL PUBLICATIONS. Although innumerable pertinent essays
in the literature have been overlooked by the abstracters, this
is a useful reference to articles in relatively obscure journals and magazines.

3733. ————, ed. INDIANS OF THE UNITED STATES AND CANADA: A
BIBLIOGRAPHY. Santa Barbara, California: ABC-CLIO Press,
1974.

This work lists articles cited about North American Indians
in AMERICA: HISTORY AND LIFE: A GUIDE TO PERIDICAL LITERA-
TURE FROM 1964 THROUGH 1972. It contains nearly 1,700 annotated entries but relatively little about the Revolution.
However, the topical arrangement by area and by tribe is
useful.

3734. Smith, Myron, J., comp. NAVIES IN THE AMERICAN REVOLUTION:
A BIBLIOGRAPHY. American Naval Bibliography. Vol. 1.
Metuchen, New Jersey: The Scarecrow Press, 1973.

This excellent bibliography contains over 1,600 entries
related to naval affairs during the war. It is particularly
useful for material about the Royal Navy.

3735. Thomas, William S. "American Revolutionary Diaries, Also
Journals, Narratives, Autobiographies, Reminiscences and
Personal Memoirs.... NY HIST SOC Q BULL, 6 (1922), 32-35,
61-67, 101-107, 143-147; 7 (1923), 28-35, 63-71.

This is a useful source for items that are often difficult
to locate.

3736. Trussell, John B.B., Jr. PENNSYLVANIA MILITARY HISTORY.
Carlisle Barracks, Pennsylvania: US Army Military History
Research Collection, 1975.

Though this work contains some references to local history during the war, it is relatively useless as a reference tool. The material on the American Revolution is disjointed, poorly organized, and it incorporates much that barely relates to Pennsylvania.

3737. Tyson, Carolyn, A., and Rowland P. Gill. AN ANNOTATED BIBLI-
        OGRAPHY OF MARINES IN THE AMERICAN REVOLUTION. Washington,
        DC: History and Museums Division. United State Marine Corps,
        1972.

Here is a very helpful guide for a general audience. It contains over seventy pages of data about campaigns, organizations, weapons, and biographies concerning the Marines.

3738. United States National Park Service. A BIBLIOGRAPHY OF THE
        VIRGINIA CAMPAIGNS AND THE SIEGE OF YORKTOWN, 1781.
        Yorktown, Virginia: Colonial National Historical Park, 1941.

Though quite outdated, this 162 page booklet contains a fine bibliography about Yorktown that has not been surpassed.

3739. Wilkinson, Norman B. BIBLIOGRAPHY OF PENNSYLVANIA HISTORY.
        2nd ed. Harrisburg: Pennsylvania and Museum Commission,
        1957.

This big (826 pages) volume provides fine coverage on virtually all aspects of the state's history. But the material on the Revolution is very brief.

3740. Wiltz, John and Nancy C. Cridland. BOOKS IN AMERICAN HISTORY:
        A BASIC LIST FOR HIGH SCHOOLS AND JUNIOR COLLEGES.
        Bloomington, Indiana: Indiana University Press, 1964.

The authors list thirty-three books on the Revolution suitable for juveniles.

AUTHOR INDEX

Abarca, Ramon E., 2104

Abbey, Kathryn T., 1088, 1089, 2877

Abbot, William W., 2809-2811

Abernathy, Thomas J., 1258

Abnernethy, Thomas P., 194, 2105

Acomb, Evelyn M., 1714

Adair, Douglas, 110, 280, 2916

Adams, Abigail, 3078

Adams, Charles Francis, 457, 558, 658

Adams, Charles T., 2260

Adams, George R., 2732

Adams, John, 3078

Adams, Randolph G., 1, 281, 943, 1280, 1883

Adams, Scarritt, 2033

Adams, Thomas, 2, 3442

Adams, Willi Paul, 2204, 3443

Adrien, Claude, 1442

Agniel, Lucien, 897

Ainslie, Thomas, 1805

Akers, Charles W., 2261, 3079, 3248, 3353

Alberts, Robert C., 3607

Albion, Robert G., 1533, 2034, 3676

Alden, Dauril, 2106

Alden, John E., 154

Alden, John R., 195, 400, 401, 433, 458, 847, 3608

Aldrich, Edgar, 2262

Aldrich, James M., 2593

Aldridge, A. Owen, 3444, 3609

Alexander, Anthony J., 1383-1385

Alexander, Arthur J., 1175, 1205, 1206, 2452, 2641

Alexander, C.B., 2733

Alexander, David E., 659, 977

Alexander, De Alva S., 2453

Alexander, Dennis W., 1706

Alexander, Edward P., 2454

Alexander, John K., 1467-1470, 3304, 3336

Allaire, Anthony, 1806

Allard, Dean C., 1629

Allard, Jean C., 3677

Allan, Herbert S., 3610

Allen, Ben, 196

Allen, Ethan, 502

Allen, Freeman H., 644

562

Coulter, E. Merton, 3102

Coulter, Jack L.S., 1700

Countryman, Edward, 2476, 3340

Covington, James W., 3201

Cowen, Bob, 857

Cowen, David, 1312, 1313, 2551, 3688

Cowing, Cedric B., 2127

Cox, William E., 858

Crackel, Theodore, 3339

Crane, Verner W., 116

Crary, Catherine S., 1406, 2477, 2478, 2953-2955, 3307, 3308

Crawley, Martha L., 3677

Cress, Lawrence Delbert, 1211

Cresswell, John, 2058

Cresto, Kathleen M., 1448

Cridland, Nancy C., 3740

Criss, Mildred, 3103

Crist, Robert G., 519

Crittenden, Charles C., 2736-2738, 3008, 3526

Cromot du Bourg, Marie Francois Joseph Maxime, 1716

Corsby, Alfred W., Jr., 2128

Course, Maurice A., 2780-2782

Crout, Robert Rhodes, 2818

Crowe, Jeffery J., 1913, 2739, 2740, 2956, 3256

Crowl, Philip A., 2650

Crowley, James E., 2599

Crown Publishers, 1560

Crowson, E.T., 906

Cruikshank, Ernest A., 2010

Cullen, George Edward, Jr., 3457

Cullen, Joseph P., 406, 438, 505, 519, 578, 665, 701, 702, 742, 816, 859, 1183, 1831, 3309

Cullen, Maurice R., Jr., 439, 3458

Culter, William R., 1487, 1488

Culturill, Robert S., 3202

Culver, Francis B., 817

Cuming, William P., 300

Cummings, Herbertis M., 1286

Cummings, Light, 1407

Cundall, H.M., 2059

Cuneo, John R., 666, 2011

Cunliffe, Marcus, 3636

Cunningham, John T., 2552

Currey, Cecil B., 301, 3369

Curry, Richard O., 209, 210, 2957

Curtis, Edward E., 1775

Curtis, George M., III, 2694

Curtis, Thomas D., 211, 1003

Curwen, Samuel, 2958

Cutler, Samuel, 1485

Cutler, William 1486, 1467

572

Dabney, Virginius, 2695

Dabney, William Minor, 1952, 2213
2783

Damon, Allan L., 1832

Dandridge, Danske, 1488

Danford, Jacob, 1833

Dangerfield, George, 3637

Daniel, J.R.V., 1184

Daniel, Majorie, 2959, 3370

Daniell, Jere, 2288-2290

Daniels, Bruce Collins, 2427

Danielson, Helga, 3104

Dann, John C., 407

Dargor, Marion, 2783

Darrach, Henry, 3105

Darrow, Jane 3638

D'Auberteuil, Hillard, 1717

David, Ebenezer, 743

Davidson, Alexander, Jr., 3459

Davidson, Chalmer C., 3639

Davidson, Philip, 302, 303, 2784

Davies, R.G., 1776

Davies, Wallace E., 1659

Davis, Andrew McFarland, 791,
2428, 2960, 3203

Davis, Burke, 907, 947, 1449, 3640

Davis, David Brian, 1314, 3257

Davis, Harold E., 2819, 2820

Davis, John, 948

Davis, Kenneth S., 506

Davis, Robert Scott, Jr., 860,
1893, 2012, 2821

Davis, Sallie J., 2741

Davis, W.W.H., 579

Dawson, Henry B., 2479

Dawson, Warrington, 1724

Day, Alan F., 2667-2669

Dayton, Elias, 949

Dean David M., 2961

Deane, Silas, 2214, 2429

Dearborn, Henry, 520

Dearden, Paul F., 772, 773

Dearing, James A., 667

Decker, Malcolm, 1408, 2480

DeFonblanque, Edward Barrington,
1834

Delancy, Norman C., 2742

Delaney, E.F., 2498

DeMond, Robert O., 2962

Department of the Navy, 1561

DePauw, Linda Grant, 3106-3108,
3310

De Peyster, J. Watts, 908

Derleth, August, 1004

Desmond, Alice C., 3109

D'Estaing, Comte, 1718

Destler, Chester McArthur, 2430-
2433

Detweiler, Philip F., 3553

578

604

Vivian, Frances, 1879, 1880

Vivian, James F., 2255

Vivian, Jean H., 1168, 2255, 2256, 2682

Von Papet, Frederick J., 2002

Wade, Herbert T., 1169

Wade, Mason, 3062

Wainwright, Nicholas B., 242

Waldo, Albigence, 1344

Walett, Francis G., 3507

Walker, Howell, 755

Walker, James St. G., 1465

Walker, Joseph B., 2334

Walker, Mabel, G., 3065

Walker, Paul K., 2683, 2684

Walker, Robert G., 3064, 3439

Walker, Warren S., 1440

Wall, Alexander J., 1959, 2541, 2542, 3508

Wallace, Arthur F.C., 3244

Wallace, Lee A., Jr., 1268

Wallace, Michael, 3549

Wallace, Willard M., 431, 1439, 3671

Wallace, William S., 3065

Waller, George M., 1077, 1078

Wallett, Francis G., 278, 3507

Walsh, Richard, 2804, 2805

Walterson, John S., 2776, 2777

Walton, Gary M., 7

Wangensteen, Owen H., 1342

Ward, A. Gertrude, 2621

Ward, Christopher L., 432, 1527

Ward, Harry M., 1170, 2730

Warden, G.B., 2386

Ware, Joseph, 551

Waring, Joseph Ioor, 1918

Warner, Oliver, 1627, 1628

Warren, Mercy Otis, 3187

Warren, Winslow, 54

Washington, Ella Bassett, 1256

Washington, George, 756, 1171

Washington, Ida, 1881

Washington, Paul A., 1881

Waters, John J., 105

Watson, Alan D., 3297

Watson, Derek H., 152, 190, 359

Watson, W.C., 552

Wattington, Patricia, 1079

Waugh, John T., 3066

Wax, Darold D., 3298-3300

Wayne, Anthony, 553, 969

Wead, Eunice, 2200

Weaver, Emily P., 2875

Weaver, Glenn, 2450, 3440

Webber, Laurence E., 2335

SUBJECT INDEX

Aberville Canal, 206

Adair, William, 2981

Adams, Abigail, 3078, 3079, 3095, 3103, 3121

Adams, James, 3468

Adams, John, 98, 326, 1578, 2148, 2164, 2341, 3078, 3619, 3668

Adams, Samuel, 140, 325, 326, 363, 3617, 3619, 3661

Agriculture, 89, 3512-3520

Aimslee, Captain, Thomas, 517, 1805

Albany Committee of Safety, 3002

Albany Congress, 99

Alexander, John, 3419

Allaire, Anthony, 1806

Allegheny frontier, 233, 1058

Allen, Ethan, 506, 512, 1494, 2308, 3655

Allen, John, 160

Allen, Colonel John, 783

Allen, Thomas, 2355

American department, 101

American economy, 321, 329, 340, 346

American officers, military, 1142-1174

American state constitutions, 2204

American strategy, 1135-1141

Ammunition, 1360, 1361, 1364, 1365, 1368

Anbury, Thomas, 1087

610

SUBJECT INDEX

Anderson, Captain Enoch, 559, 1360, 1361, 1364, 1365, 1368, 2623

Andre, Major John, 1401, 1408, 1411, 1414-1416, 1432, 1433, 1441, 1809, 1880

Andrew, John, 498, 2378

Angell, Colonel Israel, 770

Anglican Church, 248, 3370, 3372-3374, 3385, 3387, 3406, 3409-3412, 3421, 3425, 3432, 3438, 3440

Anspach, Peter, 1343

Apalachee (Fla.), 2899

Apothecaries, 1320

Armand-Tuffin, General Charles, 1245, 1250, 1255, 1257

Arnold, General Benedict, 503, 513, 517, 519, 523, 528, 533, 538, 552, 682, 685, 686, 1408, 1411, 1427, 1428, 1438, 1440, 1678, 1883, 3667, 3671

Articles of Confederation, 2222, 2227, 2239-2244

Artillery, 1266, 1269-1272

Asgill, Captain Charles, 1832, 1956

Ashe, Elizabeth, 3168

Ashe, General John, 858

Ashley, Jonathan, 2952

Attucks, Crispus, 1462, 3259

Augusta (Ga.), 854, 1709, 1909, 3034

Australia, 2144

Aylett, Colonel William, 1344

Backus, Isaac, 2235

Bahamas, 1577, 1584, 1587, 1609, 1615

Bailey, Anne, 3096

Bailey, Reverend Jacob, 2339, 2946

Baldwin, Colonel Jeduthan, 635

Cooper, Samuel, 3353

Corbin, Margaret, 3112, 3171

Cork, (Ireland), 1935

Cornwallis, General Charles, 917, 926, 934, 1852, 1891, 1892, 1901,
    1915, 1919, 3674

Cossit, Ranna, 3062

Counterfeiting, 2205, 2527, 2531, 3041

Cowpens, battle of, 899, 907, 910, 921, 923, 925, 929

Craigie, Andrew, 1327

Crane, Major John, 1258

Creek Indians, 3195, 3206, 3226

Cresap, Michael, 1046

Crevecoeur, Michael-Guillaume, 2490

Crevecoeur, St. John de, 269, 3249

Crogham, George, 242

Crosby, Enoch, 1426

Croton River, 570

Crowd behavior, 2362, 2542, 3336-3352, 3464, 3502

Culpepper Minute Battalion, 614

Cumberland Gap, 1039

Cummings, Charles, 2691

Currency Act (1764), 14, 53, 70, 71, 84, 106

Curwen, Samuel, 2958, 3002

Cutler, Samuel, 1485

Danbury (Conn.), 1850, 1862

Danford, Jacob, 1833

Darragh, Lydia, 1436, 3104, 3105, 3172

622

630

Matthewman, Lt. Luke, 1591

Matthews, George, 2707

Mecklenberg Declaration, 2770

Medical Department, 1301-1342

Medicine, 1323, 1324, 1329, 1330, 1332, 3083

Meigs, Lt. Colonel Return J., 531

Mein, John, 154

Melvin, James 532

Memphis, 1114, 1129

Mennonites, 3363, 3378, 3379, 3393

Mercantilism, 79

Mercenary troops, 1837

Mercer, George, 224

Merchant class, 27, 344

Merchant, Henry, 2408

Merchant seamen, 3318, 3319

Methodists, 3396, 3412, 3431

Michigan, 234, 235

Middlebrook encampment, 809, 1301

Militia, 1205-1244, 2786

Military exemptions, 2452

Military justice, 1386-1391, 1394-1396

Mill Prison, 1467, 1468, 1475, 1477, 1492, 1512

Minisink, 3199, 3200

Minuteman, 1214, 1217

Mississippi Territory, 1106, 2881, 2884

Mitchell, Colonel Jonathan, 781

Mohawk River, 2473, 3196

646

Shelby, Colonel Isaac, 913

Sheldon's Horse, 1252

Sherman, Roger, 2286, 2423, 3618, 3635

Ships:
    Alfred, 1588
    Andrea Doria, 1593
    Bon Homme Richard, 1540
    Confederacy, 1688
    Defense, 1640, 1643
    Empress of China, 3540
    Flora, 2090
    Franklin, 1660
    Gaspee, 2392, 2393, 2402, 2406, 2411, 2419
    General Greene, 1632
    General Lincoln, 1671
    General Sullivan, 1651
    Hannah, 1557, 1562, 1618
    Hercules, 1766
    Hero, 1635
    Holker, 1657
    Independence, 1662
    Jersey, 1493, 1495, 1505, 1506, 1508, 1509, 1511
    Lafayette, 1732
    Lexington, 1594
    Liberty, 359, 2084
    Margaretta, 1606, 2346, 2376
    Nancy, 1586
    Nautilus, 1557
    New York, 86, 1569
    Peggy Stewart, 2679
    Pilgrim, 1673
    Prince Edward, 1652
    Prosper, 1642
    Providence, 1610
    Raleigh, 1565
    Rose, 2415
    Royal George, 2033
    Royal Savage, 516
    Saratoga, 1554
    Sartine, 2045
    South Carolina, 1617, 1622, 1639
    Tartar, 1863
    Three Friends, 1633
    Vengence, 1644
    Vigilant, 2088
    Virginia, 1567

Simon, Captain, Abraham, 2830

Simpson, James, 2927

Sinclair, General Patrick, 1835

650

Villefranche, Chevalier de, 1286

Vincennes, 1004

Virginia Continentals, 1525

Virginia economy, 2689, 2697-2699, 2704-2706, 2708, 2710-2715, 2719,
    2723, 2727, 2731

Virginia Gazette, 305, 3463

Virginia navy, 1647, 1649, 1664

Virginia politics, 26, 338, 2687, 2690, 2693, 2696-2703, 2709, 2713,
    2715, 2718, 2721-2725, 2728-2730

Virginia Resolution (1776), 395

Wade, Nathaniel, 1169

Wadsworth, General Peleg, 2351, 2380

Walker, Quock, case, 3295, 3303

War Department (American), 1170

Ward, General Artemus, 447

Warner, Seth, 653

Warren, Captain Benjamin, 659

Warren, Dr. John, 386, 3628

Warren, Mercy Otis, 3119, 3129

Warren, Seth, 653

Washington, Colonel William, 1256

Washington, General George, 755, 756, 767, 1137-1139, 1143, 1149,
    1157, 1164, 1171, 3361, 3636, 3640, 3645, 3648, 3656, 3664

Wataugans, 196

Watson,Thomas, 3362

Wayne, General Anthony, 533, 778, 915, 3622

Weare, Meshech, 2277

Webster, Colonel David, 2320

Wild, Ebenezer, 555, 695

Wilkes, John, 175, 260

Wilkinson, Eliza, 3117, 3122

Willett, Colonel Marinus, 651, 2535

Willing Expedition, 1096, 1107, 1108, 3048

Wilmington, 2624

Wilmot, Captain William, 817

Winn, General Richard, 942

Winthroy, John, 446

Wister, Salley, 3157

Witherspoon, John, 3417

Women in the Revolution, 3078-3193, 3469, 3470

Wren, Christopher, 1483

Wright, Aaron, 501

Wright, Captain Job, 834

Wright, Patience, 3146

Wright, Sir James, 2826, 2835, 2843

Wright, Zaddock, 2921

Writs of Assistance, 13, 81, 105, 109

Wyoming Valley massacre, 992, 998, 1011, 1085, 3208

"Yankee Doodle," 1517

Yorke-Camden case, 238

Yorktown campaign, 943-970, 976, 1572, 1575, 1583, 1595, 1600, 1614, 1723, 1740, 1742, 1744, 1912, 1919, 2047, 2082, 2101

Young, Captain John, 1554

Young, Sergeant William, 634